Ninth Edition

AN INTRODUCTION TO HUMAN SERVICES

POLICY AND PRACTICE

Barbara Schram
Northeastern University, Emerita

Betty Reid Mandell
Late of Bridgewater State College

Paul L. Dann, Ph.D.
New England College

Lynn Peterson

Director and Publisher: Kevin M. Davis
Portfolio Manager: Rebecca Fox-Gieg
Content Producer: Pamela D. Bennett
Digital Studio Producer: Lauren Carlson
Portfolio Management Assistant: Maria Feliberty
Executive Field Marketing Manager: Krista Clark
Executive Product Marketing Manager: Christopher Barry
Procurement Specialist: Deidra Headlee
Cover Designer: Carie Keller, Pearson CSC

Cover Photo: Shutterstock/Rawpixel
Interior Design: Pearson CSC
Full-Service Vendor: Pearson CSC
Full-Service Project Management: Pearson CSC, Monica Moosang
Composition: Pearson CSC
Printer/Binder: LSC Communications, Inc
Cover Printer: Phoenix Color/Hagerstown
Text Font: Times LT Pro 10/12

Cataloging-in-Publication data is on file with the Library of Congress.

ISBN 10:   0-13-477483-3
ISBN 13: 978-0-13-477483-1

12 2023

INTRODUCTION

In the previous eight editions of this text, we have used the analogy in our preface of taking a ride on a seesaw to describe how we learn and teach about the human service field. When we sit on the end of the seesaw closer to the ground, we can observe in vivid detail a troubled individual struggling with his or her particular life circumstances. Based on this observation, we can describe the direct services and systems-change interventions that might be available to that individual in the local network of human service programs. Then we can map out the steps that need to be taken to provide that individual with the most appropriate social services and emotional support.

But as we soar high above the ground on our seesaw, we see that lone individual in less detail. Now we can see how that single life situation complements or conflicts with others in the community. From this vantage point, we can also learn about the world events and cultural or sociopolitical forces that might influence that individual's fate. At this height, we focus less on one person's struggle and think instead about the ways in which a community or a whole society can tackle the vexing problems of violence, abuse, poverty, physical or mental handicaps, and lack of opportunity. Looking at individuals in the context of society also helps us sort out, among many conflicting schools of thought, how their problems came about and how their problems might be prevented or solved. As human service providers, we are always looking at both the intimate portrait and the big picture. The direct services and the indirect services we provide can help alleviate suffering. Both are equally important. In this text, we place more emphasis on social systems than on individual psychology because we believe it is important for beginning students to understand the context of the field before they take specialized courses in counseling, psychology, and human development.

Our understanding of social problems and the social services they require is made far richer but much more ambiguous by this dual set of perspectives. Most importantly, this prevents us from accepting simplistic, one-size-fits-all solutions to complex human problems.

The seesaw analogy also expresses our feelings about the vast changes we (both clients and providers) have experienced since the first edition of our book. As we look back, we realize with surprise that in our first edition, the term *AIDS* (Acquired Immune Deficiency Syndrome) did not appear anywhere in the text. It is hard to believe that a disease that had spread so quickly and taken such a high death toll was barely recognized as a major social problem when our book first went to the printer in 1983. After many years during which AIDS was a virtual death sentence, things are finally improving, at least in developed countries. Many people with AIDS are now living several years beyond the one to two years that used to be their predicted life expectancy. New medications, public education, a societal increase in condom use, and perhaps the postponing of early sexual activity appear to be helping to contain this devastating medical and social problem.

In an earlier edition, we noted with regret that the problems of lack of affordable housing, mortgage foreclosures, and the increasing homelessness that has resulted from these situations have risen to alarming proportions. Temporary shelters have become permanent institutions, and most of us have become used to seeing people sleeping on the streets. Previous solutions to the housing crises, such as subsidized public housing, have virtually been abandoned, but neither new ideas nor the will to implement them has surfaced. We worried that the entitlements and social services designed to help people through hard times seemed to be diminishing as the cries for tax relief were becoming louder and more insistent. Now it is clear that the restructuring of welfare in the United States has done very little to solve this thorny problem.

Since our first edition, some awesome positive changes have occurred in the rest of the world. The tearing down of the Berlin Wall and the breaking up of the Soviet empire have diminished the ominous threat of nuclear destruction. We have noted with pleasure the dismantling of the racial-segregation system in South Africa and the rising emphasis in many quarters on the positive rewards of diversity in our own country. Lately, though, we have noted with alarm a growing wave of anti-immigrant and anti–minority group sentiment among large portions of our population.

In this country we have applauded the increased spirit of volunteerism that has been spreading across the land and the continued healthy growth of the self-help movement. We also have been pleased to see an increase in programs that provide a multitude of services to people who daily struggle with physical, emotional, or educational handicaps. We are also pleased that the discrimination around, and the stigma attached to, issues of gender identity and the redefinition of legal partnerships have shifted in a positive direction.

In the introduction to our last edition, we predicted that there would soon be a congressional solution to the vexing problems of delivering adequate physical and mental health care for all our citizens. We anticipated then that we would soon be writing about some new form of universal national health insurance. But we proved to be poor prophets. During the last several years, universal health care proposals had been completely wiped off Congress's agenda. Private, managed health care schemes, most of them sponsored by for-profit companies, proliferated, leaving many citizens uncovered. Finally, in 2010, after countless revisions and compromises as well as unprecedented partisan political discord, The Affordable Care Act (ACA) was passed by both houses of Congress. But, as we go to press, there are many legal and legislative efforts pending that seek to repeal or greatly weaken the health care bill. Students of human services need to closely follow the news about the current and evolving status of health care coverage, since the provisions for mental and physical care are likely to impact all of the people we serve (as well as ourselves and our families).

As we write this preface to our latest edition, we cannot help but note the alarming rise in violence in the world and in our society. Although crime statistics in many of our cities have shown a remarkable decrease, school and workplace shootings, explosions, and similar violent acts have shattered many lives and occupied the worried attention of pundits and citizens. The secure worlds of the middle class schoolyard and workplace have been irretrievably altered. Along with the loss of life has gone a substantial amount of our sense of security and comfort.

Many of the gains that have been made in civil liberties, in communication technology, and in the embrace of a multicultural society may be whittled back as our government attempts to stop further terrorist acts. We cannot even begin to estimate what losses this will bring to our clients.

Perhaps the most important message of this text in all its editions is that our work is always intimately connected with the history, current events, and future of society. Every shift in the social fabric has huge impact on the daily lives of the people you are learning to help. In our many years in the field, there has never been another time when knowledgeable, skillful human service workers have been so needed. To act with and on behalf of clients and communities, students need to understand the root causes that underpin social service interventions and social policy. As new workers enter this field, they will be called on to be generalists, to be able, for example, to counsel elderly citizens so that they can obtain the services that will sustain them in their homes. Later on, human service workers might need to advocate for them when a faceless bureaucrat decides the services are no longer needed. When day care facilities or job-training programs for teen parents lose their funding, we need to know how to create coalitions with other groups to go to the courts and legislative chambers. We need to know how to design new programs or protect existing ones. But you will also have to learn how to present your arguments in a professional way, marshaling accurate evidence of need, proposing creative strategies, and documenting the potential for success of your programs.

NEW TO THIS EDITION

- A new Chapter 6, Social Welfare Programs and Policies, combines the information from the previous edition's Chapters 6 and 7 for a more concise presentation about how social welfare programs and poverty interrelate.
- An expanded chapter on working with diversity (Chapter 7), with updated discussions of immigration and working with LGBTQ clients.
- Additional and updated interviews in Chapter 2.
- Numerous updates to reflect the current state of the field of human services.
- An increased focus on practical application.
- Updated references throughout.
- Many new photos and graphics to help illustrate chapter content and to make the chapters engaging. In addition, a new streamlined design makes the text easier to read.
- The addition of Learning Outcomes at the beginnings of chapters to let students know what they will learn by reading the chapter.
- Now available with MyLab for Helping Professions. See the separate description at the end of this preface.

ORGANIZATION OF THE TEXT

To make this book more accessible to the beginning student, we have organized the chapters into three sections. In the first, we present the context of human service work, answering the major questions students are probably asking: "What is a human service agency, what do human service workers do, and what are the barriers that keep people from using human services?" Then we describe how human service work has changed through the years, discuss different strategies, and explore the attitudes, values, skills, and knowledge that bind together all workers, regardless of their problem area or credentials. After that, we discuss the conflicts and dilemmas that are likely to occur as we try to incorporate the values of our field into our daily practice. Finally, we pose and then try to answer questions about the social welfare system. We discuss the major social welfare programs and how we can keep ourselves up to date so we can guide our clients through the ever-changing maze of rules and regulations.

In the second section, we examine in detail the ways in which human service workers implement each of the direct and indirect program strategies. This section begins with a chapter on working with diversity. Subsequent chapters describe the skills involved in interviewing, working on individual cases, working with groups, planning programs, and organizing to change or improve programs.

In the third and shortest section, we present information that human service workers need to know about the legal issues that are likely to be involved in our work. Fittingly, the final chapter offers words of wisdom about keeping your spark alive and avoiding human service worker burnout. This is an especially important chapter because in the next several years all of us will be challenged to work harder and more creatively until the current wave of slash-and-burn budget cutting has abated, if it ever does.

FEATURES OF THE TEXT

Each chapter ends with a summary, so you can review the information that has been presented. These summaries can also be read before beginning the chapter, which can be helpful to the student who likes to study a road map in advance of a journey. Questions for discussion and resources for further information on the topics just discussed are also included at the end of each chapter.

Interviews with human service workers and quotes from case records throughout the text keep it lively and help readers feel greater empathy for problems that might be distant from their own life experiences. The interviews of human service workers that are included in each of the chapters are primarily composites that include the work of several people who have held similar positions in human service agencies. The many political cartoons and photos are intended to add depth to the narrative, stimulate thinking, and raise questions for discussion.

We hope that the charts, checklists, and samples of interventions will continue to be useful as you venture out to an internship or job. All the examples have been drawn from the authors' many years of work in social service agencies. Among them, we have had experience in a family service agency, a neighborhood poverty program, a shelter for youth at risk, a large recreation center, and a research bureau. The authors have taught for many years in college human service programs. On campus and in community agencies, they have led training groups and done research on adoption, children and adults with special needs, mental health, and the social welfare system. Additionally, they have raised their own children and have struggled through the many crises and developmental milestones that families confront. They have struggled to provide support to their families and have turned to other human service workers when they needed more guidance.

This field of human services is filled with many "alphabet agencies" and jargon, so when new terms are introduced, they are highlighted and their definitions are provided in a Glossary at the end of the text.

ALSO AVAILABLE WITH MYLAB HELPING PROFESSIONS

This title is also available with MyLab Helping Professions, an online homework, tutorial, and assessment program organized around the 2015 Council on Social Work Education Educational Policy and Accreditation Standards (CSWE EPAS) and designed to work with the text to engage students and improve results. Within its structured environment, students see key concepts demonstrated through video clips, practice what they learn, test their understanding, and receive feedback to guide their learning and ensure they master key learning outcomes.

- **Learning Outcomes and Standards** measure student results. MyLab Helping Professions organizes all assignments around the 2015 CSWE EPAS and essential learning outcomes.
- **Video- and Case-Based Exercises** develop decision-making skills. Video- and Case-based Exercises introduce students to a broader range of clients, and therefore a broader range of presenting problems, than they will encounter in their own pre-professional experiences. Students watch videos of actual high-quality role-play scenarios. They are then guided in their analysis of the videos through a series of short-answer questions with expert feedback. These exercises help students develop the techniques and decision-making skills they need to be effective helping professionals.
- **Licensure Quizzes** help students prepare for certification. Automatically graded, multiple-choice Licensure Quizzes help students prepare for their certification examinations, master foundational course content, and improve their performance in the course.

- **Video Library** offers a wealth of observation opportunities. The Video Library provides more than 400 video clips of actual sessions and high-quality role plays in a database organized by topic and searchable by keyword. The Video Library includes every video clip from the MyLab Helping Professions courses plus additional videos from Pearson's extensive library of helping professionals in action. Instructors can create additional assignments around the videos or use them for in-class activities. Students can expand their observation experiences to include other course areas and increase the amount of time they spend watching expert helpers in action.

ACKNOWLEDGMENTS

We thank the following reviewers for their input on revising this edition: Natalie Cooper, Kentucky Community and Technical College; Susan Holbrook, Southwestern Illinois College; Heather Jones, Luzerne County Community College; and Tim Lindsey, Bethel College, Mckenzie.

A NOTE ABOUT THE AUTHORS OF THIS EDITION

It needs to be noted that Betty Reid Mandell, who co-authored the first eight editions of this text with me, has recently died. For this ninth edition, Paul Dann and Lynn Peterson have worked on revising the chapters for which Betty Mandell had taken primary responsibility. As current practitioners in the field of human services, they bring updated perspectives to those chapters. Also, I had the privilege of getting to know and respect them when they were Human Service majors at Northeastern University and students in the Human Service classes that I taught. I have enormous appreciation for their efforts to keep this text current and to continue our past efforts to make it highly readable and user-friendly. We all welcome each of our readers to the seesaw!

Barbara Schram, 2019
Emeritus Professor,
Northeastern University

To our clients, our students, our colleagues, and our families,
with thanks for all they have taught us.

ABOUT THE AUTHORS

Barbara Schram graduated from Antioch College, and received master's degrees in both sociology and social work from Columbia University and a doctorate from Harvard University with a specialization in education and social policy. She worked as the program direction of a large recreational and cultural organization, planning programs for children and young adults and supervising staff who delivered these services.

Barbara spent several years as the director of a community agency in a low-income urban area, helping parents become involved in their children's education and effect changes in the schools that better reflected their cultural background and values. She spent 26 years at Northeastern University, where she originated and then taught in the Human Services program. She designed appropriate courses and supervised student internships.

Barbara has done extensive volunteer work with citizen groups involved in interracial and special needs adoptions, improving services for persons with learning disabilities, and improving prison education programs.

In addition to this text she has written more than 20 articles and a book entitled *Creating the Small-Scale Social Program: From Idea to Implementation to Evaluation.*

Betty Reid Mandell was Professor Emerita at Bridgewater State College in Massachusetts. She was the editor of *The Crisis of Caregiving: Social Welfare Policy in the United States,* Palgrave/Macmillan, 2010, as well as the co-editor of *New Politics.*

Paul L. Dann, Ph.D., is the Director of the MS in Clinical Mental Health Counseling and the MS in Human Services at New England College, and has taught at the College since 1997. He teaches Cultural Foundations, Graduate Capstone, and Research Methods. Paul has his MA and Ph.D. in Human and Organizational Systems and also serves as the Executive Director of NFI North, a non-profit multi-service mental health and human services agency providing care to children, youth, families, and adults throughout New Hampshire and Maine.

Paul is and has served as a Board member of multiple non-profit and behavioral health organizations. He is a former Research Fellow at the Institute for Social Innovation and trains nationally on effective leadership development, resiliency, and culture. Paul is a dynamic public speaker, and in his free time, he's the front man for a regionally recognized blues band.

Lynn Peterson was a student of Barbara Schram's at Northeastern University, where she earned her Bachelor's degree in Human Services. The practical, hands-on approach of *The Introduction to Human Services* and *Creating the Small-Scale Social Programs* books provided her with essential skills to working in the field of human services. In her "Strategies of Intervention" class with Dr. Schram, Ms. Peterson's team planned and executed a successful human service professionals' retreat on Thompson Island. Following work as a congregate housing coordinator for Elder Services of the Merrimack Valley, Ms. Peterson earned a Master's degree in Urban and Environmental Policy and Planning at Tufts University, with a focus on affordable housing. She has worked in the affordable housing field as a planner, developer, and funder. While working at the Women's Institute for Housing and Economic Development, she developed supportive housing and education programs for low-income women. She was a contributing author to *Shut Out: Low Income Mothers and Higher Education in Post-Welfare America.*

BRIEF CONTENTS

CONTENTS

What Are Human Services?
What Do Human Service Workers Do?

Source: Rawpixel.com/Shutterstock

Learning Outcomes

- Students will be able to frame an overall statement of what human service workers do.

- By reading the three accounts of one student's struggles with her parent's alcohol use disorder, readers will be able to identify 25 different human service roles that she encountered.

- Through learning about the daily work of a person who oversees a substance use disorder program, students will be able to identify the various human service roles she fills.

- Students will be able to describe both the internal and external barriers that keep people who have problems from finding the help they need.

How do we explain what human service workers do? That is a logical question for a beginning student to ask and for an introductory text to answer. But the answers are not as straightforward as you might expect. A professor of human services described the challenge of answering this seemingly obvious question.

> While I was in college, my friends and family kept asking me, in a challenging way, "Exactly what is a human services major?" They wondered what a big guy like me was doing studying for that kind of a field. I'd try to give them a short, clear answer. They never seemed completely satisfied.
>
> That was irritating enough when I was in college, but even after I graduated with a bachelor's degree in human services, my friends and relatives kept right on asking me what I was really going to do to earn my living. If I fell back on my stock answer, about how I was in the business of helping people to help themselves, I always sounded hopelessly muddled.

How do you explain all the things you are *really* doing when it looks as if you are just "hanging out" on a street corner with a group of teenagers? As a young **outreach worker** hired by my town, "hanging out" was a large part of my job description. Sometimes I'd be playing pool or shooting baskets with the kids in the local recreation center. Later on in the day, I might spend a few hours drinking coffee with a family around their kitchen table. I took kids on camping trips. I held their hands when they ended up in the hospital with an overdose of drugs or a broken leg from a gang fight or football game. I'd chew the fat with the clerks at juvenile court and visit with my kids going in or coming out of the courtroom.

I was a sounding board for the parents, the kids, the local merchants, and the police. Of course, I can't point to an adult and say it's because of my work that he made it up and out of trouble. But I think that what I did made a difference in some of the kids' futures.

Twenty years later, one of my students complained to me that she had the same problem. How could she justify the usefulness of spending three hours sitting in front of a television set with five adults who have developmental disabilities? How could she explain what she was doing when she was eating a hamburger in a fast food restaurant or throwing a Frisbee around the park with her clients? She'd get frustrated when one of her friends would say, "You get paid for doing that? You have to go to college to learn how to do that? Now, my major"—engineering, business, computers, etc.—"that's real work!"

Helping is such a natural part of our everyday lives that it is hard to think of it as a specialized activity for which people must be trained. Think back over the past few weeks. Chances are that someone—a coworker, friend, or relative—has asked you for help. Perhaps a friend was having trouble with a love relationship and needed to talk about it. If you listened with empathy and tried to understand her view of the problem, you were giving a human service.

An attentive listener and a strong shoulder to cry on might have been all that your friend needed. However, if the same type of problem continued to occur, she might need more than a warm, accepting friend. She might need to talk with an experienced counselor who has helped other young adults juggle the conflicting needs of intimacy and independence.

PERSONAL PROBLEMS ARE A PART OF ALL OF OUR LIVES

All of us, at different times in our lives, will be on both sides of the helping process, giving support or asking for support. Problems are part of living, and no one—regardless of education, income, or profession—is immune. When the economy dips or a hurricane hits the coast, thousands of people from all walks of life lose their jobs, their homes, and their sense of security. If we live long enough, we will have to cope with the death and illness of many people we care about. And throughout the lifespan, we will face our own critical junctures, transitions, and changing capacities.

People can follow many different routes to find help. The route they choose is likely to be influenced by:

- The nature of the problem
- Someone's hunch about the causes of the problem
- The resources available in the local community
- The cost and the person's ability to pay
- The climate of the times that creates fads about "the right thing to do when you have problem X, Y, or Z"
- The history of the circumstances that person is confronting
- Luck or chance.

HUMAN SERVICE NETWORKS OR DELIVERY SYSTEMS

Referrals are sometimes made by word of mouth. When people are in pain, they often ask the advice of someone they trust. A member of the clergy, a doctor, or even a hairstylist can often inspire the courage to walk into a social service agency. Many now **Google search** the web for information about their problems and for suggestions of places to go for help. The opinions of people who have used different services are, of course, very varied. A potential client must sort through a maze of conflicting thoughts and feelings. Too much information can be just as debilitating as too little, but that is a common problem of our cyber culture. Human service workers spend a great amount of time, energy, and creativity getting accurate messages out to the public. Throughout the pages of this text and in your own work in the field, you will quickly discover that there is no simple path to finding help. Because people are complex, human service problems are multifaceted. So we have had to create a variety of social services. Programs that cluster around one particular problem area are called **human service networks** or **delivery systems**.

A paper written by Kathy Holbrook, a first-year student at Westwood Community College, paints a vivid picture of the variety and complexity of one of these networks. The assignment was called "The Helpee Paper." Kathy's instructor asked the students to think back to a time in their lives when they faced a painful personal crisis. They were asked to describe that situation and then evaluate the help they received from professionals, volunteers, family, or friends.

In the many years the instructor has assigned this paper, there has never been a student who was unable to remember a painful episode. Students have written about homesickness at camp; the death of a pet; problems with drugs, alcohol, and eating disorders; the divorce of parents; and conflicts around the choice of a college or career. Because the students select their topics, they decide how much personal information they want to reveal.

Some students choose to share their papers with the class. While listening to these stories, class members feel the intensity of the emotions that conflict engenders. They also learn about the complex barriers that surround the acts of asking for and receiving help. In addition, the students receive a true-to-life picture of the patchwork quilt of agencies and worker roles that make up each of the human service networks.

After reading about Kathy's attempts to tread her way through the human service network of alcohol use disorders, you will read about two other paths Kathy might have followed if her problems had developed differently. As you read these three accounts, try to identify all the human service agencies and workers Kathy encountered.

My Experience Receiving Help

by Kathy Holbrook

When I read the assignment for this paper, I had mixed feelings. On the one hand, it opens up a lot of wounds. On the other hand, I know that if I want to be a human service worker, I have to learn from my own experiences. And every time I talk about the problems my family had with my dad's alcoholism, it can help someone else. That's the main lesson I learned from the Alcoholics Anonymous (AA) meetings I've attended. Well, I guess I've started this paper already.

(continued)

I can't pinpoint when the problem began. As I look back, I realize the problem was always with us, but I didn't have a name for it. I thought the way we lived was just the way things were in everyone's family. We had a big house in Westwood. My father worked for years for the same stock brokerage firm. He could make or lose thousands of dollars a day of other people's money. It was high pressure all the time.

When I was little, we didn't see much of Dad. He had to work very hard to keep up with the rest of the community. People where we live keep moving: a bigger house, a pool, a summer place on the lake, a boat, Ivy League colleges for their kids. Mom was the "typical" housewife. She did all the chauffeuring to Scouts and swim team, and came to all our plays alone when Dad was in the city. The first ten years, it seemed like we were mostly like everyone else. I knew Mom and Dad always kept liquor around, because they did a lot of entertaining.

But in my first year of high school, everything got worse. Sometimes I'd get up in the morning and Dad would be asleep on the sofa with his clothes on. Sometimes he wouldn't get up for breakfast. I'd hear Mom phoning his boss, saying he was sick or that he couldn't get the car started. I began to notice that she often didn't tell the truth about Dad.

Then he started coming home during the day. He'd drink until he'd pass out, sometimes right in the living room. I'd ask Mom if I could have friends over, and she'd say I couldn't. After a while, no one was invited to our house for dinner parties anymore. I felt as if we were living in a cave with a locked door across it. Mom even kept the window blinds down in the afternoon. I think she didn't want the neighbors to see Dad at home, especially when he hadn't shaved or changed his clothes.

I tried to talk to my brothers about it, but they would blow me off. My brother Dennis and Dad got into such a bad fight that Dennis moved into his girlfriend's room at college. Chuck, my oldest brother, has always been a bookworm. He'd just crawl into his room and read or listen to music all the time. Even at dinner, we were never together anymore. If we were all there, Mom was nervous or Dad would get up and leave in the middle. She'd cook a big meal and he wouldn't come home or he'd say the food was no good and he'd yell. He never hit her, but he would slam his glass down so it would break or knock over his chair when he left the table.

My mom started to go to church a lot. The priest came to our house to talk to my dad. Finally, I came home from school one day and Mom said we were leaving. We would stay at my aunt's house until Dad packed his things and left. Then we could come back. That's when she told me that he was an alcoholic. He was sick and it wasn't his fault, but he had to make himself well if we were going to be a family again.

We stayed at my aunt's house for two weeks. Mom finally went to court and got a restraining order. The marshal made Dad leave the house, and he wasn't even supposed to visit us. The only time we got together was at the meetings with our psychologist, Dr. Hightower. I hated those sessions. My brother Dennis would shout insults, and Dad looked like he was going to cry. Chuck wouldn't say anything.

Mom and I started going to Al-Anon meetings together. That's a support group like AA, but it's for the families and friends of people who drink too much. I had one teacher at school whom I really liked, so one day I broke down and told her about Dad. She took me by the hand to see the school counselor. He was the one who got me to go to my first Alateen group. We all had problems with family members who are struggling with a substance use disorder. I went to see the counselor a few times during activities block. I liked talking to him alone in his office, but I wasn't comfortable in the group. There were kids in it I didn't trust. I was sure they would spread it around about my family being such a mess.

Dad went to an inpatient recovery center. His company wanted him back so badly that they sent someone to our home from the personnel department to convince him to go into a program. They were willing to pay for his treatment through his health insurance. We had family meetings with him at the hospital. My mom would see the same social worker because she was pretty depressed by now. I think she took medication for her nerves. He stayed there for three months. Then he went to the state rehabilitation office and got vocational counseling because he knew he couldn't go back to the tension of wheeling and dealing in the stock market. It was too stressful a place for him, and he thought that most of the people in his company drank too much at business lunches and dinners.

Last January, the whole family celebrated the seventh anniversary of Dad's sobriety. We went to his AA group. It was a terrific family reunion. Father Brian was there, too, because he had so much to do with helping my family get straightened out. The only dark spot is Dennis. He came to the party, but he is still very angry. He holds Dad responsible for all the bad times. Actually, I think Dennis is drinking now, too. He is very bitter.

I'm not glad that I had to go through this mess, but some good things came out of it. Dad is a really laid-back guy now. He sort of takes things as they come. He and Mom are closer than ever.

Through this, I got interested in the field of alcohol addiction counseling. I have paid my dues. I'd like to work in schools teaching kids about alcohol and drug abuse. I've been a member of Students Against Drunk Driving (SADD) and have become very self-confident. I can speak before groups now, and I don't feel like I have to please everyone anymore. I speak my mind.

Alternative Scenario 1: What Might Have Happened to Kathy

I came home from school one day, and Mom said we were leaving. We would stay at my aunt's house until Dad packed his things and left. Then we could come back. That's when she told me that he was addicted to alcohol. He was sick and it wasn't his fault, but he had to make himself well if we were going to be a family again.

Until then, Dad had never lifted a hand to anyone in the family, but now he was so angry with Mom, he tried to strangle her. Finally, Mom phoned a shelter for survivors of domestic violence called Renewal House. They sent a van to pick us up. Would you believe we heard about it from my aunt's cleaning woman? She had a sister who was a survivor of intimate partner violence and she lived there for a couple of months. They won't give out their address over the phone in case there is someone looking for you who might hunt you down and hurt you. They have to be secretive.

The whole thing was really humiliating and scary. But the center director was our lifeline. She told Mom about everything she needed to do. Mom started getting very short-tempered. I couldn't blame her, but it was awful for me. I didn't like living there and not being able to go to my friends' houses or to after-school clubs. All I did was go to school and come home. I went to a social worker at the Westwood Mental Health Clinic, but I didn't like him.

After two years, my folks got divorced. I have seen very little of my father, and it hurts that he doesn't call. He is remarried. Mom went back to school, so she was never around, and I hated where we lived. Dennis and Chuck have just gone their own ways.

By the time I began my sophomore year, the entire situation really got to me and I started to have thoughts of wanting to hurt myself. I called the Samaritans, a hotline for people who are thinking about suicide. The woman on the phone talked to me for a few nights and then suggested I go to Alateen at the Mt. Auburn Hospital. I stuck with that group and made a lot of friends there.

Now I am a member of ACOA, Adult Children of Alcoholics. Groups have been really important for me. There are other people out there like me, and we are tough survivors.

(continued)

I'm also active in SADD, Students Against Drunk Driving. I think when I finish my degree, I'd like to become an organizer. The women from MADD, Mothers Against Drunk Driving, are really dynamite people. I'd like to try to change the laws that make alcohol so available.

Alternative Scenario 2: What Might Have Happened to Kathy

Finally, I came home from school one day and Mom said we were leaving. We would stay at my aunt's house until Dad packed his things and left. That's when she told me that he was addicted to alcohol. He was sick and it wasn't his fault, but he had to make himself well if we were going to be a family again.

We stayed with my aunt and uncle for four or five months. I began to notice that Mom was changing. She had always had one or two drinks to keep my Dad company, but I never saw her as a drinker. She started not getting up to give me and Chuck breakfast. Some days, she didn't even get dressed.

I started not coming home so as to avoid the whole scene. I did a lot of stealing things from local stores. I always had a pocket full of change. I even tried drinking beer with the high school kids, but luckily it just made me fall asleep. I know that with both my parents being addicted to alcohol. I could easily become addicted also. I won't even take a social drink now.

The youth patrol officer would pick me up, give me a lecture, and send me home. The only things that still mattered to me were Scouts and my brothers. My Scout leader was more like a mother than Mom was. She took me to a child-guidance clinic and the worker there tried to get my Mom to come in and talk. When she wouldn't do it, they filed a complaint with the Department of Social Services. They accused her of neglecting me and took me out of my aunt's house. I was very angry, but the worker found me a foster home. I didn't have a choice, so I went. Ms. Braun is an older, single lady whose kids have grown up. She was what I needed, strict but very loving.

Ms. Braun got a lawyer from legal services, and she fought to adopt me. She doesn't always understand about this generation. At times, I resent her. I was in a group for teenagers who have been adopted. It was good to talk it over with the leader and the other kids. I found out I had it really good. The leader signed me up to get a "big sister" from Catholic Charities. I could really talk to her. She was attending Westwood Community College. Dolores is the one who convinced me I could go to college and maybe study for the same degree.

For a while, I saw a psychiatrist, and I was on antidepressant medication. I don't feel I need to use it now that I am getting on with my life.

I sometimes think about what would have happened to me if I hadn't had Dolores, my Scout leader, and my foster mother. They were able to see that even when I was acting up, I really did not want to be in trouble. Even the youth patrol officer gave me positive support. He had the right combination of toughness and caring.

Though I'm in human services now, I want a job in a business firm. I want to dress up, buy a decent car, and get away from all of these problems.

The Helpers That Kathy Encountered in the Three Versions of Her Story

In the three scenarios described in the previous section, Kathy, a young woman who could have been sitting next to you in a college class, encountered 25 different helpers. Although each had a different title and performed somewhat different tasks, they all offered human services. How many of these did you identify?

1. Priest
2. Psychologist
3. Family therapist

4. High school counselor
5. Teacher
6. Vocational counselor
7. Self-help group leaders (AA, Al-Anon, Alateen, ACOA)
8. Personnel department counselor
9. Rehabilitation specialist
10. Addiction counselor
11. Social worker (at drug clinic)
12. Shelter director
13. Shelter volunteers
14. Hotline worker
15. Organizer for a social action group (e.g., SADD, MADD)
16. Transitional assistance counselor
17. Therapist (in college counseling center)
18. Scout leader
19. Youth patrol officer
20. Child protective services worker
21. Foster parent
22. Adoption caseworker
23. Lawyer (at public legal services)
24. Psychiatrist
25. Volunteer Big Sister

All of these 25 people brought to their work a different mixture of education, training, and life experience. In Kathy's high school, there might have been a school counselor, school social worker, or school psychologist. Any one of them might have started Kathy on the path to finding services. All of them have been certified by their school boards and have advanced degrees.

The family therapist, the counselors, the rehabilitation and vocational workers, and the shelter staff director are likely to have graduated from college with two- or four-year degrees. Some might have studied beyond college, earning specialized degrees in clinical psychology, counseling, social work, rehabilitation, health education, or perhaps one of the newer fields, such as family systems therapy, addictions counseling, or human sexuality.

Several of the workers Kathy encountered had little or no formal education in the helping professions. Hotline workers, mutual aid leaders, and foster parents often have education and training totally unrelated to the helping professions. For some of these individuals, providing human services is their central career, but for most of them, it is something they do on a part-time, interim, or volunteer basis.

In the past, these part-time or volunteer workers were not always viewed as an important part of the human service network. In recent years, however, that attitude has begun to change. Now these workers are being offered on-the-job training through workshops and seminars. Often they can earn academic credits that enable them to obtain college degrees and grow in knowledge, self-confidence, and public respect.

Helpers Have Many Different Agency Affiliations, Backgrounds, and Orientations

Human service workers are found in a wide variety of settings, ranging from a storefront center to the carpeted offices of the personnel department in a high-tech firm. Some human services, especially for the middle and upper classes, are provided in the homes or offices of private practitioners. But the majority of professional human service workers are financed by the public and are found in social service departments, community mental health centers, hospitals and health clinics, college counseling centers, and ministers' or rabbis' offices. Many private nonprofit groups, such as the Family Service Association, the Jewish Family Service, Catholic Charities, the Protestant Federation, and the Salvation Army, conduct large numbers of direct-care and social change programs. Although most human services are provided on an outpatient basis, some are given in **residential treatment centers** or **community residences**.

Many valuable social services are offered by citizen groups, which conduct programs that advocate for the rights of tenants, immigrants, veterans, homeless families, or some other special population. Citizen groups often hire human service workers to educate and mobilize the public. They work toward changing behaviors such as substance use, violence, or destruction of the environment. Often they lobby public officials or the courts to change the way social programs are funded and laws are enforced.

Although there is no way to collect accurate statistics on the number of people in this country who conduct or attend mutual aid groups, it is possible that these groups are now the single largest source of human services. These groups, usually patterned on the model developed by **Alcoholics Anonymous (AA)**, tackle every conceivable emotional, social, and physical problem that affects some subgroup in the community.

Most human service agencies are entirely or partially funded through grants from the local, state, or federal government. Many others are private nonprofit groups, often sponsored by religious denominations that raise money from fees, public appeals, and philanthropic foundations.

A smaller but fast-growing type of agency is the private, profit-making one. Some of these operate on the model pioneered by the fast-food restaurant chains. Entrepreneurs develop a model for a preschool child care center or to serve people with head injuries, for example. These agencies make their profit entirely from the fees paid by consumers and insurance companies or in performing under a contract with a public agency. Opinions are many and mixed about the emergence of for-profit social services. This is a controversial topic that you will likely debate in your classes and internships. This movement is often called the "privatization of social services."

Most staff members earn a salary, but agency volunteers work just for the gratification they receive. And there are differences in the hours that workers are on duty. A family worker in a day care center has to work evening hours to telephone or meet with working parents; a counselor for a group of adults with disabilities might live in a community residence, working a few days a week around the clock.

Some agencies expect their workers, volunteer or paid, to operate within a particular treatment model or theoretical orientation. Their approach to the clients may be built on the theories of Sigmund Freud, Erik Erikson, or B. F. Skinner. You will read the work of these pioneer scholars in introductory psychology or human development classes. Other theories, such as those of Carl Rogers, Jean Baker Miller, or William Glasser, you are likely to read about in counseling courses or hear spoken of in your fieldwork (Hackney & Cormier, 2013; Okun & Kantrowitz, 2015). The **12-step** and **co-dependency** models, on which many addiction support groups are based, are currently much in vogue.

In addition, some agencies adhere to a specific set of religious or ethical principles. A staff member in a social service department of a Catholic hospital, for example, would be expected to suggest to clients only those options that are acceptable to the overarching principles of that religion. These agencies are currently referred to as "faith-based social services."

There is no overall approach that everyone in the human service field agrees is the most effective. Variations among counselors' styles make it difficult to compare their methods and outcomes. With no clear evidence that one theorist has found the best method for creating mental health or social change, most counselors evolve a method created out of bits and pieces of many theories. This eclectic approach is further refined through years of experience. Finally, styles are filtered through the individual personalities of workers and the demands of the population they work with. With the widespread movement to **managed health care** programs, for example, much of a counselor's action plan is dictated by how long the client's health care provider will pay for mental health services.

Differences in social welfare laws from state to state add more diversity to the field. As you read about the history of social welfare in the United States, you will learn about the tug of war that has been going on between the federal government and the states in responding to social needs. Diversity and uniformity of social programs exist side by side. On the one hand, you could travel from California to Maine and find reasonably similar **Head Start** preschool programs in each state. On the other hand, if you visited foster care agencies in each state as you went from west to east, you would find 50 different sets of rules and regulations. Head Start is a federal program, so the rules that govern it are made in Washington, D.C., and disseminated to each state. But foster care and adoption laws are made on the state level, so we find wide variations in these programs. These discrepancies underscore our assertion that human service workers cannot assume that they know what social services exist, even in their hometown. In order to practice their profession, they must know how to construct a current, accurate profile of the services available in each community.

Source: Marcel Mooij/Shutterstock

Many workers try to help people with disabilities engage in a wide variety of life activities. These two men are practicing for a mini-marathon they will enter the next week.

FINDING THE APPROPRIATE HUMAN SERVICES PROGRAM WITHIN ALL THIS VARIATION

Your local town hall is usually the first place to begin the search for an appropriate social service agency for a particular human problem. There you will probably find the local health, recreation, and education departments; juvenile and elder services; and the like. The workers in these departments can describe the social services they fund, monitor, or license. They might have listings of services in each area.

The next sources we turn to in exploring the human service network are the directories of social services published in hard copy or on the Internet by various private agencies. One type of directory is comprehensive; it lists a broad range of social problems and the agencies that deal with them. This sort of directory is generally compiled and distributed by the group that coordinates and raises funds for social services in a particular town. Such groups include the United Way, Community Chest, Community Council, Social Service Coalition, and Red Feather Agency. The table of contents of this kind of directory might start off looking like this.

a	b	c
abortion	bereavement support	child care centers
abuse, physical	birth control	children's services
addiction	block associations	consumer protection
adoption	bulimia	correctional institutions
aging		counseling
AIDS		

The other types of directories are problem specific; they focus on one particular service area. Individual booklets might list all the services for the developmentally delayed, addiction support groups, or early-childhood centers. Some directories are published by national organizations, which have chapters across the country; others are just for local child care centers, children's services, consumer protection divisions, or correctional institutions.

Some directories list only objective information about an agency: location, activities, costs, and eligibility requirements. Some on-line subjective directories provide a more in-depth picture by describing agency services and then evaluating their quality of service. Subjective directories are much more difficult to compile than factual listings. Each agency must be visited, all its materials must be read, and data must be found that offer feedback on the care that clients have received. And they must then be updated regularly.

Many agencies maintain hotline phone services. One can call them, for example, to get information on sexually transmitted diseases, learn about various forms of cancer, or find a service agency for stepfamilies. Another phone service, called 2-1-1, provides free and confidential assistance and referrals to local human service resources in the area of the caller. Recognizing that an aging population, as well as the growing number of young people moving from one city to another, face a host of perplexing life issues with no one to turn to for advice, this service will connect callers to agencies whose job it is to help people facing a crisis. Perhaps the weather is cold and there is no heat in the house, or perhaps a single mother cannot leave for her job because the babysitter has not shown up, or maybe there is no food in the house and a pay check or disability check will not arrive for days; now these people can dial 211 on the phone and find assistance.

Newspapers also contain information about new agencies that are opening or about the special projects and problems of agencies. The calendar page of your local newspaper often lists

1997, SEATTLE POST-INTELLIGENCER GREENBERG

Source: © Steve Greenberg/Seattle Post Intelligencer

In recent years, there has been a big push to get people out of what many deemed a "failed" welfare system. However, too often, the buck has simply been passed from federal to state and local governments with insufficient job opportunities and job training, leaving families without the money for food, shelter, and health care.

workshops, seminars, and meetings of support groups. Often notices are placed by social agencies seeking volunteers or donations. Computer bulletin boards and chat rooms on the Internet can also be rich sources of information on virtually every social problem and program. In addition, the classified section of a local newspaper as well as listings on web sites can provide clues to the social service networks in a town. A listing of services for older adults might include items such as these.

- American Association of Retired Persons (AARP)
- Congregate Living programs
- Council on Aging
- Day-activity programs
- Road Scholar educational programs
- Legal Services for Older Adults
- Exercise programs
- Homemaker/home health aides
- Meals on Wheels
- Elder living communities
- Recreation centers
- Residences
- Retired and Senior Volunteer Program (RSVP)
- Shuttle bus service
- Social action or issue groups
- Visiting nurses

INTERNAL AND EXTERNAL BARRIERS THAT PREVENT PEOPLE FROM GETTING HELP

Despite the problems caused by her father's addiction to alcohol, Kathy was quite fortunate in some ways. Her town had a variety of social services, and she was able to find and use them. For many people, things do not work out as well. Perhaps they resist seeking help or have difficulty locating, choosing, paying for, or using it.

Many barriers are encountered on the pathway to seeking help. When they are insurmountable, small problems balloon into large, often tragic ones. Because barriers interfere with our ability to serve prospective clients, we need to develop skills to recognize them and try to overcome them.

Some barriers, such as feelings of indecision and ambivalence, are inevitable. How could Kathy's father be certain that he had crossed the line that separates a social drinker from someone who is addicted to alcohol? How could he be certain that he needed professional help? How could he be sure that the hospital or group he ultimately chose was the right one for him? These kinds of feelings we call **internal barriers** to receiving help.

Other, more tangible barriers can stand in the way. Often there are no beds available in a detoxification unit when the person is ready. Frequently there is not enough money to train or pay staff to learn about a new treatment modality. The red tape of bureaucrats in government and in the insurance industry often interferes with a well- thought-out service plan. We call these **external barriers**.

We cannot always remove or mitigate the impact of internal and external barriers, but we must be aware of them. Both the people in the program and the worker interact within the constraints these barriers impose and are challenged to work creatively around them, using all the intervention strategies we will describe in Chapter 3.

Following is a list of barriers to finding and using human services. The first six are primarily internal barriers that will need to be dealt with in the therapeutic relationship. The last five are more external to the person seeking help and are most appropriately dealt with by using the strategies of organizing and advocacy. But here, as with most categories, lines do blur. Each of the first ten barriers is followed by some inner thoughts or questions that reflect them. We will discuss the last one in more detail.

1. **The Difficulty of Evaluating the Seriousness of a Problem**

   • Does my child have a learning disability that needs special help, or is she just developing a little bit more slowly than the other kids in the class?
   • Is it normal to be so furious at my parents? Are other teenagers as depressed as I am?
   • Is this kid in my class just mischievous, or is there some other more serious problem? Does he just have a high energy level, or does he actually have attention-deficit hyperactivity disorder?

2. **The Tendency to Deny the Gravity of a Problem**

   • I'm just a social drinker who sometimes has a bit too much. I can stop anytime I decide to. Can I really?
   • Well, I know he hits me once in a while. But don't all marriages go through rough spots?
   • There is no discrimination in this company; we just can't seem to find any qualified supervisors who are not white and male. No one can say I didn't try, can they?

3. **The Fear of Being Judged, Labeled, or Punished**

   • If I tested positive for HIV, will I lose my job and my medical insurance? Will my family support me?

- If I ask for an evaluation of my child's learning problems, will he be labeled developmentally delayed or be placed in a low track for the rest of his schooling?
- I know I don't have enough food in the house, but if I apply for the Supplemental Nutrition Assistance Program (SNAP), will my neighbors begin referring to me as a "welfare cheat"?

4. **The Suspicion or Distrust of Human Service Workers and Agencies**

- I know they assure you that complaints of child abuse are anonymous, but how do I know they won't give out my name? Maybe my neighbor will come after me.
- If I admit how mad I get at my child, will they try to take her away from me?
- If I agree to a voluntary commitment to the hospital for an evaluation, will I be permanently confined against my will?

5. **The Shame of Not Being Able to Solve One's Own Problems**

- I don't see any other men bursting into tears when they get turned down for a job. Why can't I act like a "real" man?
- I was always taught that you don't air your dirty linen in public; so, although I know the landlord is not giving me enough heat, won't I look like a crybaby if I complain to the rent board?
- How can I ask for help paying my medical bills? My family has always taken care of its own.

6. **Fear of the Unknown**

- If we start marital counseling and I say what I really think, will we end up in divorce court?
- Maybe this school isn't as good as it should be, but if the parents start making decisions, won't it get worse? What do they know about education?
- Living at home might be lonely for our son, who has developmental delays, but maybe when he's older we'll think about his moving into a community residence. How can we be sure he won't be hurt if he moves out into the world?

7. **The Difficulties of Choosing the Appropriate Program and Helper**

- I've heard about three programs for children with autism; how do I know which one is best?
- Our committee has interviewed six candidates for the job of hotline director, and they are all different. What kind of person (race, gender, age, degree) would make the best director?
- My family has been going to this clinic for three years, and we don't seem to be getting along any better. Whom can I talk with to see if maybe we should try another approach?

8. **The Inadequacy of Services**

- Will there be anyone in that program who understands my culture and speaks my language?
- Will any of the other staff have the same disability that I do?
- No one wants to have this prison (halfway house for people with substance use disorders, drop-in center for teenagers) in the neighborhood; should we locate it on the edge of town, even though it can't be reached by public transportation?

9. **The High Cost of Services**

- We don't have enough money for our day camp, so we have to save the spaces for those most in need. But how do you decide whom to reject?
- I know that your mom needs assisted living, but Medicaid doesn't pay the full cost, and we never get those payments on time anyway.

10. Past History, Reputation, or Public Image of a Program

- First it was the antipoverty program, then Model Cities, and now it's privatization. I've seen them all come and go. Our neighborhood never seems to get any better. Why should I participate in this new program?
- With all the taxes I pay, why do the schools still turn out kids who can't read?
- As a legislator, I'm convinced that this town does not need another shelter for the homeless. Do you think the social workers complain about problems so they can keep their jobs?

11. Myths and Lack of Information About the Human Services

Because the human service field is so broad and the barriers to finding and using help pervasive, the public can understandably be confused.

The public sees many professionals—firefighters, doctors, teachers—doing their jobs; this is not necessarily the case with human service workers. We don't wear uniforms or have any observable symbols or tools of our trade. People usually visualize the human service professional primarily in the role of therapist, counselor, or welfare investigator, working one-on-one to solve individual problems or ferret out wrongdoing. Although these are important roles, they do not show the full dimensions of human service work.

Instead of working in a one-on-one counseling relationship with Kathy, for example, some human service workers tackled the problem of substance use by trying to change the social system that supports it:

- They made speeches about the need for funding substance use education programs.
- They designed training programs for school and private industry personnel to combat substance use.
- They met with legislators to change the laws governing the advertising and sale of addictive substances.
- They conducted research to find out what kinds of prevention programs work best.
- They published newsletters, books, and journal articles that disseminated the wisdom they have gleaned about substance use prevention and treatment.
- They designed computer programs so that information about addiction could be easily retrieved.

These social change activities are just as important as the counseling interventions that the public identifies as the province of human service workers. Yet the media does little to help the public get a well-rounded picture of the varied work of the field. Television programs show the lives of doctors, emergency medical technicians, lawyers, detectives, newspaper reporters, and an occasional teacher, but rarely those of a human service worker.

Worse than the paucity of information about the field are the myths and misinformation projected by the popular media using human service workers as the objects of ridicule: "Hello," says the client. "Hmmm, now what do you really mean by that?" asks the counselor.

A PARADOX

When we consider the barriers strewn along the path to getting help, we should think about them in their current context. When placed in perspective, these barriers reveal a frustrating paradox.

Source: Courtesy of Barbara Schram

Encouraging responsible behavior and reducing the self-defeating cycle of substance use require creative approaches. This wrecked car raises frightening questions about the fate of its once-carefree driver. Change in drinking patterns is painstakingly slow, yet we believe that change is always possible.

Certainly, attitudes toward people with substance use disorders have improved. Thirty years ago, if a police officer had encountered Kathy's dad sleeping off his binge in a public park, he probably would have arrested him, and a judge might have charged him with disorderly conduct, public drunkenness, and the like. But by the time Kathy wrote this paper, many police were most likely aware that addiction is a disease.

So the barriers of inaccessibility and stigma, for example, should be toppling down for families facing the kinds of problems Kathy described. Right? Wrong! Strangely enough, this isn't happening. In this new millennium, there is controversy about whether health insurance plans should require mental health and addiction treatment coverage. At the same time, many citizens as well as those in government are questioning the effectiveness of publically funded social services and the manner in which they are delivered. In later chapters, we will return to these themes to see how they play out as human service workers try to ameliorate social problems in an ever more complex world.

CHOOSING OUR WORK ROLE IN A HUMAN SERVICE NETWORK

From one perspective, this wide range (some might call it a hodgepodge) of human service agencies can seem overwhelming to the those just starting a human service career. On the flip side of the coin, this incredible diversity offers workers a chance to find the particular combination of worker roles, agencies, people, populations, and problems that fits their unique talents.

As you read about Kathy's experiences, reflect on your own struggles to get help, or glance through directories or websites, you will probably be attracted to some human service roles and repelled by others. These are natural reactions. While one person thrives working with youngsters with cerebral palsy, another might drown in feelings of frustration or hopelessness. That same worker who cannot cope with a child with a physical disability might be able to coolly trade put-downs with the angriest teenager. One worker who can listen patiently and nonjudgmentally all day long to folks like Kathy's dad would be tongue-tied trying to convince the zoning board to let her agency purchase a building to house survivors of domestic violence, when the neighbors have organized to block the sale.

We need to tune in to our instinctive feelings of attraction or repulsion to different human service tasks and roles. But we also need to keep our options open. We often surprise ourselves by discovering that we can do work that we thought we could never tolerate. We can also find ourselves unstimulated by a work role that we always thought we wanted.

Currently many students are being trained to be human service **generalists**. A generalist is knowledgeable about a wide range of resources, strategies, and subgroups, and can operate comfortably in many agency roles. She does not necessarily identify with one human service subspecialty but works with a small number of people in need of services, helping them confront and solve the gamut of life's problems. The generalist is often a team member or an assistant whose daily tasks grow out of a job assignment that complements the role of other helping professionals.

Some students take the reverse path, specializing in a specific role from the start of their careers. Trained to work as addiction counselors or as mental health technicians, they develop depth rather than breadth. Later on they might need to expand their skills as priorities shift or as they move up the career ladder. Whichever direction students take at the start of their career, they will probably continue to do a significant amount of growing as they search for the academic degrees and experiences that suit them best.

Whether returning to school for advanced training or switching jobs, workers need to make choices about (1) the specific problems or populations they want to deal with, (2) the type of agency setting they enjoy, and (3) the strategies of intervention they are best at. These choices will be determined by:

- Personal attributes
- Lifestyles
- Ideologies
- Accessibility of certain occupational roles.

Our Personal Attributes

Many of us have been taught since childhood that talking about our good points is "bragging" or "showing off," but in the human services, we must develop insight into precisely what it is that we do best and what we do not do very well. We need to estimate what our chances of growth or change will be in a specific role.

Although the same values and attitudes are basic to all types of human service work, there are differences between the kinds of people who can do intensive, one-to-one counseling and those who fare best in the rough-and-tumble atmosphere of creating community or policy changes. Some of us are outgoing and articulate; others are more introspective and quiet. Some are comfortable filling a niche in a traditional structure; others like to be in charge or work alone. Each time we try a new field experience, meet clients and workers at different agencies, or read about human service work, we should try to visualize ourselves as full-time workers in that role. We need to figure out how its demands fit our personality and how much we are willing to change.

Our Lifestyles

Even as we start our human service education, we should think about the elements in an environment that bring out the best in us. Some of us, for example, are "night people," so working a 2:00 P.M. to 10:00 P.M. shift in a teen residence or running evening parents' groups would be a good fit. Others are "nine-to-fivers"; perhaps they will choose to work in a school or on the day shift at a hospital or mental health clinic. All jobs require some mix of time, location, and structure, dictated by the sorts of populations the agency serves.

Some people feel strongly about dressing in a certain fashion; however, that desire might not fit a particular setting or subgroup. Others insist on having privacy or a place of their own. Obviously, a live-in job in a residence might not suit them.

Although we need to compromise on certain issues, others are vital and legitimate personal needs. As our lives change, the kind of work that makes sense for us also changes. The choice of a specific role need not be lifelong. Optimally, it should support the other parts of our lives as family members and citizens. The broadness of the human service field offers a unique chance to shift gears as circumstances require.

Our Personal Ideologies

Each of us comes to human service work with a unique set of philosophies, drawn from our religion or a general ethical framework. These beliefs must be compatible with the work we do. If a person has strong religious convictions about war, contraception, suicide, special types of food, or days of rest, these must be taken into account in choosing a place to work. We must not be self-conscious about acknowledging the primacy of these issues in our lives. Usually, we can find jobs that allow their expression. Although our values will come under constant scrutiny in the course of learning about the field and though many values might change, they should never be suppressed. If we try to deny them, they may subtly affect our work.

Likewise, many of us have political beliefs about how society should be organized—our personal visions of utopia. We choose the human service work that seems to be moving the community in that direction. As long as our politics or visions do not engulf our work, they add dimension and intensity to it. Some jobs might make demands that we cannot in our own good conscience fulfill. We need to acknowledge these problems openly. Needless to say, having our own beliefs never means that we insist that our clients agree with us. If we have rigid beliefs, it may turn out that human services is not the right field for us.

Agencies in the Local Community

Throughout this text, we underscore the variety and changing nature of human service work. For example, priorities are not necessarily the same in a rural setting as in an urban center. Priorities might change as the population shifts in age or ethnicity or new inventions or technological advances affect people's lifestyles. Election results might redirect the agendas of local or national government. Some agencies might become obsolete and others expand when, for instance, the country is at war, is experiencing an economic recession, or seeks to establish better supports and programs for veterans, survivors of domestic violence, and other at-risk populations. Funding patterns can change dramatically in short periods. Sometimes the human services help to shape the political climate in the country; more often they are shaped by it.

You might, for example, read about shelters for young mothers who have AIDS. You might decide to work in one, only to discover that your state does not appropriate money for such

Source: Courtesy of Barbara Schram

As our lives evolve through marriage, raising children, caring for older parents, facing an empty nest, or perhaps moving to a new area, our work life needs to accommodate those changes.

shelters. This does not necessarily mean you won't ever work in one. Perhaps you will first have to join with others and use your organizational skills to create a public outcry for such programs. Once successful, you can retool, using your social change skills less and using your counseling or caregiving skills more.

To get a visceral feeling for the highs, lows, and realities of human service work, let's meet Stephanie Lake, a worker whom Kathy might have encountered on her college campus.

INTERVIEW WITH A HUMAN SERVICE WORKER AT WORK

Stephanie Lake, Program Coordinator, Drug and Alcohol Education Project

My work on the Drug and Alcohol Education Project at a large university began while I was a human services student; now I am a staff person. I first met the director of the project when she came to my class as a guest speaker. She was new on campus and looking for students to help get the program off the ground.

Although we have a Department of Student Counseling and a half-time counselor who specializes in helping students struggling with substance use disorders, the administration decided to put more energy into the prevention of substance use. That way, they don't just sit around waiting for the problems to come to them.

I volunteered to help the new Drug and Alcohol Specialist recruit students for a peer-counseling program called Peers Reaching Out, or PRO. We started with nine students. The first thing we did was a survey of attitudes and behavior. We walked around the student lounge for days with our clipboards. Because they knew their answers were anonymous, kids really opened up to us. We also recruited a few peer counselors that way.

The next thing we did was form a committee. This was made up of university staff from different programs and student leaders. They became a brain trust to come up with ideas about the rules that needed to be changed and make suggestions for programs. I became the secretary to the group and still am.

They suggested that we needed more awareness on campus of the problem of substance use and of the new programs we proposed. The president of the university declared a DRUG-AHOL Awareness Week. Faculty members agreed to invite speakers into their classes, and the resident assistants organized discussions in the dorms. We set up a table in the quad and took turns sitting at it every day for a week. We gave out literature on different aspects of the problem and had a drug board that showed the paraphernalia and effects of drugs and alcohol. We also had drug wheels that you could use to figure out how much alcohol it would take to make you legally drunk.

The idea I was proudest of was the display of a totally wrecked car donated by a junkyard. We had it towed right into the center of the quad. The students could see in gruesome detail what can happen when you drive drunk. They stopped and asked a lot of questions. We also had a video going constantly in the main lobby about the crash involving that car.

After I volunteered for two quarters I was put in charge of DRUG-AHOL Awareness Week, and each one has gotten better since then. At first I was afraid to speak in front of student clubs, but I eventually got over that. I wrote articles for the student newspaper and was interviewed on the student radio station. I also used all my own contacts and was able to recruit a solid group of 45 students. Some of them were in recovery themselves and some of them, like me, had alcohol use in their families. I organized the weekly training sessions, set up speakers, got videos, and stayed in touch with the peers between training sessions.

I think I've also been especially pleased with the development of the campus task force. I've gone from being a student member to being one of the professional staff to whom people turn for suggestions. We had a major problem with our senior "bash." For years it's been a tradition for the seniors to bring champagne onto the quad the last day of classes and just get totally drunk. They would destroy the grass, break the bottles, and have a series of nasty accidents. We needed to stop it, and yet, we recognized the seniors' need to celebrate. Our committee proposed that the university take over the celebration, providing the champagne, soft drinks, and plenty of food. That way, the seniors could have their party and we could help them drink in a responsible way. They grumbled the first year, but we pulled it off.

But this year the university decided we couldn't repeat it. The president felt we couldn't take the ethical or moral risk of providing liquor to students who would later drive home. So they gave them a beautiful, fancy, nonalcoholic party. Of course, the students went to the local bars right after it, but there is only so much you can do.

The other project I work on is a program called INSTEAD. From the student court, we get referrals of residents who have caused damage while drunk or who have been caught with liquor in the dorms. The university used to expel them from the dorms. Now we recognize they have an issue that needs to be addressed. They have to attend a six-session training course and do community service. I think this has helped a lot of them turn around. Some of the INSTEAD members go on to join AA. Some even stay with their volunteer work with neighborhood kids.

I have learned so much about administration and planning in this job. It is ending within the next month because the grant that pays my salary will end. This gives me a chance to explore going back to school for my advanced degree. I think maybe it's time to leave, but it's been great to grow with a program that has so much meaning for students and faculty. I am very pleased I chose to major in human services; it is a common foundation for study in many different fields. Wherever I go, I will take with me the insights I have gained through course and field work.

Summary

1. Three possible routes for a young woman looking for help with her father's alcohol use were described. By following these paths, we encountered 25 different human service roles.
2. A picture of the human service programs in any one particular town can be discovered by calling the town hall or an umbrella funding agency, searching out directories of services, calling hotlines, and searching online.
3. Although services might be available, people in need frequently have difficulty finding and using them. Barriers generated by internal and external pressures clutter the paths. We looked at a variety of these barriers by listening in on the nagging doubts and questions that reflect them.
4. The public often accepts stereotypes about who we are and what we do. People often lack accurate information about the full range of human service work.
5. The complexity inherent in human service problems leads to a proliferation of agencies and professional roles. This diversity can offer much choice to those seeking appropriate services or roles. People choose their work roles in the field by considering their own personal attributes, lifestyle, philosophy or ideology, and available programs.
6. The description of the daily work of a program coordinator for a substance use education and prevention project reveals many important roles in the human service network.
7. Although navigating the maze of the human service system can be complex and frustrating, it is never routine and is often exhilarating.

Discussion Questions

1. Some people believe that substance use is a crime best left to the criminal justice system. Others believe that addiction is a moral failing and thus should be cured by the family and the church. Others assert that it is a problem that should be dealt with by the medical establishment and human service programs networks. What do you think of each of these positions?
2. What is the situation with substance use on your campus? What approaches does the administration appear to be using if there seems to be a problem, and how effective do you think those approaches are?
3. If you were assigned to write the type of helpee paper that Kathy wrote, would you be willing to write about a personal problem? Would you be willing to share your paper with your classmates after you wrote it (if you decided to fulfill the assignment)? To what extent do you think that asking students in a human services class to share personal information with the instructor or with other students is an appropriate learning device? To what extent does it feel like an unjustified invasion of your privacy?
4. What human service workers have you personally met? Which ones do you know about in your community or on your campus? Which of their jobs seem like a set of tasks you might like to try out? Which would you prefer to avoid? When you check out the web site of your community, what human service agencies are listed?
5. Interview a staff person at a human service agency. What is her exact role, and what kind of degree is required for that role? What does the person see as the best part of the work? What does that person see as the frustrations or drawbacks of this role? Is this a role that you can imagine yourself in?

Web Resources for Further Study

Occupational Outlook Handbook, U. S. Department of Labor

https://www.bls.gov/ooh/

U. S. Department of Health and Human Services

https://www.hhs.gov

Hazelden Addiction Treatment Center

https://www.hazelden.org

The National Mental Health Consumers' Self-Help Clearinghouse

https://www.mhselfhelp.org

2

The Changing Nature of the Helping Process

Learning Outcomes

- Students will be able to characterize societal attitudes toward people with problems and how the social programs to deal with them have changed through the ages.

- Students will be able to differentiate between means-tested and universal programs and describe how poverty is defined.

- Students will be able to critique cycles of helping in the welfare, mental health, juvenile justice, and criminal justice systems.

- Students will be able to explain the history of human service work and the careers within the field.

Source: Courtesy of the Library of Congress

INTERVIEW WITH MARIE KISSEL, HOMECARE DIRECTOR, ELDER SERVICES OF THE MERRIMACK VALLEY

Marie has worked at Elder Services for over 30 years, and has seen many changes in clients needs, family structures, social issues, government funding, and delivery of services over this period of time.

Elder Services of the Merrimack Valley (ESMV) is a private non-profit agency under contract with the Massachusetts Executive Office of Elder Affairs serving elders and adults with disabilities who reside in northeast Massachusetts. Established in 1974, our mission is to support an individual's desire to make their own decisions, secure their independence, and remain living in the community safely. Elder Services case managers and nurses work with thousands of elders and family members each day to make sure they have the right services, living arrangements, and access to good health care and benefits (www.esmv.org).

Case managers carry a caseload of about 90 people and visit each person a minimum of twice per year as well as maintain contact by phone. The caseload hasn't changed in the 33 years I have been with Elder Services, but the job has gotten more complex. In 1984 the agency offered four programs: Home Care, Protective Services, Nursing Home Ombudsman, and federal Title III programs such as Meals on Wheels. Now we administer 24 programs with over 60 different contracted providers. Each program has its own funding sources, eligibility requirements, paperwork, and computer tracking systems. The biggest change in the agency over the years is that before, we basically coordinated housework, grocery shopping, laundry, and meals so that seniors could live at home independently. Now the focus is on keeping people out of nursing homes and providing the choice to live at home regardless of the complexity of their needs. We have seniors living on their own with dementia, oxygen tanks, or feeding tubes, and many who are bedridden. In the past, these clients would have been placed in a nursing home. Now they have the right to live at home with services. This client-centered approach, combined with hospitals that dis-

Source: Courtesy of Marie Kissel

charge people before they are well, means that we have to put more services in place to provide a safe environment. While we at times are providing services 24/7, it is not possible unless there is backup support from the family members.

Another way society has changed in the past 30 years, making elder care in the community more complex, is the growing problem of substance use in clients or their family members. More and more frequently we see elders who have criminal backgrounds, often the result of an addiction issue. These elders are unable to secure housing either in housing specifically for elders or in private housing because of this, and may at times be forced to go to an assisted living facility unnecessarily because there is no place else for them to live. There are also more grandparents raising their grandchildren because the parent is deceased, incarcerated, or addicted. Our Protective Services program is there to assist seniors who are being physically, emotionally, or financially abused by someone or who are neglecting themselves. We have seen our referrals to this program grow from 40 or 50 per month to over 250 per month now. Substance use is often a factor in these cases. We had two Protective Services workers when I started at Elder Services; now there are more than 20 outreach workers and interns that assist with the work.

The huge shortage of affordable housing is also a major problem. The waitlists are at least five years long in our area. As noted, clients with criminal records cannot be housed, so they have no choice but to stay in assisted living facilities. We are already beginning to experience the "Grey Tsunami" as the baby boomers become of age and begin to need senior housing and services. As the number of seniors needing services is increasing, we have a shortage in home care workers and case managers. Home care workers provide personal care, cleaning, and shopping services. Our provider agencies have a difficult time retaining home care workers because the positions don't pay well and the work is very challenging. Many of the home care workers are immigrants and may have language barriers, making caring for elders with dementia and/or hearing loss difficult. The pay is often less than working at a fast food restaurant and the work is both physically and emotionally demanding.

There is also a constant demand for case managers, particularly if they are bilingual. The case manager position requires a bachelor degree in Human Service, Social Work, or a related area. We have a hard time retaining newly hired case managers because there is a lot of competition for work-ers with the same qualifications. But we also have some case managers who have stayed with us for 10 to 20 years because for them it is a calling and a career rather than just a paycheck. In addition to having strong communication skills, organizational ability, and excellent interpersonal skills, the case managers must also be comfortable with using computer databases. The pay is not great, but there is a great deal of satisfaction in making a difference in an elder's life by enabling them to remain at home and supporting their family caregivers. If you enjoy being the facilitator of many interrelating agencies and services providing care to a consumer, such as the Visiting Nurse Association, mental health providers, and a variety of other agencies, this is a very rewarding job.

When asked what the future holds for elder services, Marie referred to the "elder-friendly com-munities" movement that aims to make all communities accessible to seniors in their physical design, housing, transportation, and services.

ESMV is already taking bold steps to make communities elder-friendly: We have partnered with a number of housing authorities to build supportive housing and worked with other partners to address the need of elders for fresh food, mental health assistance, basic necessities, and financial manage-ment services. We are proud to be one of the first agencies recognized nationally for our work with evidence-based healthy living programs to help people become better health care consumers and manage their chronic health conditions. We were also one of the first agencies in the nation to be awarded funding for a partnership with six area hospitals offering transitional care services for patients being discharged from health care settings.

CHANGES IN SOCIETY SHAPE HELPING BEHAVIOR

Attitudes toward the poor and toward people with physical and mental health issues have changed over time. Changes in attitudes, both positive and negative, are the result of media, research, social movements, and public policy. As social programs and policies evolve, so do the roles of the human service worker. In Europe in the middle ages, people believed God decreed their economic status. There were no programs to help people gain education or better employment if they were in a lower class. In other words, there was no "upward mobility." In America, economic status is tied to the notion of "rugged independence"—the belief that individuals are solely responsible for their economic situation. There is a strong belief in upward mobility, which implies that hard work will lead to opportunity. The flip side of that belief is that poor and troubled people are not working hard enough or have caused their own problems. Because of this deep-rooted belief, America has been a "reluctant" welfare state and there is a stigma to receiving assistance (Jansson, 2001). Human beings are social animals who have always helped each other (and, of course, also hurt each other). The kind of relationship that a society expects from its citizens and the way it organizes its important institutions—the family, and the system of governance and control—can either nurture or stunt people's impulses to give help to relatives, friends, and needy strangers.

If a modern society is to stay intact, it must encourage some form of mutual help. This is what the anthropologist Claude Levi-Strauss (1974) called the **principle of reciprocity**, which he considered the basic glue that holds together a society. That principle points to people's mutual obligations toward each other, based on caring and a sense of justice.

Not only do different cultures vary in their helping behaviors, but our governments, churches, and even private groups have always reacted differently to those in need of help. By

Source: Library of Congress Prints and Photographs Division Washington [LC-USZ62-11203]

Social attitudes about behavior go through cycles. Sometimes they reverse themselves from one era to another. These immigrants to the United States, landing at Ellis Island early in the twentieth century, faced adversity, but their labor was welcomed. Now, the descendants of many such immigrants vote to restrict the entry and social benefits of new waves of hopeful immigrants.

exploring a small part of the history of a few institutions that are supposed to provide help, we see this evolution in concrete form. "But," you might ask, "why must I bother studying the past in order to do my job as a human service worker in the twenty-first century?" Each new view of the way people should be helped, or not helped, has left behind its skeletons. Buildings constructed during one era are still standing many years later; people trained under outmoded theories continue to practice them in their day-to-day work. Lingering myths and misconceptions about crime, mental illness, physical disability, women's rights, multiculturalism, gender identity, and income inequality are almost impossible to stamp out, even in the face of overwhelming scientific evidence proving them wrong.

Changes in Social Attitudes Toward Helping People with Problems

Change is not an upward, linear progression. Rather, changes in social attitudes and treatment methods tend to be cyclical. Yet, although the next spin in the cycle may look familiar, it doesn't come out exactly like the previous one. The philosopher Hegel called change a **dialectical** process. First there is the idea or action (a thesis), which inspires its opposite idea or action (antithesis). Out of the struggle of these two opposites comes a new synthesis. Then the process begins all over again. We find ourselves periodically returning to the same debates about the legitimacy and effectiveness of strategies to deal with such issues as:

- Birth control
- Capital punishment
- Educational methods

- Mental health treatment
- Rehabilitation of people in prison
- Women's rights
- Gender identity issues
- Child raising techniques.

Tracing the overall history of helping in the United States as well as in western Europe reveals a tortured path, starting from the times when people who needed help were viewed as the responsibility of their families alone or perhaps were also given a little help from the church or a benevolent feudal lord, owner, or other master. Along with the shifts between private and public responsibility for helping has come a slowly changing set of social perspectives on people who need help. In feudal times, people were pretty much locked into their social status, and the rulers of society, buttressed by theologians, spread the word that the poor or people in trouble were poor because God willed it. If God willed it, the rulers argued, then it would be sacrilegious to change their status. The rich, however, could assure their own entrance into heaven by giving to the poor (Herlihy, 1973).

Sixteenth-century theologian John Calvin extolled the virtues of thrift, industry, sobriety, and responsibility as essential to the achievement of the reign of God on Earth. The Puritan moralists of New England used his ideas to reinforce the work ethic needed for the newly emerging industrialism of the United States. The moral imperative to be productive made it a stigma to be poor or handicapped.

A powerful influence on the treatment of the poor during the late nineteenth century was the adaptation of the ideas of Charles Darwin. Although Darwin did not draw any sociological conclusions from his work, Herbert Spencer, an English philosopher and one of the first sociologists, used Darwin's work to coin the phrase "survival of the fittest." According to Spencer's interpretation, the fittest people in society were those who were able to make money. Poor people were declared unfit and accorded the same treatment doled out to common criminals. This philosophy is called **Social Darwinism**.

SOCIAL DARWINISM   Spencer was one of the first to apply Darwin's theories of evolution to the human sphere. The concept of "survival of the fittest" was used to justify accumulation of wealth and disregard of the needs of the poor.

Darwin actually said that we are programmed to be cooperative and caring, according to one psychologist, Dacher Keltner, director of the Berkeley Social Interaction Laboratory. He wrote the 2009 book *Born to Be Good: The Science of a Meaningful Life,* in which he says, "Our mammalian and hominid evolution have crafted a species—us—with remarkable tendencies toward kindness, play, generosity, reverence, and self-sacrifice, which are vital to the classic tasks of evolution—survival, gene replication, and smooth functioning groups" (Keltner, 2009).

With the decline of feudalism and the rise of industrialism, the responsibility for those people who could not help themselves began to shift more and more to town governments. Official overseers of the poor gradually replaced the church and almsgivers as the primary sources of help outside the family. Eventually, providing help became a task for volunteers or trained professionals.

The beginnings of the industrial age ushered in the view that people with problems were morally depraved, almost as if they had a self-inflicted contagious disease. It was thought that they deserved punishment or removal from society. William Ryan calls that point of view **victim blaming** (Ryan, 1976). It is a point of view that has sunk roots deep into our society. Some examples of victim blaming:

- Women who report rape are blamed for provoking it by the way they dress.
- Single mothers on welfare are blamed for having children to get money from the state.
- People who are homeless are blamed for not managing their money properly.

An opposing point of view, held by the human service profession, is built on providing a counter-perspective to the blaming-the-victim ideology. It defines human problems as a result of interacting personal and social forces, often beyond the control of the individual. It looks at individuals as embedded in families and communities and in economic and political systems that exert a powerful pull on personality development, social status, and life chances. The alternative perspective:

- Women who report rape are courageous to step forward and should receive medical, emotional, and legal assistance for the trauma that they have endured.
- Single mothers receiving cash assistance or other benefits are struggling to take care of their children, often while working or in school, and their strengths should be recognized.
- Persons who are homeless may have a number of reasons for losing a house or apartment, including loss of job, or physical or mental illness.

This point of view, which looks at social systems, asserts that life situations are an inevitable part of the human condition in an industrialized society. Older adults will retire from their jobs; working parents will often need help with child care; everyone gets sick at some time; wage earners who support a family sometimes die or become disabled; women get pregnant and need prenatal care; everyone needs education in order to be a contributing member of society; many workers are injured; some babies are born with crippling diseases or develop them later in life; some people will lose their jobs. Poverty and the stresses of life have long-term health consequences, including more illnesses and shorter life expectancy (Wilkinson & Marmot, 2003). Some governments have developed strong **social safety nets** and others have weak and fragmented programs. These opposing philosophies have resulted in very different approaches to giving help. The blaming-the-victim ideology always sees character defects in individuals. At best, it results in remedial programs to "cure" those defects. At its worst, it punishes people for what it defines as perverse or immoral conduct. Entire groups of people are blamed for their behavior. The poor, for example, are assumed to be poor because they lack initiative and a work ethic. People who are homeless are thought to have brought their condition on themselves through personality defects or lack of careful planning. If you move from one country to another or from one state in the United States to another, you will find great differences in the programs offered and the funding given to social service programs (Urban Institute, March 2016).

The United States, for example, has been called a "reluctant welfare state" in comparison with most other industrialized nations (Jansson, 2001). The United States ranks twenty-fifth among developed countries on social welfare spending (cash and services) but spends considerably more on health care and education than other nations, partly due to tax credits and higher costs in these areas (OECD Social Expenditure Update, November 2014). According to a study in the *Washington Post* (Max Fischer, April 15, 2013), the United States ranks thirty-fourth out of thirty-five developed countries for child poverty rates. For a country with the means to provide a social safety net, it has been unwilling or unable to do so in a way that combats poverty.

Source: © Steve Greenberg

There is a growing inequality of the distribution of wealth in the United States, resulting in the richest Americans having a disproportionate amount of total assets.

MEANS-TESTED VERSUS UNIVERSAL PROGRAMS   People who tend to blame the victim sometimes feel superior to those in need. They assume that they could never be in the circumstances that the victim is in. They tend to separate people into "them" and "us, " **deserving versus undeserving**. They often prefer means-tested programs for all people, even those in the most precarious circumstances, and feel that before people receive aid that their financial situations should be fully investigated (Ryan, 1976).

The means-tested approach is often called the **residual philosophy of social welfare** (Zastrow, 2009). Proponents of means-tested programs generally have the opinion that benefits should be made difficult to obtain, that assistance should be tied to work, and that strict measures for determining need should be adhered to (Zastrow, 2014). Applicants must prove that they have so little money and so few assets that they meet the criteria that the agency sets for eligibility. When there are limited funds to support the programs, the means-test has higher thresholds for eligibility, in order to limit the number of people served. For example, in order to secure a shelter bed, a person who is homeless may have to obtain documentation to prove that he has no other assets, has no family members who can take him in, and was not evicted due to his own fault.

Those who look at people as being embedded in a social system, and thus having predictable developmental needs, are more likely to regard social supports as a universal right. That philosophy of social welfare is called the **institutional,** or **developmental, philosophy of social welfare**. Programs subscribing to this philosophy are called **universal programs**. Workers in these programs assume that problems are bound to occur, so they provide for people in need in a way that respects the dignity of the individual. The programs they create—unemployment insurance; workers' compensation; family and children's allowances; pensions for people who are older, who are survivors, and who have disabilities; Medicare—are given as **entitlements**, which do not distinguish between "deserving" and "undeserving." Social security comprised at least half the income of 69 percent of aged individual beneficiaries, and 48% of the income for married couples (Social Security Administration, 2018). Social security is considered an entitlement program and because beneficiaries pay into it, they often consider it earned income versus welfare even if they collect far more than they pay into the program.

Universal income supports and social services include both the affluent and the poor, and therefore have more public approval. Wealthy people who receive such aid will pay some of the cost through **progressive taxes**, whereby the rich are taxed at a higher rate than the less affluent. Universal programs are much more widely used in European countries than in the United States. For example, most industrialized countries except the United States have what they call a family allowance, which gives a certain amount of money to families for each child they have. France has universal child care for working mothers. Most industrialized countries have a national health insurance system, funded by the government from tax revenue.

Many human service workers tend to prefer universal programs, which they believe show more respect to ordinary people. Others, who view themselves as more conservative, tend to prefer **means-tested programs** (programs in which people must prove great need). People who receive benefits under universal programs are called claimants; people who receive means-tested benefits are called recipients. Claimants are claiming their rights; recipients are receiving whatever someone chooses to give them.

Defining Behaviors as Social Problems

When does a particular kind of personal or social behavior become defined as a "social problem"? Why did social-problems textbooks before the 1970s rarely mention such issues as sexism, domestic violence, incest, sexual harassment, rape, and discrimination against people with disabilities, whereas post-1970s textbooks prominently discuss these as social problems?

Behaviors become social problems when some people and organizations force those issues to the top of the public agenda. Domestic violence, rape, and discrimination based on race or gender identity were widespread before 1970, but they weren't defined as social problems until the feminist, civil rights, and LGBT movements, among others, challenged traditional assumptions (Best, 1989).

More than most other countries in the world, the United States has clung to an individualistic philosophy, believing the Horatio Alger rags-to-riches myth that anyone can make it if she works hard enough. Sociologist C. Wright Mills (1959) distinguished between "private troubles" and "public issues." Troubles happen to individuals and to the relationships between individuals. Issues, on the other hand, transcend one individual and are widespread within the community. Mills gives the following example:

> When, in a city of 100,000, only one man is unemployed, that is his personal trouble, and for its relief we properly look to the character of the man, his skills, and his immediate opportunities. But when in a nation of 50 million employees, 15 million men are unemployed, that is an issue, and we may not hope to find its solution within the range of opportunities open to any one individual. The very structure of opportunities has collapsed. Both the correct statement of the problem and the range of possible solutions require us to consider the economic and political institutions of the society, and not merely the personal situation and character of a scatter of individuals. (Mills, 1959, p. 9)

We know that as unemployment rises, so do substance use, homelessness, child abuse, divorce, domestic violence, crime and delinquency, mental illness, and other issues. The human service worker who treats each case as a personal trouble is doing a disservice to people in need, society, and the profession.

Source: GWImages/Shutterstock

Many individual social behaviors are a result of bigger social issues and problems that need to be addressed on wider basis.

Social issues of the last decade include post-traumatic stress disorder (PTSD) of veterans returning home from war in Afghanistan and Iraq, and the opioid crisis. Significant attention has been paid recently to racially motivated shootings, shootings of police officers, and people with mental disorders and illness as related to school shootings. The social behaviors have impacted an "ordinary" person, which moves the behaviors from individual to social problems. Once something is recognized as a societal problem, public policy and programs begin to respond.

CYCLES OF HELPING

To illustrate the dialectical nature of human service issues, we shall discuss four issues: welfare, mental illness, juvenile justice, and criminal justice.

Cycles in Welfare Reform

We are using the term *welfare* in the way that the public generally understands it. The government's name for the program is Temporary Aid to Needy Families (TANF).* If we called all government financial transfer programs "welfare," then financial aid grants to college students and veterans' benefits, for example, would come under that category. Although the amount spent on the TANF program has been relatively small—less than 1 percent of federal government spending and about 3 percent of state spending—it garners a huge amount of public attention, although

---

*States have given different names to TANF. In Massachusetts, for example, the program is called Transitional Assistance to Families with Dependent Children (TAFDC).

much larger grants go to the middle class and rich in the form of tax benefits. "Welfare grants" provide a good example of the cycles of reform. Frances Fox Piven and Richard Cloward (2013), two former professors of social work, wrote that welfare expands and contracts in response to changes in the economy and the political climate. Piven and Cloward argued that government officials expand public assistance in times of civil turmoil. When the turmoil dies down, they cut back on welfare. They documented the following cycles of expansion and contraction in welfare:

- Beginning of large-scale federal relief programs during the Great Depression as a response to civil turmoil
- Cutbacks during the 1940s and 1950s after the turmoil of the 1930s subsided. Welfare was often withheld from people in order to force them into low-paid agricultural and factory work.
- Expansion during the 1960s as a response to civil turmoil (and as an attempt to build a new urban base for the Democratic party)
- Cutbacks from the 1970s to the present after the turmoil of the 1960s subsided. During this period, welfare has been withheld to force women out of their homes and into the low-wage labor market (Piven & Cloward, 1993).

As welfare and other safety net programs were cut back, the criminal justice system expanded. The United States has the highest incarceration rate on the planet—five times the world's average. The United States has 5 percent of the world's population, but 25 percent of the world's prison population. There were about 2.24 million people incarcerated in federal, state, and county prisons in 2014 and another 6.8 million under community supervision (Bureau of Justice Statistics, 2014).

THE DOWNWARD SLIDE   The upward climb of social welfare expenditures reversed in 1975. Expenditures then took a downward turn for the first time in three decades, beginning with the Ford and Carter administrations, and picking up roller-coaster speed during the 1980s. Congress and the Reagan administration cut means-tested programs for the poor and near-poor. Programs for the middle class suffered also, though entitlement programs such as Social Security and Medicare were safe from cuts (Campagna, 1994; Jansson, 2015). Some states replaced the lost federal funds with state funds, but during periods of economic recession, states tend to cut social welfare and implement punitive measures. Across the nation, state legislators and governors have slashed benefits for people with low incomes. Fourteen of the 30 states with supplemental welfare programs, known as General Assistance, have cut benefits, affecting nearly half a million people.

At the same time that corporations were being restructured, social welfare programs were also being restructured. As wages went down, so did welfare payments—no coincidence. According to a principle known in welfare circles as the **principle of less eligibility**, welfare payments in the United States are almost always kept below the lowest wages in order to encourage people to take any low-wage job rather than go on welfare.

Over 25 years ago, the consumer advocate Ralph Nader warned that many politicians were engaged in a campaign to undermine people's trust in government. The results of the 2016 presidential election seemed to reinforce the idea that voters had lost trust in the government. Voters largely rejected career politicians and supported candidates who were in favor of limiting safety net programs and more strongly controlling immigration. Now we see how farsighted Nader was. When people believe that the government does not have a responsibility to provide social safety nets or to offer social programs that help people in challenging life situations, the fundamental basis of much social policy and practice is impacted. The impact might result in the removal of the "buffer" that is intended to protect people from situations such as working at a job that does not pay wages that cover basic needs, staying in abusive relationships, or becoming homeless. It seems that we have returned full circle to the 19th century in welfare reform.

Welfare is like society's lightning rod, attracting people's anxieties and ambivalence about dependence and self-reliance—about work, about race, about sex, about our responsibilities toward one another, and about the nature of a just society. It is an increasingly political hot-button issue in the United States (Gilens, 1999). Even though the welfare rolls have declined since the 1996 welfare reform, the perception that welfare dependency is rampant remains in people's minds.

Cycles of Treatment of Mental Health Conditions

The treatment of people with mental health conditions has taken many twists and turns throughout history. Again we see the similarity of present conditions to earlier times. In 1985, the president of the American Psychiatric Association, John A. Talbott, said: "In trying to reform the mental health system, we've gone from atrocious to awful. In colonial times, hordes of mentally ill people wandered from town to town. They lacked food, shelter, and care. That's exactly the situation today: We've come full circle" (Nickerson, 1985, p. 18).

Political philosopher Michel Foucault pointed out that certain behaviors are regarded differently in different cultures and at different historical periods. Foucault said that up until about 1650, "madness was allowed free reign" (1987, p. 67). Society neither exalted it nor tried to control it; in fact, in France in the early seventeenth century, there were famous "madmen" who were a great source of entertainment for the public. But "about the middle of the seventeenth century, a sudden change took place; the world of madness was to become the world of exclusion" (1987, p. 67). Throughout Europe, institutions were built to house many different categories of people. In about the middle of the eighteenth century, Europeans began to protest the widespread internment of people. A goal of the French Revolution of 1789 was to abolish internment as a symbol of ancient oppression, particularly for the poor. But this liberation did not apply to individuals who experienced mental illness and were considered dangerous. "Hence the need to contain them and the penal sanction inflicted on those who allow 'madmen and dangerous animals' to roam freely" (Foucault, 1987, p. 70). Thus, individuals who experienced mental illness were left behind in the old houses of internment.

In the 19th century, madness was thought to be contagious. Because it was thought unfair to criminals to expose them to individuals who experienced mental illness, the latter were separately confined in asylums. The doctor was not the servant of the patient but of the society. Foucault believed that the psychologization of madness that occurred in the nineteenth century was "part of the punitive system in which the madman, reduced to the status of a minor, was treated in every way as a child, and in which madness was associated with guilt and wrongdoing" (1987, p. 73).

While physical conditions are diagnosed using laboratory tests, mental health diagnosis is less precise. Except in the case of organic conditions such as brain tumors, mental illness is primarily diagnosed by observing behavior and through medication trials. For many years in the past, a person could be labelled as "mentally ill," without any diagnosis, and removed from her family and put in a hospital (Szasz, 1961). Lawsuits against hospitalizing people against their will and warehousing so many people with problems finally led to deinstitutionalization. This resulted in the closing of psychiatric hospitals that were supposed to be replaced with small community residences and outpatient treatment.

Unfortunately, when our society embarks on a positive social reform, the effort is often underfunded or incomplete, leading to new types of problems.

THE PROGRESSIVES AND THE REFORMERS   During the early 20th century in the United States, social activists known as **Progressives** were shocked by the oppressiveness of the overcrowded prisons and mental health facilities that helped so few people. They did not, however, want to abolish them; rather, they thought that each person would be cured if professionals could tailor a case-by-case treatment plan.

Modern reformers are closing the mental health facilities and returning the patients to their communities. Indeed, treatment of people with mental illness has come full circle, but now the rationale behind it is different. The colonists of early America believed in the inevitability of problems; modern reformers believe that hospitals institutionalize people but do not heal them. The latter argue for the healing power of kin, community ties, and normal, everyday routines.

INTERVIEW WITH JUDY CHAMBERLIN, MENTAL PATIENTS' LIBERATION FRONT

Judi Chamberlin was one of the founders of the mental patients' liberation movement in the 1970s. She called herself a "psychiatric survivor" of the mental health system. She not only survived but also went on to write a book about her experiences with mental illness and psychiatric hospitals. She also started an alternative service for those who had been treated and released from mental health facilities. Chamberlin was one of the leaders of the Mental Patients' Liberation Front (MPLF), an organization of people who are or have been in psychiatric hospitals and who oppose many established psychiatric practices. MPLF has established support groups and alternative institutions.

In 1988, Judi wrote On Our Own, *a book about her own experience with depression, when she was involuntarily hospitalized. That book became a kind of bible for the mental patients' liberation movement. Judi spoke at conferences all over the nation and the world, and passed away in hospice in 2010.*

When students learn about the mental health system, they only hear the views of the professionals. They seldom empathize with the mentally ill or try to understand how it feels to be on the receiving end. If they want to have an honest dialogue with the mentally ill and ex-patients, service providers have to be prepared to face their anger and mistrust. People who use services have been treated in paternalistic and controlling ways, and this understandably has made them angry.

The attitudes of service providers have caused a split between the Alliance for the Mentally Ill (AMI), a support group for relatives and friends of mentally ill people, and the Mental Patients' Liberation Front (MPLF). Parents in the AMI argue, "We love our sons and daughters and want them to get help. We may trick them if we have to, whether they say they want it or not." The patient may not want to take drugs, but relatives often think they should and complain that patients don't take their medications. (Research has shown that a high percentage of all drugs, not just psychotropics, is not taken according to the doctor's prescription.)

Judi tried to promote dialogue between AMI and MPLF.

Ex-patients and families have one thing in common: They didn't choose to be in the system. Professionals choose to be there. It is important to recognize that families have a valid perspective.

Some people accuse the MPLF of being totally opposed to drugs, but I believe in choice. Patients need to have all the facts, which are often kept from them. The professionals sometimes feel that if they give patients information, they only scare them. I tried drugs but didn't find one that helped me. For me, drugs didn't work, but I wouldn't tell anyone else what to do. The journalist Robert Whitaker wrote the book *Mad in America*. He investigated the statistics of mental illness and found that the number of people diagnosed with mental illness keeps going up and the number of people on disability keeps going up, despite all the claims that drug companies make about medication. A typical anti-psychotic drug causes severe obesity— [a gain of] 100 pounds or more—and diabetes. But it is very profitable for drug companies. The power of drug companies keeps growing. Lots of doctors are getting huge amounts of money from drug companies, and lying about it.

Drug companies and doctors have everyone convinced that the problem is biochemical, but we see it as psychosocial. Poverty is a factor. Life on SSI (Supplemental Security Income) is pretty miserable because the grant is so low. There is a "Ticket to Work" option to encourage people to try working, and to enable them to return to SSI if it doesn't work out. But people are wary of trying that because they know how hard it is to get on SSI, and they fear that they would be left with nothing if they were denied SSI. Researchers have tracked unemployment and hospital admissions, showing that mental illness rises with unemployment. Research about women in mental hospitals indicates that as many as 50 to 80 percent have been sexually abused.

Interestingly, the rate of recovery of mental patients is higher in third-world countries. I believe that is because they have stronger family and community ties. Also, traditional healers, who would be used more in third-world countries, sit with the patient, sometimes for days. In Africa, for example, a native healer spends several days observing the patient. That presence sets up a powerful therapeutic alliance. The healer does not think that it is important to ask questions but that it is important just to be there.

Ours is a strength-based model. It is important to teach people skills, and train people to be advocates and mentors. That changes how people think about themselves. Instead of making sickness his identity and saying, "I'm Joe, I'm schizophrenic," he can see himself as somebody with something to give others. We aim to put people in positions of power over their own lives. When people feel powerless, they are overwhelmed. When everyone is making decisions for them, it is not surprising that they don't have good outcomes.

RECENT DEVELOPMENTS AND PROBLEMS IN TREATING PEOPLE WITH MENTAL HEALTH CONDITIONS

1. **Deinstitutionalization, followed by a lack of funding, has caused increases in both homelessness and incarceration of individuals with mental health issues.**   Dorothea Dix, who campaigned in the 19th century to get people with mental illness out of jails and into psychiatric hospitals, would have been vexed to see that the hospitals evolved into substandard and abusive living conditions. Beginning in about 1955, the state psychiatric hospitals began to undergo **deinstitutionalization**. While the intent to deinstitutionalize may have been good, the outcome was that community facilities did not meet the demand, and ultimately most of the patients were "reinstitutionalized" into shelters, nursing homes, rest homes, or prisons. David Wagner (2005) studied this process of "reinstitutionalization" and compared the poorhouses and workhouses with present-day shelters for the homeless. He said, ". . . almshouses and shelters are generally comparable, and the six studied are probably better than most homeless shelters in regard to sleeping areas, waiting lines, food and so on"(Wagner, 2005).

   Most psychiatrists assert that deinstitutionalization was made possible by the discovery of antipsychotic drugs, which allow patients to live a stable life outside the hospital. Although it is true that these medications have helped some people return to mainstream life, Blau (1992) points out that psychiatrists have often relied too heavily on drugs in their eagerness to empty the hospitals. An overreliance on drugs can prolong social dependency and produce neurological damage. The lack of a permanent home and outpatient treatment can also prevent regular use of medication.

   Pharmaceutical companies are spending large sums to get doctors to use their medicines by giving the doctors various perks. Some psychiatrists are lured by this largesse to prescribe medications that they might not otherwise prescribe (CBS News May 13, 2017). One psychiatrist spoke out against this practice, which he himself had been doing. He said, "There's really no nice way to say it. If you're being paid to offer an opinion you're not all that confident that you believe, you're corrupt" (Goldberg, 2007a).

   The failure of deinstitutionalization to live up to its promise is an illustration of a principle that sociologists call the **unintended consequences of reform**. Sometimes a reform can become so perverted in the way it is carried out that its advocates, who held such high hopes for it, feel betrayed.

   In 1955, there was 1 psychiatric bed for every 300 Americans. In 2005, there was 1 psychiatric bed for every 3,000 (Torrey et al., May 2010). Now it is extremely difficult to find beds for people who need them. Most acute in-patient care is now available in general hospitals. Average length of stay has fallen steadily to less than 10 days (Lee, Rothbard, & Noll, 2012). Officially, patients who left the hospitals were supposed to be mainstreamed into the community, where they would receive supports. Some of the patients went home to their families and some went to halfway houses, foster care, or jail. Some were discharged to the streets or to shelters for the homeless. The rest went to nursing homes.

   According to the Substance Abuse and Mental Health Services Administration, 20 to 25 percent of the homeless population in the United States suffers from some form of severe mental illness. In comparison, only 6 percent of all Americans are severely mentally ill (National Institute of Mental Health, 2009). The Mental Retardation Facilities and Community Mental Health Centers Construction Act, signed into law by President

Kennedy in 1963, was supposed to fund 2,000 mental health centers by 1980, but only 789 were ultimately funded (Blau, 1992). Even those did not serve the chronically mentally ill in the way that was originally intended. Mental health professionals found the chronically mentally ill less rewarding to work with than the acutely ill or the neurotic. "Hence, a mere ten years after passage of the act, chronic mental patients had too few places to go, and even in those places, they were not exactly welcome" (Blau, 1992). Far too many people with mental illness wind up in the criminal justice system: An estimated 56 percent of state prisoners, 45 percent of federal prisoners, and 64 percent of jail inmates have a mental health problem (Urban Institute, March 2015). Homeless shelters and permanent affordable housing often require residents to be substance free and will not accept residents with mental illness they feel they cannot handle. The Housing First model is a permanent housing option that accepts the resident first, and then provides opportunities (not requirements) for the individual to address her behavioral and mental health issues. This model can include independent apartments or permanent supportive housing. Permanent supportive housing has proven to be both cost-effective and effective in retention of people with dual diagnosis of substance abuse and mental illness (National Alliance to End Homelessness, April 2016).

2. **Untreated mental illness has gained media attention after mass shootings.** Several bills were introduced following the mass shootings of innocent victims by people with mental illness, such as the Sandy Hook Elementary School shooting, where a 20-year-old man who had been treated for mental illness shot and killed 20 first-grade students and 6 teachers in December 2012. The tragic incident prompted outrage by parents and formation of groups such as Moms Demand Gun Reform. Their efforts resulted in requiring increased background checks in four states that did not have them before and an expansion in seven other states. However, on the federal level, gun rights were expanded with conceal and carry laws across state lines and changing the definition of "fugitives from justice" to allow people on the FBI list to own weapons. (ABC News, December 12, 2017). The tragedy also prompted a look at the mental health system and at the need for prevention services (National Council for Behavioral Health, July 26, 2018).

   The "Helping Families in Mental Health Crisis" and the Mental Health Reform Act bills were introduced in Congress in 2015 to improve prevention and treatment, and to move away from incarcerating persons with mental illness. Under President Barack Obama, the 21st Century Cures Act (Cures Act) was signed into law in December 2016. This Act includes mental health initiatives such as increasing access to behavioral health services and providing treatment before justice involvement (National Council for Behavioral Health, July 26, 2018).

3. **Socioeconomic factors are strongly associated with the prevalence of mental disorders, and women and minorities are disproportionately affected.** There are a now a disproportionate number of people of color and women who are deemed mentally ill. A disproportionate number of women and minorities are poor, and poverty contributes to stress related mental health issues such as anxiety, ADHD, depression, and suicide (Grote, et al., 2007). According to the World Health Organization, "Gender determines the differential power and control men and women have over the socioeconomic determinants of their mental health and lives, their social position, status and treatment in society, and their susceptibility and exposure to specific mental health risks." Where one lives matters when it comes to conditions that impact mental health. Some clinic staff engage in social action

to change conditions that contribute to behavioral problems. One example is the psychiatrist Matt Dumont. He practiced in a community mental health clinic in Chelsea, Massachusetts, where many people with low incomes lived. Many of the children had lead paint poisoning, which created severe neurological and behavioral problems. Dr. Dumont discovered that the paint on a bridge in Chelsea contained lead, and he engaged in social action to force the city to remove the paint (Dumont, 1992).

4. **Community facilities and least restrictive settings is the preferred housing model since deinstitutionalization.**   Medicaid stimulated the growth of private nursing homes, and was paid for partly by the federal government. This encouraged states to shift much of the financial burden to the federal government by discharging patients to private nursing and boarding homes. Patients were federally subsidized by Social Security Disability Insurance (SSDI) and Supplemental Security Income (SSI), yet money to develop community facilities was simply not allocated (Warner, 1989).

  Patients' rights advocates won significant victories in the 1960s and 1970s, establishing the right to treatment in the least restrictive setting. In 1971, a precedent-setting Florida case, *O'Connor v. Donaldson*, determined that people could not be committed involuntarily to a psychiatric hospital unless they were dangerous to themselves or others. Other states followed suit. On June 22, 1999, the United States Supreme Court held in *Olmstead v. L.C.* that unjustified segregation of persons with disabilities constitutes discrimination in violation of Title II of the Americans with Disabilities Act. The Court held that public entities must provide community-based services to persons with disabilities when (1) such services

Source: Cameron Bennett/Spare Change

A judge must decide the fate of a person who is accused of committing a crime but who also has a mental illness. Should courts be permitted to mandate treatment? Can therapy or medication be effective if its use is coerced?

are appropriate; (2) the affected persons do not oppose community-based treatment; and (3) community-based services can be reasonably accommodated, taking into account the resources available to the public entity and the needs of others who are receiving disability services from the entity (www.ADA.gov). The Supreme Court explained that its holding "reflects two evident judgments." First, "institutional placement of persons who can handle and benefit from community settings perpetuates unwarranted assumptions that persons so isolated are incapable of or unworthy of participating in community life." Second, "confinement in an institution severely diminishes the everyday life activities of individuals, including family relations, social contacts, work options, economic independence, educational advancement, and cultural enrichment."

The federal Department of Housing and Urban Development (HUD) has responded to the Olmstead Act by requiring that housing funding result in units that are integrated. The Section 811 program, which subsidizes the construction and operations of affordable housing for people with disabilities, has moved away from creating subsidized buildings for people with disabilities, and toward subsidizing a percentage of units within larger developments in order to promote integration. Some cities and states have adopted "inclusionary zoning," where a percentage of new units developed must be affordable, and some cities, such as Boston, Massachusetts, require that buildings receiving local funds designate some units for the homeless. This has prompted developers to partner with social service agencies, such as the Pine Street Inn, in order to meet the requirement and ensure services are in place for those tenants.

5. **Peer models of support are effective.**   Peer support groups have become increasingly popular, and are even accepted by mental health officials as being as effective as professional help—sometimes more so. Medicaid reimburses peer support therapy in 30 states, and private insurers cover it in some states. Massachusetts has created a new job category—certified peer specialist—meant to formalize this kind of therapy (Goldberg, 2007b).

The clubhouse model is a client-driven community center that offers people with mental illness an opportunity to work toward individual or common goals and to form relationships. The clubhouse typically provides employment assistance, meals, and social activities, with member involvement in the planning and implementation. The staff's role is not to treat the individuals but to engage with them.

Cycles in Juvenile Justice

Youth mental illness is most often in the form of mood disorders, ADHD, anxiety, depression, or eating disorders. Bipolar disorder diagnosis in youth has risen 40 times in the last decade. Suicide is the third-leading cause of death for adolescents, and 90 percent of those who committed suicide had an underlying mental health issue. Fifty percent of youth ages 14 and older with mental illness drop out of high school (National Alliance on Mental Illness, 2016).

Closely following the adult prisons and insane asylums of the late nineteenth and early twentieth centuries came the establishment of reformatories or training schools for juvenile delinquents. This **child-saving movement**, as it is often called, was also spearheaded by the Progressives. Ironically, although the Progressives were appalled at the brutality of the asylums and prisons of the 1830s, they created new asylums of their own—for children who had gotten into trouble with the law or who had no parents able to care for them.

Sociologist Anthony Platt (1977) believes that both compulsory education and the institutions of the child-saving movement (reformatories, orphanages, foster care homes, and juvenile courts) were devised by certain segments of the middle and upper classes as new forms of social control and occupational tracking. Industrialists wanted to preserve social stability, and the juvenile courts and reform schools helped to do this. Furthermore, affluent women wanted careers, and social service was a respectable career for them.

The juvenile court system was based on the belief that children who break the law should not be punished as if they were adults. Children's cases were reviewed informally by judges. Lawyers generally did not handle juvenile cases; as juvenile court is not based on an adversary model. Court-based probation officers investigated the backgrounds of the youthful offenders and reported to the judges. No jury sat in judgment, and no defense attorney and prosecutor debated.

Juvenile reformatories were supposed to protect youngsters humanely from the corrupting influences of adult criminals. Although this sounds rational, in actual practice it meant that a youth found guilty was assigned to a reformatory without a trial and with a minimum of legal protection. Legal due process was assumed to be unnecessary because reformatories were intended to reform, not punish. The judge and probation officer were assumed to be enlightened, free of self-interest, incorruptible, and always working in the best interest of the youth. Reformatories were built in rural areas, often far from the residents' homes. Inmates were "protected from idleness, indulgence, and luxuries through military drill, physical exercise, and constant supervision" (Platt, 1977, p. 54). They were required to work at industrial and agricultural jobs but were given no more than an elementary education so that they did not "rise beyond their station in life." The reformatories were supposed to teach "the value of sobriety, thrift, industry, prudence, 'realistic' ambition, and adjustment" (p. 55).

CHANGE IN THE SYSTEM Fifteen-year-old Gerald Gault challenged the fairness of the entire juvenile court procedure. He declared that he had not been treated in a humane way. In 1964, he was sentenced to a state industrial school in Arizona for six years for making an obscene telephone call. This misdemeanor carried a maximum sentence of two months in jail and a fine of $5 to $50 for adults. Gault brought suit against the state of Arizona, and in 1967 the U.S. Supreme Court declared that the juvenile court had indeed ignored the legal due process that is required by the U.S. Constitution. Speaking for the majority in the Gault case, Justice Fortas said: "However euphemistic the title, a 'receiving home' or an 'industrial school' for juveniles is an institution of confinement in which the child is incarcerated.... Under our Constitution, the condition of being a boy does not justify a kangaroo court" (Platt, 1977, pp. 27–28).

This decision finally gave juveniles certain due-process rights. Now they have a right to know the charges against them, the right to have their own lawyer, and the right to confront and cross-examine their accusers and witnesses. They must be warned about self-incrimination and their right to remain silent. (Juveniles still do not have the right to a jury trial unless they are bound over to an adult court.)

Soon after the Gault decision, a reform-minded commissioner of the Massachusetts Department of Youth Services, Jerome Miller, shut down every training school and reformatory in the state. He condemned them as unworkable and unreformable. Miller was brought in to reform the system after a series of scandals—including stories of beatings, isolation, and rape—had rocked the state's prison-like reform schools. He shifted state policy from warehousing juveniles in institutions to counseling and educating them in community-based group homes. Miller's small-scale detention centers devoted to treating and educating youth who have committed crimes was hailed by the National Council on Crime and Delinquency as a model.

Critics charged Miller with being soft on crime, and have continually called for more locked facilities, especially for repeat offenders. The 1991 "get tough on crime" climate prompted Governor William Weld of Massachusetts to file legislation calling for the prosecution of violent teenagers in adult criminal court (McNamara, 1991, p. 24). Governor Weld's call to get tough on juvenile crime was echoed throughout the nation. Many juveniles have been bound over to adult courts and put in adult prisons. Boot camps grew substantially in the 1980s and 1990s. Thousands of juveniles have been put in them, and have often been treated harshly in them. At least 31 teenagers in 11 states died at these camps between 1980 and 2001. A 14-year-old boy named Tony Haynes died in July 2001 at an Arizona desert boot camp. Investigators said they were told that before he died, counselors physically abused him and forced him to eat dirt (Janofsky, 2001).

A 13-member panel of experts convened by the National Institutes of Health reviewed scientific evidence to look for consensus on causes of youth violence and ways to prevent it. The panel concluded that scare tactics don't work; programs that seek to prevent violence through fear and tough treatment do not work. The trouble with boot camps, detention centers, and other "get tough" programs is that they bring together young people inclined toward violence who teach each other how to commit more crime. Juveniles transferred into the adult court system have higher rates of sexual abuse and suicide, and higher rates of recidivism than adult criminals. There is no proof that the laws deter others from committing crime. The panel also found that programs that consist largely of adults lecturing, such as DARE, are not effective. Programs that offer intensive counseling for families and young people at risk, however, are more promising (Meckler, 2004).

Thousands of juveniles have been sentenced to life imprisonment. In 2010, the Supreme Court ruled that teenagers may not be locked up for life without chance of parole if they haven't killed anyone. However, more than 2,000 other juveniles will have no chance for parole because they killed someone (The StandDown Texas Project, 2010). According to National Alliance for Mentally Ill (NAMI), 70 percent of the youth in the juvenile justice system have mental health issues.

Just as with adults, socio-economic factors are at the heart of mental health issues in youth. Mental health issues are higher among youth from low-income households (National Institute of Health, 2017). Fifty percent of students age 14 or older with a mental health issue drop out of school (NAMI, 2014). It is estimated that between 40 percent and 80 percent of children in the foster care system have mental health issues. As with most of our policies and programs, the approaches are less likely to be based on evidence than on public perceptions and political motivations.

In 2015, a bill was introduced to amend the 1974 Juvenile Justice and Delinquency Prevention Act; if passed, it would be a step in the right direction. The bill would require states, as a condition of funding, to adhere to the following core principles:

- Support a trauma-informed continuum of programs to address the needs of at-risk youth and youth who come into contact with the justice system.
- Implement plans to ensure fairness and reduce racial and ethnic disparities in the detention of juveniles.
- Enhance requirements for separating juveniles from sight or sound contact with adult lock-ups.
- Expand requirements for state plans for juvenile justice and delinquency prevention to include community-based alternatives to the detention of juveniles in correctional facilities, enhanced mental health and substance abuse screening, and a description of the use of funds for re-entry into the community of juveniles after release.

Cycles in Criminal Justice

In the 1960s, the goal for those who were in prison was rehabilitation. Wacquant believes that welfare reform and mass incarceration were two parts of the same policy of creating a supply of low wage labor in an unstable job market of temporary, part-time, low-paid, and flexible employment. Wacquant says that the government's policy for poor people is now "prisonfare and workfare" (Wacquant, 2009). In addition to enforcing low-wage work, politicians use "tough on crime" rhetoric to win elections, and cash-strapped rural communities build prisons to provide employment—sometimes the prison is the biggest employer in the community. The United States is the world's leader in incarceration, and has had a 500 percent increase in the number of incarcerations over the past 20 years (Prison Policy Initiative, 2016).

These trends have resulted in prison overcrowding and in state governments overwhelmed by the burden of funding a rapidly expanding penal system, despite evidence that large-scale incarceration is not the most effective means of achieving public safety (Stemen, 2017; Eisen & Cullen, 2016). Although most of those in prison are men, the number of mothers in America's state prisons has reached a record high, which has an impact on the whole family and the child welfare system (Greene, M., Chicago Tribune May 11, 2018). Prenatal care is inadequate, pregnant women are often shackled during childbirth, and there are few community-based alternatives to incarceration that enable mothers to be with their children. More women—two-thirds of whom are mothers—are behind bars today than at any other point in U.S. history as a result of mandatory sentencing for drug offenses. The National Women's Law Center has published a report, "Mothers Behind Bars," that discusses how federal and state correctional laws can better meet the needs of pregnant and parenting women behind bars (National Women's Law Center, 2010). Efforts to establish legal "personhood" for unborn foetuses, including fertilized eggs, is increasing incarceration of women for having illegal abortions, failing to heed doctor's orders, or driving without a seatbelt while pregnant. This has been referred to as the "New Jane Crow" (Paltrow, 2013).

More than 60 percent of the people in prison are racial and ethnic minorities. One in every eight black males in their twenties is in prison or jail on any given day. These trends have been intensified by the disproportionate impact of the "war on drugs," in which three-fourths of all persons in prison for drug offenses are people of color (Sentencing Project, 2010). The argument in Michele Alexander's book *The New Jim Crow* (2012) is that in the era of "colorblindness," it is unlawful to discriminate based on race, but not based on status, such as having a criminal record. Once an individual is labeled a felon, rights can be denied, such as the ability to vote, as well as benefits to housing, food stamps, and educational opportunity. Alexander makes the case that mass incarceration of black males is intended to create a racial caste system and political disengagement of black Americans.

President Clinton signed the Violent Crime Control and Law Enforcement Act in 1994, which offered states billions in funding for new prisons. The increased reach of the prison system was achieved by implementing four major penal planks: (1) "determinate sentencing," which drastically reduced judicial and correctional discretion; (2) "mandatory minimums," which established irreducible sanctions without regard for the injuriousness of the crime; (3) "truth in sentencing," which requires every convict to serve a minimum portion of his sentence before he becomes eligible for parole; and (4) "three strikes and you're out," in the form of inflexible sanctions imposed on recidivists and the implementation of life sentences—or 25-to-life when the accused has committed three specially designated felonies (Alexander, 2012).

Another reason for the increase in incarceration has been the imprisonment of undocumented immigrants. By the end of 2009, the U.S. government was admitting more than 380,000 people per year into immigration custody in approximately 350 facilities at an annual cost of more than $1.7 billion (Detention Watch Network, 2009). Some states are re-evaluating their detention policies as they face budget deficits. A 2018 study by MassINC has found that Massachusetts's spending on corrections agencies has increased despite recent decreases in the number of people incarcerated, and the spending is not going to recidivism prevention. In February 2009, a federal three-judge panel in California ordered the prison system to reduce overcrowding by as many as 55,000 inmates. New York is putting more discretion in the hands of judges and more treatment options in the hands of offenders. Michigan has repealed most of its mandatory minimum drug sentences.

People in prison have to put their lives on hold while they are in prison. There are few job training or rehabilitation programs in prisons. According to the National Center for Education Statistics, only 7 percent of incarcerated people earned a vocational certificate and only 4 percent earned an associates degree. Since 95 percent of those incarcerated will eventually be released, it is imperative that they learn job skills in order to prevent recidivism. People in prison may be required to work in prison work programs for little or no pay (Zoukis, 2017). In September 2016, tens of thousands of prisoners in over a dozen prisons across the country went on strike from their prison jobs to protest "slave labor" and prison conditions. The inmates risked harsh punishment for their actions. Little media attention was given to the strike (Blau & Grinberg, 2016).

In many states, people who have served their sentence cannot vote after they get out of prison. When they have a "rap sheet" (the FBI identification record called the Criminal History Record Information—CHRI), they are often unable to find housing or get a job. They may lose their children to state foster care. Individuals wanted in connection with a felony or for violating terms of their parole or probation (called "fugitive felons" or "fleeing felons") are prohibited from receiving SSI or TANF benefits. They were at first prohibited from receiving food stamps, but this has changed. Since 1998, they have been unable to receive federal financial aid for postsecondary education. Since 2001, veterans accused of being "fleeing felons" have been unable to receive veteran's benefits in health care, vocational rehabilitation and education service, insurance, or loan guaranty service. Some human service workers work with people who are on probation and parole or in rehabilitation programs. They can help those formerly incarcerated check their crime records to make sure the records do not contain inaccuracies. If human service workers work with people in prison, they can help children visit their parents to prevent termination of parental rights if the children are in foster care. They can help people released from prison find jobs, get into education and job training programs, and find housing. They can work to change the system by lobbying for a more humane correctional system. Many states have social action groups working on reforming the corrections system. In Massachusetts, Governor Baker signed a bill in April 2018 to overhaul the state's criminal justice system including sealing convictions after a shortened period of time so people can get jobs, eliminating some mandatory sentences, and decriminalizing some minor offenses for youth (Schoenberg, 2018).

POLITICAL AND MEDIA INFLUENCE ON SOCIAL POLICY

People get much of their information and disinformation from the media, especially from websites, and when the media distort facts, people are more likely to have distorted views. We will examine how the media dealt with substance use, AIDS, welfare, and public health to illustrate how the media can demonize a group of people or shed light on a social problem. We have seen media change from being primarily newspapers and TV news programs to now include Internet postings, podcasts, and other opinion "news" that often are geared toward promoting one specific ideology over another.

The Drug Problem

The process of defining problems and treating those problems is often more political than scientific. Both the definitions and the treatments go through cycles that depend more on the political and economic climate than on objective analysis. A two-page pamphlet by the federal Department of Health and Human Services states the following: "Our nation is in the midst of an unprecedented opioid epidemic. More people died from drug overdoses in 2014 than in any year on record, and the majority of drug overdose deaths (more than six out of ten) involved an opioid. (Rudd, R. et al., 2016). Since 1999, the rate of overdose deaths involving opioids—including prescription opioid pain relievers and heroin—nearly quadrupled, and over 200,000 people have died from prescription opioid overdoses (CDC, 2017). Prescription pain medication deaths remain far too high, and in 2017, the most recent year on record, the Department of Health and Human Services declared opioid use a public health emergency. That year, 2.1 million people had an opioid disorder and there were 47,600 deaths from opioids and 28,466 deaths from synthetic opioids. Eighty percent of opioid abuse began with misusing prescription opioids (U.S. Department of Health and Human Services, 2019).

As the opioid epidemic has reached the suburbs and started affecting middle-income white families, the government has paid attention, with some communities moving toward treatment versus incarceration.

AIDS

In his study of the way magazines dealt with AIDS, Edward Albert (1989) shows that national magazines were slow to pay attention. When they first printed news about it in 1982, they focused on sexual orientation, sometimes in a sensationalized manner. This encouraged readers to conclude that AIDS was something that happened to "them," not "heterosexual readers," because "we" don't do those things. This raised the question of whether sexual orientation and AIDS were moral or medical issues. Because the public assumed that AIDS happened to "them," a socially devalued and powerless group, they did not insist that officials pay more attention to the disease. Newspaper coverage increased in 1983, when stories appeared about children being at risk, but decreased when the Centers for Disease Control and Prevention indicated that there was no change in the at-risk populations. Media coverage increased in 1985 with the disclosure that the actor Rock Hudson had AIDS and the implication that he was gay.

When the media finally presented AIDS as a disease that could affect anyone, it began to be seen as a disease of the normal rather than just of the deviant. Increasingly, celebrities admitted to having AIDS. Arthur Ashe, a champion tennis player, got AIDS from a blood transfusion, and basketball star Magic Johnson got HIV from heterosexual contact. In the 1990s, the media became more sympathetic, speaking out against the stigmatization of AIDS victims, which was created in part by their early inadequate coverage of AIDS (Albert, 1989). By 2000, most U.S. adults were relatively well informed about the causes of AIDS (HIV-Related Knowledge and Stigma, 2001).

The AIDS epidemic had increased people's homophobia about gays and lesbians. Although AIDS is caused by a virus, the fact that in the United States it first began and spread the fastest among gay men propelled the belief that the disease was caused by their orientation. Much of the change in public perception and official response to AIDS was created by organized groups of AIDS activists working tirelessly to educate the public and to force officials to act. Most individuals living with

HIV in the United States have access to treatment. As a result of better health outcomes, individuals living with HIV are returning to employment, some working specifically within the field of HIV/AIDS, especially in peer-based services to clients. However, not all groups have benefited equally from HIV treatment. Federal and state budget cuts on support services have had an impact on clients and the agencies that serve them. Besides medical treatment, clients need income supports, housing, food, and transportation. They also need informal support from family and friends.

Welfare

Ten different public opinion polls between 1986 and 1995 showed that most Americans thought that spending should be increased to fight poverty, but at the same time, they were opposed to funding spent on welfare (Gilens, 1999). Efforts to erase the stigma of welfare were coordinated by the Welfare to Work Partnership, which was established in 1997 with President Clinton's encouragement. It included corporate executives and aimed to persuade business leaders to hire welfare recipients. It conducted an advertising campaign with the slogans "Welfare mothers make responsible employees" and "Welfare to work is a program that creates independence" (DeParle, 1997). Politicians and corporate executives, with the help of the media, were rehabilitating the image of welfare recipients.

Welfare rolls declined by 58% between 1996 and 2011. In 1996 there were 4,543,000 households receiving AFDC. In 2011 there were 1,921,000 households receiving its replacement, TANF. There are fewer people receiving income support (23 percent of who is eligible) because states can use the funds to provide services instead of income support (Floyd, Burside, Schott, 2018). In fact, extreme poverty has increased (Ehrenfreund, 2016). These facts are not frequently discussed in the media. The current anti-immigrant sentiment is further inflamed with the perception that illegal immigrants are obtaining welfare. Illegal immigrant women may be receiving food assistance and children may be receiving free or reduced lunches, depending on the state, but they are ineligible for the majority of public benefits. With the rise in use of social media over mainstream media for news, many unchecked "news" reports are circulated.

Preventive Health Care

If we all eat healthy and exercise, we should all be equally healthy, right? There is increasingly more information showing that being poor affects overall health and life expectancy. Poverty is bad for your health. A British commission named for its chairman, Sir Douglas Black, studied the health of people in several countries, including Great Britain. It found that health policy directed to individual health (regarding smoking, diet, and exercise) improved the health of middle-income and rich people but not the poor. The poor were exposed to such deleterious conditions by their work, housing, and low income that individual behaviors often could not overcome these disadvantages. The death rate of a blue-collar worker was 2.6 times higher than that of a doctor or lawyer. The Royal Commission called for a return to the **public-health approach**, which asserts that life span is more influenced by improvements in housing, living standards, and sanitation than by improvements in medical intervention, surgery, and acute care (Townsend, 1992).

During the 1970s in England, despite countrywide improvement in living standards, the gap in health between the rich and the poor widened. The Royal Commission, after studying scientific evidence, said that gap could be closed only by (1) providing better housing and adequate income to the poor, (2) increasing wages, and (3) increasing government payments to people who are older, single parents, people with disabilities, and those who are currently without work.

This same concept, now coined the **social determinants of health (SDH)**, as defined by the World Health Organization, is widely recognized among health care providers, social workers, and community development professionals. The social determinants of health are the conditions in which people are born, grow, work, live, and age, and the wider set of forces and systems shaping the conditions of daily life. These forces and systems include economic policies and systems, development agendas, social norms, social policies, and political systems. Dr. Megan Sandel, a physician with Boston Medical Center and Children's HealthWatch, calls affordable housing a "vaccine" that prevents a myriad of health problems. Without safe, decent, affordable housing, conventional medical treatments will often not be effective.

Preventative care is a feature of the 2010 Affordable Care Act, and if states utilize the Medicaid waiver component, they can propose innovative ways to address the social determinants of health with the Medicaid funds. The state of Vermont has implemented a comprehensive in-home care program for seniors, called the SASH program, which coordinates social service, housing, and health care providers to remove barriers for seniors to remain in their own homes. The Republican-controlled Congress repealed the individual mandate of the ACA in 2017, which will go into effect in 2019. The repercussions on the cost and availability of health coverage are not yet known.

Food programs, vaccination, and fluoridation are three examples of the success of preventive public-health measures. According to the United States Department of Agriculture (USDA) the WIC (Women, Infants, and Children) food program in the United States for mothers and children with low incomes has proved that providing healthy food to children and pregnant women can prevent health problems such as infant mortality, low birth weight, and low resistance to disease. Studies of fluoridation of the water has shown a 26 percent decrease in cavities in the permanent teeth of children. (Iheozor-Ejiofor, et al., 2015). Today, immunology is an accepted practice in Western society, and many diseases of a generation ago, such as chicken pox and measles, are rare today.

Source: Rob Marmion/123RF

The senior population is growing and seniors are living longer, which has increased demand for services, including home health workers.

Public health is concerned with preventive health care, and that is a concern of human service workers. Where an illness is a large-scale problem—as are black lung disease among coal miners; brown lung disease among textile workers; hypertension among black people; cancer among asbestos workers and people living near hazardous wastes; and stroke, cancer, and heart disease among the general population—human service workers deal with the problem on these levels:

1. They work to prevent the causes of illness when they are known.
2. They work to develop appropriate and adequate services.
3. They work with the victims of these public-health problems in giving health-related services.
4. They work on addressing the social determinants of health through community organizing and building partnerships with hospitals, workforce development programs, and a myriad of social programs.

THE HISTORY OF HUMAN SERVICE WORK

Human service is a broad umbrella category that includes many different kinds of work. Among the first human service workers were doctors and nurses, teachers, lawyers, and the clergy. During the nineteenth century, the people whom we generally call human service workers today began to define their work and organize themselves into professions. They have taken a variety of routes to define their work as they responded to changing definitions of problems, technological innovations, and political and economic realities. Some of the professions under the human service umbrella today are:

- Claims workers in government benefit programs—e.g., welfare, unemployment, Social Security, Medicaid, and food stamps
- Cooperative extension workers (often called extension agents or county agents)
- Counselors (school, employment, rehabilitation, and career planning and placement counselors)
- Music therapists, art therapists, and dance therapists
- Residential-care workers with children, people with disabilities, older adults, people with substance use issues, people on parole, and youth who have committed crimes
- Psychologists
- Social workers and social service aides
- Speech pathologists and audiologists
- Therapy and rehabilitation workers (occupational, recreational, and physical therapists)
- Life coaches and motivational coaches
- Health care navigators
- Resident service coordinators
- Community engagement specialists.

We shall briefly trace the history of the profession of social work as it evolved from nineteenth-century forms to the present, and the history of the newer human service profession.

The COS and the Settlement House Movement

The roots of social work were nurtured by two major wellsprings: the **Charity Organization Societies (COS)**, from which casework and counseling grew, and the settlement house movement, which pioneered group work, community and social change, and advocacy. The COS first began in England, expanding later to large cities in the United States. They tried to be orderly in their distribution of relief funds through what they termed scientific charity. Their "friendly visitors" sought to separate the "deserving" from the "undeserving" poor through case-by-case investigation of their life situations. The COS thought that poverty was perpetuated by indiscriminate relief giving, which made people lazy, or by defects in character. The present-day Family Service Societies grew out of these COS, and people who worked in them organized most of the schools of social work in the United States. The kind of thinking that dominated the COS certainly exerted an influence on the entire social work profession. The Columbia University School of Social Work (originally the New York School of Philanthropy), the first university school to award a degree in social work, opened in 1898 under the auspices of the New York Charity Organization Society.

Social work also derived from the **settlement house movement** of the late nineteenth century. Although the early settlement house workers did not call themselves social workers, social work graduate schools began in the 1940s to include group work and community organizing in their curriculums. The settlement house movement was exemplified by the work of Jane Addams at Hull House in Chicago. A young woman from a rich family who was profoundly shocked by the poverty and exploitation of immigrant families in the urban slums of Chicago, she established a community center to help immigrants solve their social, educational, recreational, and survival problems. Hull House attracted a dedicated core of privileged yet concerned young staff, mostly volunteers who "settled" (lived) in the house (thus the name "settlement house"). These volunteers helped the newly arrived families care for their young children and conducted classes in English, citizenship, and the like. Addams imprinted on the field the values of respect for cultural differences and reaching out to clients where one finds them—on the stoops of their houses, at the corner bar, in the factory, and on assembly lines. She also promulgated the belief that society needs to work in a variety of ways to conquer social and personal problems. She loved the city and understood the power of groups to give support to their own members and to apply pressure for needed changes in the laws and customs of their communities. Four labor unions were organized at Hull House. Chambers (1980) records the history of the settlement house movement. He describes how settlement leaders supported the organizing efforts of working women, walked picket lines to demonstrate labor solidarity, testified before civic groups about the needs and rights of working women, and helped raise strike funds.

The settlement workers wanted to bring together the privileged and the underprivileged to share some of the finer things of life. Music, drama, art, and dancing clubs and classes were opened to the immigrant residents. Workers, college students, and alumni could live for a time in the settlements, playing basketball, chatting on stoops, and participating in the life of poor neighborhoods.

Many of the settlement house workers were Progressives who struggled to expand the role of the state in social welfare. They sponsored reforms such as the juvenile court movement and the establishment of kindergartens. They had a vision of a more just society and believed that their reforms could create it (Berry, 1986). That thread of reform resurfaced in the New Deal of the 1930s, the New Frontier of the Kennedy era, and the Great Society of the Johnson era. Not until the liberation struggles of the late 1950s and 1960s was the view of the state as benign parent challenged and the "rights revolution" begun.

Bertha Reynolds, an outspoken advocate of social change, summed up the difference between the settlements and the COS. She commented that although the COS and settlements were interested in the same reforms, the settlements organized neighborhoods to act for themselves, whereas the charities helped families in need. A settlement worker told her:

> "You caseworkers see people only when they are in trouble and at their worst. We live with them in good times or bad, and see them at their best. It makes our attitude different. We encourage them to take social action and help them to do it effectively. We abhor charity" (Reynolds, 1963, p. 30).

As the Progressive reform movement died, so too did much of the reform thrust of the settlement houses. Workers no longer live in the houses, and often do not even live in the same neighborhood. Many settlement houses are now primarily social and recreational centers, although some are involved in social action in their communities. The sounds of square dance music and then of rap and heavy metal replaced the angry arguments of union organizers exhorting crowds of garment workers to fight for their rights. Some settlement houses, however, continued to be involved in social action in their communities, particularly during the War on Poverty. Chicago settlement houses helped to shape Chicago's War on Poverty, brought about major changes in the city's police department, and reformed the child welfare system in Illinois (Seever, 1987).

Social Work Schools

From two groups attempting in their own fashions to aid the troubled and poor emerged a profession with noble aims but built on a shaky alliance. When schools of social work developed their curriculums, the COS wielded the most influence. As social work developed its educational curriculum during the next 50 years, the casework model of the COS became a largely accepted strategy in the field. Social workers counseled families, worked in child-protective agencies, arranged foster care and adoption for children, helped the families of sick people plan for release and rehabilitation, and worked on mental health teams with psychiatrists and psychologists.

Jane Addams drew on sociological rather than psychological theory. She was well connected with the world-renowned sociology department of the University of Chicago. But at that time, clinical psychology had not yet been developed, and sociology "offered little in respect to managing face-to-face interaction with clients; and that is where psychiatry could be applied" (Specht, 1990, p. 348). The individualistic philosophy of the COS laid the foundation for social work's almost wholesale acceptance of psychiatric theory, beginning in the 1920s. The most popular of these theories were the psychoanalytically oriented theories of Sigmund Freud.

Beginning in the 1950s, social workers were increasingly influenced by the humanistically oriented psychologies of Carl Rogers (1951), Abraham Maslow, and others, and some later incorporated what Specht (1990) calls popular and New Age psychologies—"transcendental meditation, rolfing, hypnosis, and the scores of other therapies now available" (Specht, 1990, p. 19).

Although there was no return to the theory of moral depravity that held sway in the nineteenth century, the adoption of psychology as the almost exclusive theory of social work education slowly moved professionals away from the neighborhood and group work of Jane Addams. The adoption of behaviorist theory by many schools of social work, beginning in the 1960s, did little to change the individualistic focus of the profession. The introduction of social systems theory in the 1970s (Pincus & Minahan, 1973) emphasized the interaction of the person with the environment, but although systems theory is widely discussed in social work schools, the overwhelming majority of social workers are trained to work one-on-one. Group work and community organizing expanded to meet the social ferment of the 1960s and early 1970s, but contracted when the ferment subsided.

INTERVIEW: BRIAN REYNOLDS, TRANSITIONAL LIVING ASSISTANT

Brian is a recent graduate who earned a bachelor's degree in social work and started his career two years ago working with youth in the Baltimore public school system. He currently works at a cost-free, residential school that serves pre-K through twelfth-grade students from lower-income families. As a transitional living assistant at the school, Brian works with high school seniors who reside in shared apartments. He helps them gain life skills, such as grocery shopping and cooking, and guides them in their transition to college or work. In addition to group work, he meets with the students one-on-one to support them. He is careful not to impose his own beliefs and agenda, using techniques such as "reflecting back" and paraphrasing so that the students learn to reach their own conclusions.

When asked how school prepared him for his job, Brian said that one of the most relevant classes he took was "Diversity and Inequality," a course that taught cultural competency, which is recognizing and valuing differences. He has learned on the job to be cognizant of various perspectives and careful not to say anything that could be interpreted as insensitive. His thesis class instilled the concept of "dealing with ambiguity," which he has found to be a reality in this field. For example, when designing a workshop or small group project, there is no single right way to go about it. The important thing is to follow the mission and watch out for "goal displacement" or getting sidetracked. The human service field is very broad—there is such a variety of jobs with non-profit agencies, each with a different focus and approach. One school might focus mostly on building character while another emphasizes academics.

Brian plans to pursue a master's degree in social work and would like to one day work abroad.

CURRENT TRENDS IN SOCIAL WORK

As social services are becoming increasingly privatized, so is social work. As states passed licensing laws, workers became eligible to receive **third-party payment** for therapy through the clients' insurance. Social workers' reasons for preferring private practice over agency practice vary. Earning more money is certainly one of the major reasons; another is that many workers are dissatisfied with the bureaucracy and restrictions of agency practice and yearn to control their working conditions and choose the types of clients they will serve (Abramovitz, 1986). There is intense debate within the profession, and there have been pitched battles among the National Association of Social Workers (NASW), the National Institute for Clinical Social Work Advancement, and the American Board of Examiners (Battle, 1990). Many who oppose the trend believe that the rise in private practice amounts to turning our backs on the poor, who cannot afford to pay $70 to $150 per hour for therapy and cannot get insurance coverage for it. Those who favor the trend argue that social workers are as qualified to do therapy as are psychologists, and should have that choice.

College graduates with degrees in social work, psychology, sociology, or human services fill jobs in public social services. They provide care for people who are older, children who have been neglected and abused, people with disabilities, and people with mental illness, a large proportion of whom are poor and minorities.

Undergraduate social work programs were established in state colleges, mostly in sociology departments, during the Depression, to staff the new public welfare agencies created by the Social Security Act. The Council on Social Work Education (CSWE) accepted the bachelor of social work (BSW) credential in 1966, but it was not until 1970 that NASW admitted BSW workers as members. The CSWE allows graduate schools to admit BSW members with advanced standing if they choose. Thus, BSW graduates can often finish an MSW degree in one year rather than the two years usually required.

Loan Forgiveness

The NASW is promoting loan forgiveness for social workers. It supports proposals to provide loan forgiveness for social workers in child welfare and schools, as well as other practice areas. You can find out if you are eligible for these programs by contacting the U.S. Department of Education Federal Student Aid Information Center at 1-800-433-3243, You can also take a look at two bills that offer loan forgiveness for social workers and other human service workers: (1) the Higher Education Act and (2) the College Cost Reduction Act of 2007.

Another federal program that helps social workers is the National Health Service Corps Loan Repayment Program. In exchange for two years serving in an approved community-based site that has a shortage of health professionals, or Health Professional Shortage Area, this program offers fully trained and licensed clinical social workers $50,000 to repay their outstanding student loans.

The Roots of the Human Service Field

The field of human services was born in the 1950s and since then has expanded in fits and starts. The term *human service*, as opposed to *welfare*, was given the official stamp of approval when the federal Department of Health, Education, and Welfare (HEW) changed its name to the Department of Health and Human Services (HHS) in 1980.

The federal government set out to create a new profession of human service workers. Although saving money may have been one reason for this, there were also other factors at work. Some liberal federal bureaucrats saw social work as too traditional and rigid to deliver adequate services to the poor. The civil rights movement created pressure to open up service professions to minorities who had previously been excluded. Then too, there was money available for social services, and many professions wanted a piece of this action. Government expenditures on social welfare rose dramatically, nearly tripling between 1960 and 1970, and another infusion of funds came in 1975 with the passage of Title XX legislation, which funded social services. College educators from a variety of disciplines—counseling, education, special education, psychology, social work, and others—scrambled for Title XX funds.

The new human service workers included the indigenous neighborhood people ("new professionals") recruited during the War on Poverty by social agencies, schools, and hospitals; community college graduates with an associate degree and a major in human services or a related field; and graduates of four-year human service programs. The following influences have helped the human service profession to grow:

1. **The civil rights and liberation struggles.**   During the civil rights and liberation struggles of the 1960s, people of color, feminists, LGBT, and youth declared that mainstream social work was irrelevant. It was too white, too middle class, and too patriarchal. They created their own alternative self-controlled agencies: The Black Panther breakfast program, feminist health collectives, parent co-op day care centers, shelters for survivors of domestic violence, gay and lesbian counseling centers, and shelters and drug counseling centers for alienated and runaway youth. Most of these were not staffed by professional social workers, although an occasional social worker sympathetic to the agency's ideology might work with it.

2. **The OEO War on Poverty.**   In its War on Poverty, the Office of Economic Opportunity (OEO) challenged the COS mentality of established social work. The OEO set up new agencies to do battle with the social work gatekeepers to get more benefits and services for clients. Actually, because most workers in departments of welfare are not BSW or MSW social workers, OEO's war with welfare was not in a strict sense a war with the social work profession but instead with government bureaucracy. However, OEO officials tended to view the profession of social work as the enemy of change.

   Many establishment agencies eagerly accepted OEO money, and some highly professionalized agencies, such as Family Service Societies, for the first time hired "indigenous workers" from the communities they served in order to forge links between the agency and the service users. Many professional child welfare social workers were challenged, for the first time in their careers, by poverty lawyers defending parents of foster children. Poverty lawyers entered areas that had in the past been the domain of social workers.

3. **The New Careers for the Poor movement.**   The **New Careers for the Poor movement**, conceived of and best articulated by Arthur Pearl and Frank Riessman (1965), was begun as part of the War on Poverty to create human service careers for poor people. Finding that they were blocked in their quest for upward mobility by lack of credentials, one of the movement's leaders, Audrey Cohen, started the College of Human Services in New York City. She announced her intention to "change the whole pattern of credentialing as it now exists" (Houston & Cohen, 1972, p. 22).

   The **career ladder** concept, in which a worker with incomplete training could move up through on-the-job experience and training, was built into some antipoverty legislation. Many agencies and colleges drew upon antipoverty funds to set up training courses and programs.

4. **The growth of community colleges.**   The burgeoning growth of community colleges in the late 1960s and the 1970s spurred the growth of human service programs—more than 500 by 1996 (Di Giovanni, 1996). This gave the New Careers students another way to gain a credential, and—aided by antipoverty money and grants—many associate's degree graduates found jobs in agencies and schools. President Obama's administration increased funding for community colleges.

5. **Deinstitutionalization and contracting out services.**   Deinstitutionalization created a demand for workers in community residences, pre-release centers, mental health clinics, and other community settings. This, along with the increase in contracting out of services to private agencies, created new agencies that were not part of the MSW or BSW tradition. Workers came from many disciplines. Contracting out not only took some turf away from social work but also weakened public service unions, bringing down the wage scale in both the public and private sectors.

Some people consider Dr. Harold McPheeters the founder of the human services field. In the 1960s, Dr. McPheeters of the Southern Regional Education Board (SREB) applied for and received a grant from the National Institute of Mental Health (NIMH) for the development of mental health programs at community colleges in the southern region of the country. This was the beginning of the associate-level human service degree in the United States (Di Giovanni, 1996).

The National Organization for Human Service Education (NOHSE) was founded in 1975 at the Fifth Annual Faculty Development Conference of the Southern Regional Education Board. It unites educators, students, practitioners, and the people they serve in a conversation about preparation of effective human service workers. In 1976, the NIMH gave funds to the SREB to create national standards for training and reviewing human service programs (Brawley, 1980). Out of this project came the Council for Standards of Human Service Education (CSHSE), formed in February 1979. In 1982, the National Commission for Human Service Workers was incorporated to provide a national system for voluntary registration and certification of human service workers (National Commission for Human Service Workers, 1982).

NOHSE is now called the National Organization for Human Service (NOHS), and SREB is now called the Southern Organization of Human Service (SOHS). There are many four-year human service programs and two-year programs in community colleges, and there are now PhD programs. Judy Slater, the president of the NOHS, says that the NOHS is revising its Code of Ethics so that more programs will have a way to identify if they are meeting the standards of the Council. It has developed a practice-based examination for certification. The exam is based on case scenarios. A board-certified practitioner will be designated a Human Service-Board Certified Practitioner (HS-BCP). To be eligible to apply for the HS-BCP national credential, an applicant must have a degree from a regionally accredited college or university, or a state-approved community or junior college at the technical certificate level or above. Applicants must also have completed the required post-degree experience. The number of years or hours is outlined in the HS-BCP application packet.

New Disciplines

Among the first professionals to retool for the human service field were elementary and high school teachers who were faced with layoffs resulting from declining student enrollment. By 1979, more than 300 colleges or departments of education had human services programs (Vogel, 1979). One of the authors of this book, Barbara Schram, started a human service program in one of them. The American Association of Colleges for Teacher Education recommended relieving the oversupply of teachers by diversifying to produce a new kind of teacher, a human service educator.

Although psychologists have always been in the human services, a branch of psychology called professional psychology is more oriented toward counseling than toward research. The first school of professional psychology, accredited by the American Psychological Association in 1974, appears especially oriented toward health services, the field that accounts for a large proportion of the growth in social welfare spending since the 1960s.

In sociology, a specialty called clinical sociology has developed, whose practitioners, particularly family sociologists, do therapy with individuals, groups, and families. Their counseling theories include a sociological perspective that examines the difference between private troubles and public issues.

Finally, in the field of child abuse and neglect, which for decades was the almost exclusive province of social work, doctors and lawyers gained prominence. Advances in radiology in the 1960s made it easier to diagnose abuse, and the term *battered-child syndrome* was coined. Since then, many child abuse units have been located in hospitals rather than in social agencies. Lawyers also became involved in defining abuse and neglect and in representing parents, children, and states in court cases.

As a human service worker, it will be helpful to think of situations in your own life or among your family members where you or they have encountered a problem and sought assistance. How did you feel asking for help? How were you perceived or treated? Drawing on your own experiences will make you a more understanding human services worker.

Trends in Payment and Evaluation Systems Impacting the Human Services Field

The **Pay for Success (PFS) Model** reforms the payment for and delivery of social services to successful outcomes versus paying for outputs. An example of an outcome would be the percentage of people who completed a substance use treatment program and have not relapsed in 12 months. An output would be the number of people obtaining substance use treatment. It is a contractual arrangement that is becoming popular in government and philanthropy. One of its advantages is that it includes an evaluation component where the focus is on strategies and programs that are effective. This is called an **evidence-based** approach. In the Patient Protection and Affordable Care Act, the PFS model discourages the "revolving door" of hospital re-entry and creates an incentive for hospitals to do a better job of follow-up care to prevent re-hospitalization. In some of the state homeless contracts, shelter providers are paid for each successful placement in permanent housing when the individuals do not re-enter the homeless system for a period of time. For seniors, preventing placement in nursing homes by providing home care services is a successful outcome for the client and a savings for government programs such as Medicaid. The disadvantages of the model could occur when "creaming" the clients' results. Creaming is selecting the candidates most likely to succeed for the program because of the payment incentive. Another potential disadvantage of the PFS model is the elimination of services that are useful but don't provide the level of outcomes desired.

As these changes in payment structures evolve, so will the skillsets of the human services worker. This model does rely on data collection systems and training of staff in evaluation and technology.

Summary

1. People have always helped, as well as hurt, each other. The nature of a society shapes people's helping impulses. One anthropologist believes that the principle of reciprocity is the basic glue that holds a society together.

2. A review of the history of helping gives perspective on how changes in society shape the methods of helping. To understand the present, we need to know the past.

3. At the beginning of industrialization, people who needed help were regarded as morally depraved. That attitude shifted somewhat to the view that problems are often beyond the control of the individual.

4. Universal programs, such as Social Security, cover people of all social classes. Means-tested programs, such as TANF, cover only the poor and are often stigmatized.

5. Welfare gradually shifted from local to state and then to federal responsibility. In recent years, responsibility has drifted back to state and local governments.

6. During the rise of Protestantism, especially Calvinism, the poor were regarded as people who had been denied the grace of God, and were treated as criminals. They were placed in debtors' prisons and workhouses. This attitude pervaded American society well into the twentieth century.

7. During the civil rights era of the 1960s, many people redefined poverty as a result of an unjust social system. This gave rise to an opportunity theory of poverty, as opposed to a victim-blaming theory.

8. Political ideologies often define personal and social problems. Such influence characterizes,

for example, the following issues: the drug "epidemic," the response to welfare, an individual versus a systems approach to health care, and the roles and privileges of men and women.

9. The forms of helping go through cycles. For example, welfare reform, the care of those with mental illness, and the treatment of youth who have committed crimes and adults who are incarcerated have all run cyclical courses.

10. The Progressives attempted to individualize the treatment of those who were in prison with mental illness. However, given unchecked authority, professionals often violated clients' rights.

11. The contemporary response to mental illness is deinstitutionalization, which places clients in more normal settings in the community, although there are not enough community facilities.

12. Judi Chamberlin, one of the founders of the mental patients' liberation movement, talks about the treatment of mental illness.

13. The juvenile court system was more humane for children, but its failure to provide the due process of adult courts resulted in many injustices.

The Supreme Court's 1967 Gault decision gave juveniles some due-process rights.

14. The United States is the world's leader in incarceration. A disproportionate number of people in prison are black or Latino partly because of the war on drugs, which criminalized possession of small amounts of drugs.

15. The causes of people's problems can be distorted in popular culture, and policies are often based on perceptions.

16. The public-health approach, stressing preventive care, has saved more lives than medical intervention, surgery, and acute care.

17. The first professionals to do social welfare work with the poor were social workers. The two early strands of the profession were the COS and the settlement house movement.

18. The human service field began in the 1950s and since then has grown with the impact of deinstitutionalization, the War on Poverty program, the New Careers movement, and the proliferation of community colleges.

19. Some federal programs help college students to repay loans.

Discussion Questions

1. What is the federal government's responsibility toward helping the poor and in ending extreme poverty?

2. Individuals with mental illness often reside in homeless shelters or in the prison system. What alternatives are available that protect clients' rights and choices?

3. Why do you think benefits such as welfare cash assistance and food stamps are political hot buttons in the United States?

4. How do attitudes toward the poor shape human service workers' responses to their situations?

Web Resources for Further Study

National Organization for Human Services (NOHS)

https://www.nationalhumanservices.org

The National Association of Social Workers (NASW)

https://www.socialworkers.org

The National Empowerment Center

https://www.power2u.org

Planned Parenthood

https://www.plannedparenthood.org

Prison Policy Initiative

https://www.prisonpolicy.org

National Alliance to End Homelessness

https://www.endhomelessness.org

National Organization for Women (NOW)

https://now.org

Community Voices Heard

https://www.cvhaction.org

National Alliance on Mental Illness (NAMI)

https://www.nami.org

MyLab Helping Professions for Introduction to Human Services

In the Topic 1 Assignments: History of Human Services, start with Application Exercise 1.1: Identifying Historical Values and Credentialing Quiz 1.1: Identifying Historical Values.

Then try Application Exercise 1.2: What If Jane Addams Were Here Today? and Credentialing Quiz 1.2: Jane Addams and the Settlement House Movement.

3

Strategies, Activities, and Tasks of Human Service Work

Learning Outcomes

- Students will be able to describe why we need interventions that are tailor-made for individuals and their specific sets of problems.
- Students will be able to list the 14 direct and indirect strategies that human service workers use to help their clients solve their problems.
- Students will be able to identify the seven worker activities that are employed when using both the direct and indirect strategies of human service work.

Source: Monkey Business Images/Shutterstock

There Are No One-Size-Fits-All Solutions to Human Service Problems

A human services student intern in the human resource department of a large corporation wrote this entry in her fieldwork journal:

> While I was covering the reception desk yesterday, a woman who works in the employee cafeteria came into the office. She told me that her boss is sexually harassing her. I described to her all the possible places she could go to report her concerns. Then I told her my honest opinion of the benefits and drawbacks of each pathway. After a few sentences she interrupted me, saying, "Okay, enough, just tell me the best thing to do!" I gave her one of our usual yes-but-then-again answers.
>
> "Damn it!" she shouted, "Why can't you give simple answer to a simple question?"

Although the employee was frustrated by the lack of clear solution to her problem, this student knew that with personnel problems, just as with all other human service problems, there are no easy, one-size-fits-all solutions. Action plans to solve people's problems cannot be designed the way a chemist combines elements—two parts of hydrogen mixed with one part of oxygen always produces water. In our field, we never can predict exactly what the outcome of our words or actions will be. Because that reality is often forgotten, people become frustrated by the endless duplication, contradictions, and lack of clarity they find when dealing with human service problems. For every problem a person faces there are several possible ways to try to alleviate it. These ways are called "intervention strategies" and every one of them has a set of trade-offs.

Irritating as this situation may be, it is inevitable. Three basic forces create this seemingly endless diversity of approaches and consequences:

1. Value conflicts in a pluralistic society
2. Historical changes in theories and resources
3. The concept of multicausality

We will briefly explain the first two factors, but in this chapter, we will focus primarily on the impact of the concept of multicausality on the design and implementation of intervention strategies.

Value Conflicts: As you read Chapter 2 on value conflicts and Chapter 5 on working with diversity, you will find that there is very little agreement in our society on issues as basic as human nature and the legitimate functions of government. The definitions of what constitutes proper parental discipline, the appropriate roles of males and females, attitudes toward sexuality, consumerism, and even the legitimacy of social protest vary according to our race, religion, ethnic heritage, educational level, and the extent of our assimilation into U.S. society. Our socioeconomic class, sex, region of the country, ideology, age, and stage in life also exert an impact on our opinions and actions.

Historical Changes: The attitude of society toward social problems, and the helping process, undergo constant shifts. New theories on the causes of and cures for social problems keep emerging. Programs established in one era reflect the state of theory at that time. But agencies rarely change as quickly as the shifting beliefs and viewpoints. Human service workers trained at a time when certain theories or viewpoints held sway sometimes continue to operate under those theories long after they have been discarded or revised by other more current theories or viewpoints. For example, Title VII of the Civil Rights Act of 1964 defined sexual harassment as a form of sexual discrimination. Before this, there was no legal designation for sexual harassment. However, specific guidelines for what constituted sexual harassment were not established until the Equal Employment Opportunity Commission issued proposed guidelines for enforcement in 1993. The guidelines have been used as a foundation for helping companies create human resource policy as well as establish a foundation for possible legal action. That has led to human resource departments of many companies issuing written guidelines for employee conduct that specifically address sexual harassment.

THE CONCEPT OF MULTICAUSALITY

When a person sets out to solve any problem, the most logical first step would be to try to find out what has caused it. When the cause has been identified, a rational plan to solve the problem can then be designed. But as human service workers try to propose solutions to fix problems, six principles of **multicausality** make this a very difficult task.

1. *In dealing with social problems, it is difficult to prove causality with any solid degree of certainty.*   Even though we may have collected all the data we could about a person, we

still end up with a best guess, an informed hunch, or a hypothesis to explain the causes of his or her problem. For example, it is easy to make the assumption that if infants are picked up every time they cry, they will become spoiled. But it is equally possible that if infants are allowed to cry for long periods of time, they will become frustrated. As we watch a child who constantly seeks attention from a teacher, we cannot tell if the child's behavior is caused by too much or too little parental supervision at home. We also cannot tell if it is because of a genuine inability to understand the work and the child needs more instruction, or if it is because the work is too easy and the child is bored and ready to move on.

If we were to read all the books on the shelf of a library under the heading "Child-Raising Manuals," we would find many different, often contradictory views among the experts. Whether children should be spanked, breast-fed, sent to day care or kept at home, taught the alphabet early, and so forth are questions with many different answers (Breitbart & Schram, 1978). Dr. Benjamin Spock, author of a best-selling manual on raising a healthy child, did a major revision of his book several years after the first edition (Spock, 1946, 1976). If you tried to follow his parenting advice in 1946, you would have raised your little boy or girl very differently than if you read his revised book 30 years later. Spock looked back at his first book and was shocked by his own sex-role stereotyping. In his later books, he confessed that his thinking had undergone a dramatic change (Spock & Morgan, 1989).

When we read about the lives of famous people, we find every possible kind of parenting. Some have excelled in life presumably because of supportive home environments, but others have excelled despite their negative home environments. Some of these people were orphans, some were the only child in the family, and some had many siblings. The authors of biographies struggle to understand the impact of their subjects' early experiences on their adult personality and life choices, and rarely can they come up with answers. Jerome Kagan (2016), an eminent Harvard University child development specialist, has found that the more he studies, the less he is convinced that there are very many linkages between a person's early childhood characteristics and his or her personality as an adult.

2. *There is rarely one simple reason for a complex social or personal problem.*   When we observe negative behavior, either in a social system or in an individual, we can be absolutely sure that more than one factor is responsible. Beware of popular wisdom that will try to sell you simple reasons for a complex phenomenon. Headlines may shout:

> POLITICIAN DECLARES LACK OF DISCIPLINE IN HOME
> IS MAJOR CAUSE OF RISE IN VIOLENCE IN SCHOOLS

or

> SCHOOL AUTHORITIES SAY INADEQUATE CRIMINAL JUSTICE
> SYSTEM IS CAUSE OF VIOLENCE IN SCHOOLS

or

> SOCIAL REFORMERS DEMAND INCREASE IN JOBS
> TO STEM GANG MEMBERSHIP IN YOUTH

Our popular culture sometimes can lead people to simplify the causes of their problems, leading them to believe that their problems are caused by a single event in their lives—the "one cataclysmic event" after one cataclysmic event is the cause of their current pain.

For example, perhaps a television drama portrays the therapist helping a distraught woman remember the horrible experience that led, 20 years later, to her inability to cope with her mental health issues. Finally released from the confines of her repressed memory, she walks out of his office into the waiting arms of husband and children, made whole again. Veterans, refugees, and victims of violent assaults often suffer **posttraumatic stress disorder (PTSD)** from the devastating things they have seen and felt. But neither the development of their problems nor the solutions to these problems are ever that simple.

3. *Human service problems are the result of many intertwined personal pressures and social forces.*   The problem of delinquency among young men and women, for example, involves so many different developmental stresses, generated by the family, neighborhood, peer group, media, and school, that it would not be possible to overcome delinquency by changing only one aspect of a teenager's life.

   If we look behind another headline, we will find that there are no compelling research data proving that when fewer women worked outside the home, youth crime was substantially lower. Given both the current economy and the realities of many women's desire for jobs and careers, it is hardly practical to expect all mothers to stay at home.

   Although a severe lack of jobs and few prospects for their future employment might encourage youngsters to resort to criminal behavior, jobs alone do not stop crime. Youth need to be trained adequately for rewarding jobs, and the jobs offered must hold the promise of a future. In addition, if simply having a job assured honesty, we would not have the widespread white-collar fraud that has led to the downfall of many banks and other financial institutions.

THE NEW SEXUAL REVOLUTION

Source: © Steve Greenberg/Seattle Post Intelligencer

Each major social change, such as the sexual revolution, brings with it a host of both negative and positive consequences. This leads to the further proliferation of social programs to deal with them.

Too much leisure time with nothing to do may encourage some juvenile crime, but providing recreation centers alone would not account for a large reduction in crime statistics. Video arcades, movie theaters, and even sports teams do not necessarily create mentally healthy people.

Finally, there is the individual enmeshed in all these systems. Individuals bring with them their own strengths and weaknesses, some innate and some learned, as well as their unique combination of luck and chance.

Another human service problem that is the result of many complex personal and social events is child abuse. Some people might believe that child abuse is caused by poverty, or that parents who were beaten as children will become abusive parents. But these two factors account for only some unknown percentage of abuse. Not all victims of child abuse come from poor families, and many adults who were abused as children do not become abusers.

To understand the full dimension of any social problem, we must systematically analyze all the contributory causes. To do this type of multicausality analysis, we draw a circle to represent the whole problem. (See Figure 3.1). Then we divide it into several pie-shaped pieces. Each piece contributes to the whole problem.

As you study Figure 3.1, remember that many of the theories of causation are tentative. Some reasons have yet to be found, and we are not sure of the relative importance of each of the wedges to the total problem. Research in the field of child abuse reveals much contradictory data (Hilarsky, Wodarski, & Feit, 2008; Kadushin, 1980). After a few more years of study, we will probably omit one wedge or diminish its size. For example, we used

Source: Michael Candelori/Shutterstock

When we work for social change, we often become involved with others in demonstrations of their values. This is a march to protest discrimination against people based on their race, religion, gender, or country of origin.

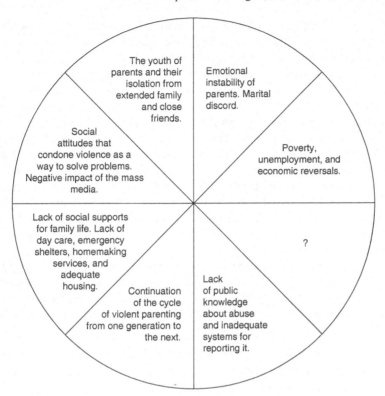

FIGURE 3.1 Possible causes of child abuse

to think that poverty and harsh working-class-style discipline were the major contributors to abuse. Then, as child abuse reporting systems improved, we became aware that child abuse was not dependent on social standing: it also occurred in many middle- and upper-class families. These families might have avoided detection earlier because they used private doctors who were less likely than those in public hospitals to diagnose a bruise as being the result of parental abuse or neglect. And in suburban schools, as opposed to inner-city schools, teachers may have discounted or rarely considered the possibility that a child's injury had been inflicted by his or her parents.

We have also realized that there are different forms of abuse and neglect. When sexual and emotional abuse are included in the definition, there is little doubt that this problem does not respect the boundaries of socioeconomic class.

As you study the pie chart, you will notice that the several reasons for child abuse described are generated from different sources. The inner psychological pressures that drive adults to hurt children are intertwined with the exterior pressures exerted by social institutions and world events.

4. *Some causes of social problems are deeply rooted, and others are more secondary.*   After we explore the many causes that lie behind a human service problem, we must try to rank them in some order of priority. Then we might try to focus our efforts for change on the causes that might have the most powerful impact. These are called the **root causes**. But usually the root causes are the most deeply buried and the hardest to deal with. Visualize a large tree you want to remove from your garden. It is held in place by a series of roots,

some close to the surface and others firmly embedded. The surface ones may be the easiest to remove, but that does the least to dislodge the whole tree.

Exploring root causes, like everything else connected with causality, is a matter of action and reflection, trial and error. For example, a woman enters counseling convinced that her depression is a result of her husband's unhappiness with their relationship. Her husband complains that she is no longer willing to go out with him or entertain their friends as they used to. After meeting with the couple together and separately, the counselor suggests that she visit a physician. The doctor diagnoses her constant lack of energy as a biological disorder called chronic fatigue syndrome. Unfortunately, there is no cure for this biological condition. Perhaps the couple's situation will remain the same for a while, but the definition of the root cause of the problem is now very different. He might still be unhappy with her inactivity, but he is likely to feel less unhappy and, perhaps, more understanding. If he is less angry, her mood is likely to improve. And if the basic commitment to each other is still strong, perhaps they can find new ways to enjoy being together as a couple and with friends.

5. *Although many people appear to have the same problem, they may have it for different sets of reasons.* If one were to visit a meeting of Alcoholics Anonymous (AA), it would be easy to assume that the participants were all there for the same reasons. True, they all have problems with alcohol. But what constellation of causes has led them to their addiction to alcohol? There are many subgroups within this seemingly homogeneous assembly:

   - Subgroup A includes people who were raised in a family with substance use issues.
   - Subgroup B includes people who are in a relationship with a lover or spouse with a substance use disorder.
   - Subgroup C includes people who have an undiagnosed and untreated biological condition such as **anxiety disorder** or **attention deficit/hyperactivity disorder (ADHD)**.
   - Subgroup D includes people who are in a profession that includes a great deal of social drinking.
   - Subgroup E includes people who have recently experienced a major life trauma, such as death, divorce, job loss, or diminished physical capacity.

If one were to observe a group of 18 third-grade students in a town-wide tutoring program, it would be easy to assume that they all have the same problems. Even though they are all labeled as having a learning disability and their scores on a standardized reading test place them two years behind their peers, we may discover after getting to know them that:

   - Three need eyeglasses and one needs a hearing aid
   - Two are very bright but have short attention spans
   - Three have a specific learning disorder, such as dyslexia
   - Five are attending a school that has large classes, inexperienced teachers, and high staff turnover
   - Two have serious problems at home that divert their energy
   - One frequently comes to school hungry, cold, or physically ill
   - For two, we can find no reasons at all. (Maybe they are just late bloomers.)

Of course, each of the causal factors just described is filtered through the screen of the child's unique personality and habitual way of coping. Just as there are no two identical faces in the world (except for identical twins), there are no two identical psychological profiles.

Figure 3.2 shows a multilayered maze that illustrates the many forces shaping our attitudes and actions. These forces begin to influence us from the moment our genetic makeup is determined by the combining of a sperm with an egg. The impact that sex, race, and physical abilities and disabilities will have on a specific child's future will be mediated by his family, culture, and neighborhood, and other significant events and groups.

6. *Even when people encounter similar experiences, they do not necessarily react in similar ways.* In a very personal account of his internment in a Nazi concentration camp during World War II, the late psychologist Bruno Bettelheim (1950) wrote about being both victim and professional observer. He described the ways inmates adjusted to life under intolerable circumstances. Many died resisting the guards, others acquiesced almost humbly, some escaped, some collaborated, and some took leadership roles for the first time in their lives. Differences among the prisoners seemed to be based on their life experiences before their internment and their personal characteristics, occupations, and skills, as well as on large doses of luck and chance.

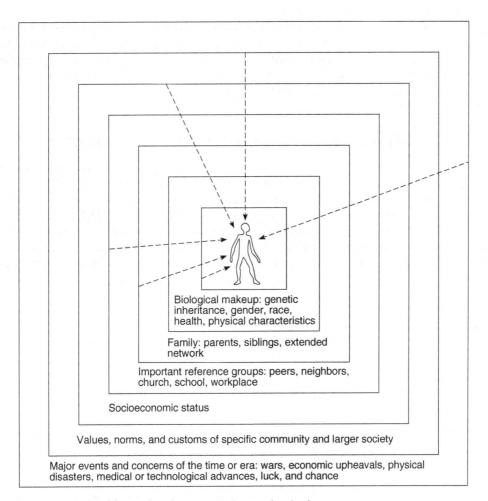

FIGURE 3.2 Six sets of forces that shape our actions and attitudes

It was impossible to predict in advance how concentration camp survivors would fare in the future. Some, like Bettelheim, gained strength from adversity and went on to have outstanding careers. Some became bitter, withdrawn, and distrustful. Still others became profoundly more appreciative of the basic pleasures of family and friends.

By not understanding this concept, social planners often propose simple—and very wrong—solutions to complex social problems. For example, those who believed that the wide availability of alcohol was the root cause of alcohol use lobbied long and hard to get it outlawed. They succeeded in passing the Eighteenth Amendment to the U.S. Constitution in 1920. The Prohibition Act banned the sale of alcoholic beverages all across the United States. Although it appeared to be a logical strategy of intervention, the act was a disaster. Criminals quickly took the place of the legitimate alcohol-producers and merchants, and we had a situation that looked very much like the drug wars that are being fought in the streets of many U.S. towns today. Formerly honest citizens became criminals and the time and energy of the police were spent in futile effort. Should we try to decriminalize drugs in the same way? What are the pros and cons of doing that? The debate rages on.

Currently both government officials and citizens who are concerned about the problem of alcohol misuse use a variety of strategies. They are working to make alcohol less available by banning alcohol advertisements in the media, raising the minimum drinking age, limiting the amount of alcohol at campus events, and teaching about the negative effects of binge drinking. Can you think of five other strategies that might be used in the battle against alcohol misuse?

THE STRATEGIES OF INTERVENTION: DIRECT AND INDIRECT

Although workers use many strategies to solve problems and they assume different roles in various settings, their actions are neither random nor idiosyncratic. The Southern Regional Education Board surveyed a large number of human service workers in the field. They identified 14 of the most consistently used worker roles or strategies of intervention. In Table 3.1 we have divided them into three categories: **direct-service strategies**, which deliver services directly to those people confronting the problem; **indirect** or **systems-change strategies**, which create, maintain, or change the institutions and groups in which services are delivered; and finally, a middle category that combines elements of both types of strategies.

TABLE 3.1 Strategies of Intervention

Direct-Service	Both Direct-Service and Systems-Change	Systems-Change
Caregiving	Group facilitating	Planning
Case managing/counseling	Outreaching	Administering
Teaching/training/coaching	Mobilizing	Data collecting and managing
Behavior changing	Advocating	Evaluating/researching
	Consulting	
	Assisting a specialist	

Source: Categories derived from Southern Regional Education Board, 1969.

An excellent way to increase one's understanding of the world, both as a worker and as a citizen, is to volunteer for a Sister City Project. Members of families in a poor village in Nicaragua work side by side with visitors from the United States to build low-cost, sturdy houses.

The boundary lines that separate one set of strategies from another and those that divide the direct-service from the indirect or systems-change strategies are fluid. A worker might shift from one intervention strategy to another over the course of a week or in the course of an hour. We warn the student that these worker strategies are not brand names like products on a supermarket shelf. Agencies may use them interchangeably or in ways that differ from the way we are defining them. But categories, although imprecise, are useful insofar as they help us visualize the two overarching goals of all human service interventions:

- Helping individuals overcome the problems that confront them
- Helping to improve the environments or organizations that might help or hinder overcoming their problem

In order to see how a human service worker uses many of the strategies we have just listed, we introduce the reader to Ruth Bork, who is the coordinator of the Disabilities Resource Center (DRC) at a large university. The interview with Ruth shows how she and her staff members use virtually every one of the direct-service and indirect or systems-change strategies. After you have read the interview, see if you can identify how she employs each of the strategies in her daily work.

Source: Jeffrey B. Banke/Shutterstock

An excellent strategy to increase the public's knowledge of the human services that are available in their community is to hold events with information tables at which staff can describe their programs.

INTERVIEW: A HUMAN SERVICE WORKER AT WORK

Ruth Bork, Administrator, Disabilities Resource Center at a large university

It is hard to believe that I've been in this job for over 30 years. I was the first staff member hired, so I had the rare opportunity of starting an agency from the bare walls. My job has grown and changed so much. I work on a variety of levels, from the individual students all the way up to the University President's office. Since the passage of the Americans with Disabilities Act (ADA), in 1990, my job has expanded even more.

My primary task is meeting the needs for supportive services and accommodations for any student or staff member at the university who has a documented disability. This includes folks who have significant visual or hearing impairments, problems with mobility, learning disabilities, or psychiatric conditions. Some of them are permanently disabled from birth or through accident or illness. Some are temporarily disabled.

Counseling begins from the moment students are accepted. They need help in finding the package of resources that can get them through the class work and social life of a large university. For example, if a student has a mobility impairment, I review his or her program to make sure that the classes needed for his or her major are held in accessible buildings. If they aren't, I get the class moved. I also have to make sure that a student in a wheelchair can get from one part of the campus to another in the class break time. Nothing is worse for the student's morale than to have the class start without him or her or to keep everyone waiting.

Sometimes I advocate with a department chairperson for changes in the student's academic program because a learning disability makes mastering certain subject matter almost impossible. Perhaps a major is very prescribed, requiring certain courses in sequence, but the student can handle only a limited number of courses at one time. The university will have to make an exception. If there is fieldwork, we may have to arrange transportation; if there is a conference with an instructor, the student might need a sign language interpreter.

The DRC hires, trains, and schedules note takers, who sit in on classes and provide the DRC student with a coherent set of notes. We have one staff member whose whole job it is to schedule sign language interpreters and note takers for students with a variety of limitations.

I'll arrange for books to be delivered if the student has a condition such as arthritis and has a hard time standing in a two-hour line at the bookstore. We make sure that the university library has the latest Braille texts and that the dorms are equipped with special alarm systems and telephones for the visually and hearing impaired. Our students have a right to anything that gives them a level playing field. . . . . Equal opportunity means many different things.

Training and orienting the faculty and staff takes up a lot of my time. They need to be aware of the needs as well as the feelings of the different segments of the population with disabilities. I run workshops and conferences. I am available to consult with faculty on individual students in their classes.

The fastest-growing segment of the population we serve is the students with learning disabilities. Their condition is invisible. It requires a lot of consciousness raising to help professors realize that being late or incomplete on an assignment can be part of a documented disability. Many of these students take untimed tests in our office, where there are few distractions. Faculty members have to change their mindset from "lazy and unmotivated" to "student who needs organizational support services."

I encourage the students to tell the faculty what their abilities and disabilities are and what it is they need in order to get the most from school. Labels don't tell us much because every student, whatever his or her disability, has a different set of circumstances and personality.

I also serve as the adviser to the DSO, the Disabled Students Organization. This is a social group, but more importantly, it is a voice for the students. One voice isn't very loud, but when several are raised all at once, the university pays attention. Sometimes the students win their demands and sometimes they have to compromise, but I still encourage them to make requests and take action. Now the DSO is protesting because the administration plans to move our office. The new space is larger, but it will be in the subbasement. Some students see that as an insult. They have felt swept under the rug in their own communities, so they want a central location. I don't think they will win this battle, but I think it is worth voicing their opinions.

We also run support groups. These are led by the students with disabilities themselves, counseling interns, and occasionally a faculty member. These groups help the students to realize that they aren't alone, and the more experienced students can pass on wisdom about the system. Instead of me deciding and telling others what needs to be changed, I can get varied opinions through the groups. They have been catalysts for improvements.

We've been working for many years to make the buildings on campus more accessible. Federal laws require that physical barriers be removed. For example, we now have chair lifts installed in the buildings, so wheelchair riders can go from one level to another. We also have published special maps of the campus so that a new student who uses a wheelchair can quickly learn how to get around. We take the barriers one at a time, and we work on a specific architectural modification. In the older buildings, that is very hard to do.

I'd like to tell you what a typical day is like, but there is no such thing. A student may come in with a problem concerning a class or an internship. I may get a call from an administrator who wants information on the cost of a chair lift. Lately the university attorney has been struggling with some lawsuits that have been brought by staff members who have disabilities and don't feel they have been treated fairly. As people with psychiatric conditions move into the mainstream, there are more students and staff on campus who present challenges to faculty and administrators. I act as a consultant on those cases.

The problems I deal with range from A to Z—from administrative problems to zero sensitivity. For example, I might advocate on behalf of one of our students who's living in a building off campus that needs to be made accessible and the landlord just wants him or her to leave. So my work isn't contained just within the school. I deal with all the facets of our students' lives if they ask me to.

Networking, referral, and resource collecting are important aspects of my work. If a student is having trouble with financial aid, the athletic department, or a roommate, that can be his or her most pressing concern. It needs to be addressed.

I also have to keep sharpening my administrative skills as the job gets more complex. I have learned how to propose and keep a budget, do annual reports, write memos and action plans, do research, chair meetings, and speak up on behalf of the students with disabilities.

As the civil rights of people with disabilities expand, my office and my job also expand.

DESCRIPTION OF DIRECT-SERVICE STRATEGIES

Caregiving

When using a caregiving strategy, the bulk of a worker's time and effort is spent meeting the client's immediate needs. In jobs such as home health aide for elders, provider of **respite care** for the family of a child with physical disabilities, or counselor in a residence, the worker gives emotional support and physical care, and helps in obtaining additional services. For example, Ruth often must find personal care attendants who can help a student with a disability get ready in the morning. She also helps to recruit workers or volunteers to help by note taking, or by reading to a student who is blind. Many entry-level and part-time jobs in the human service field require that a large percentage of worker time be spent on caregiving tasks.

Case Managing/Counseling

Case-managing and counseling interventions aim at making sure that individuals locate and obtain the services for which they qualify. Vocational rehabilitation agencies, welfare departments, family agencies, hospitals, school systems, children's protective agencies, and large institutions such as city governments or universities employ workers who use these strategies.

Sometimes the worker is referred to as an ombudsperson, a Scandinavian word for a professional go-between, a red-tape cutter who carries a person's complaints to the highest authority. Workers who do counseling or case management are assigned a number of clients—a caseload. These workers stay in touch with these individuals to make sure that services are reaching them. Because entitlements are often buried in many different laws, programs, or agencies, few people can find their way through the maze alone. Human service workers often organize hot-lines and special resource centers so that connections can be made between their clients and the programs they need.

Although human service workers provide emotional support and assist clients in finding and using services, generally they do not perform the type of insight counseling or therapy done by a more highly trained psychologist or clinical social worker.

Teaching/Training/Coaching and Behavior Changing

In recent years, more and more human service workers have been using teaching/training/coaching and behavior-changing interventions. In this role they work to prepare clients of institutions or hospitals for an eventual move into a community residence and from there, hopefully, to live on their own. Through role-playing, guided field experiences, modeling, and reward systems, they teach survival skills to people with physical or mental disabilities. These skills, which include finding and keeping a job, managing money, using public transportation, and enjoying recreational outlets, are called "the skills of daily living."

Such intervention strategies are also employed by public school staff workers as they try to mainstream (integrate) children with disabilities into regular classrooms. A special-education worker may go into the home of a family to show parents techniques that will help their developmentally delayed preschooler to do routine tasks and prepare for school. The use of an early intervention program is increasing in importance with every age group. The government agencies that fund programs have realized that money invested in solving problems early on saves a great deal of money down the line.

Human service workers often train peer leaders or mentors to help in the running of drug and alcohol awareness programs. Ruth uses these interventions when she orients new note takers and tutors or models techniques for faculty members to use when they have a student with a hearing impairment.

DESCRIPTIONS OF COMBINED DIRECT-SERVICE AND INDIRECT/ SYSTEMS-CHANGE STRATEGIES

Group Facilitating

Traditionally, YMCAs and YWCAs, Scouts, 4-H clubs, Junior Achievement groups, settlement houses, and recreation centers have used group-facilitating strategies. Group workers help members develop their leadership qualities, build confidence, and expand their skills and cultural awareness.

In recent years, the use of group techniques has grown beyond the recreational setting. The deinstitutionalization of individuals with mental illness or physical disabilities has led to the creation of many small community-based programs. There are social clubs for people with mental health issues, pre-release centers for people completing jail sentences, and group homes for juveniles who have committed crimes. Day care programs for preschool children as well as for elders and adults with disabilities also use group interventions.

Support groups bring together divorced parents, adult survivors of abuse, persons caring for an individual with AIDS, compulsive gamblers, individuals who are overweight, or older women entering the workforce for the first time. Human service workers may facilitate such a group. When able peer leaders emerge, the human service workers often withdraw, providing consultation as needed.

Many agencies use groups to orient new clients and volunteers. Some adoption and foster care agencies ask experienced parents to orient prospective ones, just as Ruth asks a junior or a senior to lead a support group for first-year students who share her disability.

Outreaching

Because she has learned that she can never simply sit in her office and wait for students or faculty to come to her, Ruth has developed many creative outreach strategies. Through meetings, phone calls, and extensive networking, she spreads the message about the DRC's services to members of the university community. She invites them to visit the office and get to know her staff.

Mental and physical health agencies, recreation centers, and both private and government youth-serving agencies often employ outreach workers to make sure the public knows about the services they offer and to encourage them to use them. Outreach workers, for example, might seek out and work with gang members in an effort to reduce inner-city violence. During the summer months, many suburban towns employ college students to mingle with the neighborhood teenagers and try to head off the problems that often develop when teenagers with too much free time hang out together. After they become accepted by the teens, the college students can plan recreational programs with them.

Outreach workers at day care centers and other early-childhood programs might visit churches and clinics to obtain referrals. They also spend their time sitting in living rooms and around kitchen tables answering questions about their programs or sharing educational techniques. Departments of social services use outreach workers—sometimes called "home finders"—to locate and monitor appropriate foster homes for children, teens, and the elderly.

Mobilizing and Advocating

There has probably never been a day in the years she has worked at the DRC that Ruth has not heard at least one complaint from a student, a faculty member, or a staff member. Complaints are warning signs that something is not going as well as it should and needs to be improved. Working in a large university, she has often had to mobilize a great deal of clout to smooth out the rough spots. Perhaps a faculty member refused to let a student use a tape recorder even after the student explained why it was necessary. Ruth might have had to go up to the next level of authority, exerting pressure through the department chair, the dean of the college, or the academic provost.

Perhaps parents are futilely demanding that the city park department clean up a rubble-strewn lot so it can be used as a safe play space. They may turn to a human service worker to learn how to mobilize enough citizen pressure to get action.

On a more sophisticated level, perhaps a citizens' task force with a human service staff person is mobilizing public sentiment to exert pressure for the reorganization of an unresponsive school board or police department. Human service workers mobilize others and advocate to bring about change. They often attend board meetings, public forums, court, and occasionally picket lines.

Consulting and Assisting a Specialist

Some human service workers share their special knowledge and skills with clients, the public, and other professionals. Ruth has been serving on a task force that monitors how well the university is complying with the ADA. If there are problems involving an employee who is deaf, she calls on her staff member who specializes in hearing impairments. If there are issues she does not know enough about, the university seeks out an expert who can share his knowledge.

Professionals from many fields tap the special knowledge of human service workers by organizing interdisciplinary teams. In the adolescent psychiatric unit of a hospital, for example, each patient is assigned a team composed of a doctor, a nurse, and a human service worker. The human service worker generally interviews or visits the family and represents their needs when the team meets to evaluate each patient's progress.

When employed by a government licensing or monitoring board such as the Office of Elder Affairs, human service workers visit nursing homes, for example, to make sure they are providing adequate care. If there are inadequacies, they share their expertise in programming, budgeting, or staff relations.

Some lawyers, doctors, and therapists employ human service workers to act as their eyes and ears with community groups or other mental health professionals. In this role, human service workers are likely to employ any one, or all, of the strategies discussed so far.

DESCRIPTIONS OF INDIRECT/SYSTEMS-CHANGE STRATEGIES

Planning

Of course, planning is an integral part of all interventions. But some human service workers develop special expertise in this role. They spend most of their time researching, designing, organizing, monitoring, and evaluating a new or expanded program to fill a gap in the human service network. You are likely to find a planner hard at work in a library, at a computer terminal, or in the office of a foundation or government bureaucracy.

In small agencies such as community residences, all the staff use planning interventions to organize fundraisers, outings, social events, and volunteer orientations. Ruth started out using mostly counseling interventions, working one-on-one with each student. But now, as her staff has grown and her expertise has expanded, she has become so adept at planning that she could move into any setting and put together a program proposal to start a new service.

Administering

Although traditional human service agencies and government bureaucracies are most likely to be administered by an experienced staff person with an advanced degree in psychology, medicine, social work, or public administration, newer, small-scale institutions assign staff with human service degrees to administrative roles. Even a recent graduate may be given the job of directing a small program for mothers with AIDS or a shelter for women who have experienced domestic violence. Although the center may accommodate only five or six women at a time, it requires the same range of skills needed to run a large hospital or school. Money must be raised and accounted for, the facility must be furnished and maintained, forms must be submitted, staff must be recruited and trained, and mailing lists and other clerical details must be completed.

Collecting and Managing Data

If a student at Ruth's university who has broken a leg on a ski trip cannot find out about the services available at the DRC, then the services are worth very little. The mushrooming of human service programs and entitlements on college campuses and in the larger community has led to new methods for finding, assessing, and utilizing resources. Compiling specialized resource booklets and designing web sites that are attractive and accessible require vital human service skills. Keeping a computer updated with information on programs for eating disorders or narcotic addiction enables a counselor at the DRC to make a useful referral.

Laws are constantly changing. They are also written in legal language and are difficult to understand. Human service workers write pamphlets that translate complex legal jargon into standard language. With this information, a mother with a sick child and no money can find out how to apply for Medicaid or file an appeal if she is denied fuel assistance or food stamps.

Evaluating/Researching

Although human service workers are likely to turn to a variety of experts to find statistics and research data, they too must be prepared to carry out a small-scale survey or a web search for up-to-date information on a particular disability or medication.

As community-based programs have become more decentralized, their funding sources have had to work harder to keep track of them. Human service workers need to learn to help design and implement evaluation plans. They collect statistics, interview clients, and write reports of program events. The funding or renewal of a program often depends on how well social workers have assessed client attitudes and needs and kept their services responsive to the population they serve.

At the end of each fiscal year, Ruth submits a budget request for the DRC for the upcoming year. She has been able to document the need for expanded budget and services through her systematic research. In addition, an outside evaluator visits the program each year, and Ruth assigns two staff members to help the evaluator assess student satisfaction with the services of the DRC.

ACTIVITIES AND TASKS WE USE FOR ALL THE STRATEGIES

The interview with Ruth showed her using all of the strategies of intervention. What you could not see, however, is the way she goes about implementing them. Whether she is counseling a student with a head injury, drafting a plan to remove an architectural barrier in a dormitory, or organizing an orientation meeting for faculty, she proceeds in an orderly way, using the same activities for all of her work.

Seven tasks must be performed in all of the work that she does:

1. Gathering data
2. Storing and sharing information
3. Negotiating contracts and assessing problems

4. Building a trusting relationship
5. Designing an action plan
6. Implementing the action plan
7. Monitoring and evaluating the work

Ruth always begins by gathering data and ends by evaluating the work she has done. Although we have listed these activities and tasks by number, we do not mean to imply that one must be completed before proceeding to the next. In actual practice, several may be done simultaneously. But the message we wish to impress on the reader is that our work is never random. There is an underlying pattern of tasks that are needed to implement each strategy. If we skip one of the following tasks, we risk a failed intervention.

Gathering Data

Ruth needs to paint the fullest picture possible of each student, faculty member, or administrator's situation. Yet it is much harder for her to collect relevant information than it would be if she were a biologist or physicist. Many of the data she collects and acts on are at best incomplete and variable. We cannot take a temperature or do a blood test to find accurate information. Sometimes a person's words may be cheerful, but the tone of voice reveals pain. To more fully understand the emotions behind words and to grasp the complexity of each person's situation, Ruth uses many data-gathering techniques. She collects data through conducting interviews, reading, doing research, and attending conferences and workshops. Only after the data have been gathered can she begin to plan how to help each student.

INTERVIEWING   Interviewing underlies all of Ruth's work. The quality of information she gathers before making a plan depends on how skillfully she conducts an interview. The first part of the interviewing process is asking appropriate questions. Through role-playing in a class or a training situation, students develop skill in phrasing questions in a way that avoids steering the listener into a preconceived path or into a verbal trap. Ruth has learned when to ask open-ended questions that provoke maximum expression. She uses focused questions to elicit accurate information about dates, times, and places. She often asks for clarification.

When asking questions and listening to a client's or colleague's responses, she uses her active-listening skills. Active listening is distinguished from the more passive kind of social listening by its total concentration. She remembers precisely what has been said and reflects back ideas and feelings to make sure she understands.

Active observing is also part of interviewing. Ruth tries to grasp the full significance of what is being said by assessing the emotional tone of the words as well as by observing facial expressions, hand movements, posture, and gestures—in other words, body language.

READING, RESEARCHING, AND ATTENDING CONFERENCES AND WORKSHOPS   Usually some background information is available for each of the tasks Ruth undertakes. The counselors at the DRC have access to their clients' test scores and high school grades as well as statements from school counselors and doctors. Records of past meetings, for example, help a new worker assigned to the support group for students with learning disabilities get oriented. Human service workers read whatever background data they can find. But all information has limitations. Records are written by people who have brought their own biases to the recording or testing process.

Much data gathering goes on at case conferences or committee meetings. Sometimes workers do their data gathering at libraries or on the web. In the professional journals, they learn about a research or demonstration project on a particular problem. They go to workshops where clients, coworkers, or professionals from allied fields gather to share information.

An integral part of data gathering is focused visiting and observation. In some programs, this involves visiting the homes, classrooms, or workplaces of clients to gain some firsthand insights into their strengths and weaknesses as they interact with the system. Visiting another program can be stimulating for workers who have been locked into the routine of their own agency.

Storing and Sharing Information

Information is never randomly jotted down. Recording has a purpose, and the DRC workers practice the skills of focused note taking. Professional recordings or minutes separate a worker's personal evaluation or judgment from the observable or verifiable data.

Careful collection and sharing of information is a direct expression of respect for clients and coworkers. It also protects workers from accusations of mismanagement. Ruth needs to document how her staff has spent money and time, and she must keep records of her clients' unmet needs.

Negotiating Contracts and Assessing Problems

Nothing defeats the helping process as much as lack of direction. For each new intervention, Ruth negotiates a working contract, which articulates mutual expectations and the rules of the road with clients, faculty, and colleagues. The contract spells out each of the actors' responsibilities and often includes goals and time frames. A contract might be written or verbal, but it must be clear. And it often changes over time as reality shapes the task at hand.

Building a Trusting Relationship

Ruth begins building a relationship with a student (or faculty member or administrator) from the first moment of contact. She continues to nurture the relationship throughout the helping process. The primary tool all workers must have is an ability to communicate warmth, concern, empathy, and knowledge. It is also vital that she assure others that she will keep their words confidential where that is required.

If Ruth cannot gain the trust of students, colleagues, and administrators, she will be ineffective, no matter what else she is able to do.

Designing and Implementing Action Plans

Many social agencies, especially those that receive public funds, require that a formal action plan be written and accepted by client and worker before any services begin. These plans commit to paper the problems, the goals, and the specific ways they will be worked on within a set period of time.

In programs that employ behavior modification approaches or in which basic survival skills are being taught, individualized service plans (ISPs) help both worker and client be clear about the small tasks that must be worked on from day to day. In Ruth's office, there is a written plan in each student's file. Both the student and his case manager sign the plan and review it periodically.

For Joan, a first-year student who has both receptive and expressive language problems, Ruth suggested the following items for her action plan:

1. For the first semester, she will take a reduced load of two courses.
2. A note taker will accompany her to class.

3. Three times a week, she will attend the DRC for skill building with a tutor and three other students.

4. She will continue seeing an occupational therapist twice a month to help her with eye–hand coordination.

5. She will attend two workshops on study skills offered by the counseling and testing center.

6. She will arrange to take some vocational preference tests at the counseling center to help her decide on a major.

7. She will check back in with Ruth five times during the semester for 15-minute sessions to evaluate each of the preceding activities.

To make sure each part of the plan is implemented, Ruth will write a memo to the staff member who schedules tutors, write a letter to the department chair explaining the need for the reduced course load, and send a referral form for testing. During the 15-minute check-in sessions, she will offer an attentive ear and a lot of encouragement.

Monitoring and Evaluating the Work

Because individuals, environments, and social interactions are in perpetual motion, Ruth becomes skilled at critically looking at and reshaping contracts, relationships, action plans, and methods of implementation. A worker who is in tune with the dynamic state of the problem-solving process is always asking questions: How is that student getting along in each class? What seems to be getting in the way of X, Y, and Z? Have I fully understood how the client feels about her situation?

In order to answer these questions, Ruth has developed a variety of evaluative feedback techniques. She uses both focused questions—asking for the facts—and open-ended questions getting at feelings. Obviously, the student is the primary source of feedback. Workers also use supervision by or consultation with more experienced colleagues to check on how their own work is progressing.

Source: A katz/Shutterstock

These young adults are members of AmeriCorps, a civic engagement program funded by the Federal Government. They are fixing up a park in an urban neighborhood.

We have just taken a quick tour through the work of Ruth, a human service administrator with an important and challenging position. From starting each program strategy by gathering data to finishing each one by evaluating her work, she proceeds to move along a well-trod pathway. In the chapters in Section 2 you will read in more detail about each of the program strategies that she and her very committed staff use to improve the lives of so many members of the University community. We have begun to answer the big question posed by the first chapter of this text: What Do Human Service Workers Do?

Summary

1. Solutions to social problems should flow from a diagnosis of the many possible causes of the problems.

2. The uniqueness of people and their problems calls for diverse, tailor-made interventions. No one-size-fits-all solution is ever possible.

3. Strategies of intervention are overall approaches to the helping process that have been identified by studying the tasks that workers perform in their daily practice.

4. All of the intervention strategies are necessary and equally important. The generalist worker uses them at different times. Some workers specialize in a few of the strategies.

5. The 14 strategies can be divided into those that directly assist the person with the problem and those we term *indirect strategies*, which are needed to maintain or change the systems within which the person interacts and services are delivered.

6. The direct-service strategies are: caregiving, case managing/counseling, teaching/training/coaching, and behavior changing. The mixed direct-service and indirect/systems-change strategies are: group-facilitating, outreaching, mobilizing, advocating, consulting, and assisting a specialist. The systems-change strategies are planning, administering, data collecting and managing, and evaluating/researching.

7. The seven worker activities used for all of the strategies are: gathering data, storing and sharing information, negotiating contracts and assessing problems, building a trusting relationship, designing an action plan, implementing an action plan, and finally, monitoring and evaluating the action plan.

Discussion Questions

1. In the discussion of multicausality, we assert that just as there are no two identical faces in the world (except for same-egg twins), there are no two identical psychological profiles. What might account for the often enormous differences in the personalities and interests of two siblings raised in the same family? For example, one might be an honor student and school council leader, while the other lives for sports and is content to be at the bottom of her class. If you have siblings, how alike are you? If there are major differences between or among you, what might account for the differences?

2. Ruth Bork provides many services for students with disabilities, many of whom have learning disabilities. Discuss the differences between equal treatment of students and equitable treatment of students.

3. How might you explain to an engineering major the reasons why organizing a bake sale to raise money for a tutoring program or organizing a dinner at a senior citizen community, which seem like such non-academic activities, are valid educational experiences for a human service class?

Web Resources for Further Study

Strategies

When you want further information on any of the strategies discussed in this chapter, you can Google the specific skill or theory you are interested in (e.g., interviewing, group work, or community organizing). There is a wealth of published material. If you want to know more about a specific field and what is required in the job, the Occupational Outlook Handbook can be an useful resource.

The National Association for Human Services

https://www.nationalhumanservices.org/ethical-standards-for-hs-professionals

For Students—National Organization for Human Services

https://www.nationalhumanservices.org/for-students

Disabilities Information

https://www.makoa.org

This site is a directory of many kinds of disability resources and links leading to accurate, informative sources. Each disability has several of its own web sites.

MyLab Helping Professions for Introduction to Human Services

In the Topic 2 Assignments: Human Systems, try Application Exercise 2.3: The Nature of Human Systems.

Attitudes/Values, Skills, and Knowledge of the Human Service Worker

4

Source: Merfin/Shutterstock

Learning Outcomes

- Students will be able to explain why both volunteer and professional workers often appear to be doing similar work in a human service agency.

- Students will be able to recall the differences between a friendship and a professional helping relationship.

- Students will be able to draw the pyramid of the helping relationship and then list the key attitudes/values, skills, and knowledge within each of the three dimensions.

- Students can describe how John, who works at a center for youth who are homeless, utilizes many of the attitudes/values, skills, and knowledge described in the chapter.

If we were to go on an around-the-clock tour of the human service agencies in Urban Center, U.S.A., we might find:

1. A young college student and a middle-aged homemaker hunched over telephones or computers in a church basement, listening to or reading with great care the words of some people who have reached out for help. One of them is a recently widowed older man talking about ending his life. The other person is a frightened teenager pouring out an anguished account of her rape.

2. In a union hall on the other side of town, an articulate, charismatic woman is holding the rapt attention of her neighbors at the weekly

strategy meeting of the Citizens United for Economic Justice. She is organizing a campaign to obtain job training programs for the poor people in this community, who have been suffering from a recent surge in unemployment. The next speaker is an outreach worker for a legal services program. He explains the intricacies of lobbying at the state house in support of subsidized, affordable health care.

3. In an old but brightly painted two-story house, a young man—a rehabilitation counselor—is teaching a cooking class to four adults with blindness who are preparing themselves for the day when they will leave this community residence to move into their own apartments.

As we continue our tour, we will meet workers who have a dizzying array of titles, qualities, styles, backgrounds, and motivations. Most typically, they will be working as parts of teams or coalitions that combine laypeople and professionals. They are working as staff members or are serving on committees and boards, sharing their expertise and uniqueness. At times, this mixture of people from different backgrounds is cooperative and supportive; sometimes, it is abrasive or adversarial. Often, laypeople and professionals work in different ways toward similar goals.

In this tour, we have described an incredible diversity in the roles, titles, agencies, and program strategies in the human service profession. Without a doubt, it is much easier to describe the work of a doctor, a lawyer, a printer, a chemist, or an elementary school teacher. Each draws on a specific body of knowledge and skill. Each works in a limited number of institutions or roles. Usually there are great differences between the abilities of these professionally trained workers and those of the ordinary "man in the street." We wouldn't feel very safe having our tonsils taken out by a garage mechanic who did a little surgery in his spare time.

This is not true in the human services. The professional with years of experience, the person who just received a degree, the hot-line volunteer counselor who makes his living as an insurance broker, and the fellow sufferer in a support group of cancer survivors all can play pivotal helping roles.

The fact that many types of people are helpers—caregivers, counselors, organizers, group leaders, and activists—does not make our profession any less dignified or prestigious. In fact, this inclusiveness is its strength.

Let's look first at the helping relationship and then at the attitudes, values, skills, and knowledge that are shared by all human service workers.

THE PROFESSIONAL HELPING RELATIONSHIP DIFFERS FROM A FRIENDSHIP

A key element shared by all human service workers is the **professional helping relationship** they build with their clients. It differs in both structure and content from the purely social relationship.

In our personal lives, we might accompany a friend to a nursing home to lend moral support as he or she visits a dying grandmother. We might take care of a child while his or her parents go out to vote or attend a school open house. In our professional role, we might talk about a baseball game with the members of a foster parent group before their meeting begins. However much these interactions might seem similar, our friendships and our professional helping relationships are uniquely different, and a competent helper is always aware of this.

The Structure of the Professional Helping Relationship

Five qualities distinguish the professional relationship from the purely social one.

1. *The professional helping relationship exists for a limited time, whereas friendships might last for many years.*   In a professional helping relationship, a time schedule may be agreed on at its inception. For example, a worker and a group of teenagers who have physical

disabilities might agree to spend six sessions discussing issues of sexuality. Or a worker in a rehabilitation agency might say, "We shall work together until my client has found a job and seems to have settled into it."

Whatever the duration of the relationship, we commit ourselves to ending the relationship just as soon as the client no longer needs it. We strike a subtle balance between setting someone adrift too soon and hanging on so long that we encourage dependency.*

Saul Alinsky (1969; 1971), a pioneering community activist, always stressed that the human service worker who built a strong neighborhood action group should expect eventually to be "thrown out" by the indigenous leadership. Once the group members develop skill and self-confidence, they are likely to view the outside professional as excess baggage. Strange as it sounds, the aim of all human service workers is to work themselves out of the professional helping relationship and maybe even out of a job!

2. *The professional helping relationship has a clear focus, whereas friendships have many purposes—some superficial, others profound, most of them vague.* Though the focus of a professional helping relationship may change as it progresses, both client and worker need to agree on an initial set of tasks, stated in action outcomes:

> "I am going to this vocational counselor because I want to find a job so I can leave the residential treatment center and be on my own."

> or

> "I came to Renewal House because I need a safe shelter from my husband, who has been beating me. As soon as I find an apartment, get some legal help, and sort out my finances, I will move out."

> or

> "I work for the Children's Protective Services and have been asked by your son's teacher to visit you to see if you can use any of our services for families."

The helper and helpee **negotiate a contract** in which tasks and goals are spelled out. Some of these initial goals are likely to change. Sometimes the contract is a grudging one. Perhaps the client has been forced to see the worker in order to earn extra privileges on the locked ward of a psychiatric hospital or to gain early release from prison.

3. *The professional helping relationship depends on a division of labor.* Although friends often complement each other in many ways, the division of roles and responsibilities in a social relationship is random. The professional helping relationship is a collaboration, but each of the parties has specified tasks. The person being helped shares expertise about the problem—basic facts as well as fears, hopes, and expectations. The helper shares knowledge of resources, alternative strategies, obstacles, and the prospects of different courses of action. Each has the right to make certain decisions. Whenever possible, most of the decisions should be made by the client, who must live with the decisions.

4. *The professional helping relationship is disciplined, whereas in a friendship each person is relatively free to act on impulse.* Of course, friends learn what to do and what to avoid if they want their relationship to last. In the professional helping relationship, much of the informal trial and error is replaced by a set of operating principles.

---

*Unfortunately, in an age of managed care and cost cutting, forces outside our own reasoned judgment may decide when the professional helping relationship must terminate. This will be discussed further in Chapter 9.

Even when the human service worker appears to be kidding around in the locker room with the basketball team member or drinking coffee with her parents, she is behaving in a conscious manner. Workers can relax, but they cannot lose track of the tasks that need to be done or the goal of the encounter. The role of the worker is not to solve the clients' problems but to be a catalyst in the problem-solving process.

Even in informal settings, everything the client says must be kept confidential. Throughout the book, we will discuss the realistic difficulties in maintaining absolute **confidentiality**. But as a general principle, workers accept this basic tenet of the helping relationship.

Although a recreation leader might have a splitting headache or a devastating family problem, on the job, his personal issues take a backseat. Disciplined workers can, to an amazing degree, ignore their own illnesses or personal troubles when working. Afterward, in the privacy of their own homes, these irritants might resurface, as annoying as ever.

5. *The professional helping relationship is built on acceptance.*   A professional helping relationship is not built on friendship. Without judging (or perhaps even liking) a client, the worker tries to understand the person's problem, accepting feelings without necessarily condoning specific acts. Of course, if a worker cannot emotionally connect on any level with the essential humanness of a client's predicament, the client should probably be reassigned to someone else.

The Content of the Professional Helping Relationship: Attitudes/Values, Skills, and Knowledge

Although the structure of the professional helping relationship sets the stage for competent human service intervention, its content—words and actions—is, of course, most important. Figure 4.1 illustrates the three components of this content.

THE PYRAMID MODEL

Professionals in every field require a combination of attitudes and values, skills, and knowledge, a constellation that has been dubbed the "ASK" concept. In Figure 4.1, we represent the three components in the form of a pyramid. Any professional who lacks one of these components will be less than satisfactory. For example, a doctor who is a brilliant diagnostician (skills and

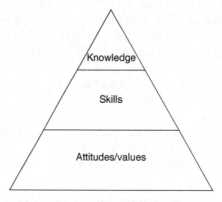

FIGURE 4.1   The pyramid model of the components of the helping relationship

knowledge) but also is cold and brusque (attitudes) and lacks a comforting bedside manner might slow down a patient's recovery. The racetrack driver who has the bravado to compete (attitudes) but has not carefully studied the engine in his new car (knowledge) is likely to lose the race or have an accident.

Not only do the attitudes and values, skills, and knowledge areas vary from one occupation to another, but so does the relative importance of each dimension. For example, in the training of doctors, knowledge and skill are stressed the most. That annoying doctor who lacks an empathetic bedside manner (attitudes) can still be elected to high office in a medical society for his or her brilliance as a diagnostician. He or she is even likely to be sought out by anxious patients willing to put up with gruffness as the price of being cured.

With human service workers, however, all three dimensions have equal weight. Their work is very holistic, but each component of their work must be built on the base of appropriate attitudes and values. For example, it is possible for a school counselor to be knowledgeable but be of no help to a student. Perhaps you have met someone like Mr. Schroder. He knows all about college requirements and the Scholastic Aptitude Test (SAT). But if he does not have the warmth to relax that shy, inarticulate student sitting before him, he may never find out what his student, Eric, really wants to do after graduation. Lacking empathy and insight (attitudes and values), he doesn't sense Eric's ambivalence about going to college. He rambles on. Eric barely hears him, and will soon forget what he has been told. Mr. Schroder never notices that although Eric has ostensibly come for college counseling, he wants to take time off from school but is worried about hurting his parents.

Attitudes and Values Form the Base of the Pyramid

Human service education and work must always start from a solid base of appropriate attitudes and values. Onto that base, knowledge and skill can then be added. Although attitudes form the base of the pyramid, they are not in themselves sufficient to help the person who must take the next steps in solving the problem. The worker at the local mental health agency who is filled with empathy (attitudes) for the family of a recently blinded child might be able to give appropriate emotional support, but if she does not know how to find the best resources for the education, recreation, and rehabilitation of children who are blind (skills and knowledge), she won't be of much assistance.

Bruno Bettelheim, an eminent psychologist, underscored this point in the title of his landmark book on working with children with mental "disturbances," *Love Is Not Enough* (1950). He asserted that human service work, like effective parenting, involves love coupled with wisdom and the skills to communicate both.

The pyramid concept is especially important to understand as you begin your training. Most human service educators visualize the pyramid in their minds even if they do not draw this diagram for their students. Their teaching style assumes that the starting point consists of attitudes and values. They often use first names, encourage students to share their backgrounds, sit the class in a circle, and stimulate discussion to elicit students' ideas on controversial topics. Although these teachers are using a method of interaction aimed at helping class members sharpen their self-awareness and self-confidence, students sometimes worry that the class is not academic enough. One faculty member expressed her surprise at the students' hesitant reactions to her teaching style.

At each of my class sessions, I would come into the classroom hoping to find the students buzzing to each other about their fieldwork or the controversial speaker we'd heard the day before. Instead, they'd be sitting seats apart from each other in the vastness of the lecture hall.

They waited for me to start, as if nothing could happen among them until I arrived. Every day I'd insist they get up, push the tables to the side, and form the chairs into a circle. Although they were much more animated when sitting in a circle, they still seemed to view the furniture moving as a pointless waste of energy. They resisted, and I got frustrated. I felt that they did not believe that listening to each other's ideas and experiences was an important part of their education.

After that disappointing semester, I got the idea of starting off my first class with a discussion of the attitudes/values, skills, and knowledge pyramid. Once the students understood that we were exploring the attitudes and values at the base of the triangle—as we played name games or argued about capital punishment—they stopped worrying about memorizing my words to repeat for the final exam. They even stopped resenting the work involved in moving chairs into a circle.

These students realized, as we hope you do, that without a firm, broad base, a pyramid will topple over!

ATTITUDES/VALUES, SKILLS, AND KNOWLEDGE: AN OVERVIEW

Table 4.1 lists the attitudes and values, skills, and knowledge areas that are of vital importance to the professional helper. We have already warned you that the categories are bound to overlap. In addition, our list is neither definitive nor exhaustive. Your course instructor or field supervisor is likely to say of us, "They have missed this vital concept," or 'They have given too much importance to that idea."

It is easy to understand differences in emphasis. If you compare the catalog description of the program you are enrolled in with a similar one at another college, you will probably find much variation in the courses offered and the competencies stressed. Because human service programs

TABLE 4.1   The Content of the Helping Relationship

Attitudes/Values	Skills	Knowledge
Patience	Data gathering	Human growth and development
Empathy	Interviewing—active looking, listening, and question asking	Abnormal growth and development
Self-awareness	Observing	The impact of society and culture on behavior
Capacity to deal with ambiguity and take risks	Researching	The dynamics of groups and organizations
Willingness to ask for help and offer feedback	Attending conferences	
	Visiting	
Belief in people's and systems' capacity to change	Storing and sharing information	The social and political forces that affect helping
	Keeping records	
Open-mindedness, skepticism, and rejection of stereotypes	Writing reports	Social problems, special populations, and resources
	Building relationships	
Humor and a light touch	Negotiating contracts	Issues of research and evaluation
	Forming action plans	
	Implementing action plans	
	Intervening	
	Referring	
	Monitoring and evaluating	
	Giving and receiving feedback	
	Constructing evaluations	

are relative newcomers on most campuses, they have grown out of, or remain under the wing of, more established behavioral fields. They take their coloration from the particular academic department that gave them life. If the program is under the wing of the Psychology Department, the course content stresses counseling and interpersonal skills, whereas course work emphasizing social, cultural, and institutional elements of mental health and treatment might take a backseat.

Before reading the descriptions of human service attitudes and values, skills, and knowledge, be assured that no human service worker ever masters all of them. Each of us understands, accepts, or integrates some areas better than others. As challenges occur, such as a new job or an unusual situation, we stretch ourselves to learn more, sharpen our skills, and explore the impact of our attitudes and values on our current tasks.

Most of us are likely to change direction several times in our careers. Sometimes the change is a response to political upheaval; sometimes it is a move to renew ourselves and avoid burning out as work becomes too draining. We may have counseled individual clients for many years and then discovered that we enjoy managing or planning an agency. Some workers start their careers by doing recreation with children who have disabilities and then later engage in advocacy with older adults or families experiencing difficulties.

In order to make the components of the model less theoretical, let's look at the work of John Torrente, a counselor at Sanctuary House, a shelter for teenagers. As you read about his work, see how many elements of attitudes and values, skills, and knowledge you can identify.

Source: Courtesy of Barbara Schram

Our beliefs about the value of people of differing classes, ethnic groups, ages, and genders begin early. These nursery school children are learning to respect varying lifestyles by taking trips around the city and being exposed to differences and similarities in the families and cultural backgrounds of their classmates.

INTERVIEW: A HUMAN SERVICE WORKER AT WORK

John Torrente, Outreach Counselor at Sanctuary House, a Shelter for Teenagers

Sanctuary is just what its name implies. It is a safe haven. Many of the teenagers here have run away from their parents' homes. Maybe there was some abuse or they felt no one wanted them around. A few are running from the consequences of some of their own antisocial actions. Some have left—with or without permission—from foster families, institutions, or community residences. There are as many stories as there are kids. You learn early on that you can't judge in advance why they left and how justified it was.

I am one of six outreach counselors at Sanctuary. This is my second year on the full-time staff. I go to college part-time during the day. I've been working on and off at the house for four years. I began as a volunteer when I was in high school as part of a community service club. I used to go one evening a week with some of my classmates, and we would help to cook dinner. In our high school, we put on dances to raise money and ran raffles and things like that.

It's easy to get hooked on this place. The woman who runs it is a sister from a Catholic religious order. She doesn't fit any of the stereotypes of a nun, though. She is one tough cookie and she has seen it all; nothing shocks her. She is a human dynamo who manages to rev us all back up again when everything looks particularly hopeless. She is a genius at wheedling money and donations out of people. It's mostly because of her that the house has grown so phenomenally. It started in a small storefront in Highland Heights, then moved to a big private house. Now we are located right in the middle of the downtown section in what was once a fancy hotel.

Starting out with three cots in 1993, we now can sleep about 70 teenagers, mostly in two-bedded rooms. In the middle of February, when it gets incredibly cold on the streets, we usually put up about 20 more young people in a dorm-style arrangement in what was once the ballroom of the hotel.

To do my kind of work, you have to be a night person. I start at about 8:30 or 9:00 P.M. three nights a week and work straight through until maybe 6:00 in the morning. Then I'm on a day shift one day over the weekend. The staff goes out in pairs, a male and a female, looking for kids who need shelter. Two teams cover the train station, the bus depot, and once in a while, the airport.

Sister Noreen never pressures the kids. If they don't want to talk, that's okay. They don't even have to tell us their names. Sister Noreen and the other counselors let them know that what matters to us is that they are safe. When and if they are ready to trust us enough to tell us what pressured them to leave home, then we'll see what can be done. Sometimes kids open up the first night, and it will all come pouring out. They'll call their folks or the place they ran away from, and we'll put them on a bus home. There is a national program run by one of the bus companies that guarantees passage back home to any runaway kid if an agency verifies his or her story.

We try to assess the situation they came out of. If they tell us there was physical or sexual abuse, we let them know that they have options. They can stay for a while at Sanctuary House or find a shelter back in their own communities. No kid, no matter what he or she might have done, deserves to be hurt so badly that he or she has to run away. Sometimes we'll call an agency for them in their hometown and a counselor will meet the kid's bus and start working with the kid and family. Often the counselor calls a priest, rabbi, or a friend who'll meet the kid's bus when they get home. When kids first run away, they often think there is no other solution. Maybe we can help them see that there are people in their own communities who can help them. Maybe then they can slowly move back home.

It's possible, though, that what they were running away from isn't much safer than roaming the streets after dark in this town. A lot of the parents seem like very troubled people themselves. Of course, some seem like ordinary folks who are going out of their minds with worry and facing marital or employment problems of their own. We never meet most of the parents, and we very rarely hear how things worked out, so all of this is guesswork.

If it seems kids are deep into alcohol or drugs, we'll invite them to stay for the night and then link them up with a rehabilitation program the next day. We can't handle teens with active substance use issues at Sanctuary. It seems like a contradiction to say we are there for the kids and then reject some of them, but Sister Noreen learned early on that if the house was filled with drugs, then no one was safe.

We tap into a broad network of services. If kids are determined to make it on their own, we can refer them to programs where they can complete their high school education. We also have counselors who try to find foster homes for them in their home city if that seems appropriate. We try everything we can to keep them from making a life on the streets.

If a kid has already been on the streets for a while, sometimes he or she develops serious health problems. We have a clinic at Sanctuary and contacts with local doctors who volunteer to see our kids. Sometimes a young woman thinks she is pregnant. Often that's the case. Many of the kids pick up sexually transmitted diseases. They even have dental problems that have grown outrageously from being neglected.

The constant problem for us is that there are plenty of other people around the terminals and on the streets who have things to offer the kids. The pimps are doing some of the same things we are. They're also trying to spot the greenhorns. But they offer them a hot meal and a bed along with a line of cocaine. Their offers come with plenty of strings attached. They will be just so generous to the kids until they have the kids in their debt, and then they show the kids how to "repay." Usually it's by turning tricks, a young woman or young man having sex with a "john." The kids have to give the pimps a large part of the money they earn through prostitution.

Sometimes I go out with the Sanctuary van. It's a soup kitchen, infirmary, and office. Most nights we have a volunteer nurse. We park in a location where a lot of street kids congregate. There is an area down by the docks that is used as a pickup spot by men who want to buy teenage boys for sex. They come driving in from the suburbs. They have their suits and ties on like they just came from work. Sometimes they arrive in their work trucks. You wonder what is going on with their families while they are down here. They look over the line-up and invite a kid into their car, go off for an hour, and then bring the kid back to the dock.

We offer the kids coffee, medical help, and conversation. If they want to go back to the center for the night, we drive them there. You have to be careful not to pressure them or they just avoid you. If they think you will call the cops every time you see something illegal, they won't tell you anything.

Of course, we have limits as to what we can ignore. If we think they have a weapon, it's always a judgment call. Can you get them to give it to you? Do you call the police? If you do, will the word get out and then will all the other kids stay away from the van? It's never easy. You need to be a good listener, try not to judge them, and take it one step at a time.

I love the work, but I can see signs that I'm beginning to burn out. You have to focus on small successes. You can't think in absolute terms, like this kid went home and everything worked out fine. Life isn't that simple. The thing that keeps me going, in addition to Sister Noreen, is the rest of the staff. We do a lot of social things together and rally around each other when there is a crisis. We are always celebrating someone's birthday or graduation or 30 days of sobriety.

ATTITUDES AND VALUES OF THE HUMAN SERVICE WORKER

Patience

As you read John's account of his work, you can see that the worker who thrives in this field understands and accepts how slow, painful, and awesome change is. John Torrente sometimes feels annoyed when kids refuse the services he offers them. Sometimes he'll spend three or four nights without any of the kids on the docks coming back to the house. He's faced disappointment many times when a kid has dropped out of a job program or has returned to substance use. But usually he manages to control his impatience. He sets small, achievable goals, taking comfort in any signs of progress.

When the frustration with two steps forward and one step backward becomes too overwhelming, he heads for a gym and works out. He spends time talking with his supervisor, and sometimes he asks to change his job assignment for a while. When he is really feeling burned out, he finds that raising funds for the house instead of doing direct work can renew his energy.

No matter how slow or discouraging the change effort, the effective worker deflects feelings of impatience away from the clients. They can't be punished for the worker's often justifiable sense of frustration.

We also need to be patient with ourselves. Our skills seem so inadequate when we watch young people nightly put themselves and others in danger and we cannot stop their downward slide. We have no magic solutions.

John has had to divest himself of the rescue fantasies he had when he came to Sanctuary. But as he learns to accept his own and other persons' limitations, he must also guard against drifting into callousness or complacency. He has seen kids and parents change, and he believes that his agency can make a difference.

Human service workers walk a tightrope between what is and what might be, and between the reality of the moment and a vision of change for the better.

Source: Courtesy of Boston Cares

Everyone can find a way to contribute their energy to improve the lives of their fellow citizens. These middle school students are helping to clean up a local park as one of the many volunteer projects their club takes on.

Empathy

John tries hard to understand the difference between sympathy—feeling sorry for another person, and **empathy**—putting oneself in the shoes of another person. Needless to say, no worker can ever really know precisely what it is like to occupy someone else's skin. It is especially hard when that other person is of a different race, gender, or age, or has a different set of abilities. (See Jackson & Samuels, 2011; Rivera & Erlich, 1998; and Schram, 1971.) But he tries hard to see the world as it might look through a set of eyes very different from his own. Empathy is a path we walk, not a destination we can ever be sure we have reached.

Empathy requires a finely tuned, intuitive sensitivity to other people, the kind that one finds in good fiction or poetry. Sometimes as we read a novel, hear a song, or look intently at a great painting, we have an amazing moment of recognition. We see our own thoughts reflected and are surprised that someone can touch us so deeply. It is this profound understanding of the human condition, with its complex and ambivalent emotions, that explains why the plays of William Shakespeare, written in the late 1500s and early 1600s, can still bring tears to our eyes today.

To sharpen empathetic understanding, John taps the well of his own experiences. He hasn't had alcohol use issues of his own, but when he's counseling a compulsive drinker, he remembers how it felt when he tried to stop overeating, quit smoking, or disengage from an unhealthy love affair. Although he has never been discriminated against because of his race or religion, he can recapture the feelings of impotence he felt as a young child being unfairly scolded by his parents or teachers. He is does not have physical disabilities but can remember times when a broken arm or sprained ankle kept him from joining his friends for bike riding or playing ball. All of us have distant memories of shoplifting, skipping school, lying, or disappointing our parents through fear, ignorance, or peer pressure. These memories can help us avoid rushing in to judge harshly a person with whom we are working.

The late therapist Carl Rogers listed empathy as one of the three vital counselor attributes that can lead to positive change. The other two are nonpossessive warmth and genuineness (Rogers, 1951). These three attitudes are important in all major counseling theories. In fact, there is accumulating evidence that therapy is effective only when these attitudes are present at high levels, no matter what the particular school of psychology or counseling method used (Okun & Kantrowitz, 2014; Nystul, 2010; Truax & Carkhuff, 1967; Truax & Mitchell, 1971).

> The empathetic counselor must see beyond conventional facades, refrain from imposing personal interpretations and judgments, and be willing to risk understanding another person's private logic and feelings, which in superficial daily contacts the counselor might view as weak, foolish, or undesirable (Hammond, Hepworth, & Smith, 1977, p. 3).

To test the strength of this value in yourself, consider how you would be able to work with a man who had murdered his own child. On most people's scales of values, that crime may be the most reprehensible. Could you work with such a man without being repelled by him?

For instance, suppose a man was charged with murdering his own baby and confessed to the crime. Unemployed, he had lived with his wife and baby in a tiny, cramped apartment. The baby had cried constantly. The man was profoundly depressed by not being able to care for his family. He cracked under the stress and hit his baby. He did not intend to kill the child, but he did. He was convicted of murder and sentenced to death. This example raises the issue of individual guilt as opposed to the guilt that society must share in the provocation of such a crime.

Many times, John has wondered how he would act if he had been the child or parent in one of the many hair-raising stories he has heard at Sanctuary House. Sometimes he even wonders what he would do if he found himself sexually attracted to young boys. Would he sneak down to the pier to buy sex in the dead of night? How would he feel on the drive back to his suburban home? Often he finds himself saying "There, but for luck and chance, go I!"

Empathy, rather than judgment, is a key human service attitude. These college students learned that prisons offer few educational opportunities that might improve the prospects of inmates when released. They decided to collect used books, read request letters from prisoners, and send them packages of donated books.

Self-Awareness

John is genuinely fascinated by his reactions to the things he sees around him. He constantly wonders about the complex forces that have shaped these feelings. He has had to be willing to reexamine all of his attitudes and values. How does he feel about money, work, marriage, war, sex, sexual orientation, and abortion? Each of his opinions has been challenged by things he has seen and heard. He has been provoked to explore whether the attitudes and values transmitted by his family are still valid for him.

John has had to find the courage to talk openly about emotion-laden topics such as rape and suicide. He believes that each woman should have a right to choose what to do about her body, so he supports legal abortion. Sister Noreen opposes it on religious and ethical grounds. They have agreed to disagree with each other on that topic. Both positions are defensible, but they must be openly acknowledged. If they are kept underground, they might subtly direct or constrict a client's own exploration of possible courses of action if she finds herself pregnant and wants to talk about what she might do.

Effective human service workers need to be clear about where their own problems and their clients' problems overlap. Many young workers, for example, are still separating from their parents. When working with teenagers, these workers have to be alert to keep their own anger or ambivalence about dependence from influencing the way their clients feel or react toward their families.

The most important part of self-awareness is being able to sketch an increasingly accurate portrait of one's own strengths and weaknesses, likes and dislikes. John has been learning how to say "I can do that task very well, but I don't feel competent in doing some other task. I need help."

Some of us can work with patience with a person with multiple disabilities; others enjoy the liveliness of children in a recreation center. Some workers cannot tolerate the slowness of people who are older; others thrive on working with this population. The ability to live with other people's emotions and express our own is not something most of us are born with. We may need to undertake some personal development work in this area. Nichols and Jenkinson (2006) suggest some questions that a worker might think about before leading a support group.

- Do you think that you are aware of and open to the flow of feelings in your daily life? Do others confirm this to be so?
- Are you able to say that you value your own feelings and allow their expression rather than strive to mask them?
- Are you able to share your feelings with a trusted companion without being defensive?
- Are you able to receive and experience the painful feelings of others in a relaxed, accepting manner without wanting immediately to placate, soothe, or distract them from expressing those emotions?
- Do you believe that if a person expresses or acts out feelings in a group, you will be able to allow this to unfold without needing to take control and return the discussion to more matter-of-fact issues?

Capacity to Deal with Ambiguity and Take Risks

None of us is comfortable with ambiguity. Uncertainty creates tension. Yet John has come to understand that when working with people, one is never sure of what has gone on in the past or will happen in the future.

The young people he works with are so complex that there can be no guarantees that a "correct" action will produce the "right" results. The expression "the operation was a success but the patient died" is often true in the human services.

When working with the general public, there are many unknowns. For instance, John organized a community meeting for prospective volunteers. He took enormous care with all the details. He double-checked the invitations for accuracy and clarity, made sure the meeting place was conveniently located, brought refreshments, arranged for child care, got a good speaker on the topic of runaway youth, and then waited expectantly for the crowd that never came. There were probably 20 different reasons that so few people showed up. One person had a household emergency; another got tickets to a World Series game. Everyone had a reason for not attending that seemed legitimate to them. So John swallowed his disappointment and did the best job he could with the few volunteers-to-be who attended the meeting. Next month he will try again.

Often John must close the book on a teenager's problem without being able to "read" the last chapter. How can he know if teenagers with substance use disorders he worked so hard with for so long will stay in recovery for six months, one year, or a lifetime? Usually the staff loses track of the young people after they leave the program. When a young person returns to her family in a distant city, John often wonders if she was able to talk out the disagreement that made her run away. But he will probably never find out.

John has to act with very little accurate background information. Sister Noreen has been around youth who are homeless a long time and has sharpened her ability to distinguish the drug abuser from the occasional user. But even she cannot be sure if a teenager is telling her the truth about where his or her money went. Was it really lost, or did he or she spend it on cocaine?

Source: Tom Prettyman/PhotoEdit*

If young children are in a supportive environment, they are more likely to be comfortable encountering differences in skin color, language, or physical abilities. In the words of a song from the musical *South Pacific* . . . you've got to be taught to hate . . . before you are 6 or 7 or 8 . . . you've got to be carefully taught.

South Pacific is a play, with music by Richard Rodgers, lyrics by Oscar Hammerstein II, and book by both Hammerstein and Joshua Logan.

When Sister Noreen was a protective service worker, she often had to decide whether to leave a child over the weekend with a family that had been accused of abuse. If she removed the child, there was no guarantee that the foster family with which she placed the child would be much better than the family the child had just left. She learned early in her career that the human service worker has to be thoughtful in making choices, carefully weighing pros and cons of each situation.

The outreach counselors live with ambiguity because their job tasks are necessarily ill-defined. They are required to make moment-to-moment decisions:

- Which park should they visit?
- What youngster should they talk to?
- At what point should they call the police when they witness a drug deal or a fight?

Each decision is a judgment call made in a split second. Phoning the police too frequently might make it impossible to build relationships with these diverse young people. Waiting too long to respond might result in another teenager or staff member getting hurt or even killed!

Capacity to Ask for Help and Offer Feedback

To increase his effectiveness while struggling with ambiguity, John has developed a positive attitude about asking for help. A burden is always lighter if someone else can carry it with you.

As he has matured and become more able to acknowledge his weaknesses, John is able to say "I don't know that, but if you give me an hour, I'll find out," or "I've tried to do that, but I wasn't able to; can you help me?"

Knowing when to ask for assistance or for an honest appraisal of his work is the mark of a self-confident human service worker. A less-secure worker needs to bluff, pretending false expertise. But the field is so vast and ever-changing that no one could ever know everything. Social welfare legislation, laws, and entitlements are evolving daily. New programs are added, old ones cut back. No matter how many years Sister Noreen has worked with youth that are homeless, if she were to shift to another problem area—perhaps working with individuals with educational or physical disabilities—she would be a novice.

Sanctuary House offers an orientation program for new staff and volunteers, and in-service training for everyone. Even staff members who have been in the field for a long time need to keep learning about the ins and outs of this particular program, population, and community.

Just as important as asking for help is the willingness to give honest feedback to others. In our personal lives, much of our social interaction is superficial. We often give stock answers to standard questions; "How are you today?" provokes the anticipated neutral answers. We are hardly going to share our inner problems with all the neighbors or tradespeople we meet during the day. But at Sanctuary, when someone asks "How did I do?" or "How could I have done it better?" they have a right to expect a thoughtful and honest reply. Sometimes a less-than-positive evaluation is momentarily painful, but if the person learns from it, then it is a gift.

Belief in the Capacity to Change

At the risk of stating the obvious, John has to be a person with a powerful belief in the capacity all of us have to grow and change. His clients need a lot of help, but most of them are not permanently stuck in destructive patterns. He knows they often resist change; they fear the unknown consequences that change may bring, no matter how painful their current reality.

As he tries to assess realistically how much growth is possible or how fast it can happen, John has to struggle to maintain his own delicate balance. On the one hand, John has energy and optimism; on the other hand, he sometimes feels rage and frustration. All the workers at Sanctuary juggle feelings of pessimism and optimism. The discouraging reality of the life they see on the streets exists side by side with their hopes for the futures of the young people. No worker ever has enough time or resources or skill.

Although our minds and bodies cannot tolerate perpetual rage, we should be intolerant of injustice wherever we encounter it. We need to hold firm to our convictions about equal opportunity and the potential of equal access. A veteran human service worker once said that she was an optimist in her heart and a pessimist in her head.

No matter how discouraged he gets, John still appreciates the astounding plasticity, flexibility, and resilience of people. Human behavior has an almost infinite range of possibilities. The brutality of human traffickers and child pornographers contrasts sharply with the altruism and decency of volunteers who give up their evenings to help out.

Because he realizes that each of us is capable of acts of cruelty as well as altruism, John rejects glib generalizations about human nature, such as:

"People are no damn good!"

"People are only out for themselves!"

"Nowadays parents don't care about their kids!"

When things are falling apart, John looks to see what forces in the environment might be inhibiting human potential. He struggles to understand the obstacles in people's paths rather than retreat into fatalistic conclusions about their inferior heredity, moral lassitude, or psychological deviance.

John also has to stop himself from feelings of hopelessness when he sees city workers who seem so overwhelmed with their caseloads that they appear to throw up their hands in defeat.

Open-Mindedness, Skepticism, and Rejection of Stereotypes

John has learned that being open-minded is a requirement of his job. Open-mindedness is often derided. A comedian once described the open-minded person as one whose head is so porous that the wind whistles through it. Others describe the open-minded person as someone whose two feet are firmly planted in midair.

Of course John has opinions, but by keeping his mind open to new information, he protects himself from casting his first impressions in concrete. He meets someone, forms a preliminary estimate of his or her situation, and then continues to change that impression as he learns more.

John must keep from generalizing about a whole group from the behavior of one person. Ethnic background, race, class, and gender play significant roles in the socialization of every child. Still, no two people, even from the same background, are ever identical. The teenagers want the staff to understand their lifestyles and stresses, but they would resent being labeled as "suburban, middle-class, teenage underachievers with domineering, divorced parents." Although that kind of labeling sounds like a caricature, John has heard a surprisingly large number of workers referring to the teenagers at Sanctuary with shorthand labels that deny the humanness and uniqueness of the runaways. But categories and labels can be important in qualifying a client for a particular service or benefit. They must be used, but used with care and only when needed and accurate.

Humor and a Light Touch

John, like many of the young people he works with, finds that laughing—sometimes even at himself—is a great way to get rid of tension. A belly laugh, like a good cry, cleanses the system, putting a difficult situation back into perspective. Because working with these very troubled kids can be fraught with so much pain, humor might seem out of place. But John has discovered that many times a serious message can be effectively communicated through good-natured teasing. He uses tact and timing to moderate his wit. By picking up on signals that he is being insensitive when he teases, makes a pun, or giggles at the absurdity of life on the streets, he can quickly back off or apologize.

Human service workers, especially in group or community settings, often socialize with their clients and coworkers at potluck suppers, holiday celebrations, and open houses, and in the after-hours of weekend workshops or retreats. They need to learn how to organize these occasions so they are not too threatening. Touchy issues will always surface when we cross the fragile boundary line between client and worker, or worker and supervisor.

Traditional mental health practitioners such as doctors, psychologists, and psychiatrists often rigidly cling to boundary lines. Human service workers don't. When they work and when they relax, John, Noreen, and the other staff confront ambiguity, take risks, and individualize every situation.

SKILLS OF THE HUMAN SERVICE WORKER

Gathering Data

Every day John is asked dozens of questions that he doesn't know how to answer:

> "Do you think Larry is telling the truth about where he got that money he has been flashing around?"
>
> "If we send her home on that bus, who will meet her at the other end?"
>
> "Where did Gloria go? I haven't seen her in a week, but I heard she was badly beaten up. Is it a rumor?"
>
> "Where can we get money to purchase a van?"
>
> "Where can we find a volunteer to teach an Introduction to Computers class?"
>
> "What do other centers do when guests are caught in each other's rooms in compromising positions?"

John often responds, "That's a good question; I really don't know." Then, because he is a conscientious worker, he goes on to say "But I'll find out what I can and call you back on Tuesday [or in an hour or other appropriate time]."

The process of finding out as much as possible about a topic is called data gathering. John has been trained to use a variety of methods. In some ways, he is rather like a detective on the trail of insight and information. The following are some of the data-gathering skills he uses.

INTERVIEWING   Throughout the time you work in human services, you will keep increasing your skill in phrasing questions that help people to think more clearly. You will learn a great deal about how to establish an atmosphere that helps the interviewee relax and become engaged in the process of information sharing. The counselors at Sanctuary must learn how and when to ask questions while preserving a young person's dignity and right to privacy.

When John conducts an interview with a young runaway's parents, he is trying to find out as much as he can about the family's situation and to assess its potential resources. Each person needs the space to tell his or her own version of the crisis that precipitated the family breakup. He will listen to each family member and try to tune in to the emotions that might be surrounding the words. The counselor discovers that everyone has his or her own story to tell, and everyone has stories that never get told. If John is lucky, he will have several interviews he can use to fill in the background.

Often John must act quickly in a crisis situation, condensing all his data collecting into a few hectic moments. A fight erupts on the docks and he must quickly decide how serious it is. Should he call the police, or try to break it up himself? He reviews all he knows about these young men. He has a brief exchange with one of the leaders to see how seriously he is taking it. Based on his past experience, John makes an educated guess as to whether the combatants are likely to have weapons and whether they are likely to use them. To an outsider, it might look as though the fight will turn violent. But after a few minutes of this process, John is able to distinguish "dissing," a street game of trading insults, from the kind of genuine anger that will leave one of the participants dead or injured.

Whether talking to a public official over the phone or at a meeting, conferring with a parent or teacher, or sharing information with a coworker about a referral, John uses the following skills.

ACTIVE LISTENING   After asking questions, John uses his skills of active listening. Each guest at Sanctuary has a unique style of communication. John has to remember for future reference precisely what has been said. He has to be able to rephrase the ideas and feelings of the speaker to make sure he has understood correctly. He counts on such data so that he can point out connections between what is said at one time and at another.

When actively listening, John also "hears" the emotion that surrounds words. He listens to the sounds of silence: words left unsaid, hesitations, pauses, and small sighs. By checking back with the interviewee, he avoids the pitfalls of overanalyzing or overinterpreting.

ACTIVE LOOKING   From his study of psychodynamics, John has learned about the theory of the unconscious mind. He knows that people do not always do and say exactly what they mean. It is not easy to put one's feelings into words. Careful scrutiny can often tell us more than any words can convey.

The workers at Sanctuary also use active looking to better understand their group or community. By absorbing the many small details of a neighborhood, for example, John can make educated guesses about the stresses and the quality of life of its residents. He can walk into the game room and notice the small signs that signal trouble is brewing.

READING, RESEARCHING, AND ASSESSING   Because John encounters his clients in random, often unpredictable ways, he usually starts out by knowing almost nothing about them. In most other agencies, workers have access to a variety of background information. Reading through a client's file is a form of research. A file might include:

- Notes from previous professionals
- Employment records
- Test scores
- Medical records
- Records of monetary grants
- The results of some type of investigation or a court case.

John has become adept at using web directories of community resources so that he can make referrals to job training, housing, and medical services. He always wondered why he had to take subjects such as statistics and research in college; they seemed so far removed from the human service field. Now he realizes how much he depends on his skills of finding information.

ATTENDING CONFERENCES AND WORKSHOPS   At least three times a week, John participates in a case conference. It might be held at Sanctuary House, the local courthouse, the mental health clinic, or the Department of Social Services. At these meetings, the teenager, the teen's family, and a variety of mental health workers pool their perspectives on the young person's problem. Learning how to gather and present information at a case conference is an important set of skills.

Occasionally John has been able to attend professional conferences and workshops. He recently went to one organized by the Coalition for Homeless Youth. He networked with other workers and came back newly energized.

MAKING HOME OR AGENCY VISITS   Only rarely can John visit a young person's home, which provides him with much material. But he can visit another social agency to gain in-depth knowledge about its services. Observing for himself, he gets insights into the strengths and weaknesses in an environment. When he visits a local health center, shelter, or school, he reads the graffiti on the walls and the notices on the bulletin boards. He can evaluate the atmosphere on first entering the front door or sitting in the waiting area. He forms initial impressions of the kind of service the agency might give his clients by the messages it projects to him.

Storing and Sharing Information

Once gathered, information about a particular client, problem, or program must be put into a useful format. John resists writing records and is often reminded by Noreen how important this skill is. At Sanctuary the workers enter a description of their daily activities in a computerized logbook. This is used for continuity from one shift of staff to the next or from one period of time to the next. If good records have been kept, a young person won't be asked to summarize in a few sentences his or her complex set of problems when a new worker comes on staff.

At the end of any major event—be it a camping trip, parent workshop, or community fair—John writes an evaluation. He describes how the money was spent, what equipment was used, and what pitfalls he encountered. If he takes the time to sit down at the computer and write a full description, the next worker who repeats that activity can build on his successes and try to avoid his failures. To start again each time from scratch would be a misuse of everyone's scarce time and energy.

An entire program can rise or fall on the quality of its administrative detail. When a budget is reviewed, the bits and pieces of paper—bills, invoices, moneys taken out and brought in—can determine whether a program will be continued or terminated (Schram, 1997).

Building Trusting Relationships

If John cannot build a trusting relationship with a child who has run away, he will never be able to help him. Gaining the trust of teenagers is especially hard. Even an adult as young as John still represents the adult world that these young people are busy rebelling against.

John has found that there are no formulas for building a relationship. Stock empathetic phrases such as "I can understand just how you feel" or reassurances such as "I'm sure everything will work out fine!" are perceived by the teenagers as patronizing and hollow. And they are!

Sometimes, even with all his skills, John just doesn't connect with a particular teenager. The elusive element of "cohesion," the bond that develops between people, just isn't there. There are workers who cannot connect with certain clients, and clients who find it impossible to trust anyone. John has had to honestly admit when he was having difficulty relating to a particular young person. If he can, he adjusts his approach. No one on the staff considers it a failure if a relationship does not gel. Of course, if John found that he couldn't build a relationship with most of the young people he worked with, he would obviously be in the wrong job.

Negotiating Contracts and Assessing Problems

The process of sorting out mutual goals, roles, and tasks is called negotiating the contract. At Sanctuary, the contract between client and worker is not actually written. Instead, it is discussed during the initial stages, when a client first begins working with a staff member.

A contract begins by stating mutual expectations. Global statements such as "I am here to help you," "We are meeting to change the way the police act toward street kids," or "I want you to make my son behave" are only starting points. The counselors break down large goals into small, do-able steps that can build, one on top of the other. The discussion of mutual expectations and consequences includes a description of who will do what in the change effort and of which consequences will follow which actions. At Sanctuary the young people are not allowed to use drugs in the house. They need to know what will happen if a worker finds them shooting up in the bathroom. They also need to review the rules of confidentiality. Will their parents be called? If they have a weapon, will it be taken away? Under what circumstances will the police intervene?

Some parents or young people expect John to solve their problems by giving advice or orders; others think he will sit back and remain mute, like the psychiatrists they have seen in movies. Of course, he does a little of both.

Constructing Action Plans

In most agencies, individualized service plans (ISPs) spell out the goals that will be worked on and the tasks that can accomplish them. At Sanctuary there are no formal, written action plans. The staff sets short-term goals with and for each resident. John tries to keep those goals in mind. They shape the choices he makes about how to spend his time.

Because so many of the teenagers have not developed the skills required to see beyond their next meal and warm bed, the staff tries to teach them how to chart a course and stick to it in a variety of ways. When planning a house dance or trip to a beach, John tries to help the residents make lists of the jobs that need to be done, by when they must be completed, and who is responsible for doing them. If they don't keep careful track of their plans, the kids often backtrack over each other's trails, leaving important pieces of work undone or rushing to do a month's worth of work in a few hours. Lack of clarity creates conflict.

By teaching them how to use an action plan, counselors seek to enable their clients to accomplish two goals: organize a successful event and, more importantly, practice a method of systematic problem solving. Translating goals into concrete actions can help clients avoid emotional overload. All these young people have had crises in their lives and have reacted by withdrawing or striking out. John tries to bring some order into their chaotic lives.

Implementing Action Plans

To translate plans into reality, John meets with a young person who is looking for a job. He offers encouragement and shows him how to use the job listings or locate an employment agency. Another of his clients has just moved into an apartment. He refers her to a day care center for her 2-year-old son and helps her apply for financial assistance. Another resident has a court appearance; John briefs her on her rights and offers to go with her. Helping clients make decisions, release emotions, and locate and use services are some ways he assists them as they implement their action plans.

Although John might spend most of his time doing one-on-one casework, he also has had to learn to run a group. Because Sanctuary is short of staff, he also has to fill other roles as needed. He teaches a small class in using the computer and coaches an occasional baseball game. All these activities help implement Sanctuary's overall goal of helping each teenager survive the transition into adulthood. Like John, most human service workers are willing to do a little bit of everything.

Monitoring and Evaluating

John has learned how to use many techniques to elicit feedback. It is not easy to be objective about one's own work. He asks his clients and coworkers how he is doing but knows that most people have a hard time being constructively critical. The Board of Directors of Sanctuary House has hired a professor from a local college to conduct yearly evaluations. She interviews the staff and residents, summarizes the agency's progress, and then helps the board and staff set goals for the next year.

BASIC KNOWLEDGE NEEDED FOR THE HUMAN SERVICE WORKER

Human Growth and Development

All college human service curricula are likely to include courses with titles such as Self and Society, The Person in the Environment, or, simply, Introduction to Psychology, or Human Growth and Development.

These courses describe the major milestones and developmental tasks that a newborn infant faces as he or she grows through childhood, adolescence, young adulthood, adulthood, and old age, and finally faces death. They discuss the basic needs shared by all human beings, regardless of their particular culture or the era in which they live. Students are challenged to think about how human beings meet their needs for association and acceptance, for work, play, sexuality, and spirituality.

Many of the major theorists disagree with each other about what causes people to think or act as they do. But the struggle to understand and synthesize their varying perspectives sharpens the intellect. It has provoked John to take a second look at many of his facile assumptions about human nature.

Abnormal Growth and Development

After studying "normal" or "typical" behaviors at different stages of life, John learned about the forces that stunt development. In class he explored the ways in which biology, genetics, and family and social relationships contribute to mental deterioration, stress, family disorganization, and various forms of physical and mental disabilities. Through the study of nontypical behavior, he began to understand the complex, intertwined issues of causality. Understanding how psychological problems develop has helped John to seek out the multiple resources needed to cope with or overcome them on behalf of the people he serves.

Sanctuary House does not base its work on one particular psychological theory. Before working there, John was an intern in a community residence for adults with developmental delays, where the staff was expected to act in accordance with a rigid program of behavior modification. John is more comfortable working in an agency in which staff has the latitude to pick and choose from a variety of approaches.

Impact of Society and Culture on Behavior

While he was studying some of the psychological, genetic, biological, nutritional, and interpersonal forces that shape human behavior, John also had to understand their social contexts. While the family is an important influence on personality formation, so too are the many groups within which individuals interact.

The study of socioeconomic class, social role and status, ethnicity, peer group, family, religious institutions, school, and community—with their norms, myths, pressures, and subtle messages—has helped John to further understand why people act as they do. In realizing how cultures place expectations on behavior and mete out punishments for nonconformity, John begins to see order in the confusing crosscurrents of our pluralistic, heterogeneous society.

The Dynamics of Groups and Organizations

Once he recognized the ways in which groups influence attitudes and behavior, John was curious about how they form and maintain themselves. In studying small groups, such as the nuclear family, the gang, or the clique, he discovered that they have much in common with larger, more diffuse organizations such as workplaces, schools, and social agencies. Groups develop patterns of predictable behavior, rules, regulations, and rituals. These eventually determine how well the members will accomplish the goals of the group.

Learning how bureaucracies form and how they can be changed has helped the staff of Sanctuary secure services and resources for clients from a panoply of often unresponsive city agencies. It has also helped them look critically at the house itself to figure out how it could be improved.

Social and Political Forces that Affect Helping

Although human service workers cannot possibly absorb all the political, economic, and sociological data about society, he or she must acquire a basic understanding of how communities are organized and how they are changed.

In anthropology and sociology courses, John has learned about variations in beliefs from one culture to another. He has learned that there are different ideas of how men and women should treat each other, how children should be socialized, and how people who are older and the young should relate to each other.

These insights drawn from history and cross-cultural analysis prepare the human service worker to suspend quick judgments about what is right and wrong. They warn us that there are no carved-in-stone ways to run a world, a community, or an individual life.

Study in this area might also include gaining knowledge about how laws are introduced, implemented, and amended. John still does not know enough about how the legislative and judicial systems affect the delivery of social services to youth that are homeless. He has some clear ideas about what he would like to see happen. He will need to keep on learning.

Social Problems, Populations, and Resources

John's human service courses and his internships introduced him to many social problems and special-population groups. He has learned a little about the problems of crime and corrections; mental and physical disabilities; hospitalized, neglected, and abused children; family relations; alcohol and drug use; death; suicide; survival in the rural or urban community; poverty; and discrimination. He has learned about discrimination based on social class, age, gender, and ethnic or religious status, and the tensions surrounding sexual identity. All are issues he sees played out in his work every day.

Although he has not learned in depth about all these issues, John has begun to understand how social problems are identified, how new problems rise to prominence on the social agenda, and how new services to deal with them come into being. He has learned that atitudes toward mental health, addiction to alcohol, aging, childhood, and male–female relations, among other issues, have changed in dramatic ways in the past several decades. Having mental health issues was once considered a moral depravity, later it was treated as a wholly psychological disturbance, and now it is viewed on a continuum with both psychological and biological roots. Definitions have shaped interventions.

John knows a bit about the general shape of the social welfare system. Now that he is a committed newspaper reader, he attempts to keep up with the ever-changing legislation in the field of human services.

Research and Evaluation

Although John is probably never going to have full responsibility for conducting formal research projects, he needs to understand the language of research. He has helped out in the formulation of some projects and tries to read reports about them as an alert consumer.

Research in the human services is particularly complex, controversial, and problematic. Human beings are infinitely unique and are perpetually bombarded with conflicting demands and environmental stressors. It is always hard to pinpoint the exact cause of any social problem or its solution. There are probably as many reasons for a youngster to leave home as there are residents at Sanctuary House.

Despite the limitations, research and evaluation studies need to be conducted in the social services. Results are sometimes used to increase our knowledge base. More often, studies are used to decide whether funding of a particular program should be sustained, increased, or terminated. See York (2009) for an excellent review of the issues.

Summary

1. It is difficult to draw a boundary line between the lay helper and the professional helper.
2. The boundary lines between professional specialties in the human services are often unclear. Work roles overlap.
3. Regardless of formal credentials or titles, competent helpers share a commitment to the content and structure of the professional helping relationship.
4. The structure of the professional helping relationship differs from that of a purely social one. The professional relationship:
   - Exists for a limited time
   - Has a clear, agreed-on focus
   - Has a division of labor
   - Is disciplined
   - Is built on acceptance rather than attraction or affection.

5. The helping relationship is composed of three components:
   - Attitudes and values
   - Skills
   - Knowledge
6. The three components of the helping relationship build on each other like a pyramid, with attitudes and values at the base.
7. Though all the components are of equal importance, the training of human service workers begins with attitudes and values.
8. The key attitudes and values are
   - Patience
   - Empathy
   - Self-awareness
   - Capacity to deal with ambiguity and take risks
   - Capacity to ask for help and offer feedback
   - Belief in people's and systems' capacity to change
   - Open-mindedness, skepticism, and rejection of stereotypes
   - Humor and a light touch.
9. The basic skills are
   - Gathering data, interviewing, and researching
   - Storing and sharing information
   - Building relationships
   - Negotiating contracts and assessing problems
   - Constructing action plans
   - Implementing action plans
   - Monitoring and evaluating.
10. The basic knowledge areas are
    - Human growth and development
    - Abnormal growth and development
    - The impact of society and culture on behavior
    - The dynamics of groups and organizations
    - The social and political forces that affect helping
    - Social problems, special populations, and resources
    - Research and evaluation.
11. No worker embodies or masters all the attitudes and values, skills, and knowledge described. They form a model that helps set goals for professional development.

Discussion Questions

1. What do you think is meant by the statement "Empathy is a path we walk, not a destination we can ever reach"? How might you prepare yourself to try to empathize with one of your classmates who comes from a different ethnic or religious background than you do, or is of the opposite sex, or has a different sexual orientation, or perhaps has a different set of abilities or disabilities than you do?
2. To what extent do you think you could work with youth who are homeless, who often might appear angry with adults or might be sexually provocative or manipulative? How do you think you would react to having to deal with the people who sexually exploit others, many of who are children? How might you react to the parents from whom they have run away—sometimes for good reasons?
3. What do you think a worker means when she says "In my heart I am an optimist but often in my mind I am a pessimist"? Are there any issues that you feel that way about?

Web Resources for Further Study

Attitudes/Values, Skills, and Knowledge of the Human Service Worker

https://www.humanservicesedu.org/human-services-professional.html

https://www.nationalhumanservices.org/ethical-standards

https://msw.usc.edu/mswusc-blog/10-skills-every-social-worker-needs/

Although this web site is aimed at social workers, there is much overlap between the professions of human service and social work.

For Students—National Organization for Human Services

https://www.nationalhumanservices.org/for-students

Homeless and Runaway Teens

The web is a rich resource of programs for runaway and homeless teens (many of whom have aged out):

https://www.acf.hhs.gov/fysb/programs/runaway-homeless-youth

https://www.covenanthouse.org/homeless-youth-programs

https://www.theharbour.org/youth-in-transition.html

https://www.congress.gov/bill/114th-congress/senate-bill/262

MyLab Helping Professions for Introduction to Human Services

In the Topic 2 Assignments: Human Systems, try Application Exercise 2.1: Using Person-in-Environment Theories When Working with Clients.

Values and Ethical Dilemmas

5

Source: Rawpixel.com/Shutterstock

Learning Outcomes

- Students will become aware of various types of value-based and ethical dilemmas that they will encounter as they work to become helping professionals.

- Students will develop an awareness of their own values and capacity for ethical practice.

- Students will develop strategies to successfully work through the ethical and value-based dilemmas they encounter.

Betty, a community support worker, is advising a welfare recipient on how to deal with a welfare worker. The worker is required by law to ask the client where her former husband is and to ask for his Social Security number. Then the worker will turn this information over to the Department of Revenue, which will pursue the man aggressively for support. The welfare recipient knows where her former husband is. She is afraid to tell the worker, however, because her husband has beaten her, and she fears he would be abusive to her again. The woman asks what she should do. Betty knows it is wrong to lie to the welfare worker, yet she also knows that it would be in the woman's best interest to tell the worker that she doesn't know where her former husband is. What should Betty tell the woman? What would you do?

Linda is a case worker in the child welfare department. A school counselor has reported a mother for neglect of her child. The child is malnourished and listless. She cannot apply herself to her studies. Linda talked with the mother and found out that she formerly received money from Transitional Assistance to Needy Families (TANF), but she reached that state's two-year time limit and was subsequently cut off from TANF. She tried to feed her child—often going hungry herself—but even with food stamps, she did not have enough money to feed the child adequately.

Linda's supervisor advised her to place the child in foster care. This was a dilemma for Linda because she knew the agency did not have enough high quality foster parents available. Part of the problem was that the reimbursement for foster parents was not enough to attract strong applicants. She could place the child in a foster home where there were already more children than the agency usually allowed, but would the child be any better off than in her own home? It would be traumatic for the child to be taken from her mother, whom she loved. Yet she would probably get enough to eat in this foster home, even though the foster mother would not be able to give her the attention that she needs. What should Linda do?

Every attitude and value carries with it the seeds of conflict and insoluble dilemmas. Debates about the **ethics of helping** are not just mental gymnastics best left to university scholars or cloistered philosophers. Human service workers face dilemmas or value conflicts of one sort or another every day, no matter what their role in an agency.

Sometimes there are conflicts between what we have been taught is correct behavior and what our clients do. For example, perhaps our parents, church, and school taught us that it is wrong for a woman to get an abortion, yet we may work with many people who do not share this value. Or perhaps, because everyone we knew said so, we might believe that most welfare recipients are lazy people avoiding work. Yet we find that assumption false when we read research on the subject. Which path do we follow when we must choose between our vision of life and our client's, between a long-held belief and research findings?

Value conflicts are often caused by the realities of our work. Within the field of human services there are specific ethical standards that should be upheld. Despite this knowledge there are often competing interests that pressure us to move away from ethical practice. A policy, for example, that focuses solely on efficiency may not be the most effective way to provide services for an individual or family. Choosing efficiency over efficacy creates a dilemma, particularly when we know our ethical practice is to do the best we can by providing the highest quality services possible. Human service workers regularly encounter ethical challenges that result from many competing pressures.

CAN WORKERS BE COMPLETELY UNBIASED?

Our social class, ethnic group, and gender have shaped many of the values we hold. These values may be very different from those of people from another group. This difference in values can create problems in the helping relationship.

Some theoreticians urge workers to be objective and "value-free," which means being careful not to impose their own values on their clients. Yet in practice, this is simply impossible. Even if one only grunts and says "uh-huh," the timing of the noises can reflect a value judgment about which of the client's statements warrant attention; inflection of the voice can give a sense of approval or displeasure. Inevitably there will be some differences between the client and the worker in attitudes toward politics, religion, sexuality, culture, social class, time orientation, or the environment, or in beliefs about human nature. Some of those **value conflicts** may not be very important. A Democrat can help a Republican, or vice versa, without needing to agree on the respective party platforms. But if the worker honestly believes that abortion is murder and the client wants help in terminating a pregnancy, that can create such a serious problem in their working relationship that a special effort is required to soften or eliminate the conflict. What's key here is that an effective human services worker must develop an awareness of his own values and beliefs so that he can reasonably manage the dynamics of difference present between the helper and the helpee.

In the following pages, we will look at some of the areas that can lead to **value dilemmas** and conflicts, either within us as workers or within society as a whole. Often the dilemmas or

Questions to Guide Decision Making

1. What values are promoted by the action?

2. What values are violated by the action?

3. Is the client competent to decide? If not, how should a decision be made? Who should make it? How should we define *competence*?

4. How does the social worker's position/power affect our evaluation of the action? How does the institutional setting affect our evaluation?

5. What alternative actions are possible? (Evaluate each in terms of questions 1 through 4.)

6. How do your own values affect the way you evaluate the action? Would your client or agency make a different evaluation?

In evaluating each course of action, consider the client's right to self-determination; such values as privacy, trust, honesty, and respect; the good or harm of the action for the well-being of the client/others/community.

FIGURE 5.1 Human service dilemmas

Source: Ethic Model of Decision Making from What Social Workers Should Know About Ethics: Understanding and Resolving Practice Delimmas by Elaine. P. Congress in Advances in Social Work, Vol.1, Number 1. Copyright © 2006 by Indiana University School of Social Work

conflicts occur simply because human situations are by their nature unclear and complex. Other times a lack of awareness about the dynamics of difference confounds our ability to be effective within the helping relationship. The choices open to our clients are all imperfect, and each carries unknown consequences. The very definition of a dilemma implies that it is a difficult situation without a readily apparent solution. We shall give some case examples and ask you to think through the values and ethics involved in each example, using the questions in Figure 5.1. Exploring each of the dilemmas in this way will help to increase your own self-awareness as well as your ability to manage difficult dilemmas.

DILEMMAS SURROUNDING THE VALUE OF SELF-DETERMINATION

What happens when one person's right to control his or her own behavior clashes with another set of rights? **Self-determination** is a value held in such high esteem in the social work profession that the National Association of Social Workers (NASW) code of ethics puts it at the top of its list of professional values:

> Social workers respect and promote the right of clients to self-determination and assist clients in their efforts to identify and clarify their goals. Social workers may limit clients' right to self-determination when, in the social workers' professional judgment, clients' actions or potential actions pose a serious, foreseeable, and imminent risk to themselves or others (Code of Ethics, 2008).

More recently, the idea of self-determination has evolved to include important ideas about family- and youth-driven practices (Wald, Zubritsky, & Jaquette, 2014). In this context, human service workers strive to advance systems of care that put the interests and needs of the family and youth first, without allowing the worker's values to become a block to the family's progress.

Lynn Atkinson, a social work professor who believes that social workers should not force their services on clients, defines self-determination as follows:

> In working with people, social workers must respect the right of individuals to choose their own life paths. Although a social worker may disagree with the choices or the values of a particular person, the social worker must respect that individual's right to believe and do as he or she wishes and honor that right by not forcing the person to do something that is against that person's will (Atkinson & Kunkel, 1992, pp. 159–160).

In a rejoinder to Atkinson, another professor of social work, O. Dale Kunkel, points out that subsections of the code of ethics on self-determination "quickly hedge by characterizing the legal conditions under which client self-determination is not primary" (Atkinson & Kunkel, 1992, pp. 157–172). Kunkel argues that social workers often must work with clients who do not come to them of their own free will because they know they have a problem and want to solve it. Social workers must investigate complaints of child abuse and neglect with or without the client's consent; they counsel people with substance use disorders who have been court-ordered into treatment; they work with youth and adults who have committed crimes and are incarcerated or on probation or parole; they treat individuals with mental health conditions who have been involuntarily committed to hospitals. Many of these people could assert that their self-determination is being abridged.

Self-Determination and Child Abuse

Child welfare agencies across the nation are under fire from groups of all ideological points of view. Many states have had lawsuits brought against them:

- From conservatives who may object to what they see as to an agency's invading the sanctity of the family
- From advocacy groups that may claim that an agency fails to protect children because it is understaffed and underfunded and does not adequately train workers
- From parents who may claim that their rights have been abused by intrusive social workers
- From parents who may claim that an agency doesn't give them the services their children need
- From foster parents who may claim that an agency does not treat them like co-professionals and does not give them enough help.

Child protection workers have little guidance from state laws about what constitutes abuse. Parents in all 50 states are allowed to hit their children. There are limits to what is allowed, but out of reluctance to legislate parental conduct, state lawmakers have shied away from getting too specific about those limits, instead letting courts consider the matter case by case. Journal articles help to illustrate the complexity of this question (see for example Coleman, Dodge & Cambell, 2010). Coleman, Dodge, and Campbell argue for example that all states allow corporal punishment as long as the act on the part of the parent falls under a standard of discipline and that the injury sustained by the child is not lasting. The complexity here is found at the point in which an act of corporal punishment crosses the threshold from a simple act of discipline to that of abuse. In some jurisdictions a bruise lasting more than 24 hours constitutes abuse while in other systems the risk of abuse is sufficient (Coleman, Dodge & Cambell, 2010, p. 120).

In 2008, Cesar Rodriguez was accused of murder for killing his 7-year-old stepdaughter Nixzmary. He admitted that he routinely beat Nixzmary with a belt, hit her with his hands using "all my force," and threw her on the floor, and that he held her head under cold water the night she died in January 2006. He admitted duct-taping her emaciated 37-pound frame to a chair and binding her with bungee cords. Rodriguez's lawyer, Jeffrey T. Schwartz, argued that Rodriguez gave Nixzmary the same kind of discipline that Rodriguez's father had given him, including hitting him a lot and holding his head under cold water. This corrected Rodriguez's waywardness and helped him grow up to be a decent father, Schwartz said: "It was done to him, and it didn't kill him" (Shallwani & Bain, 2008).

In 2014, Kosair Children's Hospital in Louisville, Kentucky posted signs indicating that its hospital was a no-spanking zone (Frazier, Liu, & Dauk, 2014). The goal was to create a safe place for children and to provide an opportunity to engage in a discussion about positive parenting techniques. Those in the helping profession have long understood that spanking and other forms of corporal punishment are far less effective than other, more positive parenting techniques. Many parents understand this as well, though their own upbringing often becomes the driving force for using spanking and other forms of corporal punishment as a way to discipline children.

Opponents of hit-free zones argue that the medical profession and other helping professions have no business telling parents how to discipline their children.

Forty-two countries have passed bans on parental corporal punishment, including Sweden, Norway, Finland, Chile, the Netherlands, New Zealand, Spain, Austria, and Venezuela.

GENUINE CHILD ABUSE VERSUS FALSE CHARGES Child protective workers are all too familiar with the challenges that can come from trying to assess whether child abuse reports are founded—which mandates they take action, or unfounded—requiring no further state involvement. In some instances, couples in the midst of divorce use allegations of child abuse as a way to express their genuine concern and distress, or as a strategy to gain custody. This phenomenon occurs across socioeconomic lines and can be seen even among society's celebrities. Brad Pitt, for example, recently found himself accused of child abuse during the breakup of his marriage with Angelina Jolie (Hjelmgaard & Blas, 2016).

Accusations of abuse, whether they are made against an average person or a well-known individual, place child protective workers in the difficult position of having to make a determination as to whether a child has been abused.

Self-Determination When Treatment Is Mandated

To regain custody of their children, some parents have been ordered to undergo treatment for their substance use and counseling for their personal issues. Under these conditions, it is very possible that a client will go through the motions of **mandated treatment** simply to gain the promised benefits or avoid punishment. But can people change if they are forced to accept help? Consider the following case, in which a mother did what she had to in order to get her children back. This is an actual case, described by Robert Ingram (1992), a social work therapist and one of the founders of Empower, a welfare rights group.

Case Example: Alice

"I was working in a nursing home as a nursing assistant. I didn't want to ask welfare for anything. It felt good. I worked from 7 to 3. My 12-year-old daughter was supposed to take my 6-year-old son to nursery school and then go to school herself. The kids were mad because I was working so they didn't go to school. They fooled around and they set the house on fire.

(continued)

> "They [the social service department] took the kids. I was missing work, and I lost the job. They said the kids were emotionally upset. Any kid would be if he were taken out of his home. They wouldn't let me see the kids. They told me that if I go to therapy, I'd get my kids back. They didn't say anything about how long I'd be in therapy. They told me it would be up to the therapist to say when the kids could come home. The therapist was like a judge. [I] went to the therapist.
>
> "All he wanted to do was talk about the past. What the . . . does the past have to do with it? The therapist said it was up to the judge when I'd get the kids back. The judge said it was up to the protective worker, and the worker said it was up to the therapist. It took me a year and a half to convince the therapist that I was well enough to have the kids at home. I was calmer because I had a job and had something to do with my time."
>
> Ingram asked her if the therapist said anything to her or gave her medicine that helped her to be calm, and she said, "No." She went to the therapist once a month at first. Ingram asked her if it wouldn't have been better to go more often to learn or do whatever was necessary to get the kids back.
>
> "I don't know," Alice said. "That's the way it was set up. I used to tell him, 'I'm doing good.' There was nothing to talk about. It got to be boring. I told him, 'I'm not trying to be rude, but I have better places to be.' He'd sit there and shake his head yes. He had no suggestions at all. After a year and a half, the therapist sent a letter to the judge, suggesting that [my] younger child should be returned home and that the therapy should continue. Then I had to go twice a month, with my son. It was a pain. I had to get him out of school early. It was messing up his schoolwork. [My] employer was concerned that I was taking time off work to go to therapy. The therapist told me I didn't have to work but he wouldn't help me get SSI [Supplemental Security Income]."
>
> Ingram asked her how she finally stopped seeing the therapist. She said that he resigned from his job. He tried to persuade her to continue with another therapist but he let her go when she insisted that she did not need to continue in treatment.

Ingram treats mandated clients, leaving the decision about whether to submit to the therapy up to the client, and recommends developing a contract with the client in the beginning. The contract certifies that the client is in treatment if she at least shows up regularly for interviews. "Once the therapist demonstrates his or her trustworthiness by adhering to the contract, the client may begin to work on the issues that attracted the attention of the mandating agency" (Ingram, 1992, p. 96).

Parents of children with mental health conditions may want their children to be hospitalized and to take psychotropic medication, even while the children resist both hospitalization and medication. In our interview with Judi Chamberlin in Chapter 2, Judi talked about how parents in the National Alliance on Mental Illness often pushed for hospitalization and medication against the wishes of their children. The Mental Patients' Liberation Front believes in complete freedom of choice. Its members develop self-help support groups and alternative treatment methods, and hope they can win voluntary membership.

Self-Determination Is Undermined When Clients Are Manipulated

Although it is not easy to know how to handle the ethical dilemmas of mandated treatment, at least both client and worker openly acknowledge that there is coercion in the relationship. But there are other types of coercion that undermine self-determination. **Manipulation** by the worker can be subtle, and harder for a client to detect and to defend against. For example, many workers possess both implicit as well as explicit bias. They may feel that they treat people equally but are unknowingly predisposed to treat people like themselves more positively. Or they may be fully aware of their own bias and treat people differently as a result. Both forms of bias result in cognitions about the client that can result in conscious or subconscious discriminatory behaviour toward them (Reihl & Hurley, 2015, *27*(4)). In these instances, the client may be directed toward service delivery or treatment options based on the worker's bias and not on what is in their best interest.

In discussing the philosophical implications of manipulation, Rhodes argues that manipulation usually should be avoided and always needs to be carefully monitored. If the worker believes that coercion is necessary, it should generally be undertaken *with the client's knowledge*. Otherwise, social workers may be able to covertly force actions on clients that society and clients would not allow if these actions were made explicit (Rhodes, 1989).

Rhodes argues that, because it is impossible to be ethically neutral in human service work, workers should be open with clients about their ethical commitments so that clients can make an **informed choice**. "How much a therapist reveals must depend upon the relationship and the client's ability to process such information" (Rhodes, 1989, p. 120).

The question of informed choice is further heightened by the need in current human service, mental health, and social work practice to obtain **informed consent** from clients prior to engaging in any treatment, service delivery, or research involving human subjects. Yeates (2015) suggests that receiving informed consent from clients who are required or ordered to undergo treatment can be challenging. For example, voluntary consent to a procedure or treatment can be difficult to assess for individuals who have been incarcerated, or who are court-involved. The dynamic is ripe for coercion that is both explicit as well as implicit. And while these situations can be complex, one important key is for the human service worker to be fully aware of the dynamics present and do his best to help support an environment that reduces any chance of manipulation or coercion.

SOME CURRENT ETHICAL CONFLICTS

Conflicts Surrounding HIV/AIDS

The issues that surround HIV/AIDS are fiercely debated. While school directors, principals, and parents have welcomed children with HIV/AIDS into their schools, knowing that such children are not a danger to the other children and that the youngsters need to live as normal a life as possible despite having a virus that can have profound health implications, public ignorance about and fear of the disease continue to exist.

HIV/AIDS has also raised debate about whether medical personnel should be routinely tested, whether condoms or clean hypodermic needles should be distributed, and even whether individuals with full-blown AIDS should be quarantined. Over time almost all human service organizations and medical providers have come to realize that fears about providing services to individuals with HIV/AIDS are overblown by people lacking proper information and relevant facts. Despite this, research shows that health care professionals would benefit from greater education on this important topic (Ljaljevic, Scepanovic, Mugosa, & Catic, 2015). As a human service professional it's important to stay current on the most recent medical information for diseases and ailments that impact the clients we serve. Public health organizations and HIV/AIDS action groups readily provide the most up-to-date information.

Source: Courtesy of Boston Cares

It is easy to fall into the trap of accepting simple stereotypes, such as assuming that all business corporations have the single-minded goal of making money. These folks, sorting grocery items at a free food bank, are employees of a large corporation that encourages its workers to help their fellow citizens while on company time.

Conflicts Surrounding the Right to Die

Some conflicts between the individual and the community spring from conflicting interpretations of morality. For example, does an individual have a right to choose to die, or does the state have the right to forbid that choice? If a person who is terminally ill wants to die, should a doctor help her do so? Do parents have the right to decide on **euthanasia** (also called assisted suicide or death with dignity) for their child who is terminally ill?

Should assisted suicide be permitted to spare the patient and family from suffering when death is inevitable? Does it make a difference whether you are deciding about a child, a young adult, or an older adult? Do you believe you would think the same way if it were your relative? What if the doctors were wrong; what if a new medication were about to be discovered that could save someone's life a few months later? How can we be sure? What about the impact of health care costs? Is there a risk that rising health care costs will motivate insurers and managed care entities to choose assisted suicide over continuing expensive medical treatments?

The debate over questions like these continues across our country. In February 2017, the District of Columbia became the sixth jurisdiction to enact legislation allowing death with dignity. Following the lead of the Oregon law, the District of Columbia joined Oregon, Washington, California, Seattle, Vermont, and Colorado in allowing physicians to provide assisted suicide for individuals with terminal illnesses. Others states though, had death-with-dignity initiatives fail to result in legislation.

No one can afford to be casual about taking human life for any reason or under any circumstances. Dangers lurk behind what seems to be an otherwise logical and compassionate policy for assisted suicide. In some states, there have been efforts to include depression and mental illness as permitted reasons for assisted suicide. It's difficult to know where to draw the line, and the grey areas in this ethical dilemma abound.

Conflicts Surrounding Reproductive Choice

Fierce battles have raged over the issue of abortion for nearly five decades. In this deeply personal and intimate area, most people have firm opinions. Because social science is never value-free, as the authors of this text we should state our biases on this hotly contested issue. Along with most other feminists, we believe that women should have the right to choose whether to have a baby, a right that the Supreme Court of the United States affirmed in its 1973 *Roe v. Wade* decision.

This decision protects a woman's right to privacy regarding what she does with her own body through the second trimester of pregnancy. Both the decision and the right have been contested ever since. The pro-choice faction fights to retain the right to abortion for all women. The anti-abortion faction works to make it illegal in the same way that murder is outlawed.

The *Roe v. Wade* decision was modified in July 1992 in the case *Planned Parenthood v. Casey*. This case involved a Pennsylvania law that required physicians to give counseling that encouraged childbirth to women seeking abortions. After the counseling, women would be required to wait 24 hours before undergoing an abortion. The law also required that the woman's spouse be notified, as well as the parents in the case of a minor teenager.

The Supreme Court upheld all the Pennsylvania requirements except spousal notification. In a narrow decision, a five-judge majority held spousal notification to be unconstitutional because it was "unduly burdensome," particularly to women in abusive or otherwise dysfunctional marriages. It did not, however, consider a 24-hour wait to be unduly burdensome to poor women. Many women cannot afford the extra travel, lodging, and child care costs they would need for an abortion. For these women, such extra costs can turn a burden into a veritable ban on access to abortion. The Hyde Amendment passed by the United States Congress House of Representatives

DUNAGIN'S PEOPLE

"DON'T WORRY. WHEN SEX EDUCATION IS PRESENTED IN A CLASSROOM SETTING, IT WILL BECOME AS FOREIGN TO THE STUDENTS AS MATH AND SCIENCE."

There is a fierce debate today about sex education, with some advocating "abstinence-only" programs (Belluck, 2018) and others arguing that young people should be told about all the options. This cartoon suggests that any sex education program given in school will not be relevant to students' actual life experiences.

in 1976, which banned using publicly funded Medicaid money for abortion unless a woman's life was were in danger, had already limited access to abortion for poor women. Many states stopped funding "medically unnecessary" abortions. Poor women could not afford abortions. In October 1977, Rosie Jiminez, a Texas woman, died from an illegal abortion in Mexico, the direct result of Texas's decision to stop Medicaid funding for abortions.

Other Supreme Court decisions also have weakened the *Roe v. Wade* decision. Several states have passed laws restricting abortion in various ways. Restrictions include requiring waiting periods, informed consent, and parental notification, and allowing abortion only in cases of rape, incest, and risk to a woman's health. Many of these restrictions have since been contested in the courts. In March 1993, the Supreme Court upheld a lower-court decision that prohibited Louisiana from virtually outlawing abortions. This affirmed that states have no constitutional right to outlaw abortions. A Colorado law that prohibited Medicaid funding for abortions in cases of rape or incest was struck down by the Supreme Court in 1995, leaving intact a federal law that forces states to provide Medicaid funding of abortions for victims of rape or incest.

Anti-abortion activists have succeeded in intimidating doctors and clinics through the use of militant, often frightening demonstrations. Doctors and other clinic workers have been murdered (Stack, L. 2015). Most doctors now do not want to risk doing abortions. In 2010, there was no known abortion provider in 87 percent of the counties in the United States, where a third of women lived (Bazelon, 2010).

In 1973, hospitals made up 80 percent of abortion facilities. After the *Roe v. Wade* decision, mainstream medicine backed away from abortions because of anti-abortion agitation. Feminist activists stepped in to set up stand-alone clinics to provide abortions. Fifteen years later, 90 percent of abortions were performed in such clinics (Bazelon, 2010). At the same time, medical schools increasingly refused to make abortion training part of their curriculum (Bazelon, 2010). However, an abortion-rights campaign, led by physicians themselves, has resulted in more medical schools training doctors to perform abortions. Jody Steinauer, an OB-GYN professor at the University of California at San Francisco, began the campaign in 1992. She organized the group Medical Students for Choice, which now has 10,000 members. The Accreditation Council for Graduate Medical Education—which represents the medical establishment—in 1995 decided, for the first time, to make abortion training a requirement for all OB-GYN residency programs seeking its accreditation. This was opposed by anti-abortion advocates, and the following year, Congress passed the Coats Amendment, which declared that any residency program that failed to obey the Accreditation Council's mandate could still be deemed accredited by the federal government. Today, about half of the more than two hundred OB-GYN residency programs integrate abortion into their residents' regular rotations. Another 40 percent of them offer only elective training.

People who oppose abortion made a further assault on the right to it through their efforts to ban what they called *partial-birth abortion*. This ban, passed by Congress and signed into law by President George W. Bush in 2003, was declared unconstitutional by Federal District Court Judge Phyllis J. Hamilton in 2004 (Preston, 2006). Hamilton said that the act creates a risk of criminal liability during virtually all abortions performed after the first trimester.

Another hotly contested issue in the abortion fight involved mifepristone (formerly known as RU 486), the drug regimen that terminates pregnancy within the first five weeks, and which can be taken by women at home. Anti-abortion forces tried to prohibit it; pro-choice forces fought to have it legalized. After much research, the Food and Drug Administration (FDA) finally approved it in 2000. During his 2000 campaign, George W. Bush pledged to sign any legislation that restricted mifepristone. In August 2002, anti-abortion groups petitioned the FDA to ban mifepristone. However, it continues to be sold legally.

The "morning-after pill," called "Plan B," has also been a hotly contested issue—even though pro-choice forces insist that it does not result in abortion, because it prevents the fertilized egg from being implanted in the wall of the uterus. In August 2006, the FDA ruled that it could be sold over the counter to women 18 and older. Plan B lowers the risk of pregnancy when started within 120 hours of unprotected intercourse.

Regardless of whether abortions are legal, women will continue to get them. One researcher says that the real public policy question is not whether we will have abortions but what kinds of abortions we will have (Miller, P. 1992). For example, in the 2007 decision *Gonzales v. Carhart*, *Roe v. Wade* was modified again when the Supreme Court upheld lower-court rulings that banned "partial-birth" abortions, saying that the lower-court rulings did not impose an undue burden on a women's right to abortion. Given this, laws in states that ban "partial birth" abortions remained in place.

In the past, the kinds of abortions performed while they were illegal were often very dangerous. In his 1953 survey of female sexual behavior, Alfred Kinsey, with Pomeroy, and Martin (1953), reported that 22 percent of his married respondents said they had had at least one abortion. Kinsey claimed that illegal abortion in the 1960s was estimated to be the third-largest money-maker for organized crime, exceeded only by narcotics and gambling, and he pointed out that most large public hospitals had septic abortion wards to treat the large number of life-threatening infections resulting from abortions performed under nonsterile conditions.

Anti-abortionists won another victory in 2010 when the Patient Protection and Affordable Care Act passed during the Barack Obama administration did not establish abortion coverage for women whose pre-existing conditions would place them in "high-risk pools" that were established through the ACA. Cecile Richards, president of the Planned Parenthood Federation of America, stated:

> The very women who need to purchase private health insurance in the new high-risk pools are likely to be more vulnerable to medically complicated pregnancies. It is truly harmful to these women that any administration may impose limits on how they use their own private dollars, limiting their health care options at a time when they need them most. This decision has no basis in the law and flies in the face of the intent of high-risk pools that were meant to meet the medical needs of some of the most vulnerable women in this country (*Our Bodies, Ourselves*. 2011).

The debate over reproductive rights continues with court decisions and laws passed by various jurisdictions with regularity. While former Senator Al Franken declared the Supreme Court's striking down of an antiabortion bill in Texas was a victory for a women's right to choose, Donald Trump ignited a firestorm when he indicated that women should be punished for having an abortion (Ziegler, 2018).

THE FETAL PROTECTION MOVEMENT   A recent tactic of the anti-abortion movement has been the campaign to protect the fetus from harm. Anti-abortion activists claim to care only about the health of the fetus, but as columnist Bob Herbert pointed out, they have a hidden agenda: to define the fetus as a person. If a fetus were defined as a person, abortion would logically become, under the law, murder (Herbert, 1998, p. 17).

In 1998, Governor Tommy Thompson of Wisconsin signed into law a bill that permitted the state to take into custody pregnant women who exhibit a serious and habitual "lack of self-control" in the use of alcohol or drugs. The bill defines *unborn child* as a human being from the time of fertilization to the time of birth and gives the state the right to appoint a legal guardian to represent the interests of the fetus.

The fetal protection movement has not made any serious effort to provide women with the treatment they need for substance use—or even adequate prenatal care. That is not part of its agenda. "When South Carolina began locking up pregnant addicts for criminal child abuse, there was no residential treatment for pregnant addicts in the entire state. Wisconsin still has long waiting lists of pregnant women seeking addiction services." (Herbert, 1998, p. 17)

In February 2017, a federal judge blocked a new Texas Department of State Health Services rule that required that women either bury or cremate their aborted fetuses. Critics of the new rule decried the effort as a thinly veiled attempt to further limit a women's right to access abortion. The Texas Attorney General, Ken Paxton, on the other hand vowed to appeal the court's order.

Anti-abortionists succeeded in getting a law passed declaring it a crime to harm a fetus, called The Unborn Victims of Violence Act. It was passed by Congress and signed into law by George W. Bush in 2004. This law gave a fetus the same rights as the pregnant woman and was an attempt to sidestep the question of whether abortion should or shouldn't be allowed. By defining the fetus as having equal rights as a person, the bill attempted to frame the debate as one person's rights against another person's rights (fetus verses mother). Kim Gandy, a former president of the National Organization for Women, made the following observations on the law:

> The sponsors of this cynical bill have devised a strategy to redefine the Fourteenth Amendment, which guarantees equal protection of the law to "persons," which has never been defined to include fetuses. The inventive language of this bill covers "a member of the species *homo sapiens* at any stage of development." Such a definition of "person" could entitle fertilized eggs, embryos, and fetuses to legal rights—ultimately setting the stage to legally reverse *Roe v. Wade* (National Organization for Women, 2004).

ATTITUDES TOWARD ABORTION ARE DEEPLY ROOTED BELIEFS When does life begin? This is an abstract philosophical question, which most of us probably answer according to our value system and not solely (or even at all) according to scientific evidence. Catholic theology holds that life begins at conception, although some believe that the Catholic hierarchy does not represent the views of most American Catholics on this issue, or the practice of Catholic women, who have abortions at the same rate as the national average for all women. Some Orthodox Jews believe that life begins with the sperm, even before it meets the egg. Other religious groups, such as the Mormons and fundamentalist Christians, also oppose abortion on religious grounds.

Many of the most militant anti-abortion demonstrators have come from the ranks of fundamentalist Christians with conservative politics (Castle, 2011). Due largely to a mistrust of government and social programs, they sponsor a few social service agencies geared to help women keep their babies. As a group they pay little attention to the policies that can make it easier for women in poverty to raise children—adequate TANF grants, affordable housing, good wages, affordable child care, and so forth (Stephens, 2016). Despite our own pro-choice stance, we have great respect for those who oppose abortion because of their deep commitment to preserve life and who express that commitment after the children are born by working for a more equal distribution of tax money and an end to war. The Catholic Workers are one such group of dedicated pacifists and social activists who oppose abortion.

Human service workers need to inform themselves thoroughly about the issues, be as clear as possible about where they stand, and make their position known to clients so that their biases do not subtly influence clients to make choices they may later regret. If you personally object to abortion, for example, it would be appropriate, given the right time and place, to share your view. Along with this, though, is the importance of keeping the best interests of the individual being served at the forefront. In the case of abortion, or not, the decision belongs to the individual, and your role is to support them as they work to make the best decision possible for their own situation and circumstance.

SEX OFFENDERS   How do you prevent sex offenders from molesting children? Pass a law to prevent them from getting near children? After the 1994 murder of 7-year-old Megan Kanka by a released sex offender living on her street, public outcry created a call for programs to provide the public with information regarding released sex offenders. Congress passed a law in 1996 called "Megan's Law," which requires all states to conduct community notification but does not set out specific forms and methods, other than requiring the creation of Internet sites containing state sex-offender information. Beyond that requirement, states are given broad discretion in creating their own policies. The law was an amendment to a previous law passed in 1994, which required convicted sex offenders to register their addresses with local law enforcement (Wright, 2014).

More than thirty states, and thousands of municipalities nationwide, have passed residency restrictions for sex offenders (Ward, 2008) and have designated areas where sex offenders are not allowed to live—near schools, playgrounds, day care centers, and other places where children congregate—in the hope of preventing repeat offenses. Does it work? There is increasing evidence that it doesn't. Studies indicate that many sex crimes are never reported (Butler, 2005), and that sex offenders often molest beyond the areas where they live. Some scholars believe that the measures could put children in greater danger, not less—because the sex offenders go underground, and because limited resources are wasted enforcing the laws (Craun & Theriot, 2009). From the author's perspective, no one who has professional experience in the management of sex offenders thinks these laws make much sense.

In addition, it's important to understand that child sexual molestation is often perpetrated upon the victim by someone that they know and trust. Sex offenders rely on a trusting relationship in order to have access to the child and in order to ensure that their acts remain hidden. Our tendency to believe first and foremost in stranger danger creates a false sense of security for family members when their children are around friends and family. The literature underscores this point. Gallagher, Bradford, and Pease (2008), for example, found that 65 percent of the children within their study who were sexually abused were abused by someone known to them. What's important here is to understand that children can be at risk from adults that surround them, families and friends, as well as strangers.

Many people ignore or minimize the issue of the civil liberties of the sex offender, believing that they pose such a great danger that their civil liberties are not important. However, the residency laws pose serious civil liberties concerns. These measures apply to convicts after they have been punished and released and have served their parole. In many cases, homeowners are exempt, while renters may be required to move. And this type of post-release regulation doesn't exist for other criminal classes. For example, arsonists are not prohibited from living near gas stations. In some cases, the strict residency restrictions have caused more issues than they have solved. Many sex offenders cannot find housing in urban areas and often are forced into homelessness (Dunlap, 2010).

One of the nation's most aggressive attempts to limit the mobility of sex offenders was struck down in Georgia in 2007 by the Georgia Supreme Court, which declared the state law unconstitutional. The Georgia Supreme Court ruled that, by forcing a sex offender from his or her home, the law violated his Fifth Amendment right to be safe from the government "taking" his or her property. The ruling said, "It is apparent that there is no place in Georgia where a registered sex offender can live without continually being at risk of being ejected" (Whoriskey, 2007). (We discuss this case more fully in Chapter 14.)

CONFLICTING VIEWS ON HUMAN NATURE

The Declaration of Independence states that people have an inalienable right to life, liberty, and the pursuit of happiness. But in daily life, no one is guaranteed a job, and no one is guaranteed an income or a home or food.

Although welfare recipients' taxes have already paid for some of the money they receive, taxes probably do not cover all of the money received. Money must come from the haves if it is to help the have-nots. This is also true of Social Security. Most people get back a good deal more than they paid into the fund. Yet the crucial question is not whether people should get back only as much as they paid but whether society as a whole has a responsibility to care for its members when they are having a hard time.

Your values about the kind of society you want to live in are partially shaped by your beliefs about human nature. Each of us has a mental picture of the "normal" child or adult, even if we have never articulated it. If we are program planners, administrators, or human service workers,

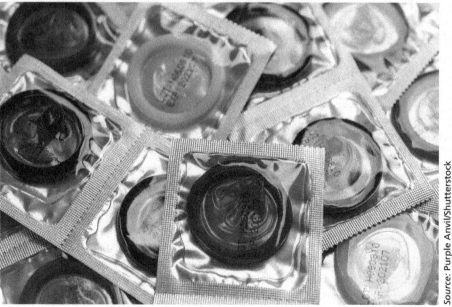

Source: Purple Anvil/Shutterstock

There are arguments for and against the New York City Department of Health and Mental Hygiene's campaign to distribute more than 1 million free condoms. Advocates argue that using condoms will reduce the spread of HIV/AIDS and sexually transmitted disease. Opponents assert that easy availability of condoms could increase sexual promiscuity, increasing transmission of the virus. What do you think?

our basic view of people will be expressed in many direct and subtle ways as we plan or implement social programs.

Discussed below are some of the most common views of human nature. Which ones come closest to yours? In what ways do your views differ from your parents', your peers', or your neighbors'?

The Belief That People Need to Be Civilized

For **Thomas Hobbes**, a seventeenth-century English philosopher, the human condition was characterized by both desire and rationality. If everyone pursued desire fulfilment, that, according to Hobbes, might lead to conflict with others and to lives that are "nasty, brutish, and short." But every rational person wants to live and to live in peace. Thus he accepts authority to regulate, and perhaps curb, desire. Considering the times in which he lived, a period of constant war, Hobbes's conclusions are understandable.

Some people have interpreted William Golding's widely read novel *Lord of the Flies* (1959) as a Hobbesian allegory. In this story, a group of English schoolboys, stranded by an airplane crash on a desert island, create a social order that looks very much like the Hobbesian scenario of dog-eat-dog survival, with restraints of authority removed. (Others point out that the boys were simply duplicating the authoritarian society of the supposedly civilized English private school from which they came.)

People who subscribe to a view of human nature similar to Hobbes's are likely to advocate a strong authority and to favor "law-and-order" approaches to human problems. Clearly, Hobbes didn't believe in self-regulation. A social worker sharing Hobbes's distrust of self-regulation might give clients vouchers rather than cash, keep careful watch over their behavior, and invoke strong punishment for deviations.

The Belief That People Are Basically Rational

While Hobbes was propounding his theories, **John Locke**, another English philosopher and scientist, had a different view. He believed that if people followed their own self-interest, a rational, just society would result. Locke rejected the traditional view that babies were born with fixed selfish ideas or brutish characteristics. He believed instead that a child came into the world with a *tabula rasa* (blank tablet) on which the world could inscribe itself through the experience of the five senses. People in the helping professions who follow a philosophy similar to Locke's would be likely to subscribe to a more environmentally oriented psychology, such as that of the **behaviorist** B. F. Skinner. The assumption in his work is that with the appropriate stimuli, correctly administered, human social behavior can be positively shaped and changed.

The Belief That People Are Corrupted by Society

Jean-Jacques Rousseau, an eighteenth-century Swiss–French philosopher, put forth the idea that people were good by nature but corrupted by civilization: "Man is born free, but is everywhere in chains." He believed that education should draw out the knowledge that people are born with, in contrast to the "banking" theory of education, which holds that knowledge should be deposited in people's empty heads. Education, according to Rousseau, should allow the free development of human potential. Paolo Freire (1970), a Brazilian adult educator, subscribed to a theory of education called "conscientization," which is similar to Rousseau's theory. According to Freire, poor people's education should begin by raising questions about their life situation, why they are so poor, and why they have been kept from getting the education they need.

The Belief That People Need to Be Connected to Each Other

Several nontraditional and feminist psychologists suggest that, in contrast to the individualistic and competitive orientation commonly found in men, women are socialized to place value on nurturing, cooperation, and nonviolence. Carol Gilligan (1982) asserts that women choose their actions when faced with a moral dilemma according to what effect their choice will have on the others who are involved, rather than by referring to abstract concepts of justice. Caring and responsibility for others are central to their moral concerns.

Psychologist Jean Baker Miller (1976) says that these "feminine" traits that have been traditionally regarded as weaknesses are, in fact, strengths. They take us beyond the "macho" succeed-at-any-cost attitude. She suggests that men as well as women need to strengthen their ability to empower each other without needing to dominate or control.

Not everyone agrees that women are naturally more caring than men. We all probably know selfish women who don't care about other people's feelings, and men who are very caring. As many feminists warn, we should avoid "essentialist" thinking, which believes that women and men have essentially different and unchanging characteristics.

CONFLICTS CAUSED BY BUREAUCRATIC DEMANDS

Most human service workers, unless they are in private practice or a small independent agency, are employed by an organization that possesses a level of bureaucracy that is required to conduct day-to-day business within the organization. Sometime this bureaucracy creates practices and procedures that are contrary to the needs of workers and clients. When this happens, the barriers created can actually pit workers against clients. A social services worker, for example, may be convinced that a TANF claimant needs more money than the grant allows but be unable to help the client because of state and federal regulations.

According to Max Weber (Gerth & Mills, 1958), a nineteenth-century sociologist, bureaucracy is supposed to make work more efficient, to substitute dependable rules for arbitrary decisions, to treat people more fairly, and to judge workers on merit rather than favoritism. But bureaucracies can also depersonalize and objectify people. They can divide work into specialized components so that no one has the satisfaction of seeing a job through to completion. They set up hierarchies of authority that can take away the autonomy of workers. One of the most pervasive problems of modern society is **bureaucratization** of work and of relationships. In human service work, this is especially serious because our work requires warm and genuine relationships between people. States and jurisdictions have long recognized that rules and regulations, while necessary at one level, often get in the way of what has to be done to meet the individual needs of the individuals we are committed to serve. As an exemplar, Colorado in 2011 repealed 850 rules within their Department of Human Services as a way to make the department better able to achieve its mission (Gillentine, 2011). The occupational hazard for workers in a bureaucracy is the tendency to "go along to get along." Many workers may want to keep their jobs and do what is required, even when it is not in the best interest of clients. Social psychologists have studied the tendency to go along willingly with authority. One of the most famous of these studies is the Milgram experiment on blind obedience, which explored the conditions under which people would refuse to obey immoral commands (Milgram, 1974). Stanley Milgram asked people to "shock" subjects with varying amounts of "electricity" each time they made an error on a task. (Subjects were not actually shocked but were trained actors who simulated being shocked.) Far more people obeyed the commands than either Milgram or others predicted. Milgram concluded

Source: Reproduced with permission of Chris Madden

that a person's conscience is diminished in a hierarchical system, and that in authority systems, people are more likely to see themselves as agents who carry out other people's wishes rather than as autonomous decision makers.

Another classic study that revealed people's willingness to go along with authority was the prison experiment that Zimbardo, Haney, Banks, and Jaffe (1982) conducted with healthy college students. Half of the students were instructed to be "prisoners," the other half "guards." In a very short time, the students were adopting the behavior of the role they had been assigned. The experiment had to be discontinued because of the sadism of some of the "guards" and because some participants, especially the "prisoners," were displaying negative effects on their emotional health.

Guidelines for Dealing With Conflicts in a Bureaucracy

The task of debureaucratizing society is an enormous one that requires the best creative thoughts and efforts of all of us. We need to accept responsibility for the ethical and political dimensions of our work. Rhodes (1989, pp. 154, 156) suggests that workers can do that by:

- Speaking out about their beliefs, showing the politics behind alternative courses of action, and pointing out inconsistencies in the way the agency does its work. Speaking out is a skill that requires as much planning and thought as the most carefully prepared case presentation
- Forming alliances with other workers and with clients to organize social action on policy issues
- Questioning the rationale behind rules and regulations rather than docilely implementing policies with which the workers disagree
- Offering expertise on legislative committees, pushing for legislative action, and educating the public about human service issues.

It's also important to understand the role that the organization's mission, vision, values, and beliefs should play in the development of its policies and procedures. Careful adherence to a clear mission and vision within the context of well-articulated values and beliefs helps to ensure that the organization can avoid becoming overly bureaucratic. NFI North, a multi-service helping organization in northern New England, for example, prides itself in having a steadfast focus on advancing its mission, which is *to empower and inspire people to achieve their full potential so that they can live successfully within their own home and community (https://www.nfinorth.com).* The organization pursues its mission in an environment of respect and support with the firm belief that people have great potential. Following its mission statement closely within the context of the organization's values becomes a litmus test for the success of its policies and procedures. Does the policy or procedure help the organization to achieve its mission? If not, then the policy and or procedure must be set aside for a more mission-focused alternative. Mission-focused organizations are generally less bureaucratic and better able to meet the needs of their clients.

Consumer-Driven/Family-Driven/Youth-Driven Practice

Within the delivery of human services, we recognize the importance of helping the people served to play the central role in determining the way in which services are driven. In a very real sense, the people served by the agency are treated as the organization's employers. The concept that the client is our employer is closely related to the value of self-determination—the belief that only clients can decide what is best for themselves. Even when the client does not pay a fee for our service, we subscribe to the belief that the service should be responsive primarily their needs, not to the workers' or agency's needs.

Today's effective human service organizations recognize the importance of working to help the people they serve to be in the driver's seat when it comes to the way their needs are met. Many organizations have institutionalized this philosophical approach by including consumers and family members of consumers on their board of directors. Others have worked to bring on peer advocacy and peer support services as important elements in their array of services. In some instances, this takes the form of hiring peer support staff that work alongside professionals. These individuals have lived experience, and as a result they bring important elements of insight and advocacy that benefit the individuals being served by the organization. In addition, most organizations conduct regular surveys of the individuals they serve in order to develop strategies for continual quality improvement. And while these strategies are firmly in place in many organizations, it's important that each agency work hard to avoid the pressures that exist to simply "process" people through the system in as short a time as possible.

It's very important as you become a human service worker that you maintain respect for and value the opinions, desires, and wishes of the people you serve. At times it can be challenging, especially when the individuals have a different world view then your own, or are living in poverty, incarcerated, or dealing with an intellectual disability or mental illness. Nevertheless, just as in a relationship with an architect, a real estate agent, or a lawyer, the client has the right to decide which problems are most pressing and which treatment methods are most acceptable.

Professionalization creates built-in conflicts about how to behave with clients. Social work comes out of a nineteenth-century paternalistic tradition. Gratitude was expected from "deserving" clients. Help was refused to the "undeserving (Backwith, 2015)." Although many twentieth-century professionals no longer hold such expectations, old attitudes linger. When money or services are defined as everybody's right, as with Social Security, beneficiaries feel entitled to the benefit and do not feel any obligation to be grateful or behave in a certain way. However, when a service is not presented as an automatic entitlement, there are ambiguous behavioral expectations. Both the giver and the recipient resent a relationship in which one person does all the giving and the other does all the taking. Mutual-aid groups derive much of their attraction from the fact that power is shared equally among the members. *The relationship of a human service worker to a client is inherently unequal because of the power differential.*

The worker is in a position to give or withhold benefits. As a result, your ability to manage the dynamics of difference in a way that helps ensure the integrity and choice of the individual being served is particularly important.

In Chapter 7 on diversity, we suggest that some cultural groups expect a very personalized helping relationship, and therefore it is important to structure the relationship to meet their expectations. A classic study of helping relationships in child abuse and neglect (Berkeley Planning Associates, 1978) concluded that two of the most important factors in helping parents were a more friendly, personalized relationship and the down-to-earth assistance given by parent aides. This was true for a wide variety of cultural groups. Rhodes concluded, after reviewing four studies of client satisfaction, that:

> Client satisfaction and client change depended to some extent on clients' perceptions of their workers as "friends." And such friendship had the following qualities: empathy, caring, flexibility, patience, suggestions rather than advice, reciprocity in the form of sharing aspects of one's personal life, and immediate concrete help in the mode requested. In addition, many small social activities were viewed as important to befriending: "calling in for a cup of tea, accepting an invitation to a party, sending cards while on holiday, extending a home-visit to play with the children" (Rhodes, 1989, p. 164).

These clients did not seem to make a sharp distinction between friend and professional when they liked their worker. If a worker was only a professional and not a friend, the worker was usually viewed with hostility or at least distrust (Rhodes, 1989).[*]

The importance of the connection between the helpee and helper has also been studied at length within the framework of the working or therapeutic alliance (Bucci, Seymour-Hyde, Harris, & Berry, 2016). When it comes to counselling relationships, the interpersonal connection between the client and the counsellor is one of the key dimensions necessary to ensure successful outcomes. Bordin (1979) is credited with articulating all three elements needed to achieve a working alliance, which he theorized as necessary to achieve positive outcomes. The first dimension is a shared goal between the helper and the helpee, the second is a shared task, and finally, as noted, there must be a bond or relationship in order to effectively pursue the desired goal. The relationship makes it possible to help the individual weather the challenges that will undoubtedly occur as the necessary tasks are pursued in order to achieve the desired goal.

The working alliance conceptual frame is helpful no matter what part of the helping profession you are engaged in. For example, as a behavioral health worker, you will find yourself working to help your client achieve a goal. Sharing that goal is incredibly helpful. Knowing the task at hand and then having a connection with that client becomes the formula for ensuring success. In our own experience, this framework has helped even when the clients are ordered to receive services. As a caseworker working with youth committed to the Department of Youth Services, I would start with the most basic of goals—i.e., "helping the youth to get me out of their life." Often this was the only goal a resistant youth and I could agree on when we first started working together. It didn't matter that the goal seemed outside of the individual service plan or care plan. The fact that we could agree to the goal became a starting point. It did ultimately help to begin a process and create a window where our connection or bond could be developed.

---

[*]Studies that Rhodes reviewed included Mayer and Timms (1970), Sainsbury (1974), Rees (1979), and Keefe and Maypole (1983).

While studies of clients' opinions of human service workers were once rare, they are becoming more and more prevalent. Many licensing, regulatory, and accreditation bodies now require that organizations measure and report back on the satisfaction of the clients they serve. The Joint Commission, for example, one of the premier accreditation bodies for hospitals as well as behavioral health organizations, requires that organizations collect, report, and act upon client satisfaction surveys (Dupont, Castro, Nahmens, Ikuma, & Harvey, 2015).

CONFLICTS DUE TO THE VARIATION IN NATIONAL VALUES IN THE UNITED STATES

Although it is as hard to generalize about national values as about individual or ethnic group values, some dominant themes stand out in each nation. At times these themes conflict with one another. In the United States, the democratic and humanitarian values expressed in our Constitution stand side by side with what is often termed the Protestant work ethic, which says that all people who work hard enough can pull themselves up by their own bootstraps (Zafirovski, 2014). Social Darwinism maintains that in society, as in the jungle, only the fittest can and should survive.

These contradictions help us understand the mixture of progressive and surprisingly punitive legislation that makes up our social welfare system. The values implicit in the punitive legislation often strongly influence public opinion and misconceptions about welfare assistance. In the United States, people in need of financial assistance often receive less help and are more stigmatized than they are in several European countries.

It is interesting to see how these values of competition and individualism, and a belief that people are in control of their own destiny, affect the views of people in the United States toward individuals with mentall illness. Jagdeo, Cox, Stein, and Sareen (2009) found that nearly 50 percent of respondents from the United States and Canada were embarrassed to tell their friends and family about their own mental illness and that 20 percent of the respondents from the United States said they probably or definitely would not seek treatment if they had a serious emotional illness.

Anthropological studies of cultural attitudes toward mental illness show that many other cultures are more tolerant than the United States and other Western societies. Those diagnosed with schizophrenia actually seem more likely to recover in less-developed countries, such as Mexico or India (Bass, 1992).

Anthropologist Janis Jenkins found that Mexican and Indian families were more likely to believe there are forces *outside* each person's control that influence their ability to ward off disease. They are, therefore, much more likely to believe that the person suffering from mental illness deserves sympathy, support, and special treatment. Latinos are also more likely than European Americans to believe that even severe mental illness is curable. When people *believe* that they will be cured, they are more likely to be cured. In the United States, on the other hand, we are more likely to stigmatize people with mental illness because of the dominant belief that people are autonomous and in control of their own destiny (Bass, 1992). Of course it's important to recognize that any culturally specific observation made here and throughout the literature is made in the broadest sense and so one cannot assume that what is true for one individual from a given culture is true for the next.

It is important though, as a human service professional, to be sure that you are wholly aware of your own cultural perspectives as well as the perspectives of the individual you are serving. Some cultures, for example are more collective in nature while others, such as western culture, have a more individualistic lens. This has a direct impact on how mental illness is viewed by a given culture, how help can be realized and who is responsible for what within the process of recovery (Abdullah & Brown, 2011). Sue and Sue (2012) not only stress the importance of knowing your cultural roots and they cultural roots of the individual you are serving, but also becoming aware of the dynamics that exist as a result. Its critical from that point to adapt your practice as a human service professional to optimize your ability to be effective.

Age and Aging

Increasing awareness of race and sex discrimination has been followed by an increased awareness of age discrimination. Robert Butler (1975), former director of the National Institute on Aging, coined the term **ageism**. In a culture that values youth, attractiveness, productivity, and activity, older people are often devalued. Professionals who work with them sometimes share society's dominant attitudes. Ageism is present throughout our service delivery system and can take the form of implicit as well as explicit discrimination. Many professionals feel less interested in treating seniors, while others' implicit beliefs may result in overtreating elderly clients (Ouchida & Lachs, 2015). Some human service workers have misconceptions about the inevitability of the degenerative process. Although there is no evidence suggesting there must always be a decline in the mental activity, responsibility, and even sexual prowess of older adults it is difficult not to be influenced by these widely held misconceptions.

Sexual Orientation

The lesbian folk singer Betsy Rose sings a song about a woman coming out to her mother for the first time. Rose's imaginary mother in the song is delighted, and says, "Darlin', I'm glad you're gay!" The song is presented humorously, and the audience laughs because it is so contrary to what often happens in real life.

Homophobia (the irrational fear and stigmatization of gay people) is deeply ingrained in society, and human service workers are not immune to it. It was not until 1973 that the American Psychiatric Association declared that being gay was not a mental illness and removed it from its list of psychiatric disorders. Two years later, the American Psychological Association followed suit.

Despite growing recognition that being gay is no more a mental health concern than heterosexuality, individuals who are gay continue to experience stigmatization and discrimination. They were one of the first groups the Nazis forced into concentration camps in Poland and Germany. They were required to wear a pink triangle as an identifying symbol, in the same way that Jews had to wear a yellow star. Because they are stigmatized, lesbian, gay, bisexual, transgender, and questioning or queer (LGBTQ) individuals have a history of having to stay "in the closet"—that is, they pretend to be heterosexual. It is often traumatic for them to publicly acknowledge their sexual orientation. It may be especially hard for older people, because the stigma was even more severe in their youth.

It is a safe bet that, whether you know it or not, you work with, learn with, or are taught by an LGBTQ individual. Your supervisor at work, the homeless mother in a shelter for domestic violence, the undocumented immigrant from El Salvador in an English as a Second Language program, the man in a nursing home with Alzheimer's disease, the runaway teenager on the street, your colleagues and friends—any of them could be gay. They are not likely to tell you until they trust you. It is important not to make any prior assumptions about a person's sexual orientation. If, for example, you are a hospital social worker and are called to help a man who was brought to the hospital because of a bicycle accident, and someone needs to be notified, you might ask him, "Could you tell me the name of someone who is close to you who could come to help you?" rather than asking "Do you have a wife I should phone?"

In June 2015, the United States Supreme Court ruled in *Obergefell v. Hodges* that state bans on same-sex couples' right to marry were unconstitutional. In the court's ruling, the denial of licenses by individual states was seen as a violation of individuals' right to due process and equal protection under the Fourteenth Amendment of the United States Constitution. Today many states are implementing laws to protect the rights of individuals who are gay. Twenty states prohibit discrimination based on sexual orientation and gender identity. And while this represents significant progress in assuring the rights of people to marry without regard to their sexual orientation, there continues to be a significant amount of discrimination based on sexual orientation. In many states, for example, employers may legally discriminate against an employee based solely on their sexual orientation as there aren't laws prohibiting this form of discrimination (Kattari, et al., 2016). Transgender individuals can experience discrimination by being banned from using public restrooms that reflect their sexual identity, and LGBTQ individuals find themselves the recipients of daily micro and macro aggressions. At some point, you might be asked to make a recommendation to a judge in a custody case. As a human service worker, you are more likely to be concerned with the capacity of parents to nurture their child than with those parents' sexual orientation.

New reproductive technologies, especially artificial insemination, have opened up the possibilities for childbearing for lesbians. Some gays and lesbians also want to become foster or adoptive parents, and many now have, as state child welfare agencies have come to realize the key is one's ability to parent and not one's sexual orientation.

KEEPING VALUES STRAIGHT IN A TIME OF SOCIAL UNREST AND STRIFE

The 9/11 attacks on the United States and the subsequent wars on Iraq and Afghanistan, the war in Syria, and the rise in terrorism sponsored by ISIS as well as other groups nationally and internationally have created value dilemmas for everyone in the country. Human service workers

Source: Shutterstock Fotos593

In 2015, the U.S. Supreme Court ruled that state bans on same-sex couples' right to marry were unconstitutional. In the court's ruling, the denial of licenses by individual states was seen as a violation of individuals' right to due process and equal protection under the Fourteenth Amendment of the United States Constitution.

share in the world's grief, bewilderment, fear, and anxiety as we try to sort out the issues. How do our core values shape our reactions to these crises? Does our profession have anything special to offer the world?

Frederic Reamer, a social work professor, looks to the core values of social work as guidance for these times, and his advice is appropriate for all human service workers (Reamer, 2001). One of the core values is respect for the dignity and worth of the person. Social workers (and all other human service workers) have a strong belief in human dignity and worth. But what about our response to an individual who has abused another? Should we also be expected to respect their dignity and worth? For example, should we as human service workers respect the dignity and worth of someone who has abused a child in our care? Questions like this are extremely difficult and require a mindful consideration of the circumstances.

Social workers are also called upon to respect individual difference and cultural and ethnic diversity. At the same time, social workers sometimes struggle to distinguish the ethical from the unethical. How does one reconcile corporal punishment as a cultural child-rearing practice with child protection standards that now exist across all 50 states? It's important to realize that not everything is subject to cultural relevance. The respect for an individual's confidentiality, for example, generally ends at the point where the individual's actions may adversely impact his own safety or the safety of others. Confidentiality has its limits, as do other areas of respect for cultural differences. Cultural actions that affect the safety or wellbeing of a child can cross the line of what is appropriate.

FINDING YOUR WAY THROUGH THE MAZE OF ETHICAL CONFLICTS

How do we find our way through the thicket of ethical dilemmas and ambiguity? It's important to consider what approach you will use to ensure that your effort results in the best ethical decision making. McAuliffe and Chenoweth (2008) have developed an approach to address ethical dilemmas that they call the Inclusive Model of Ethical Decision Making. This approach is built on four key platforms that become the backdrop for a five-step action plan for resolving ethical dilemmas. The four platforms are developed from important principles and values that include dignity, respect, and self-determination. The four platforms are accountability, consultation, cultural sensitivity, and critical reflection.

Ethical decision making is then achieved using the four platforms as a foundational stance for pursuing the five-step process:

Step One: Defining the Ethical Dilemma What exactly is the dilemma, and as a part of this, what are the competing principles involved?

Step Two: Mapping Legitimacy Who is involved in this dilemma, and based on this, who has a role in the decision making?

Step Three: Gathering Information Collecting information about the situation is important, and it is important to also gather information about the related code of ethics and the professional requirements that the situation demands.

Step Four: Alternative Approaches and Action What are the available courses of action, and how will I justify the decision I make? What are the potential consequences of each course of action, and have I considered the cultural nuances of the situation?

Step Five: Critical Analysis and Evaluation How did the situation turn out? What steps worked well, and how might I adjust my approach to resolving this sort of ethical dilemma going forward?

Summary

1. No one is value-free. Our values are shaped by many influences: families, friends, school, church, the workplace, and our social class, ethnicity, and gender.
2. The value of self-determination is important in the human service professions.
3. Despite its importance, self-determination is difficult to follow in practice, especially in work with involuntary clients.
4. Decisions about self-determination must weigh the good of the individual against the good of the community.
5. Child welfare agencies are under fire across the nation. Complaints come from biological parents, foster parents, and advocacy groups.
6. Human service workers disagree about treating clients who are ordered to receive treatment. Some refuse, believing that the client's right of self-determination is an overriding value. Others believe that they can often overcome resistance and their help will be accepted.
7. Self-determination can be violated by manipulation as well as by overtly coercive methods. Manipulation should be avoided.
8. Some current ethical dilemmas center on the treatment of individuals with HIV/AIDS, death with dignity, and reproductive choice.
9. One's view of human nature shapes the service one gives. Three views of human nature were proposed by Thomas Hobbes, John Locke, and Jean-Jacques Rousseau.
10. Bureaucracies often conflict with meeting the needs of clients and workers.
11. Workers need to take responsibility for their own beliefs and speak out about them.
12. Conflicts about national values affect policy and practice. A mixture of progressive and punitive values shapes welfare policies.
13. Clients today should be active in driving their service delivery. Consumer choice, representation, and feedback are important elements of effective practice. Feedback from clients improves practice.
14. There are misconceptions about the process of aging.
15. Conflicts about sexual orientation affect human service policy and practice.
16. It is hard to keep our values clear in a time of social unrest and strife. We offer some guidelines.
17. It's important to consider how to approach ethical dilemmas.

Discussion Questions

1. Although self-determination is an important value in human service work, it is often hard to follow in certain disciplines. In what ways could self-determination be maximized in the following situations if you were the human service worker?
   a. A parent has been reported as being abusive to a child.
   b. A person who was driving while drunk has been mandated to get treatment.
   c. A youth who has committed a crime is on probation.
2. A woman says she would rather die than go through the debilitating processes that are inevitable with her illness. She is 50 years old and has early-onset Alzheimer's disease. What are your thoughts on this?
3. You are given the job of leading a discussion between pro-choice and anti-abortion proponents. How do you structure this discussion?
4. In some open adoption arrangements, the biological parent and the adoptive parents continue to have contact with each other after the adoption, and the biological parent is allowed to have

frequent contact with the child. What are the possible advantages and disadvantages of this arrangement? Do the same issues that apply to open adoption also apply to artificial insemination when the child who is born is allowed to contact her father?

5. Why do you think that it is important for social agencies to have clients serve as members of their board of directors? What do you think is important about ensuring that social service agencies receive regular feedback from their clients?

Web Resources for Further Study

The Hastings Center

https://www.thehastingscenter.org

National Association of Social Workers (NASW)

https://www.socialworkers.org

National Organization for Human Services

https://www.nationalhumanservices.org

Self-determination theory

http://selfdeterminationtheory.org

MyLab Helping Professions for Introduction to Human Services

In the Topic 11 Assignments: Human Services Values and Attitudes, try Application Exercise 11.2: Self-determination and Worth and Uniqueness of the Individual and Application Exercise 11.3: Worth, Uniqueness, and Ability to Change.

6 Social Welfare Programs and Policies

Learning Outcomes

- Students will be able to characterize who is considered to be living in poverty, how poverty rates are determined, and how they are used to determine eligibility for benefits.

- Students will be able to explain how social welfare programs evolved in America and the concept of the "reluctant welfare state."

- Students will be able to assess how income inequality has widened in the United States.

- Students will be able to compare how income and support programs are delivered based on assumptions of "deserving" and "undeserving" poor, and conditions that must be met to qualify for the programs.

- Students will be able to distinguish between "entitlement" and "eligibility" for benefits and services.

Source: Monkey Business Images/Shutterstock

Social welfare programs encompass those goods and services that are provided by the government and private organizations for individuals in need. They include Social Security, public assistance, food stamps and food vouchers, medical care, housing and housing subsidies, child care, unemployment and workers' compensations, veterans' benefits, and personal social services.

The term *social welfare system* implies a sense of order, comprehensiveness, and rational planning. However, the major health and welfare systems in the United States can be complicated and difficult to navigate. In fact, there are 80 different social welfare programs, mostly within the 10 means-tested programs and tax credits, which provide cash payments or assistance in obtaining health care, food, housing, or education to people with relatively low income or few assets. The major programs and credits consist of the following:

- Medicaid
- The low-income subsidy (LIS) for Part D of Medicare (the part of Medicare that provides prescription drug benefits)
- The refundable portion of the earned income tax credit (EITC)
- The refundable portion of the child tax credit (CTC)

- Supplemental Security Income (SSI)
- Temporary Assistance for Needy Families (TANF)
- The Supplemental Nutrition Assistance Program (SNAP, formerly called the Food Stamp Program)
- Child nutrition programs
- Housing assistance programs
- The Federal Pell Grant program.

There are many conflicting reports about the effectiveness of the social service programs. Though the United States has been referred to as a "reluctant welfare state," its programs of assistance have raised millions of people out of poverty; given medical care to those living in poverty and the aged; provided compensatory education; and provided food, housing, and cash assistance to those living in poverty, older adults, and people with disabilities. (Sherman, November 2015). For example, spending on TANF decreased in 2005 to levels lower than in 1970, but spending on Medicaid grew over 200 percent in that same time period. While spending has increased over time, there has been a shift in funding toward people with disabilities and older adults and away from mothers who are single, children, and the very poor. (Moffitt., June 2016).

We discuss some of these programs in this chapter.

UNDERSTANDING HOW POVERTY IS DEFINED

The formula to determine the poverty level was established in 1963 based on a pre-tax income of three times the cost of a minimum food diet. It is updated annually for inflation using the Consumer Price Index and adjusted for family size, composition, and age of householder. The U.S. Census Bureau tracks poverty rates, and some programs use poverty rates to determine eligibility. Criticism of the poverty rate calculation is that it is an outdated measure of a household budget. Food is no longer the costliest budget item for a household—housing and child care costs can exceed food costs. Geographic differences in cost of living are not factored in, and the definition of "family" has not been expanded to include the many types of households prevalent today. Another criticism of the poverty rate is that people living over the poverty rate can still be poor. Therefore, poverty is highly undercounted.

U.S. DEPARTMENT OF HEALTH AND HUMAN SERVICES 2018 POVERTY GUIDELINES FOR THE 48 CONTIGUOUS STATES AND THE DISTRICT OF COLUMBIA

Persons in Family/Household	Poverty Guideline
For families/households with more than 8 persons, add $4,320 for each additional person.	
1	$12,140
2	$16,460
3	$20,780
4	$25,100
5	$29,420
6	$33,740
7	$38,060
8	$42,380

Source: U. S. Department of Health and Human Services

Some government benefits, such as fuel assistance and Medicaid, use a percentage over the poverty line for eligibility (138 percent of the poverty level.) Welfare cash assistance payments (TANF) are below the poverty line in all states, far below in southern states. Setting the percentage often becomes a struggle between advocates and legislators. In Massachusetts, for example, the eligibility level for shelter for families who are homeless in 2017 was 115 percent of the poverty line, down from 130 percent in 2010 (Massachusetts Budget and Policy Center). Whichever the level, if clients earn even a dollar more, they remain homeless. Some people must choose between either keeping their job and living on the street or leaving their job in order to access shelter—an unintended consequence of income limits. For some programs, such as publicly subsidized affordable housing, area median income is used to calculate eligibility. Each year, HUD publishes the income limits based on a percentage of area median income. These income targets are geographically specific and adjusted for household size. For example, if the area median income is $75,000 and the income eligibility for a HUD subsidized unit is targeted to households with incomes of 50 percent of area median income or below, then $37,500 would be the maximum allowable income (adjusted for household size).

A **family self-sufficiency standard** calculation takes into account the real costs of basic needs when constructing a minimum budget. This calculation was introduced in 1996 by an organization called Wider Opportunities for Women. It is a far better measure than the poverty rate for determining need, as it takes into consideration the cost of housing and child care by geography.

Source: Rafael Ben-Ari/123RF

The foreclosure crisis of 2008 that continued for several years was the result of deregulation of banks and a lack of consumer protection. Unscrupulous lending practices for short-term profit left families without homes, and entire communities lost the equity they built in a matter of months.

The **cliff effect** is the sudden loss of benefits due to an increase in income that puts the individual over-income to receive benefits. When the increase in income is not sufficient to cover the loss in benefits, there can be severe consequences, such as loss of a child care or housing voucher. One policy change that may combat the cliff effect would be a gradual decline of benefits until the individual's income could support the costs.

The **Supplemental Poverty Measure (SPM)** takes into account the value of social welfare benefits such as cash transfers, in-kind transfers, SNAP (food stamps), and tax credits in addition to pre-tax household income. Without Social Security, 26.6 million additional people would be living below the poverty level, and without the Earned Income Tax Credit, an additional 9.2 million people would be classified as living in poverty. The SPM also factors in expenses and makes geographic adjustments for housing costs. The result is higher poverty rates in high-cost states.

Who Meets the Poverty Definition?

The demographics of who is living in poverty have shifted over time. The Social Security Act has ensured that many Americans 65 years of age and older are not living in poverty. According to Pew Research (Bialek, 2017), more than half of the families living in poverty are female-headed. Women are more likely than men to work in part-time and temporary jobs that don't offer benefits or pensions. Because these women's wages are often lower, their future Social Security pensions will be lower. They will get no pay, private pension, or Social Security if they stayed home to care for their children.

The wealth gap between white households and black and Hispanic households further widened after the Great Recession of 2007-2009. Lower income white households had dramatic losses in wealth, and the wealth gaps between the highest income households and the lowest are at the widest ever (Kochnar & Cilluffo, 2017).

Income inequality is an important concept, because statistics such as the unemployment rate do not tell the whole story. Wages of the middle and working classes have not kept ahead of inflation. Real wages between 1979 and 2013 only grew by 8.7 percent, although productivity grew 64.9 percent (Bivens & Mischel, 2015). In their report, Understanding the Historic Divergence Between Productivity and a Typical Worker's Pay, Bivens and Mishel say, "If the hourly pay of typical American workers had kept pace with productivity growth since the 1970s, then there would have been no rise in income inequality during that period." The income growth of the top 1 percent between 1973 and 2013 was five times that of the middle 60 percent and the income for the bottom 30 percent actually decreased (Stone, Trisi, Sherman, & Taylor, 2018).

The Wealth Gap

The income gap is one way to measure poverty, but the wealth gap is also crucial, and racial disparities are drastically greater in terms of wealth than in terms of income. **Wealth** in financial terms is the amount of assets in excess of liabilities—in other words, what you own versus what you owe. A person's wealth might include equity in homes, savings accounts, and investments.

Some groups of people are not experiencing growth in income and have no wealth, and as a whole the nation is experiencing wider gaps between the extremely wealthy and the rest of the population. Wealth is particularly important in an economic crisis such as a job loss. It influences your ability to retire or support yourself as an older adult. Women of color had the highest foreclosure rates of any group during the 2008 recession—as a result of both their lack of wealth and their being targeted for subprime mortgages, regardless of their income level (Consumer Federation of America, 2006). "Wealth also helps people get ahead. Home equity can be borrowed against to send children to college, for example, and wealth can be passed down through the generations to provide them with more stability, access, and options. Family wealth is the biggest predictor of the future economic status of a child, giving lie to the old American 'bootstraps' mythology" (Hollar, 2010).

Barbara Ehrenreich, author of *Nickel and Dimed: On (Not) Getting By in America* (2001), decided to find out how anyone could live on minimum wage. She worked undercover—as a maid in Maine; a waitress in Key West, Florida; and a Wal-Mart clerk in Minneapolis—to get firsthand material for her book. Although she took the same kinds of jobs and lived in the same kind of housing as her co-workers, she was better off than many of them because she had no children to support and she had a car. Ehrenreich found that she couldn't afford even basic needs, such as housing or food, on her pay. She was surprised and distressed to learn about people's dire poverty, such as the maid in Maine who ate hot dog buns for lunch.

After the collapse of the real estate and financial markets beginning in 2008, a movement called Occupy Wall Street emerged in 2011 against the unscrupulous practices of Wall Street such as selling sub-prime mortgages with high adjustable rates and terms often buried in the fine print. Occupy Wall Street rallies against the concentration of wealth and power in the United States by the top 1 percent of the population. According to its web site, "Occupy

Source: a katz/Shutterstock

The concentration of wealth and power in the top 1 percent of the population fueled the Occupy Wall Street movement.

Wall Street is a leaderless resistance movement with people of many colors, genders and political persuasions. The one thing we all have in common is that the 99 percent that will no longer tolerate the greed and corruption of the 1 percent (Gautney, 2011)." The movement garnered media attention on the wealth divide, but there was not a unified voice. Bernie Sanders trumpeted the messages of income inequality and Wall Street corruption in the 2016 presidential race.

The 2014 and 2015 riots in Baltimore, Maryland and Ferguson, Missouri, erupted after what was perceived as excessive use of weapons toward unarmed black men. These two cities also have in common decades of neglect and disinvestment in communities of color. The book *Color of Law* by Richard Rothstein outlines the government policies that reinforced residential segregation (Rothstein, 2017). For example, Baltimore is racially segregated, with many neighborhoods that are 80 percent to 100 percent black. Those same neighborhoods have unemployment rates of 13 percent to 17 percent, compared with rates below 5.5 percent in predominantly white neighborhoods. A 2015 report by the Democratic staff of the U.S. Congress Joint Economic Committee showed that many African-American families were struggling—and facing troubling economic disparities. Black Americans are three times more likely to live in poverty than white Americans. The employment rate for black Americans is more than double that of white Americans, and median income is considerably lower (U.S. Congress Joint Economic Committee 2015 report).

Raising the minimum wage to a living wage, ensuring equal pay for women, and providing free community college tuition are some strategies to increase income and wealth. The federal minimum wage began in 1938 with the Fair Labor Standards Act, at 25 cents per hour. While there have been increases over time, the federal minimum wage has been stagnant at $7.25 per hour since 2009. Beginning January 1, 2017, the federal contract minimum wage increased to $10.20 an hour per Executive Order. This increased to $10.35 in January 2018. Given long stretches of no increases, minimum wage value has declined in real dollars since 1968. Most states have a minimum wage that exceeds the federal standard, and those that have no minimum wage or a minimum wage below the federal law must apply the federal minimum wage.

In *Saving Capitalism* (2014), author Robert Reich posits how the decline of the middle class is the result of corporations' allegiance to their shareholders instead of their employees. The idea that there was an agreement between employer and employee that would include prevailing wages and benefits such as pensions, has been broken since the decline of unions. Unions peaked in 1954, with 34 percent of the nation's employees unionized, compared with only 11 percent in 2013 (Dunn & Walker, 2016). Cutting the workforce and their salaries and benefits has the effect of driving up shareholder profits. In addition to seemingly cater to shareholder interests, CEOs' interests have prevailed over their workers'. In 1950, CEOs made an average of 20 times what their employees made; in 2016, CEOs made an average of 200 times what their employees made. To put this in perspective, employee Joseph earns $20,000 per year and the CEO makes $4 million. CEO pay has risen 900 percent since 1950. Corporations have gained more political power and as a result have benefited from corporate subsidies and tax advantages. Middle-class jobs have dwindled as manufacturing became automated and some jobs were shipped overseas. What remains are predominantly high-skill jobs and low-paying service sector jobs. Employees at retail jobs often rely on government programs for health insurance and food stamps (Cooper, 2016). People who meet the poverty definition increasingly are those who work full-time.

As Human Services Professionals, most of the people you will be working with will be living in poverty or close to living in poverty. We all need to examine our own attitudes about people living in poverty to avoid adopting a widespread view of that they are generally inadequate, incompetent, and in need of reform. That view shapes many service programs for people living in poverty. For example, shelters for families who are homeless have many rules to discipline the residents in ways that shelter administrators and/or welfare departments believe to be necessary, such as curfews and mandatory workshops. Prejudice against the poor has permeated social policy since the country began. It leads to creating categories of who is "deserving" and who is "undeserving." Men and women who are single and living in poverty have been regarded as less deserving of help because it is assumed that they should be working. Mothers who are low income have been regarded as more deserving but are still the objects of suspicion that they may be cheating the welfare system or may be immoral. Children living in poverty are regarded as "innocent" and more deserving of help. But they are, after all, children of parents who are low income, so the distrust of their parents sometimes leads to harming the children by denying aid to their parents.

THE HISTORY OF SOCIAL WELFARE IN THE UNITED STATES

The first social welfare programs in America were modeled after the Elizabethan fifteenth-century poor laws of England, which classified the needy into three categories: the vagrant, the involuntarily unemployed, and the helpless. Taxes were raised to deal with people living in poverty, and alms houses were created where a mix of destitute people—including older adults, individuals with disabilities, and children who were homeless—went to live. Able-bodied persons were sent to work houses or poor farms, and the stark and difficult conditions were intended to act as a deterrent to anyone wanting to use the alms houses. Jail was also used for people who refused to work. In time, the alms houses were wracked with problems and "outdoor" relief was provided instead in the form of food and clothing, which was deemed less degrading than alms houses (Wagner, 2005).

In the 1800s, the prevailing attitude toward the people living in poverty was that the condition was due to immorality. Alcoholism was considered a result of indolence. In 1841, Dorothea Dix agreed to teach Sunday school at a jail. She witnessed people bound in chains and locked in cages, and children jailed with adult prisoners. She set out on a mission to visit hundreds of jails and prisons. The shocking mistreatment of prisoners, particularly those with mental illness, led her to write a report to the state legislature. She campaigned the rest of her life and succeeded in ending the practice of putting debtors in prison and inflicting cruel punishments. She helped spawn the notion that society had a responsibility for criminal activity, and a duty to treat people with alcohol dependencies and children who were neglected.

The late 1800s and early 1900s brought waves of immigrants from Europe. Settlement houses were created to provide immigrants and people migrating to the city for work with inexpensive housing and accompanying services. Jane Addams, a pioneering social worker and sociologist, co-founded the famous Hull House in Chicago. By the 1920s, there were over 400 settlement houses in the country (Husock, 1993). Dorothy Day's Catholic Worker movement continued the settlement house model in the 1930s during the Depression; it grew to 203 houses today (Catholicworker.org).

During the Great Depression that followed the stock market crash of 1929, many social welfare programs were born. The New Deal was a series of social liberal programs enacted in the United States between 1933 and 1938, as well as a few programs that came later. They included laws passed by the U.S. Congress as well as presidential executive orders during the first term (1933–1937) of President Franklin D. Roosevelt. Programs included the Works Progress Administration, which hired unemployed people for large public works projects; the Social Security Administration; and public housing. These programs were politically possible because the middle class was suffering and the programs were not targeted only to the traditional people living in poverty. There was a sense that people were temporarily low income due to the Depression, and would not need to rely on programs centered around public works or public housing for very long.

The next wave of social programs came in the 1960s, which was a tumultuous decade marked by the civil rights movement and passage of the Civil Rights Act of 1964, the Cold War with Russia, the Vietnam War, a rise in feminism, and the invention of modern methods of birth control. During that decade, America suffered the losses of President John F. Kennedy, Robert Kennedy, and Martin Luther King, Jr., by assassinations. As Lyndon B. Johnson stepped in as president, he declared a War on Poverty. The national poverty rate was approximately 19 percent. The Community Action Program, the Food Stamp Program, Medicare and Medicaid, Head Start, VISTA, and Job Corps were among the programs he created. Poverty rates dropped to a low of 11 percent in the decade that followed, and stood at 12.7 percent in 2016 based on the U.S. Census Bureau's estimates. The calculation of the poverty rate has been criticized as not capturing the full extent of poverty. It should also be noted that while the national average may be 12.7 percent, some groups of people and geographic locations endure much higher poverty rates.

The 1960s and '70s ushered in community-based social service programs in community action agencies, which deliver social programs such as fuel assistance and Head Start, and community development corporations, which organize residents to transform communities and increase affordable housing and locally owned businesses.

In the 1960s, some social planners and theorists revived long-dormant theories that place the onus for poverty on inferior heredity (Eysenck, 1971; Herrnstein, 1971). Other social scientists have asserted that people living in poverty have a culture of poverty, a system of self-defeating beliefs passed on from parent to child. According to this theory, some groups of people stay mired in poverty because they lack basic psychological discipline. They cannot control their desires to own a TV, buy a bottle of whiskey, and have unprotected sex long enough to save enough money, study hard, or plan for their futures (Banfield, 1974). By the mid-1980s, the buzzword in poverty discourse was "underclass." Journalists Ken Auletta and Leon Dash, who had written about the underclass, emphasized that it was not just about low income, but also about destructive or anti-social behaviors such as inner-city violence and drug use, teenage sexuality, minority teenage mothers and jobless youth, and single-parent families (Sawhill & Jargowsky, 2006).

President Ronald Reagan's budget director, David Stockman, asserted that "there are no entitlements—period" (Katz, 1989, p. 151). In his book *Losing Ground* (1984), Charles Murray argued that illegitimacy, crime, and family deterioration are caused by Aid to Families with Dependent Children (AFDC) payments and rules, and he recommended the elimination of virtually all social benefits except Social Security (Katz, 1989). Since the 1980s, government has been dismantling services that it once offered citizens. When George H. W. Bush was president, he wanted volunteers to take the place of government services and called for "a thousand points of light" (Pointsoflight.org). When his son, George W. Bush, became president in 2001, he continued

Source: Thawornnurak/123RF

Between 1980 and 2015, incarceration rates in America more than quadrupled, with African Americans currently incarcerated at five times the rate of whites.

his father's efforts to increase dependency on voluntary organizations in social services. In the book *The Bell Curve* (Murray & Herrnstein, 1994), the authors attributed social inequalities among races to differences in intelligence (Williams, L., 1997). This was a highly controversial book that set off numerous studies, some of which point to societal factors—such as residential segregation and discrimination—as the causes of economic inequality. The 1990s were characterized by a recession in 1990–1991 followed by two terms for President Bill Clinton (1993–2000), which brought strong economic performance marked by low unemployment and a budget surplus. It was also a time of progressive ideology, notably the failed attempt for universal health care but also the passage of the Children's Health Insurance Program (CHIP). Conservative social policies such as welfare reform and tougher sentencing were also passed during the Clinton administration. These are described in detail in this chapter.

The 2007–2009 collapse of the real estate market due to unscrupulous lending practices and the burst of the housing bubble resulted in massive foreclosures across the country.

As previously discussed, the foreclosure crisis further exposed the social segregation and economic divide between people of color and whites. The Black Lives Matter coalition formed in 2013 as a non-violent movement to expose unfair treatment of and racism toward black Americans following the acquittal of Trayvon Martin's murderer.

The last decade in social work has seen a focus on the psychological impacts of violence and racism. Social workers have developed programs including anti-bullying programs, gay and transgender support groups, and treatment for post-traumatic stress not only for veterans, but for people who have witnessed violence in their homes, communities, schools, and workplaces. The Center for Disease Control recognizes that violence is a serious public health problem with life-long ramifications to physical, mental and emotional health. (Centers for Disease Control).

The election of Donald Trump as president in 2016 let surface the anger of low-income and middle-income white people who had not benefited from the "American Dream"—the ideal that achieving a comfortable standard of living is possible through hard work.

After the passage of the Tax Cuts and Jobs Act of December 2017, spending on federal entitlement and means-tested programs was destined to be the subject of much debate about where to cut, as tax revenues fell sharply on account of a reduction in corporate taxes. According to Philip Alston, "There is a contempt for the poor that seems to permeate the president's inner circle that seems very worrying." "It's done under the banner of providing opportunity and seeking long-term solutions, but it all seems designed to increase misery" (Thrush & Green, 2018).

Source: Mauro Pedro da Silva/Shutterstock

The Black Lives Matter movement was begun by three black women in 2013 when an unarmed 1-year-old black boy was killed by a white vigilante who was later acquitted.

Federal Means-Tested Programs

TEMPORARY ASSISTANCE TO NEEDY FAMILIES (TANF)

Cash assistance to needy families was part of the Social Security Act of 1935. The program was first called ADC (Aid to Dependent Children) because parents were not included. Mothers were not included until 1950, and fathers who were unemployed were not included until 1965, when the name of the program was changed to Aid to Families with Dependent Children (AFDC). Until 1996, the federal government set guidelines and shared program costs with the states; the states set benefit levels. Everyone who was eligible was entitled to assistance. That is no longer true. The Personal Responsibility and Work Opportunity Reconciliation Act (PRWORA) of 1996 ended federal control over AFDC and gave the states block grants to run their own programs. By ending the entitlement status of AFDC, the federal government, for the first time in 60 years, no longer guaranteed that it would help families in need. In fact, states are under no obligation to use the block grant for cash payments to low-income individuals. Conservatives in Congress proclaimed a victory; liberal Massachusetts Senator Edward M. Kennedy, who voted against the bill, proclaimed it "legislative child abuse" (Edelman, 1997).

The income support program that most people think of is welfare, also known as Temporary Assistance to Needy Families. What most people don't know is that only 23 percent of the TANF funds go to income supports for low-income families (Floyd, Burnside, & Schott, 2018). Other little-known facts include:

1. **There is a lifetime term limit of five years.** In addition, nearly half the states have a family cap, meaning no increase in payment to families with additional children.
2. **There is a work requirement.** A study by Johnson, Kalil, and Dunifon (2010) found that when work is stable and well-paid or leads to higher income and brings about

regularity of life, parents become good role models for children. However, low-wage work available to lower-skilled individuals coming out of welfare does not usually fit such a description. Children whose mothers experienced greater job instability, particularly due to being laid off or fired, had consistently worse behavior problems and poor academic progress. Fluctuating work hours and full-time employment in jobs with little wage potential are strongly associated with the probability that a worker's child will repeat a grade. The researchers conclude that "a child's behavior at a given point is determined by the quality and quantity of time a mother spends with her child up to that point."

Welfare recipients have always been in and out of the workforce. They have traditionally used welfare as a substitute for unemployment insurance, for which they are usually ineligible because much of their work is temporary or part-time. Unemployment insurance is popularly thought to be for "deserving" workers who are out of work through no fault of their own. Some people believe that if unemployment insurance were expanded to include those low-wage workers who are not now eligible for it, it could provide a more dignified income supplement to women who would otherwise have to go on welfare (Handler & White, 1999). Some states have put programs on the agenda to extend either temporary disability insurance or unemployment benefits to workers with caregiving needs (Gornick, 2001).

3. **Illegal immigrants cannot collect welfare.** The current anti-immigrant sentiment has resulted in repressive immigration laws and severe cutbacks in funding for welfare. The PRWORA was most severe toward legal immigrants, cutting off their access to any benefits except emergency health care. They were denied SSI, food stamps, and Medicaid. (Illegal immigrants never had access to those benefits.) Several states pay for immigrant benefits out of state funds, but state benefits are usually lower than federal benefits.

4. **States do not have to provide cash assistance.** The income support ranges from $300 to $900 a month based on family size and depending on the state. In some states, the payment is less than $5,000 annually, which is less than one-third the poverty limit for two people. Ever since PRWORA was enacted in 1996 and funds shifted to a block grant, the amount of income support to individuals has declined in favor of utilizing the funds for everything from child care to college tuition. (Floyd, 2016).

5. **Education and training is limited to one year.** Prior to the 1996 legislation, states were able to support activities that helped prepare people for work, such as job training, education, or rehabilitation in substance use programs. However, PRWORA has a much narrower definition of what constitutes work-related activities. Only a year of education and training is allowed, and it must be directly related to a specific job that does not require a bachelor's or an advanced degree. States could sponsor more education if they paid for it out of state funds. But in connection with the federal block grant, no more than 30 percent of a state's recipients can be in education and training. Outside this 30 percent, mothers can still undertake training, but only if they first work or look for work for at least 20 hours a week (Semuels, 2016).

One study showed that 100 percent of former recipients who earned a four-year degree did not rely on welfare again, compared to 81 percent of those with a two-year degree (Freeman, A. 2015). Since the Personal Responsibility Act was passed, there has been a precipitous drop in college enrollment among welfare recipients. This barrier to recipients' accessing college does not bode well for their future ability to climb out of poverty. While the state of Maine has very restrictive cash assistance programs, it has a very progressive and comprehensive college program called "Parents as Scholars," which supports TANF-eligible parents in college programs, providing tuition, books, child care, and cash assistance. This program is featured in the book *Shut Out: Low Income Mothers and Higher Education in Post-Welfare America*, which chronicles welfare reform and parents' pursuit of higher education (Polakow, Butler, Stormer Deprez, & Kahn, 2004).

For the first decade following the Personal Responsibility Act, very few TANF recipients had access to education and training. A 2010 study found that nationally, less than 8 percent of "work-eligible" adult TANF recipients were engaged in education or training activities (Fremstad, 2010). The training that recipients did get was largely very short-term training, often lasting three months or less. When Kentucky had more than 30 percent of recipients enrolled in vocational education, it faced penalties from the federal government. The Deficit Reduction Act of 2005 that reauthorized TANF increased the work participation rate targets for states and imposed a new and demanding requirement that all hours of participation be extensively verified and documented. (U.S. Department of Health and Human Services, 2016)

6. **There is a high rate of disability among the mothers and children on welfare.** Both the mothers on welfare and their children have a high rate of disability. This interferes with the mothers' ability to get a job, because of their own health problems and/or because they need to stay home to care for children with disabilities.

About half of TANF recipients have either a disability or a family member with a disability. Food stamp recipients have a similar prevalence of disability as TANF recipients. Some states exempt parents with disabilities and parents caring for a child with disabilities from the work requirement, but there are stiff standards for proving disability. Emotional and cognitive disabilities are especially hard to prove.

Most of the disabilities that parents have do not qualify them for SSI but still restrict their ability to work. The definition of disability under ADA rules is a physical or mental impairment that substantially limits one or more major life activities of the person (www.adata.org), while SSI is for severe disabilities that are expected to last at least 12 months or to result in death and that prevent substantial gainful activity (www.ssa.gov).

The most common mental health problems among welfare recipients are depression, post-traumatic stress disorder, and general anxiety disorder. According to one study, about 42 percent of heads of households receiving TANF funds meet the criteria for clinical depression—more than three times the national average (Solomon, 2001). What appears to many people to be "laziness" may actually be depression.

BEHAVIORAL REQUIREMENTS   Welfare reform not only aims to get people to work but also to enforce certain behaviors. The family-cap policy prohibits cash assistance for children born while the family receives TANF. "Learnfare" reduces the grant if a child truants from school, and "Shotfare" reduces the grant if parents do not get their children immunized. Wisconsin was the first state to institute Learnfare. The Wisconsin Legislative Audit Bureau found no positive effects on the attendance of teenagers in the Learnfare population but the program continued because it was politically popular (Quinn, 1997).

In an effort to control substance use, federal law stipulated that people convicted of drug felonies were prohibited from receiving a TANF block grant or food stamps for life. In all but six states, the SNAP ban for felons has been eliminated (CSG Justice Center, 2017).

Policymakers and legislators believed that the family-cap policy would reduce the birth rate of TANF recipients, but there is no evidence that it accomplished this. In fact, researchers found that family caps are harmful to children, cause lifelong damage to their learning and development, and increase the "deep poverty rate" of children by 13 percent (Donovon 1998).

THE EFFECTS OF WELFARE REFORM   The main objective of TANF was to downsize welfare rolls, and states' welfare rolls downsized dramatically. The welfare rolls declined in the 1990s as poverty rates declined, and politicians pointed to the success of the program. However, in 2007, after poverty increased, there were only 4 million recipients, as compared with 14.2 million recipients in 1994 (Edelman & Ehrenreich, 2010). Today, only 23 percent of the people living in poverty receive welfare payments. This is because TANF is a block grant to the states, and they can choose to spend the money on programs such as child care and college tuition rather than on direct payments to families (Floyd, Burnside & Schott, 2018).

Peter Edelman was an assistant for planning and evaluation at the Department of Health and Human Services in the Clinton administration, but resigned in protest when Clinton signed the PRWROA. This is how he described the implementation of the Act:

> These are the techniques of radical reduction: Shut the front door almost completely, staff the back door with the equivalent of a tough nightclub bouncer, and, in between, hassle applicants to the point where they just give up and go away.
>
> At the front door, many states just say no, evoking memories of the pre-1960s period, when unbridled discretion ruled.
>
> At the back door there is sanctioning—kicking people off the rolls because they were late to a work assignment—no excuses for sick children, late buses, or car breakdowns—or didn't show up for an appointment at the welfare office—no excuses for failure to receive notice of an appointment or inability to understand English. In some states multiple infractions of this sort can result, legally, in lifetime disqualification.
>
> In between there are requirements to bring an entire dossier of documents in order to navigate the application maze, intrusive questions about the applicant's private life, assignments to work programs that sometimes ask people to work without necessary protective equipment, regular and irregular summonses to come in for redetermination of eligibility, and much more. Many needy people refuse to undergo the hardships associated with asking for help. (Edelman, 2009)

Under the TANF program, there is no entitlement to child care, even though it is an absolute necessity if parents are to enter and stay in waged work. The cost is a major drain on a working parent's income. Patching together safe, reliable, and child-positive care is a job in itself. Under the Family Support Act of 1988, anyone in education or training was provided with transportation costs. This is not required under PRWORA, and lack of transportation is a major barrier to getting a job.

For example, a study of transit service from a point in Boston in which a high population of welfare recipients lived to the high-growth areas for entry-level employment found that more than 66 percent of existing jobs could not be reached within two hours—even though most of the city's welfare recipients live within one-half mile of public transit (Lacombe, 1997). Furthermore, public transportation services can offer inadequate hours of operation and infrequent service. And transportation is expensive.

The problem with transportation in rural areas is also severe. In many parts of Maine, for example, there are no buses.

The Portland Press Herald reported (Russell, E., 2016) that the state of Maine was sitting on $155 million of unspent TANF funds, while extreme childhood poverty has increased. Maine spends only 14 percent of its TANF grant on cash payments and has shifted the funds to other allowable TANF activities such as job training. TANF in Maine is $363 per month, or $4,356 per year, a fraction of the poverty level. The article pointed to the fact that one-third of the cases closed due to finding employment, but did not discuss what happened to the two-thirds of the cases that closed where employment was not found.

SOCIAL SECURITY If you've ever had a job, you no doubt noticed that money was taken out of your paycheck for FICA (Federal Insurance Contributions Act). That is your contribution to Social Security (officially called Old Age, Survivors, and Disability Insurance [OASDI]). The program is funded by employee and employer taxes. In 2017, employees paid 6.2 percent of their wages for Social Security and 1.45 percent for Medicare, and employers paid the same (Internal Revenue Service). Because it is a universal program and therefore politically protected by middle class voters, Social Security has so far been relatively safe from large cutbacks, although there have been cutbacks for college students, people with disabilities, and those living in significant poverty. Its administrative costs are remarkably small—only 0.5 percent of total benefits paid out.

Although there have not been large, publicly visible cutbacks in Social Security, there have been less-visible cutbacks through denying disability claims, delays in approving applications, and appeals hearings for those who have been denied SSDI.

Social Security has prevented a huge number of people, particularly older adults, from being identified as low income. In 1959, more than 35 percent of people age 65 and over lived in poverty. In 2014, approximately 10 percent of older adults (4.5 million) were living below the poverty level (Administration on Aging, n.d.). As the population is aging, the number of beneficiaries is growing:

Beneficiaries Receiving Benefits at the End of December 2016 (Social Security Administration)	
All beneficiaries	60,907,307
Retired workers and dependents	44,266,144
Survivors	6,031,093
Disabled workers and dependents	10,610

Despite the success of Social Security, however, there are efforts to dismantle it as a public program. For the past decade, conservatives have sought to privatize it by having people invest some or all of their savings in the stock market. They raised the alarm that the system will go broke as the aging population increases and the number of younger working people decreases. They proposed various ways to cut back the program, such as raising the retirement age and taxing benefits but didn't propose ways to raise the cap on the amount of money that is taxed. In 2019, only $132,900 of an individual's wages is subject to taxes for Social Security, although there is no cap on Medicare. In other words, all income earned over $132,900 is not taxed by Social Security, so a billionaire pays the same amount of Social Security tax as someone earning $132,900 (Schreiber, 2018). If the salary cap were removed and all wages were subject to a payroll tax, there would be more than enough money to keep Social Security solvent. And if newly hired state and local government workers were brought into the system, the two measures together would easily solve the long-term financing problems (Mandell, 1997).

In her book, *Pitied But Not Entitled* (1994), Linda Gordon argues that the deserving/undeserving, universal/means-tested split was built into the Social Security law at its inception. The people who built the social insurance program wanted one that workers were entitled to. They were not interested in people's character flaws. They developed the unemployment compensation system, workers' compensation, and old-age insurance. But they shaped a program that responded to the needs of working men and to the elite of the working class, those with steady jobs with major employers and professionals. According to the Social Security Administration, it left out about half the workforce, including single mothers, workers living in poverty who had low wages, and workers who were not wage earners, such as farmers, sharecroppers, and small-business owners. African Americans predominantly worked in jobs that were not covered, such as domestic and agricultural work (DeWitt, 2010). Only much later were those people included. Female homemakers were never included in their own right, only as dependents of their husbands. Wives were expected to stay home and depend on their husbands' wages. Men were expected to earn a "family wage" to care for their families (Gordon, 1994).

SUPPLEMENTAL SECURITY INCOME   The SSI program is a nationwide federal assistance program administered by SSA that guarantees a minimum level of income for older adults, people with blindness, or individuals with disabilities. It is a means-tested program that acts as a safety net for individuals who have limited resources and little or no Social Security or other income. It was created as part of the Social Security Act in 1974, consolidating two former programs called Old Age Assistance (OAA) and Aid to the Permanently and Totally Disabled (APTD). OAA and APTD were structured in a way similar to AFDC in that states provided matching funds, but SSI federalized these programs.

The monthly maximum federal amounts for 2018 were $750 for an eligible individual, $1,125 for an eligible individual with an eligible spouse, and $376 for an "essential person," which is someone considered essential to the individual's basic care. (Social Security Administration Online, 2018). Several states supplement the federal SSI payment. Some states provide a cost-of-living allowance for SSI, but some do not.

Because it is a means-tested program for people living in poverty, SSI is more politically vulnerable to cutbacks than is Social Security. People with disabilities faced severe cutbacks in their benefits in 1980 when President Ronald Reagan and Congress pushed 491,000 people off the rolls of SSI and SSDI, arguing that some people were taking advantage of the system and could go to work. As a result of protests by beneficiaries and their advocates, laws were passed that required medical proof of improvement in the condition of beneficiaries before they could be terminated from SSI. Half of the people who fought back, about 200,000, were put back on the rolls (Blau, 1992).

The second large-scale reduction to SSI came with the Personal Responsibility Act of 1996, which cut off all legal immigrants from SSI (some have since been reinstated), narrowed the definition for children with disabilities, and cut off benefits for people with substance use disorders (Davies, 2019). Conservatives argued that SSI checks were fueling addictions, while others contended that drug and alcohol addiction must be treated as a potentially fatal diseases.

Cutbacks in eligibility are not the only way to reduce the rolls. They are also kept low by bureaucratic barriers. Applying for SSI is a very difficult process. Some people have waited up to two years to have their application accepted. Advocates advise applicants to appeal denials. By the third appeal, many applications are accepted.

GENERAL ASSISTANCE   General assistance (or general relief) programs give cash grants to people who do not qualify for TANF, SSI, or Social Security. Such programs are funded entirely with state or local money, without any federal matching funds. Benefits are very low, and these programs are generally the first to be cut when states cut welfare programs. Not all states have a general assistance program. In those that do not, if people without physical disabilities have used up their unemployment insurance or if they were in a job that was not covered, there is no cash assistance at all for them. They would probably still be eligible for food stamps.

Eligibility varies among states, but in general the program is for single individuals and childless couples, including individuals living with a disability for less than a year or who are awaiting a determination of whether they are sufficiently disabled to qualify for SSI. Older adults who do not qualify for SSI or Social Security are generally eligible. Some states give general assistance to people who have exhausted their unemployment insurance, but others don't. Some families who are not eligible for TANF receive general assistance.

During the 1991–1992 recession, Michigan abolished its General Relief program, ending benefits for about 82,000 recipients. Follow-up studies in Michigan and Ohio, which ended benefits after six months, showed that relatively few former general assistance recipients became employed after their benefits were ended, and those who did were in low-wage and often temporary jobs. In Michigan, there was a 50 percent increase in homelessness. In Ohio, the ranks of the people who are homeless increased substantially (Frech, 2016).

FOOD STAMPS (SUPPLEMENTAL NUTRITION ASSISTANCE PROGRAM, SNAP)   Food stamps aren't really food stamps any more. Electronic benefit transfer (EBT) cards replaced coupons for food stamps across the nation in 2004. The official name has been changed to Supplemental Nutrition Assistance Program (SNAP), but people still generally call the program "food stamps." SNAP is a means-tested program, and all people without physical disabilities and non-elderly adults must comply with work requirements.

The food stamp program is paid for by the U.S. Department of Agriculture. Administered by state welfare departments, its purpose is not only to feed people who are low-income but also to provide subsidies to farmers. Stores and banks also receive money for participating in the program. People can buy most foods with the cards, but they cannot use the cards for non-food items such as paper goods, diapers, toiletries, and cigarettes.

According to A Short History of SNAP, published by the USDA, participation in the SNAP program grew by 70 percent between 2007 and 2011, and since 2013, coinciding with the economic recovery, participation has declined. May 2018 participation in SNAP was over 39 million persons, a decrease of over 2.1 million persons (5.1 percent) from May 2017. Legal immigrants and some non-citizens who meet certain criteria and all those under 18 are eligible for SNAP.

Like most programs for those living in poverty, those near the poverty line or those working and still considered low-income, food stamps/SNAP has been under fire at different points in history. Cuts to the program occurred in 1981, when the Reagan administration and Congress cut funds used to advertise the program for outreach. Then, between 1982 and 1986, they cut $6.8 billion from the budget, eliminating benefits for 1 million people and reducing them for the remaining 20 million recipients (U.S. Department of Agriculture, 2017).

The next large cuts in the food stamp program came with the Personal Responsibility Act of 1996. The Republicans had hoped to eliminate entitlement to food stamps, but the agribusiness lobby stopped that. Yet Congress made deep cuts, including making legal immigrants ineligible and cutting the amount of benefits. Before 2008, the food stamp program limited food stamps to three months out of every three years for unemployed adults under age 50 who were not raising children. The 2008 Farm Bill expanded eligibility and benefits.

During the 2007–2009 recession, people who were previously middle class joined people who were already poor to apply for food stamps. A boost in SNAP benefits in the 2009 Recovery Act expired in November 2013. In 2010, 6 million Americans had no other income than food stamps. Philadelphia had more than 427,000 residents—a quarter of the city—receiving food stamps in 2010, but more than 150,000 people who were eligible were not receiving them (*The New York Times*, 2010).

In 2017 and 2018 bills, such as Farm Bill H.R. 2, have been introduced that would cut the Supplemental Nutrition Assistance Program and expand the work requirements. As the program currently stands, there is a 20 hour per week work requirement. Individuals ages 18–49 are only eligible for food stamps for three months out of every three years.

HOUSING Affordable housing is not an entitlement program. Approximately one out of four households that are eligible receives a form of housing assistance. Rents are generally calculated at 30 percent of an individual's income, or as a flat rent based on an income limit. Three spending programs account for the majority of the housing assistance provided directly to low-income households:

- The Housing Choice Voucher (HCV) program—provides federally funded, portable vouchers that recipients use to help pay for housing they choose in the private market up to a rent limit.
- Project-based rental assistance (PBRA)—provides for federally contracted and subsidized rent in designated buildings that are privately owned and operated.
- Public housing—provides for federally subsidized rent in buildings that are publicly owned and operated.

Privately developed subsidized housing is largely possible through the use of the Low Income Housing Tax Credit, which is a public–private partnership. The program stipulates that the average income of households occupying the units is 50 to 60 percent of area median income. The tax credit is bought by private investors, and produces the largest number of new units for low-income households. Other funding sources for the development of housing include the HOME program, the National Housing Trust Fund (which is targeted to extremely low-income households), and a few other targeted grants and loans. Many states have their own grant and loan programs to facilitate the development of affordable housing. Non-profit community development corporations and private developers build affordable housing. The amount of affordable housing produced is always in short supply compared with the demand, given the cost to build, zoning restrictions, lack of resources, and community opposition. Housing vouchers provide mobility; however, landlords are not required to accept them, and the units must pass an inspection.

SPECIAL SUPPLEMENTAL FOOD PROGRAM FOR WOMEN, INFANTS, AND CHILDREN (WIC) The WIC (Women, Infants, and Children) program is sponsored by the U.S. Department of Agriculture. It provides vouchers to purchase specific foods, such as baby formula, milk, eggs, and fruit juice. It also gives nutrition screening and nutrition counseling to pregnant and postpartum women, infants, and children under 5 years of age.

During fiscal year (FY) 2017, the number of women, infants, and children receiving WIC benefits each month was approximately 7.3 million (U.S. Department of Agriculture, 2018). Pregnant, postpartum, and breastfeeding women; infants; and children up to age 5 are eligible. They must meet income guidelines, meet a state residency requirement, and be individually determined to be at "nutritional risk" by a health professional. To be eligible on the basis of income, applicants' gross income (i.e., before taxes are withheld) must fall at or below 185 percent of the U.S. Poverty Income Guidelines.

The USDA website claims that WIC has proven its value by reducing low birth weights, the number of infants who die, and the number born with developmental disabilities. WIC has encouraged greater use of prenatal and pediatric care. It saves Medicaid money because fewer low-birth-weight infants require hospitalization after birth. When the WIC program was started, planners made the decision to bill it as a nutrition program, rather than a welfare program, and to have it administered by health clinics in order to avoid the stigma of welfares.

Human service workers who work with pregnant women or parents of young children can make sure that their clients know about WIC. Even illegal immigrants are eligible for the program, though many are opting out of WIC, Medicaid, and SNAP benefits for their children due to fear of being deported.

SCHOOL BREAKFAST AND LUNCH PROGRAMS   The National School Lunch Program is a federally assisted meal program operating in public and non-profit private schools and residential child care institutions. It provides nutritionally balanced, low-cost or free lunches to children each school day. The program was established under the National School Lunch Act, signed by President Harry Truman in 1946 (U.S. Department of Agriculture, 2009). School breakfast and lunch programs are sponsored by the USDA, which provides states cash to administer the programs and supplies 20 percent of the food. Children from families with incomes at or below 130 percent of the poverty level are eligible for free meals. Those with incomes between 130 percent and 185 percent of the poverty level are eligible for reduced-price meals.

During the 2018 school year, the USDA reported that approximately 31 million children got a free or reduced-price lunch through the program (U.S. Department of Agriculture, 2018b). The federal government doesn't require schools to serve breakfast, but nationwide, 81 percent of the schools also provide a breakfast program.

As part of the Healthy, Hunger-Free Kids Act established in 2010, the National School Lunch Program's policies were revised to better guarantee that children receive a nutritionally sound lunch. The changes ensure that schools offer fruits and vegetables, whole-grain foods, and low-fat dairy products, and limit calories, saturated fat, and sodium (Fisk, 2017).

MEDICAL AID PROGRAMS

Medicare   Medicare is a federal universal program; Medicaid is a means-tested program. Everyone on Social Security, regardless of financial background, is eligible for Medicare at age 65 (or earlier, with some permanent disabilities), but only individuals with low incomes can receive Medicaid. In 2018, there were over 59 million enrollees on Medicare (Centers for Medicare & Medicaid Services (CMS), 2019).

Medicare helps pay the hospital and medical costs for people age 65 or older, as well as for Social Security recipients with disabilities and people with end-stage renal disease, an expansion of eligibility passed under President Richard M. Nixon. Under certain limited conditions, Medicare pays some nursing home costs for beneficiaries who require skilled nursing or rehabilitation services if the nursing home is Medicare-certified. In the 1980s, in an effort to reduce expensive nursing home care, Medicare expanded to cover home health services and hospice care. The Program of All-inclusive Care for the Elderly (PACE) provides help to people who need a nursing home level of care but would prefer to remain in their own homes with the help of their family and friends, community services, and professional care agencies. If medical expenses exceed what Medicare pays for, some elders pay for private insurance to cover the balance, or they might seek Medicaid.

In 1983, the Reagan administration and Congress—in an effort to limit Medicare expenses—created a program establishing what it termed diagnosis-related groups (DRGs). Under this program, a hospital is paid a set fee for each diagnosis. Many people were concerned that hospitals were releasing patients sooner than was medically advisable. Some complained that their managed care plans refused to pay for treatments ordered by doctors, and two patients sued. The suit went to the Supreme Court, which ruled in June 2004 that patients cannot sue in state courts when their managed care plans refuse to pay for treatments ordered by doctors. Patients can still sue in federal courts, but they can seek only reimbursement for the benefits they were denied, not compensation or punitive damages for any additional costs or harm stemming from such denials (*The New York Times*, 2004).

Medicare did not cover prescriptions until 2003, when Congress passed a Medicare bill that pays part of the costs of some prescriptions. With Medicare Parts A and B, which cover hospital services and doctor visits, the government pays providers directly. Under Part D, the government pays some 260 private insurers—including pharmacy benefit managers, HMOs, and pharmacies—to provide the coverage. If seniors want the benefit, they must buy it from one of those private carriers. Congress imposed a financial penalty for those who didn't sign up by May 15, 2006.

There are numerous different types of cards available, which can be very confusing to older adults who are signing up for Medicare. These cards offer different discounts, based on what types of medicines are purchased and where they are purchased. Millions of seniors called special hotlines set up by the Centers for Medicare & Medicaid Services, which administers those programs, but they were subject to long waits and often couldn't get the information they needed. In 2007, Medicare provided funding to all 50 states for health insurance counseling.

The Medicare Modernization Act of 2003 prohibits Medicare from negotiating for lower drug costs, as the Department of Veterans Affairs is able to do for veterans. Drug companies lobbied hard against allowing Medicare to negotiate lower prices. Representative Sherrod Brown, an Ohio Democrat who voted against the bill, said that older adults he has talked to have "an intuitive understanding that this bill was written by the drug and insurance industries" (Washington, 2004, p. A1). The drug benefit was the biggest expansion of Medicare since the creation of the program in 1965, but patients still face substantial costs.

There is no limit placed on what pharmaceutical companies can charge for prescription drugs in the United States, as there is in Canada. As a result, drugs in the United States cost two to three times more than they do in Canada. Some people are getting prescription drugs from Canada, and pharmaceutical companies have lobbied to make that practice illegal. Some states, such as Vermont, have proposed legislation to purchase bulk prescription drugs from Canada to distribute to pharmacies across the state.

Medicaid   Congress enacted Medicaid in 1965. Medicaid is the nation's largest public health insurance program, covering 70 million people. Medicaid is a joint federal–state program and is the largest source of federal grants to states. Because it is means-tested, it is more vulnerable to cutbacks than is Medicare. Although the program started as mostly a welfare program for low-income individuals, during the boom years of the 1990s, many states took advantage of rising revenues to cover those near the poverty line or those working and still considered low-income, and added benefits. However, when the economy slowed and states faced fiscal crises, many states reduced payments to hospitals and nursing homes, eliminated many services, or found ways to discourage enrollment. The most severe cutbacks were in Mississippi, which ended Medicaid eligibility for some 65,000 senior citizens with low incomes and people with severe disabilities in 2004 (Herbert, 2004).

President George W. Bush proposed to turn Medicaid over to the states in the form of block grants, but Congress did not act on that proposal. Medicaid has a more powerful political constituency than does TANF because large numbers of middle-income people have parents in nursing homes whose bills are paid by Medicaid. It is the Medicaid program, not Medicare, that pays for the bulk of nursing home care. The Medicaid program pays doctors and hospitals at levels well below those of Medicare and private insurance, and often below actual costs. Large numbers of doctors, therefore, do not accept Medicaid patients (Sack & Pear, 2010).

Officials sometimes label Medicaid a "budget buster," because as medical costs have skyrocketed, they have taken a large chunk of state budgets. Medicaid is paid for by both state and federal tax revenue. The federal government specifies the minimum services that must be offered, which states can broaden but not narrow. The recession that began in 2007 put even more stress on the Medicaid program.

The Affordable Care Act of 2010 expanded Medicaid to non-elderly individuals at 138 percent of the federal poverty level, which provided access to care to millions of uninsured people. In FY 2011, 48 percent of Medicaid beneficiaries were children, 27 percent adults, 15 percent people with disabilities, and 9 percent older adults (Kaiser Commission on Medicaid and the Uninsured, 2015). Medicaid pays for about 40 percent of all births in the United States and about one-third of all children's health care. It covers about one-third of people whose incomes fall below the poverty line. It finances about two-thirds of all nursing home stays. The ACA took the burden off of state governments as the federal government covered 100 percent of the expansion costs for three years beginning in 2014 and phasing down to 90 percent in 2020 (Medicaid.gov, 2015). The 31 states that opted for Medicaid expansion as part of the Affordable Care Act had enrolled 17 million people into the program as of December 2016. Since talk of repealing the ACA and other changes, such as the elimination of the individual mandate of the ACA and reduction in the cost-sharing payments, no additional states have opted for Medicaid expansion as of this writing.

Children's Health Insurance Program (CHIP)   In 1997, Congress started a State Children's Health Insurance Program (SCHIP; subsequently renamed Children's Health Insurance Program, or CHIP), which extended coverage to more children in families with low incomes. In 2009, Congress passed and President Obama signed a bill to expand coverage to about 4 million more children, including children of legal immigrants, with no waiting period; children of legal immigrants previously had to wait five years before getting coverage. In 2017, there were 9.4 million children in the plan according to Medicaid.gov, 2017. The program relies on a mixture of state and federal funds, combined with premiums paid by families on a sliding scale depending on income.

Patient Protection and Affordable Care Act   The Affordable Care Act was passed by Congress and then signed into law by President Obama on March 23, 2010. It brought about the Health Insurance Marketplace, a single place where consumers can apply for and enroll in private health insurance plans. The health insurance uses the private system, and states can opt into a federal subsidy program to expand Medicaid. The goal was to get 40 million people who were uninsured onto insurance plans, and as of 2017, roughly 20 million people who were otherwise uninsured or ineligible had health insurance thanks to the ACA, Medicaid expansion, and facets of the ACA law such as allowing young adults to remain on their parents' insurance through age 26.

The law required most U.S. citizens and legal residents to have health insurance. Those without coverage pay a tax penalty. The system creates state-based American Health Benefit Exchanges through which individuals can purchase coverage, with premium and cost-sharing credits available to individuals/families with income between 133 percent and 400 percent of the federal poverty level. (The poverty level was $19,530 for a family of three in 2013.) All newly eligible adults are guaranteed a benchmark benefit package that meets the essential health benefits available through the Exchanges. Small businesses can purchase coverage. One significant feature of the Affordable Care Act is called Medicaid Expansion, which extends Medicaid to 133 percent of the federal poverty level. Under current law, undocumented immigrants are not eligible for Medicaid. As of August 2018, 31 states had adopted Medicaid expansion. Some of the poorest states had not adopted it, even though they had great numbers of uninsured people. This was likely a result of negative advertising against "Obamacare" and reluctance of their elected officials to support the program. The cost of Medicaid expansion would not adversely impact the state, as it is borne primarily by hospitals and the federal government. The 2012 Supreme Court ruling on the constitutionality of the ACA upheld the Medicaid expansion, but limited the ability of HHS to enforce it, thereby making the decision to expand Medicaid optional for states (Kaiser Family Foundation Focus on Health Reform, 2012).

The main points of the ACA are

- Individuals with pre-existing conditions cannot be denied coverage
- Coverage includes adult children up to the age of 26
- Focus on preventative services: free routine check-ups, immunizations, and other preventative services
- Links payment to outcomes: Hospitals are penalized if there are re-admissions, which pushes better follow-up
- Encourages integrated health
- Increases home services versus institutionalization
- Requires hospitals to conduct community needs assessments
- Provides incentives for primary doctors in underserved areas.
- Cracks down on fraud
- Older adults get a rebate to fill the so-called "donut hole" in Medicare drug coverage, which severely limits prescription medication coverage expenditures over $2,700
- Any new plan must implement an appeals process for coverage determinations and claims
- Medicare payment protections are extended to small rural hospitals and other health care facilities that have small numbers of Medicare patients
- Chain restaurants are required to provide a "nutrient content disclosure statement" alongside their items
- Lifetime caps on the amount of insurance an individual can have are banned. Annual caps were originally limited, then banned in 2014
- The program expands eligibility for Medicaid to include all Americans regardless of age with income below 133 percent of the federal poverty level
- The program increases mandatory funding for community health centers to $11 billion over five years
- Employers with more than 50 employees must provide health insurance or pay a fine of $2,000 per worker each year if any worker receives federal subsidies to purchase health insurance.

Republicans have been threatening to dismantle the Affordable Care Act since it passed. On June 28, 2012, the Supreme Court rendered a final decision to uphold the health care law.

President Donald Trump promised to repeal the Affordable Care Act and replace it with something different. As of this writing, the ACA had not been repealed; however, the Tax Cuts and Jobs Act of 2017 repealed the individual mandate for health insurance, which could result in fewer healthier people opting to buy health insurance. The economics of the Affordable Care Act depends on healthy people in the risk pool to keep the cost of premiums down. According to the nonpartisan Congressional Budget Office (CBO), 13 million fewer people will have health insurance as a result of this change.

Fuel Assistance   The fuel assistance program, officially called the Low Income Home Energy Assistance Program (LIHEAP), is a federal program that provides eligible households with help in paying a portion of winter heating bills, as well as help in weatherizing their apartments and homes. It is a means-tested program. Eligibility is based on household size and the gross annual income of every household member 18 years of age or older. Households must apply for the program each year at the Fuel Assistance Agency.

State and local officials in cold-weather states often plead with Congress to release funds for the program. The funds are often supplemented by state funds and private charities such as the Salvation Army and churches. Some oil was donated by Venezuela through CITGO, a Venezuelan oil company, after Hurricane Katrina in 2005, continuing until 2009. At that time, President Obama's stimulus program included doubling the LIHEAP program. CITGO resumed providing oil in 2012, benefiting 400,000 households across the country.

The fuel assistance program does not have strong political support in Congress from either Republicans or Democrats. President Trump tried to eliminate LIHEAP in 2017 but Congress resisted.

Unemployment Insurance   The U.S. Employment and Training Administration and each state's employment security agency provide unemployment benefits to eligible workers who are unemployed through no fault of their own (as determined under state law) and who meet other eligibility requirements of state law. Unemployment insurance (UI) is funded by a federal unemployment tax levied on the state and federal taxable payrolls of most employers. Three states also require minimal employee contributions. The amount of benefits varies widely between states, with some states giving over twice as much as others. Some states supplement the basic benefit with allowances for dependents. In general, benefits are based on a percentage of an individual's earnings over a recent 52-week period, up to a state maximum amount. Benefits can be paid for a maximum of 26 weeks. Additional weeks of benefits may be available during times of high unemployment (U.S. Department of Labor, 2018).

There is an extended benefit program (authorized through the Social Security Acts) that may be triggered by state economic conditions. Congress has often passed temporary programs to extend benefits during economic recessions. In July 2010, President Obama signed legislation that provided an extension of federal unemployment benefits through November 2010. The extension restored unemployment benefits to the 2.3 million unemployed Americans who had run out of basic unemployment benefits (Congress, 2010).

Because unemployment insurance in the United States typically does not replace even 50 percent of the income the recipient received on the job, and because it is limited in time, the unemployed often end up using welfare programs such as food stamps or accumulating debt, and sometimes become homeless.

TAX CREDITS

Earned Income Tax Credit   The Earned Income Tax Credit (EITC) is a federal income tax credit intended to offset the loss of income from payroll taxes owed by families and individuals who are working but still live in poverty. Some states provide an additional EITC, refunding a percentage of the federal EITC.

Single or married people who worked full-time or part-time at some point in the previous year can qualify for the EITC, depending on their income:

- Workers who were raising one child in their home and had income of less than $39,617 (or $45,207 for married workers) in 2017 could get an EITC of up to $3,400.
- Workers who were raising three or more children in their home and had income of less than $48,340 (or $53,930 for married workers) in 2017 could get an EITC of up to $6,318.
- Workers who were not raising children in their home, were between ages 25 and 64 on December 31, 2016, and had income below $15,010 (or $20,600 for married workers) could get an EITC up to $515 (www.irs.gov).

Most increases in social welfare in the United States since the 1970s have been accomplished through the tax system. In 2015, the federal budget for TANF was $19.9 million and for EITC it was $60 million (Kearney, 2015).

Twenty percent of eligible workers do not receive the EITC because they do not know that they qualify, how to claim the credits, or where to find free tax-filing assistance (Wiens, 2018). The Internal Revenue Service (IRS) sponsors a Volunteer Income Tax Assistance (VITA) program to help workers with low incomes file their tax forms. Human service workers can perform a valuable service by directing their clients to this program. Some cities have established a VITA site. Some communities may have several VITA sites. Others, such as rural communities, may lack the VITA sites they need.

Human service workers can advise their clients that they can save a substantial amount of money by using a free VITA site rather than a commercial tax preparer.

The Child Tax Credit (CTC)   The CTC is a federal tax credit, like the EITC, that in 2016 provided parents a deduction of up to $1,000 for children younger than 17 years old. To be eligible, one must have taxable earned income above $3,000 and have either a Social Security number or an Individual Taxpayer Identification Number. Immigrant workers with either type of number may be able to claim the CTC refund. Human service workers can do a great service to working people by explaining benefits such as the CTC.

Child Care Tax Credit (CCTC)   The CCTC is a federal tax credit that allows working parents to deduct a percentage of their child care costs from the federal income taxes they owe if they pay someone to care for a child, spouse, or dependent. Unlike the EITC, the federal CCTC is not a "refundable" tax credit. A family may receive the CCTC only as a credit against federal income taxes owed.

VITAL-SERVICE DELIVERY PROGRAMS

Personal Social Services   The government programs that spend the most money are those for health, education, income maintenance, housing, and employment. Other personal social services account for only 6 percent of total expenditures. They nevertheless are very important to both human service workers and recipients. In fact, many graduates of human service programs will work in these programs, which include such services as:

- Day care for children of working parents
- Homemaker service and home health care for children, people with disabilities, and older adults
- Respite care to provide a breathing spell for overburdened parents, foster parents, or care-takers of people with disabilities
- Child welfare work
- Community residences for people with mental illness and/or with disabilities, and individuals who have committed crimes
- Shelters for survivors of abuse, people who are homeless, and teenagers who have run away.
- Community mental health centers
- Children's institutions
- Community services for people who are older
- Recreational programs
- Family planning counseling
- Correctional and penal programs
- Care of people with physical and mental disabilities
- Veterans' programs
- Services to the military
- Drug and alcohol programs
- Disaster relief
- Legal assistance
- Counseling in various settings for various kinds of problems
- Information and referral services.

The personal social services make up a diverse collection of programs that grew rather haphazardly in response to various social needs. They can be crucial to a person who needs help. Here are some examples:

- George has a severe mental illness and cannot work. He needs counseling and perhaps medication supervised by a psychiatrist or psychopharmacologist in order to function again.
- Laurie needs help finding day care for her child so she can take a job outside the home.
- Mary and George are unable to bear children. They need the help of an adoption agency to get a child.
- Anthony is frail but may be able to stay out of a nursing home if he has a homemaker and a home health aide to look after his needs.
- Cheryl was totally incapacitated by a stroke. She will need nursing care or intensive home care.
- Ann works 9 to 5, and her school-age children need a community center to care for them after school.

These are important services used by the middle class as well as the poor. Most of us will need some social services in the course of our lifetime.

Source: Courtesy of Boston Cares

A disaster the size of Hurricane Katrina destroys much more than houses. It uproots an entire social system and does untold damage for years to come to the people who lived in those houses.

Services for Older Adults The Older Americans Act of 1965 created a new federal agency, the Administration on Aging, within the former Department of Health, Education, and Welfare. It established or encouraged many services for older adults:

- Nutrition programs
- Housing and transportation assistance
- Homemaker and home health care
- Legal services
- Chore services
- Senior citizen centers
- Day care centers
- Telephone reassurance
- Job training and placement

Housing for older adults includes federal and state public housing, as well as subsidized housing built by non-profit or for-profit sponsors, with financial help from the federal Department of Housing and Urban Development.

The War on Poverty also created some service programs for the elderly, including:

- Retired and Senior Volunteer Program (RSVP), which seeks to match work and service opportunities with elderly volunteers
- Foster Grandparent Program, which pays the elderly for part-time work as mentors, tutors, and caregivers for at-risk children and youth with special needs
- Service Corps of Retired Executives (SCORE), which provides consulting services to small businesses.

Family Care   According to the National Alliance for Caregiving and AARP Public Policy Institute (2015), an estimated 43.5 million adults in the United States have provided unpaid care to an adult or a child in the prior 12 months. Women form the majority of caregivers, at 60 percent, but the ranks of men in caregiving roles have been growing. Nearly 1 in 10 caregivers is 75 years of age or older (7 percent). Only about half of the caregivers have another caregiver assisting them, and only about one-third have paid support in place for their loved one. The longer a person is a caregiver, the more his own health and well-being decline.

When most workers take time off from work for caregiving responsibilities, they feel the pinch. Six out of 10 caregivers for older people reported being employed, with 56 percent working full- or part-time, and having to making some sort of work-related adjustments such as going to work late, leaving early, or taking time off according to the Caregiving in the U.S. 2015 Report by the National Alliance for Caregiving. Some give up work entirely. These work adjustments can take a large financial toll.

Forty-five percent who care for a spouse and 44 percent who care for a parent reported symptoms of emotional stress and 20 percent experience decreases in their own health (Caregiving in the U.S. 2015 Report). Although most caregiving is short-term, prolonged responsibilities take a toll on the emotional and physical health of caregivers. Caregivers worry about not having enough time to spend with their spouse, partner, or children, or by themselves. These people need supportive services such as respite care.

Foster Care and Adoption   Many foster parents are married couples (63 percent), although about 30 percent are single women (Foster Coalition March 2015). Social workers are often unionized, especially in public agencies, but foster parents are not, although there is a national organization of foster parents, with state chapters. The money that foster parents receive from agencies is usually called "board payments" rather than "wages." This carries the message that foster parents are not considered to be professionals, but are doing the work out of their love of children.

Adoption became an official legal process (and not just an informal practice) in the 1850s. The number of women giving their children up for adoption decreased from 9 percent in the 1950s to 1 percent today, according to the National Center on Adoption and Permanency. One out of every 25 families has an adopted child, and 40 percent of children are adopted out of the foster care system (AFCARS Report #23, 2016), 14 percent of them from international adoptions. And over the last 150 years, the institution has evolved and changed along with society.

In 2016, there were about 427,910 children in foster care (AFCARS Report #23, 2016), of which about one-quarter were waiting for adoption. The number of emergency removals has increased in the past two decades and the primary reasons have to do with unemployment, mental illness, substance use, and domestic violence. Over half of the children removed have a reunification plan, and 51 percent are reunited with their parents or primary caretaker within one year (www.childwelfare.gov). The median time in foster care was 13 months, but the mode was 2 years, with 8 percent in care for 3–4 years and 5 percent for more than 5 years (www.childwelfare.gov, 2014) One of the most recent changes in the child welfare system has been the major growth in the number of children in state custody who are living with their relatives. About one-third of all children in foster care are living with relatives, mostly grandparents (AFCARS Report #23, 2016). The bulk of funding for foster care goes into taking children from their parents and placing them in foster homes, not in family preservation programs that could strengthen families.

From the 1950s to the present, black children have been disproportionately represented in out-of-home care nationally. Although black children comprised 13 percent of the U.S. population in 2015 (U.S. Census Bureau, 2015), 24 percent of foster children were black, while 43 percent were white (AFCARS Report #23, 2016).

The Fostering Connections to Success and Increasing Adoptions Act (H.R. 6893; the FCA or Fostering Connections Act) was signed into law on October 7, 2008. Some of the provisions include

- Promoting permanent placement with relatives
- Maintaining connections with siblings and family
- Increasing the number of adoptions for waiting children
- Improving outcomes and transitions for older youth.

MENTAL HEALTH SERVICES Fred is a psychologist in a community mental health center. He is a member of a clinical team that includes social workers, psychologists, psychiatrists, and mental health nurses. Fred has a varied caseload. He counsels people who have been recently discharged from a psychiatric hospital. Some live at home, some in a community residence. Most are comfortable with their living arrangements, but one has consulted a lawyer about suing the state for placing her in a group home rather than in a private apartment. The ADA protects people with disabilities from discriminatory treatment, and the lawyer believes that a person who is placed in a group home is being treated differently than a person who can choose to live in her own apartment.

Fred's clinic is getting more and more patients who have been "dumped" by private hospitals onto financially strapped public hospitals and community service organizations. A study showed that hospitals with managed care plans are particularly likely to reject uninsured patients and discharge patients when their insurance runs out, regardless of whether the clients are better (Kilborn, 1997). Fred's clinic is in a state that has privatized its mental health care. Public hospitals used to take everyone, but private hospitals eager to make a profit are less likely to accept seriously ill or uninsured patients.

Most of the center's long-term clients are receiving medication for mental illness, supervised by the clinic psychiatrists. Some psychiatrists check their clients often to see how they are responding; others seem casual about checking. Part of Fred's job is to alert the psychiatrists about any unusual symptoms he observes. Fred took a course on prescription medication in graduate school and keeps up-to-date on the literature. He has mixed feelings about these drugs, feeling that they do some good but are overused. He prefers to emphasize talk therapy. Not all psychiatrists agree with him, and they have most of the power in the clinic. Because Fred does not have a medical degree, he is not authorized to dispense prescription drugs or to give any official advice about them.

Some of Fred's clients suffer from what some psychiatrists call free-floating anxiety. They are able to function fairly well at their work and with their families but need Fred's support to help them function. Fred also does family therapy. Fred knows, almost by memory, the American Psychiatric Association's *Diagnostic and Statistical Manual of Mental Disorders* 5 (American Psychiatric Association, 2017) because every patient has to have a diagnosis in order for the clinic to get reimbursed by private insurance, Medicaid, or Medicare. He wishes that he did not have to label everyone, and he does not agree with all the labels, but he knows that is the way the clinic gets paid.

Fred is aware of the power of self-help groups. He often refers his clients to a local group for manic depressive and depressive patients, a widow-to-widow group, the National Alliance on Mental Illness, or the Mental Patients' Liberation Front. Fred feels that the state Department of Mental Health has not vigorously recruited minority staff or trained the present staff in cultural sensitivity. He takes courses and reads a lot about different cultures. He also tries to get to know people from different cultures. Not all the staff are as concerned as he is. He has winced at episodes of cultural insensitivity. It does not surprise him that some people of diverse backgrounds do not return to the clinic after their first visit.

MEDICAL SOCIAL WORK   Medicare legislation in 1966 stipulated that if a hospital sets up a social work program, it should be under the direction of an social worker with a Masters of Social Work (MSW.) That same legislation expanded the number of hospital social workers. More were hired after the 1978 amendments to the Social Security Act, which provided expanded benefits for patients with end-stage renal disease. To qualify for that funding, hospitals had to hire MSW social workers to treat those patients (Rossen, 1987).

Dorothy works with a multidisciplinary team of doctors and nurses, psychologists, nurse clinicians, physical therapists, occupational therapists, and patient advocates. She helps make living arrangements for patients after they leave the hospital. This is called *discharge planning*. In child welfare agencies, social workers are almost always in charge, but a social worker in a hospital is sometimes the low person in the hierarchy, unless the hospital administration establishes clear role divisions. Dorothy also helps victims of domestic violence, including victims of rape, child abuse, spouse abuse, and elder abuse. She was trained in crisis intervention and continues to receive in-service training. She has friends who work in other medical settings, such as:

- Home health care
- Hospice services
- Nursing homes
- Employee assistance programs (working with the employees of a corporation or organization)
- Health maintenance organizations (HMOs)
- Visiting-nurse associations
- AIDS clinics
- Health education
- Private practice.

All states and the District of Columbia have some form of legal regulation for social work practice. Because insurance companies grant third-party payments to licensed social workers, programs are eager to hire licensed workers.

SERVICES FOR PEOPLE WITH DISABILITIES   Individuals with disabilities won a landmark victory in 1990 with the passage of the ADA, which outlaws discrimination against people with disabilities. The ramps you see on buildings, the leveled sidewalks for wheelchair access, and the signer for the deaf at an event are all efforts at complying with the ADA. On July 26, 2015, millions of people with disabilities, their family members, and friends celebrated the 25th anniversary of the signing of the law. Based on responses to The Impact of the ADA in American Communities survey (Frieden, 2015), the largest quality-of-life changes were related to transportation and accessibility in buildings:

"Public transportation is not allowed to charge more for the paratransit bus than it does for the regular bus. I became legally blind after 22 years of teaching in my district. I do not believe I would have been allowed to continue teaching without the ADA. Nor do I think I would have been given accommodations to help me."

"As a parent who uses a wheelchair, and has two children (now 8 and 10) who have mobility impairments, the ADA's impact on 'simple things' like accessible restrooms and accessible diaper changing stations has made all the difference in my family's successful inclusion in our community."

"I am a guide dog user and the ADA has made it possible for me to enter most public spaces without encountering discriminatory behavior. When I do encounter discriminatory behavior, I feel comfortable in voicing my rights since I know that the ADA protects my access rights when I am working with my guide dog."

"[Because of the ADA,], children with disabilities are now able to access their school and neighborhood playgrounds."

More modest improvements were made in education, employment, access to government services, recreation, and other areas. Reaching economic independence is still a goal that needs attention.

January 2017 Disability Employment Statistics Ages 16 Years and Over (U.S. Dept. of Labor, Office of Disability Employment Policy)

Labor Force Participation
People with disabilities: 19.5 percent
People without disabilities: 68.2 percent
Unemployment Rate
People with disabilities: 11 percent
People without disabilities: 4.9 percent

There are other laws, in addition to the ADA, that cover individuals with developmental disabilities. The Developmental Disabilities and Bill of Rights Act of 1975 and an amendment in 1978 have defined *developmental disability* as a severe, chronic disability of a person that results from mental and/or physical impairment; begins before age 22; is likely to continue indefinitely; results in substantial limitations in functioning in self-care, language, learning, mobility, self-direction, and economic self-sufficiency; and results in the need for individually planned and coordinated services of lifelong or extended duration (Golden, 1990).

Because the law covers only severe disabilities, many people with mild disabilities are not eligible for these services. The legal limitation affects the poor disproportionately, because there is a high correlation between poverty and disability, yet often poor families have the fewest services made available to them.

The diagnosis of developmental disability used to be determined solely by scores on intelligence tests, such as the Wechsler or the Stanford-Binet. In the 1980s, the American Association of Mental Deficiency decided that adaptive-behavior tests, which showed how a person actually performed, should become a part of the diagnostic criteria for developmental disabilities (Grossman, 1984).

Later changes to the Developmental Disabilities Act have encouraged independence, productivity, and community integration for adults. They have encouraged the phasing out of sheltered workshops, which segregated individuals with developmental delays into low-paying work, and have encouraged the placing of people into regular jobs. They have also included clients with diagnoses of cerebral palsy, epilepsy, and autism.

SERVICES TO THE MILITARY There were 20.4 million living veterans in 2016, of which 9 percent are women (Bialek, 2017). The wars in Iraq and Afghanistan have focused the nation's attention on enlisted men and women and on veterans, and the kinds of services they are receiving. The Department of Veterans Affairs (VA) oversees three programs: Veterans Benefits Administration, Veterans Health Administration, and National Cemetery Administration. Poor quality of care and long waits to be seen were issues headlined in newspapers in 2007 and again in 2016. President Obama signed a $16.3 billion bill to overhaul the troubled Department of Veterans Affairs, saying the country had a "sacred duty" to protect its military service members. The bill, passed by Congress, allows veterans to seek private care outside VA facilities, and also provides money for the VA to hire more doctors and nurses. The effort came after reports that some veterans had waited months to get care from the VA. The VA operates more than 1,400 sites of care, including hospitals, community clinics, community living centers, domiciliaries, and readjustment counseling centers. The agency is moving toward an integrated community care model. From fiscal year 2015 to fiscal year 2016, total community care authorizations increased by 25 percent. Over the same period, the Veterans Choice Program (VCP) network of providers grew 67 percent to over 360,000 providers and facilities contracted (U.S. Department of Veterans Affairs, 2017).

The backlog of disability cases was 84,000 in 2017, down from 600,000 in 2013 according to the U.S. Dept of Veterans Affairs. If soldiers are rated 30 percent or more disabled, they are entitled to disability retirement pay, medical benefits, and privileges at the commissary, where prices for goods are significantly lower than in the civilian market. A rating below 30 percent means they get severance pay and no benefits.

Twenty percent of recent war veterans exhibited symptoms of a traumatic brain injury, 14 percent reported PTSD or depression, and more than 1,500 recently returned vets are amputees (RAND Center for Military Health Policy Research, 2008). This report revealed that only 50 percent of veterans with mental health issues receive treatment, which could be due to shame and stigma, availability, and long wait times for services. There is a shortage of mental health workers at many of the VA's hospitals and clinics across the country. Veterans in rural areas are particularly disadvantaged. Specialized care is concentrated in urban areas, while 6 million of the veterans live in rural areas (Tanielian, et al, 2008). The National Institute of Drug Abuse (2013) reported that substance abuse among veterans is strongly related to their exposure to combat and prescriptions to opioid pain medications. It also reported that 25 percent of returning Iraq and Afghanistan veterans showed signs of substance use disorder.

Service members can experience PTSD from a combination of combat and sexual abuse in the military. The military services received a total of 6,083 reports of sexual assault involving service members as either victims or subjects throughout fiscal year 2015, which was a 1 percent decrease over 2014. About 25 percent of U.S. military women and 1 percent of military men have experienced military sexual trauma (U.S. Dept. of Veterans Affairs, Veterans Choice Program, 2017). A study of female VA outpatients found that women who had been sexually assaulted had symptoms of current depression three times higher and symptoms of current alcohol abuse two times higher than did other women (Hankin et al., 1999). Since the Tailhook incident in 1991, which involved sexual violence against women at a naval party, the Pentagon has become more concerned about sexual assaults. The 2004 National Defense Authorization Act required investigation and reporting regarding sexual harassment and assault at the United States military academies.

Human service workers need to become aware of services available to soldiers and veterans. In addition to services on military bases, the VA has Veteran's Outreach Centers that welcome veterans home by providing readjustment services and assisting them and their family members in making a successful postwar adjustment. Veterans' Outreach Centers are non-profit agencies that receive state funds to support veterans and their families. They give financial assistance based on need. Army Emergency Relief gives financial assistance and scholarship help to soldiers and their families. The Red Cross also gives some financial assistance and provides other services.

WHERE THE MONEY COMES FROM

If you work in a human service agency, you will want to know who pays your salary and how secure it is.

Government Programs

Funding comes from different levels of government—county, city, state, and federal—and from private sources. In theory, some agencies are public, and others are private (voluntary, non-profit), but in practice, there is a complicated mix of public and private agencies. Some agencies that call themselves "private" get most of their funds from the government, and public agencies sometimes hire personnel from "private" agencies to do some of their work.

Most private, non-profit agencies were historically organized under religious auspices and were a major source of charity. Non-profit agencies have revenue coming from fees earned, public sources, and private donations. Even programs that decide not to take government funds get a subsidy in the form of a tax exemption.

Private Enterprise and Social Welfare Programs

Since the 1960s, state and local governments have been hiring more and more private corporations to do some of the work that state bureaucracies used to do themselves. This is called **contracting out**. Corporations want to make profits on human service. Public sector unions play an important role in ensuring fair wages and benefits. Some states have restricted unions' power and with the Supreme Court Janus 2018 ruling, unions cannot unilaterally charge membership fees which were used for collective bargaining (Dynarski, 2018).

Corporations have continued to enter the social welfare field, particularly since the inception of Medicare and Medicaid in 1965, when the government began paying large sums to doctors and hospitals. This **privatization** has occurred on a large scale in health care, especially in hospitals, nursing homes, and group medical care. Hospital chains such as Hospital Corporation of America and Humana sprang up in the 1970s. By the 1980s, human service corporations had established themselves in child care, ambulatory health care, substance use care, psychiatric care, home care, assisted living facilities, and continuing care. Since 2000, the number of people housed in private prisons has increased 47 percent, according to the Sentencing Project (2018).

Charitable Giving

The "faith-based" approach toward social services, initiated by President George H. W. Bush, proposed giving religious organizations more money to deliver social services and more freedom from government restrictions. This strategy is reminiscent of that of the nineteenth century, which relied on volunteers and private philanthropies to deliver services. Some officials have even suggested that we return to the practices of feudal days, when the church gave whatever help was available. Churches protest that they are not equipped to handle the job, and Catholic bishops have called for more government help for those living in poverty and oppressed (United States

Conference of Catholic Bishops [USCCB], 1986). Leaving social welfare to benevolence will may not ensure critical needs are met, particularly since the largest donations go to universities and churches rather than to the poor. The 2000s began with the terrorist attack on the World Trade Center, which led to a war that continues more than 16 years later and heightened intolerance toward immigrants, particularly people of Middle Eastern origin. Except for a generous outpouring of giving to the victims of the attacks on the World Trade Center and the Pentagon, many charities nationwide experienced sharp drops in contributions after September 11, 2001. According to Charity Navigator (www.Charitynavigator.org), the 2008 recession brought drops in giving for several years in 2008 and 2009, until 2014. According to Giving USA, Charitable giving in 2017 grew by 4% with the largest donations going to churches ($123 billion), followed by education ($60 billion) and human services ($47 billion) (Giving USA, 2017).

The trend for giving to social service non-profit organizations is increasingly tied to outcomes, in "pay for success" models where government contracts and grants are paid based on meeting contract outcomes, in some cases not until the goal is achieved versus when the service is provided. Foundations view their donations as "investments" instead of charity, and expect a social return, if not an economic return. The intent is to ensure funding goes toward effective programs and that the funds are not wasted on unproven services. One by-product of this approach could be that sometimes the social service agencies are criticized for "creaming," or taking the least needy clients, to ensure success.

Structural solutions beyond charity are needed to address poverty and social problems in America. Several large foundations are paying for cross-sector efforts to address complex issues, and non-profit organizations are serving as "back-bone" organizations bringing together public and private sector partners (Kania & Kramer, 2011).

The approach is sometimes referred to as the "collective impact model," which relies on building a common agenda and developing measurements with stakeholders including government, business, non-profit, academia, and residents and clients. Many examples addressing education and health are included in the Stanford Social Innovation Review paper mentioned above, which demonstrates the success that can be had when a commitment is made to solve seemingly intractable complex problems.

This message was once again delivered in a pastoral reflection of the United States Conference of Catholic Bishops called *A Place at the Table* (United States Conference of Catholic Bishops (USCCB), 2002), which stated that "we must come together with a common conviction that we can no longer tolerate the moral scandal of poverty in our land and so much hunger and deprivation in our world," and that the "Gospel and Catholic teaching require us to serve those in need and to work for a more just society and world."

Summary

1. Some have called the United States called a "reluctant welfare state," the argument being that it assumes people will take advantage and therefore makes benefits difficult to obtain.

2. Social welfare programs have helped millions of people, and when their value is added to the households' incomes, it is evident that many people have been lifted out of poverty.

3. The poverty level is a formula used to determine eligibility for services and to track income.

4. Most services are means-tested, based on income and sometimes other eligibility requirements.

5. The United States modeled its colonial-era social welfare practices after the Elizabethan fifteenth-century poor laws.

6. Income inequality is the gap between the people who are rich and those living in poverty. It has widened in the United States.
7. The New Deal created many programs following the Great Depression, including social security, public housing, and public works programs.
8. The War on Poverty was a series of social programs launched in the 1960s.
9. Information about the following social welfare programs is provided: Temporary Assistance to Needy Families; General Assistance; Social Security; Supplemental Security Income; Emergency Assistance; Medicaid; Medicare; the Women, Infants, and Children food program; Supplemental Nutrition Assistance Program (food stamps); Unemployment Insurance; Earned Income Tax Credit; Child Tax Credit; and Child Care Tax Credit.
10. The federal Personal Responsibility and Work Opportunity Reconciliation Act of 1996 created the Temporary Assistance to Needy Families (TANF) program, which ended the entitlement of income assistance to needy families and gave block grants to states to administer the program and set their own guidelines, within federal constraints.
11. The main goal of TANF was to downsize the rolls, which states accomplished through time limits and other requirements.
12. Entitlement programs, such as Social Security and Medicare, are social welfare programs available to all Americans regardless of financial background. Entitlement programs have less stigma and more political support than means-tested programs.
13. Some of the fields of service described include services for the older adults, foster care and adoption, mental health services, medical social work, services for individuals with disabilities, and services for the military.
14. The wars in Iraq and Afghanistan have put stresses on service men and women and their families. The Department of Veterans Affairs has a large volume of disability claims.
15. Funding for social services comes from local, state, and federal governments, as well as from private sources.
16. Social services are becoming increasingly privatized. Corporations are taking over services that were once run by the state.

Discussion Questions

1. If you were put in charge of developing an ideal system of social supports, what would your system look like?
2. Discuss the attitudes toward welfare recipients that you have encountered in your family, school, and community. How were these attitudes developed? Does your attitude differ from other attitudes you have encountered?
3. The Affordable Care Act signed by President Obama mandates contraceptive coverage. The Trump administration is working to end that mandate. They would like religious non-profits to have the final word on whether their employees get coverage for contraception on their health insurance. Do you think religious employers (e.g., religiously based hospitals and universities) should have that control? How would you counsel women living in poverty to obtain contraceptive coverage they need?

Web Resources for Further Study

Children's Defense Fund (CDF)
https://www.childrensdefense.org

Child Welfare League of America (CWLA)
https://www.cwla.org

Food Research and Action Center (FRAC)
https://www.frac.org

Center on Budget and Policy Priorities
https://www.cbpp.org

National Women's Law Center
https://www.nwlc.org

Legal Momentum
https://www.legalmomentum.org

Center for Law and Social Policy (CLASP)
https://www.clasp.org

The Coalition on Human Needs
https://www.chn.org

MyLab Helping Professions for Introduction to Human Services

In the Topic 1 Assignments: History of Human Services, start with Application Exercise 1.3: Attitudes Toward the Poor and Credentialing Quiz 1.3: Attitudes Toward the Poor.

Then try Application Exercise 1.4: Political Ideologies, Governments, and Businesses and Credentialing Quiz 1.4: Political Ideologies, Governments, and Businesses.

7   Working with Diversity

Learning Outcomes

■ Students will gain knowledge about diversity that will assist them in recognizing cultural differences within diverse populations.

■ Students will be able to describe the dynamics of difference between their own cultural experience and the experience of people who are culturally different.

■ Students will have an increased capacity to conduct analysis and develop understanding of the challenges experienced by culturally different individuals.

■ Students will develop the capacity to construct strategies for working with culturally different individuals and groups.

Source: Gino Santa Maria/Shutterstock

National polls show that there are significant differences in how racial discrimination is viewed by both Black and White adults. For example, a recent Pew Research Center poll showed that 88 percent of Black people feel the nation has more to do in order to achieve equal treatment while 53 percent of White people feel this way (Pew Research Center, 2016). White people believe that Black people have as good a chance as they do to find a job and are as well off financially and educationally as they are.

As evidenced by the aforementioned poll, the majority of Black Americans don't see it that way. Author Bell Hooks writes about her childhood as a Black girl. She learned as a child that to be safe, it was important to recognize the power of Whiteness, even to fear it, and to avoid encountering it. She remembers walking from her home to visit her grandmother:

> It was a movement away from the segregated Blackness of our community into a poor White neighborhood. I remember the fear, being scared to walk to Baba's, our grandmother's house, because we would have to pass that terrifying Whiteness—those White faces on the porches staring us down with hate. Even when empty or vacant those porches seemed to say danger, you do not belong here, you are not safe.

Oh! that feeling of safety, of arrival, of homecoming when we finally reached the edges of her yard, when we could see the soot Black face of our grandfather, Daddy Gus, sitting in his chair on the porch, smell his cigar, and rest on his lap. Such a contrast, that feeling of arrival, of homecoming—this sweetness and the bitterness of that journey, that constant reminder of White power and control. (Hooks, 1997, p. 175)

Times have changed since Black people had little intimate contact with White people, but Hooks believes that the feeling of impending danger has never completely left Black people, even when they have adopted the values, speech, and habits of White people. She says that even though it was a long time ago that she visited her grandmother, she still has associations of Whiteness with terror. "All Black people in the United States, irrespective of their class status or politics, live with the possibility that they will be terrorized by Whiteness" (Hooks, 1997, p. 175). She says that most White people don't understand this terror, and that this lack of understanding has played a role in the recent push against "politically correct" behavior. The push against politically correct speech as seen in the most recent presidential election has emboldened hate groups like the Ku Klux Klan as well as White supremacist organizations across the United States. The Southern Poverty Law Center's 2015 Annual Report documented a 14 percent increase in organized hate groups in America during a one-year period, from 784 identified hate groups to 892 (Potok, 2016). This increase of 108 organized hate groups occurred after a three-year decline, which underscores the impact of growing hate speech within our communities. After the 2016 presidential election, there were 437 incidents of reported racist and xenophobic harassment reported between Election Day, November 8, and November 14 (Okeowo, 2016).

These facts as well as those that follow contradict the belief that we have achieved equality between people of color and White people. In Chapter 6 we discuss the disparities in income and wealth. Other disparities include:

- *Home ownership and housing discrimination.* In 2009, 74.5 percent of White households owned their own homes, compared with 46 percent of Black people and 48.4 percent of Latino individuals (U.S. Census Bureau, 2009a). "Even when homeseekers contact housing providers by telephone, linguistic profiling (whereby the provider recognizes the race of the caller and provides less service to those with a recognizably Black voice) results in African Americans experiencing discrimination in efforts to buy or rent a home even when they do not even meet the housing provider" (Squires, 2006). In 2016, the U.S. Office of Fair Housing and Equal Opportunity (OFHEO) reported more than 8,000 complaints filed for housing discrimination. Of the more than 8,000 complaints, 59 percent were for discrimination against people with disabilities and 26 percent for discrimination against racial minorities, while others were targeted based on their national origin, sex, and/or family status (Office of Fair Housing and Equal Opportunity Annual Report, 2016). And while housing advocates reported significant progress under the Obama administration, there is an air of uncertainty under the Trump administration. There is a great fear that efforts to end discrimination within housing in America will be set aside or rolled back under the new administration (Greenberg, Z. 2017).
- Black people and Latino individuals lost their homes to foreclosures proportionally more than did White people; 8 percent of both African Americans and Latinos, compared with 4.5 percent of White people, had their homes foreclosed on. These disparities hold even after controlling for differences in income between the groups

(continued)

(Gruenstein, Li, & Ernst, 2010) and contribute to the wealth gap between Whites and non-White groups. The average Black person's wealth, for example, is 4.5 times less than the average wealth of a White person in the United States (Burd-Sharps & Rasch, 2015).

- *Health.* White people have lower rates of diabetes, tuberculosis, pregnancy-related mortality, and sudden infant death syndrome (SIDS) and are more likely to have prenatal care in the first trimester than Black people, Latinos, or Asians. African Americans face a higher risk than any other racial group of dying from heart disease, diabetes, stroke, or hypertension. (Orsi, Margellos-Anast, & Whitman, 2010).

  In 2016 life expectancy for U.S. White males at birth was 76.1 years compared with 71.5 years for Black non-Hispanic males, and 81 years for White females compared with 77.9 years for Black non Hispanic females (CDC, 2017).

- *Health insurance.* Historically, minorities are more likely to be uninsured than White people, even when accounting for work status. This results in lack of access to health care and more health problems. Nearly 70 percent of nonelderly White people receive employer-based insurance, while only 40 percent of Hispanics, 48 percent of Black people, and 43 percent of Native Americans/Native Alaskans receive such coverage (American College of Physicians, 2010). With the passage of the Affordable Care Act these disparities have begun to diminish (Austin, 2016), though the Trump administration's push to "repeal and replace" raises questions of whether these reductions will be maintained.

- *Professional advancement.* Black people and Latinos are underrepresented as lawyers, physicians, professors, dentists, engineers, and registered nurses (Bureau of Labor Statistics, 2017).

- *Racial profiling.* In California, since 1991, between 80 percent and 90 percent of all motorists arrested by law enforcement officials have been members of minority groups. In Maryland, although only 21 percent of drivers along a stretch of Interstate 95 are minorities, including Black people, Latinos, Asians, and others, 80 percent of those who are pulled over and searched are people of color. Racial profiling has come to be known as "driving while Black (DWB)" (American Civil Liberties Union, 2010).

- *Fatal Shootings.* The implicit bias that results in racial profiling and traffic stops has real-life consequences for Black Americans, who are 2.5 times more likely than White people to be shot and killed by law enforcement officers (Lowery, 2016).

- *Job discrimination.* White job applicants with a felony conviction on their record were more likely to get a job than comparable Black applicants with no criminal record. Applicants with White-sounding names are more likely to obtain employment than those with Black-sounding names (Squires, 2006).

- *Political representation.* In 2017, the House of Representatives was 19 percent non-White, while Latino and other non-Whites make up 38 percent of the overall population in the United States (Bialik & Krogstad, 2017). In 2014 there was only one Black governor, Deval Patrick of Massachusetts, and while there have been numerous Black candidates, as of May 2018 there were no Black governors in the United States.

- *Voting rights.* Following the election of Barack Obama states passed photo identification requirements for voting which disproportionately impacted the ability of Black people to vote (Boddie, 2016). Most convicted felons are prohibited from voting, and a disproportionate number of prisoners are people of color (Hetey & Eberhardt, 2014).

- *School segregation.* A 2010 study sponsored by Harvard School of Public Health as reported by Jackson (2010) found "gross levels of disparity" between schools that White and Black children attend. Children of color "continue to attend very different schools than White children." In Chicago, the average Black student goes to a public school that is 74 percent Black while the average White student goes to a school that is 6 percent Black. Forty-three percent of both Latino and African-American students attend schools where the poverty rate is more than 80 percent. Only 4 percent of White students do. The study concluded that "issues of persistent high racial/ethnic segregation and high exposure of minority children to economic disadvantage at the school level remain largely unaddressed" (Jackson, 2010).

AN OVERVIEW OF THE STRUGGLE FOR EQUALITY

The founding fathers of the United States—all White and Christian—did not grant the vote to women or to Black men. In fact, they gave the vote only to people who owned land. Those excluded from having a say in how the country was run have had to gain their equality through long, hard struggles. Frederick Douglass, an African-American leader who literally fought his way out of slavery, said that power concedes nothing without a struggle.

A look at history shows this to be true. The Civil War freed the slaves, and the Fifteenth Amendment of 1870 gave Black people the vote. But they were kept from using it until the civil rights movement that began in the 1950s struck down segregation laws (called Jim Crow laws) in the South. Then the Civil Rights Act of 1964 prohibited racial and sexual discrimination, and the Voting Rights Act of 1965 banned practices that disenfranchised Black people.

The first wave of the women's movement in the late nineteenth and early twentieth centuries fought long and hard for the Nineteenth Amendment of 1920, which gave women the right to vote. The second wave of the women's movement, beginning in the 1960s and continuing to the present, renewed women's struggle for equality on many fronts. Gays and lesbians began to fight for equal treatment when they resisted police repression in 1969 at the Stonewall Inn in New York City, and their struggle continues. The struggle reached a new level when Massachusetts legalized gay and lesbian marriages in 2004, followed by the *Obergefell v. Hodges* Supreme Court's ruling in June 2015 that state bans on gay and lesbian couples' right to marry were unconstitutional.

Many stigmatized groups began their struggles for equality and self-esteem in the 1960s, giving birth to advocacy groups such as the National Welfare Rights Organization, Mental Patients' Liberation Front, and Disabled People's Movement.

But power does not yield easily. The backlash against the liberation movements of the 1960s and early 1970s bubbled up in the mid-1970s, picked up steam in the 1980s, and led to a volcano of conservative repression with the Republican takeover of Congress in 1994 and their Contract with America, which essentially dismantled many of the social gains of the previous decades.

Conservatives oppose the affirmative action programs that were established in the 1960s and 1970s. There are fierce fights against immigrants, bilingual education, multicultural curricula, sex education in schools, supporting fairness and equality for all sexual orientations and abortion. In the past three decades, laws have been passed to deport illegal immigrants, cut off welfare benefits and food stamps for legal immigrants, end affirmative action for minorities, and end bilingual education. Women, on average, still earn only 77 percent as much as men with the same level of education.

Where does the human service worker fit into this political maelstrom? When the battle enters directly into the social service field, the worker has to make choices about implementing restrictive policies. For example:

- If you work in the welfare department in a state that has an English-only law and you don't know Spanish, how do you explain the regulations to a Spanish-speaking client? Policies won't be printed in Spanish, and the agency might not employ a Spanish-speaking worker.
- Massachusetts passed a law prohibiting the placement of foster children with gay or lesbian foster parents, but after years of organizing work by LGTBTQs and their allies, it then passed a law forbidding discrimination against people based on their sexual orientation. If you are a worker in a state child welfare agency and the legislature passes a law saying you can't place foster children with gay or lesbian foster parents, what will you do if you disagree? Do you obey the law, even against your convictions? If you do, how do you resolve the internal conflict this is likely to cause? Do you oppose the law, and if so, how? Do you work with the movement that is fighting against it by joining demonstrations, writing letters to the editor, or lobbying your legislators? Do you simply place a child with a foster parent whom you know to be gay but tell the foster parent to keep his sexual orientation a secret?
- If you are a human service worker in a state that has passed a law denying services to legal immigrants, what will you do? In California, some workers could not in good conscience obey such a law, and they vowed to continue to give services. Many teachers in California refused to obey a law that eliminated bilingual education and continued to teach as they had done before the passage of the law.

Some legislation may not require you to make such agonizing choices but will nonetheless affect your work environment and agency practice. If affirmative action is ended, your agency may become less diverse. If you are White, you will have fewer opportunities to work with people of color. African-American, Hispanic, Asian, and Native American clients will have less chance of working with someone who shares their culture.

Regardless of what you do about the politics of diversity, you will always need to understand how the issues affect your clients, or you will be shortchanging your clients and shortchanging yourself as an effective worker. If you belong to a group that has been discriminated against, you probably have already had personal experience that will help you to identify with a client who has also faced discrimination. If, on the other hand, you have never experienced discrimination, it may be hard for you to identify with people's reactions to it.

Understanding Oppression and Privilege

Individuals can be dominated by other individuals for a variety of reasons. Siblings often oppress each other; parents sometimes oppress their children. In this discussion, however, we are talking about social forces that hold people down, hem them in, and block their ability to lead a good life. Oppression occurs because of structural inequalities in society.

Privilege is the other side of the coin of oppression. If Group A has something of value and keeps Group B from having it, Group A is privileged and Group B is oppressed. Any individual, however, could be privileged in one respect but oppressed in another. One way to look at this was devised by Patricia Hill Collins (1990), who constructed a "Matrix of Domination" that integrates categories such as gender, race, class, sexuality, age, and ability. This matrix assumes that everyone is shaped by some combination of interacting social categories, and everyone experiences varying degrees of privilege and oppression depending upon her social location or place. In the

African-American community, for example, there are vast differences in lifestyle and outlook between affluent professionals and executives on one hand and the people on the bottom rung of the income and status ladder on the other, yet the color of their skin ensures that both groups will face some discrimination.

In all ethnic groups, women have less power than men (although the patriarchal tradition is stronger in some cultures than others). But wealthy women have more power than poor women. A rich woman who is abused by her husband is unlikely to go to a shelter for domestic violence She can afford to leave and rent an apartment or buy a house, provided that she has access to the checkbook or charge account and her psyche has not been battered to the point of helplessness.

Ethnicity is only one of the many factors that determine people's standing in society and feelings about themselves. Social class and gender are also powerful influences. Anthropologist Oscar Lewis (1966) maintained that social class was a more powerful determinant of behavior than ethnicity. He believed there was more similarity between poor people in the barrios of New York City and poor people in the favelas of Sao Paulo than between the poor Puerto Rican and the rich Puerto Rican. Although both the poor and the wealthy might share certain cultural beliefs and behaviors, their differing social class positions would result in different self-identities.

Psychologist Robert Coles (1977) studied many children in different groups, including children from wealthy families. He said that one of the most outstanding attitudes of rich children is their "sense of entitlement." They know they will inherit the country. Most poor people don't expect to inherit anything. At times it appears that all they can hope for is to win the lottery.

Since we are all participants in a society with a significant amount of sexism, racism, and homophobia, it is inevitable that we have internalized some of these cultural beliefs. We don't need to feel guilty about that, but we do need to examine our own position in society and our own attitudes. Battling discrimination is a lifelong process in which the authors of this book are also engaged.

A group of Harvard psychologists have devised a test to detect prejudice called the Implicit Association Test (IAT). The test attempts to measure "implicit prejudices"— subconscious attitudes, those that lie outside our awareness and may contradict our conscious ideas about equality and fairness. The researchers say that tests of thousands of people yield some striking results. In one study using the IAT, while White physicians denied any racial bias, most physicians reflected a preference favoring Whites over Blacks, which is consistent with research conducted with the general population for Whites (Green et al., 2007). Key here is that it matters whether people prefer one race over another, as it has a practical impact on how people engage with each other.

If you would like to know how you score on the test, simply Google Project Implicit and then once you're on the site take any of the number of sample tests that are available. The Implicit Association site is also listed in the Resources for Further Study section of this chapter.

COLOR-BLIND PRIVILEGE In a chapter about race in his satirical book *I Am America (And So Can You!)*, Stephen Colbert writes, "We're all the same. Unfortunately, not everyone sees that. They get too hung up on little things like 'appearance' and 'history' and cultural identity'" (Colbert, 2007). Pretending race doesn't matter doesn't fool anyone. Instead, experimental psychologists say, it pushes our responses down into our unconscious, where ideas we would actively reject reside. In tests of implicit association, researchers asked study participants to pair terms with faces. White people found it easier to link Black faces with guns than with tools. White participants also found it harder to see Black people as equally "American" with Whites or Asian Americans (Lehrman, 2008).

The sociologist Charles A. Gallagher maintains that color blindness "maintains White privilege by negating racial inequality" (2003). The belief that the United States is free of **racism** and discrimination, and that people get ahead only on their merits, allows White people to believe that one's race has no influence on one's economic situation. It allows White people to believe that their material success was gained only by individual hard work, determination, thrift, and investments in education, and has nothing to do with institutional racism. It also allows White people to avoid feeling any guilt about institutional racism.

People who are reading this book are likely to be college students. It hasn't been easy for many of you to get to college and it might not be easy for you to stay in college until graduation. Many of you work part-time, or even full-time. Many of you may be living in poverty and trying to work your way into a more comfortable lifestyle. You may be in debt for college tuition. If you are White and someone suggests that you are privileged because of your White skin, you may think that is ridiculous. You don't feel privileged. You have worked hard to get where you are. Yet we suggest that you examine some of the things that made it possible for you to get where you are. You might discover that you did in fact have some privilege because of your White skin. Becoming aware of your implicit biases is a critical aspect of developing your skills and abilities to work with people from other cultures and of different races.

The late playwright August Wilson spoke about attitudes toward Blackness:

> When you go to the dictionary and you look up Black, it gives you these definitions that say, "Affected by an undesirable condition." You start thinking something's wrong with Black. When White people say, "I don't see color," what they're saying is, "You're affected by this undesirable condition, but I'll pretend I don't see that." And I go, "No, see my color. Look at me. I'm not ashamed of who I am and what I am." (Lahr, 2001, p. 52)

Overt racism is easy to spot, but covert racism is subtler. Counselors who relate to minority clients as though race is unimportant are disregarding the central importance of color to the client. They also disregard the influence of their Whiteness upon the client.

Color consciousness is the opposite of color blindness. It is based on the premise that the client's problems stem essentially from being a person of color. A color-conscious counselor places too much weight on the color of the client and assumes that all problems are due to the client's ethnicity.

Impact of Prejudice on Self-Esteem

Positive self-esteem is at the core of mental health. In the following anecdotes, consider how prejudice and discrimination might negatively affect people's feelings about themselves. In education about diversity, and in particular bias, it's important to both highlight and articulate potential bias. By reviewing the examples that follow, you can begin work toward heightened awareness of your own implicit bias. In what ways to you think the individual's feelings about themselves are impacted by others' perceptions of them?

- A 70-year-old person recounted the following incident: "I was driving into a parking lot and a youngish woman was driving out. She evidently didn't like the way I was driving, because she screamed at me, 'Where do you think you're going, you old bat?'"

    The 70-year-old woman had never considered being old as the most important part of her identity, but here she encountered a woman who saw her age as the most important part of her identity and as a degraded status. The yelling woman combined her anger about a person's driving with her contempt of older adults. Because the older woman was secure in her identity, and in her driving ability, she was able to pass this incident off with a shrug. But this example of ageism is representative of the mountain of insults that older people face, insults that can wear down a shaky self-confidence.

- A lesbian student is told by one of her teachers that she has no right to wear a necklace with a cross on it because her sexual orientation is against "God's will." The teacher forces her to "come out of the closet" to the class about being a lesbian, and when she does, some class members turn on her. The student is hurt and angry, feeling that she has been emotionally violated.

- Women who have experienced domestic violence are not only physically abused, they also face a barrage of emotional insults from their abusers, often to the point of agreeing with the abusers who tell them that they are worthless.

- Two social psychologists, Claude Steele and Joshua Aronson, tested the effects of expectations on students' performance. They gave graduating Black high school students GRE exams. When they told the students that White students get better scores on those exams than Black students do, the students' self-confidence went down and, true to the prediction, on average their scores were lower than those of White students. But when they were told that the exam was not being used to evaluate ability or qualification, their scores went up and were as good as the scores made by White students (Steele & Aronson, 1995). When their anxiety about performance was removed, Black students worked up to their full potential, which is as great as that of White students. This study is one of the many that disprove the premise of the widely publicized book *The Bell Curve* (Herrnstein & Murray, 1994), that the intelligence of Black people is consistently lower than that of White people. Steele and Aronson also conducted a similar experiment with women, using math tests, and the results were the same (Steele & Aronson, 1995).

How can a human service worker combat prejudice and discrimination? We need to work on three levels—with the larger community, with small groups, and with individuals. Working for community-wide social change involves social activism. Causes that might be embraced include the women's movement, gay and lesbian liberation, welfare rights, antiracism, immigration issues, combating ageism, liberation for patients with disabilities, liberation for patients with mental health conditions, and body-image liberation.

Large-scale movements bring about the most effective change in social attitudes. Liberation movements not only change public attitudes but can also raise the self-esteem and self-confidence of oppressed people. People often internalize their oppression and come to believe that they are the way the oppressor says they are. When they join with similarly oppressed people, the very fight to free themselves raises their self-esteem. Black Lives Matter represents a group that has coalesced to fight the way in which Black people are treated by law enforcement. Gay Pride marches help restore pride to lesbian, gay, bisexual, and transgender people. The women's movement has had a profound effect on women's self-esteem, giving support to women's quest for equality with men. The welfare rights movement helped welfare recipients feel themselves to be worthy and productive people.

On an individual level, the most important job for human service workers is to understand the culture of their clients. As a part of this it's important to that human service workers also understand their own cultural lens, or the way in which they look at the world. Awareness of your own culture and the culture of your client will make it possible to understand the dynamics of difference that exists between you as the worker and the individual you are striving to help. This understanding will enable you to adapt your approach to helping and become more effective as a human service worker.

We use the word *culture* broadly. In a sense, every individual you work with is from a different culture. But in this chapter, we focus particularly on groups that have been oppressed because of their ethnicity, social class, gender, sexual orientation, or physical or emotional status.

UNDERSTANDING ETHNICITY

The Definition of Culture

There is no one agreed-on definition of *culture*. We will use the term to connote a group of people who share history, language, traditions, and networks. They may also share a minority social status. More importantly, they see themselves and others see them in a special way, although their ethnic and cultural status may have slightly varied meanings for each individual (Lukes & Land, 1990).

Theories about cultural identity have changed over time. The melting-pot theory, popular among the "establishment" of the 1960s, implicitly assumed that the White, Anglo-Saxon culture was the ideal that other cultures should aspire to. The melting-pot theory has formed the basis for the view that everyone should be treated the same and that we should be "color-blind." The theory has proven to be inadequate. Ethnic groups never totally assimilate into the majority culture, and they have asserted their right to be unique.

During the War on Poverty, some sociologists proposed a cultural-deficit theory (Moynihan, 1965), which assumed that minority cultures were inferior to the mainstream. This theory called

Source: Library of Congress Prints and Photographs Division

During World War II, the U.S. government forcibly interned thousands of U.S. citizens of Japanese ancestry. The official reason was that they might spy for Japan, our enemy. Yet the German Americans and Italian Americans, both of whose ancestral countries also opposed us, were not harassed. Why do you think Asian Americans were treated so much more harshly?

for socializing minorities into the mainstream culture. That was one of the guiding principles of the Head Start early-childhood program.

Through the organized efforts of those supposedly deficient cultural groups, the cultural deficit theory yielded to a theory of cultural difference, which focused on the uniqueness of each minority culture and implied that each was separate from the dominant culture. However, that too was inadequate, as there is much overlap between the minority and dominant cultures.

A current theory is called **bicultural theory**. It states that although people are socialized into their minority culture through their family and ethnic community, they are also influenced by the dominant culture through social institutions and the mass media. No one is quite sure how people incorporate cultures. Each person goes through the process with varying degrees of success. A totally bicultural person moves easily between two cultures, feeling at home in each, to the extent that the dominant culture allows this (Lukes & Land, 1990).

Anthropologists say that a person's ethnicity is situational, asserting itself according to the situation (Green, 1982). An African-American person might speak "Black English" with other African Americans but, when with White people, speak the dominant form of English. It is important to know how people deal with ethnicity in cross-cultural interactions as well as within their culture.

Advances in genetics and biotechnology in the past few decades have caused a dramatic shift in thinking about race. Most anthropologists now agree that race is not a biological reality at all. It is nothing more than a social, cultural, and political invention (Chandler, 1997). But that is not how the general public sees it. Many people become locked into their own personal belief systems, beliefs that have been reinforced through stereotypes that have been passed down over generations and supported by societal messages from the dominant culture. The mapping of the human genome provided scientific proof that human beings are not divided into separate biological groups. J. Craig Venter, whose company Celera Genomics mapped the human genome, said, "It is disturbing to see reputable scientists and physicians even categorizing things in terms of race. There is no basis in the genetic code for race" (Stolberg, 2001, p. 1).

While we agree that there is only one race, we go on to discuss race as a social construct because it is a concept deeply embedded in people's ideas about themselves and others.

Media Stereotypes

The media has a powerful influence in shaping our attitudes. Ahmed and Matthes (2017), for example, reviewed 345 published studies to explore how media portrays individuals who are Muslim as well as the Islamic faith. The research showed that that the majority of media reporting presents Muslims in a negative light. The Islamic faith is also portrayed negatively as a violent religion. It's important to realize that people's views as well as their behavior toward others are influenced when the messages they receive from the media are largely negative about a particular group.

The impact of negative media coverage isn't simply a phenomenon that affects individuals who are Muslim or a part of the Islamic religion; others groups also find that media coverage influences how people feel toward them. Hadden, Tolliver, Snowden, and Brown-Manning (2016) for example, researched the attitudes of people toward police violence and found that negative reporting about Black men or African Americans was associated with attitudes that support police violence. For the African-American man, media reporting matters, particularly when the impact they experience with regard to police violence can range from a loss of their liberty to death.

News reports of police shooting unarmed Black men have become more apparent within the media, and the ways in which the individuals are portrayed play an important role in not only how the situation came to pass, but also in how the death of an unarmed individual is handled. How the individual subject to a police shooting is portrayed, both by the media and the larger society, will affect whether they are seen as a thug or as a victim (Keene, 2015). With rates of shootings of unarmed Black men almost five times that of White men (Robinson, 2017), it's no wonder that many have become alarmed.

Ethnic Identity

It is risky to generalize about ethnic traits. There is much variety within each culture. For example, some of the literature on working with ethnicity points out that although the usual advice in interviewing technique is to look someone straight in the eye, that would be the wrong technique for some Asian, Latino, African and Native American groups, who might interpret that as hostility. In her autobiographical novel *The Woman Warrior* (1977), Maxine Hong Kingston shows that this advice would be wrong for an older woman, Moon Orchid, who was newly arrived from China, but right for her nieces, who were acculturated to the American tradition of looking people straight in the eye:

> "Good morning, Aunt," they said, turning to face her, staring directly into her face. Even the girls stared at her—like cat-headed birds. Moon Orchid jumped and squirmed when they did that. They looked directly into her eyes as if they were looking for lies. Rude. Accusing. They never lowered their gaze; they hardly blinked. . . Sometimes when the girls were reading or watching television, she crept up behind them with a comb and tried to smooth their hair, but they shook their heads, and they turned and fixed her with those eyes. She wondered what they thought and what they saw when they looked at her like that. She liked coming upon them from the back to avoid being looked at. They were like animals the way they stared. (Kingston, 1977, p. 133)

Stereotypes can both demean and exalt a group. For example, Asian Americans are sometimes seen as the "model minority," a homogenous group of high achievers taking over the campuses of the nation's most selective colleges. A study published by the Asian American Journal of Psychology (Gupta, Szymanski & Leong, 2011) found that stereotypes of this nature actually increased stress among Asian Americans while reducing their help-seeking behavior. An important guideline for a human service worker is to seek to understand how each individual person is affected by his ethnicity. To do that, there is no substitute for asking the person. If you were working with many people from a culture different from yours, you would be wise to read as much as possible about that culture, including the literature of the culture. That will enrich your life as well as help you in your work. If their language were different from yours, it would also help you to learn their language. We are the first to admit that this isn't easy.

The Power of Names

Before we discuss ethnicity, we need to explain some terms. You may wonder sometimes what you should call a particular group of people. The name that a group chooses to be known by is important because it reflects that group's self-identity. When a group is oppressed, the name it chooses becomes a political as well as a linguistic issue. For example, people with disabilities generally do not like to be called simply *disabled* rather than *people with disabilities* because the word *disabled* can be inferred to mean their whole self is defined by being deficient in some way.

As these name changes take place, not everyone in the group adopts them, and often the old names linger on alongside the new ones. For example, the word *colored* is still part of the name of the National Association for the Advancement of Colored People (NAACP). Many people still call themselves Mexican Americans rather than Chicanos. Although many indigenous people prefer the term *Native American* to *Indian*, some activists are now saying that both terms are reminders of colonialism. They prefer the term *First Nations* or *First Americans*, or their tribal names. *American Indian* is also an accepted term. The Census Bureau calls all Spanish-speaking people Hispanics but makes it clear that "persons of Hispanic origin may be of any race." In addition, many Hispanics prefer to be referred to as Latinos or Latinas.

As authors, we use the terms that we believe are in current usage by people who are in the forefront of their particular group's liberation struggles. When more than one term is in current usage, we use both. When you are in doubt about the term a particular person prefers, ask that person.

BROAD CATEGORIES DISGUISE LARGE DIFFERENCES Many different nations are lumped under the broad categories "Asian American" and "Latin American," which obscure enormous national differences. One could no more speak of a "typical Asian" than of a "typical European." Immigrants from Japan, China, Korea, Cambodia, Vietnam, Laos, and the Philippines all speak different languages and come from vastly different cultures. Immigrants from Colombia, El Salvador, Argentina, Guatemala, Mexico, and Puerto Rico all speak Spanish, but they too come from very different national cultures. Although Haiti and the Dominican Republic share the same Caribbean island, their people speak different languages and have different histories and cultures.

The Census Bureau has finally recognized the reality that many people are of more than one race, and in 2000 allowed people to select more than one racial category for the first time. The Census Bureau records "race" and "Hispanic ethnicity" as separate questions. Thus, a Hispanic person can be of any race. Officially, the proportion of ethnic groups in the United States in 2015 was as follows: Non-Hispanic White 61.6 percent; Black or African American 13.3 percent; Hispanic origin 17.6 percent; Asian American 5.6 percent; American Indian and Alaska Native 1.2 percent; Native Hawaiian and other Pacific Islander 0.2 percent; two or more races 2.6 percent (U.S. Census Bureau, 2015).

The Latino population has surpassed the Black population recently, and the growth of this diverse ethnic and cultural group is a trend that will continue into the future. It's predicted that this group will make up 56 percent of the population in the United States by the year 2060.

Discrimination Hurts Everybody

The college students who scrawl a swastika on a dorm door have been infected with a contagious, chronic virus. Having learned how to hate one group of people, they are likely to turn on others from backgrounds that they do not understand or that they feel threatened by.

Prejudice and discrimination have economic, psychological, and political causes. In recent years, the loss of jobs to other countries and the decline in the real value of the average worker's earnings in the United States have given rise to increased anxiety and fear about

Source: Digital Media Pro/Shutterstock

Thanksgiving, a national holiday in the United States, has a different meaning for Native Americans.

immigrants, both legal and illegal. Competition for jobs that pay a living wage has increased. Many working people look for scapegoats, and we have seen a frightening increase in hate groups such as the Ku Klux Klan, American Nazi Party, Aryan Nation, right-wing militias, and other White nationalist groups. The rise in hate crimes against minority groups noted earlier in this chapter serves as an example.

In his classical study of prejudice, psychologist Gordon Allport described a racist as a person who is suspicious and distrustful of anyone perceived as "different" and who is a "superpatriot," believing that all newcomers and those who are different from the mainstream pose a threat to an idealized and more secure past (Allport, 1954). Allport's study discovered that bigoted people go through life feeling threatened. They are insecure, cannot live comfortably with themselves or others, and are burdened by guilt. They insist on a strict code of morality in order to try to control their own instinctive feelings, which they mistrust.

Prejudice generally leads to discrimination against the feared group. It is a way to shore up the prejudiced person's weak ego by feeling that she is better than other people. It is also a way to protect privileges, by keeping other people out of jobs, housing, or other benefits they need.

Sociologist Robin Williams says that "racial ideologies developed to rationalize the social, economic, and political domination initially developed to enhance the resources and privileges of White Europeans" (1966), a domination that persists to the present day. Discrimination harms all workers. Discrimination against people of color and women enables management to pay workers low wages and governments to rationalize cutbacks in social spending. Anti-Semitism enables the power elite to use Jews as scapegoats to deflect anger away from those in control. As long as they are fighting with each other, minority groups cannot unite to bring about equality and equity for everyone.

The closing off of equal opportunities to people of color has not only caused incredible hardship to them and to their communities, but it has also created social instability that threatens all of society. Rising unemployment in the Black community has affected the structure of the Black family. Until the problems of unemployment and low income are solved, none of the other problems of the African-American community can be solved. Slavery, and the decades of racism that followed, created a workforce in which "Blacks still predominate in those occupations that in a slave society would be reserved for slaves" (Ezorsky, 1991, p. 74).

There is also a correlation between the numbers of unemployed young men and the crime rate (Sameem & Sylwester, 2018). The official response to crime has been to build more prisons, at great expense to the taxpayer. Unfortunately, this approach simply created more prisons to fill and a larger percentage of African Americans disproportionately incarcerated for crime at a huge annual cost to society and to the health and wellbeing of Black families (Western & Wildeman, 2009). Nationally our resources would have been better spent on job training and workforce development efforts.

Institutional Racism

How does institutional racism or sexism differ from individual racism or sexism? Imagine a situation in which no worker in an agency holds strong racist (or sexist) views, yet the policies of the agency are constructed so that minorities don't receive fair treatment. Such a situation is an example of **institutional racism** (or **institutional sexism**). It is larger, more powerful, and harder to change than one person's attitudes, because interconnected systems and policies perpetuate it. Even if a policy may appear fair and neutral on the surface, it can become racially discriminatory in the way it is practiced. Institutional racism is pervasive in all of society's institutions, including human services.

Institutional racism can be attacked through changing social policy and legislation. One of the purposes of a practice called "subsidized adoption," which was given federal support in the Child Welfare and Adoption Act of 1980, was to make adoption financially possible for those prospective parents who had been denied access to the chance to earn the money that qualified them to adopt. Now, more people of color and of low income are able to share their lives with those children who need a home, many of whom because of unequal opportunities are themselves from low-income and/or minority groups.

Another example of institutional racism occurs in the criminal justice system. The hypothetical stories that follow are based on research that contradicts the widespread belief that drug use is primarily confined to the Black ghetto. In actual fact, White youth sell and use drugs at higher rates than do Black youth. Institutional racism seems to be at work here:

> William Greer, an African-American youth, was picked up by the police while he was using crack on a ghetto street corner. He was unemployed and could not afford a lawyer to represent him in court. The legal aid lawyer appointed to defend him was overworked and could not spend much time with William; in fact, he talked with William for just a few minutes before court began. He advised William to plead guilty and plea bargain rather than ask for a jury trial. The judge, known to be "tough on drugs," sentenced him to a mandatory five-year prison sentence.
>
> Jack Clifford, a White college student, was sniffing cocaine at a party. He had purchased the drug in the suburbs from another student who was known as someone who always had drugs for sale. The party got wild and a neighbor called the police. Jack had to appear in court on a drug charge. His parents hired a skilled lawyer. She asked the judge to allow Jack to get psychiatric treatment for his drug habit rather than go to jail. The judge agreed, knowing that the parents were successful professionals in the community.

Generally, the deviant behavior of urban people who are low income (minorities are over-represented among the urban poor) is more likely to be defined as criminal and handled in the criminal justice system. Conversely, the deviant behavior of White people is more likely to be defined as a mental health problem and handled in the mental health system (Morales, 1978). To explain this difference, researchers look to the dynamics of institutional racism.

Research published in *Psychological Science* found that the more stereotypically Black a defendant appeared, the more likely they were to receive the death penalty (Eberhardt, Davies, Purdie-Vaughns, & Johnson, 2006). White defendants who kill White people are more likely to be sentenced to death than those who kill Black people (Petersen, 2015). All else being equal, Black people have been more likely to be sentenced to death than White people in the more than three decades since the Supreme Court reinstated the death penalty in 1976 (Liptak, 2008).

Institutional racism is pervasive in the criminal justice system. Black and Latino youth are treated more severely than White teenagers charged with comparable crimes. Due in part to the disproportionate contact that youth of color have at every step of the law enforcement process. Research has shown that minority youth are more likely than White youth to be arrested, held in jail, sent to juvenile or adult court for trial, and convicted, and are given longer prison terms. At each additional step in the juvenile justice system, things get worse for minority youth than for White youth. Here are the shocking facts (Mallett, 2018):

- Black youth, representing between 15 to 16 percent of the youth population, make up 26 percent of youth arrested, 31 percent of referrals to juvenile court, and 44 percent of the population adjudicated delinquent.
- Black youth are six times more likely that their White counterparts to be placed in detention while awaiting disposition. Latino youth are three time more likely.
- Black youth are five times more likely to be incarcerated in state facilities than White youth.

Unfortunately, the disparities within institutional racism accumulate, creating even greater barriers for members of minority groups to complete education, achieve gainful employment, and participate as full members of the larger community. The impact on the individual, and on his ability to be a successful husband and father, should not be underestimated. Across the country, a Black man is five times as likely to be incarcerated than a White man. In at least five states the rate of incarceration for black men over white men is at least ten times higher (Nellis, 2016).

The nation's war on drugs unfairly targets African Americans, who are much more likely to be imprisoned for drug offenses than White people, even though far more White people use illegal drugs than Black people. Overall, Black men are sent to state prisons on drug charges at 13 times the rate of White men. Drug transactions among Black people often are easier for police to target because they more often occur in public than do drug transactions among White people (Kain, 2011).

Despite the intention of our society's war on drugs, it's become increasingly clear that the effort has resulted in higher levels of incarceration for individuals who are not a danger to the larger community and for whom drug treatment and other rehabilitative services would make eminently more sense.

The United States has the highest incarceration rate on the planet—five times the world's average. A total of 6,741,400 people were incarcerated in 2015. The United States has 5 percent of the world's population but 25 percent of the world's prison population (Tsai & Scommegna, 2012). The Justice Department's Bureau of Justice Statistics attributes much of the increase to get-tough policies enacted during the 1980s and 1990s, such as mandatory drug sentences, "three strikes and you're out" laws for repeat offenders, and "truth in sentencing" laws that restrict early releases.

The "get-tough" sentencing laws adopted by the federal government and most states have forced judges to impose prison terms for certain crimes, including drunk driving and drug possession or selling. More than four in five drug-related arrests in 2008 were for possession of banned substances, rather than for their sale or manufacture. Four in ten of all drug arrests were for marijuana possession, according to FBI data (Eckholm, 2007). Today, with the growing success decriminalizing as well as legalizing marijuana, there is hope that this trend will be reversed.

The racial inequalities of the war on drugs also disproportionately affect pregnant women of color. Research has shown, for example, that pregnant women of color are 1.5 times more likely to be tested for illicit drugs, which in turn has grave legal consequences for the women (Kunns, et al., 2007).

These laws and practices have resulted in a disproportionate number of arrests of Black people and Latinos. The passage of the Fair Sentencing Act of 2010 has helped to reverse some this unfortunate trend, yet our country's reliance on stiff sentencing guidelines and incarceration over rehabilitation continues to disproportionally impact minorities and people of color.

The Obama administration sought to increase drug treatment as well as rehabilitation programs for people after release from prison. The Justice Department was working on recommendations for a new set of sentences for cocaine (Moore, 2009). Senator Jim Webb (D-VA) submitted a bill to Congress in 2017 to establish the National Criminal Justice Commission to study the criminal justice system and make recommendations for change. The effort to pass this legislation and to create an important review of our justice system has continued. Special interests and differing views on how to proceed kept the bill in a form of limbo, with the most recent form of the bill submitted on March 8, 2017, as S573 by Senator Gary Peters, Democrat from Michigan where it passed the Senate.

Discrimination Against Arab Americans and Muslim Americans

Discrimination against Arab and Muslim Americans has been around for a long time, especially in the workplace. The workplace can represent a point of intersection between the individual's personal and religious beliefs. In a largely westernized society, minority groups with different religious holidays, dress, and appearance can find themselves having to manage competing demands. The challenges faced by Arab Americans and Muslim Americans following 9/11 has caused an increase in the level of discrimination experienced at work, which has spread into many other areas of life (Mujtaba & Cavico, 2012).

The following basic facts will help you avoid simplistic assumptions (a.k.a. stereotypes) (Adams, 2002):

- Although some articles assert that Muslims are the second largest religious group in much of Europe and North America, it is very unclear exactly how many Muslims there are in the United States. Estimates of the number of Muslims range from a high of over 6 million to a low of 1.6 million. Why is there such a wide disparity and why does it matter? First of all, it is important to know that the U.S. Census does not ask people their religion.

Groups that hold to the higher number include those who want to assert the growing importance and/or electoral impact of this religious group. This includes many Muslim American Associations, as well as fear monger groups who decry the supposed threat they pose. Groups that espouse the significantly lower number might use that figure to minimize the relative importance and impact of the Muslim community in the overall society or to quell the fears of the alarmists.

Many people who are born into the Muslim faith do not necessarily attend a mosque, while other people are not born Muslim but have converted to the faith. In any event, this is a cautionary note—be skeptical about numbers and always think about who is making the estimates, what data they are using, and what they might gain from the information they present.

- There are 22 separate primarily Arab nations.

  There is no simple definition of who an Arab is. That word refers to those who speak the Arabic language—but some of those 22 countries' versions of Arabic are different from the others', and several Arab countries have internal ethnic groups who speak a totally different form of Arabic or some non-Arabic language. There are also several countries with large Muslim populations who do not speak Arabic or consider themselves Arabs.

- Two more terms that are often used are *Middle Easterners* and *Muslims* (not *Moslems*). The first refers to geography and the second to religion. But not all persons who consider themselves Arabs or Muslims come from the Middle East (e.g., some are from Indonesia, and others from some countries in Africa)—and not all Arabs are Muslims. There are three countries in the Middle East that are not Arab or wholly Muslim: Iran, Israel, and Turkey.

- While some Arab/Muslim Americans are very wealthy, many others are extremely poor, and there is a growing professional middle class. Arab/Muslim Americans as a whole are more highly educated than are many other ethnic groups.

- Arab/Muslim Americans are very family-oriented and often come from large families. They tend to shun social service intervention in private affairs. And while discussing concerns is a part of their culture, it's important to know that Muslims who adhere closely to the faith do not accept public touching of the opposite sex. Given this, a pat on the back or any friendly touch would not be well received.

- Most Americans know very little about the Muslim faith and the importance of their articles of clothing, such as head coverings and scarves, as well as of beards. Often the wearing of these is prohibited in schools and workplaces, and practicing Muslims may not be given the time or space for the daily prayers that are fundamental to their religion. Yet these observances are protected under the U.S. Constitution and Section VII of the Civil Rights Act.

When surveyed, more than half of Americans claim that Islam is not a mainstream religion and more than 75 percent of Muslims perceive discrimination against them (Green, 2017). In fact, only LGBTQ individuals are seen as facing more discrimination. Results of a survey among 2,010 adults revealed that two-thirds of non-Muslims say that *Islam* (another term for the religion) is very different from their own faith, although they are unsure what Muslims do believe (Pew Research Center, 2009).

But most importantly, a record number of Muslims in the United States are complaining of serious employment discrimination and harassment on the job. "There's a level of hatred and animosity that is shocking," says Mary Jo O'Neil, a regional attorney at the Phoenix office of the Equal Employment Opportunity Commission (EEOC). "I've been doing this work for 31 years and I've never seen such antipathy toward Muslim workers" (Greenhouse, 2010). Although Muslims make up about 2 percent of the population, they accounted for about 25 percent of the complaints submitted to the EEOC in 2009. During the same period, complaints by other religious and racial groups declined.

WHAT CAN A HUMAN SERVICE WORKER DO TO HELP STOP DISCRIMINATION AGAINST MUSLIM AMERICANS?

1. Learn more about the religion and customs of Muslims and Arabs, and whenever you encounter misinformation, try to set the record straight.
2. Support your clients and fellow citizens who are being denied their rights to practice their religion (as long as such practice does not endanger others) in their school or workplace by suggesting accommodations that administrators might make. When helpful suggestions fail to result in changes, encourage individuals who feel their rights are being abridged to file complaints with the top level of administration or the town or state commission against discrimination. It is always more effective if the complaints come from other members of the affected population and if coalitions are built with like-minded individuals outside of the ethnic group or religion.
3. While it is important to learn about groups other than the one you belong to, be aware that there are enormous differences both among various populations and within groups who share some characteristics. For example, some very observant Catholics oppose abortion rights and work to repeal *Roe v. Wade*, while other co-religionists reject abortion for themselves but support the legal right to choose. Similarly, some Jewish people eat only kosher foods and wear special clothes, whereas others eat what they wish and dress like the mainstream population, while still attending synagogue or special celebrations for Jewish holidays.

Anti-Semitism

There is a long history of discrimination against Jewish people. For hundreds of years in many countries of the world they have been persecuted and punished simply because they were born of Jewish parents and chose to follow their faith. In recent history, the Nazis exterminated 6 million Jews in death camps in the 1940s.

Since the end of WWII, discrimination against Jews has lessened a great deal in the United States, but they are still arbitrarily excluded from some neighborhoods, job promotions, or social clubs, causing pain and damage to their self-esteem (Phillips, 2016). American Nazi skinheads, the Ku Klux Klan, and militia groups still spread their virulently anti-Semitic messages. The Anti-Defamation League, a Jewish support organization, publishes a yearly audit of anti-Semitic assaults, vandalism of synagogues and centers, and harassment. In the first quarter of 2017 alone, there were more than 160 bomb threats against the Jewish Children's Museum and nine other Jewish institutions. In 2014, anti-Semitic acts grew a total of 3 percent over the course of one year, while assaults grew a total of 50 percent. Much of the growth in anti-Semitic expression is connected to the emboldened hate groups and the perceived legitimacy of simply speaking one's mind without regard to what is considered to be civil behavior by some and politically correct speech by others.

Jewish people constitute only about 2 percent of the entire U.S. population, and their numbers are diminishing because of low birth rates and marriage to non-Jewish people. Jewish Americans now have an out-marriage rate of 54 percent.

In contrast to people of color, no physical characteristics distinguish someone who is Jewish from someone who is not Jewish, because Jewish people have come here from every corner of the world. American Jews have no common language other than English (although Hebrew is spoken in Israel and in orthodox religious practice, and Yiddish was often spoken by an earlier generation of Eastern European Jewish immigrants). There is enormous variation in their involvement in Judaism and in their identification with its practices and culture. Although always a small percentage of the population, Jews have been in this country since the 1700s, with most coming from Eastern Europe in the 1900s.

Currently, most people of Jewish ancestry are clustered in urban areas, primarily in the greater metropolitan area of New York including the state of New Jersey, and in white-collar professions, although this was not so in their early immigrant days. They are not, as a group, economically deprived. They are also represented in most professions (Joffe, 2011).

Some Paradoxes of Prejudice Against Jewish People

Prejudice against whole groups of people is a very difficult phenomenon to understand because it serves many psychological, economic, and political purposes for those who express negative attitudes. It is difficult to eradicate these negative attitudes because the stereotypes and misinformation upon which they are built are essentially not rational. Those who hate others have some self-interest or some self-delusions in continuing to hate or act upon the hatred. The following paradoxes are issues to think about.

1. Despite the generally high level of economic security of Jews in the United States, their voting patterns have overwhelmingly supported candidates who place priority on the needs of the have-nots, women, and ethnic minorities over the demands of the haves and the industrial complex (Svonkin, 1998).

   In the 2016 presidential election, 70 percent of the Jewish community voted for Hillary Clinton. Members of Congress from Jewish backgrounds are among the most supportive of civil rights in both the Senate and House of Representatives. During the era of agitation for the end of racial segregation in the 1960s and 1970s, the Jewish community played a highly supportive role. Despite this tradition of Jewish people siding with the underdog, survey data indicate that many residents of low-income communities, predominately in urban areas, express many negative views when asked about their attitudes toward Jewish people. Residents of inner city communities considered to be low-income communities often perceive Jewish people as being the source of their exploitation in the person of landlords or employers. It is not an easy thing for people who find themselves left out of the American dream to find the source of their distress. Interestingly, minority group members with high levels of education (college and above) from the same ethnic groups hold less stereotyped opinions. With exposure to books and many different types of people, prejudice seems to lessen (Anti-Defamation League, 1998). Certainly it is clear to many people of color that Jewish people, because of their white skin, have had opportunities to disappear into the mainstream in ways that people of color rarely have the luxury of doing.

2. With the escalating violence between the state of Israel and the Palestinian refugees, and the cold war between Israel and many of the Arab nations, tensions between Muslims and Jews have grown alarmingly.

Some Paradoxes of Prejudice Against Arab Americans and Muslim Americans

It is now not uncommon for some U.S. citizens polled to suspect that members of the Muslim community in the United States are potential terrorists or terrorist sympathizers, regardless of whether they are citizens of long standing or recent immigrants. Wearing a headscarf or having a noticeably Arabic-sounding surname or "Arabic-looking" face can put a person in danger of rebuffs from neighbors, scrutiny from the authorities (the CIA, FBI, and local police), and, especially, the security screeners at airports.

In the most basic measure of negative attitudes, a 2017 Pew Research Poll asked Americans to rate their feelings about Islam and Muslims using a thermometer rating of 0–100, with 100 reflecting a warm and positive feeling about Islam and Muslims and 0 a cold and negative feeling. The results of the poll indicated that Americans rate Islam and Muslims at 48 degrees. And while this score reflects a cool feeling toward this group, it does represent a warming on the part of the American public, as the last poll rated Islam and Muslims at 40 degrees. The same poll shows that Republicans are more likely to believe that Muslims will support violence (70 percent versus 26 percent of Democrats), and together about half of those polled believe that Muslims are anti-American. At the same time, most individuals polled admit to knowing almost nothing about this religion, and most did not personally know a Muslim person. Many of the respondents based their opinions on the activities of a small number of people they learned about from various media sources.

Fighting Back Against the Rising Tide of Prejudice

There are some positive developments in resisting the rising tide of prejudice:

1. *Across the United States, groups have organized special interfaith vigils and celebrations.*   Many towns have enlarged or started human rights councils to protect the civil rights of citizens and to rally around those who have been harassed. Legal advocates have come forward to help when rights have been violated. Most importantly, conversations are taking place across religious lines (Antlitz, 2013).
2. *Many schools have begun or expanded their "teaching tolerance" curriculums.*   The Southern Poverty Law Center of Montgomery, Alabama (SPLC, Teaching Tolerance), has expanded its 20-year-old program that helps elementary and high school teachers promote tolerance in the classroom and learn how to respond to hate crimes. The classroom is one of the best places to counteract many of the misconceptions that lead children to adopt stereotypes and mistaken ideas about religious or racial groups.
3. Many colleges and adult education institutions have organized classes and seminars to teach both Jews and Muslims about their respective cultures as a way to advance understanding and acceptance of the dynamics of difference as well as the similarities each group shares. (Ari & Mula, 2017).
4. Advertisers and business owners who long ignored the substantial population of Muslim Americans are beginning to focus on ways to use the cultural aspects of the Muslim religion to help sell their products. Businesses are now recognizing that a growing middle class of Muslims in the United States as well as globally represents a vast and untapped marketing possibility to advance the sale of products and goods (Pasquarelli, 2018).

Advertisers that try to target their programs or ads to the Muslim community will face the same dilemmas they would face if selling to the Protestant, Catholic, or Jewish communities. Just what approach companies should take to reach Muslims is far from clear. The market is diverse, including African Americans, South Asians, Caucasians, and people from the Middle East, some very observant, others quite secular.

Affirmative Action

Affirmative action, a policy that gives some preference in admissions, hiring, or promotion to equally qualified members of underrepresented minority groups, is one of the mechanisms that attempt to redress the inequalities that minorities have historically encountered. African Americans have not only suffered from slavery, but also from many forms of discrimination since slavery. In housing, for example, the Federal Housing Administration—which underwrote one-third of all new housing construction from 1937 to 1972—required that all properties "continue to be occupied by the same social and racial classes". The Interstate Highway Act of 1956 directly displaced 330,000 families considered low income, mostly Black. State laws and local zoning ordinances artificially concentrated both poverty and wealth, and sharply segregated people on the basis of ethnicity and social class (Chappell, 2004).

Federal support for affirmative action has weakened since the 1980s, and the policy continues to be under fierce attack. White people who feel they have been denied opportunities because of affirmative action have fought it in court on the grounds that it violates the equal protection clause of the Fourteenth Amendment. In a case brought against the University of Michigan, the Supreme Court ruled in 2003 that colleges could consider race in admissions but must also treat students as individuals and not accept or reject them solely on the basis of their skin color. Soon after this decision was handed down, Ward Connerly, a member of the University of California Board of Regents who led successful ballot initiatives in California and Washington state that ended racial preferences, continued his campaign in Michigan to put a similar measure on the ballot there. In Colorado, the bill that would have banned affirmative action in the state was defeated by one vote in the Republican-controlled state senate. That one vote was cast by Senator Lew Entz, a Republican, who crossed party lines to deliver the deciding vote. Senator Entz had a large constituency of Latinos, who favored affirmative action (Klein, 2004). In 2016 the Supreme Court ruled in *Fisher v. University of Texas* that university admission offices may still use race as a consideration in determining acceptance, but the court indicated that affirmative action may not be allowed in all circumstances.

A 2016 Gallup poll in response to the Supreme Court ruling found that 63 percent of respondents felt that race should not be considered in college admissions. Six in ten Republicans opposed such programs, while 67 percent of Democrats favored them. However, there was broader support for programs that make special efforts to help people from low-income backgrounds get ahead, regardless of gender or ethnicity. Eight in ten favored this, with just 15 percent opposed (Dutton, 2009).

While affirmative action is often divisive and cannot by itself achieve racial equality, we believe it is still an essential device to counteract institutional barriers to minority advancement. Ezorsky (1991) reports, for example, that 80 percent of executives find their jobs through networking, and over 86 percent of available jobs do not appear in the classified ads. Given this, White men in positions of power have a leg up in their ability to network for high-paying positions, increasing their mobility while furthering the distance from and negative impact on minority populations, who interestingly enough didn't even have the opportunity to apply.

DiTomaso (2013) reports that White people receive assistance in obtaining positions through racially exclusive networks that result in 68 percent of positions obtained and up to 75 percent for

Source: © Steve Greenberg/Seattle Post Mariner

The effectiveness of affirmative action continues to be hotly debated in America today.

White males. Yet individuals who receive this type of racially biased support believe that they have attained their positions based on their own merit and good work. This "invisible" support system, as represented by the benefactor's unknowing advantages, serves to perpetuate discrimination in employment practice.

Furthermore, some hiring criteria, such as diploma requirements and standardized tests, often work against minorities. Many tests are culturally biased, drawing material from the White middle-class world. This bias can be overcome either by constructing culturally sensitive tests or by giving training in test taking. For example, the highest pass rate on the National Teachers' Exam is by graduates of Grambling University, which has a primarily African-American student body. That has been attributed in part to the fact that the university requires its students to take a test-taking course (Hacker, 1992).

Many universities have admission practices that favor people in the upper class. Critics say that a policy of "legacy admissions," which gives preference to children of alumni, amounts to affirmative action for upper-class White people. President George W. Bush was admitted to Yale University through a legacy policy, as he himself has admitted that he was not accepted to Yale on the strength of his grades. The legacy policy at Texas A&M University helped more than 300 White students qualify for admission every year but only about 30 Black people and Hispanics. After Texas A&M did away with affirmative action for minorities, the school decided that it was inconsistent to keep a legacy policy that favored White students and did away with that policy. Georgia and California have also ended legacy policies in their state schools (Talk of the Nation, 2004a).

Affirmative action has become a lightning rod that attracts people's anxieties about race. It "dominates the nation's obsession with race relations" (Holmes, 1997, p. 1) and seems to have become magnified out of all proportion to its real significance in people's lives. When public opinion polls ask White people whether they ever lost a job or a promotion or were denied college admission as a result of affirmative action, few say yes. Affirmative action costs little in comparison with social services. It hardly affects the majority of Americans. Most students who are eligible for college are accepted, regardless of affirmative action (Holmes, 1997, p. 12).

Some people argue that economic diversity is as important as racial diversity, and that we need to refocus on a new kind of affirmative action based on social class. Affirmative action helps the middle-class more than minorities who are low-income. Both White and Black People who are low-income are also disadvantaged in college admissions. In the 146 most selective universities, students with low-income backgrounds make up only 3 percent of the student body. In two-year colleges generally, about two-thirds of those from the top economic quartile go on to a four-year college, while in the bottom economic quartile, only about one-fifth do (Talk of the Nation, 2004b). This economic stratification is getting worse as colleges increasingly grant scholarship money on the basis of merit rather than need. As college tuition becomes more expensive, low-income students are increasingly priced out of college.

IMMIGRATION

As the United States celebrated the 500th anniversary of Columbus's "discovery" of the nation, people from the First Nations reminded us that they had already "discovered" this nation and had been living in it for a long time before Columbus appeared on their shores. The rest of us emigrated here from another country, and the African slaves were forcibly brought here. Some Mexican Americans came with the territory when the United States won the Mexican–American War in 1848 and annexed Mexican land in the Southwest. The following are vignettes about three children who immigrated after the Vietnam War and what it was like for them.

A twelfth-grade Lao Mien boy who emigrated from Laos at age 14 told an interviewer:

The school was so big! There was no one who could speak Mien and explain to me. My uncle had told me if I needed any help to go to the Dean. My teacher asked me something and I didn't understand her. So I just said, "Dean, Dean," because I needed help. That is how I got my American name. She was asking me "What is your name?" Now everybody calls me Dean. It is funny, but it is also sad. My name comes from not knowing what was going on.

A ninth-grade Filipino girl who immigrated with her parents declared:

Our parents don't come [to school functions] because they don't know any English. I don't even tell them when they are supposed to come. They dress so different and I don't want our parents to come because the others will laugh at them and tease us. We are ashamed.

A Cambodian boy who immigrated was reminded of his past:

In an elementary school in San Francisco, a teacher is playing "hangman" with her class as a spelling lesson. One "Limited-English-Proficient" (LEP) student, a Cambodian refugee, bursts into tears and becomes hysterical. Later, through an interpreter, the teacher learns that the student had witnessed the hanging of his father in Cambodia. (Portes & Rumbaut, 1990, pp. 180–181)

People immigrate because they need work or perhaps their own country is at war or in crisis. Sometimes, as with the legacy of the war in Vietnam, our own country has helped to bring about the crisis conditions. Ultimately the problem of immigration would have to be solved by stabilizing countries' political situation and by ending world poverty. Yet instead of alleviating poverty, some national and international policies have increased poverty in underdeveloped nations:

> The United States supported repressive military dictatorships in the Southern Cone between 1964 and 1985, leading to waves of political refugees and exiles. The U.S.'s wars against nationalist and leftist movements and governments in Central America in the 1980s set millions of migrants in motion. Then in the 1990s the North American Free Trade Agreement (NAFTA) between Canada, Mexico, and the United States had a devastating impact on the Mexican economy, ruining farmers already struggling financially who also migrated to seek work in the United States. More generally, the Washington Consensus, the regime of neoliberal globalization imposed on Latin America by the United States, the International Monetary Fund, and the World Bank, resulted in a more or less continual crisis of their economies causing high unemployment and persistent poverty, which has driven more and more farmers and workers to seek work in the United States. (La Botz, 2007)

IMMIGRATION IN THE UNITED STATES

Some Background on the Current Situation

The United States has more immigrants in the country today than at any other time since 1910, the high tide of the great European immigration that began in the 1880s. More than 13 percent of the U.S. population today is made up of foreign-born individuals—more than 43.2 million people. Over half come from Latin America, one-quarter from Asia, and most of the rest from Europe, with others from the rest of the world. Minorities now make up one-third of the U.S. population (Lopez & Bialik, 2017).

Illegal immigrants often suffer sweatshop-like working conditions and low pay because they are afraid that if they complain they will be reported to immigration authorities and deported. Sadhbh Walshe (2013) describes how some domestic workers who are undocumented immigrants are treated like slaves by rich Americans.

Fluctuations in Immigration Policy

The immigration policy of the United States has been dynamic, moving between two ends of a continuum; the country's need for labor and a level of xenophobia where citizens fear losing their jobs to foreigners. It has also been influenced by foreign policy. When the country needed workers in the nineteenth and early twentieth centuries to build the railroads, work in the mines and the steel mills, and weave cloth, it especially welcomed European immigrants for these jobs. African slaves were brought in primarily to work on southern cotton plantations. Chinese immigrants were brought in to help build the railroads in the West, especially for menial work that White men refused to do.

After the railroads were built, the country no longer wanted Chinese people, and passed restrictive legislation to keep them out. The Chinese men who had built the railroad weren't even allowed to be present when the golden spike was driven to mark the joining of the Central Pacific and Union Pacific Railroads, creating the first transcontinental railroad (Hsu, 1971). This was one example of the rising tide of racist fears that led to the United States excluding people of color. Some of the fears were fueled by competition for jobs. Organized labor feared that Chinese laborers would be used as strike breakers, which did sometimes happen.

Immigration policy in the United States has always made distinctions by race, ethnicity, and socioeconomic class. Japanese people were excluded in 1907, except in Hawaii, where they were needed as agricultural workers. In 1924, the United States adopted a national-origins system that limited admissions from each European country to 3 percent of the foreign-born population here as of the 1910 census. That resulted in favoring northern Europeans over southern and eastern Europeans for nearly half a century. Most Asians were still excluded, but there were no limits on migrants from the Western Hemisphere (Schmitt, 2001).

The eugenics-based racism that produced the restrictive 1924 immigration law increased the distance between White and Black people. White immigrants bought homes in racially restricted areas, resulting in all-White neighborhoods, and a kind of American apartheid.

The civil rights movement helped to achieve more fairness in immigration policy. The Immigration and Nationality Act of 1965 eliminated racial criteria and replaced country-by-country quotas with a system that awarded lawful permanent resident (LPR) status[*] based largely on family or employer sponsorship.

Immigration policy before 1965 used statistical data to classify the ethnic origins of immigrants, resulting ultimately in a list in 1907 that drove immigration policy by race (Weil, 2001).

But the pendulum swung again in the 1980s. The Immigration Reform and Control Act, passed by Congress in 1986, was a response to increasing concern about illegal immigration, particularly across the Mexican border, but also from other war-ravaged Latin American countries. Now employers can be fined and sentenced to prison for hiring undocumented immigrants. That is why, if you start a part-time job at a restaurant or store, your employer will ask you to give proof of your citizenship.

The act has contributed to discrimination against both legal and illegal immigrants. Many employers hire and then exploit illegal immigrants, forcing them to accept substandard wages and working conditions because they fear deportation. Employers also sometimes assume that anyone who has a Spanish name or speaks English with an accent is an illegal immigrant, and so they refuse to hire immigrants who actually have valid work permits (Hosoda, Nguyen, & Stone-Romero, 2012).

The Immigration Act of 1996 provided for "expedited removal" of immigrants and represented a major change in the country's treatment of immigrants. Columnist Robert Kuttner saw it as one aspect of a growing police state. Kuttner said that under the provisions of the act,

> People guilty of only technical lapses have been led off in handcuffs and jailed. Legitimate Canadian and Mexican business people, including corporate board members, have been barred from entering the United States and treated like common criminals because they lacked some immigration form. Other long-time legal residents have been deported abruptly because of minor legal problems decades ago. The law disdains due process, makes judicial appeal almost impossible, and reinforces the thuggish tendencies of the Immigration and Naturalization Service. Fit parents are separated from their children and caught up on a family court judicial system that in some cases actively discriminates against both documented and undocumented immigrants. (Rogerson, 2013)

The 1996 law changed the rules for about 300,000 refugees from Nicaragua, El Salvador, and Guatemala who fled civil wars in the 1980s and were given temporary protection from

---

[*]Someone with Lawful Permanent Resident (LPR) status can work without limitation, travel in and out of the country, and petition for a spouse and children. After five years as an LPR, she can apply for naturalization and become a U.S. citizen. If married to a U.S. citizen, an individual with LPR status can apply for citizenship after three years instead of five years.

deportation. The law made it more difficult for them to stay in the country ("Flaws in Immigration Law," 1997). The law made it harder for people to go back to their country of origin and re-enter this country. It also stipulated that legal immigrants who leave the country and then return—even after a brief vacation—could be subjected to harassment and imprisonment without due process if they have any criminal record. This includes the most minor infractions. Unauthorized use of cable television service, for example, can be treated as an "aggravated felony" under the 1997 law, and the Immigration and Customs Enforcement (ICE; formerly a part of Immigration and Naturalization Service, INS) may detain legal immigrants and begin deportation proceedings against them for it (*The Progressive*, 1997).

The Justice Department's attempt to speed deportations of thousands of immigrants convicted of crimes in the United States was dealt a setback in 1999 when the Supreme Court let stand the Court of Appeals decisions that gave those immigrants the right to judicial review of their cases (Vicini, 1999).

The Immigration Act of 1996 and the benefit-cutting effects of the Personal Responsibility Act created panic in the immigrant community. Immigrants and their advocates fought back through both legal and political means. Lawyers in California challenged the law's income requirement as unconstitutional and discriminatory (Lewis, N. A. 1997). The 20 members of the Hispanic Congressional Caucus mobilized their resources to fight both the immigration law and the cuts in benefits of the Personal Responsibility Act. Congress and President Bill Clinton decided that they had gone too far in attacking immigrants, and in 1997 they eased some of the immigration curbs of the law.

The fierceness of the anti-immigration sentiment was beginning to abate before the 9/11 terrorist attacks. The AFL-CIO, in a 180-degree policy turn, shifted from denouncing illegal immigrants as a threat to American workers, to calling for a general amnesty for them all (meaning they could stay and join a union). Some states granted driver's licenses to illegal immigrants. Virtually no business owners worried at all about being fined for hiring illegal immigrants. Much of the shift in attitude stemmed from the need for workers. Offering driver's licenses to illegal immigrants so they can get to work benefits not only the workers but also the employers who need them (Pertman, 2001).

After the attacks on the World Trade Center and the Pentagon, fears about terrorist attacks led the White House and Congress to move rapidly toward making immigration laws tighter. The reversal, which came just as the administration had considered loosening its policies, sent a chill through legal and illegal Latino immigrants. Maria Blanco, national senior counsel for the Mexican American Legal Defense and Educational Fund, said, "People are very disappointed that, so soon after the debate seemed to be moving forward on immigration, it has taken a few steps backwards. Latinos don't want to be tainted by this broad brush" (Sterngold, 2001, p. A20).

In 2008, Congress authorized the Secure Fence Act, a multi-billion-dollar plan to build hundreds of miles of fencing along the southern border of the United States to stem the flow of undocumented immigrants from Mexico (NOW, 2008). The bill was controversial. An organization of mayors, county commissioners, and economists, named the Texas Border Coalition, filed a federal lawsuit opposing the wall and asking for the construction to be halted. Two environmental groups, Sierra Club and Defenders of Wildlife, supported the suit. Many homeowners complained that the wall cut through the middle of their properties. The president of the University of Texas said she had not been consulted about plans to build the fence, and that it would leave the campus's technology center and golf course on the Mexican side of the fence (Archibold & Preston, 2008).

Although the Department of Homeland Security didn't build the full 700 miles of fence originally planned, it did tighten up gaps in the fence where immigrants had found easy access. During the 2016 presidential campaign, Donald Trump once again raised the spectre of building a great wall along the southern border. To cheers of "build the wall," candidate and then President Trump heralded the virtues of keeping illegal immigrants out of our country and away from jobs that belong to American citizens, a theme that continues to play a role in the Trump Administration's political- and policy-based interests.

It has become increasingly dangerous for immigrants to cross the border as they have to travel longer distances in the hot sun. Border patrol agents are aggressive in catching and deporting immigrants, sometimes killing them. On April 1, 2011, Arizona activists marched against the increasing use of excessive and sometimes lethal force against illegal immigrants, and even against Hispanic citizens. Three teens who were illegal immigrants were shot and killed while more than 440,000 individuals are detained each year due to their immigration status. Under government policy more than 34,000 beds are maintained to hold detainees in more than 200 facilities across the United States. Of the 80,000 unaccompanied immigrant children seeking entrance to the United States each year, approximately 75,000 are deported upon arrival. These children confront U.S. state and immigration officials who tend to be "oppressive and terrifying rather than reassuring and protective" (Lopez, 2010). The few who are allowed to stay are transferred to the Office of Refugee Resettlement Division of Unaccompanied Children's Services, but some children are thrown into detention facilities where they must await the outcomes of their immigration cases behind bars.

In 2017, ICE carried out increased immigration raids in factories, meatpacking plants, the offices of companies that subcontract janitorial services, and other workplaces employing immigrants. This was sparked in part by President's Trump's executive order on immigration that was quickly overturned by the federal courts, though this was denied by officials indicating that

Source: Shutterstock/B Donnellan

Immigration reform continues to be an ongoing issue bringing New Americans to the street to express their desire for effective reform.

the raids were "business as usual." ICE called the factories "crime scenes" because immigration law forbids employers to hire illegal immigrants. This made the public think of the workers as criminals, although immigration violations are civil violations, not criminal violations. Many of the workers were deported and some were separated from their children. However, the employers received only light reprimands and none went to jail. (Immigration courts are civil courts. That is why foreign nationals in deportation proceedings have no right to court-appointed counsel even though the proceedings "feel" criminal. They do have a right to due process; the Constitution protects all persons in the Unites States, not just citizens or LPRs.)

The Southern Poverty Law Center investigated **guest worker programs** that allow labor contractors to maintain blacklists of workers who work slowly or demand their rights. Guest workers, with the support of attorneys, spend years trying to receive wages owed them, and the Department of Labor almost never decertifies contractors who abuse guest workers (Southern Poverty Law Center, 2013). Workers often find themselves paying huge entry fees and become indebted to a single employer during the term of their visa, without regard to the conditions they find themselves in.

The Current State of Immigration Reform

With the election of Donald Trump as president of the United States, the landscape for immigration reform promises to undergo significant changes. In the very first days of the new administration, long-standing practices such as "catch and release," where illegal immigrants would be arrested and released until their processing, were overturned in favor of expanding the government's capacity to detain illegal immigrants. As a part of this, the administration is also considering immediate deportation while the individual's immigration case is reviewed. The practice, known as expedited removal—which had been limited by the Obama administration to individuals detained within two weeks of entering the country—has now been restored to its earlier vigor. In these instances, there isn't a requirement for a judge to hear the individual's case. Children arriving alone continue to have the right to a hearing before a judge, but the policy now contemplates prosecution for parents of children who travel alone. Advocates worry that this approach will drive parents of children who arrive here illegally further underground, leaving children without the support of their parents.

Dreamers, the children of illegal immigrants that were provided legal status under the Development, Relief and Education for Alien Minors (DREAM) Act, are for now maintaining their legal status under the current administration, though controversy abounds, as local authorities have accused some individuals of illegal activity as a way to negate their Dreamer status in order to pursue deportation. Similarly, the administration hopes to reinstitute the use of local police as de facto immigration agents through the use of a program known as 287(g). The Obama administration had previously put this program on hold due to abuses by local police departments that used this newfound authority as a way to target the Latino community through racial profiling.

In addition, the new administration is concerned with reporting on issues related to illegal immigration. Of particular interest is the amount and types of crime perpetrated by illegal immigrants on American citizens. ICE planned to release weekly reports about cities and towns that arrest and release illegal immigrants. Born of the Administration's view that illegal immigrants are the source of crime in our communities this is seen as a shot over the bow of cities and communities that have chosen to become sanctuary cities. The Trump administration believes that these reports will be a way to help build safer communities, though there is little evidence that illegal immigrants are involved in crime at a rate higher than other individuals. In fact, some studies have shown just the opposite (Perez-Pena, 2017).

Under the Bush administration, certain privacy rights were extended to illegal immigrants. Under the Trump administration, the limits on what can be shared have been lifted. This, combined with the president's efforts to build a larger ICE force, will certainly result in the detaining of more individuals and increased deportation. And while immigration advocates vow to fight these steps, the administration remains resolute.

KEY ELEMENTS IN THE IMMIGRATION DEBATE

Immigration is a very complex issue, and many people are confused about it. It engenders fierce, sometimes vitriolic debate. The following are some arguments and issues to consider as you think about the fate of immigrants in the United States.

1. *Some people compare present immigrants unfavorably to past immigrants.* Much of the anti-immigration sentiment seems to reflect a belief that there are "good" immigrants and "bad" immigrants. People whose ancestors arrived in the late nineteenth and early twentieth centuries believe that this qualifies them as real Americans. The early immigrants are remembered as good, hardworking assimilators, while the new ones are "inferior, parasitic, and implacably foreign" (Walker, 1995, p. 62). Prejudice arising from 9/11 and the rise of terrorism globally has unfortunately heighted the "unfavorable immigrant" view for individuals from Syria, the African nation of Somalia, and other largely Muslim nations, which in turn has driven the executive branch's policy on immigration practice.

Source: Courtesy of Barbara Schram

While watching a festive parade in a small Mexican village, we need to look past the colorful costumes and think about the onlookers. Many of them, unable to find work, will make the torturous trek across our borders.

2. *People who are anti-immigrant sometimes exaggerate the health problems that immigration creates.* For example, in 2005, Lou Dobbs (a popular TV commentator) claimed there had been 7,000 cases of leprosy in this country over the preceding three years and attributed it to immigration. He said, "The invasion of illegal aliens is threatening the health of many Americans." In 2007, Dobbs appeared on the *60 Minutes* TV show. Researchers for the show had checked his statement, and on the show, interviewer Leslie Stahl said there didn't seem to be much evidence for it. The official leprosy statistics do show about 7,000 diagnosed cases—but over the preceding thirty years, not the preceding three years. James L. Krahenbuh, the director of the National Hansen's Disease Program, said, "It is not a public health problem—that's the bottom line. . . . The 137 reported cases last year were fewer than in any year from 1979 to 1996" (Leonhardt, 2007).

3. *People who oppose immigration say that immigrants are costing taxpayers money and taking advantage of such programs as welfare, Medicaid, and food stamps.* Alabama politicians who believed this passed a bill called The Deficit Reduction Act, which required a birth certificate or other proof of citizenship from people before they could qualify to continue or begin receiving Medicaid. The bill resulted in more than 5,000 people losing their Medicaid coverage for failing to provide a birth certificate or other proof of citizenship. Children were the largest group affected, and Black people were disproportionately affected.

Alabama's Medicaid commissioner said that Alabama doesn't have a large problem with illegal immigrants trying to cheat the state out of Medicaid dollars. Most of the people who lost their Medicaid were not immigrants, but they were unable to provide the requested documentation. After Medicaid officials realized what was happening, people were put back on the rolls (Angus Reid Global Monitor, 2007).

A bill was filed in the Texas legislature in 2007 that would not only deny public services to undocumented immigrants but also strip their American-born children of benefits as well. The bill challenged the Fourteenth Amendment to the U.S. Constitution, ratified in 1868, which states that all persons born in the United States are citizens of the United States and of the state where they reside (Bustillo, 2007). While the measure failed to pass given the existence of the Fourteenth Amendment, it serves as an exemplar of growing legislative efforts to limit the rights of children born in the United States to undocumented immigrants.

A look at the facts contradicts exaggerated fears about the cost of immigration. The largest cost is the border control and law enforcement measures, according to a study by the Congressional Budget Office. This study concluded that legalization of immigrants would contribute tens of billions to the federal treasury (Milligan, 2007).

Illegal foreign-born residents contribute in many ways, such as paying Social Security and Medicare taxes. In 2002, illegal immigrants paid $6.4 billion in Social Security taxes for benefits that they would never receive (Steinberg, 2005). Illegal immigrants are not eligible for need-based aid, except limited emergency medical care and children's health care, as well as elementary and secondary schooling. Legal immigrants must be in the United States lawfully for five years before they're eligible for aid such as food stamps and welfare. The exceptions are refugees, including Cubans, who are immediately eligible for federal need-based aid. United States–born children of illegal immigrants are citizens and are also eligible for such assistance (Milligan, 2007).

Undocumented immigrants were guaranteed access to a free public education (kindergarten through twelfth grade) by a 1982 Supreme Court decision, but the 1996

Immigration Act prohibits undocumented immigrants from accessing any postsecondary education benefit. As a result, many states have blocked access to in-state tuition for undocumented students. An estimated 60,000 undocumented students graduate from the nation's high schools each year, and most are unable to pay out-of-state tuition at their public college, although a few states allow them to pay in-state tuition. In jurisdictions where states no longer allows in-state tuition benefits for undocumented students, research has shown that Mexican youth are 49 percent less likely to be enrolled in school (Bozick & Miller, 2014).

4. *The people who benefit most economically from immigration, aside from the immigrants themselves, are businesses and the wealthy.*   David Card, an economist who studies immigration, said that when he moved to San Francisco, he noticed some changes from his lifestyle in Princeton. "In California, a professor has at least a gardener and maybe two, someone who cleans his house, and two or three day-care workers," he said (Cassidy, 1997, pp. 41–42).

The rich, despite the law prohibiting that practice, hire many undocumented immigrants. Two prominent cases involved people who were nominated for federal attorney general—Zoe Baird and Kimba Wood. President Clinton withdrew their nominations because it became known that they had employed illegal immigrants as nannies.

Aside from the economic benefits, we all derive enormous social and cultural benefits from living in a country with a large and diverse immigrant population.

5. *Some pro-immigration advocates minimize problems with immigration, such as its effect on African Americans.*   In his article "Immigration, African Americans, and Race Discourse," Stephen Steinberg points out that African Americans have been historically disadvantaged by immigration (2005). After the Civil War, the 4 million emancipated slaves could have filled the labor needs of the North. However, businesses preferred to import White immigrants from Europe:

> Here was a missed opportunity to integrate Blacks into the industrial labor force during the critical early stages of industrialization, and the failure to do so set the nation on a path of racial division and conflict that continues to this day. (Steinberg, 2005, p. 43)

Steinberg questions whether the influx of another 25 million immigrants since 1965, and the millions more of undocumented workers, has "again made the Negro 'superfluous,' undercutting Black progress. Here was another missed opportunity to integrate Blacks into the economic mainstream" (2005, p. 44).

Steinberg makes it clear that he is not calling into question the rights of immigrants. He says, "I am the grandson of immigrants, and the new immigrants have as much right to be here as I do, and to claim all the rights of their adopted nationality" (p. 45). But, he says, the rights of immigrants should not override the rights of African Americans.

> Immigration should be part of a national manpower policy that protects the interests of immigrants and native workers alike. A laissez-faire policy that relegates millions of immigrants to the vagaries of the "free market" only throws low-wage workers in pitiless competition with each other, and closes off avenues of mobility into more desirable job sectors. As a result, current policy exacerbates existing inequalities along lines of race, ethnicity, gender, and class. (p. 53)

Some people have used the argument that immigration hurts African Americans in order to oppose legalizing it.

Fletcher points out that where immigrants are displacing African Americans, as in construction, it is happening because employers want lower-paid, non-union workers. The solution is not to oppose immigration, but to oppose the lowering of wages:

> The problem is the system. And, just as African American workers were used in certain industries as low-wage workers in the late 19th and early-to-mid 20th centuries, in order to undercut higher paid workers, this changed dramatically through a combination of unionization and the Black Freedom Movement. . . . Low-wage workers will not be competitors if they cease being low-wage workers, i.e., if they are unionized and gain power in their workplaces or jobs. (Fletcher, 2007)

Guidelines for Ethnic-Sensitive Human Service Work

People who have been discriminated against because of their skin color have reason to be mistrustful of White-dominated organizations, including (and sometimes especially) human service agencies. Unfortunately, agencies have a poor track record of eliminating discrimination. After the Civil War, such agencies were almost always segregated and poorly funded. The Charity Organization Society served very few people of color. In *The Woman Warrior*, Kingston gives an example of the feeling of alienation created by discrimination:

> Lie to Americans. Tell them you were born during the San Francisco earthquake. Tell them your birth certificate and your parents were burned up in the fire. Don't report crimes; tell them we have no crimes and no poverty. Give a new name every time you get arrested; the ghosts* won't recognize you. Pay the new immigrants twenty-five cents an hour and say we have no unemployment. And, of course, tell them we're against Communism. Ghosts have no memory anyway and poor eyesight (Kingston, 1977, pp. 184–185).

The distrust that discrimination creates affects all of us. An individual White person may never have discriminated against anyone, but the climate of fear that prejudice has created in a society may make every White person seem like a potential enemy until he proves trustworthy.

Of course, people of color can also express prejudice against White people when they believe that all White people are alike. And some light-skinned Black people are prejudiced against dark-skinned Black people.

GUIDELINES TO BUILD TRUST

1. *Learn the culture.*   You can learn a lot about a person's culture by asking sensitive questions. No matter how much you have read about a group's culture, you won't know how it affects the specific person you are talking with until you ask.

   Here is an example of an incorrect assessment of a person based on a lack of understanding of the culture:

   > A young Southeast Asian woman was ordered by the court to attend therapy for repeatedly shoplifting merchandise from a neighborhood grocery store. The young woman had been in this country less than a year and spoke minimal English. She was assigned to a White therapist who after several failed attempts to get the young woman to

---

*In this story of Chinese people in San Francisco, the Chinese regarded all non-Chinese people as "ghosts" because they seemed as alien as ghosts. Interestingly, Kingston's protagonist saw black ghosts as more friendly than white ghosts.

communicate her reasons for shoplifting informed the court that the client was withdrawn, uncommunicative, and appeared depressed.

A young Asian paralegal working in the office at the time read the case and was able to shed some light on the problem. The Asian paralegal related that the item, repeatedly stolen from the store, sanitary napkins, was not openly displayed, or sold in public markets in the country of the Southeast Asian woman. . . . In the woman's country, it was considered highly improper for women to publicly acknowledge their monthly menses. Purchasing the pads outright or explaining her reasons for taking this product would have caused this woman great embarrassment and public shame, not to mention a breach of her ethnic and cultural values on proper conduct. (Boyd, 1990, p. 160)

2. *Create a welcoming atmosphere.*   As soon as they walk in the office, people should receive the message that they are welcome. If the agency's clientele includes people who speak languages other than English, posters on the wall and informational brochures should be written in those language as well as in English. The magazine rack could include diverse reading material from local journals and newspapers.

3. *Acknowledge the validity of their suspicion of you.*   Research has shown that people from minority groups are less likely to return to a human service agency after the first interview than are people from the dominant culture.

Kingston talks of the reticence about discussing intimate affairs within the traditional Chinese culture, but she indicates that it was a much more serious offense to share secrets with the ghosts:

> They came nosing at windows—Social Worker Ghosts; Public Health Nurse Ghosts; Factory Ghosts recruiting workers during the war (they promised free child care, which our mother turned down); two Jesus Ghosts who had formerly worked in China. We hid directly under the windows, pressed against the baseboard until the ghost, calling us in the ghost language so that we'd almost answer to stop its voice, gave up. (Kingston, 1977, p. 98)

The person who suffers from discrimination feels a dreadful wound, a humiliating degradation, or tremendous rage. (Most tragically, the individual may turn the rage inward against herself.) *The Autobiography of Malcolm X* presents a vivid literary description of these feelings. An outstanding leader of American Muslims in the 1960s, Malcolm X was assassinated in 1965. He gives us a personalized account of his disillusionment as he writes bitterly about the state welfare workers who claimed to be "helping" him. In the course of his life, he encountered a good many helping agents of the state and found them wanting. When he was a young boy, his father was murdered by White people, and his mother had to struggle to keep the family together, eking out a living by cleaning houses. She hated to accept welfare assistance, but when she finally gave in, she was harassed by welfare investigators. They termed her *crazy* for, among other behaviors, refusing to eat pork, even though she was a Seventh-day Adventist and it was against her religion to do so. They also opposed her seeing a male friend, even though this made her happier than she had ever been before. Malcolm X held them partially responsible for his mother having to go to a psychiatric hospital, and he said they were as vicious as vultures (Malcolm X & Haley, 1966).

Malcolm was placed in a foster home, and this is what he thought about that:

> Soon the state people were making plans to take over all of my mother's children. . . .
> [A] Judge McClellan in Lansing had authority over me and all of my brothers and

sisters. We were "state children," court wards; he had the full say-so over us. A White man in charge of a Black man's children! Nothing but legal, modern slavery however kindly intentioned. . . . I truly believe that if ever a state social agency destroyed a family, it destroyed ours. We wanted and tried to stay together. Our home didn't have to be destroyed. But the Welfare, the courts, and their doctor gave us the one-two-three punch. And ours was not the only case of this kind. (Malcolm X & Haley, 1966, pp. 20–21)

When Malcolm was about to enter the third grade, an English teacher asked him what kind of career he wanted. Malcolm said that he wanted to be a lawyer, to which the teacher replied:

"You've got to be realistic about being a nigger. A lawyer—that's no realistic goal for a nigger. You need to think about something you can be. You're good with your hands—making things. Everybody admires your carpentry shop work. Why don't you plan on carpentry?" (Malcolm X & Haley, 1966, p. 36)

By raising people's consciousness about discrimination and pressuring organizations to change, Malcolm X and other civil rights activists helped reshape social services as well as other institutions of society. Since the 1960s, many ethnic groups have developed their own agencies and professional organizations, creating changes in the policies and hiring practices of White-dominated agencies. The National Association of Black Social Workers was formed in 1968 to improve the provision of social services to Black people and to spur the recruitment of Black social workers (McRoy, 1990).

4. *Emphasize strengths in individuals and communities.* This is especially true when working with people who have been treated as inferior because people have already focused so much on their weaknesses.

Emphasizing people's strengths is equally important when working with communities as it is when working with individuals. John McKnight (1992) believes that some professionals who claim to help others actually harm them by focusing on their weaknesses. He has developed a questionnaire designed to discover people's talents and a map called the Neighborhood Assets Map designed to highlight a community's strengths—cultural organizations, individual capacities, religious organizations, citizens' associations, home-based enterprise, social service agencies, and so on. McKnight also designed a map called the Neighborhood Needs Map, which lists pathologies—slum housing, crime, mental illness, teenage pregnancy, substance use disorders, illiteracy, and so forth. The Neighborhood Needs Map is the one that people use most often, but it ignores the strengths of a neighborhood.

The liberation movements of oppressed people have revealed their enormous strength and courage. Thousands of people have literally put their lives on the line to win their freedom. And there is the quieter but enduring strength they show by protecting their families and communities in the face of constant oppression and discrimination.

5. *Find sources of power.* Lorraine Gutierrez recommends that the worker and client together engage in a "power analysis" of the client's situation to assess the structural barriers a client faces and the potential strengths available to the client:

Clients and workers should be encouraged to think creatively about sources of potential power, such as forgotten skills, personal qualities that could increase social influence, members of past social support networks, and organizations in their communities. (Gutierrez, 1990, p. 152)

6. *Use the network of family and friends.*   The first strength of any group is family and friends. Many minority groups rely heavily on this support. Some students of Native American culture say that it is hard for Native Americans to accumulate resources, not only because of their low-wage work and unemployment but also because of their ethic of sharing with other family members.

    African-American communities have a long tradition of mutual help. Carol Stack (1974) showed that although many families in a low-income Black community in the Midwest were officially designated "single-parent" families, they were actually extended-kin networks, sharing in child care. This was more typical among the very poor. As families became upwardly mobile, they were less likely to share their resources. Urbanization and industrialization have weakened extended-family networks for all of us, though this research shows that necessity helps to drive some level of interdependence. This seems to dissipate as individuals have the income to meet their family's needs without sharing resources. Cross, Nguyen, Chatters, & Taylor (2018) expand this discussion of support by exploring the presence of instrumental support in African-American families. In their research they found that support between African-American family members extends to assistance during illness, transportation, financial support, and help with various chores, and with greater support occurring for individuals who are senior citizens or unemployed. Interestingly, the amount of support received declined for individuals who were married and as well as when their educational obtainment increases.

7. *Use the community networks.*   The ethnic neighborhood itself is a support system in which people can share their language, religion, food, memories, and experiences. Networks include neighbors; churches; political, social, and service organizations; newspapers; stores; restaurants; and bars where people gather. The church is an especially important support network in the African-American community. In some Hispanic communities, the spiritualist may be an important support to many people, and many Native Americans may turn to the tribal medicine man or woman for support and guidance. In her study of ethnicity in the social services, Shirley Jenkins (1981) found that, in general, members of minority groups prefer going to services in their own community staffed by bilingual and bicultural workers.

8. *Understand patterns of informality and friendliness.*   Many cultures share different patterns of informality and friendliness. I recall, for example, frustration felt by a close friend from Jamaica who was interested in working for my large non-profit organization as a transporter for the children's services program. When he called to express his interest, I provided him with the information for sending along his résumé to the hiring manager. I was surprised when he sounded offended. He told me that in Jamaican culture, if a friend has a job that a friend needs, then the job is secured. In western culture, if there is a job opening, usually the friend provides information about how to apply. As the executive director of the non-profit it would be inappropriate for me to call my manager and tell them to hire my friend. Different cultures have different ways of measuring and understanding friendship and patterns of informality.

    Some cultures are more likely to expect help to come in the context of a personal relationship. They expect helping roles to be diffuse rather than specific. It's important for you as a human service professional to understand the nuances of these types of cultural differences.

9. *Be willing to share yourself.*   Workers need to be willing to share something of their own lives with clients, to make the atmosphere of the agency warm and nurturing. Perhaps you could serve refreshments or coffee, be willing to accept small gifts, be flexible about time,

be willing to make an occasional home visit, and have at least one worker for walk-in clients.

10. *Understand clients' lack of resources.*   People's poverty affects how they use social services. They may not even have the carfare or gasoline to get to the agency. Research has shown that immigrants and minorities, particularly Black people, are likely to be without a car more often than their White counterparts (Klein, & Smart, 2017). Given this, clients may not be able to keep appointments due to unreliable transportation, because they can't afford babysitters, or they fear losing their job if they take any more time off from work. They may not have a checking account, so cashing a check for bus fare might be costly and time-consuming.

11. *Give concrete services and information.*   Because of their lack of resources, people living in need require concrete help. Whatever your agency's activities, your knowledge of benefit programs might be more important than any mental health counseling. One formerly homeless woman said that she was in homeless shelters for four years because the workers there did not tell her about housing vouchers or how to get welfare benefits. It was not until she discovered a welfare rights group that she learned about her rights from other welfare recipients.

12. *Learn how to empower.*   People who are oppressed often feel powerless. Women, who have less power than men, head a large proportion of poor families. Women of color make up a large proportion of the clientele in human service agencies. They struggle more than twice as much financially than White women. They are overrepresented in low-status occupations and have on average a low level of education. The stress of having poor housing or no housing, insufficient food and clothing, and inadequate access to health services takes a toll on their physical and mental health. Human service workers need to deal with the psychological effects of their clients' powerlessness and provide concrete resources to better their lives (Gutierrez, 1990).

   The literature on empowerment indicates that small-group work is the ideal method for empowerment. In these groups, members receive support, reduce self-blame, learn new skills, and provide a potential power base for action (Gutierrez, 1990).

WORKING WITH WOMEN

Many college women, even those who do not call themselves feminists, are benefiting from the gains won by the women's movement, even though they might not be aware of the struggles that other women went through to win them. Although women have many challenges before they achieve equality with men, the gains of the women's movement have been enormous. The women's movement has touched every aspect of women's lives. Women have fought for equal pay and advancement and have often won. They have defined some lower-paying jobs as equal in worth to higher-paying men's jobs, even though the jobs may be different, and won some major **comparable worth** lawsuits. They have entered fields previously defined as men's work, and some have argued that housework and caretaking, traditionally defined as women's work, should be paid wages and shared equally by women and men.

The Women's Movement and New Social Services

Some of the most dramatic changes in the helping process were brought about by the women's movement. By 1994, shelters for victims of domestic violence had been established in more than two-thirds of the 3,200 counties in the United States (Crden, 1994). Women also created rape crisis centers; women's health centers; feminist mental health services; and services for displaced homemakers, women substance abusers, older women, single parents, and ethnic minority women (Gottlieb, 1980a, 1980b).

Feminists created new social services because they believed that traditional social agencies were not in tune with women's needs. Drawing on Freudian psychology, traditional workers said that a woman who was abused by her husband might have a sadomasochistic need to be beaten. But feminists would assert:

- The husband is committing a criminal act by beating his wife and must be legally restrained
- No one has the right to beat her for any reason
- She might be staying with him because she has:

  - No place to go
  - No money
  - Children to care for
  - No marketable work skills
  - Shame because of the stigma of being abused.

- She might need supportive therapy, but she also needs:

  - A court order
  - A shelter
  - A support group
  - A job or an adequate welfare grant
  - Decent, affordable child care
  - Help in finding an apartment.

Feminists also redefined rape. Traditional common wisdom assumed that women inadvertently "asked for it" with their behavior. Feminists defined rape as an act of violence used to control women. They told women that they didn't ask for it or deserve it. They taught women how to struggle against it and how to do the healing grief work to recover from the assault. They told women that there is no "allowable" rape—forced sex by a date or by a husband is rape. They also lobbied to change the laws that made reporting of rape another form of assault on self-esteem. In fact, feminists looked at every aspect of services to women and suggested new ways to view old problems.

Feminists took a new look at depression, menopause, and premenstrual syndrome and critiqued the way the medical establishment dealt with them. Depression, for example, is much more prevalent among women than among men. Feminists believe this is due to the socialization of women rather than to any inherent female characteristics. This socialization includes:

- An emphasis on self-effacement, which leads to low self-image
- A sense of powerlessness and of lack of control over one's life
- Difficulty in asserting oneself
- An inability to cope with stress. (Gottlieb, 1980a, 1980b)

Women, socialized to be passive rather than assertive, have a much greater tendency to turn their aggression on themselves than do men. This is generally considered to be one of the dynamics of depression.

Understanding New Theories About Women

There has been a flowering of feminist theory since the late 1960s that has had a profound effect on the human services. Feminist psychologists challenged some of the traditional Freudian theory that claimed women were "naturally" masochistic, passive, and envious of men. These psychologists helped women to feel comfortable with the assertiveness they had been taught to repress since childhood.

Feminist research has helped women reclaim their sexuality by rejecting the Freudian assertion that the only "healthy" orgasm is a vaginal one. Ann Koedt showed that the vagina has few nerve endings and that the clitoris is more sensitive to sexual stimulation than is the vagina (Koedt, 1971). (Kinsey had also shown this in his research on sexuality in the 1940s, but it was not until feminists focused on female sexuality that these findings became more widely understood.)

"Women's intuition" and emotionality, which had been ridiculed as inferior to the male world of "hard facts," won a new respectability when feminist researchers, in comparing women's ways of learning about the world and relating to people with men's ways, concluded that women's ways were different but might make for a more peaceful world.

How Feminist Theory Influences Our Practice

Feminist therapy introduced a sociological and political perspective that had been lacking in most traditional therapy, helping women as well as men to realize that women's problems were not just personal troubles but also social issues. The women's movement was built through consciousness-raising groups, a model that was adopted by other mutual-aid groups.

Yet much of feminist theory and practice have been focused too narrowly on middle-class White women, neglecting issues of social class and ethnicity. Women of color have written a wealth of literature and contributed research about their lives, and some White feminists realize that the assault on women living in poverty is an assault on all women, particularly at a time when the middle class is eroding. Crenshaw (1989) in her theory of intersectionality helped build awareness about the multiple challenges facing women, particularly women of color as they found themselves dealing with racism, discrimination, and sexism. Marecek (2016) too writes of the importance of Crenshaw's theory of intersectionality, reminding us that a woman's experience goes well beyond her gender to include cultural, racial and systemic challenges. However, although the leadership of the National Organization for Women (NOW) has been militant in fighting against repressive welfare policies, most NOW members have not been involved in welfare rights struggles.

That may be changing. When more than 1 million people attended the March for Women's Lives in Washington, D.C., on April 25, 2004, there was the largest representation of women of color and women who are low-income that had ever attended a women's march. Cheri Honkala, a welfare recipient and leader of the Kensington Welfare Rights Union in Philadelphia, gave a moving speech about welfare and emphasized that choice for women involves not only the right to have an abortion but also the right to choose to have children and the resources to care for them. Toni Bond, a woman who is low-income who had been helped to get an abortion by the National Network of Abortion Funds, spoke powerfully about the importance of financial help to women who can't afford an abortion. (There has been no federal funding for abortions since the Hyde Amendment was passed in 1974.)

Feminist scholars have analyzed social policies and social services, exposing institutional sexism. Abramovitz (1988) described how Social Security regulations discriminate against women. By giving larger pensions to those who earned more in their work, women—who almost always earn less than men—receive smaller pensions. Thus gender inequality is perpetuated through the life cycle. Further, by not including caretaking work as wage earning, homemakers are unable to draw a pension of their own but must rely on their husband's record of earnings.

Recently the women's movement has become alarmed at the way the country is moving forward from a public policy standpoint. *Roe v. Wade* is seemingly under assault, and questions remain about the way in which the Supreme Court will be shaped by numerous appointments that will occur as the result of retiring justices. An expression of these concerns as well as concerns for the rights of all women was seen recently following the 2017 presidential inauguration when hundreds of thousands of women marched on Washington. Women also marched simultaneously in cities across the country. New York City reported crowds as far as the eye could see, and the marchers in Boston were so numerous that they weren't actually able to march the intended route. The protesters gathered to express their concerns for women's rights and vowed to stay involved, run for office, and continue to protest until their rights are both realized and secured under the law.

Source: Shutterstock/sirtravelalot

This woman's strength shines through her face. If she came for help, a worker would need to recognize that strength and help the woman draw on it.

A Gender Analysis of Child Welfare

More than 30 advocates employing a feminist perspective challenged the way the child welfare system treated women who experienced domestic violence and their children in New York City (Coalition of Battered Women's Advocates, 1988). This group mobilized after the widely publicized death of a child, Lisa Steinberg, and the domestic violence against her mother, Hedda Nussbaum, by the child's father, an affluent attorney.

The coalition pointed out that women are often afraid to cry out for protection to the police or social service agencies for fear that they will lose their children, or that the perpetrators of domestic violence will retaliate against them, or that no one will believe them. Often, service providers remove children exposed to domestic violence from the home where a man is abusing his wife rather than force the abusive husband to leave. This can result in children's being victimized a second time by the trauma of foster placement (Coalition of Battered Women's Advocates, 1988). Many of these women and their children become homeless when they leave the perpetrator. Subsequently, many mothers are charged with neglect, and their children are taken from them and placed in foster homes.

The advocates demanded that the police and judges take victim's complaints seriously, removing the violent individual from the house rather than the nonviolent spouse and children, and doing everything possible to prevent further harassment. They called on agencies to provide more safe, short-term emergency refuges for victims of domestic violence and asked that funds used for foster home placement be used instead to provide violence-free homes for the children. Advocates also asked that service providers receive training in domestic violence, as few know even the basic facts about it.

Child abuse does not discriminate, but is found across all segments of our society.

The advocates lobbied for more affordable housing, more community-based services such as day care, legal assistance, health care, substance abuse prevention, child abuse prevention, and job-training programs. They pointed out that undocumented abused women are especially at risk for fear of deportation, that lesbian mothers fear losing custody of their children if they ask for help, and that women of color face racist assumptions that their children are at a higher risk of abuse. Domestic violence affects women of every race and class, yet the poor—who are disproportionately non-English-speaking and/or Black—are most often victims of involuntary intervention by police and child protective workers (Coalition of Battered Women's Advocates, 1988).

WORKING WITH LGBTQ INDIVIDUALS

In Chapter 5, we discussed the value judgments people make about working with individuals who are lesbian, gay, bisexual, transgender, or questioning or queer. Here we will put forward a framework for human service competencies when working with this diverse group of individuals.

As you consider your own capacity to work with individuals who are gay, lesbian, transgender, or questioning/queer, it is important to first understand the impact that the dominant culture, which is largely heterosexual, has on virtually everything that we see, think, and do on a day-to-day basis. From the media we watch, which portrays gender- and sex-based stereotypes, to the way we dress and how we divide up the way in which we accomplish our daily tasks, the attitudes, beliefs, behaviors, and values that we either act upon or espouse within the dominant culture have a huge impact on peoples lived experience. This hetero-cultural lens informs the world that surrounds the LGBTQ individual. Your ability to develop an awareness of the impact this has on the person you serve is critical to your ability to work successfully with someone whose sexual orientation or gender identity is not part of the mainstream.

It's important to understand the impact that being lesbian, gay, bisexual, transgender, or questioning or queer can have on the individual's experiences. Imagine if you will being a middle school teacher who happens to be gay and the impact of hearing students using anti-LGBTQ slurs. Compound this with the fact that your colleagues rarely if ever speak up to address these **microaggressions**. Add to this the nagging feeling that your boss is apparently anti-gay, based on the way he talks. He's never really said that he doesn't like gay people, but your own experience tells you that his regular microaggressions risk becoming **macroaggressions** should he ever find out that you are gay. Also, we might mention that you've never really shared your sexual orientation with many people, as the risks of coming out seem far too great. In our military, for example, the Clinton era policy of Don't Ask Don't Tell became the standard that only served to further suppress gay military members. In 2011 Congress repealed the Don't Ask Don't Tell policy, though uncertainty remains about being openly gay for military members based on the risks of stigmatization and the impact of prejudice and the potential discrimination that follow.

The discrimination and isolation that result from these dynamics can be particularly challenging for individuals within the LGBTQ community. As an effective human service worker, it is important to not only understand the dynamics that are present in the larger society but also to become aware of your own biases. Are there things, for example, that you do which might be off-putting or represent a microaggression against another individual? Oftentimes we do these things unintentionally, and so considering difficult questions like this is an important part of developing your own competency as an individual within the helping profession.

Scherrer (2013) underscores the challenges faced by individuals whose sexual orientation falls outside the mono-hetero-cultural societal lens when she writes that the complexity for bisexual individuals is further compounded by the discrimination they experience from both the heterosexual as well as the gay community. Transgender individuals too experience considerable discrimination, and the battles we saw recently centred around who can use which public bathroom are simply the tip of the iceberg.

Ragg, Dennis, and Ziefert (2006) conducted research to identify the skills necessary to work successfully with LGBTQ individuals, and we believe their work provides a useful frame for the skills you will want to consider as you work to become an effective helper within the human service field. In their research they highlight three dialectical themes, or opposing views, under which they identified key skills necessary to help LGBTQ youth in care meet developmental milestones. Their work can also be used when working with a broader array of individuals whose sexual orientation and/or gender identity is different than the largely heterosexual culture.

The first dialectical frame identified is **vulnerability versus empowerment**. Within this frame is it critical that the helping professional develop skills in three areas. First, they must have the capacity to "tune in." This requires that the helping professional have an awareness of how the client is experiencing the larger cultural context that he is working through. The more one is able to develop an understanding of and have empathy for the context through which the individual is working, the greater the chance that he will be able to become empowered within the helping relationship.

The second skill identified through this research is termed "working through." Here the helping professional must be prepared to hold fast, or stay in the game as the individual works though their situation. Within this skill it is important to provide facts that are accurate and free from bias and misinformation. It's also the worker's responsibility to help the individual experience respect and to assure her of confidentiality.

The final skill necessary to advance toward empowerment is the use of advocacy on the part of the helping professional. Here the worker must become a voice against micro- and macroaggressions and actively speak out against those whose actions hurt the individual. It's critical to help mitigate circumstances when bias and injustices are foisted upon the individual. It can be challenging to "swim against the tide," but this is integral to building trust and helping the individual realize that the worker's support is genuine and can be counted upon.

There are four skills identified within the second dialectical theme of **stigmatization versus validation**. The first skill, identified as "individualizing," requires that the helping professional possess the capability to respond to the individualized needs of the person. This means working from a whole-person perspective, honoring the strengths and the individual needs of the client separate from his sexual orientation and identity. This skill relates closely to the second skill, which is "strength finding." Despite the micro- and macroaggressions experienced by the individual, it is essential that the worker identify and highlight the strengths that the individual brings to his life circumstances. This plays an integral part in helping the individual to become validated while avoiding the trap of letting stigmatization define his life's narrative.

The third skill is closely aligned with the first two in this theme of stigmatization versus validation, as it calls upon the worker to be "affirming." The capacity to affirm the individual's challenges, from an internal and external perspective, plays in important role in his ability to make sense of his circumstances and, through this move, toward feeling validated. In a like way the final skill within this thematic area is the ability to provide a "normalizing" context for the individual. Here the worker uses her skills to help the individual realize that his sexuality is completely natural, that his feelings are normal, and that he is not alone within the context of his circumstances.

The final theme identified though the research of Ragg, Dennis, and Ziefert, is **acceptance versus rejection**. Here the effective human service worker must have the ability to "remain open." We all possess implicit assumptions, and it is critical for us as workers to avoid knee-jerk reactions and instead listen carefully. Dr. Schram, one of the authors of this book, always told her Introduction to Human Services class at Northeastern University to "listen with the third ear and watch with the third eye." The underlying concept of this perhaps seemingly unusual perspective is that we all need to bring a mindfulness to the work that we do so that we might fully understand what our clients are facing in their day-to-day lives.

The second skill identified under this theme is to pursue a posture of "supportive engagement." Supportive engagement aligns closely with the ability to maintain a connection with the helpee. This is accomplished through active listening and engaging in behavior that helps the individual experience an ongoing connection that is caring and supportive.

The final skill to help the individual realize acceptance and avoid rejection is identified as "responsive exploration." This skill takes supportive engagement to the next level by working with the individual to more fully understand the context that the LGBTQ individual is confronting. Here the successful worker is able to utilize supportive and probing questions in order to help the individual better understand the connections between his internal and external experiences. Through this process the worker empowers the individual to develop problem-solving strategies. This is similar to the work of Heck, Flentje, & Cochran (2013), who believe that the use of affirming strategies becomes a useful tool from the very beginning point of the initial interview with individuals who may identify themselves as LGBTQ.

The core skills suggested by Ragg, Dennis, and Ziefert to be an effective human service worker provide some useful tips to advance your own capacity to work with individuals who identify as LGBTQ. It's important to realize, though, that you are embarking on a journey of skill development that will take time. In fact, we'd argue that the journey of skill development should be a journey that truly never ends. The field is always developing new techniques, and so it is important to keep yourself informed. In addition, the nature of our own cultural experience requires that we continually strive to become more aware of the systemic challenges the LGBTQ community face. The challenges that many LGBTQ individuals face are therefore rooted in the ways their own lives bump up against the mainstream view of gender identity and sexual orientation.

WORKING WITH PEOPLE WITH DISABILITIES

People with disabilities are an oppressed group because they have not been allowed equal access to society's benefits. They are a minority both in absolute numbers and in the political meaning of the term.

Some people with disabilities have an acronym for people who define themselves as non-disabled: They call them TABs—temporarily able bodied. This term vividly reminds us that being able-bodied is only a temporary condition. Any one of us could get hit by a car when crossing the street or get hurt when skiing or diving, and in time all of our bodies will give out due to the natural aging process. The recognition of our own vulnerability helps to lower that psychological barrier between "them" and "us," which is the biggest handicap of all.

The liberation movement for people with disabilities challenges the arbitrary distinctions people make on the basis of differences in physical or mental functioning. Members declare that the real disability lies in society's unwillingness to structure its architecture, public facilities and space, cultural offerings, and so forth to open up the entire society to everyone regardless of their level of functioning.

New Definition of Disability Influences Our Practice

Traditional models of disability focused on labeling each "disease," defining what people can do in the job market, and what functions a person can and cannot perform. The new model is a **psychosocial model of disability**. It looks at the entire environment of the person, including social attitudes, attitudes of other individuals, and the society that those without disabilities have created (Marini, Glover-Graf, & Millington, 2011). The psychosocial model of disability was recognized in public policy by Section 504 of the Rehabilitation Act of 1973, the first civil rights act for people with disabilities, as well as by the Education for All Handicapped Children's Act of 1975. That law required children with disabilities to be mainstreamed with children without disabilities as much as possible. The most sweeping civil rights law for people with disabilities was the Americans with Disabilities Act of 1990.

At different times in history and in different places, certain disabilities could be or were viewed as somewhat of an asset, not as a liability. Dostoyevsky, who had epilepsy, describes the aura preceding an epileptic seizure as a route to cosmic clarity. Julius Caesar had epilepsy in Roman times, when it was considered to be a holy disease. During the nineteenth century in the Western world, people with tuberculosis were considered especially refined, sensitive, and wise. If a character in a nineteenth-century novel was described in Chapter 1 as refined, sensitive, and wise, it was sure to be revealed by Chapter 8 that the character was dying of tuberculosis, or "consumption."

Obtaining an accurate count of how many individuals with disabilities there are is especially tricky because the number depends on whom you define as disabled. Some deaf people do not consider their deafness a disability, because they are totally immersed in the deaf culture and take great delight in it. When the deaf students at Gallaudet College for the Deaf successfully rebelled against a hearing person's being chosen as president of the college, some of them declared that their deafness should not be defined as a disability and that they were as "normal" as anyone else. Neurologist and author Oliver Sacks (1989), who described that rebellion so vividly, tells of a community on Martha's Vineyard in Massachusetts in which so many significant citizens were deaf that everyone learned sign language. With no communication barrier, life was the same for the hearing and the nonhearing.

According to the ADA Network, in 2017 approximately 54 million people in the United States had a reported disability. Given our country's population of over 325 million, this means that just over 16 percent of the population within the United States report having a disability. As of February 2017, 18.7 percent of individuals reporting a disability were within the workforce, and the unemployment rate for individuals with a disability who are actively seeking work was 9.2 percent which compared with a 4.2 percent unemployment rate for individuals without disabilities (U.S. Department of Labor, 2017). There are a disproportionate number of disabilities among older people, people living in poverty, people of color, and blue-collar workers. People with disabilities are more likely to be unemployed or underemployed and, if they are employed, are more likely to earn less than workers without disabilities. They face discrimination in the job market and often have to navigate buildings not designed for their needs.

Six Tennessee residents with disabilities achieved a victory in 2004 when the U.S. Supreme Court declared that states could be liable for not making courthouses accessible. One of the people who sued was a man who refused to crawl or be carried up to a second-floor courtroom in a county courthouse to answer a criminal traffic complaint. He sued after the state charged him with failing to appear for his hearing (Greenhouse, L. 2004).

Human service workers who work with people with disabilities need to be informed about the eligibility guidelines for both Social Security Disability Insurance (SSDI) and Supplemental

Security Income (SSI), as well as for workers' compensation, to make sure their clients get the benefits they are entitled to. Legal service lawyers who specialize in disability law can help with this.

Because applying for these benefits requires people to see and define themselves as being disabled and thus unable to work, many people do not apply. This is a dilemma for both the client and the worker. On the one hand, clients are refusing needed income; on the other hand, people's self-definition and self-esteem are critically important to their mental health. Some people will accept general assistance even when the grant is much lower than SSI because they regard general assistance as short-term temporary help until they get a job.

Summary

1. Racial inequality exists in housing and home ownership, health and health insurance, professional advancement, arrests and imprisonment, jobs, political representation, voting rights, and school segregation.

2. There has been a long struggle for equality in the United States, and the struggle continues.

3. Human service workers are faced with issues of diversity in all of their practice.

4. People who claim to be color-blind are actually ignoring an important aspect of a person's identity. They maintain White privilege by negating racial inequality.

5. Prejudice and discrimination may negatively affect people's feelings about themselves.

6. In order to fully understand people, we must understand their cultures.

7. The current theory about culture is bicultural theory, which assumes that people are socialized into their own culture and influenced by the dominant culture.

8. Having limited access to power defines a "minority group."

9. The United States has been run predominantly by White, heterosexual, Anglo-Saxon, English-speaking, middle- and upper-class men without physical disability. Those who differed have often suffered discrimination.

10. Latinos face discrimination sometimes on the basis of skin color and often because of not speaking English, or because they speak with limited fluency and/or an accent.

11. Acculturation is stressful, causing conflict between the older and younger generations in families.

12. Ethnicity, social class, and gender must be considered together.

13. In order to understand any group, we must understand its history.

14. Because minorities have been discriminated against, they are likely to be distrustful of White-dominated organizations.

15. Institutional racism is harder to change than individual racism because it involves interconnected systems and policies that perpetuate it.

16. The media often perpetuates stereotypes.

17. There are large differences within ethnic groups.

18. The drug war is a failed policy that resulted in the overincarceration of non-violent drug offenders.

19. Black men are sent to prison at 13 times the rate of White men.

20. Discrimination against Arab and Muslim Americans has risen at an alarming rate since 9/11.

21. Most Americans know very little about the Muslim faith.

22. Discrimination against Jews has lessened since WWII, but they are still discriminated against in some neighborhoods, jobs, and social clubs.

23. Affirmative action has become a lightning rod that attracts people's anxieties about race.

24. The immigration policy of the United States has fluctuated between the country's need for labor and people's xenophobia and fears of losing their jobs to foreigners.

25. The 1996 Immigration Act, which provides for "expedited removal" of immigrants, represents a major change in the country's treatment of immigrants.

26. A study by the Congressional Budget Office concluded that legalization of immigrants would contribute tens of billions of dollars to the federal treasury.

27. The Personal Responsibility Act of 1996 denied federal help to legal immigrants in the SSI, food stamp, and Medicaid programs. In 1997, some SSI and food stamp benefits were restored.

28. The immigration bill that was debated in the U.S. Senate in 2007 proposed to gradually change a system based primarily on family ties, in place since 1965, into one that favors highly skilled and highly educated workers who want to become permanent residents. Low-skilled workers would largely be channeled to a vast new temporary program.

29. It is important to emphasize people's strengths rather than their weaknesses.

30. Family and friends are the most important supports for people.

31. Most minority groups are considered low-income and therefore need concrete supports from human service agencies. Telling people about the benefits to which they are entitled empowers them.

32. Workers need to be willing to share themselves, be informal, be flexible about time, and be willing to make home visits.

33. Feminists have created alternative social agencies and new theories.

34. Feminist practice strives to be egalitarian.

35. Understanding issues that affect gay and lesbian individuals not only helps them but can also give them new insights into heterosexual behavior.

36. The Don't Ask, Don't Tell law that forbade gay and lesbian members of the military from being open about their sexuality was struck down by Congress in 2011.

37. In June 2015, the United States Supreme Court ruled in *Obergefell v. Hodges* that state bans on gay and lesbian couples' right to marry were unconstitutional.

38. The new definition of disability does not accept the medical model; rather, it sees the problem as the reluctance of society to accommodate the needs of the people with disabilities.

39. The Americans with Disabilities Act of 1990 requires sweeping changes in accommodations for people with disabilities.

Discussion Questions

1. What do you think is a good immigration policy for a nation? What guidelines would you use in setting up such a policy? The National Catholic Social Justice lobby NETWORK calls for "just reform of immigration policy" and "a just U.S. foreign policy that fosters economic equity and alleviates global poverty." What do you think would be a just reform of immigration policy and a just U.S. foreign policy?

2. The United States Supreme Court ruled in *Obergefell v. Hodges* that state denials of gay and lesbian couples' right to marry were unconstitutional. Opponents of that ruling say that it will destroy traditional heterosexual marriage. On what do they base that argument?

3. Exercise: In group discussion, name several social identity groups that you think influence people's lives. This could include race, ethnicity, gender, sexual orientation, class, physical ability, religion, age, and others. Identify where you fit in those groups in a notebook. During class discussion, share this information to the extent that you feel comfortable doing so. Discuss how (or whether) people are oppressed, or feel oppressed, because of their social identity. (No one should feel under any pressure to share personal information.)

4. Exercise: In group discussion, share information on the neighborhoods you grew up in and organizations you belonged to. How diverse were these neighborhoods and organizations? Discuss the reasons for their diversity or lack of diversity.

5. France has passed a law saying that Muslim girls are not allowed to wear head scarves in school, as this violates the principle of the separation of church and state and erodes national identity. What do you think of this law?

Web Resources for Further Study

Teaching Tolerance

https://www.splcenter.org/what-we-do/teaching-tolerance

Facing History and Ourselves

https://www.facinghistory.org

Unidos US

https://www.unidosus.org

National Association for the Advancement of Colored People (NAACP)

https://www.naacp.org

National Organization for Women

https://www.now.org

Project Implicit

https://implicit.harvard.edu/implicit/takeatest.html

LGBT social movements

https://www.apa.org/pi/lgbt/resources/history.aspx

Beyond Prejudice

https://www.beyondprejudice.com

Betsy Leondar-Wright

https://www.classmatters.org

SisterSong: Women of Color Reproductive Health Collective

https://www.sistersong.net

MyLab Helping Professions for Introduction to Human Services

Try the Topic 4 Assignments: Diversity.

Interviewing

8

Source: Rawpixel.com/Shutterstock

Learning Outcomes

- Students will learn key concepts related to effective interviewing techniques.

- Students will be able to contrast effective interviewing techniques with less effective approaches.

- Students will learn strategies to apply interviewing skills to their own practice.

- Case studies and discussion questions provide students with the ability to analyze and compare successful interviewing strategies.

CHARACTERISTICS OF AN INTERVIEW

Interviews come in many different forms. There are interviews that are conducted as an initial assessment for counseling, to determine eligibility for services, as a part of an investigation into an incident, or as a part of an effort to more fully understand the needs of a community or a particular group. No matter the circumstance, human service work will require you to develop effective interviewing skills. Every intervention that a human service worker uses—whether counseling one client or mobilizing a group to take social action—requires interviewing. All our work is built on planned, careful communication: talking and listening, making and observing nonverbal gestures, or writing and reading. In this chapter, we will discuss the basic elements and skills of interviewing.

Because this book is for the beginning human service worker, we will not focus on long-term counseling or psychotherapy interviews, or on specialized treatment of children. Nor will we discuss the skills specific to research interviewing (though many of the skills we will talk about also apply to this area). These topics require experience and training beyond the beginning level.

We define a human service interview as an interaction between people that has a consciously planned purpose, structure, and goal and requires specific communication skills.

Purposeful Communication

Social conversations need not have any conscious goal. When we are having a casual chat with a friend, we generally don't have a fixed agenda about what we discuss. The conversation often ambles at a leisurely pace from one topic to another: the weather, what happened on the way to work, how we feel, the party we went to last night, gossip about friends, and so on. You talk because you enjoy being with each other.

An interview, on the other hand, has a purpose and a goal. You may engage in some small talk with clients to establish rapport, but they usually come to you for a specific service, or you reach out to them.

Focus and Structure

In general, each person involved in a conversation expects more or less equal attention. But in an interview, the focus is on the needs of the client. We would feel neglected or angry if a friend talked endlessly about her problems without bothering to listen to us in return. In an interview, however, skilled workers know how to stay in the background and encourage clients to say what is on their minds. This does not mean that interviewers never reveal anything about themselves; in fact, research suggests that it is useful to share a moderate amount of information about one's own life (Ziv-Beiman, 2013). However, what is shared must be carefully considered, in the interests of not interfering with the meaning and purpose of your interaction with a client. For example, you might comment to a client who is late to a meeting that you too have experienced traffic on the way to the office. You wouldn't expound on this to say how your significant other caused you to be late. There is no point in sharing at this level, as it interferes with the purpose of your meeting with the client and has no bearing on making an appropriate connection with her. Of course, the interviewer is responsible for keeping the interview focused on the client.

The structure of an interview varies according to the context in which it takes place, the individual client, and the phase of the helping process. Each interview is unique, but initial interviews always include (1) the beginning process of establishing rapport (which continues to some degree throughout the helping relationship), (2) opening the interview and making the contract, (3) exploring the issues, and (4) closing the interview and looking forward to the next steps in the helping process.

CONTEXT AND ORGANIZATIONAL PURPOSE The **primary purpose** of the social agency shapes the focus and content of the interview. The focus of the Department of Welfare, for example, at the state and local level was broader before 1974, when workers were called "social workers" and could offer help for problems beyond financial need. Now workers are called "investigators" or "eligibility workers." Their function is narrowly focused on a client's financial situation. However, a multifunction agency, either a state agency or a non-profit organization such as Child and Family Services, as the title implies, can have a broader focus in an interview because it is authorized to offer counseling for a broad spectrum of clients' needs. When an agency has a narrow focus, the worker can refer a client whose needs fall outside its scope to one that serves those needs.

In agencies that work with involuntary clients, interviewers need to be particularly skilled in helping people express anger or resentment, yet they must be able to stay on course with the main purpose of the interview. A worker also needs to be skilled in sorting out the issues inherent in situations that limit self-determination and in dealing forthrightly with those issues.

The public support and **image of an agency** also influence interviews. For example, under-staffing means that clients must often wait long periods for an interview, and sometimes an interview is more rushed and mechanical than it should be. Such working conditions can be demoralizing to both clients and workers. Even though a dedicated worker can conduct a superb interview in a stigmatized or underfunded agency, the pressure of the work and the drabness of the surroundings can encourage joyless and dehumanizing treatment of clients. Of course, your skill level in conducting interviews can help to mitigate the challenges we often face when resources and space are limited.

SETTING   The focus and content of an interview are affected by the setting in which it takes place. Interviews can happen anywhere, but ideally, there should be a logical relationship between what you are going to talk about and the place where you do the talking.

Sometimes interviews take place in the home of a client with the television set blaring and the children within earshot as the parents talk about them. Even in our offices, we must often ask personal questions with little more privacy than a room divider. Although we can try to improve these conditions as a long-range strategy, we must deal with them from moment to moment the best way we can.

The following suggestions can help make an awkward situation more private and comfortable for the client:

- Try to assess the emotional state of the client to see what behavior would be appropriate. Lower the tone of your voice, lean forward, and listen intently so the client does not have to shout his information.
- If you are in an office with no privacy, apologize to the client or comment that you know he might feel uncomfortable in such a setting. Say that you're sorry about it and wish there were a more private space. When possible, arrange for a more private place to conduct the interview.
- Move your chair to the side of the desk so that it doesn't separate you from the person you are talking with. Have at your desk a plant or some objects that make it as attractive and personal as possible.
- The interview space should also be inviting. Have decorations and reading material that reflect the cultural make-up of the clients you are working with. Provide a sign that your space is a safe space for LGBTQ individuals. This can be done by hanging a safe zone ally poster somewhere visible in the space. Rainbows are stereotypical.

Skill and Awareness

Conversations and interviews differ in the level of skill each requires. It is true that people vary enormously in their interpersonal skills, and therefore some people carry on more creative conversations than others. Yet as long as we can make ourselves understood, most of us don't think we must train ourselves to carry on social conversations. In order to become skilled interviewers, however, we need to learn a great deal about how people interact with each other. We need to assess behavior—to listen carefully not only to words but to shadings and nuances of tone, pitch, and volume—and to communicate our understanding of what we have seen and heard in a clear and concise way that shows we genuinely care about that person. Indeed, much of the skill in interviewing comes from awareness:

- Awareness of your own personality and the personality of the interviewee
- Awareness of your own expectations and those of the interviewee
- Awareness of your own cultural background and that of the interviewee
- Awareness of your own attitudes and values and those of the interviewee

We will discuss each of these separately, but remember that, in practice, no one factor can *really* be separated from all the others.

AWARENESS OF PERSONALITY AND STYLE Because each interviewer and interviewee has a unique personality and style, there is no magic formula for interviewing. An outgoing person may be a more assertive interviewer than a quieter one, but both can be equally skillful. Fortunately, people are not programmed robots. Precisely because of our human capacity for spontaneity, there is always an element of uncertainty in what we will say and what others will say to us. Therefore, interviewing, depending as it does on words and gestures, can never be totally systematized in a scientific way and will always remain—to some extent at least—*an art*. We believe, however, that we can all learn to become more sensitive to others through studying our interactions and ourselves, and through continual practice in self-discovery and effective communication techniques.

Ideally, self-discovery continues for each of us throughout our lives. Unquestionably, however, some people are more sensitive than others, and a certain level of sensitivity is an absolute requirement in human service work.

Certain kinds of interviewers' behavior that could create barriers to communication include:

- Focusing on weaknesses rather than strengths
- The need to "rescue"
- Overly passive behavior
- Discomfort with emotion
- Anger
- Condescension.

FOCUSING ON WEAKNESSES. Some interviewers see the glass as half empty rather than as half full. These interviewers are less helpful than those who look for strengths. *At the core of mental health is self-esteem*, so we look for genuine ways of enhancing the interviewee's self-esteem. Sometimes we can find an interviewee's positive intentions even in undesirable actions. Then we can emphasize the intentions, not the undesirable actions. For example, you might say to a man who stole money in order to feed his family: "Although your stealing gets you in trouble, I understand that you are very worried about your family and want to help them. Let's discuss ways of supporting your family that won't get you into trouble."

NEED TO "RESCUE." An occupational hazard of human service workers is their need to rescue people, regardless of whether the clients want to be rescued. *We are supposed to be "doing with," not "doing for."* "Doing for" implies that the helper is superior and knows what is best for the helpee. "Doing with" implies a mutuality and equality.

Children and extremely dependent adults are especially likely to evoke **rescue fantasies** in us. We often have strong feelings about what is acceptable parenting, and when working with children, we must curb any tendencies to be in rivalry with the children's parents.

OVERLY PASSIVE BEHAVIOR. The amount of the interviewer's verbal activity will vary from one situation to another. Some interviewees talk easily and with little prodding; some need help in limiting or structuring their verbosity; others do not talk easily and need more encouragement from the worker. A worker who sits like a bump on a log gives the appearance of being uninterested in the interviewee or of having no structure or goal for the encounter.

DISCOMFORT WITH EMOTION.   Some interviewers are uncomfortable with emotions, which makes it harder for the interviewee to express powerful feelings. This characteristic can show itself whenever the interviewee cries or expresses anger. To avoid dealing with the emotion, the interviewer changes the subject, talks about superficial things, gives false reassurance, intellectualizes about the problems, or becomes emotionally detached.

ANGER.   Because an interview is a human encounter, there will be times when the interviewer will feel angry with the interviewee. There could be many reasons for the anger. Perhaps something the interviewee says triggers some old resentment, or perhaps some personality trait annoys the interviewer. An articulate, assertive interviewer may become impatient with a passive interviewee; a laid-back interviewer may feel annoyance at an interviewee who is a compulsive talker.

   Whatever the reason, it is important for interviewers to be aware of their anger and come to terms with it. When this happens, anger can be a useful tool. It is not helpful to express the anger impulsively and thoughtlessly to the interviewee, but anger can be used helpfully if the interviewer understands it. One author recommends recognizing "the inward side of a feeling":

> If the counselor feels bored with or angry toward a client, rather than express these feelings (the outer edge) that imply criticism or blame, he seeks to determine and to express deeper aspects of the feelings by asking himself, "Why do I feel this way?" In seeking the answer, he will discover that behind the boredom lies a positive desire to hear more personal and relevant information that can facilitate progress. Likewise, behind the anger lies disappointment in being unable to be more helpful to the client. If we similarly analyze such feelings as impatience, irritation, criticism, or disgust, we will discover that the inward side of these feelings will consist of a desire that the client have a better and more fulfilling life, a desire that can be shared safely and beneficially. (Hammond, Hepworth, & Smith, 1977, p. 224)

CONDESCENSION.   Condescension implies that the worker feels superior to the client. Workers are generally unaware of these feelings, but clients have their antennae attuned to them. A condescending attitude gives the message "I know what is good for you. The fact that you are a client automatically guarantees that you don't know as much as I do about human behavior in general and your behavior in particular. You came to me because you want my expertise, and I intend to give it to you."

AWARENESS OF MUTUAL EXPECTATIONS   When two people come together for an interview, they bring with them the sum total of their past experiences and current expectations. This is their mental set. They bring anxieties, knowledge, misinformation, and hopes to the interview. They may be from different social classes, races, or ethnic backgrounds. Their ages, gender, physical capacities, or sexual orientation may be different. All these qualities have shaped their attitudes, and will help shape the interview. Each might have a drastically different agenda for the interview. A person with depression may hope for a pill to cure the depression immediately, and the worker may have been trained to believe that medication must be supplemented by a lengthy counseling process.

   Workers and clients seem sometimes to be in two different worlds. The solution to such divergence between client and worker expectations is to clarify expectations and bring them into convergence by changing either the worker's or the client's expectations or by changing the treatment methods. At times, perhaps all these changes may be necessary. Often it helps to clarify expectations at the beginning of the interview. Sharing with the interviewee what she can expect as a part of the process while asking the individual what her expectations are helps to set the right course from the very beginning of the session.

Both the interviewer and interviewee come to the interview with anxiety, particularly if they are meeting for the first time. Everyone feels anxious in a new and untested situation. For example, remember how you felt at the beginning of a semester during the first session of your classes. Perhaps you wondered how the teachers would treat you or what they would expect from you. You might have wondered whether the teachers would be tough or easy graders. Would the classes be boring or interesting? Would the teachers humiliate you or be sarcastic if you gave a wrong answer? Would the teachers respect your individual needs and ideas?

Remember, too, how you felt when you were about to be interviewed by a prospective employer. You probably wondered whether you would measure up to the employer's expectations. Would you say the right things? Were you dressed correctly? Would the employer like you? Would you be asked questions you'd rather not answer? What parts of your experience and personality should you emphasize, deemphasize, alter, or conceal?

Inexperienced workers usually wonder whether they will ask the right questions: What if I ask the wrong question? Will it send the client into a tailspin? What if the client doesn't talk? What if the client talks too much? What if the client talks about the wrong things, or what if I talk about the wrong things? How can I keep the interview on target? Will the client like me, or will I like the client?

To move the interview along toward its goal, the anxieties of both the interviewer and the interviewee need to be dealt with. The interviewer can practice certain techniques through role-playing and can deal with personal anxieties through supervision and peer support.

Holland (2015) found that one key element necessary in order to ensure the success of the helping relationship is the presence of trust between the helper and the helpee. The different contextual lenses presented by each party, including socioeconomic factors, race, and life experiences can be a barrier to the understanding and communication that are essential to establishing the trust necessary to ensure successful outcomes. Without establishing trust within the helping relationship there can be little chance of building shared expectations, goals, and agreed upon tasks in order to achieve the desired end. In Holland's research successful counselors were able to build trust by establishing a caring relationship by consistently infusing the helpee with positive regard. Successful helpers also were able to successfully adapt their practice to the contextual needs of the helpee, choosing to see the challenges presented by the helping relationship as an opportunity to ensure a successful outcome rather than as a barrier. As an interviewer its essential for you to understand the individual you are serving and to adapt your practice to build a climate of trust.

AWARENESS OF CULTURAL BACKGROUNDS   Cultural issues are related to expectations. People from various cultural backgrounds might have different expectations of each other and might literally speak different languages. Even when the language *seems* to be the same, people who belong to a subculture within an English-speaking culture will probably have developed their own language variations.

Sometimes, words convey different meanings to different people. Slang is one example of this: *Straight* means "very proper" in one person's vocabulary; to another it means "not crooked"; to another it means "heterosexual." We should try to use language that the interviewee understands, which means that we have to learn the interviewee's particular idiom if it differs from ours. However, we should not use slang that is unnatural or uncomfortable to us. The people we serve know when you are trying to connect in an artificial way. Better always to strive to be genuine rather than trying to impress your client. It's also true that nonverbal behaviors have different meanings within different cultures. Some cultures, for example, consider direct eye contact disrespectful, while in others, the expression of emotion might be looked upon unfavorably. We have to be careful not to impose our own cultural views on our interviewees. For example, our culture considers a lack of eye contact as a sign of disrespect and a lack of expression as "bland affect," signaling that depression may be something to rule out. Of course, as noted, these two culturally based nonverbal communication patterns may have nothing to do with being disrespectful or depressed; it may simply be that the person is communicating with you in a way that is consistent with her cultural norms. For this reason, it is particularly important to understand the cultural lens that your client brings. Is she fully assimilated into the dominant culture, or has she recently emigrated from a culturally different place? (Matsumoto & Hwang, 2016)

LEARNING ABOUT A CLIENT'S CULTURE.   Anthropologists have a lot to teach human service workers about interviewing and about how to relate to people. Their job is to learn how a culture works, how people relate to each other, what kinds of organizations they create, and what their strengths are. When anthropologists do ethnographic interviews, they are the students, and the interviewees are the teachers. The anthropologists make some decisions about how to structure their interviews, but they have no preconceptions about people's problems or the way to solve those problems. The anthropologists are curious about people's lives and their relationships to others in the family and the community.

Human service workers are more likely to think they need to be in control of an interview and to have some thoughts about the nature of the problems and ways to solve these problems because they believe that they are the experts. In addition, the belief that the worker is an expert had been buoyed by the growing use of evidence-based practices also known as empirically supported interventions (ESI). Chorpita, Daleiden, & Collins (2014) raise a well-founded concern when they highlight the challenges presented by strict adherence to an ESI. It's essential that the human service professional understand the importance of making appropriate adaptions to meet the cultural and contextual needs of the people they are serving. Strict adherence to a manualized ESI can create a context where the worker is seen as the expert and where the unique needs of the individual can be overlooked.

Social work professor Irene Glasser uses these ethnographic methods in teaching students interviewing techniques. She considers any situation to be cross-cultural when the worker:

> is working with someone who views the world, defines reality, and organizes behavior differently than the worker does. This means that practically all of my social-work students are engaged in cross-cultural work whether they are working with poor people, young parents, people on probation, children in a class for emotional problems, or shelter residents. (Glasser, 1989, p. 5)

Glasser suggests that students become the "learner" of each person's culture. Some questions that might be helpful are to ask people to talk about:

- Their daily routine
- A critical period in their lives
- Their childhood
- Common expressions and jokes friends tell each other.

Listen carefully to people's words and ask for clarification when necessary. Don't be too quick to "understand." An admission of ignorance might be more productive than a facile claim to understanding. Look for recurring themes in people's conversation or behavior (Glasser, 1989).

LEARNING ABOUT YOUR OWN CULTURE. Students may find it odd when we ask them to consider their own cultural roots and the impact that these roots have on their ability to be effective as an interviewer. Many students say that they don't have any cultural roots, or that their grandparents came from Europe, but that's about it. What we do know is that we all have cultural roots and culturally based practices that inform how we engage in the world. For example, White middle-class individuals often possess what Sue and Sue, recognized experts in the field of cross cultural counseling (2016), describe as a high internal locus of control, meaning that there is a basic belief on the part of the individual that he can take things on and get things done for himself. Individuals from a lower socioeconomic minority group often possess a lower internal locus of control, meaning that there is a general belief that there isn't much they can do to impact a given situation. The outcome in this case is more informed by external situations rather than internal control. You can imagine the challenge that these two differing cultural lenses can have when they exist between the interviewer and the interviewer. If you believe as the interviewer that your client just needs to "pull himself up by the bootstraps," you'll bump up against a challenge when you realize your client feels he doesn't have "bootstraps," or that circumstances caused them to break many years ago.

Similarly, some cultures are future-orientated, while others are present-oriented. Our dominate Western culture is future-oriented, meaning that the focus is on what needs to be done next, where one needs to be, and what the schedule is for the day and the week ahead. Other cultures, on the other hand, are more present-oriented. In these instances, individuals are more focused on what is happening in the present and less concerned with what's next on the schedule. We experienced this directly in our work with Native Americans and individuals from the Caribbean Islands. Our Western culture is highly concerned with schedules and meeting deadlines, while individuals, for example, from the Wabanaki Indian tribe or the Dominican Republic might be more focused on the here and now. Our own experience is supported by others who write about the differing world views of various cultures (see, for example, Sue & Sue, 2016, p. 484). Given this, an effective interviewer understands that there may be a different level of concern for arriving to the meeting on time, or making sure that all the paperwork is completed and filed as required by the deadlines that are imposed.

As you work to develop your skills as an interviewer, it's critical that you begin a process of considering your own cultural roots. The greater your self-awareness becomes, the more adept you will be at understanding the dynamic of difference that exists between you and your client. This in turn makes it possible for you to adapt your approach to better ensure the success of the people you serve. Ensuring the success of the people we serve is at the very heart of our work.

AWARENESS OF ATTITUDES AND VALUES Interviewers set the stage for a worthwhile interview by their attitudes of active observation, physical attentiveness to the interviewee, and active listening. These attitudes are essential to productive interviews.

ACTIVE OBSERVATION. Active observation is different from the kind of looking we generally do in our everyday life. It is like the difference between being a passenger on a bus and the driver. The driver is aware at every moment of the conditions of the road, the traffic, the passengers, and the fare box. But although they might glance casually about, noting some people and incidents with mild interest, the passengers are generally preoccupied with their own thoughts.

OBSERVING NONVERBAL MESSAGES. Interviewers get clues about the people they are listening to from people's nonverbal messages. Suppose, for example, you are a human service worker in a nursing home. A middle-aged couple comes to see you about placing the husband's mother in this home. As you show them through the halls, you notice that they get quieter; their voices drop; their speech slows; they glance significantly at each other as they look at the seriously ill residents in wheelchairs, or at others walking with walkers and canes, staring into space. They look away from you and decline your invitation to see the wing of the home where the more seriously ill residents live. Observing their behavior and knowing how much stress people are under when making decisions about their sick or aged parents, you'd want to help this couple talk about their feelings about placing the husband's mother, as well as their impressions of what they have just seen.

Interviewees can give nonverbal clues about feelings: rigid posture, trembling, yawning, wringing hands, sweating palms, trembling voice, blushing, a sad look, moistening of the eyes, sighs, clenched jaws and hands, pursed lips, lowered head, and other gestures. Workers also communicate with clients through nonverbal behavior. They can express warmth with a handshake, by leaning toward the interviewee rather than sitting back, and with facial expressions. Workers can also express disapproval, contempt, or disinterest by glancing off into space, fidgeting, coming to an interview late, looking at their watches, forgetting important names or facts about the interviewee's situation, and interrupting the interview to answer the phone or talk to others.

There is disagreement in the field about how much physical contact is appropriate between an interviewer and an interviewee. Although we cannot go into a full discussion of this issue, we do believe that touching can send both positive and negative messages. When either the interviewer or the interviewee sexualizes touching, it can be abusive. Some people's natural style of relating to others involves touching. However, before you touch a client (except for a handshake), you should ask permission. Even if it is natural for you to touch people, it might make some interviewees uncomfortable. It takes experience and skill to know when, how much, and with whom physical contact will help build rapport. Few doubt, however, the usefulness of using some reassuring touch when it seems appropriate. It's also important to learn the policies and practices of the organization that you work for. Use your organization's policy book to help you learn about its specific practice and remember to always seek input from your supervisor in your supervision times about this and other important questions.

To illustrate this, we return to the case of the elderly woman whose son and daughter-in-law were choosing a nursing home for her. The woman was terrified of going into this institution, imagining it was a type of prison, even though her son and daughter-in-law saw it as a gracious, well-run home. During the intake interview, the worker in the nursing home took the woman's trembling hand in her own. Afterward, as the elderly woman recounted the interview to her children, she said, "She put both of her hands around mine and made me feel not so alone."

Looking for nonverbal clues to feelings is not a parlor game. Some people jump to quick, simplistic conclusions based on one gesture. Yet you can't tell much about the significance of a gesture if you don't know what a person's typical body stance is like. A crying child may tell you, when you ask, that nothing is wrong, but his uncharacteristically sad face and quietness tell you that something is upsetting this usually bouncy youngster.

Although intuitive understanding is important, your first reaction to a scene may not always give you accurate information. For example, you might see men without a physical disability hanging around on a street during working hours and assume that they are shiftless or chronically unemployed. In fact, the men might be construction workers who have just been laid off because a project is finished and are looking for a new job. Or perhaps they might be migrant workers waiting for the grape harvest to begin or third-shift workers enjoying their time off. To arrive at any valid understanding, your observations of any one person or incident must be put in social and historical context.

ACTIVE LISTENING. As much as we long for perfect nonverbal understanding, we communicate most of our thoughts and feelings through language. Yet our attempts to communicate with one another often seem doomed to failure. Why is this so? One reason is that language itself is too frail to carry our full meaning. In the novel *Madame Bovary*, nineteenth-century French author Gustave Flaubert expresses his tragic awareness of this fact. Madame Bovary had told her lover Rudolph that she loved him, and she meant it sincerely. Rudolph, however, felt the words were being used in a phony way, perhaps because he himself had used them that way so often that he no longer believed them. Madame Bovary could not get through to him. This is what Flaubert (1856/1959) writes:

> He [Rudolph], this man of great experience, could not distinguish dissimilarities of feeling between similarities of expression . . . as though the fullness of the soul did not sometimes overflow into the emptiest phrases, since no one can ever express the measure of his needs, his conceptions or his sorrows, and human speech is like a cracked pot on which we beat out rhythms for bears to dance to when we are striving to make music that will wring tears from the stars. (p. 165)

In many of our conversations, we are faced with the awareness that our words may not carry our full meaning. Perhaps it is because we have not chosen the right words or because the listener is not really receiving our message or because we are not sure of what we mean ourselves.

An interviewer needs to master the crucial skill of active listening to be able to grasp the complex personality and the complex situation of each person. In order to "read" the emotion behind the words of the speaker and get closer to the real meaning, we must listen carefully to each word and then remember what has been said. Careful, active listening is not a common occurrence.

Try to remember the last time someone gave you her absolutely undivided attention and listened to you talk about your concerns, without interjecting any of her own. Few people are capable of giving their undivided attention to everyone they meet. Most of us are preoccupied, worrying about a test, a dentist's appointment, or a troubled friendship.

Although some people reveal themselves easily, most of us do not pour out our innermost thoughts to total strangers. In fact, we have been taught caution. Even with good friends, we are often reluctant to speak about what is on our minds. Many people feel a special reticence when they must ask for help, embarrassed to admit that they can't handle some aspect of their lives without help. Many people raised in the United States have learned the individualistic "pull yourself up by your own bootstraps" ideology. So when a person comes into an interview at a human service agency, we need to be alert to any feelings of anxiety about asking for and receiving help.

Recurrent references to a subject may indicate great concern about that topic. The way ideas are associated with each other can give hints about feelings. For example, if a woman tells us about her daughter's beauty and then shifts to her own concern about her appearance, we might wonder if the woman's feelings about herself are mixed up with her feelings about her daughter. Sometimes people conceal their meanings by saying the opposite of what they mean. A man whose fiancee has broken their engagement may say angrily that he's glad it's over because his ego is too injured for him to admit the opposite.

CORE VALUES OF THE INTERVIEWER. Many counselors and psychotherapists regard the values of empathy, warmth, respect, and genuineness as essential for a successful helping relationship. However, although everyone probably agrees that it is essential for a helper to respect a helpee, not everyone agrees about empathy.

EMPATHY Empathy is the capacity to identify yourself with another person's feelings and thoughts, to suspend your own judgment for the moment and feel with another. It differs from sympathy, which involves feeling sorry for someone but not necessarily suspending one's own feelings to try to identify with another person.

Research indicates that the capacity for empathy may be based in biology. Italian neuroscientists studying monkeys were amazed to discover that the brain has a system of neurons, or nerve cells, that specialize in a sort of "walking in another's shoes" function. These neurons become active both when a monkey actually makes a movement and when it is only watching another monkey, or even a human, make that same movement. "It is as if the monkey is imitating—or mirroring—the other's movement in its mind" (Goldberg, 2005, p. C1).

This may help researchers understand autism:

> The discovery of mirror neurons was important for basic brain science, but now it is also proving medically relevant: Researchers are reporting . . . that malfunctioning mirror neurons appear to play a central role in the social isolation of autistic children. (Goldberg, 2005, p. C1)

Empathy is an ongoing process rather than a state that is achieved once and for all. Some people object that because it is not measurable or observable, one should concentrate on training helpers in skills of communication that can be demonstrably improved. Others argue that empathy is not important when a helper is dealing with environmental concerns, such as helping someone to find housing.

We believe that empathy without knowledge of how to work the system would be useless in helping people with environmental concerns. Yet it is also essential to identify with people's feelings about their environmental concerns in order to understand fully how to help them. For example, a person may need to file a complaint against a landlord in order to get the heat turned on. The helping person needs to understand that person's personality in order to know whether he will actually file the complaint or be too frightened to do so.

In working with a welfare-rights group for Temporary Assistance for Needy Families (TANF) recipients, the prime goal may be to increase the TANF grant; yet, on the way to doing that, we must feel the linkages between the personal and the political. We must be able to:

- Identify with the recipient's rage against an arbitrary system or a mean-spirited worker
- Identify with feelings of powerlessness
- Understand a recipient's need to identify with the oppressive welfare system when he acts superior to other recipients
- Stretch our capacity to understand when, as the group's treasurer, the recipient is tempted to steal the group's funds
- Plumb the depths of the recipient's feelings of deprivation
- Understand the female recipient's feelings of frustration when the welfare functionaries watch her like a hawk to try to suppress her sexuality
- Understand the recipient's capacity to fight the system in order to know how to buoy that capacity.

Empathy springs out of our common humanness. Although no two people have precisely the same experiences, we all go through the same life cycle and share similar feelings. This could be considered a kind of universal kinship. Kinship is not only relatedness to one's family, but "also a type of connection—biological, spiritual, emotional, social, between people" (Cottle, 1974, p. xii). Using our imagination, we form connections to our interviewees that help us experience what they are experiencing. Empathy requires a finely tuned intuitive sensitivity to other people.

Empathy may be essential for survival, according to Dr. Steven Hyman, professor of neurobiology at Harvard Medical School. Dr. Hyman believes that we are hardwired to feel empathy because it confers an "elective advantage" that allows us as individuals and as a species to have a better chance at survival (Foreman, 2003). An infant is at increased risk of perishing if the parent is not empathic.

For people in the caring professions, there are potential pitfalls when experiencing another person's pain can lead to "empathic over-arousal," according to Nancy Eisenberg, a psychologist at Arizona State University. During empathetic over-arousal, the helper's own feelings—rather than the helpee's needs—become the focus, sometimes causing the individual being helped to withdraw from the helping process (Foreman, 2003). Human service workers need to learn how to empathize with a client's feelings without drowning in those feelings and without accepting the person's assumptions that led to those feelings. In addition, working with clients' emotionally charged and difficult situations can lead to vicarious trauma where workers experience the traumatic events of their clients, causing increased levels of distress on the human service worker's part (Cohen & Collens, 2013). We explore strategies to lessen the impact of vicarious trauma in Chapter 15.

More and more inmates are being sent to prison faster than new ones can be built. Very little rehabilitation is offered to them. In the process of empathizing with those who are in, or have been in prison, counselors must identify the sources of helplessness, rage, or frustration with the criminal justice system.

RESPECT Respect is a quality that most people understand in their social relationships. It involves regarding others as important and being concerned about their welfare. It acknowledges their uniqueness and their rights to feelings and needs. Respect requires that a helper be **nonjudgmental** when trying to understand a helpee.

GENUINENESS Genuineness is also a quality that people understand in their day-to-day relationships. In the helping relationship people quickly sense whether an individual is genuine or not. Putting on airs, pretending, or being disingenuous will quickly place a divide between you and your client. When people are being helped they want to know that the person to whom they entrust their thoughts and feelings actually cares. This quality has come to be more highly valued by many helping professionals than it used to be. Classical Freudian psychoanalysis established a helping model in which the therapist acted as a "blank slate"—sitting passively behind the patient, seldom interjecting an opinion or showing strong emotions. This model was always inappropriate for helping people who had concrete environmental problems and is increasingly seen as inappropriate for most therapeutic relationships. Counselors and therapists today are more likely to express appropriate feelings openly. "By being willing to discuss personal feelings, the helper encourages the helpee to respond similarly. The helpee opens up and learns to be genuine, too" (D'Augelli, D'Augelli, & Danish, 1981, pp. 58–59).

Genuineness also involves "being non-defensive and human enough to admit errors to clients. . . . [Practitioners] must be models of humanness and openness and avoid hiding behind a mask of 'professionalism'" (Hepworth & Larsen, 1987, p. 998).

Source: Lee Morris/Shutterstock

During the interview with a new client, we try to learn about the network of family and friends that surrounds him or her. The concept of "aging in place" has recently gained much attention. This wife, although also older, is able to care for her husband at home with supports from the nearby health center.

Case Example: Jean

A woman named Jean was out of money. Her husband had been unemployed for many months, and their relatives were also struggling financially and couldn't help. She set out for the welfare office to apply for TANF for herself and her two small children.

CONTEXT AND ORGANIZATIONAL SETTING

The welfare office had once been within walking distance of Jean's apartment, but because of fiscal cutbacks, the intake departments of several neighborhood welfare offices had been consolidated and centralized in a downtown office. Jean borrowed the $5 round-trip transit fare from a friend and, with two young children in tow, set out in the pouring rain for an address that rang no familiar bell in her memory. Asking her way as she went along, by trial and error she finally found the office, marked by a sign chiseled into the stone facade: OVERSEERS OF THE PUBLIC WELFARE.

(continued)

Jean entered the lobby and winced as she saw a security guard with a gun in his holster. Because it was Monday morning, the lobby was filled with people, many of them standing, since there were not enough chairs. The once-white paint on the walls and ceiling was peeling, and it was hard to see what color the carpeted floors had been, as they were threadbare in many spots. Faded posters describing long-defunct job programs lined the walls.

The receptionist sitting behind a thick glass partition ignored Jean, continuing a conversation with the other receptionist about a party she had gone to the night before. Finally, she shoved a piece of cardboard with the number 20 scribbled on it and an application form to fill out through the half-moon in the glass. Jean filled out the form and waited, and waited, and waited. The children whined, and whined, and whined. There were no toys for them and few diversions.

PERSONALITY AND STYLE OF THE INTERVIEWER

After about an hour, an assistance payments worker came into the hall and shouted, "Number 20!" Jean and her children meekly followed the worker into a room where four other workers sat at their desks, a room as dingy as the lobby, devoid of any of those objects that personalize an office.

There was a shaky coat rack, but the worker didn't suggest that Jean hang her wet coat there, so Jean simply left it on. Although the worker did not invite her to sit down, Jean assumed she was expected to do so. The worker did not smile, nor did she introduce herself. Jean remained "Number 20" in the worker's mind, and the worker was simply an animated function in Jean's mind. These two people were to talk with each other for at least half an hour, perhaps longer.

CLIENT EXPECTATIONS

Jean had been raised to believe that any interchange that took this long called for an exchange of names. Feeling that some deep social taboo was being violated and wanting to set it right, Jean introduced herself and made a few comments about the driving rain outside. The worker looked up briefly from the application form, which had been absorbing her attention since she sat down, and mumbled, still unsmiling, "I'm Marie Klausner."

ATTITUDES AND VALUES OF HELPERS

The interview could have been conducted by a computer. In fact, Jean amused herself by turning Marie into a blinking, chiming computer in her fantasy as the questions and directives flew at her:

- How much money do you have in the bank?
- What is your bank account number?
- What is your Social Security number?
- What are your children's birth dates?
- Bring in verification of their birth dates.
- Bring in bank statements for the past 12 months.

And so on.

The worker was annoyed by the children's interruptions. After she filled out the intake form and listed the many verifications that Jean would have to bring back before Jean could be accepted for TANF, the worker finally asked if Jean was in immediate need. On hearing that she was, the worker gave her an EBT card to get food. Frantic and depressed, Jean went back home in the rain, the children begging to stop for a hamburger each time they passed a fast-food restaurant.

Jean lived in a large city, and her welfare office reflected the poverty of the inner city. Jean's friend Marian, however, had a very different experience.

Case Example: Marian

Marian lived in a smaller town, where most people knew each other and the director of public welfare had some personal contact with many of the clients or their families. The director was supportive of workers' efforts to experiment with innovative ways of getting the job done. Although the department had limited funds, the workers pooled their resources and found volunteers to set up a modest child care center in the lobby. They brought in plants to create a more cheerful atmosphere, and when they couldn't convince the town council to paint the office, they held a raffle to buy paint and organized a painting party. Workers, clients, and members of the welfare advisory board painted the lobby themselves.

On the same rainy morning that Jean visited her welfare office, Marian came to this office to apply for TANF for herself and her child. The receptionist smiled at Marian when she came in and pointed out the rack where she could hang her coat. She took the children to the volunteer who cared for clients' children, and in a short time, she escorted Marian to a worker's office. After introductions and a sociable comment about the weather, the worker asked Marian how she could help her and learned that she had come to apply for financial assistance because her husband had died recently.

ACTIVE LISTENING, EMPATHY

As she explained what benefits Marian was entitled to and what the application process involved, the worker, having learned that Marian's husband had died only a week ago, kept her emotional radar tuned to Marian's distress signals. The worker knew that her main job was to process an application for TANF; she also knew that a human being was in pain and might need solace on the way to getting financial support. She obtained the same kind of information that Jean's worker had gotten, yet she led Marian gently into the application process, taking time to let Marian talk about her grief when she needed to.

Why did Jean and Marian receive such different treatment from their respective workers? A comparison of Jean's and Marian's encounters illustrates some of the factors that shape a human service interview.

FOCUS

The focus of both interviews was to find out if the applicants were eligible for benefits and, if they were, to start the process of obtaining them. Both workers were clear about their primary purpose and did not allow other issues to distract them from the task. In that respect, they were on target. Marian's worker was skillful enough to achieve the primary goal while not ignoring the other needs of her client. Jean's worker, in her single-mindedness, accomplished her goal but with a high cost to her client's sense of self-worth.

(continued)

CLIENT EXPECTATIONS

Jean's attitude about applying for welfare was shaped by all the negative publicity she had heard through the media and the grapevine. She came to the welfare office with a mental set of shame. The dingy, crowded, impersonal setting of the office heightened it. The interviewer was in no mood to reach out to Jean and put her at ease.

CONTEXT AND ORGANIZATIONAL SETTING

Jean's worker was burned out. The entire office seemed demoralized. Demoralization is not inevitable, even in an organization with limited resources. The welfare office Marian went to was able to treat clients with respect and dignity because it was located in a small community where there was no sharp social division between those who are affluent and those who might struggle financially. Most people knew each other, and the director and workers lived in the community and regarded their average client as "one of us" rather than as "one of them." The director was a warm and imaginative person who, working with limited resources, tried to bring out the best in workers and clients.

Both Jean and Marian were entitled to dignified treatment. Yet Jean went home with a hollow, angry sensation in the pit of her stomach. She had gone through what one sociologist has termed a "successful degradation ceremony" (Garfinkel, 1965). Marian, although still worried about a future with a diminished income and scared of loneliness, did not feel such degradation. She felt less alone and was reassured that the worker at the welfare office would process her claim as quickly as possible.

Interviewing skills are needed for many aspects of group work as well as for ongoing individual relationships.

Source: Pukhov K/Shutterstock

The teenage years can be very stressful, leading to anxiety and depression. It is important that young people have a person whom they trust to discuss problems confidentially with.

STRUCTURE OF AN INTERVIEW

Like a story, an interview has a beginning, a middle, and an end. It takes place within a specific time frame. The span of interviews varies enormously, from a ten-minute hot-line conversation to the more traditional "fifty-minute hour" at an agency to an interview that could take an entire day (e.g., when a worker places a child in a new foster home). There are various ways of looking at the stages of an interview. From a broad view, the interview has three stages: (1) opening the interview, starting to build rapport, and making a contract; (2) exploring the issues and making an action plan; and (3) closing and reviewing the actions to be taken. In actual practice, these phases blend together, and elements of each phase can be found in the others.

If someone is applying for a benefit, such as food stamps, the purpose of the interview may be self-evident (although not necessarily; there may be other needs that the person is hesitant to admit to, or other help for which she might be eligible). Once it is established, for example, that obtaining food stamps is the most pressing need, the beginning of the interview consists of the interviewer asking a few questions to establish whether the interviewee is potentially eligible. If, for example, the interviewee says that she is a college student, then the interviewer will save time for both of them by asking right away if the student meets a set of criteria. If not, there is no point in continuing down that path. The interviewer then should politely explain the requirements, and ask the student if she would like to be referred to some other resource (or, if the student is interested, to some group that is seeking to improve food stamp benefits). Workers should also tell clients that they have the right to appeal the decision the worker has made.

Although most of us recoil from long, complex official forms, some forms are necessary. Yet an interview need not become machinelike. Sometimes the claimant has filled out the form while waiting to be interviewed. Then the interviewer can go over it, helping the interviewee provide additional answers. The worker can further explain the program, finding out if the interviewee needs other kinds of help.

If the form is to be filled out during their time together, an interviewer can use it as the basis for a structured conversation rather than as a script for a third degree. If information pertaining to a particular question on the form has already come out in the opening conversation, the question need not be asked again. If, however, the interviewer's time is limited and there are others waiting, then the interview will probably have to be more constricted. In general, workers should ask questions precisely as written only when the answers are needed for a very structured research project or for a medical history.

Consider how a food stamp application might be taken. Here is the beginning of an interview using the mechanical approach.

Name?

Address?

Who is in your household?

How much money do you have in the bank?

Do you have a checking account?

Do you have any insurance?

Any boats, camping trailers, land?

The following interview uses a more human approach. After the initial pleasantries, the interviewer says to the applicant, Guy LeBlanc:

> Mr. LeBlanc, the food stamp program has a lot of rules about who can get food stamps and who can't. I hope you qualify, since you must need them or you wouldn't be asking for them. Yet I have to know a lot about your living arrangements and your resources before I can determine if you are eligible. Could you tell me about who you live with, how you make your living, and things that you own, such as a car, bank account, and so on?

This question is broad enough to set Mr. LeBlanc off on a discussion of his circumstances, from which you will probably be able to get most of the information you need. You can ask questions about the things he left out, but you have given Mr. LeBlanc initiative in the interview rather than making him feel as if he were on a witness stand.

Two principles are useful guidelines for all stages of the interview: seeking concreteness and focusing on the here and now (immediacy).

Seeking Concreteness

Someone once said, "God resides in the details." It is life's details that are important, and a good interviewer knows how to go after those details. This is called *seeking concreteness* or *specificity of response*. When someone says, "She's an awful parent," you could ask the person to clarify exactly what the parent does that is awful. In this way, you help the client to be clearer, get details about significant interactions and events, and make sure that you and the client understand each other's meanings.

To help an interviewee be more concrete, the interviewer can ask about specific examples or stories as a follow-up to a general response. If the interviewee says, "I really liked it when I first got here," you can ask, "Can you give an example of something you really liked?" Or, "What was most surprising about . . .?" "What was the worst disappointment in . . .?" (Martin, R., 2001)

Immediacy

An interview should focus on the present concerns of the interviewee rather than on past or future events or concerns. This characteristic is called *immediacy*. The concerns may involve the interviewee's life situation or something happening in the relationship between interviewer and interviewee. Evans et al. (1979) give the example of the former:

> INTERVIEWEE (separated from her husband for three months): When he first told me that he was going to leave me, I was very angry, but now I'm managing by myself without his help.
> INTERVIEWER: You're really proud that you have managed by yourself.

This response focused on the interviewee's present feelings of pride in her ability to manage her life, the most important issue at the moment. If the interviewer had chosen to focus on the past, she might have said, "You were really angry when he first told you." Or, if the interviewer had chosen to focus on the future, she might have said, "In the future, you'll be glad it worked out this way" (Evans, Hearn, Uhlemann, & Ivey, 1979). Either of those comments would have deflected the interviewee's attention from her main concern at the moment.

Questions That Help People Talk

The techniques of the ethnographic interview, such as asking global questions, are useful in helping people to explore problems. **Open-ended questions** begin conversations but leave the choice of direction to the client.

If an interviewer asks a lot of closed-ended, or yes/no, questions, the interview becomes a question-and-answer period in which the interviewee passively responds. Experienced interviewers try to avoid asking too many questions, which can destroy a client's initiative. Asking the right question at the right time is an important interviewing skill. Beginning workers sometimes take refuge in the question-and-answer format as if it were a security blanket, perhaps fearing loss of control with a looser structure. One guideline to use in deciding how to ask a question is: The question should help to further the process of discovery, either of an interviewee's inner self or the outer world.

Even a question aimed at finding out if a person is eligible for a government benefit can, if combined with information, help interviewees understand the program and their place in it:

INTERVIEWER (TO A TANF RECIPIENT WHO HAS APPLIED FOR THE JOB TRAINING PROGRAM): Mrs. Leavitt, the job training program doesn't require a parent to enroll in it if she has a child age 2 or under. How old are your children?

MRS. LEAVITT: I have a 1-year-old.

INTERVIEWER: Then you don't need to apply, but you still can if you want to. How do you think the job training program might help you?

Some kinds of questions keep control in the hands of the interviewer; others give more freedom to the interviewee. The closed question allows for few options and gives minimal information:

CLOSED: Do you like your teacher?

OPEN: What's your teacher like?

CLOSED: Do you shop for bargains and use dried skim milk?

OPEN: It's hard to make a TANF grant stretch. How do you manage?

CLOSED: Do you get enough sleep with the new baby?

OPEN: How is the baby's schedule affecting you?

Another controlling question that is hardly ever helpful is the question "why?" Think about how your parents, teachers, and other authority figures frequently scolded by saying "Why did you do that?" You probably answered, quite honestly, "I dunno," and the conversation ended. It is almost always perceived as a threatening question.

The **indirect question** gives the interviewee more options and elicits more insight than the direct question. It is phrased like a statement, without a question mark, but actually asks a question. Here are some examples:

DIRECT: What jobs have you held in the past?

INDIRECT: I'd be interested to hear about your previous jobs.

DIRECT: Has your new foster child adjusted well?

INDIRECT: I imagine a lot has happened since I placed Billy here. What kind of a week did you and he have?

Door openers, a term coined by Thomas Gordon (1970), are an invitation to say more about something the interviewee has brought up. Although sometimes done by questioning, door openers are best done in the form of an open-ended request for more information:

Tell me more.

I'm interested in hearing about that.

The concept of funnel sequences is another way of looking at methods to encourage interviewees to talk (France & Kish, 1995). Funnel sequences begin with a broad probe or question, continue with reflection and possibly some open questions, then end with closed questions to fill any gaps in information you must gather.

Inverted funnel sequences take the opposite path. They begin with easily answered closed questions, then move to broader responses such as reflection and open questions. This technique is a good way to encourage a client to talk when the person is reluctant to speak with you. Here is an example of an inverted funnel sequence, used in an interaction with a 16-year-old who was hospitalized following a drug overdose suicide attempt. In response to an initial open question of "How are things going?" the patient said nothing and turned away from the interviewer. But he started to talk when the interviewer used the following inverted funnel sequence:

INTERVIEWER: Did Dr. Matthews see you this morning?

CLIENT: Mmhmm.

INTERVIEWER: Have they brought you breakfast?

CLIENT: Yeah. (Turning toward the interviewer with a disgusted look.)

INTERVIEWER: You didn't like the food.

CLIENT: It was awful. Everything was cold, and the fried eggs were all runny. It was almost as bad as that stuff they had me drink last night to make me throw up. I just want out of here.

INTERVIEWER: You'd really like to go home.

CLIENT: But they're making me stay, even though I've told them I want to go home. This place is terrible. It's boring and there's nothing to do.

INTERVIEWER: What do you think would need to happen in order for Dr. Matthews to discharge you?

Initially, this client was reluctant to talk. But two easy-to-answer closed questions evoked short responses. Then two reflections elicited animated descriptions of thoughts and feelings. Finally, an open question led the interaction toward a discussion of positive change (France & Kish, 1995).

Furthering Responses

A number of techniques can be used to explore a problem. Often they can be used in combination. One skill, called **furthering responses**, encourages clients to continue talking (Hepworth & Larsen, 1987). These include:

1. *Physical attending.* This is part of active listening and involves being there physically.
2. *Silence* (when used to indicate thoughtful attention).
3. *Minimal verbal or nonverbal responses.* A minimal response such as an attentive look of interest, a nod of the head, or a verbal "uh-huh" is often all the encouragement the

interviewee needs. Whatever is natural to the listener is usually appropriate as long as it does not interfere with the interviewee's message.

4. *Accent responses.* This involves repeating, in a questioning tone of voice or with emphasis, a word or short phrase that the client has just said. For example, "if a client says, 'I've really had it with the way my supervisor at work is treating me,' the practitioner might respond, 'Had it?' to prompt further elaboration by the client" (Hepworth & Larsen, 1987, p. 1000).

Verbal Following Responses

A number of responses let clients know they have been heard and understood and provide immediate feedback (Hepworth & Larsen, 1987). These are called *verbal following responses* and include paraphrasing or restating, clarifying, and reflecting.

PARAPHRASING OR RESTATING   **Paraphrasing** or **restating** what the interviewee has just said is similar to a minimal response in that its purpose is to let interviewees know their messages have been understood. They encourage clients to continue. There is literal restatement, such as:

INTERVIEWEE: I felt terrible.

INTERVIEWER: You felt terrible.

But there is also paraphrasing or summarizing, such as:

INTERVIEWEE: The baby cried a lot, and I've never taken care of a baby before. I just didn't know what to do.

INTERVIEWER: It was a new experience and you were confused.

CLARIFYING   **Clarifying** goes beyond a minimal response. The interviewer now seeks further understanding of what has been said or tries to clarify for the interviewee something hard to express. A question designed to help the interviewer understand might be (1) I don't understand that very well. Could you explain it again? (2) Are you saying that . . .? or (3) Do you mean . . .?

The following is an example of clarification used to help interviewees articulate their thoughts:

INTERVIEWEE: When the baby cries, I feel like I'm falling apart. I don't know what to do, I'm so mixed up. I want to be a good father, but I don't know how to. It's all so confusing . . .

INTERVIEWER: The baby's crying seems to scare you. You feel mixed up and unsure of how to care for your baby.

REFLECTING   Compared with restating, which deals with what the interviewee said, **reflecting** deals with what an interviewee feels. Adding nothing of their own, interviewers say what they empathically sense the interviewee might be feeling:

INTERVIEWEE: There's sure a lot of red tape I have to go through to apply for welfare, isn't there? Why can't you people get together? I go from one person to another answering the same old questions all over again.

INTERVIEWER: I guess you feel like you're getting the runaround, don't you? Are you pretty mad at us by now?

Nonverbal Following Responses

As you develop your interviewing skills, it's important to consider the manner in which your nonverbal communication supports your efficacy. Mandal (2014) helps us to understand that nonverbal communication is the sum total of all communication that does not involve speech. How you sit, your posture, facial expressions, eye contact, sighs, grunts, and groans all play an important part in the formula for effective communication. For example, imagine you are smiling broadly when a client is telling you about something very difficult for him. In this case, the client will doubt your sincerity. Similarly, do you keep looking at your watch, or are you intently focused on what you client is saying? Each of these behaviors denotes a particular message that is communicated readily to the client.

Albert Mehrabian's 1971 book *Silent Messages* posited that your actual words represent only 7 percent of the elements necessary to communicate effectively. This is followed by 55 percent body language and 38 percent tone and musicality of voice. Some theorists now take issue with Mehrabian's theory (see, for example, Thorne, 2010), believing that this view discounts the importance of written communication, but almost all agree that body language and vocal tones are essential to effective communication, particularly when one is focusing on person-to-person and face-to-face communication.

Given this, it is critically important for you to be mindful of your nonverbal communication. Before you begin an interview, take a moment to center yourself and strive to be fully present with your clients. Western culture generally drives us to think more about where we are going rather than where we are and what we are doing in the moment. Taking a few minutes to focus yourself will help you to avoid distractions. In addition, it's important to be mindful of your posture. Leaning toward a client generally reflects a more engaged and caring message. Eye contact in western culture denotes engagement and respect for the individual, though it's important to recognize that this can be different depending on the individual's culture. As a result, it is important to understand the culturally bound nonverbal communication practices of the client you are serving.

It's also important to understand that your nonverbal communication is largely influenced by what you are thinking and how you feel. Because of this, it is entirely possible that your nonverbal behavior reflects your internal thoughts and feelings unintentionally. You might believe that you are masking your impatience with a particular client, but it's entirely possible that your internal thoughts and feelings are "leaking" through. This is another reason to strive for mindfulness in your work with clients.

Other Ways of Responding

Some responses are not specifically geared to drawing the client out but can be useful when timed correctly and given sensitively. However, some of them are controversial. They include giving information, encouraging and reassuring, suggesting, advising, confronting, and interpreting.

GIVING INFORMATION   Clients need to know everything we can tell them about the services and benefits to which they are entitled. This information should be given when clients are ready for it, in a way that doesn't overwhelm or confuse them.

ENCOURAGING AND REASSURING   **Encouraging and reassuring** responses are too often used insensitively. In our everyday relationships, we often encourage our friends by saying "Oh sure, you can win the race," " . . . you can get that job," or " . . . you can get her to go out with you." Such statements may not always be helpful, especially if they are not true. We say such things because we can't think of anything else or because we don't have the time, emotional energy, or courage to explore the real possibilities.

Such seemingly reassuring statements can actually leave clients feeling even more frightened if they don't feel strong or qualified. We all need permission to feel weak and vulnerable and to anticipate failure, and sometimes we need someone to remind us of our strengths. It takes a great deal of sensitivity, however, to recognize when encouragement is appropriate.

The following is one example of helpful reassurance given by a foster parent to a biological parent:

> BIOLOGICAL PARENT: I always felt low. Like I was kind of an outcast. I don't know why. This is just my nature. . . . I know people think I'm a drunkard. I was in a mental hospital for two weeks, and this had a bad effect on me. So I felt both insane and poor. I had no money. And you don't look nice, and you don't feel nice, you don't perform well.
>
> FOSTER PARENT: . . . anybody who has done what you did and let your children go is a big person.
>
> BIOLOGICAL PARENT: Well, I'm glad you feel this way.
>
> FOSTER PARENT: And you yourself said you felt this way.
>
> BIOLOGICAL PARENT: I don't think my child would have ever made it to college. At least she has the chance. . . . (Mandell, B., 1973, pp. 167–168)

The following is an example of reassurance that definitely can't help anyone cope with reality:

> INTERVIEWEE: I'm feeling awful about my job. Nothing seems to work right.
>
> INTERVIEWER: Oh, don't worry. We all have job problems. It will work out all right.

SUGGESTING   **Suggesting** is a mild form of advice. If a suggestion is made tentatively, without any coercion, it can pose alternatives that the interviewee may not have been aware of:

> INTERVIEWER (TO A COLLEGE STUDENT): Since you are a junior with a 3.0 average and need money, you might consider the co-op program, where you could work for a regular salary and get six credits.

ADVISING   Giving advice assumes that one person knows what is best for another, and that is a risky assumption. An interviewer should be cautious when **advising** a client. When an interviewee asks for advice, the interviewer should first find out what the interviewee already thinks about the problem and what alternative paths are being considered. This process by itself may help the interviewee to clarify his problem.

Although many experienced interviewers try to avoid giving direct advice, when they feel it is appropriate, they do so tentatively. They make it clear that their feelings won't be hurt if the interviewee rejects it. Then they ask for feedback on what the interviewee thought about it. The following is an example of an interviewer talking with a student who is considering dropping out of college because he finds his workload too heavy and boring:

> INTERVIEWER: Maybe next semester you might want to take a lot of courses in your major with teachers whom you like and pick up the rest of your required courses later. You seem so discouraged about school that some "fun" courses might get you interested again. What do you think?

CONFRONTING One of the most emotionally loaded debates about interviewing centers on the issue of the usefulness and timing of confrontation. **Confronting** is a tactic used to call interviewees' attention to discrepancies, inconsistencies, or self-destructive tendencies in their words or behavior. It aims to help interviewees view their behavior in a different light, perhaps unmasking distortions, rationalizations, or evasions. Confrontation can be used gently, with a great deal of empathy, or it can be used in a cruelly assaultive way. There are many gradations along the gentle-to-harsh continuum. Here is an example of a gentle confrontation:

> INTERVIEWEE: I don't mind that my husband insults me and says I look like a fat pig [tears in her eyes].
>
> INTERVIEWER: You say you don't mind, yet you have tears in your eyes. Most people I know mind a lot when someone insults them. I know I do.

This is a mild confrontation, pointing out the discrepancy between the client's words and behavior. It was followed by a supportive statement, which gives permission to be upset and is concrete and descriptive ("You have tears in your eyes") rather than abstract and judgmental ("You must be a masochist"). It "universalizes" the issue by helping the client realize her feelings are common to many people.

Some counselors routinely use a high level of confrontation and intrusiveness, justifying it as a high-risk but high-yield method. One study, however, declared that this justification is a myth (Lieberman, Yalom, & Miles, 1973). It found that highly challenging and confrontational encounter group leaders were destructive in their impatient pressuring of clients to change and ignored the need to individualize treatment. Another researcher warned against the assumption that everyone benefited by "letting it all hang out." Some may, indeed, need help "tucking it all in" (Parloff, 1970, p. 203).

Another study showed that counselors whose confrontations focused on the clients' weaknesses were less effective than those who focused on strengths (Berenson & Mitchell, 1974). It also showed that more effective counselors initiated sensitive confrontation more than did less effective ones.

Some human service workers who work with street people report that a more confrontational style is expected and appreciated on the streets. One professor talks about the notion of tough love. Many street people understand 'tough love,' and feel that it works.

Other literature highlights the ongoing debate about the use of confrontation. Collins (2002) notes that there are those who believe individuals who abuse substances respond to a more confrontational approach, while others argue that a more empathic-based interviewing approach is more impactful. Similarly, in the area of intimate partner abuse, Collins points out that treatment efforts often involve a fine balance between supportive interviewing and strategically placed confrontation in order to preempt aggressive behavior and build client awareness.

INTERPRETING **Interpreting** is generally reserved for a therapeutic relationship between a counselor and a client. In general, one wouldn't use this approach as an entry-level human service worker, but it is important to understand that in time, your development within the field will lend itself to positions where interpreting is more widely used. It originated in psychoanalytic practice. Client-centered, gestalt, and some existential theories generally avoid this technique. Ethnographic interviewers would also not use it, because it puts the interviewer in the position of being the expert.

Others believe that interpretation is essential. They argue that it "encourages clients to see their problems from a different perspective, with the desired effect of opening up new possibilities for remedial courses of action" (Hepworth & Larsen, 1987, p. 1008).

The other responses we've described, if done correctly, do not go beyond what the interviewee says or feels. Interpretation, however, *speculates* on what the words might *actually* mean. If the interviewee accepts a response as an accurate interpretation, it can be helpful. However, the "expert's" interpretation is often rejected with irritation or, worse, swallowed whole without reflection. The interviewee's response is the best guide to deciding whether a worker's interpretation has been helpful. The following is an example:

> INTERVIEWEE: I don't know why the baby's crying makes me feel so helpless. My mother always knew what to do when my baby brother cried.
>
> INTERVIEWER: When you compare yourself to your mother, you feel inferior to her.
>
> INTERVIEWEE: Maybe that's what it is.

Self-Disclosure

Interviewers often have a hard time deciding when they should reveal elements in their personal lives and attitudes. At one time, that was considered strictly a no-no. Now, most researchers and helpers believe that appropriate self-disclosure can be supportive to the interviewee and creates a more honest relationship. Most of us find it easier to share thoughts and feelings with someone who is willing to risk similar sharing. When the interviewer does this, he is modeling desirable sharing behavior and showing that he, too, is human.

The guideline for deciding when the worker should disclose something about his personal life is the extent to which it brings clarity rather than burdening the client with the interviewer's concerns. *Sharing can illustrate the universality of human concerns.* The interviewers who spend too much time discussing their families, hobbies, or worries are obviously more interested in themselves than in the client. The question to ask yourself is whether what you intend to share will help facilitate the individual's move toward his desired goals or hinder it. For example, adolescents that the author works with would often ask whether she had ever done illicit drugs. One might think sharing personal information here would help connect the helper to the helpees and support their movement toward their goal of being drug-free. Just the opposite is possible as well. An affirmative answer might subtly give permission to the individual to pursue illicit drug use. The client's response to hearing that her helper once experimented with drugs might be "If my counselor did drugs, then why shouldn't I?" If you answer that you've never done drugs, then the possibility exists that the client will think you don't know what you are talking about. Given this, it is important to carefully consider what you share. Oftentimes it's helpful to answer a question with a question. "It appears that this is an important question for you; tell me why this is important for you to know." It's also important to understand the policy of the organization you are working for and to make careful use of your supervision time to ensure your strategy for sharing personal information is truly in support of the client's interests.

The following are two examples of an appropriate use of sharing feelings, viewpoints, and experiences:

> INTERVIEWER: You seem to be wondering if I can understand the problems you're having with your foster child. My wife and I cared for a friend's child for a couple of years while she was ill. I know that's not exactly the same as your situation, but the child did show some of the same problems you're having. I'm not sure that means I can understand the problems you're having, but I'd like to try.

INTERVIEWER: I just listened to you say how hard you worked on the paper—reading books on research and style, spending days in the library, and doing everything in your power to do a good job. Then you described how the teacher scribbled sarcastic comments all over the paper and ridiculed it in front of the class. You apologized for doing such a bad job and say you feel like a failure. Yet, while listening to you, I found myself feeling indignant about the teacher's behavior. I was reminded of a similar situation many years ago when I was a student. Didn't you feel some anger yourself?

Rather than pretend to an interviewee that you have no values or that you agree with the interviewee's values when you don't, it is better to be honest. This leaves both you and the interviewee free to hold on to values that are important without needing to impose them on each other. The following is an example of an appropriate use of disclosing values:

COUNSELOR: Can you try to tell me what you see as the worst problems in this marriage?

HUSBAND: Yes, that's easy. She's out fooling around with her art groups all the time and the house is a mess. I don't have clean socks and underwear in the morning and dinner is never ready on time.

WIFE: You never say anything nice to me, you never talk to me, and now that I finally, after twenty years, found interests and friends of my own, you resent it and you're continually carping at me.

COUNSELOR (TO HUSBAND): It's important to you that your laundry be done, the house cleaned, and dinner prepared when you come home.

HUSBAND: Damn right it is! That's what wives are supposed to do.

COUNSELOR: I have a hard time with this because I do not agree with your definition of a wife's obligations. However, I do see that in your view, she is not meeting the terms of the marriage contract under which you are operating. (Okun & Rappaport, 1980, p. 185)

The counselor expressed her views without deriding or punishing the husband. This seemed to help both husband and wife begin to acknowledge and evaluate some of their own values and beliefs about sex roles and marriage.

Authoritarian Leads and Responses

Although giving advice may *sometimes* be helpful, authoritarian leads and responses in interviewing are never helpful. They are generally harmful because they do not take the feelings and thoughts of the interviewee into account. They assume that the interviewer is superior, which makes the interviewee feel inferior. These leads and responses include:

- Urging
- Threatening
- Moralizing
- Contradicting
- Arguing
- Commanding
- Scolding
- Punishing
- Criticizing
- Denying

- Disapproving
- Rejecting
- Ridiculing
- Putting words in someone's mouth.

When the interviewer takes a high-and-mighty moral tone, the interviewee has a choice of mindless submission or stubborn defiance. Either way, the interviewee has not been helped to grow in awareness or independence. We have all been lectured to or preached to at some time in our lives, and it's a safe bet that we have resented it! The following are some examples:

INTERVIEWER: I thought you were smart enough to know you should use birth control.

INTERVIEWER: Stealing is wrong, so the teacher had a right to suspend you.

DOCUMENTATION AND RECORD KEEPING

Many workers would much rather spend their time on interviews than on completing documentation of their interviews. Yet most human service organizations operate under strict licensing or accreditation standards that require them to carefully document their activities. Documentation helps assure compliance with regulatory authorities' requirements, agency standards, and payment requirements for services delivery. It also helps protects you as a worker against miscommunication as well as potential liability. One licensing authority always said "If it isn't written down then it didn't happen!" Human service agencies would be in deep trouble if they did not require workers to record interviews.

1. Documentation provides continuity from one worker to another and from one session to the next. Suppose as a worker in a halfway house you learned from Mary that she planned to go home next week and needed to be driven to a job interview from her home on Wednesday of that week. If you did not record this, the staff member who came on duty after you might not learn of these plans, and Mary might not get to the interview.
2. Documentation of interviews can memorialize progress or lack of it in each particular situation. If you are working with a woman in a nursing home who is losing her memory, your periodic notations about her mental state help to assess whether her memory loss is getting worse over time, staying about the same, or getting better. Or suppose you need to show your funding source the quality and quantity of the services you have given clients. Only if you have kept careful records of referrals and interviews can you do that.
3. Good record keeping provides documentation of a client's eligibility for service. If done according to previously agreed-on and uniform procedures, recording can also be used for research and evaluation of programs and for researching the history of programs.
4. Documentation can provide important evidence in legal suits. Workers who have been accused of negligence in child abuse cases have been able to prove, through records of visits and phone contacts, that they had done everything in their power to prevent the abuse.
5. Documentation is used by some agencies as a therapeutic tool. In a few states, patients and ex-patients of psychiatric hospitals are permitted to read their own records. "One state psychiatric hospital in Washington has for several years allowed all patients to examine their own records and has found that policy to be therapeutic" (Ennis & Emery, 1978, p. 177).

Documentation, Recording Keeping, and Privacy

Today most organizations recognize that clients have the right to see their records. Given this, it's important to ensure documentation is written in a way that truly considers the potential audience.

When workers know that interviewees can read their records, they are likely to be more careful about what they write. They are much less prone to make global evaluative statements such as "The child is in danger of neglect" and more likely to make concrete descriptive statements such as "The fourth-floor windows do not have window guards and the mother has four small children to look after so cannot always keep watch over each child to prevent them from falling out the window. The landlord has not provided enough heat, so the mother turns on the gas stove for heat. This is a fire hazard."

Instead of saying "The child appeared malnourished," a more verifiable statement would be "Medical exam showed the child to be 15 pounds below the normal weight for that age and anemic."

You should strive in your recording to let a future reader see what you saw. Concrete, descriptive statements are not only more accurate, but they also force workers to be more precise, avoiding moralistic, judgmental statements. Some workers discuss with clients what the client thinks should go into a record, using this as a tool to help clients articulate their problems and progress.

We'd be remiss if we didn't acknowledge the growing use of electronic health records within social service organizations. Technology has advanced the way in which client records are maintained, stored, and shared. As a human service worker, you'll not only need to consider the content of your documentation but also the way technology has impacted the interview process. Be careful not to fall into the trap of simply staring at a computer screen as you ask your client questions. You know firsthand how off-putting it can be when you're trying to talk to your friends and they are staring at their iPhones. Imagine if you're someone seeking assistance for a difficult situation and your worker seems more concerned with their laptop than with you and your circumstances.

Summary

1. An interview is defined as an interaction between people that has a consciously planned purpose, structure, and goal and requires specific communication skills.

2. Important elements of all interviews include the location or setting; the personality, expectations, cultural background, and style of both the interviewer and the interviewee; agency sponsorship; and the attitudes and values of the interviewer. All these are interrelated.

3. The structure of an interview includes three stages: opening, exploring the issues, and closing.

4. During the opening phase, the interviewer and interviewee work out a formal or informal contract to plan their work together.

5. Interviews should focus on a person's strengths rather than weaknesses.

6. Attitudes that are essential for good interviewing include active observing, physical attention, and active listening.

7. Important values include empathy, warmth, respect, and genuineness.

8. Interviews about benefits such as food stamps can be personalized and human rather than rote and bureaucratic.

9. An occupational hazard of human service workers is a need to rescue people and do things for them rather than with them.
10. Some roadblocks to good interviewing are overly passive behavior, discomfort with emotions, and condescension.
11. Open-ended questions help people to talk about themselves.
12. Confrontation can be used gently or in an assaultive way, and should be used sparingly.
13. It is important to observe nonverbal messages and to be aware of your own nonverbal messages.
14. Personal disclosure should be used only to bring clarity rather than to burden the client with the worker's problems.
15. Authoritarian leads and responses are never helpful.
16. Documenting interviews is important for continuity of work between workers, for helping the worker remember essential facts, and for legal reasons.
17. Concrete, descriptive statements in recording force workers to be more precise.

Discussion Questions

1. *Humanizing the eligibility interview.* Obtain an application form for food stamps or TANF and study the form with the goal of humanizing the interview. How can you ask questions that will give the interviewee some initiative in the interview? How can you keep some warmth and genuineness in the interview? How can you get the information you need and, at the same time, make the clients feel that they are important and deserving of respect? After studying the questions and deciding on your strategy, role-play the interview with someone, and complete the application form. After the interview, ask the interviewee for feedback on the strengths and weaknesses of your interview.

2. *Active observing.* With one other student, go to a railroad station, to a store, out on the street, or around the campus with a notebook. Observe for 15 minutes. Then each student should write up a one-page summary of the observation. Bring yours to class without conferring with the other student. Note the differences in the pair of observations.

3. *Analyzing an observation.* In the presence of several other people—on a bus, in a subway, in a waiting room, or at a party—observe people's behavior closely. Note the relationship of elements in the environment to behavior and the interrelationships among people. Make notes on your observations, write them up, and discuss them with other students.

4. *How well can you listen?* Form a group with two other students. One student takes the role of listener and another of talker, and a third student observes. For three minutes, have the talker speak about any topic she chooses. Then the listener should repeat what has been heard. The observer should judge how accurately the listener has heard the speaker. Switch roles until each has had a chance to be talker, listener, and observer.

5. *Asking questions.* Decide on some information you want from another person. First, ask the person six controlling or closed-ended questions and write down the answers. Next, ask six non-controlling or open-ended questions about the same subject and write down the answers. Which questions gave you more information? Talk to the interviewee about how he felt about the two kinds of questions.

6. *Learning to deal with anger.* Form a group with two other students. Two students should role-play, and the third student should observe an interview in which the interviewee imagines being very angry with the interviewer, feeling the anger as genuinely as possible and expressing it heatedly. For two or three minutes, the interviewer should react defensively; then, for two or three minutes, the interviewer should react empathically. Both interviewer and interviewee should observe and contrast the difference in reactions to the two kinds of responses.

The interviewer should note how she felt about the angry attack and how the two different responses felt. The interviewee should note how the two interviewer responses felt. The observer should note carefully the nature of the feelings expressed by the two role-players, as well as nonverbal behavior that gives clues to feelings. Change roles so that each person has an opportunity to play all the roles (Hammond, Hepworth, & Smith, 1977).

7. *Dealing with a "helpless" person.* In a group, ask a volunteer to play the role of Mrs. Jones, an interviewee. All but Mrs. Jones should close their eyes and imagine that they are in an office and Mrs. Jones is seeing them for the first time. Their job is to help Mrs. Jones. She sits down (adopting a slightly helpless tone of voice and a dramatic presentation): "I am so glad you have time to see me. You are absolutely my last hope! I can just tell you will be able to help me. I've been to four other places, and they all have waiting lists, or no time, or just were not interested. I am feeling absolutely desperate and I was so relieved when you could see me right away! The others did not understand me at all; they didn't even take the time to listen to my difficulty; I only need someone to help me sort out the problem and I am sure you can do that. I am grateful that you are spending time with me." Change roles so that each person has an opportunity to play all the roles (National Center on Child Abuse and Neglect, 1979).

Web Resources for Further Study

Questia

https://www.questia.com/library/sociology-and
-anthropology/social-work/interviewing-in-social
-work.jsp

MyLab Helping Professions for Introduction to Human Services

In the Topic 7 Assignments: Client Intervention, try Application Exercise 7.3: Case Management, Intake Interviewing, and Counseling Skills and Credentialing Quiz 7.3: Case Management, Intake Interviewing, and Counseling Skills.

Then, in the Topic 9 Assignments: Interpersonal Communication, try Application Exercise 9.3: Establishing Rapport with Clients.

Direct Strategies: Working with People One-on-One

9

Source: Alexander Raths/Shutterstock

Learning Outcomes

- Students can explain why there are no universally agreed-upon definitions of the terms used for human service workers who meet with clients one-on-one. They can name five of the terms often used at agencies.

- Student can list the four major goals of the case worker whatever the problem their client is facing.

- Students will be able to list the steps in the case work process from preparation for the encounter all the way to final evaluation of the work that has been done.

- Students will be able to describe the differences between informal and formal evaluation techniques that are used at the completion of the one-on-one case process.

Thus far in this book you have met many human service workers. The majority of them were delivering direct services, spending most of their day working one-on-one with people at their agencies. Although they all were doing similar work, their human service agencies were likely to refer to these staff workers by one or another of these titles:

- Case worker
- Social worker
- Counselor
- Advocate
- Case manager
- Hot-line worker
- Family resource worker
- Addictions counselor
- Other titles unique to a particular program

All this semantic fuzziness can be confusing to the person seeking help who must figure out who to go to in order to talk about his problems. And a worker searching the job listings in the newspaper or on a website most likely cannot tell from the title of the position exactly what tasks or problem areas it will include. The general public may find it difficult to understand how a middle-aged woman with a doctorate in psychology and a young man with an associate's degree in human services can both assert that they do "counseling."

In an effort to make job titles uniform, some professionals in the human service field may believe that a distinction in title should be made according to how much the worker deals with highly charged emotional material rather than with the ordinary problems of daily life.

But we don't think that is a sensible distinction! All human service workers, regardless of their backgrounds, their job titles, or their clients' problems, must inevitably deal with inner emotions, external pressures, and available resources. Human service problems stem from the interaction of biological, emotional, and environmental stresses. If we ignore one set of forces, we get a lopsided view of a problem. And lopsided views lead to inadequate interventions.

For example, Timothy, a counselor in a residential prison-diversion program, has been asked by Barry, one of the residents, for a change of roommates. Before Timothy began to juggle rooms to accommodate Barry's request, he encouraged Barry to clarify the problem he was having with his present roommate. Timothy asked Barry about the following:

1. Barry's expectations of his present roommate and what he thought his roommate's expectations were of him
2. The similarities and differences in their habits, routines, and lifestyles
3. The extent to which they both tolerated differences in styles
4. The methods of conflict resolution they had already tried when they had a disagreement
5. The stresses of study, family, work, and social life that may have been aggravating their problem

After several conversations with Barry and his roommate, some separately and some together, Timothy suggested that the tension between them might lessen if they set up a more workable system for living in a shared space. He offered to help them design a chore chart. They also agreed to make some mutually acceptable rules about playing the radio and going to bed. Through their sessions, one of the young men realized that some of his anger at his roommate probably stemmed from his past irritations with his brother and that, in fact, there were many parts of living together that he enjoyed. They agreed to try to use the chore chart and a few rules they both could agree on for two weeks. They also agreed to check in with Timothy for ten minutes each day. Thus, both young men found possible solutions to a roommate problem that at first seemed insurmountable.

ALL PROBLEMS PEOPLE FACE ARE SERIOUS, YET IN A SENSE, ORDINARY

Some people may assert that the differences in the roles of professional helpers lie in the gravity of the problems they are assigned. But this is an oversimplification. Human problems can never be divided up on a scale ranging from very serious to less serious and then be parceled out to different workers.

All problems may appear unique and overwhelming to the people trying to cope with them, but Reid and Epstein (2001), in discussing the concept of **task-focused casework**, argue that just the reverse is true. In reality, most human problems are inevitable and widespread. No one is likely to go through life without facing many serious, painful problems. Someone we love will die, someone we need very much might leave us, and barriers will be thrown up in our paths at many junctures. In making this assertion, the authors do not mean to trivialize human problems or suggest that they are easily overcome. To the person struggling against a barrier, the pain and frustration are very real. The authors are, however, pointing out that all human service problems have two similar characteristics:

1. The person lacks the specific resources to alleviate a painful situation.
2. The person lacks the skills to cope with or overcome a painful situation.

All human service workers are likely to encounter a variety of life's problems in their work. On a first fieldwork assignment, for example, you might be coaching a basketball team in a suburban after-school program. That might seem like a pretty simple assignment until the day you take one of the youngsters home and are told that her mother has just been critically injured in a car accident. Now you will be challenged to provide some solid support both emotionally and practically.

To see how problems occur and might be dealt with, let us listen into a conversation with a counselor named Carmen Mejia. In the 11 years since she graduated from college, she has been employed by three different agencies. In each, she has been assigned a different title and has worked with a different population, but still she has seen the same types of " lacks" that face her clients.

INTERVIEW: A HUMAN SERVICE WORKER AT WORK

Carmen Mejia, Family Resource Worker

I'm really excited about talking about my current job. I've been here for four years, but my position keeps changing. I was hired as a foster care worker on a special grant from the Community Council Foundation. The child-protection social workers at the Department of Social Services (DSS) designed my position and then fought to get it funded. There were never enough foster parent homes to send children to when they had to be taken out of their family homes on a temporary basis.

My first assignment was to recruit more foster parents, especially for Latino children. When children can't speak English or they are dark-skinned, it is especially hard to place them. This county has a rapidly growing population of immigrants from El Salvador, Nicaragua, Panama, and the Dominican Republic. The families come here to escape discrimination and poverty but find a whole new set of problems. They have difficulty obtaining the "green cards" from the federal government that permit them to legally stay here. Even when they have the legal status, jobs are hard to find and pay very little. The housing they can afford is very run-down. They get frustrated from all the pressures and they lack the family support they were accustomed to in their former villages. Frustration can turn outward into violence or inward into drug and alcohol abuse.

Before I started, they often placed Latino children in any home available. The kids weren't understood, the food was strange to them, and they were often ridiculed or rejected. They went from one bad situation at home to another in foster care.

For months I went around the community speaking at churches and meeting with residents at their social clubs. I had to explain about how someone applied to be a foster parent and reassure them they wouldn't be rejected because they didn't speak perfectly. I recruited a lot of new foster families. But it was obvious that just putting kids in foster homes isn't enough. It was often like a revolving door. Either the foster parents didn't get enough help from us, or their situations changed and they had to move to another town or focus on their own children.

No matter how good their foster parents were, the kids still suffered from having too many transitions in their lives. Most of the time they wanted to return home and their folks wanted them back. Both the foster and the birth parents were pretty much ignored by the system. Sometimes children did get sent back, but it would tear your heart out to hear stories of how nothing had changed; the same abuse or neglect would start all over again.

I think both the birth parents and the foster parents felt unsupported by DSS. The social workers felt they were being unfairly pressured by lawyers and the media. Nothing seemed to get resolved and children lived in limbo year after year. Every once in a while there would be a big newspaper article about some terrible mistake we made when we took children out of their homes or returned them to a dangerous situation.

I was about to leave the agency from sheer frustration. Then a new program was initiated. It's called CAPP, Coordinated Approach to Partnership in Parenting. It grew out of the mayor's task force on **permanency planning** and **family preservation**. The aim is to reunite families when that is possible or to free children for adoption and a new permanent home. All along the way it offers help to all the parties.

I am now called a Family Resource Worker. I am part of a team composed of the foster parents, the birth parents, and the agency social worker. If the child is old enough and is able, he or she is included also. The first step in CAPP was a ten-session training program for everyone involved. We did role-plays and guided imagery and talked about our own childhoods and parenting styles. We discussed child development and alternative discipline techniques. We learned how to look for signs of learning disabilities, mental illness, depression, drugs, and sexual abuse.

This wasn't the first time there has been training for the staff, but this time it was special. For once, we were all sitting down together. Maybe some of the presentations were a little elementary for the social workers with master's degrees, but for most of the people attending it was eye-opening. I think that the morale and the understanding of this new batch of foster parents is better than most of the older ones. For the birth parents it is very supportive. They are encouraged to think of us as helpers, not as snoops who are punishing them. Some of them had pretty rough treatment when they were kids. They need new models of discipline and more understanding of children's needs.

One of the big parts of my job is to visit the birth parents and foster parents on a regular schedule. I ask them to make an agenda—topics they want to talk about so we can be sure to cover what is going on and what they need from me. Whenever there is a crisis—a child runs away or a parent goes off the deep end—I hang in with the family for as long as it takes to get the situation ironed out.

The program is still new, and there is never enough time and energy. We do endless paperwork. Every contact has to be documented, partly for the research but mostly in case there is a legal problem down the road. We have to prove that we did everything possible if we recommend that parental custody be terminated. We have to keep records so that we don't just keep trying the same things over or lose track of something important.

I still get frustrated by the lack of resources despite the fact that research shows that most of the parents believe that they would all benefit more from things like day care or homemaker services than just counseling alone. But we are always hustling to obtain summer camp placements, transportation to school tutoring programs, and competent therapists, especially ones who speak Spanish. With all the talk about family preservation, child-welfare agencies spend only 10 percent of their budgets on concrete services for the families. It makes you wonder how serious they are about keeping families together.

THE GOALS OF CARMEN'S CASE WORK

Carmen has had the same goals and has employed similar skills in each of her jobs in human service programs. She might be talking with a foster mother at her kitchen table, reporting to a young man and his family after her conference with his probation officer, or interviewing a couple who are planning care for their older relative. She asks questions and gives information and support in a way that allows the clients the space and time to clarify their situation and explore alternative courses of action. Because she believes in **client self-determination**, Carmen does not tell people what to do or how to do it. She knows she might be able to influence or manipulate a pregnant teenager into giving up her child; she knows she could pressure a young offender into going back to school. But she also suspects that as a result of that kind of worker interference, the teenage girl is likely to carry around a heavy emotional burden of loss for many years, and the young man coerced back into school is likely to drop out.

When she is working with the criminal justice system or the child-protective systems, her actions are dictated by certain rules and regulations that might conflict with her concept of the importance of self-determination. Whether the clients come to her agency on their own initiative or are mandated to do so by the courts, she works to accomplish four outcomes:

1. The clients will be able to express or change a negative emotional state.
2. The clients will increase their understanding of their situation and possible courses of action.
3. The clients will be better able to make important decisions.
4. The clients will be better able to implement a decision once it is made.

Releasing or Changing a Negative Emotional State

As Carmen encourages her clients to express their feelings, she assures them that there are no right or wrong feelings. When 14-year-old Kim is angry with her foster mother for not allowing her to go to a party, Carmen does not tell her that she should not feel angry. Feelings are valid and need to be respected. Well-meaning people often say to someone who is in a rage or a deep depression:

> You should be ashamed of yourself for being so angry (or depressed) when you have so much to be thankful for.

or

> You think you've got problems; let me tell you what happened to me.

These kinds of responses are likely to make the person feel worse! People do not want to be told that their feelings are trivial, self-pitying, or irrelevant. Workers should not try to talk people out of their feelings. Their job is to help people figure out why one particular issue provokes emotion. After Kim is allowed to express her feelings, perhaps then she can figure out how to avoid another confrontation. And if her rage at her foster mother leads her to get into a fight with her teacher at school, Carmen needs to help her find a less destructive way to express her feelings.

Understanding of One's Self and the Situation

After Kim expresses her feelings, Carmen tries to get her to put herself in the role of her foster mother or teacher. It is not easy for Kim, or any other high school students struggling to find their own identity, to tap into the feelings of powerlessness a caretaking adult might have.

Carmen also tries to provide Kim with insights into the nature of her specific life crises, developmental issues, and social problems. She encourages Kim to ask questions. Together they might explore:

- What is alcohol really doing to my body or mind?
- How realistic is the notion that I'm going to flunk all my courses, or does it just feel that way at the moment?

- What are the phases most kids go through when they lose their home and parents?
- How similar am I to other people who have faced this? In what ways am I unique?
- Why are adults so controlling?

Carmen helps clients gain perspective on their fears, hopes, and plans by sharing what she has learned from other young people and from college courses.

Making Important Decisions

When people are in crisis, they often desperately need to make a decision. Yet that is precisely when they are immobilized. Any actions they take are bound to have negative as well as positive consequences. To make the best possible decisions, they need to sort out inaccurate or conflicting bits of information about each possible choice, get in touch with their feelings, anticipate possible consequences, and then try to decide what is in their best interest. Solving problems and making decisions can be a reasonably systematic process or a frustrating and chaotic one.

Carmen works with her clients to help them make one specific decision and to develop decision-making skills that can be used again and again as new problems arise.

Implementing a Decision Once It Is Made

A-BREAKING A BIG TASK DOWN INTO SMALL STEPS   The most carefully thought-out decision a person makes is an exercise in futility if action does not follow. When a decision is made, Carmen helps her clients break a big decision into small steps. Then each small step is discussed, practiced, and evaluated.

Carmen has been working with Lila Parsikian, a mother recently released from a rehabilitation program for substance use. Lila seems stuck. She has said that she wants to eject her partner who is violent toward her and also engages in drug dealings from her home. But even thinking about confronting him with her decision makes her break out in a cold sweat. Implementing a decision involves personal risk. The possibility of failure lies close behind each new move. Carmen and Lila have been rehearsing what Lila will say. They have also discussed her sources of protection. Lila thinks that her brother would be willing to stay with her for a few days. Carmen encouraged Lila to finish the paperwork for Transitional Assistance so she could get immediate financial support and break her economic dependency on her partner.

B-GIVING EMOTIONAL SUPPORT   Carmen has to be careful with Lila as she treads the fine line between reasonable encouragement and false reassurance. She can encourage her client to feel that she is a worthy person and does not deserve violence. Carmen can explain to Lila that she has the right to get a legal restraining order that prohibits her boyfriend from harassing her. Carmen can promise to call Lila each day and can refer her to a woman's shelter if Lila wants to go that route. But she also must be honest about the fact that a restraining order does not guarantee her safety. Women have been battered and even killed by violent mates as they clutched a restraining order in their hand.

C-MODELING BEHAVIOR   When they discussed Lila's growing frustration with her very aggressive child, Carmen found out about the discipline techniques Lila uses. After suggesting some methods that avoid physical punishment, she visited Lila's home to work with her and her child. By modeling a disciplining behavior, such as a short "time out," and then staying there as the parent tries it, Carmen teaches while giving emotional support.

D-MAKING REFERRALS   Sometimes Carmen refers clients to support groups or training programs. Assertiveness training helps hesitant young women put their good sense into action. Perhaps she will tell Lila about a parenting group at a local mental health center or at a domestic violence shelter for people who are in abusive relationships.

Carmen's clients' needs for handholding, reassurance, and rehearsing vary enormously. Sometimes a little push in the right direction can set the top spinning on its own. But sometimes, resistance to taking the next step masks real discontent about a decision. If Lila is not ready to take the first step to go back to school, maybe Carmen needs to spend more time working on building her self-confidence through taking some small steps with a high probability of success. Maybe attending a one-day workshop on career choice or opportunities in information technology would be a good start.

E-OVERCOMING BARRIERS   Clients often get stuck moving a plan into action because barriers block their path. Kevin, a young man who is blind, is ready to graduate from school and attend college in his community. But the college does not provide up-to-date Braille texts, special library equipment, and enough note takers. He will not be able to succeed without those supports.

Carmen suggested that Kevin complain to the dean. Carmen might refer him to an agency that does legal advocacy on behalf of students with disabilities.

THE PROCESS OF CARMEN'S CASE WORK

1. Getting Prepared for the Person and Their Problem
2. Building a Supportive Relationship
3. Contracting
4. Creating an Action Plan
5. Putting the Plan into Action
6. Evaluating the Work

1. Getting Prepared for the Person and Their Problem

Even though she never has enough time in her day, Carmen always takes a few moments to quietly and systematically think about her next appointment before the person arrives. During the initial encounter (and each subsequent one), she will face many unknowns, but the more carefully she has prepared herself, the more she will be able to meet the challenge of each unique personality and situation. She prepares herself by tuning in to the clients and their problems both emotionally and intellectually.

USING PREPARATORY EMPATHY   We have already stressed the critical importance of empathy—putting oneself into the shoes of another person and trying to see the world out of that person's eyes. Now we introduce the concept of preparatory empathy (Gitterman & Shulman, 2005; Shulman, 2008, 2015). Of course, it would be arrogant to think that we can ever really know what another human being will feel. We can, however, sensitize ourselves to listen and watch intently for the emotions that might lie below the surface of a client's words and actions. Tuning in helps us to respond accurately to the garbled, often ambivalent messages that people send when they are experiencing a high level of stress.

To sharpen her preparatory empathy, Carmen reviews all that she knows about the emotional baggage that often accompanies a particular set of issues. Carmen has been preparing for a home visit to Laurel Schultz, the mother of a 5-year-old girl who is enrolled in a day care center affiliated with a large teaching hospital. She has never met Ms. Schultz but was asked by the center director to try to get her to agree to have her daughter evaluated. The director suspects that the youngster has attention deficit/hyperactivity disorder (ADHD), a biological condition that makes concentrating and following rules very difficult. (Hallowell & Ratey, 2011; Taylor-Klaus, 2016.) Because few people truly understand this disability, children like Ms. Schultz's daughter are likely to be high-risk students when they go on to public school. They may appear to not care, not listen, or not be trying hard enough, so they are frequently punished by authority figures and may be rejected by their peers.

ANTICIPATING MISUNDERSTANDINGS AND TENSION BETWEEN WORKER AND CLIENT

Preparatory empathy is not a parlor game in which the worker tries to outguess the client. Rather, it is a process that alerts a worker to issues that might turn out to be important. If the parents do not bring up feelings, then Carmen sends up a trial balloon. She might say:

> Some people have heard a lot of conflicting information about attention deficit/hyperactivity disorder (ADHD). I'm wondering what you might have heard about it and if you have any feelings about the way it is diagnosed and treated?

If Ms. Schultz shrugs off the question, Carmen lets it drop. Perhaps Mrs. Schultz has no questions or isn't ready yet to ask them.

READING AND EVALUATING REFERRAL MATERIAL   When Carmen starts working with a client, she usually has some background information about the person and situation. Sometimes it is a bulging file; often it is just a brief note or verbal statement from another worker. When she worked with young people who had trouble with the law, a file was likely to contain some of the following:

- An official record of the arrest and a description of the precipitating incident
- A report prepared by the probation officer on the youth's school achievement, family background, and work history
- A summary of tests that the public school administered and the school transcripts
- The results of a vocational test administered by a rehabilitation agency that was working with the youth before the arrest
- A medical report on the youth's physical condition
- Notes taken at a family interview with the court social worker

Some of this information is **objective data**. It states facts such as the dates of events, medical findings, court dispositions, work history, or any public benefits that have been received. Other pieces of data might appear objective but are open to judgment and bias. For example, the results of a battery of personality tests, although useful, are open to varied interpretations according to who administered or scored them.

Other documents are filled with clearly **subjective data**. They state opinions about the client's attitude, situation, and behavior. Carmen is always careful to be a little skeptical of this kind of data. With a lack of preparatory empathy, the worker might have described the client as "aggressive" or "hostile." But if Carmen had been the worker and had tuned in to the client's feelings, she might have interpreted the client's behavior as "appropriately anxious."

Reports can be riddled with diagnostic labels that do not have hard data to support them. Phrases such as "mentally disturbed child," "overprotective parent," "hyperactive child," and "juvenile delinquent" will frequently crop up in a client's file. We have no way to evaluate the credentials, skills, or sensitivity of the people who affixed the labels. These terms are often used imprecisely and should not be automatically accepted as an accurate depiction of a client's personality or background.

As long as Carmen is a bit skeptical, the **referral statement** can still be very useful. She learns about the client's previous experiences, which might give clues to his expectations. If it is not clear from the referral statement exactly why the client is coming to the agency, a few direct questions early in the first interview may bring clarity.

METHODS OF COLLECTING ADDITIONAL DATA ABOUT A PERSON'S PROBLEM SITUATION

There are many ways we go about collecting data. Here are some of the methods we use.

A. INTAKE INTERVIEWS

In Carmen's program, all the workers take turns doing initial **intake interviews**. They write up the information gathered and decide whether the person's needs fit in with the agency services. If they do, and there is room in the agency's caseload, the worker doing the interview decides which staff member might work best with that person. For example, one worker may have a reputation for being especially effective with angry teenagers and another worker may be known to do well with people who very shy and inarticulate.

The intake interview zeroes in on the immediate problem situation—how it came about, what has already been done to deal with it, and what specific actions the client wants to or is required to take. Though intake is usually conducted on a one-on-one basis, Carmen has experimented with group intakes both for efficiency and to provide prospective clients with emotional support.

B. HOME VISITS

Whenever possible, Carmen includes a home visit as an integral part of her data-gathering process. The home visit provides an opportunity to gain greater understanding of the patterns of interaction, support, and stress that daily confront clients and their family systems. Carmen has a few clients whom she sees regularly in their homes. Many clients welcome the less formal atmosphere, but others resist and resent it. Perhaps it makes them feel intruded upon.

Carmen usually has the flexibility to let the people she works with choose the interview setting. Any resistance a person might have is usually lessened if Carmen makes an advance appointment, sticks to a time schedule, and has a clear sense of the purpose of each encounter and explains it clearly.

2. Building Supportive Relationships

Building a supportive and trusting relationship with each client starts immediately after Carmen has been assigned to a case. When she schedules the appointment for the initial interview and greets the person for the first time, she knows that her words, tone of voice, and facial expression all communicate. Through her warmth, openness, humanness, and honesty, she shows her clients that she respects them and considers their problems important. She continues to cement the relationship by doing the following:

- Listening, observing, and accurately reflecting back feelings and thoughts
- Encouraging the full expression of emotions and ideas by helping to put them into words
- Keeping clear about the purposes of each encounter

- Raising questions for thought and suggesting alternative actions, resources, and services
- Admitting the limits of her own expertise and seeking additional help
- Protecting confidentiality or being clear about why it cannot be kept

No matter how competent she is, Carmen's relationships with the birth parents or the foster parents are likely to be stressful at some time. At no point can she sit back and say, "Well, that's done. Now we have a trusting relationship!"

At times, a particular relationship may seem very strong, but within minutes it can swing to mistrust or conflict. Carmen has to keep reminding herself that frustration, anger, and tension are inevitable when people grapple with difficult decisions.

Carmen's ability to pay close attention to details strengthens her relationships. Returning phone calls promptly, being on time for appointments, remembering the details of what has been said, and following through on promises are all concrete demonstrations of the verbal caring that she professes. Leaving a client's record carelessly lying on a desk where it can be read by anyone and missing a special event in a client's life without telephoning are actions that communicate just the reverse. Being able to count on caring that is consistent with their cultural backgrounds can give clients that extra measure of emotional support they so desperately need when facing overwhelming personal distress. (Okun and Kantrowitz, 2014.)

3. Negotiating and Refining the Working Contract

When Carmen begins an encounter with a client, she does not make any assumptions about who knows what or who wants what. All the parties in the process—client, worker, family members, and other professionals—must negotiate and then refine their own special mutual working agreement. Although contracting has long been part of the business and entertainment world, it has been widely used in casework and counseling only within the past few decades (Shulman, 2012).

Contracting grows out of the basic principle that the case process is a collaborative endeavor between the person and her worker. Through mutual agreements and joint commitments, the worker tries to minimize the helpee's fear of being caseworked, "psyched out," or manipulated by what they could see as a powerful, controlling professional.

If clients do not acknowledge problems or are not convinced that they have the strength to overcome these problems, any change effort is likely to prove futile. According to the tenets of AA, no change effort can begin until the person with the problem stands up and says, for example, "I am Susanne, and I am an alcoholic. I am an alcoholic, and I want to stop drinking."

The word "negotiating" implies that Carmen and her clients might disagree on the work that has to be done. Sometimes they start out agreeing on all aspects of their working contract, but as they gain new insights, they are likely to change their initial contract. If there are many issues to be worked on, they must set priorities.

The word "refining" acknowledges that our goals and tasks are very imprecise. They must be broken down into many smaller steps. If, for example, Carmen and a parent agree that they will work together on her daughter's problems in school, that still leaves the parent unclear about what she is expected to do and what services Carmen can offer her.

TASKS THE WORKER WILL DO   Some people who need help resist working with human service workers, but others do just the opposite: They impute magical powers to the workers. Without being cold or rejecting, we need to be honest about what actual activities we can undertake as well as our limitations. If it turns out that the client's needs are greater than our time or resources, we try to refer them to other agencies.

TASKS THE CLIENT WILL NEED TO DO   Many of Carmen's cases are mandated by the courts or the Department of Social Services. Agency regulations dictate what each party is expected to do. Carmen always makes sure that these regulations are discussed and understood early in the encounter. If people are required by law to attend a counseling session, find a job, or do some other activity, it is important that they know what the consequences will be for them if they choose not to do so.

When clients are voluntary referrals, they should know that they have the right to shop around for social services and that it is best that they do. That is what an alert consumer does when choosing a home or buying a major appliance. If the agency employs a particular theory or philosophy of helping, or if it uses behavior modification, psychoanalysis, or group therapy, certain demands will be made. The client needs a chance to say "No, thank you" without feeling guilty.

DECIDING ON THE RULES OF THE ROAD   Early in their encounter, worker and client must agree on the following rules that will govern their working together:

1. A reasonable projection of how much time or how many sessions the overall process will entail and which special activities it will include (e.g., testing, home visiting, or a case conference)
2. A schedule for sessions, visits, and so forth
3. The names and addresses of places where the encounters will occur
4. A decision about the kind of note taking or recording the worker will do and the rules of confidentiality
5. Information about the client or the worker that might help or hinder their working together
6. Information about fees and how they will be billed and should be paid

4. Creating the Action Plan

All the work Carmen has done so far has prepared the soil for the action plan. Now she will use the following techniques.

DIVIDING MAJOR PROBLEMS INTO THEIR SMALLER COMPONENTS   When they were negotiating their working contract, the most challenging task facing Carmen and the person she is working with was to state, in action terms, the exact nature of the problems and the hoped-for outcomes. When people are overwhelmed by life's demands and feel buffeted by circumstances, it is hard to see the small stumbling blocks that contribute to their overall problems of poverty, rage, or depression. Understandably, clients are impatient to tackle the problem head-on. In the action plan, we take the goals and figure out how to get to them one step at a time. For example, Ms. Lugo is a recently widowed mother who complains of profound depression. She is overwhelmed by the prospect of parenting alone. Carmen helped her decide which component parts of her current situation troubled her the most. Then they could begin to work on the parts one at a time. Together, they reviewed these aspects of her circumstances:

- Financial situation
- Social situation
- Living arrangements
- Work role
- Parenting role

Every person experiencing the loss of a mate has different priorities, depending on her socio-economic status, interests, age, location, and support system. All problems can, with skill and patience, be broken down into smaller parts.

VISUALIZING ALTERNATIVE PATHS, STRATEGIES, AND RESOURCES   Once the larger problem is seen in its component parts, Ms. Lugo can move on to choosing one piece of that larger problem to work on. Carmen encouraged her to spell out exactly what she needed in order to cope with her sense of financial deprivation. They agreed that Carmen would meet with her at home. Beforehand, Ms. Lugo would gather all the bills and receipts she could find. Carmen would go over them with her, and together they would construct a budget. Once they figured out the family finances, Ms. Lugo might need to visit a legal services center or a consumer credit counselor to deal with any debts, inheritance, or documents that needed to be transferred into her name.

The second high-priority problem identified was the burden of parenting her little girl, who had serious emotional upset. They began working on finding the following:

- Specific programs, social agencies, or "people resources" that would give Ms. Lugo some time off from parenting and give her daughter additional adults to whom she can relate
- Appropriate agencies or benefits that could pay for some respite care, camp placements, and so forth
- A counselor, support group, and network of family and friends who could be sounding boards for her questions about discipline now that there was no other adult in the home with whom to discuss things

Source: Lorelyn Medina/Shutterstock

Even preschool children can be involved in projects that teach them to ask questions of others and listen carefully to their answers. This might help them become attentive students and alert citizens in the future.

CONSIDERING THE ADVANTAGES AND DISADVANTAGES OF EACH PART OF THE PLAN   After thinking creatively about the many possible strategies and resources they could tap into, Carmen and Ms. Lugo reviewed the options to see how feasible each one was. For each possible program or resource, they had to find out the following:

- Location
- Costs
- Availability
- Eligibility requirements

Together they weighed the pros and cons of each.

MAPPING OUT THE NEXT STEPS IN AN ACTION PLAN   Once major problems have been broken into smaller issues and likely strategies have been chosen, Carmen and Ms. Lugo must put a time frame on each step. If her daughter is to attend a summer camp, they must find out when the application and medical forms need to be turned in. Then Ms. Lugo will have to find time to gather camp clothes, label them, and arrange the time off from her job to take her child to the bus depot. Ms. Lugo might decide that she wants to find a smaller apartment now that her income is reduced. Before rushing out to look for one, she needs to decide which steps in the apartment-hunting process must be done first; how long each will take; and where she will get the extra money for moving expenses, security deposit, and the last month's rent.

5. Putting the Plan into Action

Often Carmen's major contribution to the problem-solving process is to act as a sounding board. As she listens to the client's plans, she plays devil's advocate, raising questions to think about. At other times, she is like a coach, helping to recharge someone's emotional batteries. Worker and client can divide up the work. Ms. Lugo will find out about the town day camp while Carmen finds out how much money her agency might be able to contribute to the fees. They can share the work that needs to be done so that the client will not be overwhelmed. Yet Carmen should not infantilize Ms. Lugo by solving all her problems for her. Each time Ms. Lugo takes one small step, she begins to feel more confident about her capacity to successfully raise her child without her husband. Because she has worked with so many families, Carmen is frequently asked to suggest a specific program. The process of linking a person to such a resource is called making a referral.

MAKING REFERRALS   Making a successful referral is a much more complicated process than simply supplying the name of an agency and trusting that the client will connect with it. Research has indicated that many clients fall through the cracks after being referred by one agency to another. Perhaps the client's needs and the agency's services were mismatched. Or perhaps the client and the agency failed to make a solid bond with each other. To avoid this, workers try to obtain accurate data about agency services and entitlements. They also need to learn to build firm linkages with both the client and the prospective agency (Feltham & Horton, 2012).

CREATING ONE'S OWN RESOURCE FILE   Referrals can fail when a worker's information about an agency or a service is wrong or incomplete. There are often vast differences between the official description of an agency on their web site and the actual service it is able to deliver.

—GLASBERGEN—

**"I'm learning how to relax, doctor —
but I want to relax *better* and *faster*!
I want to be on the cutting edge of relaxation!"**

Source: Randy Glasbergen/Glasbergen Cartoons

In our current era, speed has become a new normal. Clients often cannot understand why there are few "quick fixes" for human service problems.

Anticipating this kind of discrepancy, Carmen has constructed her own personal resource file. Alongside the official facts about the agency's fees, waiting period, and eligibility requirements, she notes her own observations.

Perhaps the agency brochure states that all clients are seen within a two-week period, but she has heard from many clients that the waiting time is more like two months. She jots this down so she can warn the next client. Optimally, she has seen the agency in action. If that has not been possible, she relies on feedback from other workers and clients.

When Carmen has not taken the time to double-check on her referrals, she has sent clients on wild-goose chases. Once she sent a client to a legal services program for assistance in obtaining a legal separation from her husband; the agency had run out of rent money two years before. The client making that futile trip was rightfully annoyed and she then missed her next appointment at CAPP.

To build a supportive relationship, we try to find common ground. We work on developing trust according to the age and abilities of each client. Even the smallest child will hesitate to reveal a painful feeling until the worker has created an atmosphere of acceptance and safety.

If Carmen finds out that there is a long waiting list for a service, she warns clients about it. Armed with an accurate understanding of its limitations, clients can then decide whether to wait their turn or shift gears.

CEMENTING A REFERRAL   After Carmen reviews the official and informal data about a resource and decides to suggest it, several acts can prevent the client—especially a very troubled or disorganized one—from falling through the cracks. This process is called **linkage technology**:

1. Write down the referral for the client. Carmen always takes an extra moment to write down an agency's address, how it can be reached, when it is open, and any documentation that must be brought on a first visit. Then she hands the paper to her client. In the midst of an emotionally intense session, it might be hard for the client to take accurate notes or remember details.

2. Connect the client to a particular person at the agency. If possible, Carmen tries to find out the name of the worker at a referral agency whom the client will be seeing. She often writes or e-mails an introductory note preceding the visit. This can build a valuable bridge for the client. Sometimes the referral can be set in motion by the client's phoning for an appointment from Carmen's office.

3. Determine who might accompany the client. In certain cases, Carmen might decide to go with her client to a referral agency. If she cannot go but thinks that extra support is necessary, she helps clients think about who in their own network of friends and relatives might be able to accompany them.

4. Determine what other resources the client needs in order to use the referral. Sometimes Carmen's clients need money for transportation, a specialized vehicle, child care, or another resource in order to use a referral. She helps them to think through potential stumbling blocks and negotiate them in advance. If left to chance, these stumbling blocks can undermine a referral.

5. Check back on how the referral went. Carmen always asks for feedback. She often arranges an interview after a person's visit to an agency. Then she can find out if there were any unanticipated obstacles that need to be dealt with.

6. Advocate for high-quality service. As she solicits feedback from her clients, Carmen discovers instances of inadequate service. Because of red tape, bureaucratic inertia, worker turnover, or misunderstanding, clients often do not get the services they need. Clients need encouragement to take the next step to overcome obstacles. That might entail switching to another resource or finding ways to pressure that first agency to meet their needs.

6. Evaluating the Work and Deciding on the Next Steps

INFORMAL EVALUATION TECHNIQUES   There are many moments during a session when both Carmen and the person she is working with step back and review the work they have done.

Each time Carmen asks the client for feedback or shares her own reflections on their work together, she is evaluating. In addition to doing these moment-to-moment evaluations, she sets aside five minutes at the end of each session to review the progress that has been made in the last hour. If the session runs too long, and there is no time remaining for thoughtful evaluation, she phones the client before the next session.

Carmen has found that it is not easy to get honest feedback. Many of the foster and birth parents she works with are accustomed to doctors, lawyers, or school principals who rarely solicit or welcome client opinions about their services. When the clients have complained to authorities, they might have been ignored or punished for doing so. To convince them that she really wants to hear their opinions—negative as well as positive—and will seriously consider what they say, she needs to reassure them again and again. She might say:

> I really appreciate it when you stop me and ask me to explain a term or an abbreviation. I am so accustomed to using them that I forget that most people haven't a clear idea what they mean. Please stop me again if I forget, okay?

FORMAL EVALUATION TECHNIQUES   In addition to ongoing informal feedback, CAPP undergoes a yearly formal evaluation of its services by an outside consultant. The public who fund this agency have a right to know if their tax money is being used effectively.

The field of human service evaluation is very challenging. It is almost impossible to verify success or failure of case management/counseling encounters. Optimally we should be able to measure the progress of our programs by charting changes in the mental health or functioning of our clients. But rarely are we able to make cause-and-effect conclusions with a high degree of scientific accuracy.

When Carmen works to keep a family functioning, her efforts are only one factor in a vast constellation of shifting pressures. There are so many variables at work that her best efforts can be wiped out by forces well beyond her control. A poor economy makes job placement almost impossible for her low-skilled clients, so money pressures mount. Money pressures often lead to increased family tension, and so it goes.

Most personal and social problems resist arbitrary definitions of cure. How can we be sure that the improvement in the way the parents cope with their child is permanent? How can we know if any improvements we observe are a direct result of our work?

Recognizing the obstacles that keep us from fully evaluating our work should not, however, stop us from trying to do so. On a day-to-day basis, Carmen can see enormous changes in a few of her families and a little bit of change in most of them. The outside evaluation has helped to reshape the CAPP program by stimulating staff members to think how they could do their jobs more effectively.

Summary

1. Terms such as "case manager," "counselor," "advocate," and many others that various human service agencies employ are often used interchangeably. There are few universally agreed-on definitions of their roles or training requirements.
2. Arbitrary distinctions might be made on whether the worker deals with emotions or resources. We do not think that this kind of distinction is useful. All workers deal with emotions and resources.
3. All human service workers try to help people with problems to:
   a. Release negative feelings
   b. Increase their understanding of themselves and their situations

   c. Make plans and decisions
   d. Implement plans and decisions
4. A worker such as Carmen performs seven steps in each case process:
   a. Prepares for an encounter by using preparatory empathy and evaluating referral data. (Referral data are both objective and subjective.)
   b. Gathers information in a planned and focused way through conducting intake interviews, home visiting, holding case conferences, and doing direct observation. This is often called the *assessment* phase.
   c. Builds supportive and trusting relationships.

d. Negotiates a written or verbal contract with each person she is helping.

e. Creates an action plan that translates overall problems into smaller ones, visualizes alternative paths, considers constraints and consequences, sets priority tasks, maps out steps, and sets time frames.

f. Implements the action plan through giving emotional support and making referrals to resources.

g. Evaluates the process through informal requests for feedback and through more formal surveys and questionnaires.

Discussion Questions

1. Think back to when you have been in disputes with your parents over issues of spending money, curfew, use of the car, your choice of friends, and so forth. In what ways have you tried to understand their point of view? How might you apply the concept of preparatory empathy before embarking on what might be a very tense encounter with your parents, or in the future with a client who presents a very troubled picture of perhaps child or spousal abuse?

2. When you imagine a class that you are now taking (either this one or another) as a human service encounter, with the student as a client and the instructor as the worker, try to visualize the contract between the parties. What are the rules of the road in that class, both the formal ones and the informal ones? How clear are the expectations the students have of the instructor and those the instructor has of each of the students? How might this contract be made clearer or more realistic, if you think it needs to be changed?

3. Imagine that you are a young newly employed human service worker from Carmen's agency.

You are visiting a woman who has been foster-parenting a child who has severe emotional problems. This foster parent has been trying to find better ways to discipline him without making him feel rejected and more depressed. Most importantly, she has been exploring positive techniques to help him learn appropriate social behavior so he can make some friends. For the past year she has been meeting with a parent advocate with whom she has established a very warm working relationship. When you enter her apartment and announce that the previous staff member has left the agency and you are her new worker, she looks at you with displeasure and says, in a very hostile tone, "You are so young; what do you know about parenting? Do you have any children yourself?" If you were that worker and had used preparatory empathy before that home visit, what kind of feelings might you have anticipated that foster mother might have? How might you respond to her question and concerns about your ability to help her?

Web Resources for Further Study

Children's Bureau, U. S. Department of Health & Human Services

https://www.acf.hhs.gov/programs/cb/

Child Welfare Information Gateway, U. S. Department of Health & Human Services

https://www.childwelfare.gov

Foster Care and Adoption

https://www.adoptuskids.org/about-us/contact-us

MyLab Helping Professions for Introduction to Human Services

In the Topic 8 Assignments: Client Evaluation, try Application Exercise 8.2: Improve Your Practice Effectiveness.

Then, in the Topic 9 Assignments: Interpersonal Communication, try Application Exercise 9.2: Conflict Resolution.

Working with Groups

10

Source: Barbara Schram

Learning Outcomes

- Students will be able to describe some of the positives and some of the negatives of working in groups.

- Students will demonstrate an understanding of the phases of group life, explaining what must happen in the norming stage.

- Students will be able to give brief descriptions of each of the five overall categories into which groups in the human services fall.

- Students will be able to describe the three concepts of leadership and explain why the task-focused one is the most useful in human service work.

HUMAN SERVICE WORKERS ARE BOTH MEMBERS AND LEADERS OF GROUPS

Few people have neutral feelings about being in a group or working with one. Group meetings may elicit strong feelings, both negative and positive.

> "Oh, no, not another meeting!" groans Arlene, an overworked addictions counselor. "All we do when the staff gets together is waste time arguing. We listen to dull reports or the administrator asks our opinion about decisions she has already made. I'd rather be at my desk catching up on my paperwork or be out in the field visiting a client!"

or

> "Although I never have enough time in my day, I look forward to our agency meetings," says Ernesto, a family worker in an early-intervention program for preschool children with developmental

delays. "When we get together, we pool our ideas, share information, and really encourage each other. Sure we argue sometimes, but at least when a decision finally gets made, I know that I put my two cents' worth into it."

It is not surprising that there are such sharp differences of opinion about the usefulness of working in groups. When members are interacting productively, a group can be an invaluable tool for solving problems, receiving and offering emotional support, and building self-confidence. When conflict rages or goals and procedures are unclear, a group can be a seething cauldron of tension and inefficiency.

Regardless of how you feel about groups, as a staff worker in a human service agency you will probably spend a large percentage of time interacting in groups. You will be expected to be an active participant in workshops, case conferences, and staff meetings. Eventually you might find yourself doing any of the following:

1. Facilitating a meeting of new staff or prospective clients
2. Leading a support or training group
3. Mediating a staff gripe session
4. Chairing a committee that is planning the agency open house
5. Becoming active in your agency union or professional association

After your workday ends, it is likely that you will interact with members of your family—the nuclear unit as well as your extended network of relatives—and intimate friends. At some time in our lives, all of us have been members of peer groups: the Scouts, a 4-H club, the "Y," a sorority or fraternity, a church, a choral group, a civic association, or a sports team.

Some groups are formal organizations conducted according to by-laws, rules, and codes of conduct. Friendships, cliques, and gangs are informally organized, but they also develop a structure and unwritten rules called **norms**. Both types of groups play roles in our early socialization, and some will continue to influence us throughout adult life.

Groups are sources of emotional support and help shape each member's attitudes and behavior. Those groups that influence us the most profoundly are called our **primary reference groups**. Reading about the work of Beth Soline will give you a quick overview of the kind of group involvement her role requires. These are roles that you might be asked to fill in your internship or employment.

A Human Service Worker at Work: Beth Soline, a Counselor at a Community Residence

Beth Soline is a night-shift counselor at Transition House, a community residence for ten adults who have been recently released from a hospital where they were treated for various mental illnesses. Transition House's primary goal is to provide a supportive, home-like environment in which each person's life skills can be strengthened. It is hoped that the residents will eventually rejoin their families or move into their own apartments and perhaps into the workforce. The residents have Individualized Service Plans (ISPs) that describe in detail the life skills they need to work on. For example, these are the skills that two of the residents need help with:

1. For Eileen, it is travel skills: learning to locate the correct buses, making change, and staying calm during the rush hour.
2. For Miriam, it is improving her interpersonal skills and learning to express feelings constructively with words rather than through withdrawal or verbal abuse.

The counselors at Transition House spend the last hour of each shift carefully recording what transpired during the shift. In the agency log book on the computer, they note any commitments they have made to the residents. They also describe any problems that occurred on their shift and any unusual circumstances that might have future repercussions.

The log book maintains continuity from one shift of workers to the next. By reviewing the logs periodically, the agency director assesses the progress of both the residents and the staff. Troubling episodes or behaviors that are described in the log book often become agenda items at weekly staff meetings. These notes also help the director decide on topics for their monthly staff training sessions.

Beth records in more detail than many of the other staff members because this position is her human service internship. By reading these recordings, her supervisor helps her expand her understanding of what is going on in the group and how she can best use her skills.

Transition House Log Book

Worker: Beth Soline
Time: Night Shift
Date: Tuesday, May 3

Arrived at 4:10 P.M. Found Miriam, Carlos, Michael, and Viet in the den, trying to decide where to go for their social activity that evening. Helped them sort through the choices. Movies, bowling, and eating out were their first three. Got them to consider the costs, time schedule, dress requirements, and behavioral demands of each.

Carlos, Viet, and Michael wanted to eat out, but Miriam kept insisting on going bowling. She got pretty agitated when they wouldn't budge, raised her voice, and began pacing. Viet started mimicking her. I stopped the action and tried to get them to talk about what was going on. Everyone finally agreed that if we ate out tonight, we'd go bowling next Monday. Miriam accepted that, but she got very quiet, curled up on the couch, and looked tense. I'd like to use that episode as a role-play for the house meeting next week. We need to help them all talk about what it feels like when you're on the losing side. Let's see what ideas folks have about why this always seems to happen when those particular four people try to plan an event together.

Went to dinner at Charlie O's Tavern. Atmosphere got more relaxed. In fact, it was so easygoing that ordering food, eating, and conversation came naturally. I began getting that old feeling of how-am-I-earning-my-salary? But then I remembered the time Carlos threw up on the waiter the evening he changed medications. I reminded myself that I never know when I'll be needed, so that's why I'm there. Decided to enjoy myself and skip the guilt trip.

Spent the next hour sitting in on group therapy session led by Dr. Kreger. Michael, Viet, Yolanda, Tricia, and Vikki were discussing last weekend. They had each gone home, and they needed to get a lot of stuff off their chests. I didn't say much. Afterwards I spent a half hour with Dr. Kreger comparing notes on what we'd both seen and heard. I feel like he appreciates my observations. Sitting in on these sessions helps me understand the moods of the residents much better. I hope we decide to make co-leading the group a permanent arrangement.

At 8:00 P.M., I went into the living room to visit the meeting of a chapter of the Mental Patients' Alliance (MPA). They are using the house for their meetings for the next three months on a trial basis. Made sure they had enough chairs, a working DVD player, and the coffee fixings. Talked for a while with Viola, who was running the meeting that night. She complained about poor attendance. I suggested she write an article for the local newspaper about how important it is for people who have had contact with the mental health system to have a voice. She thanked me for the coffee and suggestions

(continued)

but said she'd prefer it if I didn't stay through the meeting. She thought my presence might intimidate some of the participants. They have several serious complaints about conditions at Twin Oaks Hospital and are preparing to testify at the State House hearings. I wished them well and left.

I think one of our staff should also give testimony. We have been hearing about problems at Twin Oaks for a while. I have been given the runaround several times when I've tried to get in touch with staff members about medication prescriptions for some of our residents. I am scared to speak in public, but I need the experience. If the other staff agree, I'm willing to represent the house.

At 8:30 P.M., I got together with the four residents who are employed at the sheltered workshop. We went over the schedule for the morning and decided who would cook breakfast, do wake up, and call in any absentees. There have been problems getting out on time, so we're going to try a new system for speeding up breakfast and cleanup. Norman worked out a plan for getting breakfast things ready the night before. He got a lot of support for his idea. We agreed to try it for a week and reevaluate next Tuesday.

Spent the rest of the evening in the lounge, helping ease in the two new work-study students from Ryder College. Terry played the recorder and a bunch of us had a cutthroat game of Scrabble. Evening ended with everyone but Carlos pitching in with cleanup.

When I went to Miriam's door to say good night, she wanted to talk about the blowup at dinner. She wondered if being the only woman in the group was why she was never listened to. She wanted to talk more about the male–female tension. I suggested she bring it up at house meeting. She asked me if I would do it for her. Do you think I should? Maybe we could have a discussion group for the women residents. Would it make for more or less division? Let's talk about it at the next staff meeting. I left at 11:45 P.M.

Group Leadership Roles in the Human Services Have Been Increasing

In the past, workers who felt uncomfortable assuming group leadership roles used to be able to keep them to a minimum. As counselors in a hospital or a mental health agency, they traditionally conducted most of their work on a one-to-one model. The person coming for help was seated across the desk from the "expert" human service worker, who knew the resources. Because workers rarely interacted with clients in groups, the skills of group leadership received scant attention in the mental health literature and in college courses. But now the need for skilled group leaders has risen dramatically. Several factors have accounted for this increase.

1. The increase of grassroots-type programs
2. The increased use of Mutual-Aid programs and support groups
3. The impact of deinstitutionalization
4. The development of systems theory
5. The impact of social service budget cuts

1. THE INCREASE OF GRASSROOTS-TYPE PROGRAMS   As noted in Chapter 2, the U.S. Congress passed a landmark piece of legislation in the 1960s, the Economic Opportunity Act, which launched the War on Poverty. This bill mandated that all programs for the unemployed and underemployed must include the "maximum feasible participation" of the client population. For the first time in our history, people considered low income were not to be seen as simply the recipients of services. They were recognized in federal legislation as resources who had ideas about what they needed in order to improve their life chances. No longer would they be considered passive supplicants while professionals were the sole experts (Melish, 2010).

Many of these group participants were later hired by neighborhood-based **grassroots programs**. The styles of these indigenous workers grew out of neighborhood life. They talked, ate, and lived like the client population. They felt at home with the pace and closeness of group interaction, which felt much like that of their extended families.

Although most of these programs have long since been terminated and maximum feasible participation is fast disappearing from the scene, the informal group interventions it birthed left an imprint on the field. The concept and style of client participation still persist in some human service agencies.

2. THE INCREASED USE OF MUTUAL-AID PROGRAMS AND SUPPORT GROUPS During the past several decades, the mutual-aid group model, pioneered by Alcoholics Anonymous (AA), has grown tremendously. The support group, in which members use each other as resources for problem solving, has spread from one area of addiction and dysfunction to many others. The twelve-step model of recovery designed for alcohol abuse has been adapted to help people who smoke, overeat, gamble too much, or use physical violence in relationships. It has grown at such a tremendous pace that there are now mutual-aid groups for virtually every social and medical problem one can imagine (Gitterman & Shulman, 2005). They have proliferated all around the world (American Self-Help Group Clearinghouse, 2011).

A variation of this mutual-aid model has been used to further the work of the civil rights movement and for the liberation struggles of women, the Lesbian, Gay, Bisexual, Trans, and Queer (or Questioning) (LGBTQ) community, **LGBTQ** and people with physical and emotional disabilities. Unquestionably, support groups will continue to spread in response to the increasing disintegration of the traditional extended family and workplace, as well as the decreasing roles of many religious, civic, and fraternal associations in many people's lives.

3. THE IMPACT OF DEINSTITUTIONALIZATION The community mental health movement, begun at the end of World War II, has continued to gain momentum and has firmly lodged itself in the field. It was propelled by the belief that patients with mental illness and other adults with developmental delays or children and adults with disabilities were being made even more dysfunctional by being segregated in impersonal institutions. The road to health lay in moving them out of the wards of state institutions and back into community life.

Small community residences and group homes were opened to receive them and integrate them into the mainstream. There, the residents began to perform many tasks of daily life together. These groups became natural arenas for emotional support and behavioral change. Group leaders had to be recruited and trained to staff these houses. The need for staff continues to this day, and many students are likely to do their internships and accept employment in these programs.

After being deinstitutionalized, some former patients moved back to their family homes. To avoid isolation and stagnation, day-activities programs and sheltered workshops were organized. In these settings, group interaction is prescribed as a vehicle for acquiring socialization and independent-living skills.

4. THE DEVELOPMENT OF SYSTEMS THEORY The development of systems theory has spurred interest in groups. Systems theorists believe that when any member of a group—a family, for example—has a serious emotional, physical, educational, or vocational crisis, all members of the group are intimately involved. They are part of the problem and thus must be part of its solution.

The group member who is identified as the troubled person might be acting out tensions that can be traced to the faulty interaction patterns of the whole family. A mother who drinks too much, for example, might be either the scapegoat or safety valve who keeps other family members from facing the seriousness of their own problems (Nichols, 2016; Okun & Kantrowitz, 2014). Systems theorists warn us that working with one family member in isolation from all the others is pointless. All of the members must struggle together to deal with the problem and perhaps readjust to a new way of interacting.

5. THE IMPACT OF SOCIAL SERVICE BUDGET CUTS   After most periods of expansion, there is belt tightening. Downsizing budgets in the social services began in earnest in the 1980s and continues to this day (Levey, 2017). By working with people who share similar problems in groups, rather than in a series of one-to-one encounters, agencies try to use the shrinking time and energy of trained staff more efficiently. In schools, for example, as education budgets are trimmed, the school counselors and social workers are the first to experience a reduction in force. A lone counselor, facing a caseload of hundreds of teenagers and their families with many diverse needs and life transitions, is forced to utilize group meetings and orientations. In many settings, the one-on-one interview has become a rare luxury.

Thus, from professionally sound considerations about the utility of groups as well as from practical necessity, the group model of problem solving continues to expand.

ESTABLISHING AND FACILITATING A GROUP: TEN KEY QUESTIONS TO ASK

It might seem from Beth's journal that she was simply doing what comes naturally. But establishing and facilitating a group is not a random process. Before starting out and at many junctures along the way, Beth, the residents, and the mutual-aid group leaders of the MPA must ask ten key questions. The answers to the questions will guide their actions as they organize and conduct the group meetings. These are questions that you will need to ask before you start a group. Each of these questions will be discussed in more detail:

1. What positives and negatives should we anticipate before beginning to work together as a group?
2. What phases or cycles is the group likely to pass through?
3. What is the central purpose of this group? What are its secondary purposes?
4. What kinds of activities will help this group accomplish its goals?
5. Who should be included in this group? What kinds of people and how many?
6. What kinds of structures will help this group do its work?
7. What will be the role of the designated leader? What other kinds of leadership roles will the group need?
8. In what kind of environment will this group flourish?
9. What kind of interaction will the members have with the leader and with each other?
10. In what ways can we keep evaluating how well the group is doing?

1. What Positives and Negatives Should the Group Anticipate?

After a long discussion at a staff meeting and then at the residents' council, Beth decided to start a women's discussion group at Transition House. She will need to think about the positives and negatives of her plan. Should she be dealing with issues of gender and role in a group, or might it not be better to talk things out with individual members? Would a mixed-gender or all-gender group be more useful? Would the women speak up if the men were present? Even though she might be comfortable interacting in a group, she knows that groups can be enormously intimidating places. Each member will need protection, and there is no guarantee that the group will be productive.

Before they get started, Beth and the other women need to sketch a well-rounded picture of potential **trade-offs**. What might they have to give up for the benefits they get in return?

During one of the early sessions, Beth and the members will review the pros and cons of working together as a group. Through sharing their past successes and failures in groups, they may be able to figure out traps to avoid. Although every group is a unique entity, we learn by analyzing our past experiences.

As an example of thinking about working in a group format, Beth's Human Service class members were asked to make a list of the negative and positive factors of sitting in a circle and breaking into small discussion groups in class instead of the usual lecture format of their other classes.

Positive Factors	Negative Factors
1. In a group interaction class you are figuring things out by getting involved. You learn a lot about how you react when dealing with different people and moods.	1. It's hard to do solid work in a group. People use the group for their own needs rather than for learning about the subject. When a few people take over, the person in charge can lose control.
2. You hear a lot of opinions and relate to many different personalities. You can pick and choose the people and ideas that are helpful.	2. It's hard to stick to the topic or task. There's a lot of side conversation and people go off on tangents, especially if they don't have much in common.
3. When you work in a group, sitting in a circle, you feel an emotional linkage with the other members, not just with the leader (teacher). You can see that you are not the only one who thinks a certain way.	3. People can make you feel a lot of pressure. If they disagree, you can read it all over their faces. It's hard to speak when everyone's eyes are on you.
4. The attention of the person in charge isn't always focused on you; yet, it's easy to get into the discussion when you are ready.	4. People can avoid responsibility in a group. They can sit back and complain about the others who talk too much or won't cooperate.

2. What Phases or Cycles Is the Group Likely to Go Through?

If you were to reconstruct the history of a group that you have been in for a long time, you would discover that just like a human being, the group has gone through many stages, from its beginning to its ending. Researchers who study group behavior in experimental situations and in natural settings have tried to describe and put labels on the phases or cycles through which most groups are likely to pass. Like their counterparts who study the growth and development of humans, the researchers do not all affix the same labels to each phase or agree on where one ends and the next begins. Some do not even think it is useful to label them at all. But most agree that basic tasks must be worked through at different points in a group's life. These are some of the stages most groups will go through.

1. FORMING As it is being born and moving through infancy (forming), every group must, of course, work on negotiating its contract. Decisions need to be made about its purpose. What activities will implement its goals? Who should be a member? What type of structure, environment, and leadership will it need? Essentially, the "baby" is being named, and is exploring the nursery and getting to know the rules of its own family. This is a period of tentative questioning. Members are probably asking these kinds of questions:

> What's in this for me?
>
> Is this group going to be worth the investment of my time?
>
> Who in this group might be my friend, ally, or adversary?
>
> How much can I share with these people? What about the leader? Whom can I trust?

2. STORMING In the **storming** stage, members are struggling to carve out their territory in the group. Each member might seek power, both for self-protection and to get the most he can from the group. Members might seek the approval of the leader and may vie with each other to get it. Cliques may form. Members begin to figure out ways to accomplish tasks. They test the leader and each other. Sometimes they become rebellious. Perhaps a few members decide the group is not working for them and they leave.

The group has to discover how well it can handle tension and resolve conflicts. During this period, the group is beginning to establish rules. If members keep coming in late, for example, they can decide to be realistic and change the meeting time. If the bonding of the group members has gone well and they find ways of resolving conflicts, the group will be much stronger for having weathered this turmoil. If the group cannot achieve adequate **conflict resolution**, it probably will never be very productive.

3. NORMING In the **norming**, or intimacy, stage, the group becomes more like a family, complete with sibling rivalry. Members are more able to discuss feelings about the group and their place in it. They are more comfortable with the rules they have carved out and they begin to work on group tasks together. They see the group as a place where they can grow and change. "There is a feeling of oneness or cohesiveness within the group. Struggle or turmoil during this stage leads the members to explore and make changes in their personal lives, and to examine what this group is all about" (Zastrow, 1993).

4. PERFORMING Having had a few successes and maybe having survived disagreements and personality clashes, in this stage the members should now be able to spend less time on organizational tasks and on testing each other and the leader. Now the group should be able to devote more energy and skill to program activities—to performing. It should be ready to take on more challenging tasks.

If Beth starts a women's group and it gets this far, members may now be ready to take on more leadership in the residence. Instead of withdrawing from disputes, they might support each other during a house discussion, reminding the men that their needs have equal importance. Miriam might take a risk and agree to coordinate a celebration for Women's History Month.

Beth might also discover that her thinking about the phases of group life needs to be readjusted. Linda Yael Schiller (2008) suggests that there are special qualities in the development of groups composed solely of women. If the group is composed predominantly of African-American women, Beth would be wise to read *Images of Me: A Guide to Group Work with African American Women* (Pack-Brown & Whittington-Clark, 1998). The cultural background of group members often plays a significant role in how they interact with each other as well as how they relate to the larger community. For example, many members of a group composed mostly of Black women are likely to have experienced racial discrimination in a variety of settings.

As the group moves through its adulthood, new activities or shifts in membership might provoke other periods of tension and reorganization. But the group should be able to fall back on a reasonably workable structure, an appropriate division of labor, and some mutual trust. Now, the group has a history and a shared vision of its capacity to survive and perform.

5. ADJOURNING, OR SEPARATION   Sometimes a group needs to end, for any of a number of reasons. Ending is not always easy. Some members may not want to move on. To help the members let go, the worker must be able to let go. Workers can help the members evaluate their experiences, express any ambivalence they feel about ending, and take pride in the progress that they have made. If some of the members still need the support of group members, the leader could make a referral to another similar group that is ongoing.

How long any group will keep working and whether it will need to change its direction will depend on its unique circumstances. Some groups never survive the early stages, and some perform for a while and then enter old age, becoming stagnant and eventually dying. If, for example, the women's issues group needs to reorganize or decides to go out of business, it is not necessarily a negative outcome. Perhaps it served its purpose, and to keep going would be an exercise in hollow ritualism. It is usually better to terminate a group on a high note than to let it simply wither away.

THE NEED FOR AWARENESS OF THE PHASES OF GROUP LIFE   Being aware of the phases of group life keeps everyone alert to their impact. It takes time and patience to build a solid group, and once a group is built, it may need to be frequently "renovated." Although deciding on a contract and negotiating conflicts can be very stressful, workers and members can be buoyed during those hard times by realizing that periods of struggle are often precursors to periods of productiveness. The expression "no pain, no gain" is true for many human service interventions; it is especially true for groups!

3. What Is the Central Purpose of This Group? What Are Its Secondary Purposes?

All of the strategies we employ in the human service field have a definite purpose. When a collection of people join together to form a group, the members need to articulate their goals and commit themselves to a shared purpose. This is easier said than done. Perhaps you can remember the feelings of annoyance and frustration that churned up your stomach when, after you had hurried to be on time to a meeting of your sorority or social club, someone asked:

"Hey, does anyone know what we're supposed to be doing here?"

Mild feelings of annoyance turn into rage when, after an hour spent working out the details of an event, someone says:

"Hey, wait a minute, it's not our job to do that. It's the job of the program committee."

Beth has noticed that when the members are not clear about the work their group is supposed to be doing, the members drift off—some to the refreshment table, others to the restrooms, and a few taking short naps. They start chatting with each other and arguing about trivial issues.

Each time a new activity or organizational arrangement is proposed, everyone should be able to answer the question:

"In what way will doing this activity bring us closer to our group goal?"

A mutually agreed-on purpose is the cornerstone on which a worker begins to build a group. But even after the group has articulated its central purpose, members might still come to a meeting with some different agenda items. Norman attends a meeting of the mental health group because he is genuinely angry about the overprescribing of psychotropic medications, which have left him and many of his friends with facial tics. But he is also hoping to get a date with a young woman who captured his fancy at the last meeting.

Socializing can be a legitimate secondary purpose of this social action group. Recognizing this, Beth provides name tags and refreshments. A few minutes at the end of the meeting are always left open for informal chatting. But socializing cannot fill too much of the time of this group. If it does, their goal of improving the mental health system will get lost in the shuffle.

Sometimes the secondary goals for joining a group are so important to some of the members that they cannot simply be put on the back burner. Norman's desire to expand his social contacts is perfectly legitimate. If the mental health discussion group is not helping him meet that purpose, Beth might suggest two alternative pathways. He could try to get the group to expand beyond its political action goals by organizing some purely social events where members could get to know each other better. Or he might get together with some of the members who share his priorities and start another group whose main goal is socializing. Many new groups have begun as spin-offs from previous ones.

Experienced group leaders often begin a meeting by devoting a few minutes of time to the members' own immediate concerns. Participants are invited to share with each other a brief thought or recent experience before the formal meeting agenda begins.

GROUPS CAN BE CLASSIFIED BY THEIR CENTRAL PURPOSE Although we are once again warning the reader that categories in the human services always have fluid boundary lines, it is useful to know the basic types of groups that can be organized to deal with an issue. Then, when you are in an agency and you identify a new problem area, you can carefully think about which type of group seems most appropriate to deal with it. Of course, we would all like to choose the model that seems most immediately important, but we might end up having to choose the model that is within our ability to deliver. For example, you may be able to organize a task-focused social action group for Norman and his peers, or you may be able to help them organize a purely social club, but you are not likely to have the skills to be able to lead a therapy group. Here is a brief description of each of the basic group formats at Transition House.

THERAPY GROUPS. Beth looks back with great satisfaction at the camping trip she went on with the residents of Transition House. The director commented on the sense of self-worth and competence that radiated from the campers on their return. Many successful group experiences can be **therapeutic** or **rehabilitative** for the participants.

But when we use those terms to describe a mental health therapy group, we apply it more precisely. The term "therapy group" describes a group that is composed of people who have specific emotional and/or physical problems that seriously interfere with their work, education, or social relationships. At Transition House, for example, therapy groups are led by two trained psychologists using a specific model of intervention.

Although the content of each therapy session grows out of the current and past experiences of the members, the focus of this type of group is in the hands of the therapist. The professional leader selects the participants and sets the ground rules. Most counseling or therapy groups encourage a great deal of interchange among the participants, but the leader is responsible for encouraging change in the attitudes or actions of each member.

SUPPORT OR MUTUAL-AID GROUPS.   Members who participate in a support or mutual-aid group usually share at least one characteristic or experience that is troubling or challenging them. In Chapter 1 we saw Kathy's family becoming involved with AA (Alcoholics Anonymous) for those who drink too much, Al-Anon for their families, Alateen (for teenagers), and ACOA (Adult Children of Alcoholics). Within the human service field, there are many similar groups, some based specifically on the AA 12-step program and others that develop their own unique pattern.

For example, Beth helped George and Irma Castro, the parents of one of the residents, to start a family support group that meets at Transition House once a month. The relatives of several of the residents share their pain, disappointments, hopes, and resources. They call each other between meetings when a crisis looms large and in many ways act as an extended family for each other. The group is very member-focused. Leadership rotates among the members. Every aspect of the group is shaped by its participants.

Sometimes support groups in their start-up phase are led by a professionally trained worker. Beth withdrew after this group for families was launched. It has gone from being a support group to being a genuine mutual-aid group with an indigenous leader and a self-generated agenda.

Support groups frequently form in response to the sense of alienation or dissatisfaction that many people encounter when enmeshed with faceless bureaucracies or unresponsive schools or social agencies. They provide desperately needed human services in the least threatening, most flexible manner. Through informality and dependence on each other, members vividly experience their own power to heal.

Groups can range in size from a handful of people to fifty or more members at one meeting. They are usually low-cost or free, easy to get into and out of, and have few screening mechanisms. Like the parent support group at Transition House, some are homegrown. Others, like AA and its offshoots, are chapters of worldwide organizations.

TRAINING AND ORIENTATION GROUPS.   Training and orientation groups have a clearly stated purpose and content that is established before any members are recruited. Although their goal is to educate participants and perhaps to change their attitudes and actions, they are different from traditional classes. They use experiential learning techniques. Participants can test new attitudes and behaviors in the safety of the group.

Transition House regularly conducts training groups for its new volunteers and staff. It has also organized workshops for the police department and for counselors of the local family service and vocational placement agencies. Through role-plays and other simulations, participants try to understand the barriers of self-doubt and discrimination that the Transition House residents must cope with. Workshop members also receive accurate information about mental illness that punctures their stereotypes about this population.

Transition House staff members use the same techniques to train residents in job-hunting strategies, interviewing, and on-the-job survival skills. Training groups are usually time-limited

Source: Dana White/PhotoEdit

Keeping members informed is an ongoing challenge for every group. Bulletin boards, both physical and electronic, can help do that, as long as they are kept up to date and relevant.

but intensive. They might meet every Tuesday afternoon over a period of six weeks, or for a whole weekend, or for several days in a row.

In highly focused training workshops, the leader sets up the tasks, assigns exercises, and runs the discussions. In more generalized human relations training—sensitivity or encounter groups, for example—the leader frequently sits quietly and challenges the members to carve out their own learning methods and find ways to resolve conflicts.

TASK-FOCUSED OR PROBLEM-SOLVING GROUPS.   A task-focused or problem-solving group has both a clearly specified purpose and an end product. Staff, board members, and residents at Transition House volunteer (or are drafted) for these groups on the basis of their interests or special skills.

Committees, task forces, and study groups are formed when there is a job to be done. They disband when the task is completed, perhaps to be called back into action as needed. Right now, one group of staff and board members is writing grant applications to obtain money to expand the job-training capacity of the residence. Once they have written the program proposal, they will begin sending it out to foundations and corporation executives.

Last year, Beth worked on the committee that obtained funds to send five of the house residents to a special camp program. Now she serves on another ad hoc committee to recruit and screen applicants to fill a newly funded counselor position. An ongoing task-focused committee of staff and residents publishes a monthly newsletter, Transition Times. Another group is organizing a holiday fund-raising event.

Task-focused groups work best when kept small so that everyone can share a portion of the work and keep moving at a brisk pace. Once formed, these groups select a leader, or one person is asked to coordinate. Coordinators help to delegate work and keep track of the group's progress.

SOCIAL OR RECREATIONAL GROUPS.   While task groups have very specific goals, social and recreational groups tend to have quite diffuse goals, stating their original purpose in broad generalities: to have fun, play a sport, socialize, encourage moral development, or do good works.

After working together for a while, some groups carve out a series of smaller purposes—such as putting on plays, conducting tournaments, sponsoring concerts, or giving awards—and each event has a specific goal and tasks.

Social groups at Transition House, like those at neighborhood community centers, "Y"s, or residences for older adults, might be led by paid workers, college students, or volunteers. The activities or programs that these groups conduct vary enormously, depending on the interests of the members, skills of the leader, and resources available. For example, there used to be a bowling club at Transition House, but the neighborhood bowling alley closed and now the nearest one is too far away.

4. What Activities Will Help This Group Accomplish Its Purposes?

Every group, regardless of purpose, sophistication, or stage in its organizational life cycle, must plan and carry out two kinds of activities: maintenance activities and program activities.

MAINTENANCE ACTIVITIES   Maintenance activities are the housekeeping chores that keep the group functioning so that it can accomplish its goals. These activities might include:

- Finding and setting up a meeting space
- Sending out meeting notices and minutes
- Electing officers and setting up committees
- Arranging for child care, transportation, or refreshments
- Raising money and keeping financial records.

Although these activities might seem like tedious chores to the impatient residents at Transition House, Beth has learned that if a group ignores these tasks, it rarely progresses beyond the initial stages. When maintenance tasks are taken care of, the group is free to pursue its primary reasons for being.

PROGRAM ACTIVITIES   Program activities are, of course, the primary reason for a group to exist. They include trips, plays, speakers, discussions, role-plays, and other special tasks or events through which members accomplish their goals. When Beth first began working with the residents' house council, she was not clear about what activities would be appropriate. Her supervisor told her that the acid test of any program activity was its logical connection to the primary and secondary purposes of the group. If the members could not explain in a few words why they voted to work on a particular task, it probably did not make sense to undertake it.

This advice came in handy when Beth was assigned to the World of Work Orientation group. When she took over from a previous worker, she discovered that the members had done little more than socialize and complain about their lack of jobs. They enjoyed coming to the meetings, but none of them had gotten much closer to their stated purpose of making money and moving toward independent living.

Beth suggested that they construct a long-range plan of activities to help them find work and keep a job. They could get started by inviting a speaker from the Downstate Rehabilitation Service to their next meeting. The employment specialist, Lionel Parker, could videotape them role-playing typical job interviews. When Beth first suggested it, they groaned, but she assured them that they would still have time for socializing if they started the meeting a half-hour earlier. With that assurance, they agreed.

Beth learned, in her course on group work, that even programs that are very important to the lives of the participants might not ensure those participants' regular attendance. Group sessions, especially the initial ones, should include high-interest activities, such as games, sports, dramatics, photography, and trips, in combination with the activities directly related to the more specific goals of the group. Beth has learned that delicious refreshments, especially when made by one of the members, also make a group meeting so memorable that participants eagerly anticipate the next session.

BUILDING COHESION OR GROUP BOND   Cohesion is vital to accomplishing a group's purposes. In addition to their maintenance and program activities, effective groups must develop trust among the members and between members and leaders. Trust leads to the development of a **group bond** or **cohesion**. This is the glue that keeps members coming to the group even when the going gets rough.

Trust and cohesion are not built through any single activity. They grow out of the accumulated good feelings that come from weathering small challenges and successfully completing activities and tasks. Failures that result because the group bit off more than it could chew hinder the development of trust and cohesion. The choice and pacing of activities are matters of trial and error followed by careful reflection.

5. Who Should Be Included in the Group?

There is no perfect formula for the composition of a group. The nature of the setting most often dictates exactly who will be recruited and who will be excluded. For example:

- The Orientation group at Transition House is composed of all the new staff and volunteers who have started there during the month.
- The National Alliance on Mental Illness and the World of Work Orientation groups are self-selected.
- New members of the Transition House Board of Directors are chosen for their political clout, economic resources, expertise in mental illness, and willingness to give up time and energy for scant tangible rewards.

With membership chosen by administrative fiat, chance, or self-selection, all the groups at Transition House have imbalances. One week, the NAMI chapter had only one woman out of eight participants, and no racial mix. The Parent Support Group had a preponderance of aggressive, outspoken people during its first year and of the shyest of people the next.

When the family therapy group has several names on the waiting list, Dr. Kreger, the consulting psychologist, is able to make some thoughtful decisions about which members he thinks would do well together. Most of the time, though, he accepts any of the residents' families who are willing to attend.

In some groups in the community, members are voluntary participants; in others, members are mandated to attend. Perhaps a judge requires participation in a program as an alternative to a monetary fine or jail sentence. Or perhaps a spouse has dragged her partner to the meeting. There is disagreement among human service workers as to whether they should work with a group member who has not freely accepted the contract. In any event, there are bound to be resistance, anger, and preconceived notions brought to the group by members who are forced to attend. These resistances must be brought out into the open and dealt with honestly.

Source: Creativa Images/Shutterstock

While having a family brings rewards and happy moments, there are often many challenges to parenting. If these challenges become too difficult to handle alone, many parents (and children as well) can seek out a support group with others who face similar problems.

6. What Structure Does This Group Need to Do Its Work?

Whenever people assemble to achieve a common purpose, a **group structure** or a way of working together evolves. Even a very transient group—for example, a collection of volunteers who come together to rescue flood victims—quickly develops a division of labor and a leadership pattern. If the group stays together for any length of time, the routines and rules it initially establishes will probably undergo change.

No matter how small or unbureaucratic the group is or how diffuse its purpose, all groups should decide on basic elements of structure. If they do not articulate their structure, one will emerge anyway. But if it has not been planned and acknowledged, it will be unclear. Lack of clarity creates terrible tensions. Freeman, in a classic article (1972), aptly termed this the "tyranny of structurelessness."

The structure that a group evolves must be reviewed from time to time. Sometimes members realize that a particular rule or norm stands in the way of getting their work done. Hopefully, they can then change either the rule or the way it is being administered.

Group purpose also determines structure. Training and task-focused groups often have a prearranged format that has proved workable in the past. Mutual-support groups and social clubs create their own. Counseling or therapy groups often have a structure dictated by the leader's psychological or theoretical orientation.

The secret of carving out a useful structure is to find a middle ground between mindless rigidity—"We start at 8:00 P.M., no matter who is here"—and total chaos—"Who was supposed to bring the key to the clubhouse this week?"

7. What Kind of Leadership Does the Group Need?

Over many years, the study of leaders—the kind of people they are and what they do to mobilize others—has captured the imaginations of sociologists, historians, political scientists, philosophers, and biographers (Andrews, 1995; Bertcher, 1994; Stogdill, 1948; Stogdill & Coons, 1957; Towson & Rivas, 2008). The nature of leadership is an intriguing topic. Different perspectives on leadership have held sway in different historical periods. All are still around today.

THE TRAIT THEORY OF LEADERSHIP   The "great man/woman theory" of leadership assumes that the unique, often **charismatic qualities** needed to lead others lie within the character and personality of outstanding individuals (https://www.leadership-central.com). Gifted with a natural capacity to inspire and organize others, these leaders will, in virtually any situation, leave their imprint on a group. Implicitly accepting this trait theory of leadership, many people in the United States believe that the economic reverses and national drift of the past decades resulted from a lack of outstanding leaders and statesmen. They indulge in the always-intriguing "what if" game: "What if President John F. Kennedy and Martin Luther King, Jr., both outstanding charismatic leaders, had not been assassinated?" or "What if the Supreme Court had decided in favor of Gore instead of Bush in the closest presidential election in our history?"

The house counselors at Transition House who accept this view of leadership keep their antennae out, looking for "natural" leaders among the residents. When they spot a likely candidate, they encourage him to take a position of responsibility on the house council.

THE SITUATIONAL THEORY OF LEADERSHIP   Proponents of the situational theory of leadership argue that dependence on a natural or charismatic leader encourages passivity in other members. It denies them the chance to develop their own leadership capacities.

Nichols and Jenkinson (2006) assert that some of the behaviors thought of as desirable in a leader of a governmental or business enterprise may be counterproductive in a support group. For instance, a firm insistence that one's view is the correct one is not always helpful, nor is the tendency to take control.

Situationalists assert that it is not so much the great leader who shapes the times but rather the times that make the situation ripe for the emergence of a gifted leader. They point to studies of temporary crisis situations when people who had never been viewed as leaders emerged out of the crowd. They took command during the flood or airplane crash, blending back into the background when the crisis abated.

Beth has a mostly situational view of leadership. She consciously varies the activities at the house so that each member has an opportunity to become a leader at a particular time in the group's life. Each resident has some unique capacity. She tries to set up a situation in which each member can gain status by teaching or exhibiting that specialness.

THE FUNCTIONAL OR TASK-CENTERED VIEW OF LEADERSHIP   The functional or task-centered theory of leadership concentrates on **leadership acts and roles**. It assumes that there are a series of leadership acts that are necessary for any group to maintain itself and achieve its goals.

These tasks can be achieved by all the members working together. This concept of shared leadership focuses attention on the ways in which members interact with each other in pursuit of the group's purposes.

Many group-dynamics researchers have carefully studied groups, both in laboratory settings and in real life, in order to describe specific leadership acts. Typical leadership acts they have identified include:

- Giving information
- Offering suggestions
- Seeking support
- Releasing tension
- Clarifying
- Elaborating
- Energizing
- Compromising
- Opening channels of communication
- Orienting
- Reminding the group of constraints.

Although human service workers find the functional theory the most useful in their work, all three theories help us understand and nurture leadership. By utilizing the task-focused concept, the staff at Transition House can help the group members understand that no one member, even the president or chair, should feel solely responsible for the successes and failures of the group.

The counselors at Transition House view themselves as **facilitators**, helping each of the group members improve his or her constructive leadership skills. Thus, when Brian points out that some members consistently arrive late to meetings and that keeps the meetings from starting on time, they do not react as if he is being hostile. They assume that he is performing a constructive leadership act by trying to get others to live up to the agreed upon time frame in the group contract or to revise it if it is not working for everyone.

This perspective encourages workers to design program activities and training exercises that increase teamwork and cohesion. The role of the counselor/leader is constantly changing. If someone else is clarifying a point or asking a useful question, there is no reason for Beth to intervene. She jumps into the discussion only when no one else in the group seems able to. Hopefully, everyone's leadership skills will improve as the group matures. The worker's role thus becomes less and less active over time.

THE NEED FOR A VARIETY OF LEADERSHIP STYLES Classic group-dynamics research has shown that a democratic group-leadership style is more satisfying and productive in the long run than an authoritarian or *laissez faire* **style**. But the nature of the situation might modify Beth's usual democratic leadership style. In the middle of the night, when a sudden storm threatened to overwhelm the members on a camping trip, they had to quickly pack up and move into a shelter. It was not the correct time for shared decision making. Beth assumed an appropriately authoritarian "you-do-this and you-do-that" style.

After the storm ended, everyone sat down and pooled their thoughts on what to do next. Should they stick it out another day as planned or go back to the house to dry out? During that discussion, Beth sat back, in *laissez faire* style, letting the group make it or break it on its own. Switching styles is a matter of subtle timing that develops with experience.

These politically active young people are staffing a table for a voter registration drive.

8. In What Kind of Environment Will This Group Flourish?

Just as flowers must be planted in soil that has the right nutrients, group environments can significantly impede or encourage communication, trust, and cohesion.

Try to visualize a meeting of your college's student council being held in a 300-seat lecture hall. Thirty students are spread throughout the hall, and the president is on the stage behind the lectern. Trying to form committees or conduct an open discussion about school problems in such an atmosphere would challenge the skills of the most experienced leader. If the council president is sensitive to the impact of environment, she is likely to invite everyone to come up to the first two rows or sit on the stage.

It would probably be better to meet in a medium-size room with comfortable chairs arranged in a circle or horseshoe shape. A meeting place does not have to be beautifully furnished, but it should encourage members to talk easily without having to overcome barriers of space or noise.

Setting a good atmosphere entails common sense. If child care is provided at a parent meeting, the room for it should be convenient but not so close that group members can hear the noise of children at play. If the group is doing a long-range project, it needs a safe place to store materials between meetings.

9. What Kind of Interaction Will the Members Have with the Leader and with Each Other?

All of us communicate our thoughts through our words (verbal communication) and our body movements (nonverbal communication). Even during silences, something is always going on. Whether she is interviewing one person or leading a group, Beth attempts to see and hear everything that transpires.

Communication flows in all directions during a meeting, as members look at and talk to the worker, whisper to their neighbor, or address their words to the whole group while staring intently at one particular person. While the worker is responding to a question that one member has asked, the others are out of her line of vision. The grimace on the face of one and the smile on another's are messages that she probably has not received and cannot respond to.

As Beth gets more experienced, she begins to notice the subtle patterns that have emerged among a particular group of people. She notices them and responds to the many barely audible messages crisscrossing the group. As the residents get to know each other, they will (if they have practiced their interaction skills) begin to take on more of the responsibility for responding; they, too, will pick up a look of distress or another sign that some group member needs help. Then, Beth need not be in every place at once.

The following are some of the acts Beth performs to help members understand and improve their interaction:

1. She watches to make sure that all members are part of the flow of ideas and opinions and are included in the activity if they want to be. If they are not, the worker helps members figure out what is blocking them. Perhaps the worker starts a discussion on how things might be organized better so people can move in and out of the action when they want to.
2. When conflict or confusion seems to be immobilizing the members, the worker helps them figure out where the trouble is, why it is there, and how it might be overcome.
3. She supports verbally and nonverbally those acts that increase cooperation, acceptance, and group bond.
4. She teaches a repertoire of successful communication techniques she has drawn from previous groups with which she interacted.

Some surprisingly simple techniques can help a group get over seemingly insurmountable communication blockages. At the start of the women's movement, for example, many consciousness-raising groups experimented with ways to encourage members to participate equally. Some tried a system in which all the members began the meeting with the same number of poker chips. They spent one chip each time they spoke. Although the method seems very contrived, many groups found that it helped the more assertive women to sit back while the shy ones took a larger role.

Similarly, breaking one large group into several subgroups of four or five members for a particular activity or discussion helps people speak more easily than they might when watched by 20 sets of eyes. Subgroups also permit members to experience working more closely with everyone in the group at one time or another. Increased comfort in communication leads to more productive or satisfying meetings.

10. In What Ways Can We Keep Evaluating How Well the Group Is Doing?

Every group needs a **feedback** mechanism so it can keep correcting its course. If feedback is left to chance, it develops like a fast-growing weed filled with the distortions typical of one-way communication. An informal grapevine rarely includes everyone, so complaints are never aired fully enough to be acted on in a rational manner.

By using open-ended questions, which do not constrict or channel the members' reactions, Beth tries to elicit useful feedback on how each member views group interactions and activities.

TECHNIQUES OF GIVING FEEDBACK

- **Be concrete.** Give feedback only on specific sorts of behavior that were exhibited during the meeting of the group. When our whole personality or character is judged, we become understandably defensive. Members cannot be expected to suddenly change their style of acting and reacting. They can, however, change small bits of behavior in little steps. Compare:

   I found it very disruptive to our work when you didn't show up for the meeting with the paper we needed to make the banner.

with

   You're the kind of person who always takes on a task, doesn't follow through, and keeps other members from completing their tasks.

- **Describe feelings or opinions in "I" statements rather than in "you" statements.** Most of us automatically interpret other people's behavior. Yet we really do not know for sure what they meant; we know only how it felt to us. When we start a criticism with "You did … ," we can put people on the defensive. Compare:

   You ignored me!

with

   I really felt ignored when you spoke to George and didn't say anything to me.

The "I" message in the second sentence gives the person to whom it is directed a chance to explain why he acted a certain way. Often we do not want to hurt someone's feelings, and welcome being given a chance to clear the air. It takes a bit of practice to use "I" sentences in place of "you" sentences, but it is worth the effort if it stimulates honest communication.

- **Offer suggestions for change.** When something makes us feel bad or we sense that things are not going well, most of us have an alternative vision of what we would like to have happen. It is not always easy to find a concrete suggestion that puts that vision into words, but we need to try. When discussing that thorny issue of meetings not starting on time, the following sentences capture the spirit of the search for the constructive change of a negative behavior:

   I think if we all brought our coffee into the meeting room, perhaps we could start on time.

or

   Maybe it just isn't possible for Gloria to be here at 8:00, so how about starting the meetings at 8:15?

- **Make sure you have heard a criticism correctly.** When we hear a criticism, no matter how hard we try to be receptive, we may still feel embarrassment, anger, or defensiveness. As the flush rises on the cheeks and the belly tightens, it is easy to misunderstand what someone is trying to say. So, after she finishes, it is helpful to put what was just said into one's own words. This is the process of "reflecting" back.

For example:

> I think what you're saying is that several of us didn't do our committee work and that messed up the dance.

or

> Are you saying that you actually heard me say those things about you or that you heard from someone else that I said them?

Beth's group strategies must be constantly evaluated and redesigned. By sharing her efforts to react positively to criticism, she demonstrates a model of self-growth that she hopes all of the group members will use in their own lives.

Summary

1. Groups can be powerful arenas for problem solving, giving emotional support, and building self-confidence. Groups can also be filled with tension and frustration.

2. In both professional and personal life, reference groups help to shape our behaviors and actions.

3. Workers are both group participants and leaders. Group work has expanded in the wake of the War on Poverty, the civil rights movements, community mental health centers, the mutual-aid movement, and deinstitutionalization. Systems theory, family counseling, budget cutbacks, and managed care companies withholding resources make the use of group interventions a practical necessity.

4. Organizing and facilitating groups is a systematic process built on asking and answering ten key questions.

5. The positives and negatives of a particular group need to be anticipated.

6. Groups have phases or cycles of growth.

7. Members must share a central or primary purpose as well as a limited number of individual secondary purposes.

8. The five categories of groups in the human service field are therapeutic or rehabilitative groups, mutual support and mutual-aid groups, training and orientation groups, task-focused or problem-solving groups, and social/recreational groups.

9. All groups must work on maintenance activities and program activities. They must develop trust and cohesion, or group bond.

10. Group size and composition are not dictated by a formula. The more intense and focused the goals of a group, the fewer members the group can accommodate. The more diffuse the goals, the more members the group can absorb.

11. The structure of a group must be articulated clearly and reviewed from time to time.

12. The three theories of leadership are the trait theory; the situationalist theory; and the functional, or task-focused, theory. All have validity, but the functional theory is the most useful for human service workers.

13. A group needs a system of evaluation to receive and utilize ongoing constructive criticism. Feedback must be phrased in "I" rather than the more accusatory "you" statements.

Discussion Questions

1. Beth Soline, the counselor at the residential treatment house whose log you read, is planning to have a support group for the women members. Do you think that is a good idea? Do you think it is fair to the men to be left out of the discussions? Do you think it might increase communication among the male and female house members or that it will create a wider gulf between them?

2. In a small group with four or five other students, give your personal reactions to the 2015 decision by the United States Supreme Court to legalize marriage for couples of the same gender. If there is no disagreement among the members (an unusual situation, given the American public's very split opinions on this subject), the group members should assume roles, with two students arguing for the rightness of the Supreme Court's action and two students arguing that the action is wrong and should be stopped, perhaps by the passage of a proposed amendment to the U.S. Constitution that defines marriage as between one man and one woman. After a certain amount of time, the group is required to reach a joint decision. One or two members of the group should remain out of the discussion and take notes on how the discussion proceeded and how the joint decision was reached.

3. Referring back to the leadership acts described in the text, see if you can pinpoint who performed each of them. Then discuss how well each member did at articulating his position and how well the group members listened to each other.

4. How do you think a worker should handle episodes of scapegoating in a group of teenagers? What about bullying? Do you think a young person needs to find her own ways to try combat being a victim—which would make her stronger in the future—or do you think an adult should intervene and put an end to the situation? Did you see episodes of scapegoating or bullying in your own high school? What did adults do about it?

5. What role do you usually take in various groups? Does your role differ in a purely social group or in a class discussion group?

Web Resources for Further Study

American Self-Help Clearinghouse

https://healthfinder.gov/FindServices/Organizations/Organization.aspx?code=HR1681

MindTools

https://www.mindtools.com

Social Work

http://socialworkbhu.blogspot.com/2013/12/skills-of-social-group-work.html

MyLab Helping Professions for Introduction to Human Services

In the Topic 2 Assignments: Human Systems, start with Application Exercise 2.2: Common Group Dynamics and Credentialing Quiz 2.2: Common Group Dynamics.

Then, in the Topic 7 Assignments: Client Intervention, try Application Exercise 7.4: Group Facilitation and Counseling and Credentialing Quiz 7.4: Group Facilitation and Counseling.

Planning a Human Service Program 11

Source: Rawpixel.com/Shutterstock

Learning Outcomes

- Students will be able to explain why even workers who do mostly one-on-one work with clients need to develop planning skills.
- Students will demonstrate knowledge of the tools of the planner.
- Students will be able to describe the phases in creating a plan that includes troubleshooting, magnifying, and microscoping.
- Students will show that they understand the difference between a product and a process evaluation of a program and can give an example of each kind.
- Students will be able to explain why planning any intervention in the human services is both a technical skill and a people skill.

Regardless of specific job title, at some point a human service worker will be assigned the task of creating or changing a program to better meet the needs of people with problems. It is hard to imagine a human service job that does not require **problem-solving skills** and systematic planning. In his book on management in social agencies, Robert Weinbach (2014) asserts that even caseworkers, therapists, or social workers who spend most of their day in direct one-on-one services will still be required to spend some time on management functions. Central to all those management functions is the skill of planning. He goes on to say that it is not true that managers manage, supervisors supervise, and caseworkers should be left alone to see clients. It is not "us" versus "them."

Even in an agency that uses the one-on-one, direct-service model, a worker might be assigned to:

- Compile a list of agencies that assist people living with AIDS
- Visit and evaluate the services offered by several job-training programs

- Design an outreach campaign to inform the community of the agency's services
- Recruit volunteers for a mentoring program for high school students
- Help clients put on a holiday celebration
- Assist several women who are starting a support group for people with eating disorders
- Organize an open house for a new community residence for at-risk teenagers
- Plan a staff retreat to increase cohesion and improve skills
- Prepare a public information campaign to alert people to an impending funding cutback
- Set up a child care corner in the waiting room
- Gather data to be used in an application for a grant to buy new computers
- Raise money to take a group of high school students to a conference on cyberbullying.

Although planning is a common act of daily life, a human service worker does it in a more disciplined fashion than the ordinary citizen is likely to. We will begin this chapter by looking at the work of Raquel Fenning, the coordinator of a student volunteer program at a large urban university. Then we will describe some of the basic tools of the **program design** and planning process.

A Human Service Worker at Work: Raquel Fenning, University Volunteer Coordinator

I have worked at the university doing volunteer recruitment and placement for five years now. I also help volunteers to plan and carry out many program activities in this neighborhood. The first three years, I was a student doing this work, but after graduation, I was hired as a full-time employee to lead the Office of Volunteer Placements. I am responsible for making contact with neighborhood social service agencies and finding out what their volunteer needs are. Then I draft a paper outlining the agency, its mission, its funding, and so on, and finally write a job description for prospective volunteers.

The university had previously put a low priority on student involvement in the neighborhood, so this project was sort of an "add-on" to the Human Service program. But we applied for a grant from a foundation (with help from the Human Service faculty), won it, and now [the program] is an important part of the university. As a full-time employee, I report to the Provost's office, and I have a regular budget, a staff of six student interns, and a full-time secretary. The number of students using the program has gone from dozens each term to hundreds. And the students now are from all the majors on campus. Working as a volunteer in a community group for a certain number of hours each year is now a graduation requirement. Many faculty members facilitate the volunteerism by including appropriate community work as an integral part of their courses. So the student not only does the fieldwork but also has to analyze it for a research or concept paper. I also troubleshoot if something goes wrong on the placements either from the student's point of view or from the agency supervisor's point of view.

An important part of my job description is to participate in a variety of faculty/staff committees that grapple with "hot-button issues" that affect the mental health and well-being of the student population. Since I had been a student here just two years ago and am now a trained human service worker, they place a lot of value on my input. I work on committees that deal with issues facing gay, lesbian, and **transgender** students and the uses and abuses of alcohol and drugs on campus, and on the committee that oversees political demonstrations and the like.

I have just been handed a challenging assignment! I will participate in a newly formed committee which is charged with creating programs, guidelines, and policies to deal with the hottest-button issue of recent times: Recently there has been a lot of media coverage of **cyberbullying** in high schools. Newspapers have carried stories about high school kids (and even some younger children) posting nasty things about each other on web sites or in widely distributed text messages. Some high school students have posted messages about who hates whom, which person cheated on an exam, and other really hateful messages. They've tricked people into revealing their passwords and have posted photos of victims taken on cell phones without their permission (Gunderson, 2017). This isn't just kids harmlessly fooling around. Serious consistent teasing, whether in person or—more likely—through the anonymity of the web, has resulted in several teenage suicides and deterioration of mental and emotional health.

To everyone's horror, this has moved from high school students—who one can assume are rather immature and might not know better—to college students. The committee has been told by the president of the university to develop programs to deal with all forms of the misuse of technology to harass members of the student body and staff. We are exploring the use of computer software that documents and stores offensive messages, that immediately notifies prespecified recipients of an online threat, and so forth. This way messages can be documented so that perpetrators can be located. We are also planning to hold dorm talks on the misuse of texting, social network sites, videos, and so on. In the spring we will hold a campus-wide teach-in aimed at educating students on ways to protect themselves and, most importantly, on the serious nature of what might be seen as harmless teasing, especially when done anonymously. We hope to build a community spirit that will make such behavior unacceptable. Of course, the first line of defense is always education, but we will also have to draft a set of penalties for abuse when education is not enough. This is a particularly tricky issue, since we will have to struggle to find the line where free speech ends and bullying begins.

My position is very challenging but satisfying. I am so glad I took a course that helped me learn the steps in mounting a program. I will probably stay in this position for a few more years but then I hope to get a degree in public health. I like the idea of being a health educator; it builds on many of the skills I am practicing.

BASIC TOOLS OF THE PLANNING PROCESS

No plumber or carpenter would go to a job without a bag of tools. Program planners also have their essential tools of the trade. The major ones are:

- Pencil and paper and a computer
- Internet and planning software
- Directories, schedules, and other resource materials
- Calendar or memo book
- Large sheets of paper, a chalkboard, erasable board, or smartboard.

Pencil and Paper and a Computer

Proposing that traditional writing instruments are the basic tools of the planning process seems like a very simplistic statement. Yet, surprisingly, many people do not approach planning tasks with these in hand. Lakien (1989), an organization development specialist, asserts that systematic planning is an act of writing, not simply one of thinking. We heartily concur.

When engrossed in planning an event, we think about it almost constantly. Before falling asleep at night or when waiting at a bus stop, the mind races, buzzing with details. But although our thoughts may be profound, they are often fleeting insights, half-forgotten when we wake up the next morning. Details of plans that are not committed to paper (or to a computer with a backup disk) and later double-checked for accuracy have a way of drifting out of our grasp. One supervisor we know lamented:

> When I supervised graduate community-organization students in a large public agency, I lost count of the number of times I had to stop a staff meeting in the middle of a sentence to point out that I was the only one in the group taking notes on the decisions we had just made. Knowing they lacked their own personal record of what happened at the meeting, I found myself constantly calling them during the week to make sure they remembered the details of the task they had been assigned.

In the course of our busy lives we cannot depend simply on our memories. Our heads are filled with the conflicting demands of home, school, and job. A worker who is careless about the details of tasks, names, times, dates, locations, or costs often fails to accomplish the overall goal of the helping encounter despite other excellent skills.

When conducting a meeting, even the most enthusiastic beginner can forget to circulate a lined pad or have a laptop computer at the ready, with the words NAME, ADDRESS, PHONE NUMBER (work, home, and cell), EMAIL, and FAX NUMBER written across the top of the page. Lacking an accurate list of who attended the meeting and where those people live or work, the organizer cannot send everyone the minutes of that meeting or the notice of the next event. Without accurate records, it can take several days of diligent detective work to track down the person at the meeting who volunteered to print the flyers or staff the food booth for the neighborhood fair. All the people who do not receive the next mailing or phone call confirming their assignment are left to wonder why they were neglected. A minor omission can snowball into a major problem.

It is a good practice to keep a small notebook or cell phone in your pocket, purse, or knapsack. In it you can list fleeting ideas that occur to you, and each time someone hands you a business card or tells you her phone number or email address, you have a ready receptacle for it.

Internet and Planning Software

The Internet and several types of planning software are becoming vital tools in the planning process. In fact, it is difficult to remember how we managed to go about our jobs before these modern aids became widely available.

The computer should be the trusty repository for the jottings you made in your pocket notebook when the machine was not available. If notes are transferred at the end of each day to your computer, placed in the proper file folder on the hard drive, and, of course, backed up, they guard against loss. They also change your scribblings into solid bits of data that can be used now or in a future project and easily shared with other planners.

When available, email and the Internet are invaluable tools for networking with others who are working in similar areas of the human services to generate ideas, secure resources, and build support. Through the Internet we can cast our net wide, bringing in ideas from diverse communities.

Directories, Schedules, and Other Resource Materials

Perhaps you are working with a group of teenagers at a mental health center. They are trying to decide whether to go on a camping trip or to a country music concert in the next town. You suspect that both activities are too expensive. Before they get too deep into planning the details of either outing, you suggest they obtain answers to some key questions:

- How much will each of the activities cost?
- Are camping sites or tickets available?
- How can they get there?
- How long will it take to get there?

Armed with facts rather than speculations, they can then go on to discuss whether they will be able to obtain the time, money, transportation, and permissions they will need. Then you can help them weigh the trade-offs of each option—what they might have to give up in order to get something they want.

One worker described how she used this technique of matching facts with wishes with a group of teenagers she worked with at a summer work camp:

> Several years ago I took a group of 20 older teenagers to Mexico on an eight-week work project. The members were very mature but they often pushed against the limits of their independence and my sense of caution. During the first few weeks several of them made requests that frankly overwhelmed me. "We've been invited to a wedding next weekend three towns away. Please can't we go? Some people have asked us to join them in an expedition to climb a mountain. Is that okay?" Although many of their requests seemed risky, I didn't want to arbitrarily say "no." After a while we arrived at a program-planning technique that worked wonderfully for the rest of the trip. At a group meeting, we hammered out a set of basic questions: how, what, where, when, and what if? They were not to come to me with a request until they had the facts to back up their answers to those questions.
>
> If, for example, they planned to travel by bus, I wanted to know the exact schedule and the exact cost, where it left from, and how they would get there. Many grandiose schemes were quickly put to rest after a call to the bus station or a check on the computer made it clear that in this country you simply couldn't get from point A to point B in two days on a shoestring budget. By the time a request actually came to me, it was quite feasible and I was likely to agree to it.

In this experience, teens practiced systematic problem-solving skills that helped them to formulate current plans and, hopefully, equipped them to plan in the future.

Calendar or Memo Book

Watch a group of human service workers at a case conference trying to arrange a date for their next meeting. All of them will dig into a briefcase, handbag, or back pocket and pull out a cell phone or memo book. In it will be listed daily meetings and all the details surrounding them: who is to be seen, where the encounter will take place, and any driving or public transportation directions needed. Human service workers often list the home and work phone numbers of the people with whom they have made appointments. Then, if they must cancel a meeting because of an emergency, even from home at 6:00 A.M., they are prepared. (Another opportunity to demonstrate our caring for clients and colleagues!)

A calendar device right at hand also helps a worker visualize what needs to be done and when it should happen. Thus, "Stop by and see me sometime about those new regulations" or "We'll have to get together and talk about the Kramer child someday soon" become definite half-hours on a specific day. If a worker cannot make an appointment with the foster parent who mentioned she was having a hard time with the Medicaid office, a note in the calendar book is a reminder to phone her the next day and arrange a time to talk.

Large Sheets of Paper, Erasable Board, or Smartboard

To prod our memories or map out our ideas about a project, a computer or cell phone will do quite well. But when we are planning in concert with colleagues or clients, it is more helpful to use a large writing surface. A chalkboard, an erasable board, a smartboard, or even large sheets of paper propped up on an easel work well. As members suggest an idea or take on an assignment, these can be written large enough to be seen by everyone. If there are disagreements about specific points, they can be quickly noticed and clarified.

An erasable surface communicates the message that items can be reformulated. For example, suggestions can be listed, rubbed out as the members reject them, or raised to the top or dropped to the bottom of a list of priorities. This encourages experimentation and the free flow of ideas. Paper sheets lack that kind of flexibility, but they can be kept intact after a meeting ends. When a group is involved in a planning process over a protracted period, members can save the sheets with their initial ideas. Looking back at the sheets, they can analyze how far they have progressed or notice initial ideas that were forgotten in the flurry of activity.

Clearly Focused Questions

When planning any program, you cannot function without these questions:

- Who?
- Where?
- How?
- Why?
- Why not?
- How else?
- What if?

Planning is first and foremost a process of asking and answering questions. Sometimes the questions workers ask have definite answers. Often the questions are more speculative and have several alternative answers. Workers anticipate an interview with a client or a meeting with a budget committee by asking themselves and everyone else logical, hard questions about the topic under consideration.

Keith, a staff worker at the Larkin School, which provides services for children who are deaf, blind, and have emotional concerns, has written a proposal for an expanded summer camp program. Now he is preparing himself for the much anticipated but equally dreaded moment when he must appear before the other staff members to justify his plan. To prepare his answers to the questions they are likely to ask, he puts himself in their shoes. (He uses his capacity for anticipatory empathy.) Then he rehearses his answers to the possible questions:

- Why isn't our existing summer program adequate?
- What did you find the problems to be in last summer's program?
- How do you know that the parents want a more extensive camp program?

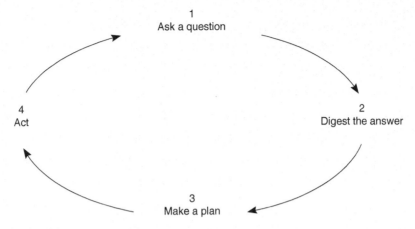

FIGURE 11.1   The information loop

- What have you done to make sure there will be sufficient enrollment to cover most of the costs?
- How safe and adaptive is the facility you plan to use for the program?
- How much will the whole program cost the agency?

Asking questions is like shining a flashlight in a dark cellar instead of simply stumbling around looking for the fuse box. Questions direct our thinking and protect us from jumping to wrong or incomplete conclusions. Even after he has designed his action plan, this process of asking, finding answers, acting, and then raising more questions continues. It creates an information loop that looks something like that shown in Figure 11.1.

THE PLANNING PROCESS

Planners wear many hats, a different one for each part of the planning process. Let's look at each of these steps and see how it is carried out.

Phase 1: Troubleshooting

STEP 1: IDENTIFYING A GAP   As shown in Figure 11.2, the planning process begins as soon as Raquel or another staff member says:

Something is wrong with how that is being done!

or

Something is missing from … !

or

Wouldn't it be wonderful if … !

or

There oughta be program for . . !

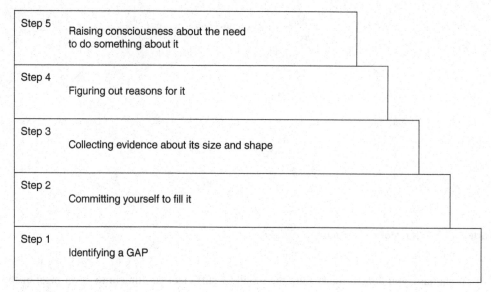

Step 5 — Raising consciousness about the need to do something about it

Step 4 — Figuring out reasons for it

Step 3 — Collecting evidence about its size and shape

Step 2 — Committing yourself to fill it

Step 1 — Identifying a GAP

FIGURE 11.2 The steps in troubleshooting a problem

Often we identify a **GAP**, without realizing we are doing so, when we are having a good gripe session.

Sometimes a gap is identified by a person who has a desperate need for a resource that he cannot locate, that does not exist, or that is functioning poorly. At other times a professional human service worker notices an unmet need and brings it to the attention of his supervisor or board.

EXAMPLE: A PROFESSIONAL IDENTIFIES A GAP. A doctor working in rural Alabama was surprised at how few patients came in to the hospital to be tested or treated for AIDS or HIV. Although AIDS is often thought of as an urban phenomenon, she knew that was not accurate. She had a hunch that people in southern rural towns, where everyone knows everyone else's business, were afraid to even ask for AIDS testing. So, dipping into her own wallet for start-up funds, she began a public education program called ASK, which stood for **A**IDS **S**upport through **K**nowledge. These are some of the outreach strategies she used:

- She set up an anonymous information telephone hot-line.
- She placed ads in newspapers.
- She sponsored a group of high school students, who performed a play about AIDS at schools and churches.

Eventually, many people who worried they might have contracted AIDS found the courage to come to the hospital for testing and care.

In *Designing and Managing Programs: An Effectiveness-Based Approach*, Kettner, Moroney, & Martin (2016) point out that many people who might need services seek them out only when the possibility of actually receiving them exists. Because people have such low expectations, they often do not even perceive that their gap is a legitimate one or that they deserve to have it filled. For example, after a rape crisis center opens in a town, instead of seeing a reduction in the rape statistics, we are likely to see them increase. It looks as if the situation is getting worse, but what might actually be happening is that victims, especially of rape, who used to feel that there was no possibility of getting justice and who endured their pain in silence are finding the courage to come forward and report the crime. Now there is a chance that they might be protected and that the abuser might be punished.

STEP 2: COMMITTING OURSELVES TO FILLING THE GAP   Once it has been stated that a gap exists, someone has to commit herself to the long, painstaking, often thankless planning tasks that can fill it. Unfortunately, gripe sessions too often end with little to show for them but shared frustration. Often people will say:

> What can I do? I don't know anything about starting up a program.

or

> But it has always been that way!

These statements express widespread feelings of powerlessness, but they do not reflect reality. Many programs have grown out of an informal discussion in someone's living room. Park benches in schoolyards where parents gather to talk about their children, their families, and their hopes for the future are often fertile fields for new program ideas.

Programs designed to fill gaps do not necessarily need vast sums of money and expertise. They grow out of someone's capacity to keep plugging away, aided by a fertile imagination, self-confidence, and a good **support network**.

STEP 3: COLLECTING CREDIBLE EVIDENCE ABOUT THE EXTENT OF THE GAP   Raquel has often noticed certain problems in the community that aren't being addressed. For example, when she visited a senior center near the university, she was surprised to discover that many of the residents didn't know about the local Meals on Wheels program that delivered cooked food to older adults who are homebound. Many of the residents also didn't know about the services that provided low-cost transportation to get them to and from medical appointments. She began to think that there was a need for some central source of information for senior services and a way to reach the seniors with that information. But she had to make sure that this was really a gap.

She began her research by collecting data at the Town Hall. She looked through directories (both hard copy and online) to find social services for the older adults, especially those that help to maintain older adults in their own homes. She decided to interview staff workers at some of these agencies to get information straight from the source. Before she interviewed anyone, though, she wrote up a list of questions to ask (see Figure 11.3).

From her interviews, Raquel decided that her initial hunch was correct: Information about available services was not getting to everyone who needed it, especially when the older adults were in crisis. Both consumers and professionals agreed that some central source of updated information, easy to access, was sorely needed. Raquel's review of the census data revealed that the elder population in this area had risen by 20 percent in the past ten years. The articles she read predicted that it would continue to grow. Now Raquel had evidence to show that increased outreach with information for the older adults was a legitimate need that wasn't being met (see Figure 11.4).

Needless to say, before any planning meeting is convened, the program planner should have a clear purpose for the gathering and a clear written agenda for the session. Both should be shared with the participants when they are invited to attend.

COLLECTING EVIDENCE ABOUT THE EXTENT OF A GAP
Services to the Elderly in Aurora

I. Questions to ask organization staff workers:

1. How many senior citizens do you have contact with, either in person or through newsletters?

2. What strategies do you use to get information out about available services to the elderly population and to social agencies?

3. What written guides do you have on elderly programs? Which of them seem most useful? What obstacles stand in the way of reaching some of the elderly?

4. Which groups of elderly citizens and their families do you feel are not being reached?

5. How great a need do you think there is for some type of information service for geriatric programs? What are your suggestions?

II. Questions to ask individual senior citizens or their families:

1. How did you hear about this particular organization (housing project, nursing home, recreational center, or whatever) you attend?

2. If you needed home care, a senior shuttle bus, meals on wheels, day care, or a nursing home, to whom would you turn for that information?

3. How easy is it to get information when you need some kind of services? If it is difficult, why do you think that is so? What are your suggestions to increase knowledge of resources?

FIGURE 11.3 Sample interview questions on services for older adults

STEP 4: FIGURING OUT CAUSALITY—THE REASONS FOR THE GAP As Raquel was collecting evidence about the size and shape of the gap in information about services, she was constantly asking all the informants "why" questions such as:

- Why do you think the public has so little knowledge about your program?
- Why do the booklets you publish seem not to reach more of the older adults and their families?
- What techniques have you used to reach out to more people who need the information?

The answers to these questions begin the difficult process of estimating the reasons for the gap. Reasons will suggest remedies. Although we can never be absolutely certain about the reasons for a problem, the process of identifying possible causes and then ranking them in importance is a vital one. It creates the foundation upon which the whole planning process is built.

Figure 11.5 shows the list of reasons Raquel created after studying the interviews and reading journal articles on the subject. See how program ideas seem to flow logically from each of them! There is no way, of course, that she could design one program that would deal with all the reasons.

STEP 5: RAISING CONSCIOUSNESS ABOUT A GAP Even after a gap has been identified; evidence about its size, shape, and causes has been marshaled; and some possible reasons for it have been outlined, the demand that it be filled still may not be addressed. Lots of other people must agree that it is a problem before it can move up to the top of the agenda for the agencies, the

---

COLLECTING EVIDENCE ABOUT THE EXTENT OF A GAP
Services for the Elderly

I. *People we will need to talk to:*

1. Citywide council on elderly affairs in the mayor's office

2. Local chapter of AARP (American Association of Retired Persons), National Council of Older Americans, or OWL (Older Women's League)

3. Nursing Home Director's Group and some residents of local nursing homes

4. The Homecare Corporation

5. The Gray Panthers (a self-help elderly social action group)

6. Project manager and residents at the Susan B. Anthony Elderly Housing Project

7. The Methodist church's friendly visitors program

II. *Publications we will need to read:*

1. Citywide and community newspapers (large-print version, if there is one)

2. Newsletters of any senior citizen clubs or groups

3. Directory of services for the elderly

4. Census data for the area

FIGURE 11.4   Sources of information about services for the older adults

bureaucrats, and the legislators. Those looking to solve the problem will need to write up a report on this unmet need, showing the results of the research, and send this report to the sources that might be able to fill the gap.

Phase 2: Magnifying

Having gathered evidence and marshaled some enthusiastic support, Raquel might now be ready to begin the **magnifying phase**. During this phase, she will collect, sort, and then choose concrete program ideas—vital components of the program-design process. Figure 11.6 shows the steps she followed.

STEP 1: CONDUCTING AN INVENTORY OF OTHER PROGRAMS   Throughout this book, we have stressed the critical importance of obtaining firsthand knowledge of program resources in the local community. But when designing an action plan, we look within and far beyond the boundaries of our own town because program ideas cross-fertilize from one region or country to another.

Sometimes program approaches are transplanted whole from one place to another. At other times, however, new program ideas leapfrog off each other. Once you see yourself as a planner, you are likely to get new program ideas almost every time you read a newspaper, watch a television show, or attend a lecture or seminar. You will not be able to act on all of them, but you can store program designs away for future use.

Source: Cartoon Resource/Shutterstock

"Frankly, I don't remember why
I called this meeting."

STEP 2: BRAINSTORMING IDEAS   Brainstorming is a very simple yet elegant planning technique that quickly produces a great many ideas, some mundane and impractical, a few marvelously creative (Michaiko, 2006). It energizes the staff members of the Office of Volunteer Placements. They do it at staff meetings in groups of three.

A time limit of five or ten minutes is set for each session. The time pressure encourages members to keep throwing out ideas. The group leader starts the creative juices flowing by suggesting a few ideas of his own—the more innovative, the better. Participants are told that there is a premium placed on far-ranging thinking. Here are some simple rules for brainstorming:

- Do not censor your ideas; let them flow. Even if you think they sound silly, impractical, or naive, they can be sorted out and discarded later.
- Do not censor anyone else's ideas by judging them or by communicating distaste, scorn, or ridicule.
- Give encouragement and support to others and expect it from others.
- Build on each other's ideas, use them, and change them.
- Move quickly and try to get as many ideas out as possible.
- List ideas on paper so that they are not lost in the flow of talk.

POSSIBLE REASONS FOR A GAP
Referral Services for the Elderly

Information about elderly services is not reaching enough people because:

1. The directories of services that do exist are all in the English language, and the print is often small and hard to read.

2. Directories of services for the elderly are not distributed widely enough. They are available only at social agencies or hospitals.

3. Directories of services for the elderly seem to be very specialized, concentrating on only one type of service. Often they don't mention alternative services available at other agencies.

4. The elderly are often homebound and use television and radio more frequently than books and newspapers to get information.

5. Often the elderly and their families don't prepare for emergencies and must do their planning when a crisis occurs, when they are least able to seek out resources rationally.

6. Many people assume that all service programs for the elderly are charity and resist exploring resources that might have a social stigma.

7. Programs change so often that staff are unaware of new ones or those which have been discontinued.

8. The best referrals are made by knowledgeable people, not directories; however, agencies are short of experienced staff.

FIGURE 11.5   Possible reasons for a gap in referral services

Step 5
  Drafting a plan and making an alternative one

Step 4
  Doing a force-field analysis of alternative ideas

Step 3
  Collecting and ranking ideas

Step 2
  Brainstorming ideas

Step 1
  Inventorying other programs

FIGURE 11.6   The process of magnifying the problem

STEP 3: COLLECTING AND RANKING IDEAS   At the student volunteer quarterly retreat, members were asked to brainstorm ways to spend the extra money they were awarded for the next semester by the Office of Student Affairs. The ideas they came up with were listed on a chalkboard and then divided into categories:

1. Senior citizen programs
2. Youth after-school programs
3. Programs for adults with developmental delays
4. Teenager programs
5. Special one-time work projects
6. Community fairs

Then the student staff edited the lists, discarding ideas that seemed impractical or that evoked little interest. They put check marks next to those that excited almost everyone. As new ideas come up, they will be added. If a Human Service major wants to do a special internship at the Fenway Project, she can look at this list to see what program ideas are waiting to be developed.

The staff also created a wish list. Staff members suggested equipment they would like to obtain if there was any money left at the end of the fiscal year. If any individuals or organizations offered to make monetary donations, the staff could refer to the wish list and suggest an item. Their current wish list looks like this:

- A laser printer, a scanner, and a digital camera
- A paint job for the office
- Slides to use for class presentations
- A catcher's mitt and a left-handed fielder's mitt
- A new coffee urn

STEP 4: DOING A FORCE-FIELD ANALYSIS   After a program idea has survived the sorting-and-ranking process, it is time to analyze its chances of success. To do this, the students use a simple but effective technique called **force-field analysis**. They first look at the forces that might help the program get started and the barriers that are likely to stand in its way. They gain confidence by reviewing the positive factors but are also alerted to the barriers posed by the negatives. They look at how the potential positives and negatives balance out.

Some of the volunteers are working with the Hi-Teens, a club of adolescents who live in the local public housing project. The volunteers have decided that the group needs a really good activity to pull the members together into a cohesive unit. They brainstormed with the teenagers and analyzed their list of ideas, and everyone agreed that they wanted a weekend camping trip. Now they must think through how likely it is that they will be able to plan and successfully carry out the idea. Systematically, they listed the positive and negative forces, as shown in Figure 11.7.

After completing the force-field analysis, the teens brainstorm strategies that might overcome or neutralize those negative forces. Now, they need to construct an action plan, making sure that potential obstacles to their camping trip are dealt with and that everything they have decided to do is clear to all the members.

STEP 5: CREATING A PROGRAM PROPOSAL AND MAKING A WORK PLAN   No matter how informal the group, it is imperative that the program plan a group hopes to implement be written down so that everyone can review it fully and those who become involved later on can be accurately

---

FORCE-FIELD ANALYSIS
Topic: Hi-Teens' Weekend Camping Trip

The Positives +
(What we have going for us)

1. We have been on several one-day trips, and they've worked out well.

2. It's January now, so we have lots of time to make a reservation at a camp site for the spring.

3. We all get along very well.

4. Our group leader has a lot of camping experience.

5. Because most of the members voted for this idea, we should get good cooperation from them.

The Negatives –
(What might get in our way)

1. We have no money in our treasury.

2. Some parents may refuse to give permission, especially if it's boys and girls together.

3. The camping sites are pretty far away, and we don't have any transportation.

4. Carlos, our group leader, has finals at college in the spring and may not have the time to take us.

FIGURE 11.7 A sample force-field analysis for the camping trip

oriented to it. The **program proposal** will be the road map. It keeps folks on course and invites others (especially funders) to come on board. Figure 11.8 lists what the proposal should include. A book the teens found useful was *Proposals That Work* (Locke, 2013).

It is critically important that all the details of the proposed plan be set down on paper. In the process of doing this, the planners themselves will become much clearer on the specifics and ultimately more persuasive. The proposal shows that they have done the homework and have a sensible plan. Although many human service workers turn to non-profit foundations or local governments for funding, there are currently many sources of small sums of money that can be found on a wide variety of web sites.

Phase 3: Microscoping

For the **microscoping** phase of the planning process, we take off our creative, think-big hat and put on the green visor of the accountant. Now the teens must focus all of their attention on each small detail of their plan for the camping trip. They must make sure that it will work as smoothly as possible. The steps to follow are listed in Figure 11.9. In this phase, we must nail down vague ideas. Using pad and paper, computers, datebooks, clocks, and web sites and directories of resources, the teenagers make checklists (and double-checklists). The mindset of the microscoper is neat and orderly, leaving little to chance.

Many experienced human service workers have adopted the anxious stance of the microscoper after several experiences in the "school of hard knocks." One of them wrote in his records:

> I still carry with me the vivid memory of facing sixty disappointed, angry adults and children on a hot street corner. Although I had booked the buses for their annual family picnic at Riverside Amusement Park, I had neglected to double-check the bus company's arrangements. The buses never showed! Many of these folks had planned their vacations around this yearly

The proposal should include:[*]

1. Title page—with name of program, who it is being presented to and by whom.

2. Abstract—a brief overview of the agency, problem (GAP) program activities, funding request, and planners. No more than one scant page, the abstract should be very tight and clear. It may be all that is ever looked at if many proposals are in a pile in a funder's in-box.

3. Table of contents—each part of the proposal should be numbered for each reference when the program is being discussed.

4. Problem statement—What (GAP) is this program trying to fill? How did the problem get identified, how long has it been going on, what are its consequences? This part would include backup data, surveys, professional articles, anecdotal evidence.

5. Background to the problem—brief information about the agency or persons making the proposal, who does it serve, how, when did it begin, staff, funding, facility, and geographic area.

6. Goals of the program—this includes hopeful outcomes spelled out very operationally and in very specific terms.

7. Proposed activities—Exactly what are you planning to do, when, and how? What staff will be needed, what facility, what equipment? This should also include a work plan or time line in this section or a separate one.

8. Budget—How much money will be needed for exactly what, and how much will need to be raised for the new program, and what in-kind donations are expected?

9. Evaluation—What methods will you use to assess how successfully your program activities have met your goals or hoped-for outcomes, over what period of time?

10. Additional supporting documents—this section would include bibliography if applicable, charts, and letters of support or concern.[**]

* Many funding agencies will have their own special format to follow.

**For a sample program proposal, see Schram (1997, pp. 220–226).

FIGURE 11.8 Writing a program proposal

outing. Few have the cars or money to take their own trips to the country. They counted on my planning ability, and I hadn't come through for them. Now I've learned to double- (or even triple-) check every time I lease a bus.

Every human service worker can recount a story of a time a mistake destroyed a program. Perhaps the DVD for the cartoon show for little kids did not work, or the CD player for a dance was broken, or the staff member in charge of food bought only half the number of hotdogs needed for the barbecue.

Mistakes creep into our work in subtle and not-so-subtle ways. Chances are you will find in your own mail at least one advertisement for a conference, a meeting, or an open house that has the wrong date on it or fails to note that baby-sitting is provided or that there are special rates for students and senior citizens. Perhaps you have encountered the frustration of receiving an invitation mailed so late that the event has already passed.

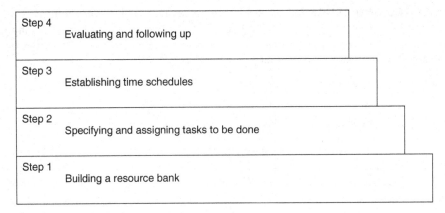

FIGURE 11.9   The process of microscoping a problem

With charts, graphs, checklists, and yellow stick-on papers on the refrigerator door, the microscoper tries to minimize small errors that can destroy months of hard work. Although there are no guarantees against errors, if we share the work of planning with others, we tap a large reservoir of energy and skills. This offers some protection.

The following anonymous poem hangs on the wall of Raquel's office as a reminder of Murphy's law: IF ANYTHING CAN GO WRONG, IT WILL.

I have a spelling checker

It came with my PC.

It plainly marks four my revue

Miss stakes I cannot sea

I've run this poem threw it,

I'm sure your please to no.

It's letter perfect in its weigh,

My checker toll me sew.

Now let's look at each of the steps in microscoping that can turn proposed programs into highly successful ones.

STEP 1: BUILDING A RESOURCE BANK   Every program needs a **resource bank**. Planners need to figure out what resources are needed and where they can get those items.

After exploring all their contacts, the members of the teen group did a resource analysis so that they could see what they were still missing. All the ideas about where to find resources had to be carefully checked out—some materialized and some fell through. The teens were surprised to find that most of the people they asked to help them said "yes." Generally, people are very willing to lend a hand if asked to donate a specific resource or service that suits their capacity and time schedule. They are more likely to continue helping if their contribution is acknowledged. We can never say "thank you" too often!

STEP 2: SPECIFYING AND ASSIGNING TASKS Many of us feel totally overwhelmed at the beginning of any new program—perhaps we are anticipating putting on a carnival, forming a tenant committee, or returning to school after twenty years of homemaking. New staff members or volunteers inevitably experience that initial panicky question:

> Can I speak in front of a room full of faculty members?
>
> Can I take fifty screaming kids to the circus?
>
> Can I walk safely through that neighborhood at night after the dance ends?

Most workers quickly learn, however, that the most important part of creating a program is breaking down the big tasks into a series of smaller tasks. Thus they will not be overwhelmed or immobilized by the enormity of what they have been assigned. When a goal is broken down into many small tasks, rank-ordered by immediacy, and then delegated to different people, the end seems attainable. Logically, each task depends on the successful completion of the one that came before. In Figure 11.10 you can see the task list that was constructed by the Hi-Teens. It demonstrated to their parents that they had done their homework and understood how much work the trip would involve.

After the list was made, each of the tasks had to be assigned to a member of the group or the leaders. Although all this list making can seem needlessly bureaucratic, especially for a group of teens, it is an absolute rule of planning that if definite assignments are not made and written down, the morale of the group can deteriorate as a result of bickering or wasted effort:

> "But I thought you were responsible for the paper goods!"
>
> "Well, whose job was it to bring the matches?"
>
> "They say they never received our reservation form for the campsite!"

TASKS THAT NEED TO BE DONE
Hi-Teens' Camping Trip

1. Get a campsite
2. Round up camping equipment
3. Get signed permission slips
4. Organize transportation
5. Plan food
6. Shop for food
7. Practice camping skills
8. Get first-aid supplies
9. Practice first-aid skills
10. Make a budget
11. Raise money
12. Plan schedule and activities for weekend
13. Decide on rules of trip

FIGURE 11.10 A sample task analysis

Every task must be thought about and followed up. As we figure out and execute the tasks of each job, nothing can be left to chance. At the risk of being a nag, we must, hopefully with charm and humor, keep after everyone and everything.

STEP 3: ESTABLISHING A SCHEDULE: FLOW CHART   Once tasks are broken into component parts and delegated, they must be put into a time framework called a **time flow chart**. Some tasks need to be done before others; some need more time than others. For example, if the teenagers use up most of their meetings planning their menu or arguing about curfew before they get around to booking the campsite, there may be no place available for the trip. First things come first! Drawing a picture of a logical sequence of events helps to visualize what lies ahead. It also gives some benchmarks along the way. If someone asks "How's it coming along?" they can say "Fine, everything seems to be moving on schedule," or "We seem to be getting bogged down by X, Y, or Z."

Nothing dooms a planning process as much as unrealistic time expectations. As we look over the chart, we notice possible stumbling blocks. We readjust our timeline to avoid those problems. If the public schools' spring vacation falls in April and all the fund-raising is planned for then, we may be set up for defeat. If we are counting on outdoor sales and fairs to raise money, we have to remember they do best in warm weather. Few of us, clients or workers, are super people. We cannot manage to complete a task in too small a time period. Anxiety and immobility can be the prices we pay for pushing too hard. In Figure 11.11 you can see the time flow chart the group constructed.

	TIME FLOW CHART Hi-Teens' Camping Trip						
TIMES							
	December	January	February	March	April	May 9	May 12–30
TASKS	Hold parents' meeting	Look for campsite Give out permission slips Make budget	Reserve campsite Slips due back Plan fund-raising	Hold fund-raising events Practice camping skills Practice first aid	Reconfirm campsite Funds all collected Plan menu Plan activities and daily schedule Decide on rules Gather equipment	Shop Leave at noon	Return equipment Send out thank-you notes Write up report on trip

FIGURE 11.11   A sample time flow chart

Of course, there are very few action plans that actually proceed as written, but a flow chart helps people organize their efforts in the best possible way. In fact, it is a general rule of thumb that everything is likely to take twice as long as you think it should.

STEP 4: EVALUATING THE PLAN AND FOLLOWING UP   Evaluation is always the final act that closes the information loop on the old plan and sets the stage for a new one. In order for the teenagers and the youth workers to learn and grow, they need a feedback system. Are they on schedule? Are things progressing well?

Record keeping and report writing are especially critical when a group has just finished a large-scale planning effort such as an annual neighborhood fair or conference. Lists of prices, the names of the bands and supply houses, and copies of receipts and permits are invaluable documents. That information, plus comments on the quality of the goods and services that were used, will help next year's staff hit the ground running. Each worker should be able to learn from his predecessor. Financial management of a program can be a vital part of its success or failure.

PROCESS AND PRODUCT EVALUATIONS.   In addition to descriptions of the events, we must also evaluate two dimensions of the activity we have planned, both the process—how we planned it—and the product—how it turned out. Sometimes the two can be different.

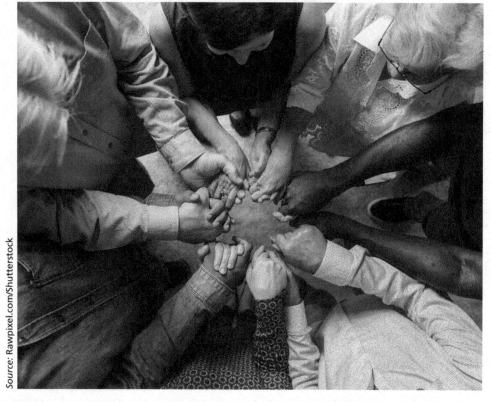

Source: Rawpixel.com/Shutterstock

The members of a group who are organizing a program need to build their teamwork so that they can support each other as they work through the details of a prospective event.

The Hi-Teens had a wonderful time on their trip. The experience helped build group cohesion, the members learned new skills, and they gained a greater appreciation for the outdoors. They rate the outcome very highly. But in the planning process, many of the young people did not keep their commitments. Carlos, the group leader, is annoyed at them. He ended up getting most of the equipment for them, checking up on the reservation, and filling in for absent members at their fund-raising car wash. The group needs to improve its process. The members must meet together in a debriefing session and discuss what went wrong with the way they delegated work and double-checked their assigned tasks. Of course, they should also be reminded to take credit for all the things they did do well.

To systematically review the process they used, members will ask each other the following:

- How accurate was their original list of tasks?
- Did they think of everything that was needed?
- Did they set realistic time limits?
- What would they repeat and what would they do differently next time?

The techniques used to evaluate depend on the nature of the program: how complicated it was, how many people were involved, and what the evaluation will be used for. For a camping trip with a group of teens, a good discussion and brief report including comments of supervisors and parents are plenty. But if we are evaluating a large conference or the first few months of operation of a community residence for teenagers, staff must conduct in-depth interviews with clients and collect statistics, questionnaires, and the opinions of outsiders. Almost any technique used with an open mind and a genuine desire to learn from experience will offer some insights.

We must be especially careful not to turn our attention away from an event before all the closure work is completed. Thank-you notes have to be written, bills have to be paid, and lost or damaged equipment must be replaced or fixed. Groups also need to spend some time saying good-bye, sharing their photos, or writing an article for a newsletter. There are always next steps to be taken.

Summary

1. The planning process used in organizing events in our personal lives is similar to, but less formal than, the one used by human service workers.
2. The basic tools of the planning process include a pen and pencil, computer, the Internet, calendar/memo book, clock, resource directories, and many thoughtful focused questions. When planning within a group, large paper sheets, a chalkboard, erasable board, or smartboard can facilitate widespread understanding and participation.
3. Accurate minutes of meetings can keep members informed about decisions and commitments that have been made.
4. Questions form an information loop that leads to action, reflection, and new action.
5. The techniques of the planner include troubleshooting (defining the problem), magnifying (seeing it with its background context and complexity), and microscoping (attending to all the details of the plan).
6. To plan successfully, we separate events into their component parts, identify the small tasks in each, set up time frames, and assign responsibilities and coordinators.
7. Evaluation of a program focuses on the product (the outcome of the intervention) as well as the process (how it was conducted from inception on).
8. Planning is both a people skill and a technical skill. Functioning within a clear structure that has a logical system brings out the best in everyone, enabling the most limited or troubled people to make whatever contribution is possible and preparing them for an event.

Discussion Questions

1. There is an old proverb that says "He has half the deed done, when he has made a beginning." What do you think this proverb is trying to convey? Do you agree with it, or do you think that it is an exaggeration? What does it have to do with planning an event or program in a social agency?

2. How much emphasis is placed by your college on volunteer service in your community? How fair is it to require volunteer service as a requirement of graduation, especially for non–Human Service majors? What do you think chemistry or math majors might contribute to a social agency in the community? What do you think they might gain that would help them be better workers in their particular fields of interest?

3. What do you see as a major gap in the services provided for students at your college? What kind of program(s) do you think might fill that gap? What evidence would you have to gather to convince the person in charge of that area or division that it is a gap that must be filled with a new program or strategy? For example, do you see any evidence of cyberbullying on your campus? If so, are there any services on campus to address this?

4. What do you think is meant by the saying "Life is lived forward but understood backward"? What do you think that saying has to do with the process of program evaluation?

Web Resources for Further Study

Strategic Planning for Nonprofits | National Council of Nonprofits

https://www.councilofnonprofits.org/tools-resources/strategic-planning-nonprofits

Find Funding | Foundation Center

http://foundationcenter.org/find-funding

GoFundMe

https://www.gofundme.com/

MyLab Helping Professions for Introduction to Human Services

In the Topic 10 Assignments: Administration, try Application Exercise 10.2: Operational Management.

Indirect Strategies: Organizing for Change

12

Source: Rawpixel.com/Shutterstock

GETTING TO THE SOURCE OF THE PROBLEM

We can think of no better way to start this chapter on organizing for change than by retelling a parable attributed to the late Saul Alinsky, who was one of this country's most imaginative and dedicated community change agents (Alinsky, 1969, 1971).

A Parable

A woman is taking a stroll along a riverbank. Suddenly she hears a cry for help and jumps into the water to rescue a drowning man. After saving the man, she is forced to jump back into the river to save another and then still another. After she has dragged four men from the river, she looks around in disgust and starts to leave. An onlooker says, "Hey, I see another guy in the water, where are you going?" She replies, "I can't hang around here all day long rescuing drowning victims. I'm going upstream to stop the son of a bitch who's pushing them all in."

Stopping Problems at Their Source

The point Alinsky is making is that it is never enough to just rescue victims from their troubles, important as that is. We have to try to change the situations that are creating their problems. Then, hopefully, we can cut off the problem at its source so that new victims are not constantly being produced.

For those of you who are mechanically inclined, visualize a machine that makes ping-pong balls. Every once in a while, it goofs and produces one that is not round enough. A worker tosses the defective balls into a bin. Later on, another worker takes the odd-shaped balls out of the reject pile and tries to round them off. But it would save time and money in the long run if they fixed the machine so that it did not make so many mistakes.

To translate this analogy into human service work, take the case of Marty, a young adult of Hispanic origin. He was raised on a run-down farm in a rural community. He attended a substandard elementary school that did not stimulate him. When his mother needed surgery and his family lost their farm because they could not pay the mortgage, Marty was forced to drop out of high school and seek employment. Marty had always tinkered with old cars and was a natural mechanic. But the garage owner held negative stereotypes about people from his community, and as a result, when a job at the garage became available, Marty was rejected.

Marty became depressed about his bleak future and found momentary relief in drugs. Once he became so frustrated that he lashed out, vandalizing the garage. He got caught and was then enmeshed in the criminal justice system. He spent two months in jail, where he was brutalized by both his cellmate and a guard. By the time the probation worker encountered Marty, he needed a whole series of direct-care and counseling strategies to overcome his addiction and rehabilitate his shattered self-esteem. Now he also had a jail record holding him back. Often a person's current problems have resulted in large part from problems in his environment and community. Thus, one-on-one direct services alone, while necessary, will not solve his personal problems or prevent others from developing similar problems.

This young man's problems might have been prevented if there had been:

- Decent housing in an integrated area
- Adequate education, both academic and vocational
- Affordable health insurance
- Mortgage assistance to save family farms
- Drug and alcohol education programs
- Job-training and -placement programs
- Protection from discriminatory employment practices
- A criminal justice system with the resources to protect and rehabilitate offenders.

The lack of these basic services helped create and maintain Marty's situation. Like a snowball rolling down a hill, his problems kept getting bigger. In their book *Social Welfare: A History of the American Response to Need*, Stern and Axinn (2018) conclude that people living in poverty too often come off as second-best—scapegoats for circumstances beyond their control.

Human service workers cannot change all the dysfunctional systems that impinge on the "Martys" of our country. Nor is it likely that they can change one system in a massive way. But all of us can, in our daily work, create small yet significant improvements in the social systems that surround our clients.

What Can One Human Service Worker Do?

When working with Marty, we might find that helping him file a complaint against a discriminatory prospective employer has two major outcomes. First, it gives him the feeling that he can take some control over his destiny. Second, if he succeeds in winning the case, not only will he get a badly needed job, but others who follow him may also find it possible to work there. If this young man joins a group of citizens who succeed in bringing bilingual and multicultural programs to the local elementary school, that might improve the life chances of his neighbor's children also.

Filing a grievance when you believe a law or regulation is not working properly, and drafting a proposal and lobbying for funds to start a program to fill an unmet social need, are examples of strategies for organizing and changing systems. They support our efforts to deliver direct services to people.

These more indirect strategies rely on the same activities and skills as do direct-service strategies. They start with carefully collecting data, contracting, and building a trusting relationship. Workers' acts need to flow out of well-designed and well-monitored action plans and are refined through reflection and evaluation. Although there are many similarities between direct-care and systems-change interventions, there are, of course, some significant differences in emphasis.

Let's listen in on this interview with Ed Wong, a human service worker who spends most of his time working on the indirect program strategies that try to improve the environment in which we all will live now and will live in the future.

A Human Service Worker at Work: Ed Wong: Staff Worker for Citizen Action for the Environment (CAFTE)

Citizen Action for the Environment (CAFTE) is a citywide, citizen-based environmental advocacy organization. Research has shown us that many of the health problems that affect people are the result of toxins in the air they breathe and the water they drink and shower in. My agency's goal is to improve the environment in which citizens live and work. For example, you can work to get health care and special educational supports for a child whose brain has been damaged by breathing in the dust or even eating the paint chips in his apartment. That is important work, but someone else has to work to eliminate the lead that is used in paint and to get the landlords to de-lead the apartments they lease to families with young children.

These are the main tasks in my job description:

- Build coalitions with local, state, and national environmental, labor, farming, and consumer organizations; identify and mobilize concerned citizens; and reach out to new constituencies to build our base of support in this town and statewide.
- Generate media attention and build public awareness. Organize at least one major news conference per month; meet with reporters throughout the town and the region; and conduct TV and radio interviews, update our blog, and conduct workshops with various groups, including schools, chambers of commerce, other merchant groups, religious institutions, and civic organizations.
- Lobby decision makers and expand our political base by building relationships with elected officials and candidates, and demonstrate broad public support for

(continued)

our positions through letter-writing drives, email activism, appearing at campaign events, and conducting meetings with decision makers.

- Build the organization by increasing membership and recruiting and orienting volunteers and other small grassroots groups that share our mission to identify and then work to lessen environmental problems in our community.

This looks like an overwhelming job description, but as with every other job in the human service field, you take it one step at a time, and of course I don't work alone. Although I am the only paid staff member of CAFTE, we have an active board and an advisory committee. Both of these groups include professors from the local colleges, engineers and architects who specialize in environment issues, sympathetic politicians, and merchants and other leaders of groups in town who really care about what is happening not only to the town of Riverside but also to the whole world.

You probably wonder how a recent college graduate who majored in human services ended up in this kind of job. Well, I have to admit I am also amazed at times by my choice. When I was a student intern and in fact during most of my teenage years, I was involved in issues of homelessness. I volunteered at a food pantry and did overnight shifts at a shelter for men and women who had no place to sleep. Some of my friends were involved in environmental issues, and frankly I thought those activities were a way to avoid dealing with the more important problems of poverty, racism, mental illness, disability, and so forth.

I have since learned that mine was a pretty typical response to the word **green**. For many years the term *green* was defined—probably by folks like me who disparaged it—as "ultraliberal," "elitist," "tree-hugging," and alarmist. Documentary films like *An Inconvenient Truth* (Gore & West, 2006) as well as popular books by Bill McKibben (2007, 2008, 2019) have pushed the terms *green, global warming*, and *climate change* onto Main Street. The reality is that the Earth's weather is changing with some alarming consequences, and the supply of natural resources, such as fossil fuels, is not endless. In some parts of the world, there isn't enough water to sustain agriculture, thereby increasing famine, and in other places, the waters are rising and threatening to flood islands. The implications of these changes are not just on a few people but also on the whole world. It might be that civil unrest will rise if these consequences continue.

My coming to understand the gravity of the situation was a result of joining the Sierra Club and the Appalachian Mountain Club because I love to hike with others. Both organizations publish magazines for members. I began to realize that although all human service issues are vital, our need to protect our forests and rivers is not "elite." It is a matter of keeping the air pure enough so we can continue to breathe and so our kids will have a livable planet.

Although my job description sounds monumental and I do work hard, it is not overwhelming. I take my job one step at a time and day by day. The members of my Board set the priorities. This keeps me from being spread too thin and ultimately not accomplishing anything. Since I cooperate with a host of other groups, their programs often determine where I will invest my energy for a period of time.

These are some of the things I have worked on in the past several months:

- Helped publicize and recruit volunteers for a townwide park cleanup day.
- Wrote an article and held three forums on ways to cut down on energy consumption both in stores and in private homes.
- Spearheaded a campaign to get the local big-box retailer to cut back on packaging on some of its products and to promote the sale of low-energy light bulbs and eliminate plastic shopping bags.

- Wrote a proposal that gained funding for the town to plant 400 trees in parts of town that are noticeably not very green. (Naturally, these were in the more economically disadvantaged areas.) This isn't just for beauty; it helps the air we breathe and creates shade in summer months.
- Attended a benefit screening of *An Inconvenient Truth* to raise money for Earth Day activities in six different locations in town.
- Participated in a demonstration by the local biking advocacy group to try to convince the town to set aside a bike lane each time they have to do construction on the streets.
- Organized a panel for the town homeowners' association on ways to insulate homes and on the use of programmable thermostats.
- Attended board meetings of the townwide recycling committee to represent our group and lend support to their efforts to increase recycling of cans, plastic, and paper.
- Gave a talk at the high school on our need to cut carbon emissions, highlighting the plans already proposed by a few cities in the United States. This was an effort to let the future generation know that the problems are not insurmountable and to encourage the students to start a green club in their school—and maybe choose Environmental Studies if they go on to college.

I use all the strategies I studied in the Human Services courses in college. Skills like active listening are essential when I am in a meeting with a company executive. I also use preparatory empathy when I am in a situation where I know I will be up against resistance. I try to go in prepared with answers to questions I think they will ask. Proposal-writing skills and research are vital in this job.

I am not sure what I am going to be doing in the future, but for now, I am very excited about the job I chose. I feel that I am working in a small way on a very monumental problem. And I still have the time and incentive to hike in the woods on the weekends.

CHECKING ON THE MENTAL HEALTH QUOTIENT (MHQ) OF A SYSTEM OR ORGANIZATION

A counselor trying to help a child who is experiencing difficulty in school begins by seeking information about the child's health, family situation, and scores on achievement and IQ (intelligence quotient) tests. Many stop at that point, only seeking out the causal factors within the child and the family. But we believe that the hunt for relevant insights cannot stop there. The competent worker must go on to look at the system in which the child is functioning. The worker must gather data about the MHQ (mental health quotient) of that student's classroom and school. We must always look at both the internal and the external sources of stress. Ultimately we will need to intervene in both sets of forces.

You can grasp this concept of the "system as problem producer" if you think back to a time when you watched people rudely shoving each other in order to grab a cab at the airport—tempers flared and anxiety levels rose as each person struggled to outmaneuver the others. Clearly, the environment—with its chaotic method of getting a cab—exerts a negative impact on otherwise reasonably polite people. If a sensible airport manager inaugurated a system in which numbers were assigned to the people who were waiting in some equitable way, everyone could relax. It might take time to get a cab, but each person would be sure that her turn was coming. A passenger could risk leaving the line for a moment to carry the luggage of an older adult or to help a harried parent with a toddler in a stroller and a heavy suitcase.

We must develop our personal method of measuring the MHQ of a variety of organizations. For example, before we begin to plan counseling interventions for the little girl who runs around her classroom fighting with her classmates, we should check the organizational climate of her classroom and school. Some places are so disorganized or mindlessly rigid that they subtly encourage disruptive behavior in a child who has some tendency in that direction. In a more sensibly organized environment, she might behave much better.

After we observe a client in a classroom or perhaps in a hospital ward, we might conclude that certain characteristics of the environment seem to be producing problems rather than solving them. Thus the system, rather than the client, should be the major focus of our change efforts. Yet despite recognition of this fact, research indicates that workers often continue to try to change the client by counseling, rather than change the environment by using organizing interventions (Brager, 2002; Brager, Specht, & Torczyner, 1987).

Ryan, in his classic book *Blaming the Victim* (1976), asserts that focusing change efforts on the client rather than on the system that is malfunctioning leads us to design social programs that are at best irrelevant and at worst deceptively cruel. Why are so many human service workers unable to confront honestly the primary causes of a client's problem? We think one reason is that workers tend to accept society's negative attitudes toward social activism, even though social activism is required if systems are ever to change for the better.

ATTITUDES TOWARD SYSTEMS-CHANGE INTERVENTIONS

As we grew up, many of us might have heard adults in our families declare:

> You can't fight city hall!
>
> It's not what you know but who you know!
>
> Good guys finish last!
>
> Well-brought-up people (especially women) don't make waves or rock the boat!

These homespun bromides encourage us to believe that working for change in a rational way is virtually impossible. Stereotypes of **change agents** encourage us to shy away from that role. One prominent stereotype depicts change agents as cartoon-character 1960s activists and bomb-throwing anarchists—bearded, grubby, and deranged. Or they are depicted as naive Don Quixotes, futilely tilting at windmills. On the other side lie the stereotypes that depict change agents as saintly crusaders—Joan of Arc or Mother Teresa, for example. Perhaps you have assumed that change agents must be charismatic leaders like the Rev. Martin Luther King, Jr., or President John F. Kennedy. That, too, is a stereotype.

When people see human service workers walking a picket line or speaking out at a school board meeting, they are often shocked by such aggressiveness. Activists are often accused by their own colleagues of behaving unprofessionally.

The late social critic George Bernard Shaw gave us a fitting answer to that accusation. He declared that reasonable people adapted themselves to the world as it was. Only the unreasonable ones persisted in trying to get the world to change. Thus, all progress depends on unreasonable people! We agree with Shaw and hope that there will be times when you decide you must take a strong stand on behalf of a client, despite an accusation that you are being "unreasonable."

To paint an accurate picture of change agents, we must discard all our preconceptions of who they are and what they do. We need to explore our ambivalent attitudes toward social change. Then we will need to replace any unrealistic attitudes with the conviction that each of us should use our skills to bring about change in a dysfunctional system, just as we do in a one-on-one direct intervention.

Working to change an unhealthy system raises unique value dilemmas for the human service worker, especially for one who is accustomed to delivering direct services to clients.

DILEMMAS OF THE CHANGE AGENT

Very Often, the Worker Must Choose Sides

If we believe that the needs of one group are being neglected and the needs of another are given an unfair advantage, or that one of our clients is being punished by an unjust rule or an unresponsive bureaucrat, we are making a judgment of right and wrong. When, for example, Ed Wong helps a group of tenants who have been living for months with no heat or hot water organize a rent strike, he is taking sides in the struggle between landlords and tenants. Although Ed realizes that the landlord will have a temporary cash-flow problem when rent money is withheld, if he is convinced that the tenants are being treated unfairly, he cannot expend much of his energy worrying about the landlord's problems. But he has been trained to be empathetic and caring to everyone!

Of course, such adversarial situations can also occur when a worker is working one-on-one with a person, but in an organizing or advocacy role they occur with alarming regularity. The pull between competing needs and outlooks is painful. It is often impossible to find a compromise. In Ed's professional role, he often feels more like a lawyer than a human service worker. Having chosen to represent the interests of the town residents who need a clean environment, he advocates for them with tenacity. He becomes adversarial when dealing with a factory owner who will not acknowledge that he has dumped industrial waste into a local stream and who refuses to clean it up.

Frequently, Workers Must Choose Among Competing Values

In addition to choosing sides between adversaries in a dispute, Ed is often forced to make almost impossible choices between competing values. This is frequently the case for social change agents. For example, in writing about their experiences as welfare rights organizers in the rural South in the 1960s, several idealistic young human service workers described how they found the maintenance needs of their organization conflicting with the service needs of individual clients (Kurzman, 1971). In order to recruit new members to the National Welfare Rights Organization, they would offer to accompany clients into their eligibility interviews, coaching them right in front of the welfare investigators. They were especially interested in recruiting articulate, energetic clients—most often young, single parents—who would be the most likely to give their time and energy to expanding the welfare rights group. Yet it was frequently the older, infirm clients who begged them for help with their welfare and disability applications or appeals. Though desperately needy, they were also bound by the old traditions and fears engendered by experiencing a lifetime of segregation. They were sometimes the least likely to sign a petition, attend a rally, or become leaders in the welfare reform movement. Striking a comfortable balance between giving services to the most needy and building up the social change group gave many workers sleepless nights.

Workers Must Overcome Resistance to Change with No Guarantees of Success

Most interventions encounter resistance. But social change efforts exert a special kind of drain on our time and energy. They follow unpredictable courses down twisting, perilous roads that lead to many dead ends. There are dubious rewards at the end of the path, and both client and worker can burn out from their seemingly futile investment of time and energy.

Many times, the clients back off from pursuing complaints, even when it looks as if they might win, because they fear that their landlords or employers will retaliate. The threat of eviction or of the landlord's shutting off their heat in the winter and other forms of harassment often abruptly terminate protests. Ed cannot in good conscience promise people that he can protect them. When a person files a discrimination complaint against an employer or agency, for example, the citizen litigant can fear being blackballed by other employers who now view her as a troublemaker. Of course, direct-service interventions also carry risks, but they are rarely as consistently perilous as those in advocacy situations.

Given Ed's slim chances of winning most of the protests his agency is involved with, one wonders why he continues with so much goodwill. But he feels that though the risks of failure may be much greater in his kind of job, so too are the rewards for success. When CAFTE wins one reform in the way industrial wastes are disposed of, for example, the eventual improvement in the quality of the lives of many people is incalculable.

Source: Diego G Diaz/Shutterstock

Many marches and meetings have been organized to build public and legislative support for the continuation of the Deferred Action for Childhoood Arrivals program, commonly known as DACA. The DACA program allowed adults brought to this country as children by their undocumented immigrant parents to receive deferred action from deportation and become eligible for a work permit in the United States.

Historically this has proved to be true. With the stroke of a pen, President Franklin Delano Roosevelt signed the Social Security Act in 1935, and since then, millions of older people have been able to look forward to some measure of financial security in their retirement years. An army of human service staff members working with each of those millions of older people, one person at a time, could not possibly have achieved such positive changes in their emotional lives.

Workers Lack Role Models of Change Agents

Systems-change skills can be difficult to learn because we lack role models in our personal and professional lives. There is also a woeful lack of written material about successful social change efforts. Not surprisingly, workers who thrive on the unstructured, rough-and-tumble nature of social change often resist sitting down and putting their thoughts on paper. Many excellent change efforts go undocumented and unrewarded. However, there are some written accounts, and we urge students to seek out those books that give firsthand descriptions of systems-change efforts (Bobo, Kendall, & Max, 2010; Boyte, 1980; Greenberg, P. 1969, reprinted 1990; Kahn, 1995; Kurzman, 1971; Miller, M., 2009; Russell, D. M., 1991; Shaw, 2001).

CHANGES IN ORGANIZATIONS CAN BE GENERATED FROM THE TOP DOWN AND FROM THE BOTTOM UP

Change flows in two directions. Like a giant waterfall, it flows from the top down, dragging the stones and sand along in its wake. Just as often, like a volcano, it simmers beneath the surface and then bubbles up from the bottom, engulfing everything in its path.

When change starts from the top of a system, it usually comes in the form of administrative or legislative fiat. A board of directors, a supervisor, or an administrator announces a new policy, or reduces or expands a budget item. It occurs when new legislation is passed. It can happen when the courts rule on a landmark case. Change can be propelled by the writing of a memo banning discrimination against one or another class of tenants, or the passage or repeal of a housing or zoning ordinance. Sometimes seemingly benign words inserted in or deleted from an official policy dramatically change the course of life for many human beings.

Clients, workers, and students usually lack the formal authority to change destructive policies. But they can force change from the bottom up through the weight of their numbers and the power that weight can mobilize. Sometimes bottom-up change comes through the ballot box. Often it comes from citizen initiative or agitation. When squatters break into a building that is boarded up and demand that city officials rehabilitate it to provide affordable housing, they are attempting to generate change.

Case histories of change efforts reveal that most of the time, struggles to create change and resistance against change are going on simultaneously, at both the top and bottom of the system. In the history of public welfare, for example, positive changes in benefits emanating from the top of the bureaucracy have often been initiated only after it looked as if the bubbling up from the bottom, from the grass roots, would spill over into uncontrolled disruptions. A fascinating analysis that links protest to reform was written by Piven and Cloward (2013).

Change efforts must be directed at all points of a system—the top, the bottom, and in between. But rarely can any one group or person spread thin enough to cover all the bases. Even if that were possible, however, different styles of organizing are needed to confront different parts of a system, for different issues, and to keep up with the changing public mood and world events.

Change agents come in two basic models: the infighter and the outside agitator. Infighters are legitimate members of the established authority who work for or administer a particular system.

They might be directors of hospitals, supervisors of social service agencies, judges, or politicians. Outside agitators are neither employed by nor beholden to any of the established systems.

Ed is an example of an outside agitator. He stands outside the bureaucracy of the public sector and private corporations. He dresses, talks, and acts differently than he would if he were working for the Department of Energy, the Environmental Protection Agency, or the Exxon Mobil Corporation. But sometimes Ed and a worker at a state agency or an employee of a corporation may share a similar change goal.

It is important to realize that if they work alone, neither enlightened leaders at the top of a system nor masses of angry people at the bottom of it are likely to create major, permanent changes.

Guarding Change

Change must be guarded after it has been won. Once instituted, it must be constantly monitored. If left unattended, a new law or policy can turn out to be totally ineffective. It can be "business as usual" unless an organized constituency monitors the process of implementation. The Supreme Court desegregation decision of 1954 is a good example of this. Although the decision made in *Brown v. Board of Education* outlawed racial segregation in every public school in the land, it has taken hundreds of individual lawsuits and the constant watchfulness of citizens' groups to achieve even the modest amount of school desegregation we now have, over decades later.* If a school is segregated and no one complains about it, it is likely just to stay that way.

Source: John S. Quinn/Shutterstock

Change agents can work either from the top down or the bottom up. Protest rallies are an effective means to mobilize for change at the grass roots level.

---

*A Look at the State of School Integration 64 years After Brown vs Board of Education." NPR March 28, 2018

Creating the Structure and the Consciousness for Change

Changes such as the Supreme Court school desegregation decision or the Americans with Disabilities Act must have two thrusts. First, change agents must create new structures composed of rules and regulations that translate the vision of change into the new reality. But that is never enough. For change to take root in a system, it must also become an integral part of the consciousness of the public.

For example, when parents are committed to overturning racial segregation in the local school system, they need to marshal the evidence that it is segregated and bring it to court. They must persuade a judge to order the school board to draw up an integration plan. If the parents, school administrators, or some other organization does not like the plan or the way it is being implemented, it returns to court to negotiate adjustments. If the school board continues its opposition, the schools might be taken over by the courts, as they once were in Boston.

However, no matter how good a plan is on paper, on the day a desegregated school opens, the attitudes of the school and town officials, parents, and teachers determine whether the elaborate plans have any chance of succeeding. Ultimately, a new law is only as effective as the feelings that swirl around it.

If women, people with mental illness, immigrants, or people with disabilities do not use the protection of the laws that guarantee their rights, those laws are worth nothing. On the reverse side, if a law is routinely circumvented by large numbers of people, it cannot be enforced. This was the case with the prohibition of alcohol in the 1920s. The usually law-abiding general public consistently violated this law. Alcohol was legally banned, which was a major structural change to the U.S. Constitution, but the desire of the population to use liquor as a means of pleasure or escape never changed.

Learning a lesson from the failure of prohibition, antismoking advocates proceed on both fronts—structure and consciousness. They have changed the structure of smoking by prohibiting cigarettes from being advertised on television and passing smoking bans in government buildings and in many public spaces, such as movie theaters, workplaces, restaurants, airplanes, and colleges. They have succeeded in placing warning labels on cigarette packages. The antismoking change efforts have also moved into courtrooms. In high-profile lawsuits, the attorneys general of several states have sued the major tobacco companies to recover the money the state health care systems have expended caring for citizens who have sickened or died from smoking-related illnesses. In many cases, they have garnered large cash settlements for both individuals and states. But, after the legal victories, alert citizen groups have had to make sure that the cash is used for public health purposes, not to fill in budget gaps in unrelated areas.

Organizers of the women's liberation movement understood that laws redressing gender inequality were a necessary first step but would not be enough to bring about major changes. Many women had to be convinced that they had a legitimate right to demand equal pay for their labor. They also needed to build up courage and group solidarity in order to press for remedies when equality was withheld from them. The current movement to address sexual aggression against women has gained in strength in recent years via the #MeToo movement. Now, on college campuses, both administrators and student activists work to change the definitions of appropriate sexual conduct. Policies defining rape and sexual and gender harassment, with stiff penalties for transgressions, have been drawn up. And seminars and workshops are conducted to sensitize students and staff to new definitions of their rights and to inform them about the way to protest if they think their rights are being abridged.

METHODS OF CREATING CHANGE IN A SYSTEM: EDUCATING, PERSUADING, PRESSURING

Educating to Create Change

When a change effort begins, Ed first points out the problems (the gaps), systematically documents them, and suggests solutions. Ed spends a large amount of his time compiling statistics about the increasing incidence of certain diseases in areas with a great deal of industrial pollution. He reads journals and checks out web sites from all over the country and goes to conferences to find out what other groups are doing to solve the problems of carbon emissions and overdependence on fossil fuels. He digests the material and helps produce a monthly newsletter that is sent to members, politicians, and businesspeople.

Ed has learned the importance of having facts ready when he visits a legislator to **lobby** for change. Often he is competing with real estate developers who have assembled their own set of data printed in a fancy booklet. Although he complained about having to study statistics and research methods in college, he has come to appreciate their power and is grateful that he can read and interpret budgets, architectural plans, census data, and other weighty documents. The volunteer lawyers who work with CAFTE do much of the actual negotiating, but he needs to understand enough to explain the CAFTE position and answer questions about it.

Sometimes, as a result of an educational campaign, people realize how destructive a certain rule, policy, or action is and agree to change it. If that happens, then the change effort is successful and it terminates. But many times, exposing an unhealthy situation and suggesting ways of dealing with it are not enough.

So the change agents turn to the second, more powerful change method.

Persuading to Create Change

Persuasion strategies use both the carrot and the stick. The "carrot" rewards constructive changes, while the "stick" threatens sanctions for continued negative practices. For example, if developers are willing to build affordable housing in low-income communities, they might be given grants-in-aid, tax abatements, and special technical assistance. Factory owners who agree to retrofit old, polluting equipment or restaurant owners who agree to eliminate trans fats from their food might be given technical assistance and even some funds to help in the switch.

If, despite all the incentives, change does not happen, then the "stick" might be threatened or used. This second level usually involves withholding money, denying permits, or causing public humiliation. For example, some towns list in the local newspaper the names of landlords and restaurant owners who have been cited for health and safety violations.

CAFTE has used persuasion by organizing public rallies supporting or opposing a proposed housing plan or industrial complex, has collected signatures on petitions, and has organized letter-writing campaigns.

Pressuring to Create Change

When education and persuasion strategies fail to bring about change, the CAFTE Board resorts to using pressure tactics. They go into court to punish, restrain, or force compliance. If these formal channels of appeal are too weak or slow, the pressure tactics of **direct action** are used. They might picket an office, conduct a sit-in and refuse to move, or find some other way to disrupt "business as usual."

ORGANIZE

Source: Bill Dobbs/Northland Poster Collection

A little fish swimming alone can easily be gobbled up. But when lots of little fish get organized, it's amazing what they can accomplish.

Believing they answer to a higher code of ethics, the agents of change sometimes take the law into their own hands. Dr. Martin Luther King, Jr., encouraged people to do this when Rosa Parks, a Black woman, was arrested for refusing to yield her seat on a bus to a White passenger. In accordance with the laws of Montgomery, Alabama, she was wrong. But she and the other members of the Black community believed that they had the right to disobey an unjust and morally repugnant law. In order to force change, they boycotted the buses for almost one year. Faced with the possibility of a bankrupt bus company as well as many bankrupt stores, the town officials capitulated, and the segregation law was changed.

Many years later, some people who believed that abortion, although legal, violated their religious or ethical principles formed a group called Operation Rescue. They used many techniques, for example chaining themselves to the doors of family planning clinics and blocking the entrances to them. They have intercepted people walking into the clinics and attempted to disrupt the functioning of these agencies in their efforts to rescue the "unborn children." As the Supreme Court and state legislatures have debated the pros and cons of legalized abortion, these activists have taken direct action on their convictions.

Choosing Which Method to Use and Who Should Lead the Struggle

We make no value judgments about which set of change strategies is better, more appropriate, or more professional. Obviously Ed, like other change agents, always hopes that exposing the facts about a problem will lead to solutions. But he knows that change comes slowly, and often encounters a great deal of resistance. An older woman soon to be evicted from her apartment or a family whose baby is eating lead paint chips cannot keep waiting for help as the wheels of a bureaucratic grievance procedure grind on.

Each strategy plays a role at a particular time with a particular problem in a change campaign. The important point to remember is that in order to maintain credibility, change agents must climb each step of the ladder before escalating to the final, most aggressive one. Each set of strategies must be carefully mapped out and executed, using the kind of planning models we have described.

When he first began his job, Ed was brimming over with energy and enthusiasm. Occasionally those wonderful qualities got in the way of careful planning. At one point, he helped organize a rally to protest the mayor's elimination of money needed to fix up three local parks, which the city council had promised. To his great embarrassment, reporters outnumbered neighborhood residents at the demonstration, and one of the speakers never showed up. Ed did not realize then that he first had to prepare the ground very well before the seeds could grow into an effective intervention. He learned that preparation consists of the following:

- Learning about the history of the problem and the systems involved in it
- Locating the sources of power and estimating their potential for change
- Getting to know the local community through both formal and informal channels of information

And, of course, he needed to learn the "rule of three": Double-check, double-check, and then double-check some more to make sure that everyone potentially involved knows the exact details of the mission and the strategy and agrees to participate.

Learning About the History of the Problem

Whatever the nature of the change we hope to bring about—more responsive routines in a day care classroom, more humane treatment for victims of domestic violence, changes in the governance of a recreation center—we need to learn about the full dimension of the problem. We accumulate the hard facts of the situation by asking questions such as the following:

- How widespread is the problem?
- How long has it been like this?
- How did this problem come about?
- Is it getting better or worse?
- What evidence backs up our estimate?
- Who benefits and who loses from this situation?
- What will happen in the future if the situation does not change?
- What solutions have others suggested? Which ones have been tried?

Locating the Sources of Power and Potential for Change

Before CAFTE begins a change effort, the members need to know just where the power lies to make the proposed changes. Ed has discovered that this is more complex than it first appears. When dealing with city government, several agencies, bureaus, and commissions have overlapping jurisdiction. Ed worked with a committee trying to clean up a vacant lot and turn it into a playground. He soon found out how Alice felt when she went down the rabbit hole into Wonderland. Everyone who answered the phone was eager to pass him along to another person. After many calls, he was right back with the first person again.

In trying to get that vacant lot cleaned up, he discovered that the Health Department was concerned about it only if he could prove it was rat-infested. (Rat bites are health hazards.) He discovered that the Sanitation Department could not clean it up because it was private property. They said they would be happy to clean it after it became a park. Finally, he discovered that the lot had been condemned for nonpayment of taxes many years earlier. In addition, no one at City Hall could find a record of who held the title to the land.

With patience, time, persistence, and lots of help from friends, CAFTE finally unraveled the threads that led to the desk of the person who could cut through the red tape and say "Okay!" A bit of green grass and trees now exists where only rubbish grew before. Ed often eats his lunch in that park and grins with pride (and scowls at children who try to pick the flowers).

POWER AND CHANGE Ed has discovered that power is in a state of perpetual flux, and change is always possible. If he gets turned down on a request one day, he tries again later, as the situation or the cast of characters changes. An election, a turnover in staff, or a downturn in the economy can change a "yes" into a "no" and vice versa.

No system is ever totally closed. Every system, no matter how rigid it appears, is vulnerable to change. When Ed gets frustrated and begins to believe the looming threat of global warming will never be addressed, he reminds himself of the dramatic international changes of the recent past. Ed's mother describes signing petitions and demonstrating for nuclear disarmament. At that time, the world teetered on the brink of nuclear destruction, as the United States and the former Soviet Union faced each other from opposite corners. But almost overnight, the Soviet empire came apart at the seams, and "Ban the Bomb" buttons became collectors' items. After seventy years of power, the "evil empire" became a supplicant, coming to the West for advice and loans.

Getting to Know the Resources of the Community

The word *community* is often used in two ways. First, it is used to describe a geographic entity. The Riverside community, where CAFTE's office is located, for example, has homes, shops, streets, and boundary lines. However, we might also use the term to describe a community of interest, a group with which we identify. It need not have a geographic boundary. Perhaps we see ourselves as belonging to the gay community, the Christian community, the university community, or the macrobiotic community. In this section we will be dealing primarily with understanding the geographic community.

Understanding the physical layout of a community as well as its spirit helps us design strategies to cope with its problems. When Ed was a student, he helped conduct an attitude survey in Riverside. Crime and vandalism had been escalating, and one summer evening a near-riot occurred when the police tried to disperse a group of teenagers congregating on a corner. When the surveys were tabulated, the researchers found that a major complaint of community members was the lack of decent public transportation. Because they could not get to the stores and factories of the nearby city, many residents had given up hope of ever obtaining steady, decent-paying employment. Hopelessness led to frustration, which then led to aggressiveness and destructiveness. When the Riverside Citizens Committee was formed, obtaining transportation was its major priority. Each community has its own agenda. Human service workers have to learn to read it.

Before scheduling any meetings, Ed needs to know how the neighbors feel about coming out at night or entering certain areas. He needs to know if, in this community, parents are likely to bring their children to meetings. If so, he needs to arrange child care. He needs to know what significant events his meetings might conflict with (such as the local church bingo game, a sports event, or ethnic holidays).

Ed needs to find out what languages people speak so he can arrange for translators, if needed. In Riverside, many senior citizens speak English but cannot read or write it, having emigrated from Greece as adults. The newest residents are Chinese, and their primary dialect is Mandarin. Ed speaks a bit of Cantonese, but the two dialects are almost totally different. He has to find some community activists to translate CAFTE's meeting notices into the languages of community residents. CAFTE has a phone message about upcoming activities it is sponsoring or supporting that is spoken in three different languages.

Even the refreshments Ed serves at meetings tend to mirror the preferences or dietary restrictions of the Greek and Chinese members. And their festivals and holidays are celebrated and acknowledged.

FORMAL CHANNELS OF INFORMATION Even though Ed had volunteered in the Riverside community and helped to conduct its community survey, when he started this job, he still had much to learn. He found many valuable sources of information at the library and on the Internet (Kjosness, Barr, & Rettman, 2004). He looked up the census data, read reports written by different city agencies, and read the town budget. He even looked back over old copies of the *Riverside News*.

Then Ed made a list of the people in town he needed to meet. His list included politicians, school board members, clergy, directors of social agencies, and especially the local heroes and town characters. Although he did not formally interview each one, he did have a series of questions he tried to work into conversations whenever he got a chance to meet a person on the list.

INFORMAL CHANNELS OF INFORMATION The formal channels of information were valuable, but Ed found that walking and driving slowly on the community's streets was just as important. Often the official version of the economic or recreational life of the community contradicted what he saw with his own eyes.

The boarded-up stores he observed, and the neighborhood park strewn with beer bottles and sleeping men and women, told him more about the community's spirit and daily life than did the statistics on parks and unemployment. Through the use of the senses—looking, listening, feeling, smelling—human service workers can round out their profile and identify glaring gaps in services.

Whenever possible, Ed drops in to a service at a local church, attends a parents' association meeting, or stops by the American Legion fair or the police versus firefighters challenge baseball game. He makes a point of doing his laundry near the office because the laundromat is a great place to chat with folks, and it has a bulletin board full of notices about events he might never hear of otherwise.

PLANNING AND IMPLEMENTING A CHANGE EFFORT

Reaching Out to the Public

No matter how brilliant our ideas, they may be destined to fail if we do not have active, broad-based support. We always seek coalitions with groups of clients and their families, influential community members, other human service workers, and the ordinary, not-to-be-ignored taxpayers.

Imagine that you were assigned the job of establishing a new family residential center in the Riverside community for mothers who have AIDS. First, you found the latest information on AIDS treatment and committed yourself to keeping current. You went to the state capitol and spent days meeting with your legislators. You helped organize a sit-in demonstration on the steps of the capitol with people with AIDS. Finally, a bill was passed and funds were appropriated. Your group has written a program proposal. It wants to manage one of the three facilities that will be funded. Now you should be able to start the program. Well, not quite yet!

Assuming that you are lucky enough to find an affordable building in an accessible location, you still must negotiate a complex maze of obstacles. You will need to use all your understanding of the formal and informal power systems of the community to obtain the permits and licenses needed to transform a private house into a nonprofit group home. You will have to get permits from the Building Department to make renovations. You will have to meet the Fire and Health Department regulations. The Police Department will probably be concerned about neighborhood safety and the extra cars the center will bring into a narrow street with limited parking.

You and your group (and your lawyer) will have to appear before the town Zoning Board to convince them to grant a variance to their rule that prohibits anything but a private home in a residential neighborhood.

Then you will have to face the members of the block association. They are planning to protest that the proposed center will lower the values of their houses. They are also terrified that their children might get AIDS from the children who will live at the house. At an emotional meeting, they pour out their fear and rage. Renting or buying a house for a community-based human service program is almost always a politically sensitive issue. Inevitably you will run up against the NIMBY syndrome—"I agree that those people need a place to live, but

NOT IN MY BACK YARD."

Anticipating all these obstacles, you and your board have carefully laid the groundwork to defuse the protests. For six months, you have been actively reaching out to everyone who might be an ally. These are some the actions you might take:

- Speak at every church, mosque, and synagogue in the community.
- Appear in a panel discussion about the proposed residence on local cable television.
- Run public service announcements on the radio.
- Recruit an advisory committee of local influential people.
- Set up an interview with the local newspaper.
- Run a series of workshops at the local high school.
- Speak at a parent–teachers association meeting.
- Convince a famous sports figure or entertainer who is HIV-positive to speak at a neighborhood rally.
- Organize a walkathon to raise money for AIDS research.
- Speak to the Chamber of Commerce to assure them that the center will patronize local businesses.
- Publish a monthly newsletter of your activities and progress.
- Organize and keep current a web site about the house.

Even after successfully working your way through red tape and most of the resistance, you will need to continue to stay in close touch with the community. Some of the typical ways social programs do that are the following:

- Have an open house.
- Become members of the block association and other civic groups in town.

- Offer free, anonymous AIDS tests or another benefit to the neighborhood.
- Encourage the Boy Scouts, Girl Scouts, and other groups to use your backyard for their fund-raising events or to use your living room for meetings.

By keeping the channels of communication open in all directions, you will be able to accomplish several of your goals. Your staff will:

- Receive constant, current feedback so that complaints can be dealt with before they explode into conflicts
- Recruit volunteers and obtain donations of materials and services to supplement the scanty budget of the program
- Obtain referrals of clients
- Mobilize supporters for your grant renewal or to protect the program when budget cuts are threatened.

INVOLVING THE PUBLIC IN THE DECISION-MAKING PROCESS The most potent vehicle for creating significant change is the ongoing, genuine participation—the give and take of ideas—of those who will be affected. As change agents, we encourage people to tell us their complaints and visualize solutions. These are the reasons we work hard to listen to the public.

1. *Client and citizen involvement is efficient and effective.* Time and again, clients complain that social researchers spend needless time and money arriving at conclusions about social causation that the clients themselves could have supplied gratis. Although this is a pretty cynical view, it carries a kernel of truth. No matter how troubled or disorganized they may be, clients do have enormous insights into their problems, aspirations, culture, and lifestyle. No matter how skillful we are at understanding systems, clients undoubtedly know their world better than we ever can.
2. *Client and citizen involvement has therapeutic and protective value.* Many of the people who arrive at the doors of human service agencies have already been overwhelmed by bureaucracies, unresponsive institutions, urban ghettos, or suburban isolation. Feeling alienated and vulnerable—one small ant on a very big hill—they desperately yearn to play a significant role in the systems that affect their lives. When we work one-on-one with people who have problems, we carefully guard their right to choose their own path; we must also do that as we work with them to pursue change.
3. *Client and citizen involvement in decision making is both a moral right and a legal obligation.* Juggling the rights of individuals and neighborhoods with the rights of the larger society requires the wisdom of Solomon.

The public can vote to change policies, and they can vote for candidates who espouse their positions. Thus, participation is built into our system at every level, either directly or indirectly.

Many special education, health, and environmental laws require the approval of "consumers." Social welfare and housing laws require advisory or review panels of citizens. These panels periodically review the work of public agencies and have some say in whether their funding is expanded or downsized.

Encouraging Participation in Decision Making

Citizen decision making is essential in a democracy, but both skeptics and supporters of participation agree that many barriers stand in its way. Citizens often lack time, self-confidence, specialized knowledge of resources and alternatives, articulateness, and objectivity. No less an authority

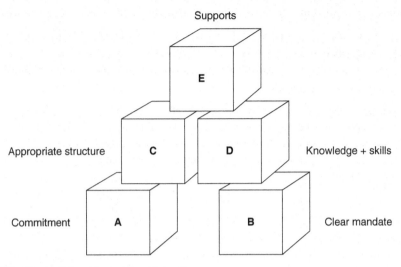

FIGURE 12.1   The building blocks of participation

than Thomas Jefferson, however, offered an answer to the public's unreadiness to assume power. He said: "I know of no safe repository of the ultimate powers of this society but the people themselves; and if we think them not enlightened enough to exercise their control with a wholesome discretion, the remedy is not to take it from them, but to inform their discretion." In Figure 12.1, the building blocks of participation are shown.

A. *Commitment.*   After the third board meeting in a row of a citizen's group, when a vote cannot be taken on a grant proposal because there is no quorum, the social agency director might be tempted to throw up her hands and yell, "Damn it, I'll decide myself!" But even if shared decision making is not working very well, it cannot be abandoned.

The agency director mandated to check out proposals with a citizen's advisory board must grit her teeth and try a new approach to solicit the opinions of the members. She could call each one and take a telephone poll, or she could write a letter (and enclose a stamped, self-addressed postcard) and ask for written feedback. She must continue to believe that six hesitant citizens will eventually make a sounder decision about the proposal than she could make alone. She understands that there are low points in every group's participation history.

B. *Clear mandate.*   Participation has the best chance of working when the contract governing the process is clear. Discussing all the details of by-laws or personnel practices seems to most of us like tedious nitpicking. However, carefully written rules of the road are the backdrop against which rational participation can take place. Vague generalities doom shared decision making. Compare the following statements in the by-laws of two different community residences for adults who are in recovery from drug addiction. The clarity of the second statement offers residents more of a chance of gaining significant participation than the generality of the first:

"Residents will play an active role in running the house."

Compare that vague mandate with this very clearly specified process of decision making:

> "Once a week, there will be a two-hour meeting during which activities for the next seven days will be planned. Each member will have one vote. All activities must get the majority of votes and must fall within the recreation funds allocated for that week."

C. *Appropriate structure.*   Every participation effort needs a tailor-made participation structure. The format must be the right one for the mix of purpose, participants, and set of tasks. Unfortunately, most of us know of few alternative models of structure. We drift into the familiar: elections for president, vice president, secretary, and treasurer. Then we establish a weekly or monthly meeting.

But not all groups need the same kinds of officers, nor do they need to meet on a regular, arbitrary schedule. Some decisions need the face-to-face interaction of a meeting; many just need a polling of opinions in any of a variety of ways. Some tasks need not be done by everyone but can be delegated to committees.

Some committees can be ad hoc, taking on one task and then disbanding when it is completed. Ed has found that it is much easier to ask a resident to take on a task if it has a beginning and an ending time attached to it. Although she turned down the job of chair of the fund-raising committee, for example, Ms. Kazantakis was willing to run two bake sales a year. That was a role that did not overwhelm her.

Carving out a structure is like sculpting a face. No two are identical. Experimentation and imagination are the keys to success. But if the structure is not designed, an informal one will evolve anyway, with all its attendant fuzziness and potential for conflict.

D. *Knowledge and skills.*   Few of the citizens in Riverside have ever made the kinds of decisions that organizing a social change movement entails. Ed has often passed on to the members the knowledge and skills he has learned in college courses as well as the skills he has acquired from volunteering in local political campaigns.

When the citizen members of board of CAFTE were hiring an architectural consultant and an engineer to help evaluate a developer's plans for an affordable housing building, Ed used the role-playing technique he had learned in counseling classes to prepare them for the interview. He has also brought in sample budgets from other groups to show them what is usually included. When they wrote their by-laws, he invited a guest speaker from an older, established neighborhood association who had already gone through the process.

E. *Supports that enable participation.*   No matter what the issue—a tenant council is lobbying for legislation to control the spread of condominiums in a low-income area, or a community residence for adults who were formerly homeless is planning its first open house—some people will inevitably invest more time, energy, and enthusiasm than will others. Those who do the work need to be warmly thanked, whether with a letter of appreciation, a dinner, or a certificate of appreciation.

Resources can support the growth of democracy. Perhaps if child care were provided during meetings, more people might come. Ed has found that if he rotates the locations and schedules of meetings, it becomes easier for some folks to attend. Sometimes he suggests to one member that she carpool with someone he knows is coming. He always makes it a point to offer rides to members because very few of them can afford to maintain a car, and walking long distances at night can be frightening.

Ed also tries to remember that as important as CAFTE is, each member and coworker has a personal life outside the organization, and that life also needs to be nurtured. Ed builds time into meetings so members can swap news of job openings or available apartments.

Changing the Rules, Regulations, and Power Arrangements of a System

Just as every worker has a boss, so every public or private organization has some type of governing body. Decisions are generally made in a boardroom, courtroom, or legislative chamber. It is to these groups that the members of CAFTE turn when they become frustrated trying to cope with a problem that is not getting solved at the local level. After they determine where the next level of power lies, they try to educate, persuade, or pressure those officials.

For many years, the citizens in Riverside had been complaining about garbage collection that was very sporadic. When garbage was collected, the empty cans were often thrown in the street, where buses would reduce them to junk metal. The smell of garbage, especially in the summer, hung over their neighborhood. Parents feared that their children would be bitten by rats that were attracted to the garbage in the streets. Letters written to the manager of the Sanitation Department got polite answers but no improvement. A petition demanding regularly scheduled and more careful sanitation service was circulated. More than 200 people signed their names, but nothing changed. So, for three weeks, a senior homebound CAFTE volunteer sat by her window, marking down the times the trucks arrived on her corner and what the sanitation workers actually did. She noted their license plate numbers so drivers could be held accountable.

Armed with all this credible data, Ed helped to arrange a meeting with the regional director of sanitation, who listened courteously and promised to discipline his staff. For two months the situation improved, but it drifted back to its original sorry state. Summer came, and the stench of garbage increased. The fear of rat infestation increased along with it.

APPEALING TO ELECTED OFFICIALS   Ed realized they had to go over the head of the regional sanitation director. One of the experienced members of CAFTE suggested that the group members appeal to their local town council. Ed made an appointment with Councilor Irene Haupt, who represented the Riverside neighborhood. The committee members practiced stating their demands. They went in with a written agenda, with evidence collected by a homebound volunteer, and with their petitions. Ms. Haupt, anticipating an upcoming hotly contested reelection campaign, seemed very impressed with the 200 signatures. Each of those signatures represented a potential vote she might capture.

Although they might think of themselves as apolitical, human service workers cannot be. They visit their statehouse when legislators are discussing budgets. If they do not lobby for the funding of social welfare programs, perhaps no one else will! The opponents of affordable housing, humane correctional programs, or domestic violence shelters are likely to be there, demanding that money be diverted from social programs to fund their priorities. They too will have research documents and signatures on petitions.

TURNING TO THE COURTS FOR HELP   Although the sanitation complaint was resolved on the legislative level, at other times Ed has needed to follow the path to the courthouse. If he is convinced that an inequity in the wording or practice of a law stands in the way of citizens getting

Source: AP Images

To remove the "Whites Only" signs in public accommodations in the southern states, advocates went all the way to the U.S. Supreme Court.

fair treatment, CAFTE either tries to get the law repealed or asks a judge to change the way it has been interpreted or implemented.

Lawyers from nonprofit legal-services programs bring these cases into court. The most outstanding group of civil rights lawyers work for the American Civil Liberties Union (ACLU). They work on behalf of both individuals and communities, especially when they are convinced that their civil rights or health and safety are being violated.

The Rewards of Social Change Interventions

Most human service jobs do not require as much time, energy, and skill at creating social change as Ed's role at CAFTE. But all workers will, at some point, encounter an unyielding barrier that stands between the people with problems and the services they need. Then, even on a very small scale, the worker acts as a change agent. As the federal government continues to shift away from publicly funded programs and the slack is picked up by the private sector, human service workers will have to continually monitor the output of social programs. Would you stand by quietly if:

… a disoriented older woman you counseled were being evicted from her home because the landlord wanted to sell her apartment as a condominium?

… a young man just released from prison wanted to find work as an electrician, and the union representative told him the union would not take anyone with a prison record?

... the mother of a troubled teen were told that she would have to wait six months for an educational assessment because the school psychologist was too busy?

... a person were running for office in your town on a platform of cutting out all the frills and were targeting the only teenage recreation center, a Meals on Wheels program for homebound senior citizens, and a van to transport adults with physical disabilities to their sheltered workshop?

We hope your answer is a resounding, "Of course not!" Walking a picket line and knocking on a stranger's door to explain a community problem can at first be intimidating. Licking stamps, stuffing envelopes, handing out leaflets, and making endless phone calls are tedious. And losing a struggle after months of hard work can be devastating. Ed does all these tasks and has faced many disappointments. Yet he has also had incredible highs when desperately needed services were begun or reinstated after being cut back. The day the first tenants move into the demonstration "green" housing development he has worked on for so long will be filled with indescribable joy.

Every organizer can tell stories about coworkers or citizens who, after experiencing a new sense of their own power, went back to school to finish their degree, took on a more responsible job, conquered an addiction, or returned home feeling more hopeful about their children's futures.

Summary

1. The problems with which people struggle are often caused by factors rooted in their social environment.
2. Changes in the social environment might help one troubled individual and, more importantly, can help solve or prevent the development of similar problems for others.
3. Indirect organizing and change strategies employ the same activities and skills as direct-service strategies. They begin with data collection and terminate with evaluation.
4. Before forming an action plan to help the person with a problem, the human service worker must check out the mental health of the systems within which that person lives and works.
5. Human service workers need to explore their ambivalent or unrealistic attitudes toward change agents.
6. Momentum for change generates from the top down through legislative or administrative fiat. It also generates from the bottom up through the actions of organized citizens. Often it comes from both the top and bottom of the system at the same time.

7. Human service workers attempt to change both the structure of an unhealthy system and the consciousness of the people in it.
8. The three escalating methods of organizing for change are education, persuasion, and pressure.
9. Before a change effort begins, organizers research the background of the problem and locate where the power to make change really resides. They need to prepare a community profile to assess resources and understand the lifestyles of the people involved in the organizing.
10. Organizers use outreach techniques to solicit public support and participation in generating ideas and making decisions, and to overcome resistance to change.
11. Citizen participation depends on obtaining strong commitments; clear mandates; and appropriate structure, knowledge, skills, and participation supports.
12. To change the rules, regulations, and power arrangements of a system, organizers disseminate information, rally support, lobby decision makers, and take direct action when other techniques have not worked.

13. Working to change systems is time- and energy-consuming, frustrating, and often fruitless. But even very small changes can result in dramatic improvements. The potential rewards of all our advocacy efforts can affect many people's life situations.

14. Change efforts can be undertaken by anyone and can bring great satisfaction to both those who initiate them and those who benefit from them.

Discussion Questions

1. George Bernard Shaw, a social critic of his times, is reported to have said that only unreasonable people will not accept the world as it is, and that therefore all change depends on "unreasonable people." How do you feel about that statement? Does it make sense to you? Would you feel comfortable in the role of "an unreasonable person"? Can you think of some famous people who might fit that description?

2. With what kinds of change efforts have you been involved within your own hometown or on your college campus? Who started them, what techniques did they use, and how did the efforts work out? Remember that these change efforts need not be major campaigns. If you can't think of any change efforts in your own experiences, what kinds of change efforts have you heard of or seen in your community or on your college campus? Have you seen or read about any groups that asserted their position for or against a woman's right to an abortion or for or against gun control? What kinds of tactics did they use to influence the public or legislators?

3. Is there any form of student governance on your campus? If so, how widespread is the participation? If it is not very widespread, how might you increase it? Where would you go to find the sources of power that might be able to change a rule or regulation that you feel is unfair or not fairly implemented in your academic department? What is the power hierarchy in your college or university—who reports to whom? What is the power hierarchy in your town?

Web Resources for Further Study

Interaction Institute

http://interactioninstitute.org/training/facilitative-leadership-for-social-change/

NetAction

https://www.netaction.org/about/index.html

Understanding Legal Issues

13

Source: Zolnierek/Shutterstock

Learning Outcomes

- Students will recognize key legal issues within the field of human services.
- Students will gain an understanding of how legal issues impact their role as a human service worker.
- Students will identify strategies to apply key legal concepts in their human service work through advocacy and other supportive strategies.
- Students will develop their ability to evaluate issues related to human services and the law.

In an effort to control the presence of individuals who are homeless, some cities have begun a practice of forbidding, through law or ordinance, the feeding of homeless individuals without receiving expensive permits (Dum, Norris, & Weng, 2017). The regulations often include hard and fast restrictions on where free food can be served, and advocates for the homeless complain that the fees associated with receiving the permits are unnecessarily cost prohibitive. Rather than addressing the causes of homelessness, some jurisdictions have chosen instead to try to control the presence of people who are homeless in their cities or towns by restricting efforts to assist them.

LEGAL ISSUES THAT CAN CONFRONT A WORKER

The preceding is one example of the many kinds of legal issues, such as city ordinances and state and federal laws, that a human service worker might deal with. It is impossible in one chapter to cover all the legal issues that affect human service workers. Not only can they seem overwhelming, but no human service worker knows the ins and outs of every issue. However, it is vital that we be sensitive to legal rights and dilemmas and that we seek further help when on shaky ground. Knowing where to turn and being willing to ask for help are strengths of a conscientious worker.

To begin your thinking about legal issues, take the following quiz. We would be surprised if you knew all the answers. Legal issues in the human services can be complicated.

Question 1: An 18-year-old high school student began to wonder just what her teachers had been writing in her record since she started school. She asked her homeroom teacher if she could look at her cumulative school record. The teacher said no, because it would violate the confidence of all those teachers who had counted on some measure of confidentiality. Did the teacher break the law?

Question 2: In 1974, the state of Georgia set up a central computer bank to store mental health information about its citizens. State officials requested that all clinics and community mental health centers send in the following information for each new patient: background data, Social Security number, the nature of the patient's primary disability, previous mental health services, and diagnosis. A human service worker at a community mental health clinic asked all her clients to sign this medical release authorization, which read:

> The state wants to keep a record of name, Social Security number, and the type of problem of every person who comes for mental health services. The reason why the state wants this information is so that it can keep track of mental health services and clients throughout the state. If you sign this paper it means that you give us permission to send your name, Social Security number, and diagnosis to the state offices in the capital, where it will be placed in the mental health computer file. (Rosen, 1976, p. 285)

Was the worker correct in the way she explained the situation to the consumers?

Question 3: Felicia, a 23-year-old woman who had been adopted, wrote to the state registrar of vital statistics in New Hampshire to request a copy of her original birth certificate, knowing that this would be a source, as a pre-adoption document, for her birth parents' names. After receiving it, she went to the agency that had placed her with her adoptive parents to ask for help in finding her biological parents, who were named on the birth certificate. The adoption worker agreed to help her with this search (Weidell, 1980). At the same time, Felicia's 21-year-old brother Paul, who had been placed for adoption in Washington, D.C., where his biological mother had moved from New Hampshire, wrote to the District's registrar of vital statistics for his original birth certificate, and officials refused to send it to him. He went to the adoption agency, which also refused to help him.

Why did the adoption agency in New Hampshire help Felicia, whereas the agency in Washington, D.C., refused to help Paul?

If you knew the answers to these questions, you are better informed about legal issues than a good many experienced human service workers. One study found, for example, that a significant proportion of mandated reporters of child abuse didn't fully understand the laws with respect to their responsibilities to report suspected abuse (Kenny, Abreu, Helpingstine, Lopez, & Mathews, 2018). Until recently, legal issues either have not been taught at all in human service training programs or have been dealt with superficially.

What Is Wrong with What the Worker Did?

Here are the answers to the questions:

Answer 1: Yes, the teacher broke the law. According to the Family Educational Rights and Privacy Act, often called the Buckley Amendment, educational institutions that receive federal aid must make students' records available to them if they are 18 or older and to their parents when they are minors (Bershoff, 1975, p. 367).

Answer 2: The state of Georgia, which requested this very personal information for its computer records, did not show sufficient concern for its citizens' right to privacy. Some states have adopted progressive privacy laws, and some states have constitutional provisions protecting the right to privacy. However, clients did not have to sign that medical release authorization in order to receive service from the clinic. The mistake the worker made was not telling clients this. A study showed that when clients were told the following in addition to the first part of the statement, the majority of them chose not to sign the statement:

> If you do not sign this paper, this identifying information will not be sent to the state offices in the capital and will only be kept locally. The services you get will not depend on your choice. In other words, if you don't sign, you will get the same services from us as if you did sign. (Rosen, 1976, p. 285)

The principle of consent assumes that people are informed about what they are giving consent to and that it is freely given, without any real or implied threats. For this reason, we talk about the importance of providing "informed consent." If people think they will be refused services if they don't sign the consent form, most will sign. This, though, is ethically unsound practice, and highlights the need to ensure that the individual giving consent has been presented with a full and complete understanding of what providing consent means for them.

Answer 3: The New Hampshire agency helped Felicia in the search for her biological parents, whereas the Washington, D.C., agency refused Paul because New Hampshire passed a law that allowed adoptees who are at least 20 years old to obtain their original, preadoption birth certificate if the biological parents have consented to the search. Washington, D.C., law does not allow birth records to be revealed for such a search.

Variations in the Law

Notice as you read those questions and answers that some laws apply equally to everyone in the United States (e.g., letting students see their records), while other laws (e.g., opening adoption records) vary from state to state. As you read this chapter, some of the laws we discuss are probably already in the process of being changed by state or federal legislatures or by a court decision. Even lawyers must do constant research to keep abreast of current law in a particular field. Although most human service workers cannot know the law in the same way, they should strive to keep abreast of the particular body of law that applies to their agency population.

THE LAW AS RESOURCE

Laws can give people rights and resources, and therefore, workers need to know them. Suppose that a human service worker is helping a child with blindness and the child's family to find an appropriate school. If the worker did not know that the Education for All Handicapped Children Act requires that children with disabilities be placed in the least restrictive setting, the worker might try to find a placement in a residential school for the blind rather than in the local school system.

This process of finding information, evaluating it as it applies to a particular problem, assessing the needs of the person or group with which you are working, and finding the correct fit between person and resource is the same problem-solving process that human service workers use in all the interventions discussed in this book.

Street-Level Bureaucracy

Although laws are passed at various government levels—federal, state, and local—most beginning human service workers will encounter those laws that affect their practice at the level of the agency in which they work. A law sets the broad outlines of a program, but the face of the law that clients see is the face of the agency worker who delivers the service. Moving up the bureaucratic ladder, the worker sees the face of the law in the face of his supervisor and the agency director, who interpret how regulations shall be put in practice in that particular agency. In a large government agency, the state officials of that bureaucracy have written those regulations according to the way they interpret the law.

Regulations: Bureaucratic Interpretations of Law

After laws are passed, they cannot affect anyone's life until the money is appropriated and the regulations spelling out how to implement the laws are written. Agencies don't make laws, but their regulations define how the law will be put into practice. These regulations end up having the same force as a law. For example, the U.S. Congress passed amendments to Title IV-E, the act that provides federal payments to states to support their respective foster care systems. The changes driven by the amendment were tucked away in a massive spending bill signed into law by President Trump. The regulations make sweeping changes in how revenue can be used to support families in need of foster care services, allowing for the first time the use of resources under Title IV-E for prevention efforts (Wiltz, 2018). The states now have to work with their counterparts at the federal level to implement rules related to how these prevention dollar will be utilized.

While the changes are lauded by some as helpful, others are concerned that the positive nature of increased flexibility in the use of funding for prevention will be offset by the 8 billion dollar reduction in federal foster care funding and by delivery system requirements that are predicted to have an adverse impact on the existing child welfare system (Kelly, 2018). Changes of this nature often throw the delivery system into a state of uncertainty while each state works with the Department of Health and Human Services to establish the necessary rules to implement the law.

Regulations are generally more specific than laws. For example, a law about licensing day care centers may say that centers shall be operated with "due regard for health and sanitation." But it is the regulations that specify a minimum number of toilets and the water temperature for dishwashing (Brieland & Goldfarb, 1987).

Sometimes, in order to save money, officials make regulations that do not conform to the law, or they break their own regulations. This happened in 1981, when the Reagan administration ordered accelerated reviews of Social Security disability cases using what a Minnesota federal district court called "arbitrary," "capricious," and "irrational" standards to evaluate applicants' eligibility for the benefits (National Association of Social Workers, 1983). Thousands of eligible people had their benefits terminated before Congress reviewed the process, slowed the rate of review, and provided for continuation of benefits during the appeals process. An attorney for the Mental Health Law Project, which brought suit in Minnesota on behalf of the disproportionate numbers of people with mental illness whose benefits were terminated, contended that the Social Security Administration, in its eagerness to reduce disability rolls, had been systematically violating federal law as well as its own regulations.

In Maine, early efforts to reduce the use of residential placement for youth and the contraction of community based services has resulted in children being stuck in psychiatric hospitals, more children being served out of state, and greater numbers of youths being committed to the youth correctional facility (Stone, 2018). Despite federal mandates for the delivery of child welfare services, the state of Maine's policy is seen by many as being driven by fiscal constraints that has resulted in a scenario where many youth with mental health challenges bounce between acute psychiatric hospitals and the community, where necessary services are lacking.

"CATCH-22" REGULATIONS   Regulations can put clients in a catch-22* a situation in which they are damned if they do and damned if they don't.

Suppose that a toddler has outgrown her crib and needs a child-size bed. In the state where the child lives, the Welfare officials who drew up the regulations decided that public money should not be spent on beds. Therefore, the 3-year-old will stay crammed in the crib or sleep on the floor, which runs the risk of being seen as neglectful or abusive on the part of child welfare workers.

Or suppose that a woman has been told by her landlord that she must leave her apartment. She agrees and then asks Welfare for money to pay a security deposit on another apartment. The officials who wrote the regulations, however, specified that she must show the worker a court eviction order or already be evicted before the Welfare Department can help her pay the security deposit.

CONFLICTING JURISDICTIONS AND REGULATIONS   The different levels of government involved in the same program may further complicate the picture. This catches the client in a web of conflicting jurisdictions and regulations. Fuel assistance for people considered low income is one such example. A federal program provides money that some states supplement. If a state requires a client to apply first to a federal antipoverty agency for fuel assistance before applying to the state Welfare Department, the client can get a bureaucratic runaround and perhaps will have to live in a freezing home until the confusing tangle is unraveled.

States and localities often implement programs that are not federally mandated. Sometimes they even challenge federal regulations. For example, at one time, a federal drug-abuse program had a regulation that required all states receiving money from the program to put personal data on patients into a centralized computer. Massachusetts refused to do so on the grounds that it would violate patients' confidentiality. Some states have stronger privacy laws than does the federal government.**

---

*The term *catch-22* refers to a novel of the same name by Joseph Heller (1961) and describes dilemmas that are impossible to solve because of contradictory requirements.

**The federal law regarding disclosure of drug information was later changed to prohibit it in all states.

If the foregoing discussion has been confusing, imagine what it feels like to be a client. You might have only a dim understanding of who gives the money and makes the regulations. When you complain, you are told, "We don't make the regulations. The 'feds' (state, county, city) make them." Local, state, and federal bureaucrats sometimes fight each other about policies and regulations, passing the buck from one to the other when clients complain. Advocating for clients in these situations requires patience, tenacity, and the concerted efforts of many people and organizations.

AMBIGUOUS WORDING Regulations are sometimes worded so ambiguously that citizen groups or individual clients challenge them, claiming they give a false interpretation of the original intent of the law. Sometimes the laws themselves are ambiguous and loosely written. When a confusing regulation is stacked on top of a confusing law, conscientious workers are also caught in a bind. How can one interpret them? Many bureaucrats are becoming increasingly aware of the immobility caused by ambiguous intent or language, and now and then agency workers are pleasantly surprised to find on their desks a revision of agency regulations written in *plain, easy-to-understand language*. Sometimes these regulations give examples, which can make complex rulings easier to comprehend. Some people argue that the ambiguity of regulations is intentional. When clients don't understand what they are entitled to, they are less likely to ask for those rights.

Learning the Regulations

Few things are more frustrating to a consumer than being served by a poorly informed worker. Think of how you feel when you ask for information about housing, financial aid, or degree requirements from a college employee and are given the runaround! A worker who is confused by the full meaning of a regulation should discuss it with a supervisor or a colleague. If the confusion persists, it is best to turn to a lawyer who specializes in this area. Most large agencies, such as a Department of Social Services or a Department of Vocational Rehabilitation, have legal divisions. In addition, there are many public-service law groups that specialize in children's rights, welfare reform, the needs of the individuals with physical and developmental disabilities, and so forth. When a new law is passed or a regulation promulgated, memos and newsletters are distributed and conferences are organized to help workers and consumers understand and use its provisions.

Without these forms of public information, none of us—human service worker, client, or lawyer—would be able to keep clear about the endless changes and refinements in social service law.

Unfortunately, the federal government has been cutting back on legal services for people considered low income since the Nixon administration. President Reagan tried unsuccessfully to eliminate them altogether. As recently as May 2017, the Trump administration has proposed eliminating the Legal Services Corporation, which provides legal assistance to individuals that cannot afford a lawyer in non-criminal proceedings (Ray, 2017). Bureaucrats and public officials resist protests against their rules and try to weaken organizations that challenge them. Because there are not nearly enough legal services for all the people who need them, human service workers will need to learn more than ever about the law in order to be able to help their clients.

Deciding exactly what are the limits of protests is a challenge for constitutional scholars and community residents. These members of the White supremacist Ku Klux Klan can march in Washington, D.C., but may no longer hide their faces behind their sheets.

THE LAW AS RESTRICTION

Laws provide resources and rights; they also limit them. City councils and state and federal legislatures create programs; they also cut them. Delinquency and correctional programs and agencies that investigate child abuse and neglect are examples of the government policing people's behavior. Human service workers in these programs need to be sensitive to the *stigmatizing* effects that such programs have on the clientele. They work to combat the **stigma** through social action and sensitive individual and group counseling. People may need to be stopped when their behavior is endangering themselves or others, but social stigma cripples rather than rehabilitates.

Human service workers work with many stigmatized clients:

1. When parents have been accused of child abuse and a child-protection worker goes to their home to investigate, the parents inevitably feel stigmatized, regardless of whether they actually abused their child.
2. When a child has been labeled a "delinquent," that label becomes a stigma that can create a self-fulfilling prophecy.
3. When people in a drug or an alcohol abuse program have their names put in a centralized computer, they have legitimate fears about how this information will be used.
4. When people test positive for HIV, they have legitimate fears that they will be discriminated against.

LAWS EVERY WORKER NEEDS TO KNOW

These are some areas of law that all human service workers need to understand:

- Confidentiality
- Privileged communication
- Privacy
- Due process

Some laws affect one specific field of practice. For example, only those involved with the courts need a thorough understanding of the probation and parole regulations of their particular county or state.

Confidentiality, privileged communication, and privacy, however, affect all fields of service delivery. What do they mean as legal concepts to human service workers? To summarize, a human service worker promises confidentiality to a client in order to protect privacy and develop trust between them. In a few human service relationships, the law treats those confidences as privileged communication, protected from being divulged in court. The only times that information should be shared with others outside the worker–client relationship are when the client gives informed consent and in instances where the worker believes there is a threat of harm to the individual or the community. We shall discuss these concepts further in the sections that follow.

Confidentiality

Confidentiality is important in order to build trust. People are not likely to reveal anything embarrassing or intimate if they cannot rely on the helping person to keep secrets. *Confidentiality* means protecting a person's privacy and respecting that person's autonomy. Some people have such strong feelings against exposing their lives to public view that they will ask for help or reveal themselves only in dire circumstances.

Most people want the right to control information about themselves. People don't like having secret files about them that they can't look at or having credit records given out that might damage their ability to get a loan or buy a car. People get angry when they talk to someone in confidence and that person spreads their secrets to others without permission. We feel betrayed if a person violates our trust.

The psychotherapeutic relationship depends on confidentiality. People need to feel free to express their most private thoughts, feelings, and impulses. Some psychotherapists have gone to jail rather than testify in court about their patients. Some therapists have stopped including highly personal material in their notes in order to protect clients' confidences in case a court subpoenas the notes.

Social agencies usually have a specific policy on confidentiality, but these statements are often vaguely worded, containing many *ifs*, *ands*, and *buts*, which create many loopholes. In practice, many agencies freely give out information about clients to other agencies, human services data banks, police or court officials, schools, employers, landlords, and researchers from both public and private groups. One experienced worker laments:

> It is not unusual for intake workers to have their new clients routinely sign a handful of blank consent forms "to make it easier for everyone." These forms authorize the agency to seek or release information about the client to almost everybody at any time under any circumstances. With the client's signature already obtained, the worker can fill in the blanks later when a need arises to disclose data. This system doesn't allow the client to maintain any meaningful control over the content of his case record. Thus, many settings (and federal regulations) are requiring that the client's consent be "informed." (Wilson, 1980, pp. 189–190)

This violation of confidentiality is not ethical, but in many instances it is legal. Two lawyers who studied the daily practices of public agencies concluded that clients of welfare or other social service agencies have no legal right to privacy and no legal way to fight a breach of confidentiality except where the federal Privacy Act or a state privacy act covers the agency's operations (Hayden & Novik, 1980). On the other hand, best practices dictate that the practice of having clients simply sign blank forms falls outside of many accreditation standards and the rules promulgated by various state licensing agencies. In Maine, for example, releases of information, allowing agencies to share information between individuals and other social service or governmental organizations, are all time-limited (Authorization to Release Information, ND).

Privileged Communication

Privileged communication gives legal protection to some human service workers against having to reveal a client's confidences in court, unless the client consents. It has historical roots in the privileged communication of the lawyer–client relationship, which held that confidences told to the lawyer must be kept secret to protect not only the client but, more importantly, to protect the right of all clients to be represented by counsel. Privileged communication is essential to ensure that clients will confide in their lawyers.

However, some states have freed lawyers to violate a client's confidentiality if they believe doing so could prevent injury or death to another person. California passed such a law in 2003, which states that the attorney–client privilege can be broken when a lawyer "reasonably believes" that disclosure is necessary to prevent a criminal act by any person, including a client, that could result in death or substantial injury. While disclosure is discretionary, not mandatory, the law was opposed by many lawyers and by the San Diego County Bar Association, which feared that it would "discourage clients from being forthright and complete" ("State Bar to Allow Lawyers to Break Confidentiality," 2004).

Privileged communication has been extended to other relationships in which trust is of the utmost importance—husband and wife, priest and penitent, psychiatrist and patient, journalist and source, and sometimes psychologist and client and social worker and client. Although it protects certain professionals from having to reveal confidences in court, it is not an absolute privilege. In fact, there is considerable disagreement and debate about this concept, even among lawyers. Some argue that privileged communication should be restricted when there is a threat to society, as when a client tells about a crime she has committed or is contemplating.

Human service workers are sometimes caught in an agonizing bind when they are subpoenaed by a court to testify. The worker may have promised clients that the information given her was confidential, honestly believing that she could guarantee confidentiality, but the state she works in does not provide the legal protection of privileged communication. DeCino, Phillip, Waalkes, and Matos (2018) underscore the importance of school counselors understanding the challenges and limitations to confidentiality that are present when they are subpoenaed to court. One important strategy as a professional is to carefully inform your clients about how information will or could be shared in the event of a court action. Knowing ahead of time the limitations to what you are able to keep confidential and communicating that clearly with your client will go a long way toward resolving unforeseen legal binds.

1. Some states have passed laws to help bolster the level of confidentiality available to clients. Women's crisis intervention agencies in Maine, for example, scored a victory for confidentiality in 2004, when the state enacted a law to protect victims of domestic violence attempting to elude their assailants. The law established a program that provides a

designated address that is unknown to the abuser and includes a first-class mail-forwarding service that has no relationship to the participant's actual address. As a result of the program, victims of domestic violence, sexual assault, and stalking are able to interact with businesses, government agencies, and other organizations without disclosing their actual address (Higgins, 2004).

A majority of state legislatures have enacted legislation privileging the communication between rape crisis counselors and sexual assault victims.

Some research projects have been charged with violating confidentiality. For example, a research project that involved drug testing of high school athletes in Oregon did not protect the students' confidentiality; students who refused to participate in the research or who tested positive for drugs came to the attention of coaches and principals, were prohibited from engaging in school sports, and could be suspended from school:

> Considering the profound social and psychological importance of peer relationships among adolescents, the loss of confidentiality results in humiliation as well as the public airing of drug-using status, assuming that the test result is a true positive. Confidentiality requires that the consequences of trial participation not be subject to publicity of any form in which individuals are reasonably at risk of identification. (Shamoo & Moreno, 2004)

Agencies sometimes invoke confidentiality as a way of avoiding public scrutiny of their failings. Child welfare agencies have legitimate reasons for assuring their clients that information will be kept confidential. Many people would not report child abuse if their identity were known; people who have been charged with abusing children do not want publicity. Yet when an agency is failing to protect the children who are in its care from abuse, it may not be possible to correct the agency's failings unless the public is informed and presses for change through the legislature. In 1999, two children ages 11 and 9, who had been in the custody and care of the New Jersey Division of Youth and Family Services (DYFS) for more than five years, brought a class action suit which alleged a systemic failure of the agency to protect them and 20 other children from harm.

Since then, the tragic death of a foster child, Faheem Williams, and the abuse of his siblings, who were known to DYFS, encouraged the plaintiffs and interveners to request a modification of the existing confidentiality order in the class action suit. They asked for public disclosure of materials pertaining to child fatality and near-fatality cases. The *New York Times* and the *Newark Star-Ledger* joined the suit, requesting permission to publish the information. The U.S. District Court of New Jersey ruled that because DYFS is a public agency, the public has a right to know some relevant information regarding the health and safety of the children. The court gave the newspapers the right to review about 10 percent of the agency's files related to child death reports and other substantiated reports, but not identifying information about children currently in the custody of DYFS. The court attempted to ensure a balance between the privacy rights of the individual and the public's right to know (Jones & Kaufman, 2003).

PROFESSIONS AND PRIVILEGED COMMUNICATION   Although privileged communication protects both the client and the professional, the confidence belongs only to the client, and only the client can waive it. Some states grant the privilege to clinical psychologists and to social workers. Human service professionals try to get broader legal coverage and stricter laws.

The confidentiality of a patient's communications with a psychotherapist was guaranteed on the federal level in a 1996 Supreme Court decision, *Jaffee v. Redmond*. The Health Insurance

Portability and Accountability Act of 1996 (HIPAA) required rules to be drawn up governing the privacy of health and mental health information. The rules were four years in the making, and in 2001 the Department of Health and Human Services (HHS) announced them. The rules now:

- Require clients' consent in order to disclose health information for the purpose of treatment, payment, and health care operations
- Preserve state laws' stronger privacy protections, where they exist
- Recognize that psychotherapy notes require a greater level of protection than other types of health records (Moss, 2001)
- Prohibit employers from receiving personal health data, except for the administration of health plans
- Subject people who misuse private medical records, such as by selling them, to fines or imprisonment (O'Harrow, 2001).

However, the rules allowed doctors, hospitals, other health services, and some of their business associates to use personal health records for marketing and fund-raising. In response to customer concerns that the marketing provision in the law did not protect privacy, HHS modified the law in August 2002 to prohibit selling lists of patients or enrollees to third parties without an individual's prior authorization. However, marketing to doctors is still permitted.

The new rules also say that sick patients will not be required to visit a pharmacy themselves to pick up a prescription but can send a family member or a friend instead (Code of Federal Regulations - Title 45, 2003).

The Act applies to medical records only if a health care facility maintains and transmits records in electronic form. A great deal of health-related information exists outside of health care facilities and the files of health plans, and thus beyond the reach of HIPAA (Privacy Rights Clearinghouse, 2014).

You have probably seen the effects of this law when your doctor or hospital handed you a "Notice of Privacy Practices" brochure and asked you to sign a form saying that you had read it. You may notice greater privacy in the reception room and changes in sign-in sheets so that patients can't see each other's names.

Despite this law, a national survey showed that an overwhelming number of Americans fear that their psychological health records are not kept confidential, particularly from their employers. And most people are not aware that many insurance plans require a diagnosis of mental illness to cover ongoing counseling. Many people are reluctant to seek psychological health care for fear their psychological health records may be shared with their employers or others. Two-thirds of Americans would not be likely to tell their employer they were seeing a mental health professional, and 70 percent would not tell their work associates. Half of Americans said they would hesitate to see a counselor if a mental illness diagnosis were required.

If human service workers do not have the protection of privileged communication, they must decide, with the help of their agencies, what to do if they are subpoenaed to appear in court with certain information. Even though a subpoena looks impressive, even frightening, you need not automatically comply with it. You can challenge its validity or relevance, or the information it requests. You can contest it, with the help of a lawyer, by claiming privileged communication or other legal protections. Most agencies have legal consultation.

LIMITS ON PRIVILEGED COMMUNICATION There are certain legal limits on privileged communication. Privileged communication laws do not grant protection from reporting child abuse. All 50 states have passed some form of mandatory child abuse and neglect reporting law.

Some highly publicized cases of priests and church youth workers sexually abusing children have helped to create public demand for applying these mandatory reporting laws to priests. In Massachusetts, a youth worker at a church pleaded guilty to dozens of child sex abuse and pornography charges, and a former priest was accused of repeatedly molesting children during a 27-year career in the church. Two dozen of the priest's 77 alleged victims sued Cardinal Bernard F. Law for transferring the priest from parish to parish.

Some states have extended the reporting requirement to include reporting the abuse or neglect of people who are disabled or incompetent, particularly older adults who are dependent (Gothard, 1995).

Most states have passed laws mandating that police arrest a person who abuses another person and have also passed laws that mandate treatment programs for those convicted of domestic violence. Work with batterers poses dilemmas regarding confidentiality because counselors are required to report on the progress of the treatment to the court. Most treatment programs for batterers have a written contract explaining that because both the court and the agency want the victim to be safe, they will contact both the court and the victim to inform them of the batterer's progress in treatment. Participants are required to sign this contract before they begin treatment (Buttell, 1998).

Probation and parole officers and counselors who work with prisoners cannot assure their clients of confidentiality because they are required to report violations of probation, parole, or prison rules to the authorities. Clients should be informed immediately of the many limitations of confidentiality.

Workers in agencies receiving federal funds are prohibited by federal regulations from disclosing information about a client's substance use without the client's consent. But even the federal code of regulations allows disclosure of confidential information in cases involving such offenses as child abuse, homicide, rape, or aggravated assault (Landers, 1998).

PRIVILEGED COMMUNICATION AND INDIVIDUAL AND COMMUNITY RIGHTS Laws often require a professional to break confidentiality if there is a possibility of a crime being committed. In a landmark 1974 case, *Tarasoff v. California Board of Regents*, an 18-year-old high school senior told the school psychologist in a therapy session that he planned to kill a girl when she returned from a midsemester vacation with her parents. The psychologist agonized over the ethical dilemma she was in. Should she break the confidence of the therapy relationship? Was the murder threat genuine? Convinced that it was, she called the campus police and asked them to take the student into custody for possible commitment. The police took him in, but—convinced that he was rational—released him on his promise to stay away from the girl. The psychologist wondered if she should warn the young woman but, following her interpretation of the American Psychological Association Code of Ethics*, did not do so. The student carried out his threat eight weeks after he had confided in the psychologist. The parents of the dead girl sued the psychologist,

---

*APA's Principle 4.01 Maintaining Confidentiality: Psychologists have a primary obligation and take reasonable precautions to protect confidential information obtained through or stored in any medium, recognizing that the extent and limits of confidentiality may be regulated by law or established by institutional rules or professional or scientific relation. Principle 4.02 Discussing the Limits of Confidentiality: Psychologists discuss with persons (including, to the extent feasible, persons who are legally incapable of giving informed consent and their legal representatives) and organizations with whom they establish a scientific or professional relationship (1) the relevant limits of confidentiality and (2) the foreseeable uses of this information generated through their psychological activities (American Psychological Association, 2010, Ethical Principles of Psychologists and Code of Conduct, https://www.apa.org/ethics/code/index/aspx).

the school, the psychologist's supervisor, and the campus police. The parents charged them with negligence in failing to warn the girl of the student's threat. The court ruled that the psychologist was negligent in failing to warn the young woman.

There are no easy answers. If you know that you will not be able to keep everything you learn in an interview confidential, tell the client in advance. Discuss with the client what you must reveal. If you are a probation officer working with juvenile delinquents, you are legally required to tell the court if a juvenile has violated parole. If you are an assistance payments worker in the Department of Welfare, you are required to act if your client has broken welfare regulations. If your clients know these rules, they can make their own decisions about what to tell you.

Privacy

Privacy can be defined as the "right to be left alone." In many state constitutions, it is defined as an individual's right to decide how much to share private thoughts, feelings, and facts of one's personal life. A person has a right to privacy unless the private information centers on an immediate risk to the individual or the safety of others or the community. If you hear, for example, that a client intends to harm herself or others, you have a duty to break confidentiality and in effect impact their privacy in order to assure the individual receives assistance and that the community remains safe. With this exception in mind, before a human service worker gives information about a client to someone outside the relationship, the client must give informed consent. This means that the client understands *exactly what the consequences of the consent will be* before giving it and that *consent is given willingly*, without any coercion or fear of reprisal.

Most human service professional societies have codes of ethics that are intended to provide their members with guidance on how to protect clients' privacy. However, these codes are rarely revised often enough to keep up with changing circumstances. They are not always helpful guides to the legality of any one particular action. Here are two examples:

1. *Research project on drug use violates privacy.* In a junior high school in Pennsylvania, a consulting firm wanted to administer questionnaires for a study designed to identify potential drug users. The school psychologist, seeking guidance from the codes of ethics of the American Psychological Association and the National Association of School Psychologists, followed what she interpreted as their guidelines in requesting the consent of the research subjects. Some parents, however, sued the school to prohibit the research study, and the U.S. District Court (*Merriken v. Cressman*) agreed with them. The court concluded that even if the subject signed a release, it did not constitute *informed consent* because the students and parents were not given enough facts about the reasons for the test or the ways in which the test was going to be used to identify and counsel potential drug users. In balancing the right of an individual to privacy and the right of any entity, public or private, to invade that privacy for the sake of the public interest, the court struck the balance on the side of individual privacy, believing that "there is too much of a chance that the wrong people for the wrong reasons will be singled out and counseled in the wrong manner" (Bershoff, 1975, p. 367).

2. *Court says that state agencies giving records to each other violates privacy.* The question of whether state records in one bureaucracy should be made available to another without client consent was tested in Massachusetts in 1979, and the client won. Jose Torres, represented by the Juvenile Law Reform Project, was the plaintiff in a class action suit against the state's Department of Mental Health and Department of Education.

   The suit was brought in an attempt to obtain services for Torres and other adolescents with emotional disturbances. In preparing the state's defense, the attorney general obtained information about Torres that was in the state's Department of Social Services files. When Torres and his lawyer contested this action, the Massachusetts Supreme Judicial Court ruled that this disclosure of information about Torres amounted to "an unwarranted invasion of his privacy". The attorney general was wrong to assume that you give up your rights when you sue the state ("Privacy and State Records," 1984).

Since the shooting massacre at Virginia Tech in 2007, colleges have been on the alert to spot students who might pose a threat to other students. At Virginia Tech, a student gunman killed 32 people and committed suicide. There were several people who knew that the student had problems, but because of privacy and other issues, they didn't talk to others about it. Seung-Hui Cho, the Virginia Tech gunman, was ruled a danger to himself in a court hearing in 2005 that resulted from a roommate's call to police after Cho mentioned suicide in an email. He was held overnight at a mental health center off campus and was ordered into outpatient treatment. But he received no follow-up services, despite his sullen behavior and his violence-filled writings.

College officials had traditionally been reluctant to share information about students' mental health for fear of violating privacy laws. But since Virginia Tech, some colleges have initiated programs to deal with potential threats. At the University of Kentucky, a committee of deans, administrators, campus police, and mental health officials began meeting regularly to discuss a watch list of troubled students and decide whether they need professional help or should be dismissed from college. Patricia Terrell, vice president of student affairs, who created the panel, said, "If a student is a danger to himself or others, all the privacy concerns go out the window" (McMurray, 2008).

Virginia Tech has added a threat assessment team since the massacre there. Bryan Cloyd, then a Virginia Tech accounting professor whose daughter, Austin, was killed in the rampage, welcomed the efforts to monitor troubled students, but stressed he doesn't want to turn every campus into a "police state." "We can't afford to overreact," Cloyd said, but "we also can't afford to underreact" (McMurray, 2008).

Schools are also dealing with issues of student rights and invasion of privacy. There is a growing conflict between administrators' goals of running safe schools and students' legal rights. Civil libertarians say that with police officers routinely assigned to many schools, the legal boundaries between schools and law enforcement have blurred. Amy Reichbach, an attorney with the American Civil Liberties Union of Massachusetts, said, "There are a number of schools calling the police for things like arguments in the hallways (Touti, 2008)."

COMPUTER DATA AND PRIVACY   The federal Privacy Act of 1974 says that people have a right to control information that federal agencies collect about them. Personal information collected by federal agencies cannot be accessed or used beyond its intended purpose without an individual's consent. Yet, in their eagerness to find fraud, some welfare departments are routinely doing computer matches with bank records and records of other benefit programs, such as Social Security; unemployment compensation; searches of social media sites; and so forth without the consent of the recipients.

In Massachusetts, for example, the Department of Welfare in 1982 gave the Social Security numbers of all welfare recipients to 117 Massachusetts banks. When the department received the list of people whose assets were over the allowable limit, it immediately sent out benefit termination notices to all the people on the list, without first discussing it with the recipients. John Shattuck, the national legislative director of the American Civil Liberties Union, pointed out that this was a violation of the Fourth Amendment to the Constitution, which prohibits unreasonable searches and seizures. Computer matches of unrelated files have generally been "fishing expeditions" directed against large numbers of people on the chance that something will turn up (Shattuck, 1984). Further, Shattuck says, they violate the legal principle on which law is based in the United States, that *a person is innocent until proven guilty.* Many of the people on the list were in fact innocent of fraud.

CRIMINAL RECORDS AND PRIVACY   Gelbspan (1986) says that a seven-year study of FBI criminal history files gives us cause to worry about the use of records to invade our privacy. According to professor Kenneth Laudon, an expert in information systems at New York University who conducted the study, there is a persistently high error rate in criminal history records within a large unregulated and unaccountable system. Criminal history files have kept thousands of people from the following:

- Employment
- Housing
- Loans
- Insurance
- Entrance to college
- Becoming guardians or foster parents (Massachusetts Alliance to Reform CORI, 2007)

Private and government employers who screen job applicants increasingly use records. Because the records are often inaccurate, every year several million Americans are unjustly denied jobs. The most common flaw involves records that list arrests but fail to distinguish between people convicted of crimes and those who were never brought to trial or who were acquitted. The impact of this falls hardest on Black and Latino men and people living below the poverty line because they experience a disproportionate number of arrests that are later dismissed.

This issue is particularly important for human service workers. People can be denied employment, housing, or other civil rights if they have a criminal record, whether or not the record is accurate. They may work in an agency that will not hire anyone who has a criminal record. People who have been denied employment and other civil rights based on a criminal record include:

- A grandmother who has been caring for her grandchildren while their mother recovered from drug addiction, and who was discovered to have a criminal record. She had given the children excellent care, and the mother was not yet ready to take them back, but when the agency considered paying her as a foster parent, they discovered that she had a criminal record and removed the children. The grandmother's "crime" was possessing some marijuana in her youth.
- A Black daycare worker was stopped and arrested for "driving while black" (DWB) and taken to the police station. The police discovered that his car registration had expired. The charges were eventually dismissed, but it remained on his record, and he lost his job.
- Sandy, a woman who is now homeless, was arrested when her boyfriend used her apartment to sell drugs to an undercover police officer. The judge in her case ruled that she was not involved in the drug transaction and therefore dismissed her case. The arrest, however, remained in her criminal record and became the basis of her being denied housing and employment (*Rosie's Place Spring Newsletter*, 2007).

- Tina and her children lost their home to a fire. Due to their income and housing situation, Tina's family was eligible for public housing. However, when the housing authority performed a CORI (Criminal Offense Record Information) check, she was denied housing due to a 15-year-old arrest for public drinking, a misdemeanor. In the years since her arrest, Tina had taken charge of her life by becoming sober and eventually working two jobs, yet her CORI continued to haunt her (*Rosie's Place Spring Newsletter*, 2007).

The human service and social work professions are quite concerned about the criminal record checks because they sometimes prevent workers from doing good work. Schools of social work are debating how to handle these checks when they place students in a fieldwork agency.

Human service workers can join in efforts to reform the program. Some legal services agencies are helping people to correct their criminal records, and some states have reform movements to get their legislators to change the system.

CLIENT ACCESS TO RECORDS   In order to protect privacy, people need to know what has been said about them and to have the opportunity to correct misinformation. Clients of human service agencies sometimes ask to read their records. Some states have privacy laws regulating this. The Privacy Act of 1974 and the Family Educational Rights and Privacy Act (Buckley Amendment) are the two main federal privacy laws.

The Privacy Act of 1974 gives certain rights of privacy to clients of federal programs, particularly the right to read and copy one's own record and to insist that it be corrected or updated if its accuracy is questionable. The client must give consent for the record to be used for any purpose other than that for which it was specifically compiled. The heaviest public demands for information have been made of the CIA, FBI, and Department of the Treasury. Federal social service agencies, such as the Department of Veterans Affairs (VA), are also subject to the Privacy Act.

When a program is partially or totally federally funded, as with Medicaid and the Title XX social services programs, clients who have appealed an agency action and have a scheduled hearing have a right to examine their case files before the hearing. The Privacy Act provisions for client access and correction cover any federally administered social service program, such as the Supplemental Security Income program.

OPEN ACCESS TO RECORD KEEPING   Some professional organizations, including the National Association of Social Workers (NASW), favor open access to records, but there is debate about this within all the human service fields. Our own position is that an open-record policy encourages honesty between worker and client. That makes for a trusting relationship. We like this guideline that one author offers:

> Pretend that your client is sitting beside you reading everything as you write in his record. Consider consciously what should and should not be documented, and figure out the most effective way of wording what has to be said. Be aware of things that might upset the consumer, but that must be recorded, and be prepared to deal with your client's reaction. (Wilson, 1980, p. 197)

PRIVACY FOR WELFARE RECIPIENTS   When people have been stigmatized and treated in a demeaning manner, they are also likely to have their privacy invaded; all of these things erode peoples' pride. Welfare applications, for example, ask detailed personal questions to aid the decision of whether the applicant is eligible. The federal–state Parent Locator Service (PLS) of the

Child Support Enforcement Program has been especially prone to use "police state" tactics in its zeal to track down fathers who don't pay child support:

> In some states PLS paternity investigations have required women to complete questionnaires revealing all of their sexual relationships, including dates and places and the names of witnesses, and to take polygraph [lie detector] tests (Hayden & Novik, 1980, pp. 68–69).

The privacy of welfare recipients in Michigan was invaded by mandatory drug testing of all state welfare benefit applicants. Michigan led the way as one of the first states to institute a policy of mandatory drug testing of welfare recipients, although the 1996 Welfare Reform Act authorized (but did not require) states to impose mandatory drug testing as a prerequisite to receiving welfare assistance. This policy was opposed by physicians, social workers, public health workers, and substance abuse treatment professionals, who filed an *amicus curiae* brief with the U.S. Court of Appeals in January 2001. The brief argued that mandatory drug testing is a marked deterrent on the willingness of individuals, particularly pregnant and parenting women, to access essential medical and social services (Vallianatos, 2001).

The brief stated that this invasion of privacy was not justified by any special need to protect public safety. It identified other shortcomings of the policy:

- The use of drug testing is narrow in scope and fails to detect obstacles to employment and problematic family relationships.
- Drug testing does not detect child abuse or neglect.
- Suspicionless drug testing erodes the trust between welfare recipients and benefit workers—such as by promoting the fear that drug testing will result in removal of children from the home (Vallianatos, 2001a).

A federal appeals court upheld the Michigan program in 2002, but in 2003, the ACLU reached a settlement with the Family Independence Agency of Michigan which states that the FIA can now require drug testing of welfare recipients only where there is a reasonable suspicion that the recipient is using drugs (American Civil Liberties Union, 2003).

In 2009, some Republicans in the Michigan state legislature put forward a proposal to implement random drug testing for those who receive food and cash assistance, make college students who apply for a card show proof they can't be claimed as someone's dependent, and add photo identification to the cards. Democratic Rep. Robert Dean said those bills are "partly election-year posturing that sounds good to voters," and some people cautioned that those stiffer requirements could hurt those in need of help (Scott, 2010).

As of 2017, 15 states required drug testing in order to qualify for public assistance.

PRIVACY IN A TIME OF WAR   Shortly after the terrorist attack of September 11, 2001, the Justice Department submitted to Congress a law dubbed the "USA PATRIOT Act," an acronym for "Uniting and Strengthening America by Providing Appropriate Tools Required to Intercept and Obstruct Terrorism." It was rushed through Congress in several days, no hearings were held, and it went largely unread. The PATRIOT Act contains provisions that increase the ability of federal officers of the executive branch to enter and search a person's house; to survey private medical records, business records, library records, and educational records; and to monitor telephone, email, and Internet use. It struck most heavily against noncitizens. It permitted the incarceration of noncitizens for seven days without charge, and for six-month periods indefinitely without access to counsel if the attorney general determined release would endanger either the country or individual persons. Many argued that the PATRIOT Act imperiled democracy by invading people's privacy and promoting governmental secrecy.

In 2007, a federal judge in Oregon ruled that crucial parts of the PATRIOT Act were not constitutional, because they allowed federal surveillance and searches of Americans without demonstrating probable cause. Shortly after that, however, President Obama asked to "make a slight change in a law to make clear that we have the right to see the names of anyone's e-mail correspondence and their Web browsing history without the messy complication of asking a judge for permission." A *New York Times* editorial said, "Yet the change he asked for was not slight, but would allow huge numbers of electronic communications to be examined with no judicial oversight" (*New York Times*, 2010). In 2011, President Obama signed a four-year extension of the act, and on June 2, 2015, President Obama signed the USA Freedom Act, which restored key provisions of the PATRIOT Act, which had expired the day before.

From a human services perspective, the sweeping changes to privacy represented by the USA PATRIOT Act and the USA Freedom Act have impacted those who work with immigrant and refugee populations that are now often referred to as New Americans. Ahmadi (2011), for example, argues that 9/11 and the PATRIOT Act have played a central role in anti-Muslim feelings as well as in a further reduction of Muslims' civil rights here in the United States.

Due Process

Due process means that, under the Fifth and Fourteenth Amendments to the U.S. Constitution, individuals are entitled to "due process of law"—including notice of the charge, an open trial, and right to counsel—before they can be deprived by the government of life, liberty, or property. In recent years, due-process protection has been extended to include some social agency practices. This was done to curb "the broad discretion available to officials and employees of public agencies and institutions and the arbitrary or illegal acts that have sometimes resulted" (Dickson, 1976, p. 274).

If someone does something to you that you think is unfair, you naturally want to find out why, give your side, and rectify the wrong. You may want others to support you—perhaps a lawyer. Clients of human service agencies want the same. They often disagree with agency policy and workers' actions. They need some protection against arbitrary decisions.

FULL AND PARTIAL DUE PROCESS   There can be either full or partial due-process procedures. In situations in which a person might be seriously damaged by a decision, full due-process proceedings are usually allowed. These include representation by a lawyer, the right to present evidence and witnesses, the right to cross-examine witnesses, the right to a written statement of findings, and the right to a trial by judge and/or jury.

When there is less potential harm to an individual, or when a full-blown judicial hearing would be costly, laws provide partial due process. Generally, they grant an administrative hearing and notice of charges, and perhaps assistance in preparing and presenting the case (Dickson, 1976).

Most human service organizations give partial due process in a dispute with a client. Clients generally have a right to appeal an agency decision, and the agency holds an administrative hearing before an impartial examiner. Agencies sometimes allow legal assistance or an advocate from another human service organization or an advocacy support group, or even a well-informed friend.

DUE PROCESS IN HUMAN SERVICE ORGANIZATIONS Clients of most human service organizations had few legal rights to appeal an agency decision before 1970. In that year, the U.S. Supreme Court decided, in *Goldberg v. Kelly*, that the due-process amendments of the Constitution applied to welfare hearings. Eventually the same principles were applied to schools; prisons; parole proceedings; Title XX (federally financed) social services; mental hospitals; and institutions for people with intellectual disabilities, severe and persistent mental illness, physical disabilities, minors with a criminal history, and other service consumers.

Soon after the *Goldberg* ruling, there was a sharp rise in administrative hearings. Many people who did not agree with this expansion of entitlements began to attack those procedures, saying they were going too far. There were demands for change, and certain due-process procedures were made less stringent. Welfare hearings were made more informal, and in the 1976 case *Mathews v. Eldridge*, the Supreme Court allowed disability benefits to be cut off before a hearing, although the *Goldberg v. Kelly* decision had stipulated that a hearing be held before adverse action was taken.

The Personal Responsibility and Work Opportunity Reconciliation Act of 1996, which began the Temporary Assistance to Needy Families (TANF) program, ended entitlement to welfare, and clients no longer had the due-process rights that they had when it was an entitlement. Welfare departments often use arbitrary means of denying TANF to clients, and clients often had no recourse to an appeal process. A number of states have "no entitlement" language in their TANF statutes. However, in 1999 a Colorado state court ruled that due process applies to TANF benefits despite the "no entitlement" language. The court challenged sanction notices as inadequate and in violation of federal and state due-process requirements. The court ruled that the plaintiffs have a property interest in which due process applies because, under the state's welfare program, benefits must be provided to those who meet the state's requirements, and does not allow unfettered agency discretion in determining who gets benefits (National Center for Law and Economic Justice, 2010).

In the Supplemental Security Income and Social Security Disability Insurance programs, the Social Security Administration often denies that a person is disabled. In a large number of such cases, an administrative law judge grants disability benefits to clients who appeal (Heller, 1981).

Although children gained some due-process rights in the *Gault* case, in which the Supreme Court determined in 1967 that constitutional due process rights apply to children as well as adults (Lahey, 2017), they do not have the right to refuse institutionalization against their parents' wishes. The Supreme Court decided in the 1979 case *Parham v. J. L. and J. R.* that parents have the right to institutionalize their children without the children's consent. Justice Brennan, one of three dissenters, argued, "It is a blind assumption that parents act in their child's best interests when making commitment decisions" (Frank, 1980, p. 379). Should parents be given full control over their children? Until what age? Under what circumstances?

HELPING CLIENTS GET THEIR LEGAL RIGHTS

During the 1960s and early 1970s, clients' rights were greatly expanded through the organizing of grassroots groups, including the following:

- The Welfare Rights Organization
- The Mental Patients' Liberation Front
- Feminist health collectives
- Children's rights advocates

Although the rights they gained still don't necessarily fulfill all their needs, clients are slightly less powerless. In recent years, however, the government has been whittling down those gains. Federal legislation has cut out or weakened client-participation provisions that gave social service consumers a way to monitor and change programs that affected them.

Title I of the Elementary and Secondary Education Act, which provides enriched resources for educationally disadvantaged children, used to give parents a share in the schools' decision making. But recent legislation has weakened their role and only gives them a watered-down advisory role. Title XX of the Social Security Act, which provides for social services, has also weakened its consumer-participation provisions. Class action suits, which represent an entire class of clients rather than just one individual, have been severely curtailed.

Due process rights were significantly eroded in 1996 by both the Immigration Reform and Control Act and the Personal Responsibility Act. Immigrants who are deported or imprisoned have no right of appeal, and recipients of TANF are not guaranteed a right of appeal against unfavorable decisions by the federal law, although states may still allow it.

The Individuals with Disabilities Education Act (IDEA) also includes due process rights for parents to address disputes when it comes to the services provided to their children through the Individualized Educational Program, or IEP. Due process under the act provides a formal way for parents and guardians to address complaints about the special education plan for their child. The due process protections under the IDEA are specific to the right of special education students and do not apply to students involved in general education. As a part of the process, parents or guardians have the right to a formal hearing in front of an impartial hearing officer, during which evidence and testimony may be presented. And while many disagreements are resolved informally, it's important to understand that any clients that you have with special education needs have this formal due process available to them.

Strategies

Human service workers, on the front lines with clients, must devise ever more ingenious strategies to help them secure their rights. Following are descriptions of some of these strategies:

1. *Human service workers need to be fully informed about their clients' legal rights, and they need to clearly inform their clients.*   Reciting clients' rights at the beginning of your working relationship is rarely enough. Clients are under stress when applying for benefits or services. They might not hear or understand your full meaning. They frequently need to be told about their rights again, in other contexts and with fresh emphasis.

   Some advocacy groups publish booklets that spell out the rights of their constituents in clear, easy-to-understand language. If none exists in your area, consider helping your clients to write one.*

   Legal services groups sometimes publish manuals, and welfare rights activists in several states are publishing newspapers to inform people of their rights. There are also

*Survivors, Inc. (http://www.survivorsinc.org), a welfare rights group in Massachusetts, publishes a newspaper that includes a section called "Survival Tips," which gives information about benefits and rights.

nationwide advocacy groups that publish useful information about legislation and people's rights.*

2. *Even if you are convinced that you are correct in denying a particular benefit, you must remember that the client has the right to appeal a worker's decision.* A conscientious worker reminds the client of that right. Perhaps new evidence will come to light. Perhaps you made a mistake. An appeal is an opportunity to make sure a decision has been fair. If another agency has denied benefits to the client, the primary worker might investigate that denial, urging the client to appeal if there is a shadow of a doubt about the decision. The client may need help from a lawyer or an advocate to prepare or pursue the appeal. An updated resource file of legal services, advocates, and consumer groups is invaluable.

3. *The worker should encourage clients to learn as much as they can about their rights.* There are never enough low-cost legal services, so people will often need to defend themselves. Find out if there is a relevant self-help group that your clients can join. Welfare recipients, people with mental illnesses, adoptees, birth parents, adoptive families, divorced partners, survivors of domestic violence, people who are disabled, skilled nursing facility residents, prisoners, families and friends of prisoners, and many others have advocacy groups that go to bat for clients.

4. *Human service workers can help in due-process hearings by interviewing participants, collecting evidence, and helping in the preparation of cases.* They also serve as **expert witnesses**, testifying in court on the basis of their specialized knowledge or experience in the field. If, for example, there is a question about whether a specific patient can manage his life outside the hospital, a worker in a community residence for people with mental illness could compare that patient with the residents she works with, establishing the likelihood of success or failure.

5. *Welfare rights advocates often advise welfare recipients to take someone with them to all their interviews at the welfare office.* A welfare recipient should take along a friend or advocate to lend support and to ensure fair treatment by the welfare worker.

6. *Workers who believe that an agency practice is harmful to a client must decide whether to challenge the agency or "go along to get along."* Often a professional organization will support the worker in challenging the agency. For example, the NASW gave a Whistleblowers Award and some legal assistance to a social worker who sued the U.S. Public Health Service (PHS). The worker, Donald Soeken, was forced to retire from PHS due to what he described as substantial animosity from his supervisors after he testified on behalf of a patient's family that the patient at St. Elizabeth Hospital was not treated in a timely fashion after the diagnosis of cancer ("Two Cases Given Legal Aid Grants," 2001).

---

*In the area of children's services, the Children's Defense Fund (https://www.childrensdefense.org) publishes *CDF Reports*. The Gray Panthers (http://www.graypanthersnyc.org/) have been progressive activists in the field of aging and social justice since the 1960s. (This is actually an intergenerational organization.) The Older Women's League (OWL—http://www.owlsf.org) focuses on social justice issues affecting older women. Food Research and Action Center (http://www.frac.org) publishes information on food programs, including food stamps and school breakfast and lunch programs. The American Civil Liberties Union (ACLU—https://www.aclu.org) defends people and organizations against various kinds of injustice. The National Center for Law and Economic Justice (https://www.nclej.org—formerly the Welfare Law Center) focuses on economic justice for low-income families. Legal Momentum (https://www.legal-momentum.org) is sponsored by the Women's Legal Defense and Education Fund. They focus on women's poverty, immigrant women's rights, reproductive rights, the social safety net, and other women's issues.

Source: Courtesy of Boston Cares

Human service workers in a training session about legal issues and agency regulations

In an innovative program called the Medical–Legal Partnership, lawyers have teamed up with doctors to help solve clients' problems. Dr. Barry Zuckerman, head of Boston Medical Center's pediatric department, started the program in 1993. It is now a national phenomenon, used in nearly 300 hospitals and clinics, with 190 participating law firms and 52 law schools in 41 states. The program first started in pediatrics, but it has expanded into cancer care and geriatrics, areas that involve extremely vulnerable patients.

For instance, cancer patients are legally entitled to less strenuous jobs when they are receiving and recuperating from treatment, but many are still forced to choose between their workday and their appointment for radiation. Older people may be subject to abuse in nursing homes or by family members (Weintraub, 2010).

The lawyers help in various ways. For example, lawyers connected to a hospital or clinic might write a letter encouraging a landlord to replace moldy carpeting that's triggering asthma attacks, assist families in getting food stamps and other government benefits, and obtain power of attorney for the parents of a child with severe disabilities who is turning 18. Dr. Peter Loewinthan Binah, a pediatrician at Dorchester House (a community center), said he used to send letters to landlords or a school district on behalf of patients. But when the law firm of Ropes & Gray sends out a letter, it gets more attention. He said, "If you're some landlord who isn't fixing up your apartment and get a letter from Ropes & Gray stationery, you know that one of the major law firms in Boston is going to stick it to you if you don't clean up" (Weintraub, 2010, p. B6).

SOME CURRENT LEGAL ISSUES

There are some hotly contested issues in the human services that, although they do not apply equally to all workers, have wide-ranging implications and should be thought about. These include the **right to treatment**, the right to treatment or education in the **least restrictive setting**, and the **right to refuse treatment**.

Right to Adequate Treatment

The patients' rights movement of the 1960s and 1970s asserted that psychiatric hospitals and institutions for people with disabilities were more like prisons than hospitals. Patients, ex-patients, and their advocates turned to the courts for relief. The first "right to treatment" case, *Wyatt v. Stickney*, was tried in Alabama in 1971. The court ordered the state social service officials to provide a specified quality of treatment for institutionalized people with disabilities. The court argued that when a person is involuntarily committed without the same type of due process given even to criminals, that person has a *constitutional right to receive adequate treatment*.

A 1974 Florida decision, *Donaldson v. O'Connor*, asserted that if a person were dangerous, she could be committed involuntarily. But the state had a responsibility to give that person adequate treatment. Some other states followed suit, prohibiting involuntary commitment to a psychiatric institution unless the person is a clear danger to self or others.

On June 18, 1982, the U.S. Supreme Court made a decision in *Youngberg v. Romeo* that established, for the first time, constitutional rights for people committed to institutions for people with disabilities. It guaranteed a minimum level of training and development (Barbash, 1982).

The impact of these as well as other court decisions has helped to drive the way that institutions as well as state and federal policy makers have worked to address the clinical and mental health needs of individuals who find themselves held against their will any number of county, state, or federally run facilities. Some argue though that our service system hasn't done enough to support the individual's right to treatment. Seigafo (2017) for example argues that the high level of recidivism among the more than 2 million men and women within our country's prison system is due largely to the lack of effective and appropriate rehabilitative services within the institutions.

The idea that people have the right to adequate treatment has also expanded to include thinking about how behavioral health services are made available to the general population through the passing of the Mental Health Parity Act (MHPA) by the federal government in 1996. The law was strengthened in 2008 through the passage of the Paul Wellstone and Pete Domenici Mental Health Parity and Addiction Equity Act of 2008 (MHPAEA) and then again when the Affordable Care Act was passed in 2010 (The Center for Consumer Information & Insurance Oversight, ND). Simply stated, the Mental Health Parity Act prohibits insurance providers from providing less favourable behavioral health and substance use disorder benefits than their plan's medical health coverage. And while some insurance plans have attempted to appeal these requirements, the courts continue to uphold the law (Linker, 2018).

When clients and parents or guardians know their rights, they can help to ensure that organizations and institutions take steps to adequately address concerning practices. When clients exercise their rights, they will often succeed in making the agency more responsive, so they don't have to go to court. When organizations are not responsive, they know that clients, parents, and guardians have a legal basis for a lawsuit if they chose that route. Legal suits that establish precedents through court rulings make it easier for people to address their concerns and bring about change without having to resort to using the courts. In the case of state agencies, the initiation of a lawsuit will often result in their coming to an agreement with the plaintiffs. This is called a consent decree. A consent decree is a document that the court approves outlining the agreed-upon changes in practice.

Right to Treatment in the Least Restrictive Setting

The right to be treated in the least restrictive setting means that the conditions should allow the most possible freedom. Implicit in the right to treatment is the constitutional issue of whether the state has the right to *force* treatment on people. The Fifth and Fourteenth Amendments to the Constitution specify that a citizen's liberty shall not be deprived except in accord with due process of law. When the state decides to provide a service for a particular group of citizens who have emotional, intellectual, educational, mobility, or psychological needs, it must do so in a manner that restricts their basic liberties as little as possible.

In deciding what treatment to use, an agency and its workers must consider which treatment will do the least to restrict the client's full growth. Courts have applied this concept to residential mental health as well as facilities for individuals with intellectual disabilities, juvenile justice institutions, and educational facilities in accordance with the Individuals with Disabilities Education Act (IDEA). Perhaps you've sat next to a pupil with a learning disability or someone who was other-abled. It is this act that gave the student the right to occupy that seat.

IDEA requires that all children be served in the least restrictive environment possible and that whenever possible they should be mainstreamed into regular educational and classroom settings. **Mainstreaming** means that schools must make every effort to put special-needs students in mainstreamed classroom settings. Many hard-fought battles have raged between parents and their advocates and school systems, arguing about the definition of "the best setting" for a particular child. Teachers who aren't used to teaching children with disabilities have had to develop new skills. States and school systems have spent a great deal of money developing the facilities and expertise to incorporate children with diverse needs into public schools.

The Supreme Court ruled in 1999, in what is called the "*Olmstead* decision," that states may be violating the Americans with Disabilities Act if they provide care to people with disabilities in an institutional setting when those individuals could be appropriately served in a home or community-based setting. This decision was made in regard to two women with developmental disabilities and mental illnesses who were residents of a psychiatric hospital, but it has been interpreted to extend also to people with physical disabilities, to those in skilled nursing homes and assisted living and other institutional settings in addition to psychiatric hospitals, and to those who live in the community and are at risk for institutionalization (General Accounting Office, 2001).

Right to Refuse Treatment

Efforts to force treatment on clients are problematic. Can the state insist on counseling as a condition for obtaining a divorce or retaining custody of a child, even though counseling requires trust and a readiness to change? There will be many court cases before this issue is resolved—if it ever is.

Individuals with Severe and Persistent Mental Illness (SPMI) have challenged the states' right to commit them to an institution and employ psychosurgery, shock therapy, aversion therapy, seclusion, restraints, drug therapy, or behavioral modifications that withhold food and privileges. Courts consider whether the patient was legally competent to be involved in a treatment decision, and if so, whether the institution obtained the patient's informed consent. Courts also consider whether the treatment is experimental or traditional, and how intrusive and potentially dangerous it is. Psychosurgery, aversion therapy, and electroshock therapy, for example, are considered much riskier than other behavioral strategies.

The Importance of Written Plans

Written documentation of a treatment plan is often required. The Individuals with Disabilities Education Act is very specific about such plans. Also, the Developmental Disabilities and Rights Act requires program plans for institutions and for individuals in community programs that receive federal funds. Whether or not the law requires a written plan it is helpful to have one because it ensures continuity of service, and research has shown that fidelity to the identified plan helps to ensure more successful outcomes (Cook, Mayer, Wright, Kraemer, Wallace, Dart, Collins, & Restori, 2012). This is particularly true given the importance of documentation as outlined in Chapter 9 of this text, on interviewing.

Summary

1. Many human service workers are unaware of their legal obligations. Human service training programs have often omitted such issues or have treated them superficially.

2. Federal laws apply equally to all states. Other laws vary from one state to another. Because laws change frequently, a human service worker needs to keep up to date on changes.

3. Laws are a resource; many human service programs were created by laws. In order to help clients obtain their entitlements, workers need to understand these laws.

4. After laws have been passed, a government agency draws up the regulations, which are the bureaucratic procedures that put the law into practice.

5. Some regulations are so restrictive that they make life very difficult for clients.

6. Some programs are governed by several government jurisdictions, and clients often get a bureaucratic runaround.

7. Some regulations are worded ambiguously, either intentionally or because bureaucrats are unable to write clear English. If clients do not understand their rights, they are not likely to claim the rights.

8. People enmeshed in the legal system are often stigmatized. Human service workers need to combat this stigma.

9. There are some laws that every worker needs to know. These include laws concerning confidentiality, privileged communication, privacy, and due process.

10. In order to protect privacy, clients need to know what is said about them in records so they can correct the records if they want to.

11. Agencies comply with privacy laws to varying degrees. Those that are covered by federal privacy laws are more likely to allow open access to records, but they do not always comply with the law or inform clients of their right to read their records.

12. Open access to records causes workers to be more careful in their recording. There are pros and cons to an open-access policy. The authors favor open access.

13. Individuals receiving public assistance have few legal guarantees of privacy. The Parent Locator Service is an example of a particularly intrusive strategy.

14. Privileged communication protects the confidences of the client–worker relationship in some cases, but it is not complete protection, nor is it extended to all professions in all states. The privilege belongs to the client, not to the worker.

15. The USA PATRIOT Act, passed shortly after 9/11, thought by many to imperil democracy by invading people's privacy and promoting

governmental secrecy, continues today as the USA Freedom Act.

16. Due process assures a client the right to disagree with a worker's decision. Most clients of human service agencies are granted only partial due-process procedures.

17. Human service workers should help clients appeal adverse decisions, which might be reversed on appeal.

18. Federal legislation is weakening or eliminating provisions that allow clients decision-making power in federal programs; therefore, self-help advocacy groups are increasingly important.

19. Workers should learn about clients' legal rights and inform clients about them.

20. Current legal issues that human service workers should be aware of include the right to obtain adequate treatment, the right to treatment or education in the least restrictive setting, and the right to refuse treatment.

21. Written plans are often required by law, as is client involvement in writing them.

22. Criminal records frequently contain errors that make it impossible for people to get jobs and housing.

Discussion Questions

1. Should parents be given full control over their children? If so, until what age? Under what circumstances?

2. What are the pros and cons of allowing clients to read their own records?

3. The state makes many intrusions into the privacy of welfare recipients but very few into the lives of children and their parents who receive Social Security. Why do you think this is? Do you think the state has the right to investigate the personal behavior of welfare recipients?

4. People with criminal records can be kept out of public housing and many kinds of jobs. They can also be prevented from voting. What do you think of this?

5. Do you agree that human service workers should be advocates for their clients' rights? What steps will you take to become an advocate for your clients?

Web Resources for Further Study

National Women's Law Center

https://nwlc.org

Legal Momentum

http://www.legalmomentum.org

Center for Law and Social Policy (CLASP)

https://www.clasp.org

Medical–Legal Partnership

https://medical-legalpartnership.org/

National Center for Law and Economic Justice

https://nclej.org

Find Law for the Public

https://consumer.pub.findlaw.com

MyLab Helping Professions for Introduction to Human Services

In the Topic 11 Assignments: Human Services Values and Attitudes, start with Application Exercise 11.1: The Least Intrusive and Least Restrictive Environments and Credentialing Quiz 11.1: The Least Intrusive and Least Restrictive Environments.

Then, in the Topic 9 Assignments: Interpersonal Communication, try Application Exercise 9.1: Clarifying Expectations.

Avoiding Burnout

14

Source: Elias Kordelakos/Shutterstock

Learning Outcomes

- Students will develop knowledge about what causes burnout and the impact of burnout.
- Students will successfully compare and contrast strategies to manage the phenomenon of burnout.
- Students will develop practical approaches to prevent burnout.
- Students will successfully analyze which strategies for managing burnout work best for their personal needs and interests.

The word *crispy* may not refer to crackers when human service workers use it; it may describe a worker who is experiencing stress and fatigue due to the demands of their work in the helping profession. Some have come to call this phenomenon *burnout*. One of the authors first heard the term *crispy* at a college human service career day:

> I had invited two of my former students to talk about their human service jobs. The first, Kathie, was all fired up and spoke energetically about her work in child protection and foster care. Sure, she said, her job had its hard moments, but that did not stop her from doing a good job or figuring out ways to solve the problems.

The second speaker, Brian, whom I remembered as a bright and enthusiastic student, talked in a depressed monotone about the problems of his job that he felt were insurmountable. He droned on about his work as a probation officer in a juvenile court, complaining about large caseloads, ungrateful and manipulative people, inadequate resources, coworkers who goofed off, other agencies that refused referrals, insensitive judges, and mountains of paperwork.

After the speeches were over, I commented to Kathie about Brian's lack of enthusiasm. Kathie replied, "He's not just burnt out, he's crispy—for sure!"

Human service work draws on our deepest impulses to form important relationships and on our curiosity about what makes us think, feel, and act the way we do. It gives us a chance to laugh and play with people, to solve problems with them, to cry and grieve with them, to share the joy of their successes, to share their anger at injustice, and to work with them to change unjust systems. What job can be more important than that?

In fact, there is evidence that by helping others, people improve their own mental health, their physical well-being, and even their longevity. A University of Michigan study that followed 423 older couples for five years found that the subjects who reported helping others—even if it was just giving emotional support to a spouse—were only about half as likely to die within those five years as those who did not. Another study of 2,000 Presbyterians found that improved mental health seemed to be more closely linked to giving help than to receiving it. A study of older people who volunteered in the Experience Corps to mentor elementary school pupils found that tutoring led to measurable benefits for the volunteers, who showed that they were less sedentary, more physically active, and healthier than other adults of similar age and demographics who did not engage in helping behavior (Associated Press, 2010).

Similar benefits were seen in another study where individuals who had suffered a cardiovascular disease (CVD) event were less likely to suffer a second CVD event when they were involved in helping behavior within their community. Interestingly, the benefits of this helping behavior appeared to diminish when the demands of the helping crossed a particular threshold of demand on the individual's time (Heisler, Choi, Piette, Rosland, Langa, & Brown, 2013). This finding is consistent with the work of Goldberg (2003), who found that constant or exhausting demands actually reverse the positive effects of altruistic behavior.

Any work is exciting only as long as we are growing in it—expanding our self-awareness, learning more about the job, feeling good about our ability to do it, gaining more power over the conditions of work, and getting some measure of success from it. In order to grow, we need the following supports from our environment:

- Working conditions that make it possible to do our best
- Support and respect from our peers and supervisors
- Freedom from unconstructive criticism and control
- Ability to share in decision making with a true sense that we have a voice at the table
- Some stability

It is the same with flowers: They grow luxuriously only when they have the right conditions of sun, soil, and water; if those conditions are lacking, they wilt and die. Continual change in the human service field brings excitement and adventure as well as tension. When the change is too rapid or when it brings a political climate that is unsympathetic, it is hard for workers to do their best work.

BURNOUT

The term *burnout* and the slang terms for its varying degrees of intensity have been coined to describe the mood that human service workers sink into when they have lost their spark. The concept has—to coin a pun—caught fire. Newspapers print articles about it, workshops and conferences are held on it, teachers' unions devote entire issues of their professional journals to it, books are written about it, and there are now "burnout experts." On October 8, 2018, there were about 115,000,000 references for "burnout" returned in .33 seconds on Google.

Burnout has been described and discussed now for more than 35 years. The phenomenon has caught the interest of many human service practitioners, given the impact that this has on the workforce needs within the field. We believe that Maslach, Leiter, and Jackson (2012) provide an important conceptual frame for understanding exactly what burnout is and the steps that one can take to avoid or reverse this phenomenon. In their work, they write about burnout as a fundamental relationship between the individual and her job that exits along a continuum. Burnout lives at one end of the continuum while engagement lives at the other. Burnout is manifested by exhaustion, cynicism, and inefficacy, while engagement is found to be characterized by energy, involvement, and efficacy. Maslach, Leiter, and Jackson believe that the most valuable interventions to address burnout are those that help to move the individual from burnout to engagement. As a result, interventions that help to build excitement, a sense of active participation in the workplace, and successful mastery over duties with positive results ultimately help to prevent or reverse the phenomenon of burnout. It's helpful to keep the idea of this continuum in mind as you read through this chapter. As you'll see, the strategies we provide are designed to help you understand the phenomenon of burnout as well as avoid or in some cases recover from its impact.

Two terms that are related to and sometimes used interchangeably with burnout are *vicarious traumatization* and *compassion fatigue* (Halevi & Idisis, 2018). Vicarious traumatization is specific to trauma, and results from empathic engagement with traumatized clients and their reports of traumatic experiences. A worker may experience both vicarious traumatization and burnout, and each has its own remedies. *Compassion fatigue*, also known as a *secondary traumatic stress disorder*, is a term that refers to a gradual lessening of compassion over time. It is common among victims of trauma and individuals who work directly with victims of trauma. We explore this in greater detail when this chapter reviews the impact that working with clients can have on the human service worker (Borenstein, 2018).

Symptoms of Burnout

As cited in the NEA Reporter (1979), Grey examined stress in teachers and identifies five overall symptoms of stress that are common and these have stood the test of time:

- Difficulty in sleeping
- Irritability
- Upset stomach
- Headaches
- Shortness of breath

Burnout may lead human service workers to stop caring about the clients they work with, perhaps to sneer at them, laugh at them, label them, or treat them in derogatory ways. It causes workers to exaggerate differences between clients and themselves, seeing clients as "less good, less capable, and more blameworthy than themselves" (Maslach, 1978, p. 113).

Some workers escape their job by drinking or taking drugs, or staying away from work—calling in sick or pretending to be at work when they are not (Griner, 2013). In place of enthusiasm, a sense of futility sets in. Some workers develop a callousness and cynicism to protect them from feeling anything. Behind this callousness may be an idealist who became overwhelmed by the job and stopped caring. Starting out with empathy for victims, the worker ends up being a victim blamer who is both alienated and disengaged from the very reason he chose this important profession. Ultimately, burnout is associated with poorer quality services and client safety (Johnson, Hall, Berzins, Baker, Melling, & Thompson, 2018).

One woman who worked at a shelter for court ordered youth watched this process happen in herself. She said that when she first started working at the shelter as a counselor, she was fired up with enthusiasm about helping the young people. But the team always seemed short-staffed, and the challenging behaviors presented by the youth created a great deal of stress. It wasn't long before she began to have trouble sleeping, consistently waking with concerns about her job and the experiences she'd had during the previous shift. In time she began to resent the young people for their demanding and challenging behavior. She started to call in instead of working her shift as well as to procrastinate while at work. She never in her life dreamed that she would be feeling this way when all she wanted was to become a helping professional.

CAUSES OF BURNOUT

Burnout impacts the individual helper's ability to work effectively and sometime to even remain within their chosen profession. Described by Maslach, Leiter, & Jackson, (2012), three empirically derived factors related to burnout, identified as emotional exhaustion (EE), depersonalization (DP), and reduced personal accomplishment (PA) adversely impact the energy required for the individual within the profession to fulfill their role of helping others.

There are numerous factors that have been identified which contribute to the phenomenon of burnout. For example, many human service professionals find themselves with an ever-increasing workload. Staffing shortages can contribute to growing stress, which in turn contributes emotional exhaustion. In some instances, the risk for burnout is heightened through the presence of inadequate leadership within a given organization or a lack of training necessary for the human service professional to fully execute their responsibilities (Willard-Grace, Hessler, Rogers, Dubé, Bodenheimer, & Grumbach, 2014).

Working to help others can be both rewarding as well as challenging work. Sometimes supporting people with significant problems can cause the helper to experience emotional fatigue. At other times human service workers finds themselves in potentially dangerous situations or working with individuals who are at serious risk of harming themselves (Letvak & Buck, 2008). Burnout can affect anyone in any kind of work and with any status. One of the earliest researchers on it, Christina Maslach, says that today hedge fund managers are as likely to be burned out as any do-gooders: "In 21st-century New York, the 60-hour week is considered normal. In some professions, it's a status symbol. But burnout, for the most part, is considered a sign of weakness, a career killer" (Senior, 2007). While it may be true that anyone can experience burnout, it's important to explore the nature of burnout within the human service field. By doing so human service professionals can prepare themselves to both avoid as well as address the adverse impact of burnout.

Source: Randy Glasbergen/Glasbergen Cartoons

**"I'd like to schedule a time management seminar on
my calendar...as soon as I find time to buy a calendar. "**

Psychological Conflicts

The powerful emotional stress and thorny problems that human service workers deal with daily
often touch deep responsive chords in them: A worker who was neglected as a child may impute
neglect when parents are merely casual in their parenting style; one whose parents were extremely
strict may see with fury clients they perceive as overdemanding parents. Many beginning workers are still dealing with their own issues of dependence and independence from family, mate,
religion, and cultural group. Often it is difficult for them to sort out where their own struggles end
and those of their clients begin. For young workers, identification with the problems of teenagers
or young adults can easily cross the line into **overidentification**.

Sometimes the goals of the work itself cause ambivalence and anxiety, even when the
worker basically agrees with the agency's mission. You can feel strongly about the importance of
protecting children from abuse, but accusing parents of perpetrating that abuse, and even removing
children from their homes, can cause intense anxiety.

Conflicting Social Values

Combined with these very personal stresses are the even more serious strains induced by the
ambivalent values of our social system, which gives only grudging support to universal social
services. Public assistance workers are in the front line of this conflict. They are charged with
determining benefits for needy individuals, having to make decisions about who will receive
benefits as well as who won't. They may find themselves working to assist individuals whose
values are different from their own. Similarly, they are charged with following a set of guidelines
that reflect the current funding and political realities of their state's welfare laws. This means that
they sometimes have to cut someone off from assistance despite feeling a great deal of empathy
for the individual and his circumstances.

In a like way, other human service workers are called upon to engage in work activities that
highlight the values they hold and how they differ from the values of the system that has been
built to serve their clients. In our own experience, restrictions on the length and amount of service

provided to clients based on the advent of managed care within the human service and mental health fields have meant having to restrict service for deserving individuals. Circumstances such as these can build a level of ongoing stress for the individual worker.

The Bind of the Double Message

The human service profession is built on a **humanitarian ethos**, but not everyone in our society fully subscribes to it. And therein lies the conflict. Communities rarely provide the full resources of money, time, and caring to allow the human service worker to do the kind of job that needs to be done. One writer says that the structure of the modern welfare state has converted the ideal of service into cynicism or self-serving behavior **careerism** (building your career at the expense of other values). The impact of this is that some professionals find themselves alienated from their work. Research has shown that alienation is positively correlated with increased careerism (Chiaburu, Diaz, & De Vos, 2013). This in turn makes it less likely that agencies will be able to effectively maintain a workforce that is mission driven and committed first and foremost to meeting the needs of the people they are there to serve. Instead, there is a danger that heightened careerism will result in the organization's failure to achieve its intended purpose.

Workers face many mixed messages in this country. They are continually in conflict about whether to help clients summon their energies for change or to make the clients more obedient in order to fit better into the agency's way of "helping." They may want to advocate for their clients to get more services, but the agency, with an eye on the budget, probably wants to limit services. Workers may want to work with clients as allies in shaping the policies and practices of the agency, but the agency does not encourage input from clients or alliances between workers and clients. Although the agency proclaims its desire to "help," that help may merely mean manipulation. All of these contradictions mirror the ambivalence society has about its people living in poverty.

The great recession of 2008 continues to impact human service programs as states strive to reduce expenditures and funding levels. Many services have been eliminated completely, and some others have had severe cutbacks in staff. A medical social worker in a hospital says that the most frustrating part of her job is the fact that there are so few services to which to refer people when they are ready for discharge from the hospital.

Increased Administrative Burdens and Bureaucratization

One significant pressure on today's human service worker is the ever-growing administrative expectations that have found their way into the helping relationship. Documentation of service delivery is an important aspect of the work, though the demands for recording the delivery of services have grown in response to the changing funding mechanisms and funders' increased expectations for the various services that individuals receive. Many human service organizations find that reimbursement now comes through funding streams that are rehabilitative in nature. Rehabilitation requires that that a licensed medical practitioner certify that the work is medically necessary in order to receive reimbursement. Of course, documenting the delivery of these medically necessary services is key to ensuring that the helping organization can withstand a federal, state, or county audit of its practice. For the worker, the practical impact of this is the need to carefully document the delivery of care. Most organizations now utilize electronic health records (EHRs) requiring that service delivery notes be entered directly into a confidential electronic health record for each individual client. Many funding sources also require that documentation of treatment services be uploaded into an EHR; the challenge is that they have their own systems for documentation, which can require the worker to enter information twice. Situations such as these create additional burdens on the worker and play a role in the growing bureaucratization of the human service professions.

Increased bureaucratization means more policies and procedures that workers are required to follow, less flexibility for those in the human service profession, greater credentialization, more hierarchical control, larger workplaces, and decreased autonomy for workers. DeHart-Davis and Pandey (2005) confirmed the adverse impact of bureaucracy when they found that the presence of "red tape" actually alienates workers. Alienated workers in turn are less committed to their organization and the work they are asked to do. Given this, it's important to use some of the strategies we discuss later in this chapter to learn how to effectively manage the stress that additional administrative burdens bring to the human service profession.

Insurance and Government Reimbursement

When insurance companies dictate the kind of treatment to be given and the way of giving it, workers no longer decide how the work gets done. This affects social workers in private practice as well as in agencies. Private insurance companies reimburse only for psychotherapy, diagnosis, and evaluation. They do not reimburse for marital counseling unless the client is given a diagnosis from what has become the "bible" of diagnosis, the *DSM-5*—the *Diagnostic and Statistical Manual of Mental Disorders*, fifth edition. In addition, many state governments have moved to a managed care delivery system for working with the neediest individuals. In these cases, as well as with insurance companies, every request for reimbursement in any field of practice must be accompanied by a diagnosis from *DSM-5*. This means there are times when our work is not reimbursable, including shelter services, foster care, client-related meetings, and advocacy.

Even when a practice is reimbursable, the funding sources set the time limits. Workers make cynical jokes about "sixty-day miracle cures" for people in psychiatric care. They are discharged as "cured" from the hospital when the insurance runs out, whether or not they act or feel cured. Initially, with the passage of the Patient Protection and Affordable Care Act, or ACA, there was great hope that the United States would achieve universal health care coverage and that insurance caps on coverage would become a thing of the past. Recent changes, though, have caused uncertainty about the scope and nature of health care coverage in the United States.

Workers may not be able to choose the method of treatment because approval processes used to determine "medical necessity" may limit the amount or type of treatment allowed. Chuang, Well, and Alexander (2011) found that while publicly contracted managed care organizations did not limit access to behavioral health services, the number of sessions approved was typically smaller than non-contracted managed care health plans. This creates a dynamic where the human service professional finds himself juggling the competing interests of the managed care funding source and the critical needs of the clients he serves.

Lack of Resources Outside the Agency

Even if workers are lucky enough to be at an agency with enough money to hire competent staff, keep caseloads to a manageable size, and provide good supervision and a supportive environment, they are not home free. As long as other agencies are not as lucky, the impact is still felt by the clients and workers of all agencies. This county's rising opioid and substance use crisis is a case in point. Many states have yet to sign on for Medicaid reimbursement for opioid treatment programs. While applications are pending with the Center for Medicaid and Medicare Services, many some states do not allow Medicaid to cover opioid addiction. As of 2016, there were 16 states without Medicaid coverage for opioid treatment (Knopf, 2016). When a state doesn't have Medicaid coverage, the only way to access opioid treatment is for the client to self-pay, which results in fewer service providers and fewer options for the consumer. Even if your organization is well funded, an external inability to access funds for a growing social concern can create a backlog of client need.

Lack of Support from the Agency

Resources are limited, and outcomes are necessary to prove the value of an organization's efforts to funding sources. A worker's frustrations in the face of inadequate resources can be eased when the agency goes to bat for its workers, helping them do the job despite challenges. But if the agency *blames* the workers for its own inadequacies (as sometimes happens), workers are likely to feel angry, guilty, and depressed. Some government funding sources and agency bureaucracies have tried to deal with their workload problems by introducing management methods that stress **accountability** and sped-up work. This can cause employees to become disengaged and alienated from the organization as well as from the work itself.

And while it's true that many agencies are increasingly under the gun for accountability and effectiveness, a good organization knows the importance of engaging its employees to become true stakeholders in the day-to-day work and problem-solving strategies. Despite these pressures, many high-quality organizations know that they rise and fall based on the investment, commitment, and capabilities of their workforce. As a human service professional, it's important for you to fully explore the type of organization that you will work for. Is there a positive culture that supports individuals in their work, or does the organization seem to disregard the employee's input and potential for contribution to the overall mission? Choose carefully, as this will have a huge impact on your professional experience.

Pressures Exerted by Clients

Workers are not the only ones who become angry and frustrated when resources are inadequate or rules are restrictive. Clients feel the same way and often express their negative reactions to the worker, because that is the person with whom they have contact. The legislators who voted the inadequate funding are far removed from the on-the-ground experience that policy has helped to shape. Today, the worker not only has to face clients' frustration and anger but also has to face a continual struggle to meet the needs of the individuals she is there to serve.

INVOLUNTARY CLIENTS Some clients are angry because they never asked to be clients, and they fight their client status every step of the way. Such **involuntary clients** include parents accused of child abuse and neglect, juvenile or adult offenders who are imprisoned or on probation, involuntarily committed individuals struggling with mental illness, individuals with traumatic brain injuries, individuals with Alzheimer's, children in treatment programs, and people caught driving under the influence of alcohol. Through patient and empathetic work, many of these people can be encouraged to participate, and some end up being genuinely grateful for the worker's intervention. Some continue to resist even the most patient and caring of workers.

WORKING WITH CLIENTS WHO HAVE EXPERIENCED TRAUMA As a future human service worker, it's safe to say that you have a big heart. Most of us have entered this profession because we care deeply for people and we feel that we have the capacity to make a difference in their lives. Some of us have also had our own difficulties growing up, and so we may know what it's like to have experienced any number of challenges faced by our clients. The fact that we care so deeply and that we may have our own lived experience can serve as a real asset when it comes to connecting with and helping our clients. Our work, though, requires that we learn of and hear firsthand the many difficult and often traumatic events our clients have experienced. To have a client recount his sexual or physical abuse at the hands of an adult parent—a parent who should have been there to help him, not cause him harm—is difficult and challenging work. In the field of human services, we recognize the difficulty associated with this, and we know that one possible outcome from the ongoing exposure to our clients' traumatic events is something known as vicarious trauma. Vicarious trauma (VT) results from the exposure an individual has to another's traumatic events, which in turn causes changes to the individual's identity, memories, and beliefs (Trippany, White Kress, & Wilcoxon, 2004). Helpers affected by VT experience discomfort, stress, and sometimes life-altering changes in the way they view situations.

One key to effectively managing the traumatic events you are exposed to through your work with traumatized clients is to actively use your supervisor within your organization to have regular supervision time. These meetings serve as an opportunity to discuss the impact that your clients' trauma has on you. In these discussions, you can expect to work with your supervisor to develop strategies to manage the intense feelings that may arise from your clients' sharing. This is particularly true if the clients' experiences are at all related to your own experiences growing up. It important in these instances to use your supervision time to explore areas of potential VT.

Resilience, defined as the ability to bounce back, becomes that road to your clients' capacity to work through the trauma that they have been exposed to in their lives. Understanding your own self and your ability to be resilient will also help you to manage even the most difficult material presented by your clients' lived experience. In fact, some theorists now write about the concept of vicarious resilience, where the resilience of your client as she works through traumatic events

Source: John S. Quinn/ Shutterstock

Understanding yourself will also help you to manage even the most difficult material presented by your clients' lived experience.

in turn provides you as the helper with an appreciation of how resilience is possible, even in the most difficult circumstances (Hernandez-Wolfe, Killian, Engstrom, & Gangsei, 2014).

Stigma, Discrimination, and Status Ranking

People who are economically disadvantaged, individuals with intellectual or physical disabilities, people with mental illness, and those who are incarcerated are often stigmatized by the larger society. People who work with them find that some of that stigma rubs off on them. Workers may often discover this when telling their friends or relatives about the nature of their jobs. Perhaps they have just gone on a home visit in a very marginalized section of town, or they have just gone to court with a youthful offender accused of a violent crime. People may say, "Why do you want to help him?" Some people can brush off these remarks, which only reinforce their commitment. Yet such constant reminders of the low social esteem in which their daily tasks are held can be demoralizing.

The public often makes distinctions between and within groups of people, continuing the age-old stereotypes of "deserving" and "undeserving" clients. Among the least stigmatized are the more affluent clients who take their interpersonal problems to the offices of private psychiatrists. Among the most stigmatized are those with substance use disorders who live and socialize on the streets. Because human service workers are part of the same society that creates these stigmas, they also sometimes measure their clientele by the same yardstick.

A stigma is effective only if you believe it. There are many workers who refuse to accept the stigma that society puts on clients and the people who work with them. They see all people as equally valuable and do not divide clients into "deserving" and "undeserving." Nor do they consider their social status diminished because they work with stigmatized clients. We believe that this approach, matched with a view that treats all people with dignity and respect, is an approach that falls squarely into a list of "best practices."

Status is another piece of the puzzle when considering the challenges that face the human service professional. There are often sharp and painful status differences between professionals within an agency. A worker with an associate's degree from a community college may be doing exactly the same work and doing it just as competently as a worker with a Bachelor of Social Work (BSW) degree from a four-year college; yet the pay for the associate's degree worker will probably be less and the possibility of being promoted without further credentials may be nil.

Dealing with Danger

Human service workers usually work with people living in poverty, and some of them live in neighborhoods that witness some violence. Naturally, a worker wants to avoid violence, yet needs to work in those neighborhoods. When a worker shows excessive anxiety about it, disproportionate to the reality, clients can interpret that as contempt or hostility toward all the people who live in the neighborhood. Yet some caution is realistic, and clients know that better than anyone else. They can give you good advice about taking precautionary steps. It is important to establish collegial relationships with neighborhood people so they trust you and show concern for your safety, just as you are concerned for their safety.

Human service workers have sometimes been assaulted by their clients, and even murdered. Health care and social services workers have a high incidence of assault injuries. Zelnick, Slayter, Flanzbaum, Butle, Dominigo, Perlstein and Trust (2013) found in their research of more than 40 human service organizations across Massachusetts that workplace violence is in fact prevalent within the field of human services. Violence takes numerous forms and includes physical assault, verbal threats, verbal abuse, and property damage. Direct care workers were found more likely to be at risk than clinical staff and in many cases abuse acts against workers went unreported.

Child-protection work is especially dangerous because parents sometimes react violently when a worker threatens to take away their children. On average, 50 percent of child protection workers (CPWs) report that they have met with at least one hostile or intimidating parent each week (Littlechild, Hunt, Goddard, Cooper, Raynes, & Wild, 2016). CPWs working in residential settings have a greater risk of violence with one study, for example, finding that 37 percent of child protection workers had experienced some form of physical violence in the prior year (Alink, Euser, Bakermans-Kranenburg, & van IJzendoorn, 2014).

Most agencies offer their staff strategies to stay safe. Increased violence against workers has also caused some agencies to heighten their security measures. The Massachusetts Department of Child and Families (DCF) for example, has increased the presence of police within their agency's offices. They've also worked to expand training for workers in safety protocols and used the expertise of the Massachusetts State Police to conduct safety audits of all their area offices. In addition workers are being provided with training to advance their capacity for self defense. (Anderson, 2015).

Workers often deny that they can become victims at the hands of their clients, thereby overlooking the potential for danger. Because workers believe it's a part of the job, they often underestimate the level of risk they may be exposed to. In addition, workers often develop what are called *attributions* to explain their clients behavior (Lamothe, Couvrette, Lebrun, Yale-Soulière, Roy, Guay, & Geoffrion, 2018). By attributing the client's behavior to a particular theory or belief about the client, the worker can misinterpret and as a result underestimate the risk that they are exposed to. This leaves them more vulnerable because they do not take realistic steps to protect themselves, and it also denies the agency information that it could use to help protect workers. Your agency has a responsibility to keep you safe and you should expect, even demand, practices that protect you from possible danger and that give you support when you encounter a threatening situation. You should expect support from your supervisor and from your colleagues. Sometimes colleagues are not as supportive as they should be because they want to deny that they too could be the victim of violence at the hands of their clients. None of us is invulnerable, and we all need support.

Hazards of the Work

Most human service workers go into the field because they have ideals and a vision about helping people and optimism about the possibilities of change. This is an absolute requirement for the work; when ideals die and turn to cynicism we call that burnout. Yet an occupational hazard for human service workers is that the desire to be of help can turn into a rescue fantasy—a belief that they have to do it all, and if clients don't change in a desired way, the worker has failed.

Even workers who do not succumb to rescue fantasies or the need to be omnipotent in clients' lives can be dragged under by the sheer weight of people's problems, many of which may be essentially unsolvable. Sometimes the feelings of helplessness and of being overwhelmed come from the simple fact that life is often painful and that some pain cannot be removed, some problems cannot be solved, and the best you can do is simply to reach out and show that you care. Here is an account of one student's feelings about the pain of the human drama in her fieldwork:

> Sometimes when I go into the home and I haven't been there for a while, I'm almost afraid to ask, "Well, how are things with you, Mrs. J.?" I know that she'll begin to catalog all the things that are wrong with her. Her health is really in a terrible state, and it's hard for her to get used

to all the tubes and bags and the feeling that she can't do anything by herself. And then she'll tell me that her son didn't show up after he swore he would. And, damn him, why can't he visit once in a while? She seems like she's such a decent person and she really cares about him. A visit would make such a difference in her morale, but I can't drag him in, and what can I say to her to make it okay—that he is just too busy with his own life to visit a sick old lady, the person who raised him and looked after him when he needed it?

For all of us, there is often a wide gap between what we wish we could do and what we can do. As human service workers, this gap can be particularly painful when we feel we are behaving differently with our clients than we were taught to behave in our college classes. We often encounter people at their worst, when they are the most abusive, discouraged, depressed, overwhelmed, and angry. Frequently they have already had their problems for many years. Inadequate housing, poor schools, bad marriages, and destructive parenting patterns did not appear overnight and will not disappear overnight, so several things happen. Our clients often slip back into destructive patterns of behavior even after they see other possibilities. An adult with a substance use disorder may make a hundred vows that will probably be broken and cover each with a hundred excuses—the same ones we ourselves use when we explain why we have abandoned our exercise program again or have broken our diets. Sometime our clients simply rationalize their circumstances:

- I'm not really hooked.
- I'll just do it one more time to get me through this hard stretch.
- When things calm down, I'll stop drinking.
- Just one more binge, and then I'll quit!

Often when our clients are feeling better about their lives and possibilities, they take off, and we never know just how well they are doing and how well we did with them. Sometimes they even need to deny that we were of any help to them at all. Sometimes we encourage them to feel their own sense of power by minimizing the contributions we may have made. But being human, we can at times get angry at them when they fall back into old behaviors or seem to be rejecting us or putting down the help we have given them.

Some days being a human service worker can be a thankless task. You have to look in the mirror and say, "Hey, I just did a great piece of work!" You'll probably have a supervisor, coworker, or good friend who gives you strokes for your good work just in case you don't get them from anyone else. We shouldn't need to be constantly thanked and fussed over, but we all are human and need a small pat on the back from time to time.

STAYING ALIVE—POSITIVE ADJUSTMENTS

The organization that you will work for has a responsibility to help each employee manage his stress. It is responsible, for example, for implementing and maintaining the policies and practices that ensure employees have the resources they need to be effective in their work. In addition, the agency ensures that you are paid, provides clear job responsibilities, and trains you to be successful at accomplishing all the duties identified within your job description. It is important, though, to realize that there are things that you as a human service professional can and should do to manage stress and avoid burnout. In the following section we explore some of the strategies that are available to you in order to manage your own stress and avoid the pitfalls of burnout.

Combating Stress

Stress is the number one contributor to burnout within the human services profession. Stress not only can be a cause of burnout; it also can contribute to many other psychological and physiological difficulties. Nixon, Mazzola, Bauer, Krueger, and Spector (2011) identified no fewer than eight physical symptoms that become manifest from ongoing work stress, including lack of sleep, fatigue, loss of appetite, and depression. Given these serious ailments, it behooves all human service professionals to learn how to effectively manage stress.

The first consideration for stress management is understanding the source of the stress. The answer to workplace stress seems readily apparent: work, of course! In fact, the answer to where the stress comes from is not quite that simple. Laurence, Fried, and Raub (2016), for example, point out that workplace stress—while existing within the context of work—could originate from the worker and not necessarily from the organization or management of the agency. Think of it this way: When you are stressed about a test, the source of the stress could be the fact that the professor is known to be tough, with high expectations. On the other hand, the source of the stress could reside in the fact that you've put off studying now for most of the semester and you don't see how you can manage to cram all that information into your head in time for the exam.

By understanding the source of the stress and the role that you play in its presence, you become better able to reduce and otherwise manage a stressful situation. Pursuing stress management from this perspective requires that we possess a level of awareness that in turn will make it possible to take action steps to reduce stress.

Self-care is an important element of stress management. Collins (2005) describes self-care as the ability to balance personal, professional, physical, emotional, spiritual, and mental aspects of our lives in order to have the energy necessary to manage stress. From a practical standpoint, this means that you continually work to keep a healthy balance between your work and your personal lives—that you eat well, ensure that you get enough exercise and sleep, and manage the day-to-day tasks associated with work and home effectively.

McGarrigle and Walsh (2011) suggest that one important way to ensure self-care is through mindfulness practice or meditation. Meditation is a stress management strategy that has proven to be successful time and time again. For example, mindfulness exercises have been shown through research to reduce stress as well as result in better physical and mental health (Creswell & Lindsay, 2014; Hülsheger, Alberts, Feinholdt, & Lang, 2013). Following are a few mindfulness exercises drawn from Alfred James's book titled *Pocket Mindfulness* (2013) that are easy to do on your own and only require that you have a few minutes in a quiet space to yourself.

MINDFUL BREATHING   In this exercise, find a quiet place to sit. You can close your eyes or you can choose a focal point. Breathe in through your nose and then exhale though your mouth. Focus on your breathing. Listen to the rhythm of your breathing and allow yourself to let go of all the other things in your mind. Feel how the breath fills your lungs through your nose and then exits through your mouth.

MINDFUL OBSERVATION   Find a place to sit and allow yourself to observe something from the natural environment—perhaps a tree as its leaves rustle in the wind, or a flock of birds. Devote your attention to this and consider its beauty. Let go of all of the other thoughts that typically surround your day-to-day activities.

MINDFUL AWARENESS Consider something that you do as a routine every day. Now, as you pursue this activity, stop and consider carefully what the experience is like. How does the physical environment feel, what are you thinking, and how do you feel? Take a moment to appreciate how you feel. You can also use this time to label and dismiss negative thoughts that might occur.

MINDFUL APPRECIATION In this exercise, the goal is to consider five things you are appreciative of that you normally take for granted. Do this over the course of your day. You might think about an important person or relationship in your life, perhaps a pet, the work that you do, or even a physical object. Once you've identified your five things, make a point of understanding how these things contribute to your well-being and the happiness you experience in life.

Each of these mindfulness activities takes but a few moments out of your busy day, and each of these activities will yield a huge benefit in the area of stress reduction. One of the authors uses these exercises with graduate students who are studying to become therapists. Working to become a therapist can be very stressful, particularly when it's time to actually begin counseling individuals and families. The use of mindful meditation activities for just a few minutes prior to each counseling session helps the counseling students to center themselves and be prepared to successfully engage in a counseling session with their clients. Our personal favorite, and the one that our students report liking the best, is the breathing exercise.

Other strategies that help reduce stress include time management, keeping lists, prioritizing activities, limit setting, and knowing your own limits. We've found, for example, that it helps to keep a running list of things that need to get done at work. Today you can use the task function in your Outlook program to help not only build your list but also include electronic reminders. Or you can choose to make your list using the old-school method of pen and paper. In either case, a running list of activities that have to be accomplished, along with their relative importance, will help ensure that you can avoid feeling overwhelmed. When the list gets too long, that's when it's time to reach out for support and seek the assistance of others to pursue a problem-solving strategy.

Problem Solving

Human service workers have to be effective problem solvers. After all, the bulk of their time is spent helping to solve the complex problems that other people are experiencing in their lives. The skills you have as a human service worker in support of clients' needs can be used to help address the needs of the organization, the team, and your own professional experience. Using these same skills, workers can involve their colleagues in analyzing agency problems and helping to work together to craft positive solutions. This gets workers beyond incessant criticism of the agency that goes nowhere, and it helps them gain mastery of agency problems (Bramhall & Ezell, 1991).

The best-run organizations in today's human service field recognize the power of engaging employees to help solve problems. Organizations that work to fully engage their employees as partners in pursuing the agency's mission are also organizations that work together to help solve the challenges that create stress and unnecessary burnout. One agency, for example, recently worked with its employees to craft an optional four-day workweek as an alternative to the traditional five-day workweek. This effort was crafted though input from all levels of the organization and now provides employees with another option for managing their work–life balance.

Meeting family responsibilities while working is stressful and can contribute to burnout.

As you prepare to enter the field, remember that you possess many problem-solving skills that can help you and your team craft strategies to reduce stress that can cause burnout. It's also important to carefully vet any organization that you hope to work for. How does it support its employees, and is there room at the table to contribute to problem-solving strategies that ultimately help the employees to move the organization's mission forward? Be sure to sign on with an organization with your "eyes wide open."

Gaining Power Through Knowledge

Knowledge is power, and the more that you learn about your organization, the program, the services that you are employed to provide, and the responsibilities associated with your position, the better you'll be able to manage the challenges that will no doubt come your way. Most organizations have extensive literature about their purpose, including the mission, vision, and values of the organization. In addition, your supervisor is a source of important information. She, for example, may be able to provide a copy of the contract that states that the organization has to provide the service that you are employed to provide. The contract typically includes the deliverables that are required as well as details about how the program is to be organized. The best organizations readily share this type of information, as they know that an engaged workforce is a productive workforce.

In addition to service contracts, laws and rules guide most of the work that we do now in human services. The delivery of community case-management services for individuals with intellectual disabilities in Maine, for example, is guided by enabling legislation as well as administrative rules that have been promulgated in order to ensure that provider organizations deliver the service using consistent standards. This is true in almost every state and for almost any type of service that is being delivered. If you work in a homeless shelter, for example, there are licensing rules that set forth the minimum standards for health, safety, and record keeping. Becoming familiarized with the laws and administrative and licensing rules for the service you help provide will allow you to understand more fully how the system works and what is readily possible within the existing system. Incidentally, all of these laws, rules, and regulations can be found by searching the web.

Another strategy for gaining power through knowledge is participating in agency- or industry-sponsored training opportunities. As a general practice, you should avail yourself of any training that is offered or available. Professional training will not only help you to do your job more effectively, it will also help raise your standing within the team. Individuals who are trained in speciality areas, for example, often become the go-to people for other members of the team. In all, professional training is an important way for you to develop your capabilities and sense of efficacy in the work that you do. We know that people who develop skills feel more effective, and through this they are better able to manage stress and avoid burnout (Cohen & Gagin, 2005).

Your attitude about your work also becomes an important factor in whether you can use knowledge to gain power within the organization. Serendipity, defined as the faculty of making fortunate discoveries by accident, was said by Louis Pasteur to only visit the prepared mind. This means that your lens or attitude toward something plays an important role in the possibilities that present themselves. Two colleagues who started out as foster care workers provide an exemplar. The first individual often shared his frustration with the organization and the work that he had to do. "This place is nowheresville!" he'd exclaim. His colleague would look surprised and respond, "Really, I think there's so much happening here and there's such potential." Her colleague would just look at her incredulously and shake his head. Twenty years later, the young man—now a middle-aged case manager—still felt there was limited opportunity at the organization, while his female colleague had become the executive director of the agency. Your view informs what is possible. Be ready to take on new opportunities, and don't be shy about trying something new. All new things involve a risk, but remember: Nothing ventured means literally nothing gained. Besides, new adventures and opportunities help to keep your energy high and your commitment to the work strong. Remember: Serendipity only visits the prepared mind!

Getting Support

SUPERVISION   Human service agencies have traditionally relied on supervision to train workers and to give them support in their work. The profession of social work has probably relied heavily on, and has a rich history of utilizing, one-to-one supervision as a key means for advancing the practitioners' skills (Sewell, 2018). Although it can have its benefits, not all human service workers are happy with the quality of the supervision they receive. High-quality supervision is a key to your professional development as well as your ability to effectively manage the challenges that this important work can present.

Your supervision is one of the key ways in which you can receive support as a worker and as an individual. Wonnacott (2011) identifies four key purposes for supervision that you should be sure to be aware of. First, supervision plays a critical role in helping you to manage your day-to-day responsibilities. Your regular meeting with your supervisor is a time for communicating about job duties, challenges, and areas for improvement. Working closely with your supervisor in these areas can help provide you with direction as well as problem-solving strategies. It's through supervision that you should receive essential feedback on performance-related issues. Your supervisor will work with you to set work-related expectations as well as develop strategies to help ensure your success.

The second thing you should expect from high-quality supervision is the opportunity to map out your professional development. In collaboration with your supervisor, you'll identify areas in which you'd like and need additional training. The best supervisor also wants you to explore your future goals. Where do you see yourself in five years, and how might your current work connect you to your midterm and longer-term goals? As practitioners, the authors love when their employees set professional development goals for themselves. We don't worry that the long-term goal might actually mean the individual won't be in their current position forever, as we know that when someone has aspirations and feels supported to pursue them, they will give their all along the way. The organization itself is better for it, and we're better able to pursue our mission. Feedback is a critical part of each of the elements of effective supervision, and it is particularly important here. Feedback means that there is an open dialogue between you and your supervisor about important ideas. Done well, it requires that there be a high degree of trust and respect between the two of you.

The third element of supervision that Wonnacott writes about is the personal support function found within effective supervision. Your supervisor knows that your work involves complex situations that have the potential to draw heavily on your emotional and psychological energy. In addition, life is happening for you and all employees, which means that everyone occasionally experiences personal issues—the loss of a family member or divorce, for example. Given this, a good supervisor knows that providing personal support to you is important, and as an employee, you have the right to expect this. This is different than thinking of your supervisor as a counselor or therapist, as that wouldn't be appropriate. It's more akin to their being a coach or playing a supportive role. A strong supervisor does this without crossing professional boundaries by becoming a quasi-therapist or negatively impacting the expectations about the need to fulfill your job responsibilities.

Your supervisor will play both a supportive role and a restorative one so that you can be successful within your work. An effective supervisor knows too when to help you seek assistance for personal concerns that exist outside of the work setting. It also means that your supervisor will help you to identify techniques and strategies to deal with support needs that arise while conducting the work responsibilities. This might mean providing some strategies for dealing with a difficult situation, co-worker, or client. It could also mean circling back to identify professional development and training opportunities to assist you in your quest for success.

The final purpose for supervision is to ensure that your connection to the larger organization remains healthy and productive. This aspect of supervision often appears as a form of mediation for you with the agency. It might mean helping you to be sure that you take your earned time off. It could also mean helping to be sure that any glitches with your benefits or pay are worked through. In both cases, as in others related to the supervisory purpose, it's important to recognize the key role that your supervisor plays in assuring that your experience with the organization is both positive and productive.

For these reasons, we recommend that you shop carefully as you consider an organization for employment. Ask them how often supervision happens. (You should receive regular sit-down supervision no less that once every other week, and preferably weekly.) Ask how professional development goals are established and what the organization's protocol is for annual evaluations. Be sure to be an informed professional as you make important decisions about your career choices.

OTHER FORMS OF SUPERVISION   Another form of supervision is group supervision, which includes **case conferences**, core evaluations, group supervisions, and staffings, in which the workers concentrate on one particular client's problem or on one key issue affecting groups of clients. A study of children with hyperactivity disorder concluded that the child was less likely to be prescribed medication and that satisfaction with service delivery was increased when the work was done using multidisciplinary teams (Bor, Heath, Heussler, Reuter, Perrett, & Lee, 2013). Using such teams, which might include teachers, homemakers, lay therapists, social workers, psychologists, nurses, and doctors, helped workers learn how to better handle a given case and similar cases in the future. Workers also do better when they have case conferences in which two or more workers reviewed their progress on a case once every three months and when they used outside consultants from different disciplines on more complex cases.

Formal and Informal Groups

Formal and informal groups serve as an important resource for the human service professionals to develop and maintain their skills. Research has shown that performance is enhanced by the effective use of formal as well as informal group resources (Soda & Zaheer, 2012). Knowing this, it makes sense for you to carefully participate in an array of both formal and informal groups in order to support your professional development as well as your capacity to be effective within the field. A number of ideas for both formal and informal groups are included in the following section.

INFORMAL NETWORKS   The informal conversations we have with our friends and coworkers are the most common way of sharing experiences. These take place during coffee breaks, over lunch, after work on the telephone, at each other's homes, and during shared entertainment. These conversations give us the emotional support to keep at our demanding jobs. They are one way to check out, add to, and revise our store of knowledge about our work. Sometimes they can improve our practice. We may share innovative ideas, but we may also share ignorance, prejudice, and stereotypes. If the conversation stays on the level of griping, it can increase anxiety and keep people mired in helplessness. One needs to gripe, but if one never moves on to analysis and action, complaining can be counterproductive.

Informal networks are essential for survival on the job. Sociologist Howard Polsky (1962), in his classic research, studied a residential treatment center for youthful offenders and found that the live-in cottage parents felt like they were—and in fact were—the most isolated and vulnerable of all the staff members because they did not have a reference group: friends they could go home to and share ideas and feelings with. The social workers, on the other hand, commuting together back to New York City and spending evenings with family and friends, returned to work the next day emotionally replenished for their bouts with the rage, wisecracks, con games, and sadness of these youngsters who had been taken from their homes by the state. The cottage parents' lack of an alternative status reference group had a negative impact on the treatment they gave to the teenagers in their care:

> Lacking an alternative status reference group, the cottage parent becomes dependent upon, and conforming to, the boys' delinquent orientation and eventually adjusts to it by taking over and utilizing modified delinquent techniques. The extreme concern with cottage loyalty and the violent condemnation of "ratting" cement the cottage parent to the boys' subculture and perpetuate a vicious circle, which insulates the cottage from the rest of the therapeutic milieu. (Polsky, 1962, p. 135)

PROFESSIONAL ORGANIZATIONS   A professional organization forges links between people in the same field. Collectively, these people share their values and their knowledge, and support each other in job searching and in other concrete ways. Most organizations have at least one professional journal that provides a platform for workers to carry on their professional debates and to share their research and practice experiences. Most human service organizations have a code of ethical practice. Workers often derive support by holding on to their professional values, even though these may at times be in conflict with those practiced in the agency. The profession often uses the clout afforded by its numbers to improve agency practice and to lobby for better social services.

UNIONS   There is often no sharp distinction between a professional organization and a union; some professional organizations, such as the National Education Association (NEA) and the American Association of University Professors (AAUP), started as professional associations but have gradually taken on the traditional functions of a trade union. Generally, professional organizations do not engage in contract negotiations or in job actions such as slowdowns or strikes.

   As the country's workforce has increasingly moved into service occupations, professionals such as teachers and human service workers are unionizing much more often now than in the past. Public social agencies generally pay workers more than private agencies pay because public social agency workers are more unionized. The literature has shown that the higher rates of pay for teachers that are unionized is in the 2 to 4.5 percent range annually (Merkle & Phillips, 2018).

   One of the most important reasons workers give for leaving human service agencies is their lack of control over their working conditions. Unions are often perceived as the most powerful tool to wrest some of that control from management. Some social service unions have a vision that is more limited in scope, bargaining mainly for wages, hours, and fringe benefits, while others struggle for a greater worker role in decision making and for changes in systems. A spokesperson for the American Federation of State, County, and Municipal Employees (AFSCME), which has organized many human service workers, tells of his union's concern for those broader issues. Professionals often want representation at the planning or policy level. For example, social caseworkers, who are often overburdened with high caseloads, work for policies that lower their caseloads (Curtin, 1970, pp. 12, 15).

   If your agency is not unionized and the workers want a union, a group of you can work on it. Study all the unions that could represent you. Find out their track records on organizing and bargaining; check out what salaries their staffs earn. (There's no reason union bureaucrats should be living in luxury while human service workers scrimp.) See what issues they are willing to take a stand on; ask how elitist or hierarchical they are in their own decision making. Who do they believe should call the shots—the membership or the union staff? How much are the dues? Do they have a fund to tide you over if it comes to a strike? Can they give you legal assistance and help in bargaining? Give ample time for each person to share her concerns about what might happen to the clients if there were a work stoppage, and what she is prepared to do if the organizing or contract negotiation gets sticky. Don't be surprised if the agency management is not happy about the prospect of workers organizing. Even human service supervisors can have serious misgivings and fears of turmoil and conflict.

Some organizations play on workers' fears in order to reduce union activity—fear of being fired, skipped over for promotion, or disapproved of. Sometimes the fears are justified. One reason for the recent decline in union membership is that employers have fired union organizers, which has made people more afraid to organize. Find out from the union leaders in your area whether this has been happening in the human service field and, if so, what you can do about it.

Often there will be resistance from some agency colleagues who believe that it is unprofessional to organize. As the economic reality of the decline in liveable wages hits more middle-class people, however, they tend to look for a union's protection. Finally, if workers are in a small private agency that contracts out work from the state, they may find they need to form coalitions with fellow workers in similar small agencies before unionizing in order to grow large enough to influence management.

Service Employees International Union (SEIU) has organized workers often considered "unorganizable," especially low-wage service-sector workers, in what is often called "social movement organizing." Many of these service-sector workers are minorities, immigrants, and women. Some of the union's organizing campaigns include:

- Justice for Janitors (janitors)
- Stand for Security (security officers)
- Invisible No More (home care workers)
- Clean Up Sodexo (outsourced services)
- National Health Care Workers Union (health care providers)
- SEIU Kids First (child care)
- Quality Public Services (public workers)
- Everybody Wins (public workers) (SEIU, Local 503)

Creative Ways of Working

One way of keeping the spark alive on the job is to experiment with new ideas. It may be hard to think of new ways to do your work when so many people are telling you "But we've always done it this way." Yet well-thought-out experimentation is often worth the risks it might entail. Clearly, it keeps people enthusiastic.

Working with people in groups rather than as individuals can sometimes save time. You might make an overly large caseload more manageable through such devices as conducting group intakes for adoption applicants. Foster parents can be trained in groups to care for children; they can also help the worker recruit other foster parents. Group counseling for unemployed people and support groups for parents, teens, families of people dealing with substance use disorders, and others can all be both time-saving and more effective compared with individual work. One study found that treatment of abusive and neglectful parents was most effective when parents were involved in mutual support groups such as Parents Anonymous and when parent aides were used (Berkeley Planning Associates, 1978). Encouraging and supporting clients to help themselves and each other cuts down on your caseload and pressures while strengthening your clients' abilities.

If you can get enough support from your colleagues, clients, and community, you might persuade your agency to change the way it does the work. One staff member of a sheltered workshop for people with intellectual disabilities said this in her letter of protest to the agency board:

> While I was told that teaching clients would be at least a part of my job, this has not been the case so far. In the weeks I've been at [the workshop], I've spent a total of half an hour working on money skills with a client, and that was only because I put other things aside and took initiative to do so. In reality, my job consists of fixing and counting chess pieces and mascara brushes, inspecting bathrooms, opening boxes of calculators. How about if I spend two hours a day teaching clients to do these tasks? I understand they must be done but think it is a ridiculous use of my skills. From 10:00–12:00 I could work on routine sorting tasks and from 1:00–3:00 hold a money management workshop. I'd like six weeks to stick with this schedule and then I'll report back on how it's working.

Programs that allow scope for creativity make space for workers and clients to grow. The ultimate goal of any human service work is the mutual empowerment of clients, workers, and the community. Workers can reach out to clients and the community to explore and discuss alternative modes of service.

Varying the Work

A good way to survive on the job is to vary the work by rotating duties with other workers, alternating between intense involvement with clients and less emotionally draining administrative work, or taking time out from regular tasks to do a special project or attend a course or conference. Workers often break a cycle of defeat by figuring out which clients are the most draining on them and making trade-offs with other workers who have different kinds of tolerances and bring a new insight to a stalled group or individual case process.

Sharing Ideas

One of the most important ways of enjoying your work is to know you are doing a good job. That is a good reason to continue to sharpen your skills throughout your career. It is stimulating to share ideas with others, both orally and in writing. You can be part of the "community of scholars" at work, in the community, and in your profession by writing letters to the editor of your local newspaper, composing practice notes and accounts for your professional journal, and, if you have a bent for more formal research and theoretical speculation, producing articles that present your thinking and research.

Setting Limits on Self and Others

Finally, you need to know how to protect yourself from the unrealistic demands that people make on you. You need to learn to recognize your limits and let others know when you have reached them. Learn to say "no" without feeling guilty. Take time out when you're feeling drained. If you've just had a nerve-wracking experience with a client and your knees are shaking, let your supervisor know that you need to take a walk or talk it out. If you're exhausted after a few years on the job, try to take a leave of absence if you can afford it. You may come back refreshed, with new ideas.

You need to learn how not to take your work home with you, and you need to take good care of yourself outside the job. There are lots of ways to do this. Our list would include good nutrition, regular exercise, rest, recreation, reading, and friendships. Some people find meditation, relaxation techniques, or biofeedback helpful. However we manage to do it, we must keep our spontaneity and spirit of play alive. If we lose our joy, how can we bring joy and hope to our clients?

Summary

1. Human service work can be a very exciting career, but only as long as one can grow in the job and feel successful in it.
2. Growth requires support from peers, supervisors, and the society that sponsors your agency.
3. If support is not forthcoming, a human service job can create stress, which leads to burnout.
4. Symptoms of burnout can include sleep problems, irritability, upset stomach, headaches, and shortness of breath. Workers may become cynical and hard-hearted, stop caring about the clients, and treat clients with contempt.
5. Burnout can be caused by both psychological and environmental stress.
6. The human service profession is built on a humanitarian ethos, but in practice that ideal sometimes turns into cynicism or careerism.
7. When managed care entities and insurance companies dictate the kind of treatment to be given and the way to give it, human service workers are restricted in their choices.
8. When there is not enough time, the helping impulse may become extinguished.
9. Government cutbacks in services restrict the kind of help that workers can give.
10. Agencies that serve the poor seldom have enough resources.
11. Clients exert pressures on the worker when resources are restricted.
12. Work stress is increased when the client has not chosen to come to the agency, as in child-protection work.
13. Dealing with clients' traumatic situations can cause vicarious trauma. Developing your own resilience through mindfulness and supervision is key.
14. Clients of agencies are often stigmatized by society. Those who work with them are sometimes included in this stigmatization.
15. Some human service work is dangerous, and workers need help from their agencies to protect themselves.
16. Hazards of human service work include workers' rescue fantasies, the fact that some problems cannot be solved, and the enormity of the problems.
17. Taking control of one's work situation involves understanding the social and political structure of the agency and its relationship to the larger society.
18. Informal support groups, professional organizations, and unions are important sources of support.
19. A supportive supervisor can help workers function at their full potential.
20. One of the most important qualities of a good supervisor is the ability to allow workers freedom in and responsibility for their own work.
21. Individual methods of change include finding more creative ways of doing the work, varying the work, improving one's competence, and joining the "community of scholars" by contributing to the dialogue of the profession.
22. Unions can give workers more control over the conditions of their work.
23. Workers need to protect themselves from impossible demands and learn how to say *no* without feeling guilty.
24. Taking care of oneself includes good nutrition, regular exercise, rest, recreation, reading, and friendships.

Discussion Questions

1. If you were in charge of a social agency, how would you structure it to avoid worker burnout?
2. Imagine that you are a worker who wants to form a union to improve wages and working conditions. The administrator of your agency calls a meeting to warn workers about the dangers of unions and makes a veiled threat that workers might be fired if they try to form a union. How would you respond to this?
3. What are some examples of federal and state laws that might contribute to worker burnout?
4. What are some examples of agency regulations that might contribute to worker burnout?
5. Describe what you would consider to be the ideal supervisor and the ideal method of supervision.

Web Resources for Further Study

American Federation of State, County, and Municipal Employees (AFSCME)

https://www.afscme.org

U.S. Department of Labor

https://www.dol.gov

Service Employees International Union (SEIU)

https://www.seiu.org

Employee Assistance Plans

http://workplacementalhealth.org/Mental-Health-Topics/Employee-Assistance-Programs

---

MyLab Helping Professions for Introduction to Human Services

In the Topic 12 Assignments: Self-Development and Self-Care, try Application Exercise 12.4: Self-Care and Credentialing Quiz 12.4: Self-Care.

GLOSSARY

acceptance versus rejection As a human service worker it is critical that one remain open when working with individuals from a different culture to avoid the pitfalls of implicit assumptions by remaining mindful of one's potential bias.

accountability A requirement, usually imposed by a funding source, that an agency perform according to a certain set of standards.

advising Telling the interviewee what to do. Used with caution, if at all, in interviews because it incorrectly assumes that one person knows what is best for another.

ageism The practice of discriminating against people who are older; attitudes associated with the practice.

Alcoholics Anonymous (AA) A self-help organization that uses a specific 12-step program for recovery from addiction to alcohol.

anxiety disorder A biological condition in which feelings of extreme fear, tension, and dread often overwhelm the person, even when there is no apparent threat to his well-being.

attention deficit/hyperactivity disorder (ADHD) A biological condition with early onset and often long duration that interferes with a person's capacity to focus and sustain interest, especially when the agenda is set by an outside authority, as in a school or work setting.

behaviorist A theorist who believes that behavior can be shaped or changed by the systematic application of rewards for behavioral compliance with the demands of the caregiver or therapist.

bicultural theory A theory asserting that although people are socialized into their minority culture through family and ethnic community, they are also influenced by the dominant culture through social institutions and the mass media.

bureaucratization Increased organizational centralization, hierarchical control, larger workplaces, and decreased autonomy for workers.

career ladder A specific path of jobs that relates accomplishment and tenure to upward mobility.

careerism A single-minded preoccupation with getting ahead in a career to the exclusion of other interests or values.

case conferences Conferences about a particular client in which staff members pool their information and share resources.

change agents Workers who use their skills to bring about change in an unhealthy agency or situation, either alone or in concert with others.

charismatic qualities Qualities of a person who profoundly influences others through the dynamism of her personality.

Charity Organization Societies (COS) The earliest professional social work agencies, organized first in England and later in the United States; they claimed to deliver "scientific charity" through case-by-case work of "friendly visitors."

child-saving movement A term used to describe the efforts of reformers in the late nineteenth and early twentieth centuries to rescue children from "unwholesome influences." The movement led to the development of children's institutions, foster care, and the juvenile court.

clarifying Seeking further understanding of what has been said in an interview.

client self-determination A profound belief that the person who has the problem must make her own decision on the next steps.

cliff effect The sudden loss of benefits due to an increase in income that puts the individual over-income to receive benefits.

co-dependency A mutually destructive relationship between a person who is addicted and his significant other, who helps to continue, rather than break, the addiction.

community residences Small living units, houses, or apartments located in communities that serve people who have disabilities or other special situations that render them unable to live on their own (also known as halfway houses or group homes).

comparable worth A practice of describing and paying wages for jobs according to their inherent difficulty and worth in order to help equalize women's wages with men's.

confidentiality The concept that what a client reveals to the worker is kept from others unless there is a legal reason to reveal it.

conflict resolution The way in which a group handles sharp differences in opinion or digressions from accepted standards.

confronting A tactic used by an interviewer to point out to interviewee discrepancies or inconsistencies in the interviewee's words or behavior.

contracting out A system whereby a government agency contracts with a private agency to do some specified work for pay.

cyberbullying The use of cyber communication technology to deliberately and repeatedly spread hostile opinions or other data intended to harass a targeted victim.

deinstitutionalization A large-scale reform movement that took people out of institutions and hospitals and returned them to their community with special services to aid their reintegration.

deserving versus undeserving The discriminatory classification of people into higher and lower categories, considering some people to be worthier of receiving benefits and services than others.

dialectical Refers to the principle that an idea or event (thesis) generates its opposite (antithesis), leading to a reconciliation of opposites (synthesis) and a continuation of the dialectical process.

direct action An action that interferes with the orderly conduct of a system that is the target of change.

direct-service strategies Worker actions that deliver services directly to clients.

door opener An invitation to say more about something that an interviewee has brought up, preferably in the form of an open-ended request for information.

due process Procedural mechanisms that secure or protect a person's legal rights.

empathy An attempt to put oneself in the shoes of another person, to feel or think of a problem from another perspective.

encouraging and reassuring When the interviewer provides a message of hopefulness in an attempt to inspire confidence, sometimes without regard to what a person is actually feeling.

entitlements Benefits and services that people have a legal right to, as compared with those that are given at the discretion of officials. Medicare and Social Security are entitlement programs available to everyone who has worked and paid into them.

ethics of helping An ethical commitment to help others rather than engage in dog-eat-dog competition.

euthanasia Active intervention in hastening death, usually made by a doctor with the permission of the dying person or her family.

evidence-based approach A delivery of services where there is an evaluation component and where the focus is on strategies and programs that are successful.

expert witness A person who is especially knowledgeable in a particular field and who is asked to give testimony based on that knowledge in a court trial.

external barriers Barriers in the environment that make it difficult for a person to receive help.

facilitators People involved in helping to move group members in the direction of their goals.

family preservation A commitment to provide the resources and supports that can hold together or reunite a family unit, especially to provide stability to the children.

family self-sufficiency standard A calculation of income needed to afford basic needs when constructing a minimum budget. It is based on real costs for a geographic area.

feedback Both positive and negative critical comments on particular actions, statements, or other factors.

force-field analysis A systematic way of looking at the negatives and positives of an idea or event in order to understand it fully, anticipate problems, and estimate chances of success.

furthering responses Any response, either verbal or nonverbal, on the part of the interviewer that encourages the interviewee to continue to talk or expand on what they are sharing.

GAP A necessary service or resource that is lacking in a program or in services that might help solve a problem.

generalist A worker who is knowledgeable about a wide range of resources and subgroups and who can use a variety of helping interventions.

Google search Clicking onto a web search engine owned by Google Inc., which is one of the most-used search engines on the web, receiving millions of queries and postings each day.

grassroots programs Programs started by people who do not hold the official decision-making positions within a system but have a stake in the outcome of its services or policies.

green Those products, services, or activities that exert no negative impact on the health of people or on the environment.

group bond or cohesion A complex set of forces that weld each member to the group and to each other.

group structure The sum total of rules and regulations that govern how a group organizes itself to do its work.

guest worker programs Programs that contract immigrants to work for a specified time in the United States for a particular job, but do not hold out any promise of citizenship.

Head Start A federally funded preschool program that aims to increase the readiness for public school of children from low-income families. It was begun by the War on Poverty in the 1960s.

homophobia An unreasoning fear or loathing of people who have intimate sexual relationships with people of the same sex.

humanitarian ethos A dedication to promoting the welfare of humanity, especially through the elimination of pain and suffering.

human service networks (or delivery systems) Programs and entitlements that offer help in dealing with different but complementary parts of an overall problem.

image of an agency The reputation that a social agency has established in its community.

indirect or systems-change strategies Acts aimed at helping clients by creating or improving the organizations that are necessary to deliver services to them.

indirect questions This type of question provides an opening for an interviewee to talk about a topic without actually directly questioning the individual on the topic. For example, "Can you tell me how things are going?"

informed choice A choice that is made after a person has been given all the relevant information about the issue.

informed consent An agreement to do something or to allow something to happen, made with complete knowledge of all relevant facts, such as the risks involved or any available alternatives.

Institutional, or developmental, philosophy of social welfare A philosophy that looks at people as being embedded in a social system and as having predictable developmental needs.

institutional racism (or institutional sexism) Discrimination against a racial group (or gender) practiced by an organization or an institution, usually perpetuated by an interconnected system of policies and practices.

intake interviews An interview (form) that solicits relevant information before the delivery of a service begins.

internal barriers Emotions or attitudes within a person that make it difficult for him to seek help.

interpreting A form of response used by the interviewer that speculates on the meaning of an interviewee's statement or behavior.

involuntary clients Clients who are forced to use a social service, usually by a court.

laissez faire style A leadership style in which the worker allows the process of the group to flow with a minimum amount of leader direction.

leadership acts and roles Influential behavior (feelings, acts, or words) that moves a group toward its primary purposes and/or maintains the group.

least restrictive setting The type of treatment and location that provide the greatest amount of freedom to a client (who often has a specific disability).

LGBTQ Abbreviation for the community of lesbian, gay, bisexual, transgender, and queer (or questioning) persons.

linkage technology The acts involved in referring a client to another agency, worker, or resource.

lobby To attempt to convince decision makers to support one's ideas or proposed actions.

macroaggressions Large-scale or overt aggression toward those of a different race, culture, or gender.

magnifying phase Looking at a program or problem within the larger context of the community, laws, professional field, and so forth.

mainstreaming Placing people who have emotional or physical disabilities into the mainstream of society as much as possible. The Individuals with Disabilities Education Act (IDEA) requires that all children be taught in non–special education settings, such as public school settings, whenever possible.

managed health care A health care system in which an individual must choose among the doctors included in a particular plan, such as a health maintenance organization. It generally stresses preventive health care but is often used as a cost-cutting measure.

mandated treatment Treatment that is legally required by the courts or by government officials.

manipulation Attempts to influence someone's behavior or thoughts by covert, unstated methods rather than open, explicit methods.

means-tested programs Programs that are available only to those whose assets fall below a certain set eligibility level.

microaggressions Brief and commonly placed daily verbal, behavioral, or environmental indignities, whether intentional or unintentional, that communicate hostile, derogatory, or negative slights against people of color or other marginalized groups within the society.

microscoping Looking at a program or problem and seeing within it all the component parts and steps of action needed.

multicausality The view that personal or social problems are caused by many interacting factors, often too complex to allow a precise assessment of causality.

negotiate a contract To forge an agreement between a helper and a helpee about what will be included in their work together.

New Careers for the Poor movement A movement that began in the 1960s to train workers who do not have extensive formal credentials for human service jobs.

nonjudgmental Describes an attitude that withholds moral judgments on another person's behaviors, attitudes, or values.

norming A process of arriving at mutually acceptable rules, regulations, and standards of behavior.

norms Mutually acceptable rules, regulations, and standards of behavior.

objective data Data based on unbiased facts, not affected by personal feelings or prejudice.

open-ended questions Questions that provide an opening for the interviewee to expand on their thoughts and feelings. For example, an open-ended question would be, "Tell me about your experience."

outreach worker A human service worker who explains the work of her agency and encourages those who need the services to participate.

overidentification The process of relating so completely to another person's feelings and/or experiences that one cannot separate oneself from the other person.

paraphrasing, or restating Putting an interviewee's words in another form without changing the content in order to encourage the interviewee to go on speaking.

Pay for Success Model Reforms the payment for and delivery of social services to successful outcomes versus paying for outputs.

permanency planning An attempt to create, in a timely fashion, a plan for a child that will return him safely to his family of origin or legally free him to be adopted.

posttraumatic stress disorder (PTSD) A common anxiety disorder that develops after exposure to a terrifying event or ordeal in which grave physical harm occurred or was threatened. Family members of victims also can develop the disorder. PTSD can occur in people of any age, including children and adolescents.

primary purpose The main goal of an agency that determines the work it does.

primary reference groups Groups in which a person is intimately involved, including family and friends who influence one's attitudes and values.

principle of less eligibility The principle that the amount of welfare given to people should be less than the lowest wage so that people will not be tempted to take welfare rather than get a wage-earning job.

principle of reciprocity The principle that social relationships are based to some extent on an analysis of trade-offs that determine what each person must give to the relationship in order to get back certain benefits.

privacy The right to be left alone.

privatization Changing the funding and administration of social welfare programs from the public to the private sector.

privileged communication Legal protection of confidences revealed in certain specified relationships.

problem-solving skills Systematic techniques that aid in achieving a goal in the most efficient and effective manner.

professional helping relationship A relationship between a worker and client(s) that follows a pattern determined by the goals and ethics of the human service field.

program design The thoughtful mapping out of a program so that it includes an analysis of tasks, strategies, resources, responsibilities, schedules, a budget, and an evaluation plan.

program proposal A proposal for a program including the thoughtful mapping out of the necessary tasks, strategies, resources, responsibilities, budget, and evaluation plan.

Progressives Members of the Progressive party in the early twentieth century who favored social reforms such as abolition of child labor, juvenile courts, and more individualized treatment of those with mental illnesses.

progressive taxes Taxes that tax the rich at a higher rate than those who are less affluent. Income taxes with gradual rates based on income are progressive, while a flat tax on income is considered regressive.

psychosocial model of disability A model that looks at the entire environment of the person, including social attitudes, attitudes of other individuals, and the society that the able-bodied have created.

public-health approach A preventive approach to social problems as opposed to a remedial approach. It implements large-scale programs to meet people's basic health and nutritional needs in order to prevent illness.

racism Hatred or intolerance of another race or other races. Belief that one's own race is superior.

referral statement An initial verbal or written statement that explains the reasons a client is being sent to or has chosen a specific resource, person, or agency.

reflecting An interviewer response that puts into words what the interviewer thinks the interviewee might be feeling.

rescue fantasies Fantasies that envision saving someone from his fate.

residential treatment center A facility providing mental and physical services for a specific problem population which requires that the person being treated stay within its walls for a specified period of time.

residual philosophy of social welfare A philosophy that views the problem requiring help as not a "normal" social need but one that arises from special circumstances brought about by individual deficiency.

resource bank People, places, services, or written materials that help people meet a program's needs and reach their goals.

respite care Care in which a paid worker relieves a person who is a primary caretaker so that the caretaker can pursue outside tasks or have some free time.

right to refuse treatment Legal protection granted to a person who does not want treatment that is prescribed by professionals.

right to treatment Legal assurance that a person who is placed in an institution that purports to give treatment does, in fact, receive treatment.

root causes The critical causes of a particular problem that seem to have contributed most significantly to its emergence.

self-determination A person's right to determine his own life plan without interference.

settlement house movement A movement of the late nineteenth and early twentieth centuries that established agencies in city slums of England and the United States, where professionals gave group services and engaged in social action on behalf of the slum dwellers.

Social Darwinism The application of Charles Darwin's theories of evolution to the human sphere by sociologist Herbert Spencer. The concept of "survival of the fittest" was used to justify accumulation of wealth and disregard of the needs of the poor.

social determinants of health (SDH) The conditions in which people are born, grow, work, live, and age, and the wider set of forces and systems shaping the conditions of daily life.

social safety net The collection of services provided by governments and institutions to help individuals from falling into poverty, or to some unacceptable level of poverty.

Social welfare programs State or federal programs that are designed to provide assistance to at-risk and vulnerable individuals, including those with lower income, older citizens, and those with disabilities.

stigma Something that detracts from the character or reputation of a person or group; a mark of disgrace or reproach.

stigmatization versus validation Working from a whole person perspective, the helper must understand the individualized experience from the lens of the individual being served. From this point, the helper is able to both affirm and normalize the experience of the individual being helped.

Storming Debating and arguing different views.

subjective data Personal opinions about the client's attitude, situation, and behavior that may or may not be objectively true.

suggesting When the interviewer gives a mild form of advice, generally made tentatively.

Supplemental Poverty Measure (SPM) An income threshold calculation that takes into account the value of social welfare benefits such as pre-tax income, cash transfers, in-kind transfers, SNAP (food stamps), and tax credits, in addition to household income.

support network The people and places in our lives that offer ongoing practical as well as emotional help.

task-focused casework A method of helping a person with a problem by focusing on the immediate priorities of the client and the small steps involved in realizing, or seeking to realize, the ultimate goal.

therapeutic or rehabilitative Characterizes groups whose members usually have in common a mental or physical problem of some magnitude; usually led by a professionally trained leader.

third-party payment A payment made by an insurance company or a government program for medical expenses incurred by an individual.

time flow chart A diagram of the tasks that need to be done in a certain period of time by specific individuals.

trade-offs Those things that must be sacrificed to obtain another hoped-for benefit.

transgender Appearing, acting, or actually becoming (by means of medical procedures) the opposite gender from the one a person is identified as at birth.

12-step program A program of healing activities designed by the founders of Alcoholics Anonymous.

unintended consequences of reform Events that occur as a result of reform measures that were not planned or anticipated by the reformers.

universal programs Programs that provide income supports and social services to both the affluent and the poor. Public education is an example of a universal program.

value conflicts Disagreements brought about by differences in values between people.

value dilemmas Situations in which competing values make it difficult, if not impossible, to determine the correct response.

victim blaming Blaming a person for her own misfortune rather than considering the social forces that contributed to her problem.

vulnerability versus empowerment. In the helping relationship it is essential for the helper to fully understand the experience of the individual being served, to understand just how vulnerable they are so that it is possible to fully support a process of building on their strengths through empowerment.

wealth In financial terms this is the amount of assets in excess of liabilities—in other words what you own versus what you owe. A person's wealth might include equity in homes, savings accounts, and investments less any debt owed.

REFERENCES

A blow to health plan patients. (2004, June 23). *The New York Times.*

A Look at the State of School Integration 64 Years After Brown vs Board of Education. All Things Considered. NPR, March 28, 2018.

Abdullah, T., & Brown, T. L. (2011). Mental illness stigma and ethnocultural beliefs, values, and norms: An integrative review. *Clinical Psychology Review, 31*(6), 934–948.

Abramovitz, M. (1988). *Regulating the lives of women: Social welfare policy from colonial times to the present.* Boston: South End Press.

ADA National Network. *What is the definition of disability under the ADA?* Retrieved from https://adata.org/faq/what-definition-disability-under-ada

Adams, M. (2002, November). Showing good faith towards Muslims. *Human Resources Magazine, 45,* 11.

Administration on Aging online. *A Statistical Profile of Older Americans.* Retrieved from https://acl.gov/sites/default/files/news%20 2017-03/A_Statistical_Profile_of_Older_ Americans.pdf

Ahmed, S. & Matthes, J. (2017). Media representation of Muslims and Islam from 2000 to 2015: A meta-analysis. *International Communication Gazette, 79*(3), 219–244

Albert, E. (1989). AIDS and the press: The creation and transformation of a social problem. In Joel Best (Ed.), *Images of issues* (pp. 39–54). New York: Aldine de Gruyter.

Alink, L. R., Euser, S. Bakermans-Kranenburg, M. J., & van IJzendoorn, M. H. (2014). A challenging job: Physical and sexual violence towards group workers in youth residential care. *Child & Youth Care Forum, 43*(2), pp. 243–250.

Alinsky, S. (1969). *Reveille for radicals.* New York: Vintage Books.

Alinsky, S. (1971). *Rules for radicals: A practical primer for realistic radicals.* New York: Random House.

Allport, G. (1954). *The nature of prejudice.* Reading, MA: Addison-Wesley.

American Civil Liberties Union. (2007). *Education not incarceration.* Retrieved from https://www.aclu.org/cases/driving-while-black-maryland

American College of Physicians. (2010). *Racial and ethnic disparities in health care,* updated 2010. Retrieved from http://www. acponline.org/advocacy/where_we_stand/ access/racial_disparities.pdf

American Psychiatric Association. (2017). *DSM-5—The diagnostic and statistical manual of mental disorders, 5th edition.* Washington, D.C.: American Psychiatric Association Publishing.

American Psychological Association (2010). *Ethical Principles of Psychologists and Code of Conduct.* Retrieved from https:// www.apa.org/ethics/code/index.aspx

American Self-Help Group Clearinghouse (2011). *The Self-Help Support Group Directory: Your Guide to Local New Jersey, National and Online Groups, 26th Edition.* Dover, NJ.

Andrews, H. B. (1995). *Group design and leadership.* Boston: Allyn & Bacon.

Angus Reid Global Monitor. (2007). *Another immigration myth bites the dust.* Retrieved from http://latinalista.com/palabrafinal/ by_now_the_vast_majority

Anti-Defamation League. (1998, September). *Anti-Semitism in America, highlights from an ADL survey.* See www.adl.org.

Antlitz, K. M. (2013). Do we worship the same god?: Jews, Christians, and Muslims in dialogue. Miroslav Volf (Ed.). Grand Rapids, MI: Wm. B. Eerdmans Publishing Co.

Archibold, R. & Preston, J. (2008, May 21). Homeland Security stands by its fence. *The New York Times.* Retrieved from http://www.nytimes. com/2008/05/21/Washington/21/fence

Ari, L. & Mula, W. (2017). "Us and them": Towards intercultural competence among Jewish and Arab graduate students at Israeli colleges of education. *Higher Education, 74*(6).

Associated Press. (2010, April 5). Tutoring found to help mentors, too. *The Boston Globe,* p. A2.

Atkinson, L. & Kunkel, O. D. (1992). Should social workers participate in treatment only if the client consents to such treatment freely and without coercion? In E. Gambrill & R. Pruger (Eds.), *Controversial issues in social work* (pp. 157–172). Boston: Allyn & Bacon.

Austin, A. (2016). Obamacare reduces racial disparities in health coverage. Center for Global Policy Solutions.

Authorization to Release Information (ND). Department of Health and Human Services. Retrieved from Maine.gov

Banfield, E. (1974). *The unheavenly city.* Boston: Little, Brown.

Barbash, F. (1982, June 19). Justices rule for mentally retarded. *The Boston Globe,* p. 13.

Bass, A. (1992, February 3). Illness coupled with stigma. *The Boston Globe,* p. 16.

Battle, M. (1990). In *Encyclopedia of social work: 1990 supplement* (18th ed., pp. 232–233). Silver Spring, MD: National Association of Social Workers.

Bazelon, E. (2010, July 14). The new abortion providers. *The New York Times.* Retrieved from https://www.nytimes.com/2010/07/18/ magazine/18abortion-t.html

Belluck, P. (2018, April 23). Trump administration pushes abstinence in teen pregnancy programs. *The New York Times.* Retrieved from https://www.nytimes.com/2018/04/23/health/ trump-teen-pregnancy-abstinence.html

Berenson, B. G. & Mitchell, K. M. (1974). *Confrontation: For better or worse!* Amherst, MA: Human Resource Development Press.

Berkeley Planning Associates. (1978, August). Evaluation of child abuse and neglect demonstration projects, 1974–1977 (Vols. 1 and 2, DHEW Publication No. (PHS) 79-3217-1). Hyattsville, MD: National Center for Health Services Research, U.S. Department of Health, Education and Welfare.

Bershoff, D. N. (1975). Professional ethics and legal responsibilities: On the horns of a dilemma. *Journal of School Psychology 13,* 359–376.

Bertcher, H. J. (1994). *Group participation: Techniques for leaders and members (2nd ed.).* Thousand Oaks, CA: Sage.

Best, J. (Ed.). (1989). *Images of issues.* New York: Aldine deGruyter.

Bettelheim, B. (1950). *Love is not enough: The treatment of emotionally disturbed children.* Glencoe, IL: Free Press.

Bialek, K. (2017, October 6). American deepest in poverty lost more ground in 2016. Pew Research Center. Retrieved from http://www.pewresearch.org/fact-tank/ 2017/10/06/americans-deepest-in-poverty-lost-more-ground-in-2016/

Bialik, K., & Krogstad, J. M. (January 24, 2017). 115th Congress sets new high for racial, ethnic diversity. Pew Research Center. Retrieved from http://www.pewresearch.org/ fact-tank/2017/01/24/115th-congress-sets-new-high-for-racial-ethnic-diversity/

Bivens, J., & Mishel, M. (2015, September 2). Understanding the historic divergence between productivity and a typical worker's pay. Economic Policy Institute. Retrieved from https://www.epi.org/publication/ understanding-the-historic-divergence-between-productivity-and-a-typical-workers-pay-why-it-matters-and-why-its-real/

Blau, J. (1992). *The visible poor: Homelessness in the United States.* New York: Oxford University Press

Blau, M., & Grinberg, E. (2016). Why US inmates launched a nationwide strike. Retrieved from https://www.cnn.com/2016/10/30/us/us-prisoner-strike/index.html

Bobo, K., Kendall, J., & Max, S. (2010). *Organizing for social change (4th ed.).* Washington, D.C.: Seven Locks Press.

Boddie, E. C. (2016). Adaptive discrimination. *North Carolina Law Review, 94*(4), 1275.

Bor, W., Heath, F., Heussler, H., Reuter, R., Perrett, C., & Lee, E. (2013). Can a multidisciplinary assessment approach improve outcomes for children with attention deficit hyperactivity disorder? *Australasian Psychiatry 21*(5), 499–503.

Bordin, E. S. (1979). The generalizability of the psychoanalytic concept of the working alliance. *Psychotherapy: Theory, Research and Practice, 16*(3), pp. 252–260.

Borenstein, M. (2018). Compassion fatigue and vicarious trauma in caregivers. *Soins. Pediatrie, Puericulture 39*(304), 13–15. Retrieved from https://doi-org.nec.gmilcs. org/10.1016/j.spp.2018.07.003

Boston Women's Health Book Collective & Norsigian, J. (2011). *Our Bodies, Ourselves.* New York: Simon and Schuster.

Boyd, J. A. (1990). Ethnic and cultural diversity: Keys to power. In L. S. Brown & M. P. Root (Eds.), *Diversity and complexity in feminist therapy* (pp. 151–167). New York: Harrington Park Press.

Boyte, H. C. (1980). *The backyard revolution: Understanding the new citizen movement.* Philadelphia: Temple University Press.

Bozick, R., & Miller, T. (2014). In-state college tuition policies for undocumented immigrants: Implications for high school enrollment among non-citizen Mexican youth. *Population Research and Policy Review 33*(1), 13–30.

Brager, G. (2002). *Changing human service organizations.* New York: The Free Press.

Brager, G., Specht, H., & Torczyner, J. L. (1987). *Community organization (2nd ed.).* New York: Columbia University Press.

Bramhall, M., & Ezell, S. (1991, Summer). How agencies can prevent burnout. *Public Welfare,* 33–37.

Brawley, E. A. (1980, March). Emerging human service education programs: Characteristics and implications for social work education and practice. [unpublished report prepared for the Joint Board Committee of the National Association of Social Workers and the Council on Social Work Education].

Breaking a promise on surveillance. (2010, July 29). *The New York Times.* Retrieved from https://www.nytimes.com/2010/07/30/opinion/30fri1.html

Breitbart, V., & Schram, B. (1978, September). Rocking the cradle without rocking the boat: An analysis of twenty-four child-raising manuals. *Bulletin of the Council on Interracial Books for Children 9*(6 and 7), 4.

Brieland, D., & Goldfarb, S. Z. (1987). Legal issues and legal services. In *Encyclopedia of social work* (pp. 29–33). Silver Spring, MD: National Association of Social Workers.

Bucci, S., Seymour-Hyde, A., Harris, A., & Berry, K. (2016). Client and therapist attachment styles and working alliance: Attachment and working alliance. *Clinical Psychology & Psychotherapy, 23*(2), 155–165.

Burd-Sharps, S., & Rasch, R. (2015, June). Impact of the US housing crisis on the racial wealth gap across generations. Social Science Research Council.

Bureau of Justice Statistics. Estimated number of persons supervised by U.S. adult correctional systems, by correctional status, 1980–2014. Annual Probation Survey, Annual Parole Survey, Annual Survey of Jails, Census of Jail Inmates, and National Prisoner Statistics Program, 1980–2014.

Bureau of Labor Statistics (2017). Labor Force Statistics from the Current Population Survey. Retrieved from https://www.bls.gov/cps/cpsaat11.htm

Bustillo, M. (2007, March 4). Texas bill targets benefits of immigrants' children. *The Boston Globe,* p. A12.

Butler, D. (2005). 92% of sexual assaults go unreported: Final edition. *The Gazette.*

Butler, R. N. (1975). *Why survive? Being old in America.* New York: Harper & Row.

Buttell, F. (1998, Spring). Issues and ethics in social work with batterers. *The New Social Worker, 5,* 7–9.

Campagna, A. (1994). *The economy in the Reagan years: The economic consequences of the Reagan administrations (contributions in economics and economic history).* Westport, CT: Greenwood Press.

Carden, A. (1994). Wife abuse and the wife abuser: Review and recommendations. *The Counseling Psychologist 22,* 539–582.

Caregiving in the U.S., 2015. The National Alliance for Caregiving (NAC) and the AARP Public Policy Institute. Retrieved from http://www.aarp.org/content/dam/aarp/ppi/2015/caregiving-in-the-united-states-2015-report-revised.pdf

Castle, M. (2011). Abortion in the United States' Bible belt: Organizing for power and empowerment. *Reproductive Health, 8*(1), 1–1.

Centers for Disease Control. (2017). Prescription Opioid Data. Retrieved from https://www.cdc.gov/drugoverdose/data/prescribing.html

Centers for Medicare and Medicaid Services. (2015). *Number of Children Ever Enrolled Report.* Data Source: Statistical Enrollment Data System (SEDS) forms CMS-21E, CMS-64.21E, CMS-64.EC (06/01/2016).

Chambers, C. A. (1980). *Seedtime of reform: American social service and social action 1918–1933.* Westport, CT: Greenwood Press.

Chandler, D. L. (1997, May 11). In shift, many anthropologists see race as social construct. *The Boston Globe,* p. A30.

Chappell, D. (2004, May 8). If affirmative action fails . . . what then? *The New York Times.* Retrieved from https://www.nytimes.com/2004/05/08/books/an-essay-if-affirmative-action-fails-what-then.html

Chiaburu, D. S., Diaz, I., & De Vos, A. (2013). Employee alienation: Relationships with careerism and career satisfaction. *Journal of Managerial Psychology 28*(1), 4–20.

Childwelfare.gov. (2014). Retrieved from www.childwelfare.gov

Chorpita, B. F., Daleiden, E. L., & Collins, K. S. (2014). Managing and adapting practice: A system for applying evidence in clinical care with youth and families. *Clinical Social Work Journal, 42*(2), 134–142.

Chuang, E., Wells, R., & Alexander, J. A. (2011). Public managed care and service access in outpatient substance abuse treatment units. *The Journal of Behavioral Health Services & Research 38*(4), 444–63. doi: 10.1007/s11414-010-9230-y

Coalition of Battered Women's Advocates. (1988, November 1). Position paper on child welfare [unpublished manuscript].

Code of Ethics. (2008). National Association of Social Workers. Retrieved from https://www.socialworkers.org/About/Ethics/Code-of-Ethics

Code of Federal Regulations—Title 45—Public Welfare, 2003. Retrieved from https://www.govinfo.gov/content/pkg/CFR-2003-title45-vol1/xml/CFR-2003-title45-vol1-sec164-510.xml

Cohen, K., & Collens, P. (2013). The impact of trauma work on trauma workers: A meta-synthesis on vicarious trauma and vicarious posttraumatic growth. *Psychological Trauma: Theory, Research, Practice, and Policy 5*(6), 570–580. doi: http://dx.doi.org.fgul.idm.oclc.org/10.1037/a0030388.

Cohen, M., & Gagin, R. (2005). Can skill-development training alleviate burnout in hospital social workers? *Social Work in Health Care 40*(4), 83–97. doi: 10.1300/J010v40n04_05

Colón, S., Finger, B., Harrison, T., Hirsch, M., Holmstrom, N., Botz, D. L., & Schulman, J. (2017). Trump takes office, resistance takes to the streets. *New Politics 16*(2), 3.

Colbert, S. (2007). *I am America (and so can you!).* New York: Grand Central Publishing.

Coleman, D., Dodge, K., & Campbell, S. (2010). Where and how to draw the line between reasonable corporal punishment and abuse. *Law and Contemporary Problems 73*(2), 107–165.

Coles, R. (1977). *Privileged ones: The well-off and the rich in America.* Boston:Little, Brown.

Collins, P. H. (1990). *Black feminist thought: Knowledge, consciousness, and the politics of empowerment.* London: Harper Collins.

Collins, S. (2002). Confrontation of clients and users—for better or worse. *Practice, 14*(3), 31–50. doi: 10.1080/09503150208411532

Collins, W. L. (2005). Embracing spirituality as an element of professional self care. *Social Work & Christianity 32,* 263–274.

Congressional Budget Office. (2017, November 8). Repealing the Individual Health Insurance Mandate: An Updated Estimate. Retrieved from https://www.cbo.gov/publication/53300

Consumer Federation of America. (2006, December 7). Women More Likely to Receive Subprime Home Loans, Disparity Highest for Women with Highest Income. Retrieved from https://consumerfed.org/press_release/women-more-likely-to-receive-subprime-home-loans-disparity-highest-for-women-with-highest-income/

Cook, C. R., Mayer, G. R., Wright, D. B., Kraemer, B., Wallace, M. D., Dart, E., Collins, T., & Restori, A. (2012). Exploring the link among behavior intervention plans, treatment integrity, and student outcomes under natural educational conditions. *The Journal of Special Education 46*(1), 3–16.

Cooper, D. (2016, February 3). Economic Policy Institute, Balancing Pay Checks and Public Assistance. Retrieved from https://www.epi.org/publication/wages-and-transfers/

Cottle, T. J. (1974). *A family album.* New York: Harper & Row.

Craun, S. W., & Theriot, M. T. (2009). Misperceptions of sex offender perpetration: Considering the impact of sex offender registration. *Journal of Interpersonal Violence 24*(12), 2057–2072.

Crenshaw K. (1989). Demarginalizing the intersection of race and sex: A Black feminist critique of antidiscrimination doctrine, feminist theory, and antiracist politics. *University of Chicago Legal Forum 14*, 538–54.

Creswell, J. D., & Lindsay, E. K. (2014). How does mindfulness training affect health? A mindfulness stress buffering account. *Current Directions in Psychological Science 23*(6), 401–407.

Cross, C. J., Nguyen, A. W., Chatters, L. M., & Taylor, R. J. (2018). Instrumental social support exchanges in African American extended families. *Journal of Family Issues 39*(13)

Curtin, E. R. (1970). *White-collar unionization.* New York: National Industrial Conference Board.

D'Augelli, A. R., D'Augelli, J. F., & Danish, S. J. (1981). *Helping others.* Monterey, CA: Brooks/Cole.

DeCino, D., Waalkes, P., & Matos, C. (2018). "Be Ready for It": School Counselors' Experiences With Subpoena and Testifying in Court. Professional School Counseling. American School Counseling Association. Sage.

DeHart-Davis, L., & Pandey, S. K. (2005). Red tape and public employees: Does perceived rule dysfunction alienate managers? *Journal of Public Administration Research and Theory: J-PART 15*(1), 133–148. doi: 10.1093/jopart/mui007

DeParle, J. (1997, September 11). As rules on welfare tighten, its recipients gain in stature. *The New York Times*, pp. A1, A28.

Detention Watch Network. (2009). About the U.S. detention and deportation system. Retrieved from http://www.detentionwatch-network.org/aboutdetention

DeWitt, L. (2010). The Decision to Exclude Agricultural and Domestic Workers from the 1935 Social Security Act. *Social Security Bulletin 70*(4), 2010.

Di Giovanni, M. (1996, April 17). Speech at the New England Organization of Human Service Educators.

Dickson, D. T. (1976, July). Law in social work: Impact on due process. *Social Work 21*, 274–278.

Dinarski, S. (2018, July 6). Fresh Proof That Strong Unions Help Reduce Income Inequality. *The New York Times.* Retrieved from https://www.nytimes.com/2018/07/06/business/labor-unions-income-inequality.html

Directory of Catholic Worker Communities. Retrieved from http://www.catholicworker.org/communities/directory.html

DiTomaso, N. (2013). *The American non-dilemma: Racial inequality without racism.* New York: Russell Sage Foundation.

Donovon., P. Guttmacher Report. Retrieved from https://www.guttmacher.org/sites/default/files/pdfs/pubs/tgr/01/1/gr010110.pdf

Drivers of Growth in the Federal Prison Population. (2015, March). Urban Institute. Retrieved from http://www.urban.org/sites/default/files/publication/43681/2000141-Drivers-of-Growth-in-the-Federal-Prison-Population.pdf

Dum, C. P., Norris, R. J., & Weng, K. (2017). Punishing benevolence: The criminalization of homeless feeding as an act of state harm. *Critical Criminology 25*(4), 483–506.

Dumont, M. (1992). *Treating the poor.* Belmont, MA: Dymphna Press.

Dunlap, K. (2010, January 25). Sex offenders after prison: Any place to call home? Find Law. Retrieved from https://blogs.findlaw.com/blotter/2010/01/sex-offenders-after-prison-where-to-find-a-place-to-call-home.html

Dunn, M., & Walker, J. (2016, September). Union Membership in the U.S. Department of Labor. Retrieved from https://www.bls.gov/spotlight/2016/union-membership-in-the-united-states/pdf/union-membership-in-the-united-states.pdf

Dupont, A., Castro, M., Nahmens, I., Ikuma, L., & Harvey, C. (2015). Client satisfaction surveys: Administering and reporting in public health units. IIE Annual Conference. Proceedings, p. 1760.

Dutton, S. (2009, June 29). Polling shows support for affirmative action. CBS News. Retrieved from https://www.cbsnews.com/8301-503544_162-5122472-503544.html

Eberhardt, J. L., Davies, P. G., Purdie-Vaughns, V. J., & Johnson, S. L. (2006). Looking deathworthy: Perceived stereotypicality of Black defendants predicts capital-sentencing outcomes. *Psychological Science 17*(5), 383–386.

Eckholm, E. (2007, June 8). Veterans' benefits system needs overhaul, panel says. *The New York Times.* Retrieved from http://www.nytimes.com/2007/06/08/us/08vets.html

Edelman, P. (1997, March). The worst thing Bill Clinton has done. *The Atlantic Monthly*, 43–58. Retrieved from https://www.the-atlantic.com/magazine/archive/1997/03/the-worst-thing-bill-clinton-has-done/376797/

Edelman, P. (2009, Fall). Welfare and the poorest of the poor. *Dissent.* Retrieved from https://www.dissentmagazine.org/article/welfare-and-the-poorest-of-the-poor

Edelman, P., & Ehrenreich, B. (2010, April 10). What really happened to welfare. *Nation*, 15–17.

Ehrenfreund, M. (2016). How welfare reform changed American poverty, in 9 charts. The Washington Post. Retrieved from https://www.washingtonpost.com/news/wonk/wp/2016/08/22/the-enduring-legacy-of-welfare-reform-20-years-later/?utm_term=.bc48f45ef9f4

Ehrenreich, B. (2001). *Nickel and dimed: On (not) getting by in America.* New York: Metropolitan Books.

Ennis, B. J., & Emery, R. D. (1978). *The rights of mental patients: An American Civil Liberties Union handbook.* New York: Avon Books.

Eysenck, H. (1971). *The IQ argument.* Freeport, NY: Library Press.

Ezorsky, G. (1991). *Racism and justice: The case for affirmative action.* Ithaca, NY: Cornell University Press.

Fast Facts January 2019. Centers for Medicare & Medicaid Services (CMS). Retrieved from https://www.cms.gov/research-statistics-data-and-systems/statistics-trends-and-reports/cms-fast-facts/index.html

Feltham, C., & Horton, I. (Eds.) (2012). *The SAGE handbook of counseling and psychotherapy.* London: SAGE.

Fermstad, S. (2010, May 13). Written statement submitted on May 13, 2010 for inclusion in the record of the April 22, 2010 hearing on the role of education and training in the TANF program, Subcommittee on Income Security and Family Support Committee on Ways and Means, U.S. House of Representatives.

Fischer, M. (2013, April 15). Map: How 35 countries compare on child poverty (the U.S. is ranked 34th). *The Washington Post.* Retrieved from https://wapo.st/2U4UqAF

Fisk, M. (2017, Oct. 3). What are the benefits of healthy school lunches? Livestrong Foundation. Retrieved from https://www.livestrong.com/article/289100-what-are-the-benefits-of-healthy-school-lunches/

Flaubert, G. (1959). *Madame Bovary.* New York: Bantam Books (original work published 1856).

Flaws in immigration law. (1997, September 29). *The New York Times*, p. A1. Retrieved from https://nyti.ms/2JABrJV

Floyd, I. (2016). TANF at 22: Still failing to help struggling families meet basic needs. Center on Budget and Policy Priorities. Retrieved from https://www.cbpp.org/blog/tanf-at-22-still-failing-to-help-struggling-families-meet-basic-needs

Floyd, I., Burnside, A., & Schott, L. (2018, November 28). TANF reaching few poor families. Retrieved from https://www.cbpp.org/research/family-income-support/tanf-reaching-few-poor-families

Foreman, J. (2003, July 29). A little empathy please! *The Boston Globe.* Retrieved from https://www.newspapers.com/newspage/442970194/

Foster Coalition. (Updated March 2015). Foster parents: Who are they? Retrieved from http://www.fostercoalition.com/who-are-foster-parents-demographic

Foucault, M. (1987). *Mental illness and psychology.* Berkeley, CA: University of California Press.

France, K., & Kish, M. (1995). *Supportive interviewing in human service organizations: Fundamental skills for gathering and encouraging productive change.* Springfield, IL: Charles C. Thomas.

Frazier, E. R., Liu, G. C., & Dauk, K. L. (2014). Creating a safe place for pediatric care: A no hit zone. *Hospital Pediatrics 4*(4), 247–250.

Frech, R. (2016, August 12). What happened to general assistance in Ohio? Retrieved from https://www.communitysolutions.com/what-happened-to-general-assis/

Freeman, A. (2015, August 18). Single moms and welfare woes: A higher-education dilemma. *The Atlantic.* Retrieved from https://www.theatlantic.com/education/archive/2015/08/why-single-moms-struggle-with-college/401582/

Freeman, J. (1972). The tyranny of structurelessness. In A. Koedt, E. Levine, & A. Rapone (Eds.), *Radical feminism* (pp. 285–299). New York: Quadrangle.

Freire, P. (1970). *The pedagogy of the oppressed* (M. B. Ramos, Trans.). New York: Continuum.

Frieden, L. (2015, July 23). The impact of the DA in American communities. The University of Texas Health Science Center at Houston.

Gallagher, B., Bradford, M., & Pease, K. (2008). Attempted and completed incidents of stranger-perpetrated child sexual abuse and abduction. *Child Abuse & Neglect 32*(5), 517–528.

Gallagher, C. (2003). Color-blind privilege: The social and political functions of erasing the color line in post race America. *Race, Gender & Class 10*(4) 22–37.

Garfinkel, H. (1965, March). Conditions of successful degradation ceremonies. *American Journal of Sociology 61*, 420–424.

General Accounting Office. (2001). Long-term care: Implications of Supreme Court's Olmstead decision are still unfolding. Statement of Kathryn G. Allen at hearing before the Special Committee on Aging, U.S. Senate, Washington DC, September 24, 2001. Serial No. 107–15. Washington, D.C.: U.S. Government Printing Office.

Gerth, R. H., & Mills, C.W. (Eds.). (1958). *From Max Weber: Essays in sociology.* New York: Oxford, Galaxy.

Gilens, M. (1999). *Why Americans hate welfare: Race, media and the politics of antipoverty policy.* Chicago: University of Chicago Press.

Gillentine, A. (2011). Colorado department of human services to repeal 850 rules, regulations. *The Colorado Springs Business Journal* (Pre-June 2, 2012).

Gitterman, A., & Shulman, L. (Eds.) (2005). *Mutual aid groups, vulnerable populations, and the life cycle (3rd ed.).* New York: Columbia University Press.

Glasser, I. (1989). Techniques for teaching anthropology to social work students. *Practicing Anthropology 11*(3), 5–10.

Goldberg, C. (2003, November 28). For good health, it is better to give, science suggests. *The Boston Globe,* p. B5.

Goldberg, C. (2007a, May 7). "No" to drug money. *The Boston Globe,* p. C1.

Goldberg, C. (2007b, June 8). Mental patients find understanding in therapy led by peers. *The Boston Globe,* p. A1.

Golden, D. (1990, November 11). Halfway to where? *The Boston Globe Magazine,* pp. 49–50.

Golding, W. (1959). *Lord of the flies.* New York: Capricorn Books.

Gordon, L. (1994). *Pitied but not entitled: Single mothers and the history of welfare.* New York: Free Press.

Gordon, T. (1970). *Parent effectiveness training.* New York: Peter H. Wyden.

Gore, A., & West, D. (2006). *An inconvenient truth.* [DVD]. Paramount.

Gornick, J. C. (2001, Summer). Cancel the funeral. *Dissent,* 13–18.

Gothard, S. (1995). Legal issues: Confidentiality and privileged communication. In *Encyclopedia of Social Work (19th ed.).* Washington, D.C.: National Association of Social Workers.

Gottlieb, N. (Ed.). (1980a). *Alternative social services for women.* New York: Columbia University Press.

Gottlieb, N. (Ed.). (1980b). Women and mental health. In *Alternative social services for women* (pp. 3–22). New York: Columbia University Press.

Green, A. R., Carney, D. R., Pallin, D. J., Ngo, L. H., Raymond, K. L.,Iezzoni, L. I., & Banaji, M. R. (2007). Implicit bias among physicians and its prediction of thrombolysis decisions for Black and White patients. *Journal of General Internal Medicine 22*(9), 1231–8.

Green, J. (1982). *Cultural awareness in the human services.* Englewood Cliffs, NJ: Prentice Hall.

Greenberg, P. (1969, reprinted 1990). *The devil has slippery shoes.* Los Angeles: Youth Policy Institute.

Greenberg, Z. (2017, January 27). Advocates of fair housing brace for a tough four years. *The New York Times.*

Greene, M. (2018). Number of moms in U.S. prisons on the rise, but each time that happens 'you incarcerate the whole family,' Chicago woman says of experience. *Chicago Tribune.* Retrieved from http://www.chicagotribune.com/news/ct-met-incarcerated-mothers-day-20180511-story.html

Greenhouse, L. (2004, May 18). States can be liable for not making courthouses accessible. *The New York Times,* p. A20.

Greenhouse, S. (2010, September 23). Muslims say they face more discrimination at work. *The New York Times.* Retrieved from http://www.nytimes.com/2010/09/24/business/24muslim.html

Grey, N. (1979, October). Tucson teachers initiate stress counseling program. *NEA Reporter 18.*

Griner, P. F., M.D., M.A.C.P. (2013). Burnout in health care providers. *Integrative Medicine, 12*(1), 22–24.

Grossman, H. (1984). *Manual on terminology and classification in mental retardation.* Washington, D.C.: American Association on Mental Deficiency.

Grote, N. K., Zuckoff, A., Swartz, H., Bledsoe, S. E., & Geibel, S. (2007). Engaging women who are depressed and economically disadvantaged in mental health treatment. *Soc Work 2007; 52*(4), 295–308. Retrieved from https://www.ncbi.nlm.nih.gov/pmc/articles/PMC3025777/

Gruenstein, D., Li, W., & Ernst, K. (2010, June 18). Foreclosures by race and ethnicity. Retrieved from http://www.responsiblelending.org/mortgage-lending/research-analysis/foreclosures-by-race-executive-summary.pdf

Gunderson, J. (2017). *Cyber-bullying: Perpetrators, bystanders and victims.* CreateSpace Independent Publishing Platform.

Gupta, A., Szymanski, D. M., & Leong, F. T. L. (2011). The "model minority myth": Internalized racialism of positive stereotypes as correlates of psychological distress, and attitudes toward help-seeking. *Asian American Journal of Psychology 2*(2), 101–114.

Gutierrez, L. M. (1990, March). Working with women of color: An empowerment perspective. *Social Work 35,* 149–153.

Hülsheger, U. R., Alberts, H. J., Feinholdt, A., and Lang, J.W. (2013). Benefits of mindfulness at work: The role of mindfulness in emotion regulation, emotional exhaustion, and job satisfaction. *Journal of Applied Psychology 98*(2), 310–325.

Hacker, A. (1992, April). Speech at the Socialist Scholars Conference in New York City.

Hackney, H. L., & Cormier, S. (2013). *The professional counselor: A process guide to helping, Plus MyCounselingLab with Pearson eText—Access Card Package, 7th Edition.* Upper Saddle River, NJ: Pearson.

Hadden, B. R., Tolliver, W., Snowden, F., & Brown-Manning, R. (2016). An authentic discourse: Recentering race and racism as factors that contribute to police violence against unarmed Black or African American men. *Journal of Human Behavior in the Social Environment 26*(3-4), 336–349.

Halevi, E., & Idisis, Y. (2018). Who helps the helper? Differentiation of self as an indicator for resisting vicarious traumatization. *Psychological Trauma: Theory, Research, Practice And Policy 10*(6), 698–705. Retrieved from https://doi-org.nec.gmilcs.org/10.1037/tra0000318

Hallowell, E., & Ratey, J. (2011). *Driven to distraction: Recognizing and coping with attention deficit disorder from childhood through adulthood.* First Anchor Books Edition. New York: Anchor Books.

Hammond, C., Hepworth, D. H., & Smith, V. G. (1977). *Improving therapeutic communication.* San Francisco: Jossey-Bass.

Handler, J. F., & White, L. (1999). *Hard labor: Women and work in the post-welfare era.* New York: M. E. Sharpe, Inc.

Hankin, C., et al. (1999, October). Prevalence of depressive and alcohol abuse symptoms among women VA outpatients who report experiencing sexual assault while in the military. *Journal of Traumatic Stress 12*(4), 601–612.

Hayden, T., & Novik, J. (1980). *Your rights to privacy.* New York: Avon Books.

Heck, N. C., Flentje, A., & Cochran, B. N. (2013.) Intake interviewing with lesbian, gay, bisexual, and transgender clients: Starting from a place of affirmation. *Journal of Contemporary Psychotherapy 43*(1), 23–32.

Heisler, M., Choi, H., Piette, J. D., Rosland, A., Langa, K. M., & Brown, S. (2013). Adults with cardiovascular disease who help others: A prospective study of health outcomes. *Journal of Behavioral Medicine 36*(2), 199–211. doi: 10.1007/s10865-012-9414-4

Hepworth, D. H., & Larsen, J. A. (1987). Interviewing. In *Encyclopedia of social work.* Silver Spring, MD: National Association of Social Workers.

Herbert, B. (1998, June 14). Hidden agendas. *The New York Times,* p. 17.

Herbert, B. (2004, June 11). Punishing the poor. *The New York Times.*

Herlihy, D. (1973). Three patterns of social mobility in medieval history. *The Journal of Interdisciplinary History*, 3(4), 623–647. doi:10.2307/202686

Hernandez-Wolfe, P., Killian, K., Engstrom, D., & Gangsei, D. (2015; 2014). Vicarious resilience, vicarious trauma, and awareness of equity in trauma work. *Journal of Humanistic Psychology* 55(2), 153–172. doi: 10.1177/0022167814534322

Herrnstein, R. (1971, September). I.Q. *Atlantic Monthly* 228(3), 43–64.

Herrnstein, R., & Murray, C. (1994). *The bell curve: Intelligence and class structure in American life*. New York: Free Press.

Hetey, R. C., & Eberhardt, J. L. (2014). Racial disparities in incarceration increase acceptance of punitive policies. *Psychological Science* 25(10), 1949–1954.

Higgins, A. (2004, May 14). Program bolsters violence, victims' confidentiality. *Bangor Daily News*.

Hilarski, C., Wodarski, J. S., & Feit, M. D. (Eds.). (2008). *Handbook of social work in child and adolescent sexual abuse*. New York: Haworth Press/Taylor & Francis Group.

HIV-related knowledge and stigma. Morbidity and mortality weekly report. (2001, March 14). *Journal of the American Medical Association 10*, 285.

Hodgkinson, S., Godoy, L., Beers, L. S., & Lewin, A. (2017). Improving mental health access for low-income children and families in the primary care setting. *Pediatrics 2017, 139*(1). doi: 10.1542/peds.2015-1175

Holland, M. M. (2015). Trusting each other: Student-counselor relationships in diverse high schools. *Sociology of Education* 88(3), 244–262.

Hollar, J. (2010, June) Wealth gap yawns—and so do media. Retrieved from https://fair.org/extra/wealth-gap-yawns8212and-so-do-media/

Holmes, S. A. (1997, December 21). Thinking about race with one-track mind. *The New York Times*, pp. 1, 12.

Hooks, B. (1997). Representing whiteness in the black imagination. In R. Frankenber (Ed.), *Displacing whiteness*. Durham, NC: Duke University Press.

Hosoda, M., Nguyen, L. T., & Stone-Romero, E. F. (2012). The effect of Hispanic accents on employment decisions. *Journal of Managerial Psychology* 27(4), 347–364.

Houston, L. P., & Cohen, A. C. (1972, Fall). The college for human services: A model for alternative professional education. *New Generation 54*(4), 22–23.

Hsu, F. L. K. (1971). *The challenge of the American dream: The Chinese in the United States*. Belmont, CA: Wadsworth.

Husock, H. (1993). Bringing back the settlement house. *Public Welfare* 51(4), 16–25.

Iheozor-Ejiofor, Z., Worthington, H. V., Walsh, T., O'Malley, L., Clarkson, J. E., Macey, R., Alam, R., Tugwell, P., Welch, V., & Glenny, A. (2015). Water fluoridation to prevent tooth decay. Retrieved from https://www.cochrane.org/CD010856/ORAL_water-fluoridation-prevent-tooth-decay

Information and Technical Assistance on the Americans with Disabilities Act. U.S. Department of Justice, Civil Rights Division. Retrieved from https://www.ada.gov/olmstead/olmstead_about.htm

Ingram, R. (1992, April). When therapy is oppression. *Transactional Analysis Journal* 22(2), 95–100.

Internal Revenue Service. (2019). Social Security and Medicare withholding rates. Retrieved from https://www.irs.gov/taxtopics/tc751

IRS online. Earned income tax credit eligibility. Retrieved from https://www.irs.gov/credits-deductions/individuals/earned-income-tax-credit/do-i-qualify-for-earned-income-tax-credit-eitc

Jackson, K. F., & Samuels, G. (2011). Multisocial competence in social work. *Social Work* 56(3), 235–245.

Jagdeo, A., M.D., Cox, B. J., PhD, Stein, M. B., M.D., F.R.C.P.C., M.P.H., & Sareen, J., M.D., F.R.C.P.C. (2009). Negative attitudes toward help seeking for mental illness in 2 population-based surveys from the United States and Canada. *Canadian Journal of Psychiatry* 54(11), pp. 757–766.

James, A. (2013). Pocket Mindfulness—The Complete Series. Kindle Edition. Amazon Digital Services LLC.

Janofsky, M. (2001, July 15). States pressed as 3 boys die at boot camps. *The New York Times*, pp. A1, A13.

Jansson, B. S. (2001). *The Reluctant welfare state: American social welfare policies: Past, present, and future (with InfoTrac)*, 4th Edition. Brooks/Cole

Jansson, B. S. (2015). *The reluctant welfare state: American social welfare policies: Past, present, and future (8th ed.)*. Boston, MA: Cengage.

Jenkins, S. (1981). *The ethnic dilemma in social services*. New York: Free Press.

Joffe, A. H. (2011). American Jews beyond Judaism. *Society* 48(4), 323–329.

Johnson, J., Hall, L. H., Berzins, K., Baker, J., Melling, K., & Thompson, C. (2018). Mental healthcare staff well-being and burnout: A narrative review of trends, causes, implications, and recommendations for future interventions. *International Journal of Mental Health Nursing* 27(1), 20–32.

Johnson, R. C., Kalil, A., & Dunifon, R. E. (with Ray, R.) 2010. *Mothers' Work and Children's Lives: Low-Income Families after Welfare Reform*. Kalamazoo, MI: W.E. Upjohn Institute for Employment Research.

Jones, R. L., & Kaufman, L. (2003). New Jersey opens files showing failures of child welfare system. *The New York Times*. Retrieved from https://www.nytimes.com/2003/04/15/us/new-jersey-opens-files-showing-failures-of-child-welfare-system.html

Kadushin, A. (1980). *Child welfare services (3rd ed.)*. New York: Macmillan.

Kagan, J. (2016). *On being human: Why mind matters*. New Haven, CT: Yale University Press.

Kahn, S. (1995). *Organizing: A guide for grassroots leaders*. Washington, D.C.: NASW Press.

Kain, E. (2011, June 28). The war on drugs is a war on minorities and the poor. *Forbes*. Retrieved from https://bit.ly/2UWhej0

Kaiser Commission on Medicaid and the Uninsured and Urban Institute estimates based on data from FY 2011 MSIS. (2015, December 10). Retrieved from http://kff.org/medicaid/issue-brief/medicaid-per-enrollee-spending-variation-across-states/

Kaiser Family Foundation Focus on Health Reform. (2012, August). A guide to the Supreme Court's decision on the ACA's Medicaid expansion. Retrieved from https://kaiserfamilyfoundation.files.wordpress.com/2013/01/8347.pdf

Kania, J., & Kramer, M. (2011). Stanford Social Innovation Review. Collective Impact. Retrieved from https://ssir.org/articles/entry/collective_impact

Kattari, S. K., Whitfield, D. L., Walls, N. E., Langenderfer-Magruder, L., & Ramos, D. (2016). Policing gender through housing and employment discrimination: Comparison of discrimination experiences of transgender and cisgender LGBQ individuals. *Journal of the Society for Social Work & Research* 7(3), 427–447.

Katz, M. B. (1989). *The undeserving poor: From the war on poverty to the war on welfare*. New York: Pantheon.

Kearney, M. (2017, July 25). Welfare and the Federal Budget. *EconoFact*. University of Maryland.

Keefe, T., & Maypole, D. E. (1983). *Relationships in social service practice: Context and skills*. Monterey, CA: Wadsworth.

Keene, S. (2015). Victim or thug? Examining the relevance of stories in cases involving shootings of unarmed Black males. *Howard Law Journal* 58(3), 845–856.

Kelly, J. (2018). Fast tracked federal overhaul of child welfare financing gets mixed reactions. *The Chronical of Social Change*. Retrieved from https://chronicleofsocialchange.org/subscriber-content/familyfirstact29826/29826

Keltner, D. (2009, February 28). Darwin 2C: The evolutionary logic of kindness. Retrieved from http://www.sciam.com/article.cfm?id=kindness-emotions-psychology

Keneally, M. (2017, December 12). *How gun laws have changed in the 5 years since Sandy Hook*. https://abcnews.go.com/US/gun-laws-changed-years-sandy-hook/story?id=51668726

Kenny, M. C., Abreu, R. L., Helpingstine, C., Lopez, A., & Mathews, B. (2018). Counselors' mandated responsibility to report child maltreatment: A review of U.S. laws. *Journal of Counseling & Development* 96(4), 372–387.

Kettner, P. M., Moroney, R. M., & Martin, L. I. (2016). *Designing and managing programs: An effectiveness approach*. Newbury Park, CA: SAGE.

Kilborn, P. (1997, December 10). Mentally ill called victims of cost-cutting. *The New York Times*, p. A20.

Kingston, M. H. (1977). *The woman warrior: Memoirs of a girlhood among ghosts.* New York: Alfred Knopf.

Kinsey, A. C., Gebhard, P. H., Martin, C. E., & Pomeroy, W. B. (1953). *Sexual behavior in the human female.* Philadelphia, PA: W. B. Saunders.

Kinsey, A. C., Pomeroy, W. B., & Martin, C. E. (1948). *Sexual behavior in the human male.* Philadelphia, PA: W. B. Saunders.

Kjosness, J., Barr, L. R., & Rettman, S. (2004). *Research navigator guide: The helping professions.* Boston: Allyn & Bacon.

Klein, A. (2004, April 9). Affirmative-action opponents suffer setbacks in Colorado and Michigan. *Chronicle of Higher Education.* Retrieved from https://chronicle.com/article/Affirmative-Action-Opponents/32016.

Klein, N. J., & Smart, M. J. (2017). Car today, gone tomorrow: The ephemeral car in low-income, immigrant and minority families. *Transportation 44*(3), 495–510.

Knopf, A. (2016). Lack of Medicaid reimbursement limits access to opioid treatment programs. *Alcoholism & Drug Abuse Weekly 28*(40), 1–3. doi: 10.1002/adaw.30736

Kochnar, R., & Cilluffo, A. (2017, November 1). How wealth inequality has changed in the U.S. since the Great Recession, by race, ethnicity and income. Pew Research Center. Retrieved from http://www.pewresearch.org/fact-tank/2017/11/01/how-wealth-inequality-has-changed-in-the-u-s-since-the-great-recession-by-race-ethnicity-and-income/

Koedt, A. (1971). The myth of the vaginal orgasm. In *Liberation now: Writings from the women's liberation movement* (pp. 311–320). New York: Dell.

Kunins, H. V., Bellin, E., Chazotte, C., Du, E., & Arnsten, J. H. (2007). The effect of race on provider decisions to test for illicit drug use in the peripartum setting. *Journal of women's health (2002), 16*(2), 245–55.

Kurzman, P. A. (1971). *The Mississippi experience: Strategies for welfare rights action.* New York: Association Press.

La Botz, D. (2007, Summer). The immigrant rights movement: Between political realism and social idealism. *New Politics, XI*(3), 24–33.

Lacombe, A. (1997, June 2). *Welfare reform and access to jobs in Boston.* Boston: Bureau of Transportation Statistics.

Lahey, J. (2017). The children being denied due process. The Atlantic. Retrieved from https://www.theatlantic.com/education/archive/2017/05/the-children-being-denied-due-process/527448/

Lahr, J. (2001, April 16). Been here and gone. *The New Yorker*, p. 52. Retrieved from https://www.newyorker.com/magazine/2001/04/16/been-here-and-gone

Lakien, A. (1989). *How to get control of your time and your life.* New York: The New American Library (Signet Division).

Lamothe, J., Couvrette, A., Lebrun, G., Yale-Soulière, G., Roy, C., Guay, S., & Geoffrion, S. (2018). Violence against child protection workers: A study of workers' experiences, attributions, and coping strategies. *Child Abuse & Neglect 81*, 308–321.

Landers, S. (1998, May). Balancing confidences, laws, and ethics. *NASW News*, p. 3.

Laurence, G. A., Fried, Y., & Raub, S. (2016). Evidence for the need to distinguish between self-initiated and organizationally imposed overload in studies of work stress. *Work & Stress 30*(4), 337–355. doi: 10.1080/02678373.2016.1253045

Lee, S., Rothbard, A., & Noll, E. (2012, September 1). Length of inpatient stay of persons with serious mental illness: effects of hospital and regional characteristics. *Psychiatric Services 63*(9), 889–895. Retrieved from https://www.ncbi.nlm.nih.gov/pubmed/?term=22751995

Lehrman, S. (2008). *Omitting race: Politically correct or good crime reporting?* Indianapolis, IN: Society of Professional Journalists.

Leonhardt, D. (2007, May 30). Truth, fiction and Lou Dobbs. *The New York Times.* Retrieved from https://www.nytimes.com/2007/05/30/business/30leonhardt.html

Letvak, S., & Buck, R. (2008). Factors influencing work productivity and intent to stay in nursing. *Nursing Economics 26*, 159.

Levey, N. (2017, March 16). Trump budget envisions big cuts for health and human services. *Los Angeles Times.*

Levi-Strauss, C. (1974). Reciprocity, the essence of social life. In R. L. Coser (Ed.), *The family: Its structures and functions* (pp. 3–12). New York: St. Martin's Press.

Lewis, N. A. (1997, April 2). With immigration law in effect, battles go on. *The New York Times*, p. 1.

Lewis, O. (1961). *The children of Sanchez.* New York: Random House.

Lieberman, M. A., Yalom, I. D., & Miles, M. B. (1973). *Encounter groups: First facts.* New York: Basic Books.

Linker, I. S. (2018). Mental health parity act precluded restricting treatment for mental health patients, Ninth Circuit concludes. *Employee Benefit Plan Review 72*(10), 19.

Liptak, A. (2008, April 29). A New Look at Death Sentences and Race. *The New York Times.*

Littlechild, B., Hunt, S., Goddard, C., Cooper, J., Raynes, B., & Wild, J. (2016). The effects of violence and aggression from parents on child protection workers' personal, family, and professional lives. SAGE Open. https://doi.org/10.1177/2158244015624951

Ljaljevic, A., Scepanovic, L., Mugosa, B., & Catic, S. (2015). HIV/AIDS education of health care providers. *Sanamed 10*(1), 31–35.

Locke, I. S., Spirduso, W.W., & Silverman, S. J. (2013). *Proposals that work (6th ed.).* Thousand Oaks, CA: Sage.

Lopez, A. (2010, May). Alternatives to detention: Unaccompanied immigrant children in the U.S. immigration system. Pace University. Retrieved from https://digitalcommons.pace.edu/honorscollege_theses/97/

Lopez, G., & Bialik, K. (2017). *Key findings about U.S. immigrants.* Fact Tank. News in the Numbers. Pew Research Center.

Lowery, W. (2016, July 11). Analysis: More Whites killed by police, but Blacks 2.5 times more likely to be killed. *Chicago Tribune.*

Lukes, C. A., & Land, H. (1990, March). Biculturality and homosexuality. *Social Work 35*(2), 155–161.

Malcolm X., & Haley, A. (1966). *The autobiography of Malcolm X.* New York: Grove Press.

Mallett, C. A. (September, 2018). Disproportionate minority contact in juvenile justice: today's, and yesterdays, problems. *Criminal Justice Studies 31*(3), 230–248. doi: 10.1080/1478601X.2018.1438276.

Mandal, F. B. (2014). Nonverbal communication in humans. *Journal of Human Behavior in the Social Environment 24*(4), 417–421. doi: 10.1080/10911359.2013.831288

Mandell, B. (1973). *Where are the children? A class analysis of foster care and adoption.* Lexington, MA: D. C. Heath.

Mandell, B. (1997, Winter). Downsizing the welfare state. *New Politics*, 33–46.

Marini, I., Glover-Graf, N. M., & Millington, M. J. (2011). *Psychosocial aspects of disability: Insider perspectives and strategies for counselors.* New York: Springer Publishing Company.

Maslach, C. (1978). The client role in staff burnout. *Journal of Social Issues 34*(4), 111–124.

Maslach, C., Leiter, M. P., & Jackson, S. E. (2012). Making a significant difference with burnout interventions: Researcher and practitioner collaboration. *Journal of Organizational Behavior 33*(2), 296–300. doi: 10.1002/job.784

Massachusetts Alliance to Reform CORI. (2007). Retrieved from http://unionofminorityneighborhoods.org/programs-and-initiatives/seal-your-cori/

Massachusetts Budget and Policy Center. (2017). Emergency assistance—family shelters and services. Retrieved from http://children.massbudget.org/emergency-assistance-family-shelters-and-services

Matsumoto, D., & Hwang, H. C. (2016). The cultural bases of nonverbal communication. In D. Matsumoto, H. C. Hwang, & M. G. Frank (Eds.), *APA handbooks in psychology: APA handbook of nonverbal communication* (pp. 77–101). Washington, D.C.: American.

Mayer, J., & Timms, N. (1970). *The client speaks: Working class impressions of casework.* Chicago: Aldine Publishing.

McAuliffe, D., & Chenoweth, L. (2008). *Leave no stone unturned: The inclusive model of ethical decision making. Ethics and Social Welfare 2*(1), 38–49.

McGarrigle, T., & Walsh, C. A. (2011). Mindfulness, self-care, and wellness in social work: Effects of contemplative training. *Journal of Religion & Spirituality in Social Work: Social Thought 30*(3), 212–233. doi: 10.1080/15426432.2011.587384

McKibben, B. (2007). *Fight global warming now: The handbook for taking action in your community.* New York: Holt Paperbacks.

McKibben, B. (2008). *Deep economy: The wealth of communities and the durable future.* New York: Times Books/Henry Holt & Co.

McKibben, B. (2019). *Falter.* New York: Henry Holt & Co.

McKnight, J. (1992, April 22). Speech at Foundations Affecting the Future of Massachusetts' Communities Forum on Community Organizing.

McMurray, J. (2008, March 29). Colleges keep closer watch on students. *The Boston Globe*, p. A2.

McNamara, E. (1991, December 26). "Last one over the wall": Battling youth crime with compassion. *The Boston Globe*, p. 24.

McRoy, R. G. (1990). A historical overview of black families. In S. Logan, E. M. Freeman, & R. McRoy (Eds.), *Social work practice with black families* (pp. 3–17).White Plains, NY: Longman.

Meckler, L. (2004, October 16). 'Get tough' programs for youths criticized. *The Boston Globe*, p. A3.

Mehrabian, A. (1971). *Silent messages*. Belmont, CA: Wadsworth Publishing Company.

Melish, T. J. (2010). Maximum feasible participation of the poor: New governance, new accountability and a 21st century war on the sources of poverty. *Yale Human Rights and Development Law Journal 13*, 133.

Merkle, J. S., & Phillips, M. A. (2018). The wage impact of teachers unions: A meta-analysis. *Contemporary Economic Policy 36*(1), 93–115.

Michaiko, M. (2006). *Tinkertoys: A handbook of creative thinking techniques*. Berkeley, CA: Ten Speed Press.

Milgram, S. (1974). *Obedience to authority: An experimental view*. New York: Harper & Row.

Miller, J. B. (1976). *Toward a new psychology of women*. Boston: Beacon Press.

Miller, M. (2009) *A community organizer's tale: People and power in San Francisco*. Berkeley, CA: Ten Speed Press.

Miller, P. (1992). *The worst of times*. New York: Harper Collins.

Milligan, S. (2007, June 5). Fiscal lift, burden in immigrant legislation. *The Boston Globe*, p. A1.

Mills, C. W. (1959). *The sociological imagination*. New York: Oxford University.

Moffitt, R. A. (2015). The deserving poor, the family, and the U.S. welfare system. *Demography 52*(3), 729–749. Retrieved from http://doi.org/10.1007/s13524-015-0395-0

Moore, S. (2009, April 30th). Justice Dept. seeks equity in sentences for cocaine. *The New York Times*, p. 17.

Moss, M. S. (2001, May). HHS gets additional comments on privacy rules. *NASW News 46*(5), 4.

Moynihan, D. P. (1965). *The Negro family: The case for national action*. Washington, D.C.: U.S. Department of Labor, Office of Policy Planning and Research.

Mujtaba, B. G., & Cavico, F. J. (2012). Discriminatory practices against Muslims in the American workplace. *Journal of Leadership, Accountability and Ethics 9*(1), 98.

Murray, C. A. (1984). *Losing ground: American social policy 1950–1980*. New York: Basic Books.

Murray, C., & Herrnstein, R. (1994). *The bell curve: Intelligence and class structure in American life*. New York: Free Press.

NAMI. Mental health facts children and teens. Retrieved from https://www.nami.org/getattachment/learn-more/mental-health-by-the-numbers/childrenmhfacts.pdf

National Alliance for Caregiving and AARP Public Policy Institute. (2015). *Caregiving in the U.S. 2015*. Retrieved from https://www.aarp.org/content/dam/aarp/ppi/2015/caregiving-in-the-united-states-2015-report-revised.pdf

National Alliance on Mental Illness. (2016). *Mental Health By The Numbers*.Retrieved from http://www.nami.org/Learn-More/Mental-Health-By-the-Numbers

National Alliance to End Homelessness. (2016, April 20). *Housing First*. Retrieved from https://endhomelessness.org/resource/housing-first/

National Association of Social Workers. (1983, February). Congress, district court chop rate of disability cutoffs. *NASW News 28*(2), 9.

National Center on Child Abuse and Neglect. (1979, September). Resource materials, OHDS, Children's Bureau, DHEW, Publication No. 79-30221. Washington, D.C.: Department of Health, Education, and Welfare.

National Commission for Human Service Workers. (1982, July). *Registration and certification of human service workers*. Paper prepared and distributed by the National Commission for Human Service Workers (NCHSW). Atlanta.

National Council for Behavioral Health. (2018, July). Shelley Starkey House Panel Examines 21st Century Cures. Mental Health Initiatives. Retrieved from https://www.thenationalcouncil.org/capitol-connector/2018/07/house-panel-examines-21st-century-cures-mental-health-initiatives/

National Institute of Mental Health. Statistics online. Retrieved from https://www.nimh.nih.gov/health/statistics/index.shtml

National Organization for Women. (2004, March 26). NOW fights right-wing assault on abortion rights, urges supporters to march on April 25th. Retrieved from https://now.org/resource/reproductive-rights-historical-highlights/

National Organization for Women. (2008, August 15). The Border Fence. *PBS*. Retrieved from http://www.pbs.org/now/shows/432/

National Women's Law Center. (2010, April). Women's lower wages worsen their circumstances in a difficult economy. Retrieved from www.nwlc.org/pdf/lowerwageshurtwomen.pdf

Nellis, A. (2016, June 14). The Color of Justice: Racial and Ethnic Disparity in Prisons. *The Sentencing Project*. Retrieved from https://www.sentencingproject.org/publications/color-of-justice-racial-and-ethnic-disparity-in-state-prisons/

Nichols, K., & Jenkinson, J. (2006). *Leading a support group*. Berkshire, UK: Open University Press (McGraw Hill Co).

Nickerson, C. (1985, March 10). Reformers' dream that went astray. *The Boston Globe*, p. 21.

Nixon, A. E., Mazzola, J. J., Bauer, J., Krueger, J. R., & Spector, P. E. (2011). Can work make you sick? A meta-analysis of the relationships between job stressors and physical symptoms. *Work & Stress 25*(1), 1–22. doi: 10.1080/02678373.2011.569175

Nystul, M. (2010). *Introduction to counseling: An art and science perspective*. Upper Saddle River, N.J.: Pearson.

Occupy Wall Street online. http://occupywallst.org/

Office of Fair Housing and Equal Opportunity. (2016). OFHEO Annual Report.

O'Harrow, R., Jr. (2001, January 21). Medical privacy: Exception to a rule. *The Boston Globe*, p. A13.

Okeowo, A. (2016, November 17). Hate on the rise after Trump's election. *The New Yorker*. Retrieved from https://www.newyorker.com/news/news-desk/hate-on-the-rise-after-trumps-election

Okun, B., & Kantrowitz, R. E. (2015). *Effective helping: Interviewing and counseling techniques (8th ed.)*. Stamford, CT: Cengage Learning.

Okun, B., & Rappaport, L. (1980). *Working with families: An introduction to family therapy*. North Scituate, MA: Duxbury Press.

Orsi, J. M., M.P.H., Margellos-Anast, H., & Whitman, S., PhD. (2010). Black-White health disparities in the United States and Chicago: A 15-year progress analysis. *American Journal of Public Health 100*(2), 349–356.

Ouchida, K. M., & Lachs, M. S. (2015). Not for doctors only: Ageism in healthcare. *Generations 39*(3), pp. 46–57.

Pack-Brown, S. P., & Whittington-Clark, L. E. (1998). *Images of me: A guide to group work with African American women*. Boston: Allyn & Bacon.

Paltrow, Lynn. (2013, January 1). National Advocates for Pregnant Women. Roe v Wade and the New Jane Crow: Reproductive Rights in the Age of Mass Incarceration. *American Journal of Public Health 103*(1), 17–21.

Parloff, M. B. (1970). Sheltered workshops for the alienated. *International Journal of Psychiatry 9*, 197–204.

Pasquarelli, A. (2018). Modest Goes Mainstream; A growing Muslim middle class spurs fashion lines with broad appeal. *Adage 89*(5), 22.

Pearl, A., & Riessman, F. (1965). *New careers for the poor*. New York: Free Press.

Perez-Pena, R. (2017, January 26). Contrary to Trump's claims, immigrants are less likely to commit crimes. *The New York Times*.

Pertman, A. (2001, May 20). Still illegal, but . . . *The Boston Globe*, p. D2.

Petersen, N. D. (2015). *Cumulative Racial Inequalities within Death Penalty Institutions* (Doctoral dissertation, UC Irvine).

Pew Research Center. (2009). Views of Islam and Violence, September 9, 2009. Retrieved from http://www.pewforum.org/2009/09/09/publicationpage-aspxid1398-3/

Pew Research Center. (2016, June 27). On Views of Race and Inequality, Blacks and Whites Are Worlds Apart. Retrieved from https://www.pewsocialtrends.org/2016/06/27/on-views-of-race-and-inequality-blacks-and-whites-are-worlds-apart/

Phillips, B. A. (2016). Not quite White: The emergence of Jewish 'ethnoburbs' in Los Angeles, 1920–2010. *American Jewish History 100*(1), 73–104, 168.

Pincus, A. H., & Minahan, A. (1973). *Social work practice: Model and method.* Itasca, IL: F. S. Peacock.

Piven, F. F., & Cloward, R. A. (2013). *Regulating the poor: The functions of public welfare.* Updated edition. New York: Random House.

Platt, A. M. (1977). *The child savers: The invention of delinquency.* Chicago: University of Chicago Press.

Polakow, V., Butler, S., Stormer Deprez, L., & Kahn, P. (2004, August 2). *Shut out: Low income mothers and higher education in post-welfare America.* Albany, NY: State University of New York Press.

Polsky, H. W. (1962). *Cottage six—The social system of delinquent boys in residential treatment.* New York: Russell Sage Foundation.

Portes, A., & Rumbaut, R. (1990). *Immigrant America.* Berkeley, CA: University of California Press.

Potok, M. (2016, February 17). *Annual Report.* Southern Poverty Law Center.

Preston, J. (2006, February 1). Partial Birth Abortion Act ruled unconstitutional by US courts. *The New York Times.*

Prison Policy Initiative. (2016). *Mass Incarceration: The Whole Pie 2016.* Retrieved from www.prisonpolicy.org/reports/pie2016.html

Privacy and State Records. (1984, February 4). *The Boston Globe.*

Privacy Rights Clearinghouse. (2014). Medical Records Privacy. Retrieved from https://www.privacyrights.org/consumer-guides/health-privacy-outside-healthcare-environment-health-records-job-available

Puente, M., & Blas, L. (2016, September 22). Brad Pitt, accused of child abuse, is under investigation. *USA Today.* Retrieved from https://www.usatoday.com/story/life/people/2016/09/22/reports-brad-pitt-accused-child-abuse-under-investigation/90825098/

Quinn, Lois M. (1997, January). Evaluation of the impact of Wisconsin's learnfare experiment on the school attendance of teenagers receiving Aid to Families with Dependent Children. Author's Note. Retrieved from https://www4.uwm.edu/eti/pages/surveys/each/learn292.htm

Ragg, D. M., Dennis, P., & Ziefert, M. (2006). Slamming the closet door: Working with gay and lesbian youth in care. *Child Welfare 85*(2), 243–265.

Ray, C. (2017). *President Trump's Proposed Cuts to the Legal Services Corporation Would Increase the Justice Gap.* Center for American Progress. Retrieved from https://www.americanprogress.org/issues/courts/news/2017/05/17/432553/president-trumps-proposed-cuts-legal-services-corporation-increase-justice-gap/

Reamer, F. (2001, October 15). Social work values resonate, inspire in wake of recent tragedies. *Social Work Today*, 22–23.

Rees, S. (1979). *Social work face to face.* New York: Columbia University Press.

Reich, R. (2016). *Saving capitalism: For the many, not the few.* New York: Vintage Books

Reihl, K. M., Hurley, R. A., & Taber, K. H. (2015). Neurobiology of implicit and explicit bias: Implications for clinicians. *The Journal of Neuropsychiatry and Clinical Neurosciences 27*(4), A6–253.

Reynolds, B. (1963). *An uncharted journey.* New York: Citadel.

Rhodes, M. L. (1989). *Ethical dilemmas in social work practice.* Milwaukee, WI: Family Service America.

Rivera, F. G., & Erlich, J. L. (Eds.). (1998). *Community organizing in a diverse society (3rd ed.).* Boston: Allyn & Bacon.

Robinson, M. A. (2017). Black bodies on the ground: Policing disparities in the African American community—An analysis of newsprint from January 1, 2015, through December 31, 2015. *Journal of Black Studies 48*(6), 551–571.

Rogers, C. (1951). *Client-centered therapy.* Boston: Houghton Mifflin.

Rogerson, S. (2013). Lack of detained parents' access to the family justice system and the unjust severance of the parent-child relationship. *Family Law Quarterly 47*(2), 141–172.

Rosen, C. E. (1976, July). Sign-away pressures. *Social Work 21*, 284–287.

Rosie's Place. (2007). 2007 Spring Newsletter, p. 2. Boston.

Rossen, S. (1987). Hospital social work. In A. Menahan (Ed.), *Encyclopedia of social work (18th ed.)* (pp. 816–820). Silver Spring, MD: National Association of Social Workers.

Rothstein, R. (2017). *The color of law: A forgotten history of how our government segregated America.* New York: Liveright Publishing Corporation, a division of W. W. Norton & Company.

Rudd, R.; Aleshire, N., JD; Zibbell, J. E., PhD; & Gladden, R. M., PhD. (2016). Increases in Drug and Opioid Overdose Deaths — United States, 2000–2014. Retrieved from https://www.cdc.gov/mmwr/preview/mmwrhtml/mm6450a3.htm?s_cid=mm6450a3_w

Russell, D. M. (1991). *Political organizing in grassroots politics.* Lanham, MD: University Press of America.

Russell, E. (2016, October 23). Maine sits on millions in federal welfare dollars, yet poverty rises. *Portland Press Herald.*

Ryan, W. (1976). *Blaming the victim.* New York: Random House.

Sack, K., & Pear, R. (2010, February 18). States consider Medicaid cuts as use grows. *The New York Times.* Retrieved from http://www.nytimes.com/2010/02/19/us/politics/19medicaid.html

Sacks, O. (1989). *Seeing voices: A journey into the land of the deaf.* Berkeley, CA: University of California.

Sainsbury, E. (1974). *Social work with families: Perceptions of social casework among clients of a family service unit.* London: Routledge.

Sameem, S., & Sylwester, K. (2018). Crime during the business cycle: Urban-rural differences. *Applied Economics 50*(22), 2500–2508.

Sawhill, I., and Jargowsky, P. (2006, January 1). The Decline of the Underclass. Brookings Institution. Retrieved from https://www.brookings.edu/research/the-decline-of-the-underclass/

Scherrer, K. (2013). Culturally competent practice with bisexual individuals. *Clinical Social Work Journal 41*(3), 238–248.

Schiller, Linda Yael, LICSW. (1997). Rethinking Stages of Development in Women's Groups: Implications for Practice, Social Work with Groups, *20*:3, 3-19, DOI: 10.1300/J009v20n03_02

Schmitt, E. (2001, July 29). You can come in, you stay out. *The New York Times*, p. 5.

Schram, B. (1971). The conscious use of color. In P. Kurzman (Ed.), *The Mississippi experience: Strategies for welfare rights organization* (pp. 66–83). New York: Association Press.

Schram, B. (1997). *Creating the small scale social program: Planning, implementation and evaluation.* Thousand Oaks, CA: Sage.

Schreiber, S. (2018, November 6). Social Security wage base set for 2019. *Journal of Accountancy.* Retrieved from https://www.journalofaccountancy.com/news/2018/nov/social-security-wage-base-2019-201820059.html

Scott, M. (2010, March 11). Michigan Republicans propose drug testing, other rules to stop public assistance fraud among Bridge Card users. *The Grand Rapids Press.* Retrieved from https://www.mlive.com/politics/index.ssf/2010/03/michigan_republicans_propose_d.html

Seever, F. S. (1987). (Review of the book Professionalism and social change: From settlement house movement to neighborhood centers, 1886 to the present). *Social Service Review 64*(1), 163.

Seigafo, S. (2017). Inmate's right to rehabilitation during incarceration: A critical analysis of the United States correctional system. *International Journal of Criminal Justice Sciences 12*(2), 183–195.

Semuels, A. (2016, July 11). The Near Impossibility of Moving Up after Welfare. *The Atlantic.* Retrieved from https://www.theatlantic.com/business/archive/2016/07/life-after-welfare/490586/

Senior, J. (2007, October 24). Can't get no satisfaction. *The New York Times Magazine.* Retrieved from http://nymag.com/news/features/24757

Sentencing Project. (2010). *Incarceration.* Retrieved from http://www.sentencingproject.org/template/page.cfm?id=107

Sentencing Project. (2018). *Capitalizing on Mass Incarceration: U.S. Growth in Private Prisons.* Retrieved from https://www.sentencingproject.org/publications/capitalizing-on-mass-incarceration-u-s-growth-in-private-prisons/

Sewell, K. M. (2018). Social work supervision of staff: A primer and scoping review (2013–2017). *Clinical Social Work Journal, 46*(4), 1–14.

Shallwani, P., & Bain, B. (2008, March 18). Stepdad guilty in Nixzmary Brown killing. Newsday.

Shamoo, A. E., & Moreno, J. D. (2004). Ethics of research involving mandatory drug testing of high school athletes in Oregon. *American Journal of Bioethics 4*(1), 25–31. Retrieved from https://doi-org.nec.gmilcs.org/10.1162/152651604773067316

Shattuck, J. (1984). In the Shadow of 1984: National identification systems, computer-matching, and privacy in the United States. *35*(6). *Hastings Law Journal*. Retrieved from https://repository.uchastings.edu/cgi/viewcontent.cgi?article=2834&context=hastings_law_journal

Shaw, R. (2001). *The activists' handbook: A primer for the 1990s and beyond.* Berkeley, CA: University of California Press.

Sherman, A. (2015, November). Safety Net Programs Lift Millions from Poverty, New Census Data Show. Center on Budget and PolicyPriorities. Retrieved from https://www.cbpp.org/blog/safety-net-programs-lift-millions-from-poverty-new-census-data-show

Shulman, L. (2008). *The skills of helping individuals, families, groups, and communities (6th ed.).* Pacific Grove, CA: Brooks/Cole Cengage Learning.

Shulman, L. (2012). *The skills of helping individuals, families, groups, and communities (7th ed.).* Belmont, CA: Brooks/Cole Cengage Learning.

Shulman, L. (2015). *The skills of helping individuals, families, groups and communities (8th ed)* Boston, MA: Cengage Learning.

Social Expenditure Update. (2014, November). *Social spending is falling in some countries, but in many others it remains at historically high levels.* Insights from the OECD Social Expenditure database (SOCX).

Social Security Administration Fact Sheet. (2018). Retrieved from https://www.ssa.gov/news/press/factsheets/basicfact-alt.pdf

Social Security Online. (2018). Retrieved from https://www.ssa.gov/policy/ https://www.ssa.gov/oact/cola/SSI.html

Soda, G., & Zaheer, A. (2012). A network perspective on organizational architecture: Performance effects of the interplay of formal and informal organization. *Strategic Management Journal 33*(6), 751–771.

Solomon, A. (2001, May 6). A cure for poverty. *The New York Times Magazine*, pp. 112–117.

Southern Poverty Law Center. (2013). Close to slavery: Guestworker programs in the United States. 2013 Edition.

Specht, H. (1990). Social work and the popular psychotherapies. *Social Service Review*, 64(3), 19-24.

Spock, B. (1946). *Common sense book of baby and childcare.* New York: Meredith Press.

Spock, B., & Morgan, M. (1989). *Spock on Spock. A memoir of growing up with the century.* New York: Pantheon Books.

Squires, G. (2006, Winter). Reintroducing the black/white divide in racial discourse. *New Politics, X*(4), p. 111.

Stack, C. (1974). *All our kin: Strategies for survival in a black community.* New York: Harper & Row.

Stack, L. (2015, November 29). A brief history of deadly attacks on abortion providers.

The New York Times. Retrieved from https://nyti.ms/2TvFBT5

State bar to allow lawyers to break confidentiality. (2004, May 14). *The Recorder.* Retrieved from https://www.law.com/almID/900005539049/

Steele, C. M., & Aronson, J. (1995, August). Stereotype vulnerability and the intellectual test performance of African-Americans. Paper presented at the American Psychological Association.

Steinberg, S. (2005, Summer). Immigration, African Americans, and race discourse. *New Politics, X*(3), 45.

Stephens, R. J. (2016). "It has to come from the hearts of the people": Evangelicals, fundamentalists, race, and the 1964 Civil Rights Act. *Journal of American Studies 50*(3), 559–585.

Sterngold, J. (2001, October 7). Legal residency hopes of millions dashed. *The New York Times,* p. A20.

Stern, M., & Axinn, J. (2018). *Social welfare: A history of the American response to need (9th ed.).* Boston: Pearson.

Stogdill, R. M. (1948). Personal factors associated with leadership: A survey of the literature. *Journal of Psychology 25*, 37–71.

Stogdill, R. M., & Coons, A. E. (1957). *Leader behavior: Its description and measurement.* Columbus, OH: Bureau of Business Research, Ohio State University.

Stolberg, S. G. (2001, May 13). Shouldn't a pill be colorblind? *The New York Times*, pp. 1, 3.

Stone, M. (2018, June 8). LePage's plan to put kids in a new kind of psychiatric institution. *Bangor Daily News.* Retrieved from https://bangordailynews.com/2018/06/08/mainefocus/lepages-plan-to-put-kids-in-a-new-kind-of-psychiatric-institution/

Sue, D. W., & Sue, D. (2016). *Counseling the culturally diverse: Theory and practice.* Hoboken, New Jersey: Wiley.

Svonkin, S. (1998). *Jews against prejudice: American Jews and the fight for civil rights.* New York: Columbia University Press.

Szasz, T. S. (1961). *The myth of mental illness.* New York: Harper & Row.

Talk of the Nation. (2004a, January 15). National Public Radio.

Talk of the Nation. (2004b, April 15). National Public Radio.

Tanielian, T., Jaycox, L. H., Schell, T. L., Marshall, G. N., Burnam, M. A., Eibner, C., Karney, B., Meredith, L. S., Ringel, J. S., & Vaiana, M. E. (2008). Invisible Wounds Mental Health and Cognitive Care Needs of America's Returning Veterans. Rand Corporation. Retrieved from https://www.rand.org/pubs/research_briefs/RB9336.html

Taylor-Klaus, E. (2016). *Parenting ADHD now!: Easy intervention strategies to empower kids with ADHD.* Berkley, CA: Althea Press.

The Center for Consumer Information & Insurance Oversight. (ND). Center for Medicaid and Medicare Services. Retrieved from CMS.gov

The Progressive. (1997, November 8).

The StandDown Texas Project. (2010, May 17). Supreme Court rules in juvenile sentencing.

Retrieved from https://standdown.typepad.com/weblog/2010/05/supreme-court-rules-on-juvenile-sentencing.html

Thompson, D. (2017, May 3). Survey reveals how many doctors receive money, gifts from drugmakers. Retrieved from https://www.cbsnews.com/news/doctors-receive-money-gifts-from-drugmakers-pharmaceutical-companies/

Thorne, P. (2010). Debunking the body language myth. *Training and Development in Australia 37*(5), 18.

Thrush, G., & Green E. (2018, June 21). Trump's proposal to reorganize government places target on social-welfare system. *Seattle Times.* Retrieved from https://www.seattletimes.com/nation-world/trumps-proposal-to-reorganize-government-places-target-on-social-welfare-system/

Torrey, E. F., Kennard, A., Eslinger, D., Lamb, R., & Pavle, J. (2010, May). More mentally ill persons are in jails and prisons than hospitals: A survey of the states. Treatment Advocacy Center, Arlington, VA.

Townsend, P. (1992, April 25). Speech at the Socialist Scholars Conference, New York.

Towson, R. W., & Rivas, R. F. (2008). *An introduction to group work practice.* Boston: Allyn & Bacon.

Trippany, R. L., White Kress, V. E., & Wilcoxon, S. A. (2004). Preventing vicarious trauma: What counselors should know when working with trauma survivors. *Journal of Counseling and Development 82*(1), 31–37.

Truax, C. B., & Carkhuff, R. R. (1967). *Toward effective counseling and psychotherapy.* Chicago: Aldine.

Tsai, T., & Scommegna, P. (2012, August, 10). *U.S. Has World's Highest Incarceration Rate.* Population Reference Bureau (PRB). Retrieved from https://www.prb.org/us-incarceration/

Two cases given legal aid grants. (2001, February). *NASW News 46*(2), 12.

U.S. Census Bureau. (2009). *Current Population Survey. People in families by relationship to householder, age of householder, number of related children present, and family structure: 2008.* Washington, D.C.: Government Printing Office.

U.S. Census Bureau online. (2015 data). Retrieved from https://www.census.gov/

U.S. Conference of Catholic Bishops. (1986). *Economic justice for all: Pastoral letter on Catholic social teaching and the U.S. economy.* Washington, D.C.: United States Catholic Conference.

U.S. Conference of Catholic Bishops. (2002, November). *A place at the table: A Catholic recommitment to overcome poverty and to respect the dignity of all God's children.* Issued by USCCB.

U.S. Congress. (2010). H.R. 4213—Unemployment Compensation Extension Act of 2010. Retrieved from https://www.congress.gov/bill/111th-congress/house-bill/4213

U.S. Department of Agriculture. (2009). *National school lunch program.* Retrieved from NSLPFactSheet.pdf

U.S. Department of Agriculture. (2017, November 28). *A Short History of SNAP.* Retrieved from https://www.fns.usda.gov/snap/short-history-snap

U.S. Department of Agriculture. (2018a). *WIC program: Total participation.* Retrieved from https://fns-prod.azureedge.net/sites/default/files/pd/26wifypart.pdf

U.S. Department of Agriculture. (2018b). *Child nutrition tables. National School lunch—participation and meals served.* Retrieved from https://fns-prod.azureedge.net/sites/default/files/pd/slsummar.pdf

U.S. Department of Health and Human Services. (2016). *Supporting career pathways for TANF recipients.* Retrieved from https://www.acf.hhs.gov/ofa/resource/tanf-acf-im-2016-05

U.S. Department of Health and Human Services. *AFCARS report #23, 2016.* Retrieved from https://www.acf.hhs.gov/cb/resource/afcars-report-23

U.S. Department of Health and Human Services. (2019). *What is the U.S. opioid epidemic?* Retrieved from https://www.hhs.gov/opioids/about-the-epidemic/index.html

U.S. Department of Labor, Bureau of Labor Statistics. (2017). *Selected labor force indicators for people by disability status, 2009–17 annual averages.* Retrieved from https://www.bls.gov/spotlight/2018/labor-force-characteristics-of-people-with-a-disability/home.htm

U.S. Department of Labor, Office of Unemployment Insurance, Division of Legislation. (2018, June). *Unemployment Compensation, Federal-State Policy.* Retrieved from https://oui.doleta.gov/unemploy/pdf/partnership.pdf

U.S. Department of Veterans Affairs. (2017, January 30). VA statement about Office of Inspector General review of implementation of the Veterans Choice Program. Retrieved from https://www.va.gov/opa/pressrel/pressrelease.cfm?id=2857

Urban Institute. (2016, March 7). *Assessing Fiscal Capacities of States: A Representative Revenue System–Representative Expenditure System Approach, Fiscal Year 2012.* Retrieved from https://www.urban.org/research/publication/assessing-fiscal-capacities-states-representative-revenue-system-representative-expenditure-system-approach-fiscal-year-2012/view/full_report

Vallianatos, C. (2001). Association backing given in two cases. *NASW News 46*(14), 11.

Vicini, J. (1999, March 9). Justice Department attempt to speed deportations is set back. *The Boston Globe*, p. A5.

Violence Prevention. (2018). Centers for Disease Control. Retrieved from https://www.cdc.gov/violenceprevention/index.html

Vogel, R. (1979, November 11). Teachers' colleges shift their focus to 'related fields.' *The New York Times*, p. 32.

Wacquant, Loïc. (2009). Punishing the poor: The neoliberal government of social insecurity. Durham, NC: Duke University Press.

Wagner, D. (2005). *The poorhouse: America's forgotten institution.* New York: Rowman-Littlefield Publishers. Retrieved 3/20/19 from http://socialwelfare.library.vcu.edu/issues/poor-relief-almshouse/

Wald, H. P., Zubritsky, C. D., & Jaquette, N. (2014). Measuring system of care core values in a behavioral health system of care. *Community Mental Health Journal 50*(3), 275–280.

Walker, R. (1995, January–February). California rages against the dying of the light. *New Left Review 209*, 42–74.

Walshe, S. (2013, March 13). Stop allowing the wealthy to treat undocumented immigrants like slaves. *The Guardian, US Edition.* Retrieved from https://www.theguardian.com/commentisfree/2013/mar/13/wealthy-use-illegal-immigrants-as-domestic-workers

Warner, R. (1989). Deinstitutionalization: How did we get where we are? *Journal of Social Issues 45*(3), 17–30.

Washington, W. (2004, May 31). Bush takes spotlight off Medicare drug benefit. *The Boston Globe*, p. A1.

Weidell, R. C. (1980, February). Unsealing birth certificates in Minnesota. *Child Welfare 59*, 113–119.

Weil, P. (2001). Races at the gate: A century of racial distinctions in American immigration policy (1865–1965). *Georgetown Immigration Law Journal 15*(4), 625. Retrieved from https://bit.ly/2U7E9e3

Weinbach, R., & Taylor, L. M. (2014). *The social worker as manager: A practical guide to success (7th ed).* Boston: Pearson.

Weintraub, K. (2010, May 10). Putting lawyers on the case. *The Boston Globe*, p. B6.

Western, B., & Wildeman, C. (2009). The Black family and mass incarceration. *The Annals of the American Academy of Political and Social Science 621*(1), 221–242.

Whoriskey, P. (2007, November 22). Ga. Court rejects sex offender law. *The Boston Globe*, p. A28.

Wiens, Annalese. (2018, January 26). Complicated earned income credit eligibility means 1 in 5 don't claim the valuable tax credit. HR Block. Retrieved from https://www.hrblock.com/tax-center/newsroom/filing/credits/claiming-earned-income-tax-credit-and-eligibility/

Wilkinson, R., & Marmot, M. (2003). *The Social Determinants of Health, The Solid Facts (2nd ed.).* World Health Organization. Retrieved from http://www.euro.who.int/__data/assets/pdf_file/0005/98438/e81384.pdf

Willard-Grace, R., Hessler, D., Rogers, E., Dubé, K., Bodenheimer, T., & Grumbach, K. (2014). Team structure and culture are associated with lower burnout in primary care. *The Journal of the American Board of Family Medicine 27*, 229–238.

Williams, L. (1997). *Decades of distortion: The right's 30-year assault on welfare.* Somerville, MA: Political Research Associates.

Williams, R., Jr. (1966). Prejudice and society. In J. P. Davis (Ed.), *The American negro reference book* (pp. 727–730). Englewood Cliffs, NJ: Prentice Hall.

Wilson, S. (1980). *Recording: Guidelines for social workers.* New York: Free Press.

Wiltz, T. (2018). This New Federal Law Will Change Foster Care As We Know It. Stateline Article. The PEW Charitable Trusts. Retrieved from https://www.pewtrusts.org/en/research-and-analysis/blogs/stateline/2018/05/02/this-new-federal-law-will-change-foster-care-as-we-know-it

Wonnacott, J. (2011). *Mastering social work supervision.* London: Jessica Kingsley Publishers. Retrieved from https://bit.ly/2UWwRqW

Wright, R. G. (2014). *Sex offender laws, second edition : Failed policies, new directions.* New York: Springer Publishing Company.

Yeates, K. (2015). Informed consent in probation and parole settings. *Journal of Criminal Psychology 5*(4), 279.

Zafirovski, M. (2014). The protestant ethic and the spirit of democracy: What is the democratic effect of calvinism? *The International Journal of Sociology and Social Policy 34*(9), 634–653.

Zastrow, C. (1993). *Social work with groups (3rd ed.).* Chicago: Nelson-Hall.

Zastrow, Charles. (2014). Brooks/Cole Empowerment Series: *Introduction to Social Work and Social Welfare, 11th edition.* Belmont, CA: Brooks/Cole.

Zelnick, J. R., Slayter, E., Flanzbaum, B., Butler, N. G., Domingo, B., Perlstein, J., & Trust, C. (2013). Part of the job? Workplace violence in Massachusetts social service agencies. *Health & Social Work 38*(2), 75–85.

Ziegler, M. (2018). Some form of punishment: Penalizing women for abortion. *The William and Mary Bill of Rights Journal 26*(3), 735–788.

Zimbardo, P. G., Haney, C., Banks, W. C., & Jaffe, D. (1982). The psychology of imprisonment. In J. C. Brigham & L. Wrightsman (Eds.), *Contemporary issues in social psychology (4th ed.)* (pp. 230–245). Monterey, CA: Brooks/Cole.

Ziv-Beiman, S. (2013). Therapist self-disclosure as an integrative intervention. *Journal of Psychotherapy Integration 23*(1), 59–74.

Zoukis, C. (2017). *Nearly half of prisoners lack access to vocational training.* Retrieved from https://prisoneducation.com/prison-education-news/nearly-half-of-prisoners-lack-access-to-vocational-training/

SUBJECT INDEX